THE
ENCYCLOPEDIA OF
MOVIE AWARDS

THE
ENCYCLOPEDIA
OF
MOVIE AWARDS

★ ★ ★

MICHAEL GEBERT

St. Martin's Paperbacks

The terms ''Academy Award(s)®'' and ''Oscar(s)®'' are registered trademarks and service marks of the Academy of Motion Picture Arts and Sciences. This book is neither endorsed by nor affiliated with the Academy of Motion Picture Arts and Sciences.

Excerpts from the *Harvard Lampoon* Movie Worst Awards are owned and copyrighted by the Harvard Lampoon, Inc. Their use is by permission.

Sight & Sound International Critics Surveys © Copyright *Sight & Sound*, The British Film Institute, 1995.

Box office figures reprinted by permission of Variety, Inc. © Copyright *Variety*.

THE ENCYCLOPEDIA OF MOVIE AWARDS

Contents

Acknowledgments

Many of the organizations listed in this book were extremely helpful in providing lists of their awards and in clearing up long-persisting errors and gaps. Thanks to Howard Prouty at the Margaret Herrick Library at the Academy of Motion Picture Arts and Sciences; Chuck Warn and Laraine Savelle at the Directors Guild of America; Harry Medved at the Screen Actors Guild; Kathryn Hammond at Don Mischer Productions/The People's Choice Awards; Tracey Dodd at the British Academy of Film and Television Arts; Dario Ventimiglia, Marina Mottin, and the Press Office of the Venice Biennale; the Internationale Filmfestspiele Berlin; R.J. Millard at the Sundance Film Festival Press Office; Matthew Waldman at the Independent Feature Project/West; librarian Michael H. Schur and the Trustees of the *Harvard Lampoon*; and John Wilson at the Golden Raspberry Awards Foundation. (P.S. Anyone who finds an error still surviving here is encouraged to write me c/o St. Martin's, or by e-mail at DrMovieGuy@aol.com.)

J.B. Kaufman, a true film scholar and one experienced in the ways of film archives, helped in too many ways to count. Richard T. Jameson provided his witty memories of National Society of Film Critics deliberations and other kindnesses. Charles Silver of the Museum of Modern Art's Department of Film and Video kindly searched his archives to bring one of my Holy Grails, the very first

National Board of Review awards, to light for the first time in 65 years. Lastly, I must thank Meredith Bernstein and Elizabeth Cavanaugh for selling the book, and Shawn Coyne and Todd Keithley for buying and editing it. And most of all, my wife, fellow typist, and moviegoing companion Susan Snyder, to whom I dedicate this book.

THE
ENCYCLOPEDIA OF
MOVIE AWARDS

Introduction

The Academy Awards may have been created as a public relations tool for the movie industry, but their greatest public relations success has been selling themselves. No one agrees with them, at least all of the time, but everyone who's interested in the movies pays attention to them—if only to make fun of them.

As a result, there's no shortage of reference books that record for all posterity the most obscure Oscar choices of the past. On the other hand, other awards appear out of nowhere, and disappear just as quickly. You may see something about the National Society of Film Critics, the Directors Guild award, or the Cannes Film Festival prizes over the course of the year, but as soon as the Oscars are handed out, they're forgotten . . . sometimes, even by the groups who give them. Yet often these lesser-known awards actually have more to do with what we see and don't see at our local movie theaters than the Oscars do—and they have *everything* to do with what Oscar finally ends up honoring or not honoring each March.

The fact is, Oscar is really just the end of a long line of awards throughout the movie year—and arguably not the most important one. An Oscar may add millions to a movie's take at the multiplex, but winning a Palme d'Or at Cannes or a Sundance Jury Prize is why an independent film like *Pulp Fiction* or *sex, lies, and videotape* or *The Brothers McMullen* made it to your local multiplex in the first place— and something else didn't. Critical attention and awards also play a more significant role than is generally recognized,

especially for actors. When an obscure young actor like
Leonardo DiCaprio gets a nomination and suddenly becomes
the hottest new face in town, it *isn't* because all those
80-year-old Academy voters actually left their Beverly Hills
homes to see *What's Eating Gilbert Grape?* in a theater,
or even watched the free screening cassette that they received
from the studio. It's because of the buzz that critics, and
critics' groups, created around him.

This book represents the first time that 20 of these awards
have been gathered in one place. You'll find the Oscars
here, sure, but you'll also find the Golden Globes; the most
influential critics' groups from New York and Los
Angeles; the awards from the four film festivals which have
been consistently successful in launching films and international
careers; and two awards, parallel in structure to the Oscars,
which offer perspectives different from mainstream
Hollywood's—the British Academy Awards and the
Independent Spirit Awards for independent films.

To offer a fully rounded picture of each year's favorites,
I also include awards chosen by the general public—like
the People's Choice Awards and even the MTV Movie
Awards—and, for fun, the two best-known "Worst
Movie" awards, the *Harvard Lampoon*'s and the Golden
Raspberries. Finally, for each year, I include the honor
that is the final arbiter of everything in Hollywood—the
box office scores, from *Variety.* While some of these
awards have been reprinted before, no one has ever collected
all of these in one place—and wherever possible I've
gone back to contemporary sources, to provide the most
complete and accurate listings possible.

There are plenty of interesting surprises to be found just
perusing the listings—James Bond's Miss Moneypenny
as most promising newcomer of 1948? Hugh Grant and *In
Living Color*'s David Alan Grier as prizewinners at
Venice and Berlin, years before anyone ever heard of them?
But since each year does produce its handful of consensus
award winners, I've taken advantage of the videocassette
revolution of the last few years to actually *watch* most
of the major ones—in order to provide my own critical take
on them and why they won. Many of these have long
been more written-about than seen, so this is the first book

to offer the movie and home video buff a 1-to-5-star guide to which award winners are worth seeking out—and which are better left on the shelf.

Finally, for each year I offer—with the benefit of 20–20 hindsight—my own annual winners for the major categories: Gebert's Golden Armchairs, even including worst film awards for the last 15 years. The idea of doing this isn't to suggest that my armchair critic's choices are on an equal footing with the Academy's or a Cannes jury's—it's to say that everybody's are. Feel free to scribble your own choices in next to Oscar's, Vincent Canby's, and mine, and start arguments of your own about what's best and what isn't. There are no right choices—though as all of the groups cited here prove from time to time, there are certainly wrong ones.

—Michael Gebert

Note

A couple of notes on form. Given the obscurity of many of them, I've tried to give the country of origin and director for all festival winners (and have supplied far more of this information than any previous printed source), though a few cases have still proven impossible to track down so many years later and miles away. I haven't added director or other information to films listed under the mainstream U.S. awards, figuring that if a film received commercial release in the U.S., it's findable in comprehensive reference works—if not in a capsule movie guide like Leonard Maltin's or Leslie Halliwell's, at least in the collected *New York Times* or *Variety* reviews or *The Motion Picture Guide*, all found in libraries.

And note that the year a film is eligible for the Oscars is not necessarily the same year that it played at Cannes, or even the same year that the New York critics saw it (as in *Casablanca*'s case); the awards for many films are spread out over two or more years—and chapters.

Rating System for Major Award-Winners

***** The perfect choice for that award, and essential viewing.

**** A well-deserved honor, and well worth seeking out.

*** A perfectly respectable (and watchable) choice.

** They could have chosen better then; you could do better now.

• An outright blunder—and to be avoided.

Abbreviations follow the titles of major award-winners, indicating which award groups gave major honors to that film or performer. These abbreviations, which are also used in the index, are:

AAW	Academy Awards	**MTV**	MTV Movie Awards
GLO	Golden Globes	**BAA**	British Academy Awards
DGA	Directors Guild of America	**CAN**	Cannes Film Festival
SAG	Screen Actors Guild	**VEN**	Venice Film Festival
NYC	New York Film Critics Circle	**BER**	Berlin Film Festival
SOC	National Society of Film Critics	**SUN**	Sundance Film Festival (U.S. Film Festival)
LAC	Los Angeles Film Critics Association	**IND**	Independent Spirit Award
BOR	National Board of Review	**HAR**	*Harvard Lampoon* Movie Worsts

PHO *Photoplay* Gold Medals

PEO People's Choice Awards

RAZ Golden Raspberry Awards

Who Are These People Giving Out Awards, Anyway?

"You buy a bag of peanuts in this town and they write a song about you," said Charles Foster Kane about New York. In Hollywood, the same purchase would get you a gold-plated trophy for Distinguished Consumption of Motion Picture Concessions. The Hollywood social calendar is full of everything from awards for animal actors to Service to Humanity awards . . . given to any celebrity willing to appear at the banquet at which they're awarded. If this book wasn't going to be bigger than Joel Silver's hospitality suite at Cannes, some kind of rigorous selection process had to be applied to weed out the trivial awards from the, well, *glamorously* trivial ones.

The easiest way was to go by the two things that have always mattered most in show business: fame and money. There are undoubtedly other honors that are more intelligently or perceptively awarded than some of those here. But on the whole, these are the awards shows that get the most publicity, the critical groups that truly make up Oscar's short list, the film festivals that have consistently launched films and filmmakers on international careers.

What follows is some basic background on the history, viewpoint, and procedures of each of the annual awards listed in the book. In addition to these annual awards, I've included at various points throughout the book other awards that aren't given to a particular year's films, such as the AFI Life Achievement Awards. These are described

7

where they appear, and a list of them appears in the table of contents.

The Academy of Motion Picture Arts and Sciences
1927–28 to present

The brainchild of MGM czar Louis B. Mayer, the organization that hands out the Oscars was originally planned as a company-controlled union and social club; the awards were just a sideline and the winners weren't even kept secret before the ceremony until 1931. In the mid-'30s Academy president Frank Capra, facing the threat of boycott against the Academy from the newly formed writers, directors, and actors guilds, got it out of the union business and moved it toward the more or less nonpartisan, public relations role it has held ever since. (He was rewarded for his efforts with three directing Oscars in five years.)

The precise awards have often changed over the years; the first year there were two separate Best Picture awards, as well as separate awards for Drama and Comedy Direction and one for Title Writing, a job that was soon to disappear in Hollywood. Supporting acting awards were added in 1936 (Walter Brennan won three of the first five); documentaries got an award of their own in 1941, right about the time that Hollywood directors started making documentaries for the war effort; and a foreign-language film award was finally established in 1956, after special awards had been given off and on for several years. A separate Oscar for color cinematography was added in 1939, just in time for *Gone With the Wind* to win it, while 28 years later it was the black-and-white Oscars for cinematography, costumes, and art direction that were finally eliminated. And a number of special and honorary awards have been given over the years, including the Irving G. Thalberg Memorial Award for producers and the Jean Hersholt Humanitarian Award (named for the star of *Greed*) for good works.

Voting and membership rules also changed frequently during the early years. In the first two years the awards were actually decided by a group of five Mayer cronies called the Central Board of Judges, but after a scandal over the second year's awards, the voting body was widened to about 600 members. Since the majority of them were under contract to a few major studios, however, Mayor Daley of Chicago had nothing over Mayer Louie of MGM when it came to getting the rank-and-file to turn out the vote the way he wanted. Indeed, many of the earliest awards were, to put it bluntly, fixed. As part of his reforms, in 1937 President Capra opened voting to 10,000-plus members of the major guilds, whether or not they belonged to the Academy, and as a result from the late '30s on the Oscars were basically clean and won the American way—by manipulation of public opinion, not the voting process. (Voting was again restricted to Academy members in the '50s, but by that time they were so numerous and their ties to specific studios were so much looser that the studio bosses never regained control.)

Today there are about 5,000 members, representing every area from acting and directing to sound recording, chosen for distinction in their fields (and, as a result, tending to be the older and more established members in their fields). In the nominating process members vote only for Best Picture and for the nominees in their own field; the entire membership then gets to vote for all the winners, with the exception of the short film, documentary, and foreign-film categories, which require attendance at special screenings. While it's nicely democratic that everyone gets to vote for the big awards, the fact that people not trained in fields like costume design, sound recording, or editing get to choose the winners in those categories means that those awards often go to the showiest example in their category, not necessarily the most skillful. (Actually, the winners in the lower categories often give a clue to what the night's big winner is going to be, since many voters wind up voting a straight *Last Emperor* or *Schindler's List* ticket.)

Each year the Academy issues warnings urging members not to be swayed by the gaudy publicity campaigns waged by nominees in the pages of *Variety*—and in fact, some such campaigns have backfired. They also disapprove, for no very good reason that I can see, of the one recent innovation in Oscar campaigns that really seems to be a benefit to all concerned—the mass distribution of videocassettes to members who might not have worked up the energy to catch a particular movie in a theater. The Academy urges members to regard the act of voting as a sacred trust and to fill their ballots out personally and privately, but it's impossible to believe that spouses, children, secretaries, and personal trainers don't occasionally fill out the ballot for their more famous and busy relatives and/or employers.

The Academy has always been firmly middlebrow, vaguely liberal politically, mostly conservative artistically. It's no great friend to radicals who try to push the medium forward—Martin Scorsese, Stanley Kubrick, Robert Altman, and David Lynch haven't got a Direction Oscar between them, but Robert Redford, Warren Beatty, Kevin Costner, and Sir Richard Attenborough all do. Some people feel the Academy is also prejudiced against women filmmakers, and there has been a tendency for female directors of Best Picture nominees such as Penny Marshall and Barbra Streisand to not be nominated themselves. However, the directors' branch is generally more highbrow than the other branches, and it may just be that they didn't agree that *Awakenings* or *The Prince of Tides* were award-worthy work. (Most recently, Jane Campion did get a nomination for *The Piano*—joining another foreigner, Lina Wertmuller, as the only women directors ever nominated.)

For an actor, a handicap (Cliff Robertson in *Charly*, Daniel Day-Lewis in *My Left Foot*, Al Pacino in *Scent of a Woman*) is a sure ticket to an Oscar; for actresses, it's playing an ordinary person and looking your age (Maggie Smith in *The Prime of Miss Jean Brodie*, Sally Field in *Norma Rae*, Shirley MacLaine in *Terms of Endearment*). Being English is a help (thus Day-Lewis beat out the similarly handicapped Tom Cruise in *Born on the Fourth of July*), and the next best thing, as it usually is in America, is a preppy alma mater—just ask multiple winners Katharine Hepburn (Bryn Mawr), Meryl Streep (Yale), and Jodie Foster (ditto). The Academy being mostly older folks, when it comes to actresses cute, perky, and unthreatening (Goldie Hawn, Marisa Tomei) easily beats mature, feminist, and forthright (Glenn Close, Susan Sarandon). Overall, however, the single best way to win an Oscar is to have been around a while, been nominated before, and been a good sport about it. Of the 40 Best Actor and Actress winners between 1975 and 1994, all but 11 had been nominated previously.

While it's rare that a real dog wins Best Picture these days (at worst, there's the occasional high-minded bore), other categories have been dogged by controversy. The foreign-language category nearly always goes for feelgood fluff like *Madame Rosa* or *Mediterraneo* over the latest foreign masterpieces, and its archaic system of requiring films to be nominated by a single producing country and to have substantial "content" from that country has led to the disqualification of multinational co-productions like *Europa, Europa* (which was perfect Oscar material otherwise) and *Red*. As several critics have pointed out, if the same criteria had been applied to the Best Picture category, many recent winners (Polish-filmed *Schindler's List*, Australian-directed *Driving Miss Daisy*, Chinese-shot, British-and-Hong-Kong–financed, Italian-directed *The Last Emperor*) would have been disqualified.

The documentary category has been even more contentious, with complaints that a single distributor of documentaries, Direct Cinema's Mitchell Block, who depends on the prestige of nominations and wins to sell the films he distributes to the educational market, has managed to manipulate the process to shut out any film which attracts enough attention to move out of his price range—such as *Roger & Me*, *The Thin Blue Line*, or, most notoriously, *Hoop Dreams*. Personally, I sort of admire Block for having found a way to manipulate the system in the old Mayer fashion—and certainly for a better cause than Mayer's—but clearly it's time for reform. And in 1992 the Academy nearly eliminated the short film awards on the grounds that short films were no longer a typical part of the theatrical moviegoing experience. True enough— they hadn't been since the '50s. But the Academy, with its usual razor-sharp timing, had decided to drop the categories just as short films were enjoying their widest exposure in years through programs like the Tournée of Animation, and as filler on cable channels.

All of which is to say, the Oscars are to be taken with a liberal grain of salt—but then anyone who ever watched the three-hour orgy of flubbed lines and manufactured suspense known as the Oscar telecast already knew that. Nominations for the Oscars are announced in early February; the Oscars are given in late March or early April.

Since the Oscars (unlike the other awards I list) are widely available elsewhere, in this book I have edited down the lists of winners in categories like set decoration, sound recording, etc., as well as the producing credits for Best Picture, shorts, and documentaries, to show only names that most movie buffs might recognize or want to know (e.g., Edith Head, but not her assistants). For Best Picture, I have listed studios first and producers second, without attempting to untangle to what degree projects were, say, in-house Columbia productions or Castle Rock productions merely picked up by Columbia. I have also annotated short winners, figuring that most people don't care that a cartoon was A Leon Schlesinger Production (the standard Academy listing) but might be much more interested to know that it was a Bugs Bunny cartoon by Chuck Jones. The technical awards, which are really a separate effort, and the medals of commendation for service to the Academy are not listed here for space reasons.

The Golden Globes
1943 to present

For every genuinely glamorous thing in Hollywood, there is a tackier, brassier cousin, and the Golden Globes have long been exactly that to the Oscars. The creation of the Hollywood Foreign Press Association, they follow the Academy Awards in major categories, except that since journalists are mainly interested in stars, they give twice as many acting awards (in both comedic and dramatic categories), along with awards for debuts, longevity, and everything in between.

The Association's membership is much, much smaller than the Academy—around 85 voters—and there's long been controversy over just how genuine the journalistic credentials of many of the people who belong are. When pressed about members' actual professions by *Variety* in 1993, Association president Mirjana Van Blaricom replied, firmly but not entirely reassuringly, "I do not know *one* member that is a waiter. They work as teachers, or they write books. Maybe someone used to work at a hotel, but *not* as a waiter." (In addition to filing Tinseltown stories for Yugoslavian newspapers, Van Blaricom runs Mirjana, a Beverly Hills boutique and beauty salon.)

Given the smaller and less affluent body of voters, there is general agreement that you can schmooze your way to a Golden Globe. Members readily admit that they favor stars who cooperate and make nice; "when they don't show up at the press conferences, we don't give them the goodies," is how one put it. The Globes are sort of what the Oscars would be like if they paid no attention whatsoever to outside critical opinion, and decided everything on the basis of favoritism, sentiment, and mutual back-scratching. Only the Golden Globes, given a choice between the popular hit *Butch Cassidy* and the critical favorite *Midnight Cowboy*, could wind up picking *Anne of the Thousand Days*.

Yet even the Globes could go too far. At the 1981 Globes, Pia Zadora won the New Star of the Year award—after her then-husband, Menahem Riklis, had treated nearly the entire membership to a few days in Las Vegas. "The Pia Incident" sparked not only a wave of derisive publicity, but even an FCC investigation that led for a time to the removal of the Globes show from network television. Many wondered if the Association would survive the scandal. In response, the group embarked on a general housecleaning, eliminating the more questionable awards, hiring Ernst & Young to tally the votes, and monitoring attendance at screenings to make sure that members have actually seen the movies they vote for—which, it only seems fair to point out, is more than the Oscars do. (Still, one can be forgiven for wondering if, say, the three-way tie in the Dramatic Actress category in 1988 was merely an amazing coincidence.)

While Hollywood's attitude has long been, in Warren

Beatty's words, that "the Golden Globes are fun—the Oscars are business," in the last decade their record as a predictor and possible influencer of Oscar success and box-office bonanza has led the industry to at least pretend to take them more seriously. Top stars who wouldn't have been caught dead attending the ceremony a decade ago are now happy to do so; one reason is that unlike the long and often pretentious Oscar telecast, the relaxed and bubbly Golden Globes ceremony is actually fun for the people who attend it (it even includes dinner and drinks). But the main reason for the Globes' post-Pia rise in stature is the timing of the ceremony—they're now given out at the precise moment in late January that Academy members receive their ballots, and a strong showing at the Golden Globes is considered a sure way to build momentum behind a candidate. As publicist Peggy Siegal recalled of one Globes ceremony, "When *Dances With Wolves* got three major awards and three standing ovations, Helen Keller could have told you that it was going to sweep the Oscars."

Directors Guild of America
1948 to present

The Directors Guild's main award, for best director, is rightly seen as far and away the most reliable predictor of Oscar night success. Since 1951, when the DGA began following the same calendar year as Oscar, the Best Direction Oscar and the DGA award have matched up in every year but 1968, 1972, and 1985. And the DGA winner's film has gone on to win Best Picture in all but eight of those 44 years, an .818 average. The reason, of course, is that virtually every member of the Academy's directing branch is also in the DGA, so the two voting bodies are nearly identical.

Things weren't always this cozy between the two organizations—when the DGA was founded in 1936, it was with the avowed intent of driving the Academy out of business. At the time the Academy was still functioning as a company union, and the fledgling Directors Guild attempted a boycott of the 1935 Oscars to discredit it. The Academy won that battle, but the DGA and the other guilds ultimately won the war, achieving recognition as the sole bargaining representatives for their fields while the Academy withdrew to its present public relations role.

The DGA began giving awards in 1948 on a quarterly basis and, uniquely among the awards listed here, in some years it even gave an award for distinguished film criticism. It has given a life achievement award called the D. W. Griffith Award on and off since the '50s, and has awarded Honorary Lifetime Memberships to both directors and nondirectors since the 1930s. (For the record, honorary lifetime members before the direction awards began were D. W. Griffith in 1938, Mabel Walker Willebrandt in 1939, Marshall Neilan in 1940, Frank Capra in 1941, Maurice Tourneur in 1945, and Tod Browning in 1948.) The DGA also gives a number of television awards, not listed here. The DGA awards are announced in March, a couple of weeks before the Oscars.

Screen Actors Guild
1994

The Screen Actors Guild has existed even longer than the Directors Guild, so it's surprising that it took until 1994 for them to launch an awards show. Actually, back in the '30s, SAG gave *monthly* acting awards (there actually were enough movies made then to make that possible), and since 1962 they've given a Life Achievement award. But the new Screen Actors Guild awards (for both movies and television, the latter not listed here) mark SAG's full entry into the world of awards shows, since they came complete with a network TV show—a breezy affair punctuated by amusing clips of winners' and presenters' earliest acting jobs—and with a controversy.

The first batch of nominees significantly omitted British performers (who don't, generally, belong to the Hollywood union), as well as films made outside the U.S. and thus outside Hollywood union control—including Ralph Fiennes and Paul Scofield in *Quiz Show*, Nigel Hawthorne and Helen Mirren in *The Madness of King George*, and Hugh Grant in *Four Weddings and a Funeral*. All were considered leading candidates by other award-giving groups. ''You could say that union membership has spoken in favor of union movies made in America," spokesman Harry Medved told *Variety*.

It remains to be seen what effect this controversy will have on this newest of the movie awards in its formative years—and what influence they will come to have over the other award the better-known SAG members help choose. If nothing else, it is to be sincerely hoped that the trophy, which has simply been dubbed "The Actor," will gain a better nickname (C'mon, guys! The Hammy, Sir Larry, something). The SAG awards were first given on February 25, 1995, and broadcast on NBC.

The New York Film Critics Circle
1935 to 1961, 1963 to present

The oldest major critics' group, the New York Film Critics Circle began in the mid-'30s as an effort by New York critics to influence and uplift Hollywood by promoting more artistic and socially relevant films—the *Citizen Kane*s and *Grapes of Wrath*s over the *Great Ziegfeld*s that Oscar favored. As Donald Lyons recently observed in *Film Comment*, "From its inception in 1935 until the late Sixties . . . the New York Film Critics Circle had a cachet second only to that of the Academy Awards, whose corrective conscience it was often perceived as being."

In fact, the Circle not only corrected Oscar's choices, it strongly influenced them. During the period (1940–1967) when it was dominated by the *New York Times*' lead critic Bosley Crowther, 18 of the Circle's 27 Best Motion Picture choices went on to win Best Picture Oscars—many of them precisely the kinds of pictures the group had been formed to champion, such as *The Lost Weekend* and *On the Waterfront*. Which means that you could argue that Bosley Crowther, more than anyone else, decided most of the Oscar winners during Hollywood's golden age— though since only three of Crowther's personal #1 choices for the year won the Circle's top award, it has to be admitted that his role was more that of a consensus builder than a cultural dictator.

The group was launched in late 1935 amid controversy over whether magazine critics as well as newspaper reviewers should be eligible for membership. It was finally decided to restrict membership to daily papers—as a result of which *The Morning Telegraph*, a racing sheet, had a staffer in the group, while two of the best working critics in America, *The New Republic*'s Otis Ferguson and William Troy of *The Nation*, were kept out. (You might suspect a political motive in barring the reviewers from two left-leaning publications, but the Communist *Daily Worker* held a seat from 1936 to 1951.) Initially winners were decided on a simple two-thirds majority basis, with reviewers switching votes frequently after each ballot to help speed the selection of a winner. After 1940, however, when it took a record 23 ballots to settle on Charlie Chaplin for Best Actor for *The Great Dictator*, a system was devised where movies receiving only one vote were dropped from subsequent ballots, and if no film had received a two-thirds majority after five ballots, the highest vote-getter of the sixth ballot would be made the winner.

That sort of system meant that a bloc representing less than half of the votes in a scattered field could decide a winner, just by holding out long enough. The *Times* bloc always had three or even four votes of their own, and in that era when movie reviewing was one of the few suitable employments at a newspaper for a college-educated female, there was also a faction of "lady reviewers"—led by the *Daily News*' troika of Kate Cameron, Wanda Hale, and Dorothy Masters—who held enough power to block anything they considered unseemly, such as Marlon Brando in *A Streetcar Named Desire*.

By the late '50s, the group's crusade for grown-up filmmaking had calcified into the ratification of cause-of-the-week movies like *The Defiant Ones* and pseudosophisticated entertainments like *Around the World in 80 Days*. As Donald Lyons wrote of the group's zenith in the '50s, "They were never more influential, [yet] what dreary commands New York laid down. . . . This is a group that started out honoring Ford and Hitchcock, but [had] now become blind to *The Searchers* and *Vertigo*." Bosley Crowther, often blamed for all of the group's ills, actually represented the more progressive faction in an ultraconservative group—leading losing battles to choose

Dr. Strangelove over *My Fair Lady* and *Who's Afraid of Virginia Woolf?* over *A Man for All Seasons*.

What initiated the process of reform was the newspaper strike of 1962, which thinned the ranks of newspapers (and thus newspaper reviewers) in New York, and forced the group to admit a few of the more mainstream magazines. In 1966 a group of higher-browed magazine critics founded the National Society of Film Critics, with the avowed aim of providing an opposing voice to Crowther's. Even in his last year, Crowther was reportedly powerful enough within the group to have singlehandedly denied *Bonnie and Clyde* the Best Film award. But after 1967 the *Times* retired him, and his successor, Renata Adler, was so dismayed by the way the system encouraged consensus to settle on mediocrity that she even joined the highbrows in a walkout against the very machine her paper had helped establish.

It took voting reforms the next year to finally change the character of the group. On the first ballot, critics vote for one choice each. If a candidate receives a clear majority, it wins. If nothing gets a majority, on subsequent ballots voters list three choices, the top one receiving three points, the second two points, and so on. To win, a candidate must receive the highest number of points—*and* it must appear on the ballots of at least half of the voters. This ensures that the winner truly represents the overall opinion of the group—but also enables one critic's rabid enthusiasm to count for more than another's lukewarm admiration. (Incidentally, the *Times* critics now participate only as nonvoting members.)

As a result of all the changes in rules and membership, the Circle became much more highbrow, picking foreign films for Best Film through much of the early '70s (ironically, a period when American filmmaking and Oscar's taste had improved considerably), and agreeing with Oscar on Best Picture only seven times since 1969.

So if they don't predict the Oscars, what good are the critics' awards? While few would claim that the awards directly affect ticket sales, members of all three major critics' groups are well aware that critical honors can help smaller films get the public's and the Academy's notice—or even get picked up for distribution at all. As a result, often awards are given less for purely aesthetic reasons than because they will help a particular worthy film in the marketplace.

In turn, the studios have even started sending cassettes to the critics, just as they do to Academy members, in the hopes that a critical award will translate into an Oscar—and *that* will translate into ticket sales. While at first glance that might seem farfetched, given how rarely the critics' picks match up with Oscar's final winners, you have to remember that the Academy has a lot of nomination slots to fill, and the critics play a major role in narrowing the field and in bringing attention to good performers in minor movies. (And of course, this year's nominee often becomes the hot new face who gets next year's Oscar-winning part.)

The critics' groups can also help to validate the Academy's choices. Would Academy voters, for instance, really have felt sure enough of themselves to pick a Clint Eastwood western over a gilt-edged prestige picture like *Howards End*—if two of the critics' groups hadn't already made the genre film a respectable choice?

The New York Film Critics Circle awards are announced in mid-December and awarded at a banquet in January.

The National Society of Film Critics
1966 to present

Fed up with the tradition of middlebrow quality represented by the newspaper reviewers' New York Film Critics Circle, in 1966 a group of mostly younger and uniformly higher-browed magazine-based critics including Pauline Kael, Stanley Kauffmann, Andrew Sarris, and Richard Schickel started up their own group. That year the Circle named the costume drama *A Man for All Seasons* as Best Film; the National Society picked *Blowup*. Ever since the Society has been a more raucous and provocative group, often (and often rightly) snubbing American films entirely to pick foreign films as the best films of their years.

Despite the group's name, for the first several years the membership was still mainly New York–based; not until 1972 did the Society begin in earnest to recruit members from around the country like Charles Champlin from Los Angeles and Roger Ebert from Chicago, causing one founding member, John Simon, to resign in protest at what he felt was a lowering of the group's standards. (There are even rumors of fisticuffs between Simon and another member.)

Simon may have had a point then, given that membership had grown rapidly and somewhat indiscriminately. But today the group displays a remarkably high intellectual level for a group of mostly newspaper- and mainstream-magazine–based critics—it's hard to believe that there are this many highbrow reviewers in America, making a living by quoting Godard rather than by providing quotes for *Beethoven's 2nd*. (The editorial pages should be so learned.) While New York is still strongly represented by the likes of Sarris, Schickel, David Denby (*New York*), Terrence Rafferty (*The New Yorker*), and J. Hoberman (*The Village Voice*), the roster also includes many critics who at least made their reputations beyond the Hudson, such as Kenneth Turan, Kevin Thomas, and Michael Wilmington (from Los Angeles), Dave Kehr and Jonathan Rosenbaum (Chicago), Richard T. Jameson (Seattle), and Michael Sragow (San Francisco).

Like the Circle, the National Society uses a weighted voting system and series of ballots to encourage consensus to build around the most popular titles. There are a couple of oddities in the voting procedures, however. One is that voting on Best Foreign-Language Film and Best Documentary is held off until Best Film has been chosen; if the winner *is* foreign or a documentary, there's no separate award in that category. (Actually, no documentary has ever won Best Film, though foreign films often do.) And curiously, actors are first voted on without being tied to specific films; only after somebody wins is there a vote to determine which of his or her films that year will be cited in the prize.

The deliberations are held, appropriately enough, at the Algonquin Hotel, and there's more than a little of the old Algonquin Round Table in the politicking and (mostly) good-natured bitchiness that marks the selections. For years the main rival blocs were the diehard auteurists (or Sarrisites), with their devotion to French film theory, and their mortal enemies, the Paulettes (led by Kael and including Denby, Sragow, and others), who rejected theory in favor of a sort of doctrine of whatever-moves-ya. Though auteurism was a more-or-less shared theoretical underpinning for the entire group, there's no question that through the late '80s the Paulettes dominated not only the National Society but the Critics Circle as well—especially since Kael, taking the whole business far more seriously than anyone else, reportedly lined up support for her choices by phone before the voting.

With Kael retired—we are all Paulettes now—and Sarris moving from rebel to mandarin in old age (the man has even made his peace with Billy Wilder!), a splinter radical-auteurist cell consisting of Kehr, Hoberman, and Rosenbaum has staked out a new position farther to the left, campaigning and bloc-voting for avant-garde works their fellows haven't even heard of. (They actually constitute an official Experimental Film Committee whose recommendations are taken pretty much as is.) As a result of its highbrow orientation, the National Society has the worst record in predicting Oscar winners, matching only three Best Pictures in 29 years (and two of those in 1992–93), though as noted before, that's far from the only measure of critical influence—let alone intelligence.

The National Society is the last of the major critics' groups to give its awards, actually waiting until early January before announcing their picks—which still leaves time to influence the Oscar nominations, of course.

The Los Angeles Film Critics Association
1975 to present

The Los Angeles film critics' group is the youngest and least well-known of the three big critics' groups, and also the one with the least restrictive membership criteria—with primarily only local media to draw on, the group includes in its ranks a number of freelancers and even (gasp) broadcast-based reviewers. Nevertheless, in the last few years it has become the most influential of the critics' groups and, after the Golden Globes, the award group which has the most direct influence on Oscar. In fact, you could argue that the L.A. critics are even more influential than the Globes, since the Globes mainly build support behind an existing candidate, while the critics often bring a candidate to Oscar's attention in the first place—the L.A. critics can point to several nominees who would never have gotten to the Oscar show without their support, most notably Jessica Lange's Best Actress–winning performance in the virtually unseen *Blue Sky*.

Founded in 1975, the group's initial intention was to provide a critical voice from the industry's own backyard—and also, one suspects, to raise the profile of critics in the industry's hometown. Hollywood has never regarded its local reviewers as having even the minimal influence over the public that the New York critics have, while at the same time it regards any sign of independent thinking as treason against the hometown's best-known industry.

The Association seems to have gone through three distinct phases in its politics. During its first several years, it was not only in tune with popular taste, it seemed to be *more* in tune with the public's taste than the Oscars were— the L.A. group was the only award-giving organization to even *dream* of giving its top award to *Star Wars* in 1977, to honor Kathleen Turner in *Romancing the Stone* over Meryl Streep in *Sophie's Choice*, or to pick *The Road Warrior* for best foreign film in 1981 over more traditional art-house choices like *Das Boot* or *Mephisto*. In the mid-'80s, with best film choices like *Brazil*, *Little Dorrit*, and *Do the Right Thing*, it seemed to be deliberately thumbing its nose at the studios and siding with its fellow critics' groups. Studio executives were said to have exerted pressure on the group to be more supportive of the local product, and were satisfied that they had had some effect when the L.A. critics came to agree with Oscar on choices like *Unforgiven* and *Schindler's List*.

In reality it may have been the other way around—it was clearly Oscar who had followed the critics' group's lead not only in honoring Lange for *Blue Sky*, but in giving several nominations to the little-known *Atlantic City* in

1981, favoring Sally Kirkland with an out-of-nowhere Best Actress nomination for the utterly obscure *Anna* in 1987, honoring Mercedes Ruehl with a Best Supporting Actress win for *The Fisher King* in 1991, and giving young Leonardo DiCaprio a nomination for *What's Eating Gilbert Grape* in 1993, among others.

The L.A. critics give the longest list of awards of any critical group, including awards for music, animation, a life achievement award for veterans, and the New Generation award for new talent, and an independent/experimental film prize (which lately might as well be called Best Gay Film). The awards are announced around the second week of December.

The National Board of Review
1929 to present

Today best known as the publisher of the movie buff's magazine *Films in Review*, the Manhattan-based National Board of Review actually goes back further in film history than Hollywood itself—to 1909 and the first center of the film industry, New York City. Responding to a wave of governmental movie censorship in the early years of the century, the National Board of Censorship of Motion Pictures was founded by representatives of the major studios (meaning at the time, Edison and the other Patents Trust companies), in league with progressives opposed to censorship on art-for-art's-sake grounds. Its mission, to protect children without restricting what adults could see, was similar to that of today's MPAA ratings system—but with neither the power nor the inclination to do anything more than loftily disapprove of salacious films, it was widely derided as an ineffective industry front group.

As governmental censorship boards proliferated anyway, in 1915 it changed its name to the National Board of Review of Motion Pictures, releasing lists of morally recommended films ("Motion Picture Aids to Sermons" was one) and, beginning in the late teens, giving out awards of one kind or another in the hopes of improving the industry's image. In the meantime the industry shifted to Los Angeles, and when the new moguls formed the Hays

Office to oversee motion picture content in 1922, the National Board of Review was eclipsed, a relic of the prehistoric Patents Trust age.

Deprived of its main Hollywood function (though the phrase "Passed by the National Board of Review" appears in opening credits well into the '50s), the Board evolved into a cinematic cultural organization, promoting both better Hollywood movies and an awareness of European films. For many years it was the only award group routinely honoring foreign actors, Soviet films, and other staples of the film society movement. Membership was mainly New York literary and society figures—its officers included Freud's translator, Dr. A. A. Brill, publisher Robert Giroux, and the book illustrator Lynd Ward; and the main reviewer for the Board's magazine, James Shelley Hamilton, was otherwise best known as the author of the Amherst College song (!). The group was not entirely elitist, however—other reviewers included the Marxist critic Harry Alan Potamkin and Iris Barry, shortly to co-found the Museum of Modern Art's film library.

When the world of diehard film enthusiasts was small, the prestigious National Board of Review was at its center, and *Films in Review*—the latest incarnation of many Board magazines—was its primary journal. With the explosion of art films, college film courses, and serious film writing and magazines in the late '50s and '60s, however, the Board was again eclipsed by younger competitors. Though it is often lumped with the critics' groups, the fact is that few of its members' names today would be familiar outside the pages of *Films in Review*. It is really a one of a kind in the awards world, a club of gentleman–amateur film fans whose tastes—artistically archconservative, politically Roosevelt-liberal, and relentlessly Anglophilic—clearly reveal their Upper West Side–New York social milieu. (A Screening Group of about 70 members picks its own awards, but the awards which receive publicity are those chosen by a 15-member panel called the Exceptional Photoplay Committee.)

Though the Board of Review published lists of as many as 40 exceptional photoplays each year beginning in 1920, the first awards in the modern sense were the lists of

the ten best American films and five best foreign films
published beginning in 1929. Titles were listed
alphabetically until 1934 and ranked afterwards, with the
top choice on each list being publicized as Best Film or
Best Foreign Film. Acting and directing prizes were
added in 1945, and a documentary prize was added in 1992
(some were also given during World War II). The Board
announces its prizes in December, and awards them in New
York in February or early March.

Photoplay Medal of Honor/Gold Medal
1920 to 1939, 1944 to 1968

Today *Photoplay* is remembered, if at all, as a supermarket
gossip rag that ultimately proved too tame to compete
with the *National Enquirer*s of the world, and expired in
1980. In its heyday in the late teens and '20s, however,
under editor James R. Quirk, it was the best movie magazine
in the English-speaking world, strikingly similar to
today's *Premiere* in its combination of starry-eyed celebrity
pieces and clear-eyed, often bemused examinations of
the workings of the movie business. Along with its dozens
of imitators, it played a pivotal role in creating the star
system and the cult of celebrity. And in 1920, it created the
first major American movie award, which, though forgotten
today, strongly influenced the criteria by which the Academy
Awards and nearly all subsequent awards would be given.
Writing amid mounting calls for regulation and
censorship, Quirk felt that movie producers should be
left free to make what they liked—but he also believed that
it was the duty of moviegoers to encourage producers to
raise the moral and artistic standards of the screen by
supporting superior pictures. As a result, when he
conceived the idea of a prize for the best motion picture of
the year, he strongly believed it should be decided not
by critics but by the votes of his moviegoing readers—as
he rather grandly put it, "like Abraham Lincoln's ideal
government, the photoplay is by, of and for the people." At
the same time, the criteria for voting included not only
the lavishness of the production or the quality of acting,
direction, photography, and so on, but "the ideals and

motives governing its production . . . the worth of its dramatic message." And because the producer was the one who truly decided what kind of pictures were made, the award was given to him, rather than to the director or the distributor.

All of that sounds very much like the way Academy Awards were given a few years later—and also familiar is the self-important tone: within two years Quirk was claiming the Medal of Honor was "rightly recognized as the supreme mark of distinction in the world of the motion picture," and routinely referring to it as "filmdom's Croix de Guerre" or "Nobel prize." The medallion itself, showing the masks of comedy and tragedy, was described as "a thing of beauty . . . solid gold, weighing 123½ pennyweights. It is two and one-half inches in diameter and is made by Tiffany and Co., of New York." (Kind of makes you wonder what happened to them all.)

Through the '20s *Photoplay* maintained its position on top of the movie magazine heap, and the award can be taken as a reasonably valid expression of the overall moviegoing public's taste at this time, the winners including such hits as *The Covered Wagon* and *The Big Parade*. (Like Academy voters, *Photoplay* readers equated bigness with greatness.) By the mid-1930s, however, other sources of movie star news were proliferating on radio and in newspapers, and with Quirk having died in 1932, *Photoplay* had become just another fan magazine. By this point the readership was nearly all female—as shown by the predominance of Norma Shearer and Jeanette MacDonald vehicles among the winners—and as you might expect, its influence in masculine Hollywood correspondingly declined. After the 1939 award (to *Gone With the Wind*, natch), the Medal of Honor was dropped.

Enter Dr. George Gallup. Seeking to expand his success as a political pollster into the entertainment field, Gallup formed Audience Research Inc., and in 1944 persuaded *Photoplay* to revive the Gold Medal, replacing Quirk's homely write-in campaigns with his own scientific polling of the American populace, sliced up by sex, age, frequency of moviegoing, and various other criteria. Besides a best film, the Gallup-era *Photoplay* awards included awards for male and female stars—based on overall popularity, not specific performances, which is how Bing Crosby won the male award for the first five years straight.

Photoplay and Gallup discontinued their association in the early '50s, but the awards, again based on polling of *Photoplay* readers, continued to be given for some years, announced on *The Tonight Show* by Steve Allen and later by Johnny Carson. By the '60s the results had a distinctly teenybopperish air, and showed the influence of television (the most popular male stars included *Dr. Kildare*'s Richard Chamberlain and *The Man from U.N.C.L.E*'s Robert Vaughn). The awards apparently continued to be given through the rest of the magazine's history; unfortunately, after 1968 the magazine's coverage of the awards had fallen so far behind the timing of the TV broadcast that the magazine didn't even bother to print complete sets of winners, and so no record appears to exist of the last, forgotten years of the very first pioneer among movie awards.

The People's Choice Awards
1974 to present

The Oscars may give actors and actresses a global soapbox, but this awards show has an even closer connection to soap—it was launched in the mid-'70s by Procter & Gamble, the home products giant, which does so much advertising that it has its own program production arm. In the mid-'70s someone at P&G or the networks noticed the enormous ratings popularity of awards shows— and also noticed that as star-studded TV specials went, you couldn't get much cheaper than a single-set awards fest with a few production numbers thrown in.

The awards, which are also given to TV shows and recording artists (not listed here), might seem like the epitome of the made-up award show, but they do have one distinction: like their predecessor, the *Photoplay* Medal of Honor, the winners really are chosen by the public, via statistically sound research conducted by the Gallup Organization. As a result, they provide a sort of benchmark of the general public's taste to compare against the other awards—though, as with the *Photoplay* awards, the awards

for actors are based on popularity, not specific roles, and
may or may not coincide with a particular movie that year.

The polling actually has two parts: first a sample is polled
by telephone to name, without any suggestions from the
interviewer, their favorites in each category, producing three
nominees for each. Then another group is polled to choose
winners from those three nominees. Methodologically,
there's no particular reason for this two-part structure,
but it does allow for the traditional award show nominations-
and-winners format. The polling is also scrupulous
enough to count results that fall within the standard deviation
as ties—no doubt despite the occasional urging of
network types to settle things with a coin toss. The People's
Choice Awards are given in March, shortly before the Oscars.

The MTV Movie Awards
1991 to present

Like a high schooler turning in a term paper months after
the school year is over, the MTV Movie Awards lope
into view in June, well after the regular award season has
come to its climax with the Oscars. Sort of the "Young
People's Choice Awards," the MTV Movie Awards aim to
commemorate the way MTV viewers really consume
movies—besides Best Movie and Best Male and Female
Performances, the categories include things like Best
Kiss, Most Desirable Male and Female, and Best Villain.

There's no doubt that MTV viewers see the movies a little
differently from other people—in 1994 an obscure actress
named Alicia Silverstone was nominated for Most Desirable
Female, Best Villain, and Best Breakthrough
Performance for a little-seen independent film called *The
Crush*. How did she do it? Well, to be honest, if few
viewers had seen her in that, lots of them had apparently
gone schwing! for her in her three Aerosmith videos.
Likewise, it's not terribly surprising to see that in the minds
of MTV voter-viewers, Best Female Performance and Most
Desirable Female seem to be essentially the same thing.
(Interestingly, females have so far dominated the Best
Villain category as well—draw your own sociological
conclusions.) On the other hand, the kids have shown on

at least a few occasions that they can be as serious-minded as Oscar—they picked the serious ghetto drama *Menace II Society* for best film one year, and Tom Hanks in *Philadelphia* the same year (for Best Actor, that is, not Best Kiss).

The MTV Movie Awards are chosen by viewers on a write-in basis in the first half of each year and are announced on a star-filled, half-serious, half-ironic telecast in June.

The British Academy of Film and Television Arts
1947 to present

The British Film Academy was founded after World War II by a group of British filmmakers to honor and promote their home film industry, which was at a particular high point then in the heady days of *Henry V, The Red Shoes, Brief Encounter*, etc. In 1948 it began giving awards (for films of 1947), modeled on the Oscars and officially called the British Academy Awards. (A nickname, the Stellas, didn't stick.) In 1959 it merged with a television group to take its present name, and it has since opened a branch in Los Angeles as well.

Where most national awards shows only honor their own country's output, the British Academy has always officially opened its awards to the rest of the world. Nevertheless, most years still showed strong favoritism for the local product—Peter Finch alone won *five* of the Best Actor awards between 1956 and 1976. But since the mid-'80s, the awards have been increasingly dominated by Hollywood and the continent—a fact that has fed Britain's perennial insecurity about the health of its national film industry. The low point had to be 1990, when Billie Whitelaw's supporting nomination for *The Krays* was the only major nomination to go to *any* British film.

Yet conservatism on the part of the Academy's membership has to be blamed, too, for the fact that relevant and artistically important British films of the '80s, such as *My Beautiful Laundrette, Distant Voices, Still Lives, The Draughtsman's Contract*, and *High Hopes*, were overlooked in favor of such lighter-weight entries as *Educating Rita, Jean de Florette*, or *Dead Poets Society*. If British

filmmaking could claim *anything*, it was good writers
like Dennis Potter, Hanif Kureishi, and Richard Curtis—
and yet Woody Allen managed to win five of the ten
original screenwriting awards between 1977 and 1986. (To
be fair, some of those more adventurous films were
produced for Britain's Channel Four, and competed on the
television side of the awards.) The irony of all this, of
course, is that Hollywood has never been so Anglophilic as
during the '80s and early '90s, with Oscars by the
truckload going to movies like *Chariots of Fire*, *Gandhi*,
and *Howards End*, and to players like Ben Kingsley,
Anthony Hopkins, Daniel Day-Lewis, and Emma
Thompson. As Oscar-winner Michael Caine recently put
it, "The British film industry is alive and well and living
in Los Angeles."

The awards are usually given in March or April. The
British Academy Awards duplicate most of the categories of
the Oscars, including technical awards and short films, plus
(as noted) awards for television; for space reasons this
book lists only the picture, acting, directing and writing
awards, along with notations of short or documentary
film winners when the winners are well-known. Special
awards also listed include a life achievement award called
the Academy Fellowship, first given to Hitchcock, and the
Michael Balcon Award, named for the longtime head of Ealing
Studio, given for "outstanding British contribution to
cinema."

Cannes International Film Festival
1946 to 1947, 1949, 1951 to 1967, 1969 to present

There is a film festival each year where, after appreciative
screenings of the finest in international film, members of
the public retire to their favorite cafés to discuss the art of
cinema in fluent French. It's called the Montréal World
Film Festival, and it's held every August in that charming
city. On the other hand, Cannes, the most famous film
festival in the world, is to the movies what a convention in
Vegas is to any other industry: a gaudy, giddy orgy of
self-promotion, wheeler-dealing, and public drunkenness—
only with foreign films thrown in.

Everywhere, from the bars in the hotels along the Croisette to the yachts anchored offshore, Italian brokers try to convince Peruvian TV executives to take their Israeli-made TV series with fading American stars. At the state-of-the-art Palais des Festivals (aka "Le Bunker"), a black-tie crowd snoozes and schmoozes through the latest masterpieces, while in the smaller theaters in town, exploitation films run nonstop in what Roger Ebert has called "a tribute to the industry's unflagging optimism that new ways can be found to combine tits, ass, and machine guns." Everywhere you look, press and paparazzi are yapping and snapping away with an intensity that would make a Kennedy feel neglected. And somehow amid all this frenzy, a small jury of distinguished filmmakers and critics manages to find time to screen the two dozen or so films in competition and award the most prestigious film festival prize in the world, the Palme d'Or (Golden Palm).

The first Festival International du Film got off to a bad start, running behind schedule . . . seven years behind, to be exact. It was set to begin September 1, 1939; Hollywood stars like Gary Cooper, Tyrone Power, and Mae West crossed the Atlantic to attend, and a replica of the cathedral from *The Hunchback of Notre Dame* was erected on the beach, inaugurating a Cannes tradition of surreally oversized promotional structures (*Pirates*' ship, *The Last Action Hero*'s inflatable Arnold, Edy Williams). In fact, *Hunchback* would be the only film shown—Hitler had invaded Poland that morning, and the festival was called off the next day. They tried again in 1946 and managed to get through the whole two weeks that time, but the early years were often plagued by money troubles and disputes within the French film industry, and the festival failed to happen at all in two of its first five years.

The seminal event in making Cannes' reputation came in 1954, when French starlet Simone Sylva dropped her bikini top and used Robert Mitchum's torso to conceal her charms from the cameras. The photo was reprinted (or at least described by the more bashful papers) worldwide, and established Cannes as a happening place, a sort of United Nations of movies where films and filmmakers from all over the world could meet (and party) on neutral ground. Festival director Robert Favre Le Bret, horrified at the salacious reputation his serious film event had gained, recruited Grace Kelly to bring some female class to Cannes the next year—a PR gambit that paid off beyond his wildest dreams: during her visit she met Prince Rainier of nearby Monaco, and the next year Cannes was held early so that festival goers could also attend their wedding. More serious trouble struck in 1968: Cannes' schedule put it smack in the middle of the May 1968 student uprising, and as turmoil swept through France (and France's top directors ran to join the students at the barricades), the festival shut down halfway through, awarding no prizes. The next year it went on as if nothing had happened.

Until 1972 films in competition were chosen by the entering countries—with the result that Hollywood often tried to force big commercial potboilers on the festival, inevitably denouncing the festival as anti-American or rigged when they failed to beat Fellini for the Palme d'Or. Today the films in competition are all chosen by one man, festival director Gilles Jacob, equal parts dictator in his running of the festival and diplomat in his wooing of stars and directors. As at most festivals, only those films entered in the competition (or Official Selection) can compete for the jury prizes, and often more interesting films are to be found in the sidebar series. The best known of these are the Quinzaine des Réalisateurs, or Directors' Fortnight, for new filmmakers—the main legacy of the '68 protests; the Critics' Week; and Un Certain Regard, which translates roughly as Your Movie Isn't Quite Good Enough for the Competition, But We'll Show It Anyway in the Hope That You'll Be Back with Something That Is.

Hollywood wisdom has long held that there is less to be gained commercially from winning the Palme d'Or than there is to be lost by trying for it and publicly failing, and American films often opt instead for the safer prestige of being the Opening or Closing Night selection. Spike Lee, however, has added a new wrinkle to this by getting more publicity out of twice losing the Palme d'Or than most winners get for winning it.

Spike aside, America has done well at Cannes in recent years, winning the Palme d'Or three years straight in

1989–91 and again in 1994. But those winners were mostly independent films, and there has been concern about the shortage of big Hollywood films the last couple of years—in competition or out. In 1994 there was even the suggestion that a backlash against French protectionist measures was responsible for American movies staying home, but the real reason is probably simpler. The major studio pictures that are ready to be screened in May are generally the big summer blockbusters. They're unlikely to win anything to begin with, and worse than that, they have everything to lose if they turn out to be dogs—and that fact is revealed to the international press several weeks before their U.S. release. (There has been talk recently of moving the festival back to the fall, when more quality American films would be available.)

Cannes' prize structure seems impenetrable at first glance, but it's actually fairly simple. The jury awards the Palme d'Or (simply called the Grand Prize until 1955) and the Grand Special Jury Prize (shortened to Special Jury Prize here, to avoid confusion). Officially the Palme d'Or is for the best film overall, while the Special Jury Prize is for the most original or innovative film—but usually it's seen as simply first and second place. Along with the two best film prizes, the jury gives awards for acting, direction, and the like, as well as one or two plain-vanilla Jury Prizes, which can go to a film, a person, or whatever they choose. The custom is to spread the awards around to as many worthy films and countries as possible; when *Barton Fink* became the first film to take the Palme d'Or, Best Actor and Best Direction prizes, it wasn't just that it had made Cannes history, but that the jury had deliberately broken one of the festival's main unwritten rules. The award presentation itself is a legendarily embarrassing event, pulled off with all the élan of a cable-access show, and controversial selections are often accompanied by boos from the audience.

Every major festival is accompanied by a host of semi-official awards given by groups ranging from movie magazines to ecumenical organizations; there are three such awards at Cannes which are well-established enough to also be worthy of inclusion here. The most prestigious is

the Camera d'Or for best first feature, open to any film
shown but usually won by something in the Directors'
Fortnight, since it's for new filmmakers. It originally
involved the presentation of an actual 16mm camera to the
winner; today it includes a cash prize put up by Kodak.
Also highly regarded is the award for technical achievement,
given by the French Technical High Commission. And
third, FIPRESCI, the international organization of film
critics and journalists, gives International Critics Prizes
to films in and out of competition; the critics' prizes are
often seen as a more objective corrective to the jury prizes in
years when the jury may have been influenced by politics
more than aesthetics. (There's also a parallel jury prize
structure for the short-film competition; I've listed only the
better-known winners of these.)

If you've always dreamed of going to Cannes, you should
know that while it is a wildly entertaining circus, it is
also first and foremost a business event. Almost any other
film festival on earth is more inviting to non-industry
types—not to mention more accommodating to the business
of seeing and appreciating good movies. But if you do
decide to go, at least remember this crucial piece of advice:
it's pronounced "can," not "con," or, God forbid,
"cans."

Venice International Film Festival
1932, 1934 to 1942, 1946 to 1968, 1980 to present

Though not the first film festival in history, the Mostra
del Cinema held on Venice's Lido is by far the oldest
film festival still active today, and the prototype of the
modern film festival. Which makes Benito Mussolini the
rarely acknowledged father of the film festival movement.

One of Mussolini's favorite PR showcases for his new
Italy was the Venice Biennale, a biennial festival of the
arts which had been founded in the late 19th century.
Totalitarians usually having a keen appreciation for the
power of cinema as a popular art form, in 1932 he added
film to the Biennale's program. And so it was arguably
here that movies for the first time were given equal stature
with painting and music as an art form, though even here

movies weren't on *quite* the same intellectual footing—distinguished art critics judged the paintings, but the attending masses got to vote on the best movies. (The actual idea for a film festival is usually credited to Count Volpi, a Venetian civic leader and head of the Biennale who also happened to own the Excelsior, the Lido hotel that is still the festival's nerve center.)

The film festival proved to be so popular that after its second Biennale appearance in 1934 it was spun off as its own annual event; in 1937 the film festival even got its own Palazzo del Cinema, where many of the films are still shown today. As the world moved closer to World War II, however, controversy erupted over favoritism toward German and Italian films (though it's hard to argue, at least aesthetically, with the Mussolini Cup to Leni Riefenstahl's documentary *Olympia*). Angered also by Mussolini's restrictions on American films in Italy, U.S. studios refused to participate in 1939, and once war erupted, it became strictly an Axis event, finally being suspended after 1942.

After the war, with international attention focused on Italian neorealist filmmakers like Rossellini and De Sica, Italian cinema experienced a great resurgence, and in 1946 the festival resumed, finding its niche over the next few years as a more serious, artistically oriented alternative to the blatantly commercial Cannes. Perhaps its most impressive early achievement was helping to popularize Japanese cinema by, among other things, giving the top prize to Kurosawa's *Rashomon* in 1951. Rediscoveries were also a hallmark of Venice: von Stroheim had a near-complete retrospective in 1958, just months after his death, Tod Browning's *Freaks* had its first showing off the exploitation circuit in decades at the '62 festival, and in 1965, just months before his death, Buster Keaton received a standing ovation from a capacity crowd.

In the early '60s festival director Luigi Chiarini alienated Hollywood by rejecting American films (notably Robert Rossen's *Lilith*) which he felt didn't measure up to Venice's aesthetic standards; the result was simply to drive Hollywood more firmly into Cannes' open arms. Following the aborted Cannes festival of 1968, the Venice festival decided to stop giving awards (ranking films against each other seemed so *bourgeois*) and to focus strictly on exhibition and retrospectives. With no awards to aim for, filmmakers and distributors had even less reason to send their films to Venice. The ongoing political turmoil in Italy through the '70s made the festival an erratic affair, and in 1972 it basically expired, replaced through most of the '70s by other, smaller film events of often merely local interest.

In 1979 a new director, Carlo Lizzani, relaunched the festival (though only critics' groups gave awards that year). But Venice is still trying to regain its former prestige. It is hampered by the lack of an attached film market (instead, there's MIFED a few weeks later in Milan), by screening facilities hardly changed since 1937, and by the fact that its top posts were until very recently political appointments. In the early '90s Hollywood was also miffed by the fact that Venice served as the center for much of the European film industry's protectionist talk. Faced with an angry Hollywood, festival chief Gillo Pontecorvo, director of the anticolonialist classic *The Battle of Algiers*, worked hard to placate the California conquistadors—a task in which he has been aided by a quirk of American movie production: with Hollywood producers reluctant to expose many of their $100-million summer blockbusters to the world press at Cannes in May, Venice's September slot has become a natural place to showcase the more serious-minded and prestigious releases of the fall. (And the Lido *is* awfully nice that time of year.)

As noted above, Venice's first prizes were the results of an audience poll; 1934 was the first year that awards were chosen by a professional jury. The best film prizes during 1934–42 were often known as the Mussolini Cup; in 1950 the top prize became known as the Leone d'Oro or Golden Lion of St. Mark, after Venice's patron saint, while the acting prizes are Volpi Cups, named for that patron saint of rather more recent vintage, and the directing, writing, and cinematography prizes are the Osella d'Oro. Venice's official award structure is fairly straightforward compared to Cannes', but it seems safe to say that no festival has ever spawned more unofficial honors—by 1968 there were more than 20 hangers-on, given by everyone from the City

of Venice to the Italian movie magazine *Cinema Nuovo*.
The only ones of any particular note are the Gold Medals
given by the Italian Senate, the International Critics Prizes
given by FIPRESCI, and the assorted Italian Critics Prizes,
including some named for the documentary filmmaker
Francesco Pasinetti. Besides the film awards, Venice gives
awards to everything from children's films to TV
commercials; only the major film awards are listed here.

Berlin International Film Festival
1951 to 1969, 1971 to present

Germans having a reputation for efficiency, the
Internationale Filmfestspiele Berlin—or Berlinale as it
is known, punning on the Venice "Biennale"—is widely
regarded as the best-run of the major festivals, combining
Venice-quality programming at the festival proper with
Cannes-style wheeling and dealing at the adjacent
European Film Market. The festival was founded in 1951,
and benefited in its early years from the encouragement
of the American occupying authority and, later, the State
Department, which took considerable interest in the
health and well-being of the West German metropolis located
deep within the borders of East Germany.

On the other hand, Berlin's growth in its early years was
hampered by FIAPF, an international film producers'
organization which, at a time when film festivals were
sprouting everywhere, was attempting to maintain Venice
and Cannes' monopoly as the major competitive festivals.
Without FIAPF's imprimatur, Berlin could not assemble
a first-class international jury, and in its early years it gave
mainly audience awards. Finally FIAPF blessed Berlin
as the third major stop on the festival calendar (resulting in
the replacement of the audience awards with a jury in
1956), and as Venice self-destructed in the '60s and '70s,
Berlin came to be recognized, as it is today, as the second
most important international festival.

Perhaps because the German commercial film industry
was so moribund during Berlin's first two decades, Berlin
early on acquired a reputation as a key showcase for
independent filmmakers, short films, and other

noncommercial areas of cinema. Berlin's status as a buffer zone between the West and the Soviet bloc also led it to give political and leftist films a prominent place they did not always enjoy at other festivals, though the Eastern bloc was barred in the early years and most of those countries continued to boycott it until 1975 (only a few Eastern bloc rebels, such as Yugoslavia, participating).

Berlin has had its controversies. In 1970, a controversy over *O.K.*, a German film about a rape-murder by American soldiers in Vietnam, led to the jury disbanding and the Berlinale closing down, as Cannes had two years earlier. In 1979 it was an American film about Vietnam, *The Deer Hunter*, that caused the Soviet bloc to walk out, just four years after they'd finally started attending the festival. In 1982, with the Eastern bloc carefully wooed back, the festival turned down *Night Crossing*, a minor thriller about a family escaping East Germany by balloon, for the prestigious opening-night slot (a decision justifiable on either diplomatic or artistic grounds), only to find the film's producer and the right-wing Springer press cynically exploiting the festival's "censorship." And in 1986, jury member Gina Lollobrigida, of all people, tried singlehandedly to prevent the awarding of the Golden Bear to *Stammheim*, a film about the Baader-Meinhof terrorist trial which she felt to be of purely German interest.

But overall Berlin's history has been reasonably uneventful—with the exception of its unfortunate move in 1978 from balmy June–July to chilly February (mainly to give the Market a more competitive spot on the calendar). Besides the competition, Berlin includes a very highly regarded series similar to Cannes' Directors' Fortnight, the Forum of Young Cinema (like the Cannes event, a response to the turmoil of the '60s), which has given early exposure to filmmakers like Wim Wenders, Nagisa Oshima (whose *In the Realm of the Senses* was briefly confiscated by the Berlin public prosecutor), Jim Jarmusch, and, in perhaps its finest moment, Claude Lanzmann's epic Holocaust documentary *Shoah*. And there is a retrospective series, which among other things had the splendid idea in 1983 of honoring actors who had fled Hitler in 1933 (including *Casablanca*'s Curt Bois and Wolfgang Zilzer—the pickpocket and the man shot for having no papers).

The top film prize is the Golden Bear, and the awards for runners-up and for acting, directing, etc., are Silver Bears. (In this book, "Silver Bear" indicates a runner-up film prize, while the other prizes are simply listed as Actor, Director, etc.) Like Cannes, Berlin has a parallel short-film prize structure; only the more familiar and noteworthy winners are listed. And as at Cannes, there are the international critics' prizes awards given by FIPRESCI, the critics' association, for films both in and out of competition.

Sundance Film Festival (U.S. Film Festival) 1978 to 1979, 1981 to present

In the last few years, the Sundance Film Festival has emerged from the pack of smaller film festivals to become the key film event for independent films, as important a stop on a studio executive's calendar as Cannes or Aspen over Christmas. That's not a bad trick for a festival that was originally founded as a *retreat* from market pressures for independents—more a workshop than a festival.

Sundance got its start as the United States Film Festival in Salt Lake City in the fall of 1978, but it really got going in 1981 when it moved to January and to the tiny ski town of Park City, Utah. The obvious model for its organizers (including Robert Redford, whose Sundance Institute would be founded two years later) was the Telluride Film Festival, an intimate, uncommercial, and retrospective-oriented event that had been founded in *that* hippie ski town precisely because its remoteness and lack of Beverly Hills–level amenities would keep the hardcore limousine crowd out. Park City offered the same benefits of scenery and seclusion, as well as a neat irony: nearby is the silver mine that launched the Hearst family fortune— and thus, indirectly, launched the patron saint of independent filmmakers, Orson Welles, on his career with *Citizen Kane*.

The offerings at the U.S. Film Festival in its first decade tended to be the kind of independents associated with the Sundance Institute and PBS's *American Playhouse* series—small, character-driven dramas about rural life, ethnic culture, and young girls coming of age, like Richard Pearce's *Heartland*, Wayne Wang's *Chan Is Missing*, and Joyce Chopra's *Smooth Talk*. As well-made as many of these films were, and as pleasant as it was to see films about teenagers that weren't *Animal House* clones (or to see films about ethnic Americans at all), with their conservative styles and subject matters these films often reinforced, rather than challenged, how marginal non-studio filmmaking was to the movie business.

Certainly none of these films had the impact on the public or critics of '60s independent groundbreakers like Robert Frank's and Jack Kerouac's *Pull My Daisy*, John Cassavetes' *Shadows*, or *Easy Rider*; they were closer to harmless "little film" art-house hits such as *The Little Fugitive* or *Lilies of the Field*. Ex-independents such as David Lynch, Philip Kaufman, and Martin Scorsese were making more artistically adventurous films within the studio system (*The Elephant Man*, *The Right Stuff*, *King of Comedy*) than their old comrades were on the outside; and when a stylistically fresh film did come along, like Jim Jarmusch's *Stranger Than Paradise*, it found funding not from American public television but from West German TV.

1989, the year the festival finally changed its name to Sundance, is usually considered the watershed year; I think that the real turning point was 1985, a year after the Sundance Institute took over management of the festival. That year the Grand Jury Prize went to a stylistically audacious genre film, Joel and Ethan Coen's *Blood Simple*, which said nothing about life on a farm (except maybe to make sure your victim is dead before you bury him on one), but everything about how much fun the crime genre could be in the hands of a couple of ingenious movie buffs. The Coens' stress on style was still the exception at the U.S. Film Festival, however. 1989's reputation as the year that *made* Sundance stems from the fact that it saw Sundance's first real commercial success: Steven Soderbergh's *sex, lies, and videotape*, in many ways the ultimate Sundance film, on the one hand an intelligent, character-driven regional drama—and on the other, a stylish,

commercially canny exercise in up-to-the-minute
kinkiness, with a cast of attractive yuppies.

Picked up by Miramax, *sex, lies, and videotape* ultimately
grossed over $100 million worldwide, and established
Sundance as the place where Hollywood could discover the
next hot thing. Among the next hot things to follow were
House Party, *Slacker*, and *Reservoir Dogs* (which polarized
the festival with its very unSundancelike violence, and
left without an award). Today, late January sees Park City
swell to bursting with Hollywood types eager to spot the
latest trend, sign the latest Tarantino, and otherwise pick up
deal-making conversations where they left off at
Morton's.

That has led to criticism that Sundance has turned into a
purely Hollywood event, where fresh young talent
eagerly parades for the chance to be snapped up and ruined
by the studios. Indeed, more and more, the so-called
independents include consummate insiders: in 1995, the
young "unknowns" whose short-film debuts were on the
program at Sundance included Lyle Lovett, David Koepp—
better known as the screenwriter of *Jurassic Park*—and
Tom De Cherchio, who had already been hired to direct
what was then *Ace Ventura Goes to Africa*. Likewise, the
festival's two greatest successes have spawned their own
minigenres of wannabes—if the typical film of Sundance
'85 was a rural farm drama like *Stacking*, the typical film
today is either a watered-down slacker talkfest like
Bodies, Rest & Motion or an imitation-Tarantino art-house
shoot-'em-up like *Things to Do in Denver When You're
Dead*, in either case designed less to express its filmmaker's
vision than to get him a Hollywood job.

In short, Sundance has become such a spectacular success
that it may be about to collapse of its own weight.
Screening facilities are so limited (relative to the crowds)
that the real bigwigs don't even bother to see the movies
there; the moguls screen what's going to be at Sundance
ahead of time in their own screening rooms, and spend
the festival itself schmoozing and skiing. And competition
for a slot at one of the few screening facilities has gotten
so fierce that in 1995 a group of rejected filmmakers launched
a rival event, Slamdance, screening their films in a hotel's

conference room. (Sundance officials were torn between dismissing the rivals as no threat and envying them for having the old Sundance spirit.)

Redford and fest director Geoff Gilmore have talked about pulling the plug on Sundance when it stops serving the filmmakers and only serves Hollywood. But what really seems to be happening is that as Sundance's brand of independent becomes increasingly the mainstream, a second festival is growing up inside it which still serves the original Sundance goal of giving commercially marginal films exposure. Gay film has been an increasingly high-profile area at Sundance, with everything from the feelgoodish lesbian comedy *Go Fish* to Gregg Araki's outrageous, bitter *The Living End*. And documentaries have remained important; in addition to *sex, lies,* Sundance '89 also showcased the most talked-about documentary of recent times, Michael Moore's *Roger & Me,* and more recent documentary successes have included *Hoop Dreams, A Brief History of Time, Paris Is Burning,* and *Crumb.* It would not be at all surprising if, in the next few years, Sundance's split personality manifests itself in an actual split between the commercially minded Sundance of *Reservoir Dogs* and the more iconoclastic Sundance of *The Living End.*

While the focus remains on American independents, the festival has also started showcasing selected foreign films in various side series (*Four Weddings and a Funeral* had its U.S. debut there in '94), and for several years an assortment of each year's best has traveled to Tokyo for a mini-Sundance in that city. (A Beijing version was launched in 1995.) Until 1988 Sundance's only awards were juried awards—a Grand Jury Prize and assorted Special Jury Prizes, which could go to actors, cinematographers, and the like. Beginning in 1989 the festival was divided into a dramatic and a documentary competition—though only about 20 of the nearly 100 films screened each year actually compete—and a number of other awards have been added. The tiny four-member jury has often taken a rap for favoring the obscure over the popular (isn't that what festival juries are for?), and the Audience Awards, voted on (rather unscientifically) after screenings by anyone who chooses to stick around and fill out a ballot, may be more revealing—if not of what was actually best at Sundance, at least of what the biggest buzz was about. (Certainly the Audience Awards' track record in predicting subsequent theatrical success is a good deal better than the jury prizes'.)

Other prizes include a Filmmakers' Trophy, chosen by prominent filmmakers at the festival, a cinematography award, a screenwriting award named for veteran screenwriter Waldo Salt (*Midnight Cowboy*), and the Freedom of Expression award for documentaries. The complete Sundance awards are printed here for the first time anywhere.

Independent Spirit Awards
1985 to present

Sundance honors only those American independent films which appear at the festival (admittedly, a pretty high proportion of the total); the Independent Spirit Awards honor the whole range of American independent filmmaking throughout the year. Though little-known to the general public—apart from those who've caught their award ceremony on the Bravo cable channel—in the decade that they've existed, the Spirit awards have become an increasingly visible and trendy Hollywood event, attracting many of Hollywood's hipper figures (Holly Hunter, Danny Glover, Oliver Stone) to serve as presenters and honorary chairs, and routinely selling out an awards show which has been staged everywhere from the Hollywood Roosevelt Hotel to a tent on Santa Monica beach.

The awards are given by the Independent Feature Project/ West, the California branch of an independent filmmaking advocacy and support group. The Spirit awards have their roots in an earlier award, the FINDIE ("Friends of Independents") awards, launched in 1984 by the IFP and others. Despite a witty trophy (a shoestring in Plexiglas, symbolizing what independent filmmakers make their films on), the FINDIE awards didn't take off, and so they were relaunched in 1986 (for the 1985 film year) as the Independent Spirit Awards with the organizational help of the L.A. film festival Filmex. (The shoestring trophy was replaced at this time by a more conventional sculpture of a bird clutching a strip of film.) Buck Henry began a regular gig as emcee the next year, establishing an irreverent, free-speaking atmosphere for the awards, which has undoubtedly done much to make them a popular social event—thank too many people in your acceptance speech, and Henry will hit his buzzer to send you offstage. Among the distinguished figures who have kicked off the evening with a keynote speech honoring the struggle of the independent filmmaker are Neil Jordan, Kevin Costner, David Puttnam, Louis Malle, and Martin Scorsese (twice).

Awards presently are given in twelve categories—besides the expected ones, they include Best First Feature, First Screenplay, and Debut Performance, as well as a Foreign Film award (which lately might as well be called the Jane Campion's Latest Film award). Where Sundance was set up to promote the traditional low-budget and regional-based indie film, the Independent Spirit's focus has always been more toward medium-budget independents such as *Platoon* and *The Player*—what might more accurately be called "alternative" Hollywood films, films that are made outside Hollywood's mainstream but within the industry's definition of what constitutes a commercially releasable feature film. (The "feature" part is taken seriously, too— unlike at Sundance, there are no awards for shorts or documentaries.)

In fact, the precise definition of either "independent" or "foreign" has caused some problems in recent years, especially since prominent "independents" like Miramax and Fine Line/New Line have now actually become subsidiaries of entertainment conglomerates like Disney and Turner. In 1993, Gramercy Pictures' *A Dangerous Woman* was yanked from the ballot when it was revealed that a major studio had contributed to its financing; the recognition that the disqualification of Miramax in particular would decimate the indie scene led the next year to the adoption of looser guidelines which allow quasi-independent films made with some measure of big-studio backing. The establishment of the three "first film" categories has enabled traditional no-budget indies like *El Mariachi* and *Straight Out of Brooklyn* to compete for those prizes, while keeping the group's focus on films like *Pulp Fiction*, which have more commercial opportunity to benefit from the attention.

Eyebrows were also raised when, for 1994's awards, the Taiwanese-made *Eat Drink Man Woman* earned five nominations (including Best Picture), rather than being consigned to the Foreign Film category; the reason was that with a Taiwan-born U.S. citizen for director and Americans among the producers and co-writers, the film did meet official criteria stating that at least two out of the three major creative areas be filled by Americans.

Taken all together, these controversies suggest that American independent status is less a fact than a state of mind. The membership of the organization votes on all prizes with the exception of the Someone To Watch award, a $20,000 cash prize given to a promising new filmmaker. The Independent Spirit Awards are given in late March, and broadcast on Bravo; the complete awards are published here for the first time.

Harvard Lampoon Movie Worsts
1939 to 1941, 1944 to 1946, 1948 to 1983, 1990, 1992, 1994

On Bow Street in Cambridge sits a brick building that looks like the unnatural offspring of the Sphinx and a fireplug. At first glance, it might be one of those secret Ivy League societies that trains tomorrow's CIA functionaries; actually, it's probably training tomorrow's writers for the David Letterman show. It's the home of the *Harvard Lampoon*, the oldest humor magazine in America, whose alumni have included William Randolph Hearst, E. L. Thayer (author of "Casey at the Bat"), John Reed, Robert Benchley, John Updike, *Spy* co-founder Kurt Andersen, most of the founders of the *National Lampoon*, and, most recently, Conan O'Brien. More to the point, it's the home of the oldest worst movie awards in America, which were given almost every year from 1939—when *The Wizard of Oz* won the "Most Colossal Flop" prize— to 1983.

Each year the *Lampoon* named its ten worst films and gave out worst acting awards named in honor of Kirk Douglas and Natalie Wood, plus, depending on the whims of the writers, such august honors as the Charles Manson Memorial Scalpel for worst editing, the Please-Don't-Put-Us-Through-DeMille-Again for the picture "which best embodies the pretentions, extravagances and blundering ineffectiveness of the traditional Screen Spectacular," the Handlin Oscar (named for a famous Harvard history professor) for the film which most distorted history, and the Golden Glob for sex scenes.

At times the sense of humor was preppy–white-guy–snotty and could border on cruel—especially in the way they went after certain actresses year after year. But at their best—the '50s through the '70s—the *Lampoon* awards displayed intelligence and a considerable consistency of satiric purpose in going after the overblown pretensions of Biblical epics, Cinemascope soap operas, illiterate literary adaptations, and alleged art films—not to mention the pretensions of award shows and critics who honored such things. (It's also fortunate that the *Lampoon* lists are next to the box office charts in this book, since they often have the most in common with each other.) Once or twice, Hollywood attempted to show that it could take the joke; both Natalie Wood and Elizabeth Taylor were among the stars who actually traveled to Cambridge to accept their Worst Acting awards. Instead of a trophy, they received a grown, hairy man in a gold lamé leotard.

For many years the *Lampoon* had the Movie Worsts field to themselves, but by the mid-'80s the world was flooded with such things, and after the '83 awards the 'Poonies pooped out. There have been only a few halfhearted or facetious attempts since—as the *Lampoon*'s librarian described it, "all sort of meta-Worsts, in that they express the unwillingness we have to dredge up this tired premise one more time for the sake of tradition." Another reason might be that with the *Lampoon* sensibility having traveled (via the *National Lampoon*) into movies and TV, '80s and '90s 'Poonies have aspired toward Hollywood more than they wanted to skewer it—note, in 1982, the awarding of "The Embarrassing *Lampoon* Graduates Certificate" to *Airplane II*: *The Sequel*.

Since the awards often ran for pages (and nothing is deader than a 40-year-old joke about a forgotten dog), in this book I've narrowed them down to the ten worst films list and the worst actor and actress awards (when given), plus a sampling of the most entertaining awards from each year. For subscription information, write the *Harvard Lampoon*, 44 Bow Street, Cambridge, MA 02138.

The Golden Raspberry Awards
1980 to present

Like the Oscars taking over from the *Photoplay* Gold Medal in the late '20s, in the last 15 years the Golden Raspberries have filled the breach left by the *Harvard Lampoon*'s Movie Worsts to become the most widely publicized bad movie awards. At a nobody-studded affair, held the night before the Oscars each year at locations that have included the Hollywood Roosevelt Hotel (site of the very first Oscars), the Golden Raspberry Award Foundation gives the largely uncoveted Razzie—a gold spray-painted *faux* raspberry attached to a super 8 reel, standing atop a 35mm film core covered in genuine woodgrain shelf paper and attached to a base made from a Lipton can lid. As the group's founder, Los Angeles copywriter John Wilson, proudly points out, the Razzie—with a street value estimated at $1.97—is "the only *other* award ever given to Pia Zadora."

Recognizing that it's all too easy to pick on no-budget straight-to-video garbage, the Raspberries' main targets are the big-budget dogs—the films that had every advantage studio money could buy and still turned out deliriously awful, the stars who get enormous sums for embarrassingly bad performances. (Although I think that at least two of their choices—*Mommie Dearest* and *The Color of Night*—were intentionally that way.) One particular target, Sylvester Stallone, is said to have left Wilson an angry phone message talking about his films' box office performance after one of the numerous times the group has honored his work.

On the other hand, while Wilson can still only look

forward wistfully to the day that anyone actually accepts a
Razzie in person at the ceremony, a very few celebrities
have been good enough sports to actually want their
Razzies, once they've heard they've won. *Christopher
Columbus'* King Ferdinand, Tom Selleck, received his
(appropriately enough) on the equally disastrous *Chevy
Chase Show*, and Bill Cosby was so taken by his multiple
awards for *Leonard Part 6* that he commissioned a jeweler
to reproduce the $1.97 trophy in considerably more costly
materials. (Bo Derek also accepted one, graciously but
involuntarily, on a British TV program.)

The Golden Raspberry Foundation amusingly chronicles
the world of bad film year-round in its newsletter;
members, who reportedly include many lower-level industry
personnel, actually get to vote on the awards—which,
as Wilson notes, means that his group has several times the
voting base of the Golden Globes. The Razzies are collected
and reprinted here for the first time. For membership
information, write the Golden Raspberry Award
Foundation, P.O. Box 56931, Sherman Oaks, CA 91413.

The Box Office
1942 to present

Of course, when it comes down to it, the award that
matters most to any producer is the one that turns up in
Variety each week—the box office results. And not only to
producers: we live in an age when the talk about movies
usually revolves around their grosses, and even around such
arcana as per-screen averages—the kind of information
that was considered strictly fodder for the trade papers a
decade ago, but now turns up in mainstream newspapers
and on TV shows. (Well, it's not like there's much else to
talk about with most movies today.)

It wasn't always this way, and the reporting of box office
figures has often been a fairly haphazard affair—not to
mention inconsistent in what the figures from different times
actually represent (grosses? rentals?) All the same, in order to
give some idea of the most popular movies, stars, and genres
over time, I have reprinted *Variety*'s listings of the top
ten moneymakers of each year, and added my own selection

of titles from the remainder of each year's list—so that
you can watch Martin & Lewis rise and Abbott & Costello
fall in popularity, say, or track the rise in importance of
the youth audience in the '50s, '60s, and '70s. Note that—
unlike other places these figures have been reprinted—
these are the *original* box office figures, without the benefit
of reissue revenues at inflated prices (which especially
tend to make Disney films look much more successful than
they were at the time).

There's a lot of movie (and even social) history to be
found between the lines in the lists. Certainly no change
in Hollywood's own structure or temperament has had more
influence over what kind of movies get made than the
simple fact that in the '30s, '40s, and '50s it was wives who
dragged their husbands to movies (which is why Jeanette
MacDonald was a star), and today it's young men who drag
their girlfriends to their choices (which is why Steven
Seagal is one). And forget the decline of the western or the
musical—the most remarkable change of the last 40 years
is how the biblical epic went from being the king of kings
at the box office to absolute extinction in the late '60s
and '70s . . . and how sci-fi, perhaps fulfilling a similar
cultural need, went from being drive-in trash to the top of the
heap in the same period.

Since the way in which the lists are compiled has changed
over the years, you should use the following glossary
and guide when comparing figures from different years.

Gross. All money taken in at the box office.

Rentals. The studio's share of the gross—for practical
purposes, roughly half.

Domestic. U.S. and Canada. All figures shown here are
domestic; you can roughly double to approximate
worldwide figures, though triple might be closer for action
films.

1942 to 1963. From 1942 to 1963, *Variety* reported
anticipated domestic rentals—that is, the studio's own
best guess as to what the total rentals would eventually be,
often based simply on how a film did at one or two major
downtown theaters in major cities. In the '40s and early
'50s this was enough of an exact science that the estimates
were usually fairly credible; by the '60s, with the growing

youth culture producing drive-in hits that nobody had ever heard of at the rapidly dying downtown houses, it became increasingly difficult for them to guess reliably.

1964 to 1984. Beginning in 1964, *Variety* began ranking and listing films by *actual*, not anticipated, *domestic rentals* to date. I have added figures from subsequent years in cases when that would significantly affect a film's standing (e.g., after winning an Oscar).

1985 to 1992. Beginning in 1985, *Variety* began listing only *actual domestic rentals* for the previous *calendar* year. Note that this means that a movie like *Aladdin* could open around Thanksgiving, play for months, and become the highest-grossing film of its time—but never place higher than #4 on either of the two lists that it appeared on, since each would show only that calendar year's totals. I have reprinted the rankings for these years exactly as they appeared in *Variety*, but again made a note of additional revenues where that would make a significant difference in a movie's ranking.

1993 to present. With the mainstream press generally reporting grosses rather than rentals, in 1993 *Variety* made the inevitable switch to *actual domestic grosses*—again, only for the calendar year, and again annotated by me in some cases. So to roughly compare, say, 1994's *The Lion King* against 1991's *Beauty and the Beast*, divide the 1994 film's gross in half.

Incidentally, if you're curious about films before *Variety* started listing box office performance in 1942, here are *Variety*'s best modern estimates of the top box office hits of the silent and early sound era—based on their initial runs, and excluding reissue revenues. Note that early films such as *Birth of a Nation* weren't distributed by modern methods, and the "rental" figures shown may be merely equivalents for comparison purposes, based on estimated total admissions. Inconsistent revenue reporting in the early '30s may be responsible for the overrepresentation of late '30s films and the absence of mid-'30s hits like *King Kong*, *It Happened One Night*, and *Mutiny on the Bounty*—though it's also true that, despite the legend of a rise in moviegoing during the Depression, overall attendance went down in the

worst of the Hoover era, and only went up again with the
New Deal recovery of the mid-to-late '30s.

Box Office 1912–1929

The Birth of a Nation (1915)	$10,000,000	Epoch
The Big Parade (1925)	5,121,000	MGM
Ben-Hur (1925)	4,579,000	MGM
The Ten Commandments (1923)	4,100,000	Paramount
The Covered Wagon (1923)	4,000,000	Paramount
What Price Glory? (1926)	4,000,000	Fox
Hearts of the World (1918)	3,900,000	Griffith
Way Down East (1920)	3,900,000	United Artists
The Singing Fool (1928)	3,821,000	Warner Bros.
The Four Horsemen of the Apocalypse (1921)	3,800,000	Metro
Wings (1927)	3,800,000	Paramount
The Gold Rush (1925)*	3,500,000	United Artists
Paul J. Rainey's African Hunt (1912)	3,000,000	Laemmle
The Thief of Bagdad (1924)	3,000,000	United Artists
The Broadway Melody (1929)	3,000,000	MGM

*May include estimated $1,000,000 from 1942 reissue

Box Office: 1930s

*Gone With the Wind** (1939)	$22,600,000	Selznick/MGM
Snow White and the Seven Dwarfs (1937)	4,500,000	Disney/RKO
Modern Times (1936)	4,000,000	United Artists
San Francisco (1935)	3,786,000	MGM
Hell's Angels (1930)	3,500,000	United Artists
Lost Horizon (1937)	3,500,000	Columbia
Mr. Smith Goes to Washington (1939)	3,500,000	Columbia
Maytime (1937)	3,400,000	MGM
The Hurricane (1937)	3,200,000	Goldwyn
City Lights (1931)	3,000,000	United Artists
The Great Ziegfeld (1936)	3,000,000	MGM
Boys Town (1938)	3,000,000	MGM
Love Finds Andy Hardy (1938)	3,000,000	MGM
Marie Antoinette (1938)	3,000,000	MGM
Sweethearts (1938)	3,000,000	MGM

*Includes revenues from initial road-show release (at raised prices) through
neighborhood engagements in 1941–42

Before 1927

That the *Photoplay* awards helped influence the criteria by which the Academy Awards came to be chosen is demonstrated by this fact: so many of the pre-Oscar winners sound so plausible as the films that *would* have won Best Picture—if the Oscars had existed then. King Vidor's *The Big Parade*, the *Best Years of Our Lives* of World War I, certainly would have won, and so would the pioneer epic *The Covered Wagon*, since one of its lesser descendants, *Cimarron*, did. Frank Borzage's *Humoresque* was based on the same book of Fannie Hurst short stories as the 1946 film *noir* of the same name, though this version skews the emphasis toward mother-love sentimentality— a favorite Oscar subgenre in those days; Henry King's *Tol'able David* was as nostalgic and beloved in its evocation of the simpler country life as *Forrest Gump*, and though none of the Lincoln biopics of the 1930s equaled the awards of the now utterly forgotten *Dramatic Life of Abraham Lincoln*, other costume biographies (Zola, Pasteur, Disraeli) did.

The only place they clearly would have parted company is in the adventure genre, which Oscar has never favored— 1930s versions of *Robin Hood* and *Beau Geste* didn't win major Oscars. The most interesting thing about the list, however, is that *Photoplay* readers, like Academy members, took it for granted that "best picture" equaled "best drama"; you will look in vain for the movies of the period that we love best today, the likes of *The Gold Rush, The General,* or *Safety Last.*

1920
***Photoplay* Medal of Honor**
Humoresque, produced by William Randolph Hearst/ Cosmopolitan Pictures

1921
***Photoplay* Medal of Honor**
Tol'able David, produced by Inspiration Pictures

1922
***Photoplay* Medal of Honor**
Robin Hood, produced by Douglas Fairbanks

1923
***Photoplay* Medal of Honor**
The Covered Wagon, produced by Famous Players–Lasky Corp.

1924
***Photoplay* Medal of Honor**
[*The Dramatic Life of*] *Abraham Lincoln*, produced by Al and Ray Rockett

1925
***Photoplay* Medal of Honor**
The Big Parade, produced by Irving Thalberg/Metro- Goldwyn Mayer

1926
***Photoplay* Medal of Honor**
Beau Geste, produced by Herbert Brenon/Paramount

1927–28

The first Best Picture Oscar winner is . . . None of the Above. There *wasn't* a Best Picture Academy Award in 1927–28.

In 1930 the Academy decided that 1927–28's award for Most Outstanding Production, which went to the WWI aviation melodrama *Wings*, was the equivalent of the subsequent Best Picture award. But that was basically an award for Most Popular Movie, Best Big Hit. The award that comes closest to today's true definition of "best picture" was the award for Most Artistic Quality of Production, to *Sunrise*. *Jurassic Park* would have won the first one; it's the second that would have gone to *Schindler's List*. And considering that Oscar's father, Louis B. Mayer, went to great lengths to screw one of his own studio's pictures (*The Crowd*, which he thought was depressing) out of it in order that it should go to something high-toned and European like *Sunrise*, it's clear that *he* considered the artistic award the most important prize of the evening.

Academy Awards/ 1927–28

NOTE: In the first three Academy Awards presentations, awards were given to individuals without being tied as closely to specific films as they are today. Thus, the Best Actor prize should be taken to read "Emil Jannings was honored as Best Actor for his work in 1927–28; his films during this period included *The Last Command* and *The Way of All Flesh*." In the case of the cinematography award, the award clearly was given to both winners because of the one film on which they collaborated, *Sunrise*, but their other individual work for the period is also shown.

*** *Wings* AAW
The so-called first Best Picture winner (see above), a WWI yarn with planes in the air and Clara Bow on the ground. The *Top Gun* of its day—exciting, but airheaded.

Most Outstanding Production
Wings (Paramount, Lucien Hubbard)
The Last Command (Paramount, J. G. Bachman, B. P. Schulberg)
The Racket (UA, Howard Hughes)
Seventh Heaven (Fox, William Fox)
The Way of All Flesh (Paramount, Adolph Zukor, Jesse L. Lasky)

***** *Sunrise* AAW
*** **Janet Gaynor** AAW
F. W. Murnau's masterpiece is an exquisite fable of a farm couple separated and then reconciled in the big city, set in a universalized world and told with more fancy camerawork than a week of MTV. The silent film at its most poetic—and artificial; winningly naive

53

performances by Janet Gaynor
(one of three cited in her Best
Actress award) and George
O'Brien keep its feet on the
ground.

Most Artistic Quality of Production
Sunrise (Fox)
Chang (Paramount, Merian C.
Cooper, Ernest B. Schoedsack)
The Crowd (MGM, King Vidor)

**** Emil Jannings in *The Last Command* AAW
An exiled Russian general turns
up as an extra in Hollywood—
where a radical he'd once
pursued is now a famous
director. The better known of
the two films which won the
first Best Actor Oscar for Emil
Jannings, an ox-like performer
whose full-body acting is out of
style and can seem hammy
today, but is still powerful.
Imagine the acting of the
young Brando—in the body of
the older one.

Actor
Emil Jannings, *The Last Command*, *The Way of All Flesh*
Richard Barthelmess, *The Noose*, *The Patent Leather Kid*
Charles Chaplin, *The Circus* [see note on special award]

Actress
Janet Gaynor, *Seventh Heaven*, *Street Angel*, *Sunrise*
Louise Dresser, *A Ship Comes In*
Gloria Swanson, *Sadie Thompson*

Dramatic Direction
Frank Borzage, *Seventh Heaven*
Herbert Brenon, *Sorrell and Son*
King Vidor, *The Crowd*

Comedy Direction
Lewis Milestone, *Two Arabian Knights*
Charles Chaplin, *The Circus* [see note on special award]
Ted Wilde, *Speedy*

Writing/Adaptation: Benjamin
Glazer, *Seventh Heaven*
Writing/Original Story: Ben
Hecht, *Underworld*
Title Writing: Joseph Farnham,
*Telling the World, The Fair Co-
ed, Laugh, Clown, Laugh*
Cinematography: Charles
Rosher, Karl Struss, *Sunrise*
[also Rosher: *My Best Girl, The
Tempest*; Struss: *Drums of Love*]
Interior Decoration: William
Cameron Menzies, *The Dove*,
The Tempest
Engineering Effects: Roy
Pomeroy, *Wings*
Special Awards: Charles Chaplin,
for *The Circus* [Chaplin's name
was removed from competition in
the Actor and Comedy Direction
categories owing to his unique
stature as a comic artist]
Warner Bros. for *The Jazz Singer*

Photoplay Medal of Honor/ 1927
Seventh Heaven, produced by
William Fox

Photoplay Medal of Honor/ 1928
Four Sons, produced by William
Fox

Gebert's Golden Armchairs
Oscar and I get off to a cordial
start honoring *Sunrise* and Jannings,
but my choice for foreign film and
Best Actress is a different
German director's work: G. W.
Pabst's drama of a femme fatale
who destroys every man she
touches, starring the American

starlet Louise Brooks. Brooks turns the tables on this paranoid male fantasy by playing Lulu as an innocent who can't help the foolish things men do over her, winning the picture a Special Golden Armchair for Best Feminist Film of 1928 (And Thirty Years in Either Direction).

Best American Film: *Sunrise*
Best Foreign Film: *Pandora's Box*
Best Actor: Emil Jannings, *The Last Command*
Best Actress: Louise Brooks, *Pandora's Box*
Best Director: F. W. Murnau, *Sunrise*

1929

In its first year, the Academy's insiders had been careful to spread the wealth around, but in 1928–29 their award lust won out—Warner Baxter was the only winner that night who *wasn't* a founding member of the Academy. The biggest stink was raised by the Best Actress award to Mary Pickford (wife of Academy President Douglas Fairbanks), since even at the time no one thought much of her performance. But perhaps because the first Best Actress award had gone to someone (Janet Gaynor) who was widely regarded as a younger, more contemporary version of herself, Pickford had campaigned hard to win one of her own, at one point inviting the members of the Central Board of Judges over to Pickfair for tea to press her case in person. 1929's awards shook the credibility of the fledgling organization so much that the Board of Judges was abolished, and direct voting by the members—who were, admittedly, still hand-picked by Mayer, et al.—was established the next year.

Academy Awards/ 1928–29

See note on award citations in 1927–28 chapter.

** *The Broadway Melody*
AAW
The first musical (and first talkie) Best Picture Oscar–winner is admittedly no *Singin' in the Rain*—though several of its songs ended up in that classic. But even if it's a little too antique for modern audiences, you can see why 1929 audiences responded to it—it offers one aural novelty after another, from banjos to tap dancing to a comic stutterer (now *there's* the promise of sound fulfilled, Mr. Edison). It also has the first good talkie performance, Bessie Love's

gutsy if somewhat cloying turn as the ambitious older sister.

Production
The Broadway Melody (MGM, Harry Rapt)
Alibi (UA, Roland West)
Hollywood Revue (MGM, Harry Rapt)
In Old Arizona (Fox, Winfield Sheehan)
The Patriot (Paramount, Ernst Lubitsch)

Actor
Warner Baxter, *In Old Arizona*
George Bancroft, *Thunderbolt*
Chester Morris, *Alibi*
Paul Muni, *The Valiant*
Lewis Stone, *The Patriot*

• Mary Pickford in *Coquette*
AAW
This stage vehicle (for Helen Hayes) about a Southern belle who takes up with a lower-class

man, forcing her deah ole daddy to shoot him, was the sort of ridiculous Southern claptrap that no one could have done much with. But Pickford's acting (and accent) is on the high school level. Sad to say, the worst Best Actress Oscar winner—though worth noting as the first winning example of a very popular subgenre for Oscar in its early years, especially in this category: the society melodrama, about women who either romance above their class (*Kitty Foyle*, *Mildred Pierce*) or stray below it (*A Free Soul*, *To Each His Own*).

Actress
Mary Pickford, *Coquette*
Ruth Chatterton, *Madame X*
Betty Compson, *The Barker*
Jeanne Eagels, *The Letter*
Bessie Love, *The Broadway Melody*

Director
Frank Lloyd, *The Divine Lady*, *Weary River*, *Drag*
Lionel Barrymore, *Madame X*
Harry Beaumont, *The Broadway Melody*
Irving Cummings, *In Old Arizona*
Ernst Lubitsch, *The Patriot*

Writing Achievement: Hans Kraly, *The Patriot*
Cinematography: Clyde DeVinna, *White Shadows in the South Seas*
Interior Decoration: Cedric Gibbons, *The Bridge of San Luis Rey*, *The Hollywood Revue*

** *The Passion of Joan of Arc*
BOR
The most acclaimed foreign film of the year—you'll find it not only on 1929 lists, but also on most of the *Sight & Sound* critics' polls of the best films of all time—was a French silent directed by a Dane, Carl Theodor Dreyer. Like *Citizen Kane* a decade later, it thrilled critics and aspiring filmmakers with its restless, audacious camerawork; the historical subject matter helped give it high-art respectability, too, and as a result it played a major role in giving the movies that respectability. However, I think Dreyer's bag of camera tricks is badly dated—like *Intolerance* and *The Cabinet of Dr. Caligari*, it's one of those works which advanced the medium by showing the things you *shouldn't* do.

National Board of Review
Best American Films: *Applause*
Broadway
Bulldog Drummond
The Case of Lena Smith
Disraeli
Hallelujah!
The Letter
The Love Parade
Paris Bound
The Valiant
Best Foreign Films:
Arsenal
The Passion of Joan of Arc
Ten Days That Shook the World [*October*]
Piccadilly
Homecoming

***Photoplay* Medal of Honor**
Disraeli, produced by Warner Bros.

Gebert's Golden Armchairs

The last silents look much better than the first talkies to me—especially in the case of Hitchcock's *Blackmail*, which exists in both versions and is far better as a sleek, disturbingly adult silent than a creaky talkie. For his last silent, Doug Fairbanks had the inspired idea of filming the sequel to his 1923 hit *The Three Musketeers*, showing the Musketeers in old age; there's no fonder farewell to the silent era and to its best-loved action star than *The Iron Mask*.

Buster Keaton's last independent comedy offers both solid dramatic pathos and a stunning solo comic turn in a hurricane; and Garbo's (and MGM's) last silent is easily her best one, the one straight drama among a host of lurid melodramas.

Best American Film: *The Iron Mask*
Best Foreign Film: *Blackmail*
Best Actor: Buster Keaton, *Steamboat Bill, Jr.*
Best Actress: Greta Garbo, *The Kiss*
Best Director: Alfred Hitchcock, *Blackmail*

1930

The Academy's reforms of the previous year didn't entirely eliminate favoritism—Mrs. MGM, Norma Shearer Thalberg, didn't go empty-handed for one—but there's no denying that in the Best Picture category, at least, members put aside studio politics to honor what was clearly the best picture of the year, regardless of its origins.

Universal was an outcast among the major studios—an A-sized studio which mostly made B westerns. But production head Carl Laemmle, Jr. yearned for the prestige enjoyed by other Hollywood princes such as Irving Thalberg (who had passed through Universal on his way up), and he found the vehicle for his ambitions in Erich Maria Remarque's novel *All Quiet on the Western Front*, producing (with a host of imported talent) the best sound film yet made anywhere in the world. It would prove a short-lived triumph; after another prestige picture flopped, the Laemmles were forced out in 1936, Universal set its sights back low again—and apart from *Hamlet*, which it only distributed, the studio wouldn't have another Best Picture Oscar–winner until *The Sting*.

Academy Awards/ 1929–30

NOTE: As in 1927–28 (see note in that chapter) and 1928–29, all of an actor's work from the eligibility period was listed in official nomination citations—so George Arliss is nominated for *Disraeli* and *The Green Goddess*, and Norma Shearer for *The Divorcée* and *Their Own Desire*. However, in both cases the final awards cited only one film—possibly, the Academy's historians believe, because voters had shown a preference for those films (*Disraeli* and *The Divorcée*) on their ballots. (The Academy switched the next year to today's system of nominations for specific, individual films.) The winning film is shown in boldface, while the other is shown in standard italics.

***** *All Quiet on the Western Front* AAW PHO BOR
A unanimous choice across the award groups, and rightly so. A little dust has settled on the acting and dialogue, but the war scenes, which director Lewis Milestone shot as if they were silent, remain stunning— men swarming over trenches like beetles and being slaughtered in droves, Milestone's moving camera hurtling over the carnage like the eye of an angry god, the microphone picking up the ceaseless clatter of weapons and

the agonized howls of men fighting and dying.

Production

All Quiet on the Western Front (Universal, Carl Laemmle, Jr.)
The Big House (MGM, Irving G. Thalberg)
Disraeli (Warner Bros., Jack L. Warner, Darryl F. Zanuck)
The Divorcée (MGM), Robert Z. Leonard)
The Love Parade (Paramount, Ernst Lubitsch)

*** George Arliss in *Disraeli* AWW

"Mr. George Arliss" (as his credit reads) was one of the first and least likely new stars to be produced by talkies, an aged English ham doing movie versions of his stage hits in which he played some great man— Hamilton, Richelieu, Voltaire—taking time out from solving the world's problems to see that the juvenile leads wound up together. (Voltaire!) With his plastered hair, long pinched face, and constant winking at the audience, Arliss suggests the Uriah Heep from an all-chimp production of *David Copperfield* but considering that some of his vehicles had had thirty years in front of audiences, it's easy to see why his polished and well-paced productions stood out in the talkies' awkward early days.

Actor

George Arliss, *Disraeli, The Green Goddess*
Wallace Beery, *The Big House*

Maurice Chevalier, *The Big Pond, The Love Parade*
Ronald Colman, *Bulldog Drummond, Condemned*
Lawrence Tibbett, *The Rogue Song*

** Norma Shearer in *The Divorcée* AAW

The Queen of MGM won her only Oscar for this realistic marital drama, in which she flings with Robert Montgomery to make straying husband Chester Morris jealous. MGM often cast her as a woman pushing the bounds of societal propriety, and frankly, I think she was just too clean-cut and ordinary to carry it off convincingly. (She's like Hugh Grant's straining-to-be-decadent minister in *Sirens*.) However, I can see why she won this Oscar—unlike a lot of early talkie players, she knows that you can't just stand there and talk, you have to *do* something. And good or bad, she's always doing *something*—tossing her head back, biting her lip, forcing an unconvincing madcap laugh.

Actress

Norma Shearer, *The Divorcée, Their Own Desire*
Nancy Carroll, *The Devil's Holiday*
Ruth Chatterton, *Sarah and Son*
Greta Garbo, *Anna Christie, Romance*
Gloria Swanson, *The Trespasser*

Director

Lewis Milestone, *All Quiet on the Western Front*

Clarence Brown, *Anna Christie,
Romance*
Robert Z. Leonard, *The Divorcée*
Ernst Lubitsch, *The Love Parade*
King Vidor, *Hallelujah!*

Writing Achievement: Frances
Marion, *The Big House*
Cinematography: Joseph T.
Rucker, Willard Van Der Veer, *With
Byrd at the South Pole*
Interior Decoration: Herman
Rosse, *King of Jazz*
Sound Recording: *The Big
House*

National Board of Review
Best American Films:
*All Quiet on the Western Front
Holiday
Laughter
The Man from Blankely's
Men Without Women
Morocco
Outward Bound
Romance
The Street of Chance
Tol'able David*
Best Foreign Films:
*High Treason
Old and New* [*The General Line*]
Soil [*Earth*]
*Storm Over Asia
Zwei Herzen im 3/4 Takt* [*Two
Hearts in 3/4 Time*]

Photoplay Medal of Honor
All Quiet on the Western Front,
produced by Carl Laemmle, Jr./
Universal

Gebert's Golden Armchairs
No reason to disagree with the
Academy this year on *All Quiet*
(I would only add its German
companion piece, G. W. Pabst's
equally harrowing *Westfront
1918*). But we part company on
performers. Ronald Colman was
nominated for Best Actor for
two films, but the main reason was
his 1929 talkie debut, an
adaptation of one of Sapper's
thrillers. The movie is creaky,
but Colman, energetic and
debonair, shows himself the first
actor to understand how to act in
talkies, and he would have been
a better choice than George
Arliss—especially given what
he, Colman, eventually won for.
The most memorable female
performance was Marlene
Dietrich's; she isn't quite an
actress yet, if she ever really was
(in her early days she was just
cheekbones; later she had great
presence), but there's no one that
year to compare with the
impression she made—especially
on drag queens.

Best American Film: *All Quiet on
the Western Front*
Best Foreign Film: *Westfront 1918*
Best Actor: Ronald Colman,
Bulldog Drummond
Best Actress: Marlene Dietrich,
The Blue Angel
Best Director: Lewis Milestone,
All Quiet on the Western Front

1931

Cimarron is often said to be the only western to win the Best Picture Oscar until *Dances With Wolves* in 1990. Is this the sign of a western? After the Oklahoma land rush, Richard Dix and Irene Dunne marry and settle in a growing town. But Dix has wanderlust, and he leaves Dunne in search of adventure, at which point the movie—*forgets about Dix and follows Dunne's rise in local society over the next 50 years.*

This isn't a western. It's a soap opera, a women's picture, to use the genre terms of the time. Let it be shouted from the hilltops: no *real* western won Best Picture until 1990. (Or maybe 1992.)

Academy Awards/ 1930–31

• **Cimarron** AAW BOR PHO Sentimental, poky, and overlong, the soap-western *Cimarron* is today the least watchable Best Picture winner of all—though note that, far from being an aberration of Oscar's (as is sometimes written), it was popular across the board—including among the general *Photoplay*-reading public.

Picture
Cimarron (RKO Radio, William LeBaron)
East Lynne (Fox, Winfield Sheehan)
The Front Page (UA, Howard Hughes)
Skippy (Paramount, Adolph Zukor)
Trader Horn (MGM, Irving G. Thalberg)

** **Lionel Barrymore in *A Free Soul*** AAW
Barrymore plays the alcoholic lawyer who defends Leslie

Howard for shooting gangster Clark Gable for sleeping with Barrymore's daughter Norma Shearer; he gets Howard off (and wins an Oscar) with the final scene, a ripsnorting speech to the jury which ends with him dropping dead. Drunk scenes, dying-for-a-drink scenes, tearful family reunions, a courtroom speech (with coronary occlusion for a socko finish)—you can almost see Barrymore holding back, as if he knows that giving all these opportunities for hamming it up to a Barrymore was like giving drink to . . . well, a Barrymore.

Actor
Lionel Barrymore, *A Free Soul*
Jackie Cooper, *Skippy*
Richard Dix, *Cimarron*
Fredric March, *The Royal Family of Broadway*
Adolphe Menjou, *The Front Page*

*** **Marie Dressler in *Min and Bill*** AAW
The famous but little-seen teaming of Beery and Dressler

as wharf rats is less the brawling comedy it appears than the first Oscar winner in the popular (but indigestible) '30s genre of maternal-sacrifice yarns— *Madame X, Madelon Claudet, Stella Dallas*, etc. Dressler and subtlety last saw each other during the Spanish-American War, but the old gal's performance does have a lot of heart; an early example of the no-glamour roles that would become an Oscar staple in the 50's.

Actress
Marie Dressler, *Min and Bill*
Marlene Dietrich, *Morocco*
Irene Dunne, *Cimarron*
Ann Harding, *Holiday*
Norma Shearer, *A Free Soul*

Director
Norman Taurog, *Skippy*
Clarence Brown, *A Free Soul*
Lewis Milestone, *The Front Page*
Wesley Ruggles, *Cimarron*
Josef von Sternberg, *Morocco*

Screenplay: Howard Estabrook, *Cimarron*
Original Story: John Monk Saunders, *The Dawn Patrol*
Cinematography: Floyd Crosby, *Tabu*
Interior Decoration: Max Ree, *Cimarron*
Sound Recording: Paramount Sound Dept.

***** *Tabu* AAW BOR
F. W. Murnau's last film—he died in a car accident the week before its premiere—is a location-filmed tale of doomed love between two South Seas natives, the most beautiful and haunting of all the ethnographic documentary-dramas of the period. Cinematographer Floyd Crosby (father of David, incidentally) won the last Academy Award to go to a silent film.

National Board of Review
Best American Films:
Cimarron
City Lights
City Streets
Dishonored
The Front Page
The Guardsman
Quick Millions
Rango
Surrender
Tabu
Best Foreign Films:
Die Dreigroschenoper [*The Threepenny Opera*]
Das Lied vom Leben [*The Song of Life*]
Le Million
Sous les Toits de Paris [*Under the Roofs of Paris*]
Vier von der Infantrie [*Westfront 1918*]

***Photoplay* Medal of Honor**
Cimarron, produced by Louis Sarecky/RKO

Gebert's Golden Armchairs
It was pro-talkie prejudice that kept Chaplin's masterfully poignant (and universally acclaimed) *City Lights* off the Oscar ballots that year, but I can't imagine *what* was responsible for the absence from Oscar's Best Actor nominees of Edward G. Robinson, who gave the year's star-making performance—especially when Richard Dix, broad as a barn in *Cimarron*, did get a nomination. I would argue that as of 1931, more than half of all the *good*

female talkie performances had been given by Barbara Stanwyck, and the early Capra film *The Miracle Woman* is merely one of many. And the director doing the best job of turning sound's disadvantages into advantages was the German Fritz Lang—the most chilling talkie moment yet was in *M* when the sound of children playing suddenly stopped, leaving us with the crackle and hiss of an empty soundtrack and the knowledge that child-murderer Peter Lorre had struck again.

Best American Film: *City Lights*
Best Foreign Film: *Tabu*
Best Actor: Edward G. Robinson, *Little Caesar*
Best Actress: Barbara Stanwyck, *The Miracle Woman*
Best Director: Fritz Lang, *M*

1932

With celebrities ranging from Mussolini and Pirandello to Adolph Zukor and Will Hays, and with films ranging from *Grand Hotel* and *Frankenstein* to *A Nous la Liberté* and *Mädchen in Uniform* (but not, you'll note, *Little Caesar*), the first Venice Film Festival would match any that has followed for glamorous attendees and glittering gala receptions. And as at so many festivals to follow, the *film* part of the film festival seems to have been almost an afterthought. The films were shown outdoors, on a makeshift screen on the Excelsior Hotel's terrace; *Variety*'s Robert Hawkins, who would cover so many of the postwar festivals, attended Venice *uno* with his parents as a boy and recalled sixty years later that "it was all very genteel. Garden chairs were laid out where the Excelsior's pool is now. You couldn't afford to walk out or be late—the crunch of feet on the gravel paths was a dead giveaway."

The attending audience was allowed to vote for its favorite films and stars, and the winners included Helen Hayes for the soap opera *The Sin of Madelon Claudet*—which incidentally refutes one of Oscar's persistent stories. Some years later Irving Thalberg reportedly approved some other trashy soap opera with the words, "Let's face it, we win Academy Awards with crap like *The Sin of Madelon Claudet*." That has led some Oscar historians to claim that Hayes' was merely another engineered award, like Pickford's for *Coquette*, for a movie that nobody liked. It was indeed engineered (to encourage stage great Hayes to stay in Hollywood), but it was *not* a film nobody liked. The crowds at Venice had also picked *Madelon Claudet*—and in the early '30s, it was Oscar that was fixed, and Venice that was run on the up and up.

Academy Awards/ 1931–32

**** *Grand Hotel* AAW
This first-class soap opera features most of MGM's top stars at their peaks—if not the peak of subtlety, certainly the peak of actorly competition. John Barrymore and Greta Garbo give indelible performances— but it's the dark horse, little Joanie Crawford as the lower-class secretary hungrily alive to all the luxury around her, who comes from behind to steal the picture.

Picture
Grand Hotel (MGM, Irving G. Thalberg)
Arrowsmith (UA, Samuel Goldwyn)
Bad Girl (Fox, Winfield Sheehan)
The Champ (MGM, King Vidor)

Five Star Final (First National, Hal B. Wallis)
One Hour with You (Paramount, Ernst Lubitsch)
Shanghai Express (Paramount, Adolph Zukor)
Smiling Lieutenant (Paramount, Ernst Lubitsch)

*** Fredric March in *Dr. Jekyll and Mr. Hyde* AAW VEN
*** Wallace Beery in *The Champ* AAW

Oscar's first tie. *Dr. Jekyll* is a startling and fascinating film, full of raw Freudian-Darwinian notions, and March's performance is imaginative— it's sort of like *Dr. Jekyll and Johnny Rotten*. But considering his competition around this time (Karloff and Lugosi), it's hard to see how March deserves to have the only Oscar for a horror part until Anthony Hopkins'. By comparison, *The Champ* is sheer tearjerking corn, both improbable and shameless—but there's real chemistry and magic between Beery's boozy old boxer and Jackie Cooper's adoring little tyke. I look forward someday to reducing my own kids to maudlin blubbering with it.

Actor
Wallace Beery, *The Champ*
Fredric March, *Dr. Jekyll and Mr. Hyde*
Alfred Lunt, *The Guardsman*

• Helen Hayes in *The Sin of Madelon Claudet* AAW VEN
Not remotely deserving of an Oscar, but so fast-paced and

ridiculous that it's a lot of fun (it helps that at 73 minutes it's the shortest major Oscar winner ever). Hayes plays ze French farm lass who is seduced and abandoned by ze American artist, and falls from high-toned mistress to Parisian streetwalker in order to pay for medical school for her beloved son (Robert Young). Hayes, a legendary stage actress, clearly takes this hokum exactly as seriously as it deserves, but she does earn a place in Oscar history for combining two of the character types which would most often lead an actress to an Oscar—the self-sacrificing mother, and the whore with a heart of gold.

Actress
Helen Hayes, *The Sin of Madelon Claudet*
Marie Dressler, *Emma*
Lynn Fontanne, *The Guardsman*

Director
Frank Borzage, *Bad Girl*
King Vidor, *The Champ*
Josef von Sternberg, *Shanghai Express*

Screenplay: Edwin Burke, *Bad Girl*
Original Story: Frances Marion, *The Champ*
Cinematography: Lee Garmes, *Shanghai Express*
Interior Decoration: Gordon Wiles, *Transatlantic*
Sound Recording: Paramount Sound Dept.
Short/Cartoon: *Flowers and Trees* (Walt Disney/Silly Symphonies)
Short/Comedy: *The Music Box* (Laurel & Hardy)

Short/Novelty: *Wrestling Swordfish* (Mack Sennett/Cannibals of the Deep)
Special Awards: Walt Disney, for creating Mickey Mouse

National Board of Review
Best American Film: *I Am a Fugitive from a Chain Gang*
As You Desire Me
A Bill of Divorcement
A Farewell to Arms
Madame Racketeer
Payment Deferred
Scarface
Tarzan the Ape Man
Trouble in Paradise
Two Seconds
Best Foreign Films:
A Nous la Liberté
Der Andere
The Battle of Gallipoli
Golden Mountains
Kameradschaft
Mädchen in Uniform
Der Raub der Mona Lisa
Reserved for Ladies
Road to Life
Zwei Menschen

Photoplay Medal of Honor
Smilin' Through, produced by Irving Thalberg/Metro-Goldwyn Mayer

**** *A Nous la Liberté*   BOR VEN
For decades *Under the Roofs of Paris*, *A Nous la Liberté*, and *Le Million*, French director René Clair's trio of whimsical early talkie musical-comedies flavored with a drop of Surrealism, were regarded as among the best films ever made—and if few would say that today, they're certainly among the most delightful and playful early talkies.

Venice Film Festival
(public referendum)
Most Amusing Film: *A Nous la Liberté* (René Clair, France)
Most Touching Film: *The Sin of Madelon Claudet* (Edgar Selwyn, USA)
Most Original and Fantastic Film: *Dr. Jekyll and Mr. Hyde* (Rouben Mamoulian, USA)
Most Convincingly Directed: *The Road to Life* (Nikolai Ekk, USSR)
Favorite Actor: Fredric March
Favorite Actress: Helen Hayes

Gebert's Golden Armchairs
Venice didn't go for *Grand Hotel*, but it's certainly the quintessential *something*. The nasal motormouth Lee Tracy isn't remembered as one of the great screwball stars, and he could be obnoxious, but he has a tailor-made role as a Winchell type in the racy *Blessed Event*. My foreign film choice is admittedly something no one could have picked in '32, since even Venice didn't invite the Japanese until later in the decade: *I Was Born, But*, a silent comedy-drama about a child's adoration of his father, is one of the best films about children ever made—and a surprise to those who only know Yasujiro Ozu for his much more solemn and static dramas of the '40s and '50s. This one proves he was not only the equal of Kurosawa but of the Little Rascals, too.

Best American Film: *Grand Hotel*
Best Foreign Film: *I Was Born, But*
Best Actor: Lee Tracy, *Blessed Event*
Best Actress: Joan Crawford, *Grand Hotel*
Best Director: Yasujiro Ozu, *I Was Born, But*

1933

For many years the least-seen, least-remembered Best Picture Oscar–winner, Noël Coward's *Cavalcade* was finally released on video in 1993—too late, alas, to enjoy rediscovery. It's a stiff. But it is worth remembering, if only as the prototype for a whole class of award-winner—the Brit-lit costume picture, represented in its heyday by MGM (who followed it with the likes of *David Copperfield, Anna Karenina,* etc.), and today by the Merchant-Ivory team.

Ironically, this serious (if reactionary) film about the social changes of the first third of the century wound up spawning a whole genre of plush Oscar winners whose main appeal is their *escape* from reality into an idealized past. (After all, who really leaves *A Man for All Seasons* thinking about the separation of church and state?) Oscar in particular has been very good to costume pictures—and costume parts; nothing reveals the banality of the Academy voters' conception of quality more than their exaggerated respect for "historical" acting.

Put Winona Ryder in black jeans and let her give a dead-on funny portrait of screwed-up teen intelligence in *Heathers,* and the Academy never gives her a glance. Put her hair in a bun in *The Age of Innocence* and let her stumble over Edith Wharton's bejeweled sentences like she's translating from the Finn, and she's the odds-on favorite for an Oscar.

(Yeah, I know that she ultimately lost. To a ten-year-old in a hoop skirt.)

Academy Awards/ 1932–33

• *Cavalcade* AAW
Noël Coward's London stage hit was an "upstairs, downstairs" story chronicling life in Britain from the Boer War to the Depression. The downstairs family leaves service and goes into business for themselves, winding up rich enough for their daughter to consider marriage to one of the upstairs sons—a social horror luckily prevented by a German bullet (for him, not her). The pacifist sentiments (very much of their time) are fascinating, but the class snobbery is impossible for modern Americans to stomach—Diana Wynyard doesn't seem half so disturbed by her son's death in World War I as she is by the fact that her former maid (Una O'Connor) has a mink coat and expects to be offered tea.

Picture
Cavalcade (Fox, Winfield Sheehan)

A Farewell to Arms (Paramount, Adolph Zukor)
42nd Street (Warner Bros., Darryl F. Zanuck)
I Am a Fugitive from a Chain Gang (Warner Bros., Hal B. Wallis)
Lady for a Day (Columbia, Frank Capra)
Little Women (RKO Radio, Merian C. Cooper, Kenneth MacGowan)
The Private Life of Henry VIII (UA, London Films/Alexander Korda)
She Done Him Wrong (Paramount, William Le Baron)
Smilin' Through (MGM, Irving Thalberg)
State Fair (Fox, Winfield Sheehan)

**** Charles Laughton in *The Private Life of Henry VIII* AAW
The international hit that put England and producer Alexander Korda on the map is a much wittier costume drama than *Cavalcade*. The technique is primitive, making it a little harder to watch than some of its follow-ups (*Rembrandt*, *Fire Over England*, etc.), but Korda's art director brother Vincent and cinematographer Georges Périnal managed a lavish look on a beer-and-skittles budget— and both Charles Laughton as Henry and Elsa Lanchester as Anne of Cleves (the one wife who got the best of Henry) give delightfully wry performances.

Actor
Charles Laughton, *The Private Life of Henry VIII*
Leslie Howard, *Berkeley Square*

Paul Muni, *I Am a Fugitive from a Chain Gang*

• Katharine Hepburn in *Morning Glory* AAW
As Eva Lovelace, the naive young actress who dreams of fame and talks an incredible line of pretentious nonsense to the Broadway types she pursues, Katharine Hepburn was like no other actress the talkies had produced—that angular face, the Boston Brahmin accent, the theatrically unnatural delivery, words that should be drawn out all rushed together and vice versa. (The only other star with such a stylized delivery was Bela Lugosi.) All those things were startlingly different— but they weren't anything more than affectations, yet. I suspect what really cinched the Oscar for her was the scene in which, drunk at a party, she recites Hamlet's soliloquy—drunk scenes were an Oscar staple, and doing a little Shakespeare would become one, but doing both while talking like Katharine Hepburn was the true mark of virtuosity.

Actress
Katharine Hepburn, *Morning Glory*
May Robson, *Lady for a Day*
Diana Wynyard, *Cavalcade*

Director
Frank Lloyd, *Cavalcade*
Frank Capra, *Lady for a Day*
George Cukor, *Little Women*

Screenplay: Victor Heerman, Sarah Y. Mason, *Little Women*

Original Story: Robert Lord, *One Way Passage*

Cinematography: Charles Lang, *A Farewell to Arms*

Interior Decoration: William S. Darling, *Cavalcade*

Assistant Director [given to one from each studio]: Charles Barton (Paramount), Scott Beal (Universal), Charles Dorian (MGM), Fred Fox (United Artists), Gordon Hollingshead (Warner Bros.), Dewey Starkey (RKO Radio), William Tummel (Fox)

Sound Recording: *A Farewell to Arms*

Short/Cartoon: *The Three Little Pigs* (Walt Disney/Silly Symphonies)

Short/Comedy: *So This Is Harris* (RKO Radio Special/Phil Harris)

Short/Novelty: *Krakatoa* (Educational) [NOTE: Educational was a studio, not a description]

National Board of Review

Best American Film: *Topaze*
Berkeley Square
Cavalcade
Little Women
Mama Loves Papa
The Pied Piper
She Done Him Wrong
State Fair
Three-Cornered Moon
Zoo in Budapest
Best Foreign Films:
Hertha's Erwachen
Ivan
M
Morgenrot
Niemandsland
Poil de Carotte

The Private Life of Henry VIII
Quatorze Juillet
Rome Express
Le Sang d'un Poète [*Blood of a Poet*]

Photoplay **Medal of Honor**

Little Women, produced by David O. Selznick, Merian C. Cooper, Kenneth MacGowan/RKO

Gebert's Golden Armchairs

Kong is any former 10-year-old boy's best picture of 1933, and I thought about giving Kong Best Actor, too—but settled on Groucho, feeling that being able to quote most of a performance is a pretty good sign that it's the most memorable of the year. Miriam Hopkins, ordinarily a brittle and bitchy actress, gives far and away her best performance as a city girl who finds herself (in more ways than one) on her ancestral farm in King Vidor's *The Stranger's Return*; and Frank Borzage, the dime-store poet of '30s cinema, makes a surprisingly erotic Hooverville variation on his Oscar-winning *Seventh Heaven* out of the romance between hoboes Spencer Tracy and Loretta Young.

Best American Film: *King Kong*
Best Foreign Film: *The Private Life of Henry VIII*
Best Actor: Groucho Marx, *Duck Soup*
Best Actress: Miriam Hopkins, *The Stranger's Return*
Best Director: Frank Borzage, *Man's Castle*

1934

During the era when Hollywood was the peerless manufacturer of flawless silver dreams, every once in a while a movie would come along that would let the perfection crack just a little—*Casablanca*, with its what-the-hell plotting; the Road movies, with their in-jokes and breezy air; *A Hard Day's Night*. Before any of them, there was *It Happened One Night*—a movie that broke out of the backlot to show us the real America of buses and motels, the real Americans who would cheat you out of a nickel if they could but were still what made this crazy country great, the real sexual attraction between a man who didn't wear an undershirt and a woman who wore men's pajamas. MGM tried to imitate it several times (*Libeled Lady*, *Love on the Run*), but they could never get the same free and easy air out of Gable—because they were the Dream Factory at its most factory-like. Capra had only himself and a tiny budget, and he made a movie as relaxed and playful as Chaplin's early shorts or the first films of the French New Wave. It was a true popular success, and on Oscar night, the industry gave Capra and his second-rate studio an unparalleled triumph for reminding them of the freedom they'd traded for perfection.

Academy Awards

NOTE: Beginning this year the writing award was changed to screenplay award and a separate one for original stories; films could be eligible for both.

***** *It Happened One Night*
AAW BOR
**** **Clark Gable**   AAW
*** **Claudette Colbert**   AAW
Capra's triumph is as fresh as ever; Gable was never happier and therefore, never more likable; but if truth be told, Colbert was better elsewhere—notably in Preston Sturges' spoof-salute to the Capra classic, *The Palm Beach Story*. Her win (and *Night*'s grand slam) came about

mainly because Jack Warner, miffed at Bette Davis for demanding to be allowed to do *Of Human Bondage* (and even more for getting the best reviews of her career for it), put out the word that she was not even to be nominated.

Picture
It Happened One Night
(Columbia, Harry Cohn)
The Barretts of Wimpole Street
(MGM, Irving Thalberg)
Cleopatra (Paramount, Cecil B. DeMille)
Flirtation Walk (First National, Jack L. Warner, Hal Wallis, Robert Lord)
The Gay Divorcée (RKO Radio, Pandro S. Berman)
Here Comes the Navy (Warner Bros., Lou Edelman)

The House of Rothschild (20th Century/UA, Darryl F. Zanuck, William Goetz, Raymond Griffith)
Imitation of Life (Universal, John M. Stahl)
One Night of Love (Columbia, Harry Cohn)
The Thin Man (MGM, Hunt Stromberg)
Viva Villa! (MGM, David O. Selznick)
The White Parade (Fox, Jesse L. Lasky)

Actor
Clark Gable, *It Happened One Night*
Frank Morgan, *The Affairs of Cellini*
William Powell, *The Thin Man*

Actress
Claudette Colbert, *It Happened One Night*
Grace Moore, *One Night of Love*
Norma Shearer, *The Barretts of Wimpole Street*

Director
Frank Capra, *It Happened One Night*
Victor Schertzinger, *One Night of Love*
W. S. Van Dyke, *The Thin Man*

Screenplay: Robert Riskin, *It Happened One Night*
Original Story: Arthur Caesar, *Manhattan Melodrama*
Cinematography: Victor Milner, *Cleopatra*
Score: *One Night of Love*, Victor Schertzinger
Song: "The Continental," *The Gay Divorcée*, m: Con Conrad, l: Herb Magidson
Editing: *Eskimo*
Interior Decoration: Cedric Gibbons, *The Merry Widow*
Assistant Director: John Waters,

Viva Villa! [*not* the director of *Pink Flamingos*]
Sound Recording: *One Night of Love*
Short/Cartoon: *The Tortoise and the Hare* (Walt Disney/Silly Symphonies)
Short/Comedy: *La Cucaracha* (RKO Radio Special) [NOTE: first three-strip Technicolor live-action film]
Short/Novelty: *City of Wax* (Educational/Battle for Life)
Special Awards: Shirley Temple

National Board of Review
Best American Film: *It Happened One Night*
The Count of Monte Cristo
Crime Without Passion
Eskimo
The First World War
The Lost Patrol
Lot in Sodom
No Greater Glory
The Thin Man
Viva Villa!
Best Foreign Film: *Man of Aran*
The Blue Light
Catherine the Great
The Constant Nymph
Madame Bovary

Photoplay Medal of Honor
The Barretts of Wimpole Street, produced by Irving Thalberg/ Metro-Goldwyn Mayer

**** *Man of Aran* BOR VEN
Robert Flaherty's *Nanook of the North* made him the "father" of the documentary film, though what he actually made were fictional dramas in which the natives of an area played themselves (or, in this case, their grandfathers, since life on these rocky Irish islands had advanced slightly from what was shown in this film). Flaherty

tended toward self-consciously artistic photography and compositions few documentarians would indulge in today; but for all that some people have accused him of prettying (or hoking) up his subjects, his films are always engrossing entertainment and, by the standards of the day, respectful toward the cultures shown. The last British champion at Venice until *Hamlet*, *Man of Aran* was popular enough in the U.S. that—60 years before *Hoop Dreams*—it campaigned for a Best Picture Oscar nomination; it didn't get it, but it wouldn't be long before documentaries would get categories of their own.

Venice Film Festival
Foreign Film: *Man of Aran* (Robert Flaherty, UK)
Mussolini Cup/Italian Film: *Teresa Confalonieri* (Guido Brignone)
Actor: Wallace Beery, *Viva Villa!* (USA)
Actress: Katherine Hepburn, *Little Women* (USA)
Director: collectively to the Czech directors (Gustav Machaty, *Ecstasy*; Josef Rovensky, *Young Love*; Tomas Trnka, *Hurricane in the Tatras*; Karel Plicka, *Zem Spleva*)
Story: *Maskerade* [*Masquerade in Vienna*] (Willy Forst, Germany)
Cinematography: Gerald Ruttenberg, *Dood Water* (USA)
Animated Film: *Three Little Pigs* (Walt Disney, USA)
Documentary: *Manovre Navall*
Best First Screening: *The Private Life of Don Juan* (Alexander Korda, UK)

Best State Entry: USSR
Largest Industrial Entry: Motion Picture Producers and Distributors of America

---

Gebert's Golden Armchairs
Among actresses, it was Myrna Loy's portrayal of a sexy, smart married woman in *The Thin Man* that was the year's real revelation—both for establishing a new character type and for breaking the exotic-looking Loy out of silly Oriental temptress roles. As for Gable, *Night* is undoubtedly his best performance, but I can't rank it above W. C. Fields in his best film, which manages to be both paralyzingly funny (often with the most fleabitten material) and bitterly sad in its portrait of a man turned into a mouse by marriage and middle-class conformity. (That's W. C. Fields, folks—vaudeville's answer to Eugene O'Neill.) And the best foreign film is a French companion piece to *It Happened One Night*—not a road romance, but a river one, Jean Vigo's erotic, anarchically funny *L'Atalante*, about a couple spending their honeymoon on a barge.

Best American Film: *It Happened One Night*
Best Foreign Film: *L'Atalante*
Best Actor: W. C. Fields, *It's a Gift*
Best Actress: Myrna Loy, *The Thin Man*
Best Director: Frank Capra, *It Happened One Night*

1935

The New York Film Critics Circle's first Best Film choice was a unanimous one—one of only two in the group's history (de Havilland, *Snake Pit*). And the influence of the new group on the Oscars was equally unambiguous, since in their first time at bat they succeeded in propelling a low-budget production—which even its own studio didn't much like— into the company of *Mutiny on the Bounty* and *David Copperfield*, winning Oscars for both its star and its director.

The film was John Ford's *The Informer*, and the reason the critics fell so solidly behind it was that choosing it made a clear statement about the new group's artistic viewpoint. Ford's tale of a simple lug who betrays a friend to the British police may have been set in Ireland, but otherwise it was an exact imitation of a '20s German Expressionist silent—from the shadowy b&w cinematography to star Victor McLaglen's Jannings-like hulking walk. To the critics, who still had the late silent-era reverence for things German, that made it art— unlike Ford's other, more conventionally American films, or much of anything else Hollywood produced. The same attitude would have a lot to do with *Citizen Kane*'s rapturous reception by the critics a few years later—by which time, ironically, Ford would be Oscar's safe choice against the radical innovations of Orson Welles.

Academy Awards

**** *Mutiny on the Bounty*
AAW
This $2 million sea epic was by far the best of its type (whatever type you want— MGM super-productions, Bounty movies, Frank Lloyd movies). The spectacle for once at MGM is subordinate to the adventure, and if Laughton's forceful Captain Bligh is a bit one-note, Gable's confidence and regular-guy heroism keeps the picture together.

Picture
Mutiny on the Bounty (MGM, Irving Thalberg)
Alice Adams (RKO Radio, Pandro S. Berman)
Broadway Melody of 1936 (MGM, John W. Considine, Jr.)
Captain Blood (Warner Bros.–Cosmopolitan, Hal Wallis)
David Copperfield (MGM, David O. Selznick)
The Informer (RKO Radio, Cliff Reid)
The Lives of a Bengal Lancer (Paramount, Louis D. Lighton)
A Midsummer Night's Dream (Warner Bros., Henry Blanke)
Les Misérables (20th Century/UA, Darryl F. Zanuck)

Naughty Marietta (MGM, Hunt Stromberg)
Ruggles of Red Gap (Paramount, Arthur Hornblow, Jr.)
Top Hat (RKO Radio, Pandro S. Berman)

*** Victor McLaglen in *The Informer* AAW

As the big dumb ox who informs on an IRA buddy, McLaglen gives the performance of Wallace Beery's career.

Actor
Victor McLaglen, *The Informer*
Clark Gable, *Mutiny on the Bounty*
Charles Laughton, *Mutiny on the Bounty*
Franchot Tone, *Mutiny on the Bounty*

*** Bette Davis in *Dangerous* AAW

Bette Davis was shafted out of an Oscar nomination for *Of Human Bondage* in 1934, and the usual story about Davis' win the next year for the little-known *Dangerous* is that it was a mere stand-in for *Bondage*—she would have won if she'd played a paramecium in *The Story of Louis Pasteur*. Davis got good reviews in *Bondage* for her versatility—she used an accent (Cockney) and she dressed cheaply and unglamorously to play the waitress who ruins medical student Leslie Howard. But the movie is stodgy and suffers from Leslie Howard's uncanny ability to suck the life out of anything he's in. *Dangerous*, in which she plays a great actress turned drunk who is rehabilitated by Franchot Tone and then proceeds to wreck his life for him, is no classic, but at least it's fast-paced and Davis gets to cut loose in her classic manner. What's more, in *Dangerous* she not only has a drunk scene—which in the '30s was the surest path to an Oscar—but, like Hepburn in *Morning Glory*, she recites Shakespeare during her drunk scene! I don't doubt that Academy voters were predisposed toward Davis in 1935 because of what had happened in 1934, but the traditional view is wrong— *Dangerous* is no mere stand-in. It had the elements to win an Oscar on its own.

Actress
Bette Davis, *Dangerous*
Elisabeth Bergner, *Escape Me Never*
Claudette Colbert, *Private Worlds*
Katharine Hepburn, *Alice Adams*
Miriam Hopkins, *Becky Sharp*
Merle Oberon, *The Dark Angel*

Director
John Ford, *The Informer*
Henry Hathaway, *The Lives of a Bengal Lancer*
Frank Lloyd, *Mutiny on the Bounty*

Screenplay: Dudley Nichols, *The Informer*
Original Story: Ben Hecht, Charles MacArthur, *The Scoundrel*
Cinematography: Hal Mohr, *A Midsummer Night's Dream*
[NOTE: the only write-in winner in Oscar history]
Score: *The Informer*, Max Steiner

Song: "Lullaby of Broadway," *Gold Diggers of 1935*, m: Harry Warren, l: Al Dubin
Editing: *A Midsummer Night's Dream*
Interior Decoration: Richard Day, *The Dark Angel*
Dance Direction: David Gould, "I've Got a Feeling You're Fooling," *Broadway Melody of 1936*; "Straw Hat," *Folies Bergère*
Assistant Director: Clem Beauchamp, Paul Wing, *The Lives of a Bengal Lancer*
Sound Recording: *Naughty Marietta*
Short/Cartoon: *Three Orphan Kittens* (Walt Disney/Silly Symphonies)
Short/Comedy: *How to Sleep* (MGM/Robert Benchley)
Short/Novelty: *Wings Over Mt. Everest* (Educational)
Special Award: David Wark Griffith

** *The Informer*   NYC BOR
Interesting enough to see once, but just an experiment, of the kind that film school students (and Woody Allen) try every day, and not nearly so good as any fifty other Ford films.

New York Film Critics Circle
Picture: *The Informer*
Actor: Charles Laughton, *Mutiny on the Bounty*, *Ruggles of Red Gap*
Actress: Greta Garbo, *Anna Karenina*
Director: John Ford, *The Informer*

National Board of Review
Best American Film: *The Informer*
Alice Adams
Anna Karenina

David Copperfield
The Gilded Lily
Les Misérables
The Lives of a Bengal Lancer
Mutiny on the Bounty
Ruggles of Red Gap
Who Killed Cock Robin? [Disney cartoon]
Best Foreign Films:
Chapayev
Crime and Punishment [France/Chenal version]
Le Dernier Milliardaire
The Man Who Knew Too Much
Marie Chapdelaine
La Maternelle
The New Gulliver
Peasants
Thunder in the East
The Youth of Maxim [*The Childhood of Maxim Gorky*]

Photoplay Medal of Honor
Naughty Marietta, produced by Hunt Stromberg/Metro-Goldwyn Mayer

**** *Anna Karenina*   VEN
As an adaptation of Tolstoy it's merely an efficient boiling-down, but as a Greta Garbo vehicle it shines—a literate, grown-up tragedy about a woman who gives up her family for love and then is ground beneath society's wheels. Garbo, giving her best performance, also won the first New York Critics actress award—the first of two she'd win while Oscar ignored her.

Venice Film Festival
Foreign Film: *Anna Karenina* (Clarence Brown, USA)
Mussolini Cup/Italian Film: *Casta Diva* (Carmine Gallone)
Actor: Pierre Blanchar, *Crime and Punishment* (France)

Actress: Paula Wessely, *Episode* (Austria)
Director: King Vidor, *Wedding Night* (USA)
Screenplay: Dudley Nichols, *The Informer* (USA)
Cinematography: *The Devil Is a Woman* [Josef von Sternberg, Lucien Ballard] (USA)
Music: *Bozambo*
Animated Film: *The Band Concert* (Walt Disney, USA)
Best Color Film: *Becky Sharp* (Rouben Mamoulian, USA)

Gebert's Golden Armchairs

A more stylishly Germanic film than *The Informer* is James Whale's spooky-poetic Frankenstein classic (which also proves that a gay subtext in horror movies long predates *Interview With the Vampire*). My foreign choice would be another Yasujiro Ozu silent from Japan (no, I *don't* know how I would have seen it in 1935), probably inspired by King Vidor's *The Crowd* and just as powerful a slice of realism. And if we define "acting" as not merely talking but whatever a performer does on screen, there's no pair of performances to equal the stars of the best musical of the '30s.

Best American Film: *The Bride of Frankenstein*
Best Foreign Film: *An Inn in Tokyo*
Best Actor: Fred Astaire, *Top Hat*
Best Actress: Ginger Rogers, *Top Hat*
Best Director: James Whale, *The Bride of Frankenstein*

1936

Without a doubt, the crookedest Oscars were 1936's—fixed over the grave of Louis B. Mayer's rival Irving Thalberg. In the outpouring of grief that followed the "boy wonder" producer's death at age 37, it was widely expected that one of his last productions, *Romeo and Juliet*, would win Best Picture as well as Best Actress for his widow, Norma Shearer.

Well, grief is grief, but business is business, and Mayer had $2 million invested in *The Great Ziegfeld* and its Austrian female star, Luise Rainer. Meanwhile, Jack Warner badly wanted an Oscar for Paul Muni, whose *The Story of Louis Pasteur* took George Arliss' costume pictures and gave them a Frank Capra spin—one man against the world, fighting for the germ theory. So Mayer and Warner struck a deal: MGM would back Muni for Best Actor, and Warner would throw his studio's support behind *The Great Ziegfeld* and Rainer. Even if MGM's own ranks split between love for Thalberg and fear of Mayer, the Warner bloc would be enough to turn the tide and ensure the outcome Mayer wanted. And so, on Oscar night—well, let's just say the performance of the year would have been Louis B. Mayer acting surprised at anything that happened.

Academy Awards

• *The Great Ziegfeld* AAW
• *Luise Rainer* AAW NYC
MGM's super-stupendous life of the reckless showman Flo Ziegfeld is a lavish, stupefying bore—a three-hour musical epic destined to be boiled down into a five-second clip in a *That's Entertainment!* montage. (Just what exactly *did* our grandparents find exciting about a four-story wedding cake with 500 ant-sized dancers on it, moving like a lace-covered barge, anyway?) As for Rainer, she's pretty and delicate in a Loretta Young–Maureen O'Sullivan kind of way, but her part is treacly, and her big

Oscar-grabbing scene—in which she bravely congratulates Flo on his second marriage over the phone while fighting back her sobs—doesn't just jerk tears, it blasts for them and runs three shifts pumping them out.

Picture
The Great Ziegfeld (MGM, Hunt Stromberg)
Anthony Adverse (Warner Bros., Henry Blanke)
Dodsworth (UA, Samuel Goldwyn)
Libeled Lady (MGM, Lawrence Weingarten)
Mr. Deeds Goes to Town (Columbia, Frank Capra)
Romeo and Juliet (MGM, Irving Thalberg)

San Francisco (MGM, John
Emerson, Bernard H. Hyman)
The Story of Louis Pasteur
(Warner Bros., Henry Blanke)
A Tale of Two Cities (MGM, David
O. Selznick)
Three Smart Girls (Universal,
Joseph Pasternak, Charles
Rogers)

*** **Paul Muni in** *The Story of
Louis Pasteur* **AAW VEN**
The *other* biographical film of
1936 holds up infinitely better
than *The Great Ziegfeld*. The
Great Scientist formula may
be a little naive, but Paul Muni's
first prestige picture hasn't
forgotten all the things Warner
Bros.' assembly–line pictures
knew about narrative drive and
colorful supporting characters.
Muni hoped that the film would
show the world that he was a
great actor—and in his mind
from this point, great acting
became synonymous with fake
beards, accents, and speeches
fit for the League of Nations. In
fact he's entirely superficial,
but he does know how to put it
over like the experienced stage
ham that he was.

Actor
Paul Muni, *The Story of Louis
Pasteur*
Gary Cooper, *Mr. Deeds Goes to
Town*
Walter Huston, *Dodsworth*
William Powell, *My Man Godfrey*
Spencer Tracy, *San Francisco*

Actress
Luise Rainer, *The Great Ziegfeld*
Irene Dunne, *Theodora Goes Wild*
Gladys George, *Valiant Is the
Word for Carrie*

Carole Lombard, *My Man
Godfrey*
Norma Shearer, *Romeo and Juliet*

Supporting Actor
Walter Brennan, *Come and Get
It*
Mischa Auer, *My Man Godfrey*
Stuart Erwin, *Pigskin Parade*
Basil Rathbone, *Romeo and Juliet*
Akim Tamiroff, *The General Died
at Dawn*

Supporting Actress
Gale Sondergaard, *Anthony
Adverse*
Beulah Bondi, *The Gorgeous
Hussy*
Alice Brady, *My Man Godfrey*
Bonita Granville, *These Three*
Maria Ouspenskaya, *Dodsworth*

Director
Frank Capra, *Mr. Deeds Goes
to Town*
Gregory La Cava, *My Man
Godfrey*
Robert Z. Leonard, *The Great
Ziegfeld*
W. S. Van Dyke, *San Francisco*
William Wyler, *Dodsworth*

Screenplay: Pierre Collings,
Sheridan Gibney, *The Story of
Louis Pasteur*
Original Story: Pierre Collings,
Sheridan Gibney, *The Story of
Louis Pasteur*
Cinematography: Gaetano
[Tony] Gaudio, *Anthony
Adverse*
Score: Erich Wolfgang Korngold,
Anthony Adverse
Song: "The Way You Look
Tonight," *Swing Time*, m:
Jerome Kern, l: Dorothy Fields
Interior Decoration: Richard
Day, *Dodsworth*
Editing: *Anthony Adverse*
Dance Direction: Seymour Felix,
"A Pretty Girl Is Like a
Melody," *The Great Ziegfeld*

Assistant Director: Jack Sullivan, *The Charge of the Light Brigade*
Sound Recording: *San Francisco*
Short/Cartoon: *Country Cousin* (Walt Disney/Silly Symphonies)
Short/One-Reel: *Bored of Education* (Hal Roach/Our Gang)
Short/Two-Reel: *The Public Pays* (MGM/Crime Doesn't Pay)
Short/Color: *Give Me Liberty* (Warner/Broadway Brevities)
Special Awards:
The March of Time for having revolutionized the newsreel
W. Howard Greene, Harold Rosson, color cinematography, *The Garden of Allah*

**** *Mr. Deeds Goes to Town*
NYC BOR

The quintessential Capra film (not least because both *Mr. Smith* and *Meet John Doe* are virtual remakes), and the one in which the formula—as well as the increasingly folksy Gary Cooper, beginning his mid-career switch from pretty boy to old oaken bucket—is freshest and most appealing.

** Carnival in Flanders [La Kermesse Héroïque] NYC BOR VEN

When the men of a 17th-century Dutch village hide in terror from the "visiting" Spanish army, the women wine and woo the Spaniards and save their village from pillage. Jacques Feyder's film was a huge international critical and box office success in the 1930s, because of its frank and honest treatment of bawdy subject matter and Lazare Meerson's authentic, un-Hollywooden re-creation of Brueghel's Holland. Alas, neither of those things easily impresses modern audiences raised on location-shot historical films like *Barry Lyndon* or *Dangerous Liaisons*, and the idea of sleeping with an invading army obviously lost some of its charm as the 1930s went on, too. Françoise Rosay's gutsy performance is what has lasted the best.

New York Film Critics Circle
Picture: *Mr. Deeds Goes to Town*
Foreign Film: *Carnival in Flanders* [*La Kermesse Héroïque*]
Actor: Walter Huston, *Dodsworth*
Actress: Luise Rainer, *The Great Ziegfeld*
Director: Rouben Mamoulian, *The Gay Desperado*

National Board of Review
Best American Film: *Mr. Deeds Goes to Town*
The Story of Louis Pasteur
Modern Times
Fury
Winterset
The Devil Is a Sissy
Ceiling Zero
Romeo and Juliet
The Prisoner of Shark Island
Green Pastures
Best Foreign Film: *Carnival in Flanders* [*La Kermesse Héroïque*]
The New Earth
Rembrandt
The Ghost Goes West
Nine Days a Queen
We Are from Kronstadt
Son of Mongolia
The Yellow Cruise

Les Misérables
The Secret Agent
[NOTE: *Rembrandt* also appears
on 1937 list]

Photoplay **Medal of Honor**
San Francisco, produced by John
Emerson, Bernard Hyman/
Metro-Goldwyn Mayer

Venice Film Festival
Mussolini Cup/Foreign Film:
Der Kaiser von Kalifornien
(Luis Trenker, Germany)
Mussolini Cup/Italian Film:
Squadrone Bianco (Augusto
Genina)
Musical: *Schlussakkord* [*Final
Accord*] (Detlef Sierck [Douglas
Sirk], Germany)
Actor: Paul Muni, *The Story of
Louis Pasteur* (USA)
Actress: Annabella, *Veille
d'Armes* (France)
Director: Jacques Feyder, *La
Kermesse Héroïque/Carnival in
Flanders* (France)
Cinematography: Max
Greenbaum [Greene], *Tudor
Rose* (UK)
Political/Social Film: *The Road
to Glory* (Howard Hawks, USA)
Documentary: *Jugend der Welt*
(Hans Weidemann, Germany)

Gebert's Golden Armchairs
If not the funniest screwball
comedy, *My Man Godfrey* has
the most backbone of any of
them—and it has Carole
Lombard's wonderful, froozy
performance as a scatterbrained
(but not stupid) heiress.
Hitchcock's *Sabotage* isn't as
much fun as some of his other
British films, but it's the only
one besides *Blackmail* that hints
at the psychological complexity
of his best American work to
come. It also looks back to Fritz
Lang's conspiratorial thrillers—
and Lang, after half a decade on the
run from the Nazis, made an
auspicious Hollywood debut
with a raw, powerful anti-lynching
melodrama with a hardbitten
lead performance by Spencer
Tracy.

Best American Film: *My Man
Godfrey*
Best Foreign Film: *Sabotage*
Best Actor: Spencer Tracy, *Fury*
Best Actress: Carole Lombard, *My
Man Godfrey*
Best Director: Fritz Lang, *Fury*

1937

The Good Earth had everything MGM's money could buy, including an Oscar-winning star, a locust invasion, thousands of extras, and an entire Chinese village shipped home and reconstructed on the backlot. But I suspect that even then, people had the feeling that I had watching it recently: the second unit went to China, and all I got was this lousy melodrama? It's the one about the big-time rancher who dumps the wife who stood by him for a pretty young thing, and raises sons who are no damn good—*Dallas* in yellowface.

The Good Earth was MGM's most expensive movie since the silent *Ben-Hur*—and like its big-budget predecessors *Mutiny on the Bounty* and *The Great Ziegfeld*, it probably counted on a Best Picture Oscar. But despite the fact that most of them had probably been *in* it, the thousands of extras who had just been made Academy voters in President Capra's cleanup of the Academy just couldn't see their way to voting it Best Picture, and instead they picked the Paul Muni costume picture that *moved*. It was the first sign of the Academy's escape from the moguls' control.

Academy Awards

**** *The Life of Emile Zola*
AAW NYC
Despite the title, the real subject of the film isn't Zola's life but the Dreyfus case, in which the popular author risked his reputation and fortune to prove that the Jewish Dreyfus had been framed for espionage committed by a Gentile. As a courtroom drama it's one of Hollywood's best, expertly sketching the backscratching perfidy of the French officers, the desperation of saintly Dreyfus' plight, and the exhilaration of Zola's fearless, hypocrisy-puncturing crusade. I still wouldn't call Muni a great actor, but he's a good show.

Picture
The Life of Emile Zola (Warner Bros., Henry Blanke)
The Awful Truth (Columbia, Leo McCarey, Everett Riskin)
Captains Courageous (MGM, Louis D. Lighton)
Dead End (UA, Samuel Goldwyn)
The Good Earth (MGM, Irving Thalberg, Albert Lewin)
In Old Chicago (20th Century–Fox, Darryl F. Zanuck, Kenneth MacGowan)
Lost Horizon (Columbia, Frank Capra)
100 Men and a Girl (Universal, Charles Rogers, Joseph Pasternak)
Stage Door (RKO Radio, Pandro S. Berman)
A Star Is Born (UA, David O. Selznick)

** **Spencer Tracy in** *Captains Courageous* AAW
Tracy had given any number of terrific, naturalistic performances in pictures like *Man's Castle*, *20,000 Years in Sing Sing*, and *San Francisco*, and he'd given one of the decade's best in *Fury* the year before. So it's too bad that instead he won his first Oscar for his one excursion into Paul Muni territory, *Captains Courageous*, in which he played a Portuguese sailor complete with an accent and curly black Harpo wig. The movie itself is one of Hollywood's best family films, but if it has a weakness, well . . . it's the part of the movie that won the Oscar.

Actor
Spencer Tracy, *Captains Courageous*
Charles Boyer, *Conquest*
Fredric March, *A Star Is Born*
Robert Montgomery, *Night Must Fall*
Paul Muni, *The Life of Emile Zola*

** **Luise Rainer in** *The Good Earth* AAW
As the unglamorous first wife, Luise Rainer wears no makeup and for that matter hardly speaks through most of the first half. As *The Piano* recently demonstrated, exotically silent suffering is a good way to win an Oscar, and if Rainer's performance doesn't have a lot of range, even her monotony is a sign of integrity—she never cheapens the part by trying to sneak a little sympathy.

Actress
Luise Rainer, *The Good Earth*
Irene Dunne, *The Awful Truth*
Greta Garbo, *Camille*
Janet Gaynor, *A Star Is Born*
Barbara Stanwyck, *Stella Dallas*

Supporting Actor
Joseph Schildkraut, *The Life of Emile Zola*
Ralph Bellamy, *The Awful Truth*
Thomas Mitchell, *The Hurricane*
H. B. Warner, *Lost Horizon*
Roland Young, *Topper*

Supporting Actress
Alice Brady, *In Old Chicago*
Andrea Leeds, *Stage Door*
Anne Shirley, *Stella Dallas*
Claire Trevor, *Dead End*
Dame May Whitty, *Night Must Fall*

Director
Leo McCarey, *The Awful Truth*
William Dieterle, *The Life of Emile Zola*
Sidney Franklin, *The Good Earth*
Gregory La Cava, *Stage Door*
William Wellman, *A Star Is Born*

Screenplay: Heinz Herald, Geza Herczeg, Norman Reilly Raine, *The Life of Emile Zola*
Original Story: William A. Wellman, Robert Carson, *A Star Is Born*
Cinematography: Karl Freund, *The Good Earth*
Score: *100 Men and a Girl*, Universal Studio Music Dept., Charles Previn, head
Song: "Sweet Leilani," *Waikiki Wedding*, ml: Harry Owens
Interior Decoration: Stephen Goosson, *Lost Horizon*
Editing: *Lost Horizon*
Dance Direction: Hermes Pan, "Fun House," *A Damsel in Distress*
Assistant Director: Robert Webb, *In Old Chicago*

Sound Recording: *The Hurricane*
Short/Cartoon: *The Old Mill* (Walt Disney/Silly Symphonies)
Short/One-Reel: *Private Life of the Gannetts* (Educational)
Short/Two-Reel: *Torture Money* (MGM/Crime Doesn't Pay)
Short/Color: *Penny Wisdom* (MGM/Pete Smith Specialities)
Irving G. Thalberg Award: Darryl F. Zanuck
Special Awards:
Mack Sennett
Edgar Bergen
The Museum of Modern Art Film Library for collecting films and making them available for the study of film as a major art form
W. Howard Greene for color photography, *A Star Is Born*

*** *Mayerling*   NYC
A decidedly timely French hit for 1937—the story of the heir to a throne who gave it up for the woman he loved. Rather than Edward VII, however, Charles Boyer plays the Hapsburg prince Rudolf who, deprived of his young mistress (Danielle Darrieux) and any meaningful role in the running of the empire, committed suicide with her in 1889. No great psychological insights into immature royalty, but a well-made doomed romance on a technical and artistic par with a good Greta Garbo picture—and it made an international romantic star out of Boyer, quickly cast in (you guessed it) a Greta Garbo picture, *Conquest.*

New York Film Critics Circle
Picture: *The Life of Emile Zola*
Foreign Film: *Mayerling*

Actor: Paul Muni, *The Life of Emile Zola*
Actress: Greta Garbo, *Camille*
Director: Gregory La Cava, *Stage Door*

National Board of Review
Best American Film: *Night Must Fall*
The Life of Emile Zola
Black Legion
Camille
Make Way for Tomorrow
The Good Earth
They Won't Forget
Captains Courageous
A Star Is Born
Stage Door
Best Foreign Film: *The Eternal Mask*
The Lower Depths
Baltic Deputy
Mayerling
The Spanish Earth
Golgotha
Elephant Boy
Rembrandt
Janosik
The Wedding of Palo

Photoplay Medal of Honor
Captains Courageous, produced by Louis D. Lighton/Metro-Goldwyn Mayer

Venice Film Festival
Foreign Film: *Un Carnet de Bal* (Julien Duvivier, France)
Mussolini Cup/Italian Film: *Scipio l'Africano* (Carmine Gallone, Italy)
Actor: Emil Jannings, *Der Herrscher* (Germany)
Actress: Bette Davis, *Marked Woman, Kid Galahad* (USA)
Director: Robert Flaherty, Zoltan Korda, *Elephant Boy* (UK)
Italian Director: Mario Camerini, *Il signor Max*
Screenplay: Sacha Guitry, *The Pearls of the Crown* (France)

Cinematography: J. Peverell Marley, *Winterset* (USA)
Best Artistic Ensemble: *Grand Illusion* (Jean Renoir, France)
Best First Screening: *Victoria the Great* (Herbert Wilcox, UK)
Best Film With Colonial Subject: *Sentinelle di Bronzo* (Romolo Marcellini, Italy)
Best Film Interpreting Natural and Artistic Beauties: *Condottieri* (Luis Trenker, Germany)
Documentary: Walter Ruttmann, *Mannesmann* (Germany)
Animated Film: Walt Disney, *Hawaiian Holiday*, *Music Land*, *The Old Mill*, *Alpine Climbers*, *The Country Cousin*, *Mickey's Polo Team* (USA)

Gebert's Golden Armchairs

The most romantic title in movie history is *History Is Made at Night*—it's supposed to refer to the Titanic-like shipwreck ending, but we all know it really means what happens between an estranged wife (Jean Arthur) and a headwaiter (Charles Boyer) when they run away together on her tycoon husband's ocean liner. Jean Gabin, the French Bogart, was also très romantique in the French *Casablanca*, *Pepe le Moko*; and three years before her Oscar for *Kitty Foyle*, Ginger Rogers proved that she was a real actress, thank you *very* much, in *Stage Door*, opposite her RKO rival K. Hepburn.

Best American Film: *History Is Made at Night*
Best Foreign Film: *Pepe le Moko*
Best Actor: Jean Gabin, *Pepe le Moko*
Best Actress: Ginger Rogers, *Stage Door*
Best Director: Frank Borzage, *History Is Made at Night*

1938

Venice had grown steadily more politicized as the decade went on; 1936 saw the top prize go to a German film amid grumbling of favoritism, and though a French film won in 1937, it wasn't the French film everyone expected—Jean Renoir's internationally acclaimed *Grand Illusion*, which was too pacifist for the politicos, found itself with only a minor acting award instead, as the prize went to *Un Carnet de Bal*.

Venice '38 took place in the shadow of the Munich Conference a month earlier. Seeing his ally Hitler suddenly poised to take half of Central Europe, Mussolini decided to curry favor with a gift—and improbable as it may seem, a Mussolini Cup at Venice was apparently just the thing for one movie-mad dictator to give another. The prize—for Leni Riefenstahl's *Olympia*—prompted an immediate outcry from American and British producers, who considered the film nothing more than Nazi propaganda. Stung, the ministry of culture hastily announced a whole host of consolation prizes, with at least one for every country attending (including Czechoslovakia—not much consolation for what happened at Munich). It didn't help; American producers, finding it harder and harder to get Germany and Italy to accept films with democratic themes (or Jewish stars) anyway, pulled out of Venice after 1938, and the next year a rival festival was launched—briefly—at Cannes.

Academy Awards

**** *You Can't Take It With You* AAW

Capra's second (and last) Best Picture Oscar–winner isn't quite as well-remembered as some of his others, and the thing that he most obviously added to Kaufman and Hart's play—a Capraesque interlude in which industrialist Edward Arnold gets his comeuppance—sticks out like a sore thumb. Otherwise, though, this is a first-rate adaptation of a surefire stage comedy, with a great cast of lovable eccentrics led by Lionel Barrymore, Ann Miller, Mischa Auer, and Donald Meek.

Picture
You Can't Take It With You (Columbia, Frank Capra)
The Adventures of Robin Hood (Warner Bros., Hal B. Wallis, Henry Blanke)
Alexander's Ragtime Band (20th Century–Fox, Darryl F. Zanuck, Harry Joe Brown)
Boys Town (MGM, John W. Considine, Jr.)
The Citadel (MGM, Victor Saville)
Four Daughters (Warner

Bros.–First National, Hal B.
Wallis, Henry Blanke)
Grand Illusion (R.A.O., World
Pictures)
Jezebel (Warner Bros., Hal B.
Wallis, Henry Blanke)
Pygmalion (MGM, Gabriel
Pascal)
Test Pilot (MGM, Louis D.
Lighton)

*** Spencer Tracy in *Boys Town* AAW

When Newt Gingrich made
Boys Town a front-page topic
by suggesting that it offered a
solution to the welfare
problem, no one seemed to
notice that *Boys Town* itself
was pure Hollywood liberalism.
It was co-written by the
quintessential Tinseltown
liberal, Dore Schary (future
producer of *Crossfire* and
Sunrise at Campobello). And
it's full of liberal notions on the
social causes of crime:
Spencer Tracy's Father
Flanagan gets the idea of
starting Boys Town when he
meets a young man on Death
Row, who says he wouldn't
have been there if he'd had a
proper home as a child; while
Boys Town itself is built on
precisely the kind of keep-'em-
off-the-streets social programs
whose modern forms (like
midnight basketball) Gingrich
campaigned against.
Ah well, the strangest
bedfellows of all are when politics
and entertainment shack up.
Taken as a movie, *Boys Town*
is an extremely effective piece
of sentimental drama, and I
wouldn't mind if it started

turning up on TV every
Election Day. Father Flanagan
is far from the juiciest part that
Spencer Tracy had, though, and
I believe he won because of
the subject matter, the film's box
office success, and his own
popularity—not because he
particularly plumbed his own
actorly depths here.

Actor
Spencer Tracy, *Boys Town*
Charles Boyer, *Algiers*
James Cagney, *Angels With Dirty
Faces*
Robert Donat, *The Citadel*
Leslie Howard, *Pygmalion*

** Bette Davis in *Jezebel* AAW

Davis didn't get the part of
Scarlett O'Hara, so she had
Jack Warner go right out and
buy her one just like it. Only
it isn't; it's a mossy old thing
that doesn't have a bit of
Margaret Mitchell's (or David
Selznick's) panache. She's
okay, but it was mainly the fact
that it was the first time she'd
been given a really lavish
production that carried her to her
Oscar win over New York's
favorites, Margaret Sullavan
and Wendy Hiller.

Actress
Bette Davis, *Jezebel*
Fay Bainter, *White Banners*
[NOTE: first performer nominated in
both categories in same year]
Wendy Hiller, *Pygmalion*
Norma Shearer, *Marie Antoinette*
Margaret Sullavan, *Three
Comrades*

Supporting Actor
Walter Brennan, *Kentucky*
John Garfield, *Four Daughters*

Gene Lockhart, *Algiers*
Robert Morley, *Marie Antoinette*
Basil Rathbone, *If I Were King*

Supporting Actress
Fay Bainter, *Jezebel*
Beulah Bondi, *Of Human Hearts*
Billie Burke, *Merrily We Live*
Spring Byington, *You Can't Take It With You*
Miliza Korjus, *The Great Waltz*

Director
Frank Capra, *You Can't Take It With You*
Michael Curtiz, *Angels with Dirty Faces*
Michael Curtiz, *Four Daughters*
Norman Taurog, *Boys Town*
King Vidor, *The Citadel*

Screenplay: George Bernard Shaw, adaptation: Ian Dalrymple, Cecil Lewis, W. P. Lipscomb, *Pygmalion*
Original Story: Eleanore Griffin, Dore Schary, *Boys Town*
Cinematography: Joseph Ruttenberg, *The Great Waltz*
Original Score: Erich Wolfgang Korngold, *The Adventures of Robin Hood*
Score: Alfred Newman, *Alexander's Ragtime Band*
[NOTE: new category distinction allows nomination of scores using existing themes]
Song: ''Thanks for the Memory,'' *Big Broadcast of 1938*, m: Ralph Rainger, l: Leo Robin
Interior Decoration: Carl J. Weyl, *The Adventures of Robin Hood*
Editing: *The Adventures of Robin Hood*
Sound Recording: *The Cowboy and the Lady*
Short/Cartoon: *Ferdinand the Bull* (Walt Disney)
Short/One-Reel: *That Mothers Might Live* (MGM Miniatures; directed by Fred Zinnemann)

Short/Two-Reel: *Declaration of Independence* (Warners Historical Featurette)
Irving G. Thalberg Award: Hal B. Wallis
Special Awards:
Deanna Durbin and Mickey Rooney, youth actors
Harry M. Warner for the production of historical short subjects
Walt Disney for *Snow White and the Seven Dwarfs*
Oliver Marsh, Allen Davey, color cinematography, *Sweethearts*
For special photographic and sound effects, *Spawn of the North*
J. Arthur Ball for the advancement of color photography

*** *The Citadel*   NYC BOR
MGM's answer to *The Story of Louis Pasteur*. Robert Donat is the English doctor who goes from idealist in a mining village to wealthy physician of rich hypochondriacs, then recovers his ideals in time to defend himself for working with an unlicensed TB researcher. A solid and engrossing drama which, alas, turns preachy at the end—a mistake Warner Bros. rarely made.

**** *Grand Illusion*   NYC BOR VEN
Long ranked among the best films of all time—see the *Sight & Sound* lists—Jean Renoir's pacifist tale is certainly a very fine drama, though its central notion (solidarity cutting across class lines) doesn't shock the way it did in 1937–38, and it doesn't have the complexity of his

masterpiece, *The Rules of the Game*. Unlike that masterpiece, you could teach this one in high school film class, if there was such a thing.

New York Film Critics Circle
Picture: *The Citadel*
Foreign Film: *Grand Illusion*
Actor: James Cagney, *Angels With Dirty Faces*
Actress: Margaret Sullavan, *Three Comrades*
Director: Alfred Hitchcock, *The Lady Vanishes*
Special Award: *Snow White and the Seven Dwarfs*

National Board of Review
Best English-Language Film:
The Citadel
Snow White and the Seven Dwarfs
The Beachcomber
To the Victor
Sing, You Sinners
The Edge of the World
Of Human Hearts
Jezebel
South Riding
Three Comrades
Best Foreign Film: *Grand Illusion*
Ballerina
Un Carnet de Bal
Generals Without Buttons
Peter the First
Professor Mamlock

Photoplay Medal of Honor
Sweethearts, produced by Hunt Stromberg/Metro-Goldwyn Mayer

**** *Olympia*   VEN
Leni Riefenstahl's documentary of the '36 Berlin Olympics is a thrillingly assembled salute to athletic perfection, beginning with a prologue set in ancient Greece full of beautiful bodies throwing things in skimpy togas (the inspiration for numerous homoerotic Calvin Klein ads), and concluding with a diving sequence edited by the avant-garde filmmaker Walther Ruttmann in which the images are so dazzlingly put together that you have no idea who won. Despite the controversy, *Olympia* really was the best film at Venice; Riefenstahl's artistry is undeniable—but her notions of physical perfection would be intellectually dubious (and a bit kitschy) even if they weren't tied to Nazi ideology.

Venice Film Festival
Mussolini Cup/Foreign Film: *Olympia* (Leni Riefenstahl, Germany)
Mussolini Cup/Italian Film: *Lucianno Serra Pilota* (Goffredo Alessandrini, Italy)
Actor: Leslie Howard, *Pygmalion* (UK)
Actress: Norma Shearer, *Marie Antoinette* (USA)
Great Art Trophy: Walt Disney, *Snow White and the Seven Dwarfs* (USA)
Special Mention Medals:
Artistic Ensemble: *A Woman's Face* (Gustaf Molander, Sweden); *Vivacious Lady* (George Stevens, USA); *Alla en el Rancho Grande* (Fernando de Fuentes, Mexico); *Fahrendes Volk* [*Les Gens du Voyage*] (Jacques Feyder, Germany); *Jezebel* (William Wyler, USA)
Acting: *The Rage of Paris* (Henry Koster, USA); *Hanno Rapito Un Uomo* (Gennaro Righelli, Italy); *Der Mustergatte* (Wolfgang Liebeneiner, Germany)
Technique: *The Goldwyn Follies* (George Marshall, USA); *Sotto*

la Croce del Sud (Guido Brignone, Italy)
Story: *Break the News* (Rene Clair, UK); *Geniusz Sceny*
Direction: Carl Fröhlich, *Heimat* (Germany); Karl Ritter, *Urlaub auf Ehrenwort* (Germany); Marcel Carné, *Quai des Brumes* (France)
Minister of Popular Culture Awards: USA: *The Adventures of Tom Sawyer* (Norman Taurog), *Marie Antoinette* (W. S. Van Dyke), *Mother Carey's Chickens* (Rowland V. Lee), *Jezebel, Test Pilot* (Victor Fleming); UK: *The Drum* (Zoltan Korda), *Pygmalion* (Anthony Asquith); Japan: *Five Scouts* (Tomotaka Tasaka); France: *Prisons sans Barreaux* (Léonide Moguy); Italy: *Giuseppe Verdi* (Carmine Gallone); Czechoslovakia: *Panen Kutnahorskych*; Germany: *Heimat*

Gebert's Golden Armchairs

You Can't Take It With You is a more than usually deserving

Best Picture–winner for this erratic period in Oscar's life, but it's still aced out in my book by Errol Flynn in the greatest adventure movie ever made. What is *King of Alcatraz* with J. Carrol Naish, you ask? A little 56-minute B thriller, in which one of those I-know-the-face-but-what's-the-name character actors from the late show turns in just one of his dozens of terrific performances, to resounding silence from critics and award-giving groups. And five years after *Morning Glory*, Katharine Hepburn's affectations *are* finally more than just affectations in *Holiday* (yes, *Holiday*, not *Bringing Up Baby*).

Best American Film: *The Adventures of Robin Hood*
Best Foreign Film: *Grand Illusion*
Best Actor: J. Carrol Naish, *King of Alcatraz*
Best Actress: Katharine Hepburn, *Holiday*
Best Director: Michael Curtiz, *The Adventures of Robin Hood*

1939

David O. Selznick didn't have a studio of flunkies he could send out to vote him up an Oscar win. He had to do it a new way, through publicity. Did he ever; it was *Gone With the Wind*'s four-year-long publicity campaign, not the movie itself, that was Selznick's masterpiece.

The artillery barrages of hype were so thick and relentless that Frank Nugent, writing in *The New York Times* the very *morning* after the New York premiere, felt obliged to pose and (somewhat nervously) answer the question: "Is it the greatest motion picture ever made? Probably not, although it is the greatest motion mural we have seen and the most ambitious film-making venture in Hollywood's spectacular history." (Imagine *The New York Times* feeling compelled to field that question the day after a modern masterpiece of hype—*Batman*, say—opened.) Even the New York Film Critics, who might have been expected to turn up their noses at it, deadlocked between it and *Mr. Smith* for 14 ballots before settling on *Wuthering Heights* as a compromise candidate. There was no escaping Selznick's *Wind* in 1939.

Academy Awards

**** *Gone With the Wind*
AAW PHO
***** **Vivien Leigh** AAW
NYC
Alice Adams, remade on the scale of *Ben-Hur*. Though the production is never less than impressive, the story falls apart in the second half (let's see, who's dying now), just pulling it together for the finale. Which is all the more reason to be glad Selznick got the cast he did—especially Vivien Leigh's unimprovable Scarlett, perfect enough to make every other possibility seem a ghastly mistake. Try to imagine Hepburn attempting that satisfied meow the morning after Rhett ravishes her—or Davis tearing turnips out of the earth without laughing.

Picture
Gone With the Wind (MGM, David O. Selznick)
Dark Victory (Warner Bros., David Lewis)
Goodbye, Mr. Chips (MGM, Victor Saville)
Love Affair (RKO Radio, Leo McCarey)
Mr. Smith Goes to Washington (Columbia, Frank Capra)
Ninotchka (MGM, Sidney Franklin)
Of Mice and Men (UA, Hal Roach, Lewis Milestone)
Stagecoach (UA, Walter Wanger)
The Wizard of Oz (MGM, Mervyn LeRoy)
Wuthering Heights (UA, Samuel Goldwyn)

*** Robert Donat in *Goodbye, Mr. Chips* AAW
A fine, whimsical performance of great charm, though it pushes tweeness when he's made up to be an old man.

Actor
Robert Donat, *Goodbye, Mr. Chips*
Clark Gable, *Gone With the Wind*
Laurence Olivier, *Wuthering Heights*
Mickey Rooney, *Babes in Arms*
James Stewart, *Mr. Smith Goes to Washington*

Actress
Vivien Leigh *Gone With the Wind*
Bette Davis, *Dark Victory*
Irene Dunne, *Love Affair*
Greta Garbo, *Ninotchka*
Greer Garson, *Goodbye, Mr. Chips*

Supporting Actor
Thomas Mitchell, *Stagecoach*
Brian Aherne, *Juárez*
Harry Carey [Sr.], *Mr. Smith Goes to Washington*
Brian Donlevy, *Beau Geste*
Claude Rains, *Mr. Smith Goes to Washington*

Supporting Actress
Hattie McDaniel, *Gone With the Wind* [NOTE: first African-American winner]
Olivia de Havilland, *Gone With the Wind*
Geraldine Fitzgerald, *Wuthering Heights*
Edna May Oliver, *Drums Along the Mohawk*
Maria Ouspenskaya, *Love Affair*

Director
Victor Fleming, *Gone With the Wind*
Frank Capra, *Mr. Smith Goes to Washington*
John Ford, *Stagecoach*
Sam Wood, *Goodbye, Mr. Chips*
William Wyler, *Wuthering Heights*

Screenplay: Sidney Howard, *Gone With the Wind*
Original Story: Lewis R. Foster, *Mr. Smith Goes to Washington*
Cinematography/B&W: Gregg Toland, *Wuthering Heights*
Cinematography/Color: Ernest Haller, Ray Rennahan, *Gone With the Wind*
Original Score: Herbert Stothart, *The Wizard of Oz*
Score: Richard Hageman, Frank Harling, John Leipold, Leo Shuken, *Stagecoach*
Song: "Over the Rainbow," *The Wizard of Oz*, m: Harold Arlen, l: E. Y. Harburg
Interior Decoration: Lyle Wheeler, *Gone With the Wind*
Editing: *Gone With the Wind*
Sound Recording: *When Tomorrow Comes*
Special Effects: *The Rains Came*
Short/Cartoon: *The Ugly Duckling* (Walt Disney/Silly Symphonies)
Short/One-Reel: *Busy Little Bears* (Paramount Paragraphics)
Short/Two-Reel: *Sons of Liberty* (Warner Historical Featurette; dir. by Michael Curtiz)
Irving G. Thalberg Award: David O. Selznick
Special Awards:
Douglas Fairbanks, first president of the Academy
The Motion Picture Relief Fund; presented to Jean Hersholt, President, et al.
Judy Garland, screen juvenile
William Cameron Menzies, for the use of color for the enhancement of dramatic mood in *Gone With the Wind*

The Technicolor Company for three-color feature production

• *Wuthering Heights* NYC
No *Gone With the Wind*—the Brontë book is reduced to a contrived piece of romantic twaddle which forces two great stage actors (Laurence Olivier and Geraldine Fitzgerald) to play second fiddle to a less-than-great movie star (Merle Oberon).

*** *Harvest* NYC
The hottest new French filmmaker of the '80s, the joke went, was dead—novelist-filmmaker Marcel Pagnol (1895–1974), whose books about life in rural France were adapted into *Jean de Florette/Manon of the Spring* and *My Father's Glory/My Mother's Castle*. By the '80s Pagnol's picture of French peasantry, all whimsical characters and crafty sneaks, would be pure nostalgia for the filmmakers who appropriated it. Pagnol may play up the whimsical side, too, but in his own films he was close enough to the real thing to convey a whiff of sweat and dung—and close enough to other '30s filmmakers like Clair and Vigo to convey some of the same earthy eroticism and anarchic spirit. This is a good, if not the best, example: a hulking but tender hermit (Gabriel Gabrio) living in an abandoned village proves to be just the charge the battery of female itinerant Orane Demazis needs, and soon

they're in the fields, sowing symbolic wheat together.

**** **James Stewart in** *Mr. Smith Goes to Washington* NYC
Stewart jumped from light leading man to great American actor with his powerhouse performance in Frank Capra's more ominous revamp of *Mr. Deeds*.

New York Film Critics Circle
Picture: *Wuthering Heights*
Foreign Film: *Harvest*
Actor: James Stewart, *Mr. Smith Goes to Washington*
Actress: Vivien Leigh, *Gone With the Wind*
Director: John Ford, *Stagecoach*

National Board of Review
Best English-Language Film:
Confessions of a Nazi Spy
Wuthering Heights
Stagecoach
Ninotchka
Young Mr. Lincoln
Crisis
Goodbye, Mr. Chips
Mr. Smith Goes to Washington
The Roaring Twenties
U-Boat 29
Best Foreign Film: *Port of Shadows*
Harvest
Alexander Nevsky
The End of the Day
Robert Koch

Photoplay Medal of Honor
Gone With the Wind, produced by David O. Selznick

Venice Film Festival
Foreign Film: none awarded
Italian Film: *Abuna Messias* (Goffredo Alessandrini, Italy)

Cups of the Biennale:
End of the Day (Julien Duvivier, France)
Robert Koch, der Bekämpfer des Todes (Hans Steinhoff, Germany)
Four Feathers (Zoltan Korda, UK)
The selection of Swedish films as a whole: *Gläd dig i din ungdom* (Per Lindberg), *En Handfull Ris* (Paul Fejos, Gunnar Sköglund)
Cinematography: Ubaldo Arata, *Dernière Jeunesse* (France-Italy)
Special Mention Awards:
Margarita, Armando y su Padre; *Tulak Macoun* (Ladislav Brom, Czechoslovakia); *Jeunes Filles et Détresse* (G.W. Pabst, France); *Veertig Jaren* (Edmond T. Gréville, UK); *Boris Istvan, The Golden Harvest of the Witwaterstrand, The Mikado* (Victor Schertzinger, UK)

Harvard Lampoon Movie Worsts

Ten worst pictures:
The Rains Came
Hollywood Cavalcade
Winter Carnival
St. Louis Blues
Five Little Peppers
Bad Little Angel
The Fighting 69th
Idiot's Delight
20,000 Men a Year
The Man in the Iron Mask
Worst Actor: Tyrone Power, *The Rains Came*
Worst Actress: Norma Shearer, *Idiot's Delight*
Most Consistently Bad Performances: Dorothy Lamour, Don Ameche
Most Colossal Flop: *The Wizard of Oz*

Gebert's Golden Armchairs

Leigh aside, my 1939 list looks like a whole different year—the year the movies started growing up: Howard Hawks' hard silver poem of flying and dying, *Only Angels Have Wings*; John Ford's supercharged reinvention of the western, the *Road Warrior* of its day, *Stagecoach*; Burgess Meredith's haunting performance as a bundle of raw nerve endings named George, with a big dumb friend named Lenny; and from France, Jean Renoir's masterful dissection of society's ruthless operating principles, *The Rules of the Game*.

Best American Film: *Only Angels Have Wings*
Best Foreign Film: *The Rules of the Game*
Best Actor: Burgess Meredith, *Of Mice and Men*
Best Actress: Vivien Leigh, *Gone With the Wind*
Best Director: John Ford, *Stagecoach*

1940

Today *The Grapes of Wrath* seems as obvious a choice for a Best Picture Oscar as *Schindler's List*—a serious picture about social problems which realizes its noble intentions just about perfectly. But that's because we've had fifty years to think of those as being the preferred qualities for a Best Picture–winner. In 1940, a Best Picture–winner was *The Great Ziegfeld* or *Gone With the Wind*—an expensive, unchallenging crowd-pleaser. *The Grapes of Wrath*, on the other hand, was not only strong, grim medicine—the most unglamorous major Oscar contender since *The Crowd*—but it also hit perilously close to home for Hollywood, since its implied targets were big California landowners (including one big landowner whom Hollywood knew very well indeed, William Randolph Hearst). At the last minute, David Selznick gave the Academy a way out by heavily promoting *Rebecca* at Oscar time—but if *Wrath* lost the battle, in the end it won the war, paving the way for a new class of realistic, seriously intended Oscar winners like *The Best Years of Our Lives*, *Gentleman's Agreement*, and *On the Waterfront*.

The social-concern faction would come to be associated in the '50s and '60s with gray old Bosley Crowther, but in his first year as leader of the *Times* bloc, the overeager kid became the cause of the critics' group's only scandal. Best Actor had gone a record 23 ballots between Charlie Chaplin in *The Great Dictator* and James Stephenson in *The Letter* before Crowther broke the deadlock—by suggesting that Chaplin would be a bigger draw for the radio broadcast of the awards ceremony. *Daily Mirror* critic Lee Mortimer finked on Crowther's machinations a few days later in his paper, and Chaplin, hoping to preserve his Oscar chances, became the only person ever to decline a Critics Circle award.

Academy Awards

**** *Rebecca* AAW
A thinking person's black-and-white *Gone With the Wind*, with the downbeat psychological dimension Margaret Mitchell's tale lacked. It's about as good as its kind gets—but it also suggests that director Alfred Hitchcock had a close escape; he could easily have been stuck in Hollywood making nothing but this sort of above-average soap opera thriller, one *Suspicion* after another instead of *Shadow of a Doubt* and *Strangers on a Train*.

Picture
Rebecca (UA, David O. Selznick)
All This, and Heaven Too (Warner Bros., Jack L. Warner, Hal B. Wallis)
Foreign Correspondent (UA, Walter Wanger)
The Grapes of Wrath (20th Century–Fox, Darryl F. Zanuck, Nunnally Johnson)
The Great Dictator (UA, Charles Chaplin)
Kitty Foyle (RKO Radio, David Hempstead)
The Letter (Warner Bros., Hal B. Wallis)
The Long Voyage Home (UA, Argosy-Wanger, John Ford)
Our Town (UA, Sol Lesser)
The Philadelphia Story (MGM, Joseph L. Mankiewicz)

*** James Stewart in *The Philadelphia Story* AAW
The screwball comedy grew up in this mature, beautifully well-made comedy. But why did Oscar single out Stewart from a cast that is all at a remarkably high level—but from which, if you had to pick an actor, the actor would be Cary Grant? The reason was to make up for '39—when Stewart lost to Robert Donat, making up for *him* not winning for *The Citadel* in '38. What tangled webs Oscar weaves.

Actor
James Stewart, *The Philadelphia Story*
Charles Chaplin, *The Great Dictator*
Henry Fonda, *The Grapes of Wrath*
Raymond Massey, *Abe Lincoln in Illinois*
Laurence Olivier, *Rebecca*

** Ginger Rogers in *Kitty Foyle* AAW
Ginger Rogers was probably the most underrated actress of the '30s, and when she finally got herself a plum dramatic role, she went after an Oscar with everything she had, doing love scenes, self-sacrifice scenes, comedy scenes, maternal tragedy scenes—everything, that is, *except* sing and dance. She deserved an Oscar for something, but *Kitty Foyle* is just too much. It announces at its start that it's going to be about the new, modern white-collar female—so of course it instantly turns into the most traditional kind of feminine melodrama, in which our average Philadelphia working girl is torn (like most average working girls) between a wealthy Main Line heir and a poor but decent doctor, both of them big strappin' hunks. This is really the last gasp of the Norma Shearer/Helen Hayes society movie, in which it becomes harder than ever to make believable the scene in which his parents tell her, the ultra-competent office manager, that she's not good enough for their idiot son. The next time we saw that scene, in a Ross Hunter production of the '50s with Lana Turner, it was camp and it knew it.

Actress
Ginger Rogers, *Kitty Foyle*
Bette Davis, *The Letter*
Joan Fontaine, *Rebecca*

Katharine Hepburn, *The Philadelphia Story*
Martha Scott, *Our Town*

Supporting Actor
Walter Brennan, *The Westerner*
Albert Basserman, *Foreign Correspondent*
William Gargan, *They Knew What They Wanted*
Jack Oakie, *The Great Dictator*
James Stephenson, *The Letter*

Supporting Actress
Jane Darwell, *The Grapes of Wrath*
Judith Anderson, *Rebecca*
Ruth Hussey, *The Philadelphia Story*
Barbara O'Neil, *All This, and Heaven Too*
Marjorie Rambeau, *Primrose Path*

Director
John Ford, *The Grapes of Wrath*
George Cukor, *The Philadelphia Story*
Alfred Hitchcock, *Rebecca*
Sam Wood, *Kitty Foyle*
William Wyler, *The Letter*

Original Screenplay: Preston Sturges, *The Great McGinty*
Adapted Screenplay: Donald Ogden Stewart, *The Philadelphia Story*
Original Story: Benjamin Glazer, John S. Toldy, *Arise, My Love*
Cinematography/B&W: George Barnes, *Rebecca*
Cinematography/Color: Georges Perinal, *The Thief of Bagdad*
Original Score: Leigh Harline, Paul J. Smith, Ned Washington, *Pinocchio*
Score: Alfred Newman, *Tin Pan Alley*
Song: "When You Wish Upon a Star," *Pinocchio*, m: Leigh Harline, l: Ned Washington
Interior Decoration/B&W: Cedric Gibbons, *Pride and Prejudice*
Interior Decoration/Color: Vincent Korda, *The Thief of Bagdad*
Editing: *Northwest Mounted Police*
Sound Recording: *Strike Up the Band*
Special Effects: *The Thief of Bagdad*
Short/Cartoon: *The Milky Way* (MGM/Rudolph Ising)
Short/One-Reel: *Quicker 'N a Wink* (MGM/Pete Smith Specialties)
Short/Two-Reel: *Teddy, the Rough Rider* (Warner Historical Featurette)
Special Awards:
Bob Hope
Colonel Nathan Levinson for making possible the mobilization of industry facilities for Army training films

***** *The Grapes of Wrath*
NYC BOR
The Grapes of Wrath completely fulfills every hope a reader of the novel could have had, bringing Steinbeck's flights of poetry to believable life in the mouths of plain, dusty people. It also fulfills every promise of John Ford's earlier work, creating (unlike *The Informer*) an authentically American mythic style out of his German Expressionist borrowings—and it would be churlish not to mention here cinematographer Gregg Toland, who would also shoot the best German-American film of 1941, *Citizen Kane*.

**** *The Baker's Wife*   NYC BOR
In the most perfectly formed of Marcel (*Harvest*) Pågnol's whimsical, risqué peasant comedies, the French actor Raimu plays a baker whose wife runs off with a shepherd, plunging him into a depression so deep he can't bear to make his bread—provoking action on the part of his hungry fellow villagers.

New York Film Critics Circle
Picture: *The Grapes of Wrath*
Foreign Film: *The Baker's Wife*
Actor: Charles Chaplin, *The Great Dictator* [award declined]
Actress: Katharine Hepburn, *The Philadelphia Story*
Director: John Ford, *The Grapes of Wrath*, *The Long Voyage Home*
Special Award: Walt Disney, *Fantasia*

National Board of Review
Best English-Language Film:
The Grapes of Wrath
The Great Dictator
Of Mice and Men
Our Town
Fantasia
The Long Voyage Home
Foreign Correspondent
The Biscuit Eater
Gone With the Wind
Rebecca
Best Foreign Film: *The Baker's Wife*
Best Documentary: *The Fight for Life*

Venice Film Festival
Mussolini Cup/Foreign Film:
Der Postmeister (Gustav Ucicky, Germany)
Mussolini Cup/Italian Film:
L'assedio dell'Alcazar (Augusto Genina)

Harvard Lampoon Movie Worsts
Ten worst pictures:
The Howards of Virginia
Swanee River
The Great Victor Herbert
One Million B.C.
I Take This Woman
My Son, My Son
Green Hell
Lillian Russell
Typhoon
Boom Town

Gebert's Golden Armchairs
The Oscars rightly belonged to *The Grapes of Wrath* and to a curiously overlooked Henry Fonda, the rock on which that movie was built. But my affection lies with a matched set of wildly ambitious, slightly daft Technicolor follies: Alexander Korda's answer to *The Wizard of Oz*, and Walt Disney's answer to the Renaissance.

Best American Film: *Fantasia*
Best Foreign Film: *The Thief of Bagdad*
Best Actor: Henry Fonda, *The Grapes of Wrath*
Best Actress: Katharine Hepburn, *The Philadelphia Story*
Best Director: George Cukor, *The Philadelphia Story*

1941

You might expect *Citizen Kane* to be the perfect example of a highbrow masterpiece which New York recognized and Oscar rejected. The reality is, Oscar didn't exactly reject it (it got nominations by the score); and New York took six ballots to give it the nod, on a simple majority vote, over *How Green Was My Valley*—and *Sergeant York*. (Admittedly, Pearl Harbor *had* happened just days before.)

The usual explanation for Oscar's choice of *Valley* over *Kane* is that fear of Hearst made Hollywood chicken out of honoring its greatest product. But the actual reason may have been more personal: Welles' image, that of the young man who blows into a stodgy town and by sheer force of genius makes a better first movie than anybody else's fiftieth, went against everything Hollywood, and especially 15,000 struggling, Academy-voting extras, believed in. 1941 gave the masses the choice between honoring a director who'd paid his dues—*Valley*'s John Ford, whose *Grapes of Wrath* had been screwed the year before—or a genius who said paying dues was for suckers. Each time Welles' name was read in nomination, there were boos. In the end, he collected precisely one-half of one Oscar—the other half of the screenwriting award won by another longtime dues-payer, Herman Mankiewicz, and the only piece of one he'd ever have.

Academy Awards

*** *How Green Was My Valley* AAW
Labor troubles in California hit too close to home for you? How about labor troubles in turn-of-the-century Wales instead? A rich, appealing slice of Ye Auld Sod nostalgia from John Ford, with a lot less blarney than *The Quiet Man*; but no *Grapes of Wrath*—or *Kane*.

Picture
How Green Was My Valley (20th Century–Fox, Darryl F. Zanuck)
Blossoms in the Dust (MGM, Irving Asher)
Citizen Kane (RKO Radio, Orson Welles)
Here Comes Mr. Jordan (Columbia, Everett Riskin)
Hold Back the Dawn (Paramount, Arthur Hornblow, Jr.)
The Little Foxes (RKO Radio, Samuel Goldwyn)
The Maltese Falcon (Warner Bros., Hal B. Wallis)
One Foot in Heaven (Warner Bros., Hal B. Wallis)
Sergeant York (Warner Bros., Jesse L. Lasky, Hal B. Wallis)
Suspicion (RKO Radio)

*** **Gary Cooper in *Sergeant York*** AAW NYC
Cooper won his first Oscar for this prewar morale booster, in

which he plays a backwoods yokel who overcame his pacifist upbringing to do his duty in WWI, winning the Congressional Medal of Honor. Less a war movie than one of Howard Hawks' very few attempts at Fordian mythmaking, it isn't intellectually coherent (a pacifist should fight because, well, he just should, that's all), and it seems a little simpleminded next to a real war movie like Hawks' *Air Force*. As Gary Cooper, which is by now a role in itself and not merely the name of an actor, Gary Cooper is perfectly cast.

Actor
Gary Cooper, *Sergeant York*
Cary Grant, *Penny Serenade*
Walter Huston, *All That Money Can Buy* [*The Devil and Daniel Webster*]
Robert Montgomery, *Here Comes Mr. Jordan*
Orson Welles, *Citizen Kane*

*** Joan Fontaine in *Suspicion* AAW NYC
Touching off one of Hollywood's longest-lasting family feuds, Joan Fontaine beat her sister Olivia de Havilland for an Oscar in her second Hitchcock film. Joan's certainly the best thing in this fairly minor melodrama about the mouse who married the tomcat and doesn't want to believe the obvious. But she's hardly the one you'd pick to win the only Oscar won by any actor in any Hitchcock film—not next to the likes of Norman Bates, Mrs. Danvers, Uncle Charley, Bruno Anthony, and so many other more colorful and twisted characters. Much more so than *Rebecca*, it's minor women's magazine stuff.

Actress
Joan Fontaine, *Suspicion*
Bette Davis, *The Little Foxes*
Greer Garson, *Blossoms in the Dust*
Olivia de Havilland, *Hold Back the Dawn*
Barbara Stanwyck, *Ball of Fire*

Supporting Actor
Donald Crisp, *How Green Was My Valley*
Walter Brennan, *Sergeant York*
Charles Coburn, *The Devil and Miss Jones*
James Gleason, *Here Comes Mr. Jordan*
Sydney Greenstreet, *The Maltese Falcon*

Supporting Actress
Mary Astor, *The Great Lie*
Sara Allgood, *How Green Was My Valley*
Patricia Collinge, *The Little Foxes*
Teresa Wright, *The Little Foxes*
Margaret Wycherly, *Sergeant York*

Director
John Ford, *How Green Was My Valley*
Alexander Hall, *Here Comes Mr. Jordan*
Howard Hawks, *Sergeant York*
Orson Welles, *Citizen Kane*
William Wyler, *The Little Foxes*

Original Screenplay: Herman J. Mankiewicz, Orson Welles, *Citizen Kane*
Adapted Screenplay: Sidney Buchman, Seton I. Miller, *Here Comes Mr. Jordan*
Original Story: Harry Segall, *Here Comes Mr. Jordan*

Cinematography/B&W: Arthur Miller, *How Green Was My Valley*
Cinematography/Color: Ernest Palmer, Ray Rennahan, *Blood and Sand*
Dramatic Score: Bernard Herrmann, *All That Money Can Buy* [*The Devil and Daniel Webster*]
Musical Score: Frank Churchill, Oliver Wallace, *Dumbo*
Song: "The Last Time I Saw Paris," *Lady Be Good*, m: Jerome Kern, l: Oscar Hammerstein II
Interior Decoration/B&W: Richard Day, Nathan Juran, *How Green Was My Valley*
Interior Decoration/Color: Cedric Gibbons, Urie McCleary, *Blossoms in the Dust*
Editing: *Sergeant York*
Sound Recording: *That Hamilton Woman*
Special Effects: *I Wanted Wings*
Short/Cartoon: *Lend A Paw* (Walt Disney/Pluto)
Short/One-Reel: *Of Pups and Puzzles* (MGM Passing Parade Series)
Short/Two-Reel: *Main Street on the March* (MGM)
Documentary: *Churchill's Island* (National Film Board of Canada)
Irving G. Thalberg Award: Walt Disney
Special Awards:
Rey Scott for producing *Kukan*, documentary on war in China, under difficult and dangerous conditions
The British Ministry of Information, *Target for Tonight*
Leopold Stokowski and his associates for their unique achievement in the creation of a new form of visualized music in *Fantasia*
Walt Disney, William Garity, John N. A. Hawkins and the RCA Manufacturing Company, for [stereo] sound, *Fantasia*

***** *Citizen Kane* NYC BOR
Everything everyone said it was—including its enemies: a serious, completely grown-up drama of power and failure, made by an energetic 26-year-old who thought a movie studio was the best train set a kid could have.

New York Film Critics Circle
Picture: *Citizen Kane*
Actor: Gary Cooper, *Sergeant York*
Actress: Joan Fontaine, *Suspicion*
Director: John Ford, *How Green Was My Valley*

** *Target For Tonight* AAW BOR
One of the first of many realistic British war documentaries— but not, at this distance, one of the best. A matter-of-fact account of a British bombing mission from target selection to the bomber's return, it's so low-key and stiff-upper-lip ("A peach of a target, sir") that it verges on Pythonesque self-parody.

National Board of Review
Best English-Language Film:
Citizen Kane
How Green Was My Valley
The Little Foxes
The Stars Look Down
Dumbo
High Sierra
Here Comes Mr. Jordan
Tom, Dick and Harry
The Road to Zanzibar
The Lady Eve

Best Foreign Film: *Pépé le Moko*
Best Documentary: *Target for Tonight*

The Forgotten Village
Ku Kan
The Land

Venice Film Festival
Mussolini Cup/Foreign Film:
Ohm Krüger (Hans Steinhoff,
Germany)
Mussolini Cup/Italian Film: *La
Corona di Ferro* (Alessandro
Blasetti)
Actor: Ermete Zacconi, *Don
Buonaparte* (Italy)
Actress: Luise Ullrich, *Annelie*
(Germany)
Director: G.W. Pabst,
Komödianten (Germany)
Cups of the Biennale:
Lettere d'Amore Smarrite
Alter ego (Frigyes Bán, Hungary)
Marianela (Benito Perojo, Spain)
Ich Klage an [*I Accuse*] (Wolfgang
Liebeneiner, Germany)
I Mariti

Harvard Lampoon Movie Worsts
Ten worst pictures:
Hudson's Bay
Wild Geese Calling
Belle Starr
Navy Blues
Honky Tonk
You Belong to Me
This Woman Is Mine
Lady Be Good
Aloma of the South Seas
Smilin' Through
Worst Performer: Betty Grable
Worst Discovery: Veronica Lake
Most Unattractive Actress:
Jeanette MacDonald

**Fastest-on-the-Downward-Pass
Award:** Alice Faye and Nelson
Eddy

Gebert's Golden Armchairs
If there is directing before and
after *Kane*, there is acting before
and after Bogart's smart, callous
yet charismatic and, above all,
modern Sam Spade. In Preston
Sturges' screwball comedy *The
Lady Eve*, Barbara Stanwyck
plays a slinky con-woman with
her eye on wealthy scientist and
snake-collector Henry Fonda,
and gives off an erotic charge that
would straighten a boa
constrictor. And the best foreign
film of the year was *49th
Parallel*, a Hitchcockian thriller
about a U-boat crew on the run
in Canada that signaled the arrival
of an extraordinary team from
Britain: Michael Powell and
Emeric Pressburger. (Actually,
it didn't signal them until 1942 in
America, where, as *The
Invaders*, it would be up for a
couple of Oscars.)

Best American Film: *Citizen Kane*
Best Foreign Film: *49th Parallel/
The Invaders*
Best Actor: Humphrey Bogart,
The Maltese Falcon
Best Actress: Barbara Stanwyck,
The Lady Eve
Best Director: Orson Welles,
Citizen Kane

1942

A successful wartime documentary was called *Know Your Ally: Britain*, and that was what MGM set out to achieve with its first major contribution to the war effort, *Mrs. Miniver*. What that meant in practice was that Britons were to be depicted as being as much like Americans as possible. The Minivers live in a house that would be more at home in Bakersfield than their town of Belham; they begin the picture by buying a new car for him and a new hat for her (which would have marked them as damn near gentry in Mr. Churchill's Britain), and while Dad (Walter Pidgeon) is off rescuing the lads at Dunkirk, Mom captures a German parachutist in her kitchen with his own pistol (it's a wonder she doesn't subdue him with a judo flip, too).

It's all too easy now to make fun of *Mrs. Miniver*—what's wrong with it is that it doesn't really deliver the picture of the "real" Britain that it promises; what was right with it was that it worked. It was a huge hit because it satisfied Americans' curiosity about what their ally was like—even if it did so falsely. Hollywood dutifully rewarded it with six Oscars, a total then second only to *Gone With the Wind*.

The New York critics, on the other hand, didn't give the middlebrow *Miniver* a single vote, preferring the genuine English article—Noël Coward's and David Lean's naval drama *In Which We Serve*, which won out 12–7 over its only serious competition, *Wake Island*. Yet there was more of Hollywood in it, too, than they recognized at the time. We'd last seen Coward at the awards shows with the snobbish *Cavalcade*; nine years later, it was evident that he'd absorbed Hollywood's notions of democracy and reversed his opinions on the mixing of the classes, because *In Which We Serve* is the quintessential officers-and-men-we're-all-in-this-together movie, in which the survivors of a torpedoed ship share the stories of their lives in flashback while awaiting rescue. In its own veddy-British, stiff-upper-lip way, it was a model for the many melting pot Hollywood war pictures to follow, with their bomber crews mixing cowboys and cab drivers. Mr. Coward, Know Your Ally: Brooklyn.

Academy Awards

** *Mrs. Miniver* AAW
*** **Greer Garson** AAW
Accept its basic propagandizing and it's a well-crafted, well-acted little saga; if Garson and Teresa Wright deserve their Oscars for anything, it's for giving their plaster-saint

103

parts the conviction of real people.

Picture
Mrs. Miniver (MGM, Sidney Franklin)
The Invaders [*49th Parallel*] (Columbia, GFD/Ortus, Michael Powell)
Kings Row (Warner Bros., Hal B. Wallis)
The Magnificent Ambersons (RKO Radio, Mercury, Orson Welles)
The Pied Piper (20th Century–Fox, Nunnally Johnson)
The Pride of the Yankees (RKO Radio, Samuel Goldwyn)
Random Harvest (MGM, Sidney Franklin)
The Talk of the Town (Columbia, George Stevens)
Wake Island (Paramount, Joseph Sistrom)
Yankee Doodle Dandy (Warner Bros., Jack Warner, Hal B. Wallis, William Cagney)

***** James Cagney in *Yankee Doodle Dandy* AAW NYC
Cagney's dance-your-heart-out performance in Warner Bros.' best musical was an easy pick for both the Academy and the critics: the Circle, which had taken nine ballots to give Cagney its award for *Angels With Dirty Faces* in 1938, gave it to him here on the first ballot by one of their highest ratios, 13–2 (the two were for Bogart in *Casablanca*, a '42 release in New York).

Actor
James Cagney, *Yankee Doodle Dandy*

Ronald Colman, *Random Harvest*
Gary Cooper, *The Pride of the Yankees*
Walter Pidgeon, *Mrs. Miniver*
Monty Woolley, *The Pied Piper*

Actress
Greer Garson, *Mrs. Miniver*
Bette Davis, *Now, Voyager*
Katharine Hepburn, *Woman of the Year*
Rosalind Russell, *My Sister Eileen*
Teresa Wright, *The Pride of the Yankees*

Supporting Actor
Van Heflin, *Johnny Eager*
William Bendix, *Wake Island*
Walter Huston, *Yankee Doodle Dandy*
Frank Morgan, *Tortilla Flat*
Henry Travers, *Mrs. Miniver*

Supporting Actress
Teresa Wright, *Mrs. Miniver*
Gladys Cooper, *Now, Voyager*
Agnes Moorehead, *The Magnificent Ambersons*
Susan Peters, *Random Harvest*
Dame May Whitty, *Mrs. Miniver*

Director
William Wyler, *Mrs. Miniver*
Michael Curtiz, *Yankee Doodle Dandy*
John Farrow, *Wake Island*
Mervyn LeRoy, *Random Harvest*
Sam Wood, *Kings Row*

Original Screenplay: Michael Kanin, Ring Lardner, Jr., *Woman of the Year*
Adapted Screenplay: George Froeschel, James Hilton, Claudine West, Arthur Wimperis, *Mrs. Miniver*
Original Story: Emeric Pressburger, *The Invaders* [*49th Parallel*]
Cinematography/B&W: Joseph Ruttenberg, *Mrs. Miniver*

Cinematography/Color: Leon Shamroy, *The Black Swan*
Dramatic or Comedy Score: Max Steiner, *Now, Voyager*
Musical Score: Ray Heindorf, Heinz Roemheld, *Yankee Doodle Dandy*
Song: "White Christmas," *Holiday Inn*, ml: Irving Berlin
Interior Decoration/B&W: Richard Day, *This Above All*
Interior Decoration/Color: Richard Day, *My Gal Sal*
Editing: *The Pride of the Yankees*
Sound Recording: *Yankee Doodle Dandy*
Special Effects: *Reap the Wild Wind*
Short/Cartoon: *Der Fuehrer's Face* (Walt Disney/Donald Duck)
Short/One-Reel: *Speaking of Animals and Their Families* (Paramount/Speaking of Animals)
Short/Two-Reel: *Beyond the Line of Duty* (Warner Broadway Brevities)
Documentary: *Battle of Midway* (U.S. Navy), *Kokoda Front Line* (Australian News Information Bureau), *Moscow Strikes Back* (Artkino), *Prelude to War* (U. S. Army Special Services/*Why We Fight* Series)
Irving G. Thalberg Award: Sidney Franklin
Special Awards: Charles Boyer for establishing the French Research Foundation in Los Angeles as a source of reference for the industry
Noël Coward for *In Which We Serve*
MGM for representing the American way of life in the *Andy Hardy* series of films

**** *In Which We Serve* NYC BOR
Though Noël Coward is credited as co-director, the one really responsible for the crisp, *Kane*-influenced visuals and editing is his assistant, David Lean. The best fiction war film made during the war (assuming, that is, that despite the presence of Yvonne the second front, *Casablanca* doesn't count).

***** Agnes Moorehead in *The Magnificent Ambersons* NYC
Perhaps the most revolutionary thing Orson Welles ever put on film was this character—a spinster aunt who wasn't a comic relief biddy but a full-blooded, Jamesian tragic figure, brilliantly and scarily realized by Agnes Moorehead.

New York Film Critics Circle
Picture: *In Which We Serve*
Actor: James Cagney, *Yankee Doodle Dandy*
Actress: Agnes Moorehead, *The Magnificent Ambersons*
Director: John Farrow, *Wake Island*
Best War Fact Film: *Moscow Strikes Back*

National Board of Review
Best English-Language Film: *In Which We Serve*
One of Our Aircraft Is Missing
Mrs. Miniver
Journey for Margaret
Wake Island
The Male Animal
The Major and the Minor
Sullivan's Travels
The Moon and Sixpence
The Pied Piper
Best Documentary: *Moscow Strikes Back*

Native Land
World in Action

Venice Film Festival

Mussolini Cup/Foreign Film:
Der grosse König (Veit Harlan,
Germany)
Mussolini Cup/Italian Film:
Bengasi (Augusto Genina, Italy)
Actor: Fosco Giachetti, *Un colpo
di pistola*; *Bengasi*; *Noi Vivi* [first
half of *We the Living*] (Italy)
Actress: Kristina Soderbaum,
Der grosse König, *Die goldene
Stadt*

**International Film Chamber
Color Prize:** *Die goldene Stadt*
(Veit Harlan, Germany)
**International Film Chamber
Technique Prize:** *Alfa Tau*
(Francesco de Robertis, Italy)
Animated Films: *Anacleto e la
Faina* [*Anacleto and the Polecat*]
(Roberto Sgrilli, Italy); *Nel Paese
del Ranocchi* [*In the Land of
Frogs*] (Antonio Rubino, Italy)
[Prizes were also given to eleven
documentaries from Axis and
neutral countries]

Box Office (Domestic Rentals)

1	*Mrs. Miniver*	$6,000,000	MGM
2	*Reap the Wild Wind*	5,200,000	Par
3	*Yankee Doodle Dandy*	5,000,000	WB
4	*The Road to Morocco*	4,000,000	Par
5	*Holiday Inn*	3,750,000	Par
6	*Wake Island*	3,500,000	Par
7	*The Black Swan*	3,000,000	Fox
	Somewhere I'll Find You	3,000,000	MGM
9	*How Green Was My Valley*	2,800,000	Fox
10	*Louisiana Purchase*	2,750,000	Par

Other films of note:

	They Died With Their Boots On	2,550,000	WB
	Now, Voyager	2,200,000	WB
	Gentleman Jim	2,000,000	WB
	In This Our Life	1,700,000	WB
	The Palm Beach Story	1,700,000	Par
	Across the Pacific	1,300,000	WB
	Sullivan's Travels	1,150,000	Par
	The Magnificent Ambersons	1,000,000	RKO
	The Gold Rush [reissue]	1,000,000	UA

*MGM's British-Allies soap opera and a grim film about our defeat at Wake Island
were signs of the reality of war in a top ten list otherwise dominated by escapism.
Yankee Doodle Dandy was far and away Warner Bros.' biggest hit of the year, and
as the chart shows, even after* The Maltese Falcon, *Humphrey Bogart in* Across the
Pacific *was no match at the box office for Errol Flynn or Bette Davis among Warners'
stars. Lastly, RKO may have dumped Orson Welles and chopped up* The Magnificent
Ambersons, *but even so it pulled in a perfectly respectable million dollars.*

Gebert's Golden Armchairs

A tough (and admittedly ridiculous) choice between *The Magnificent Ambersons*—Orson Welles' second film, which is in many ways more mature and profound than *Citizen Kane*— and the greatest screwball comedy ever made, *The Palm Beach Story*, in which Preston Sturges takes *It Happened One Night* and twists it into a pretzel. The winner is the one I'd rather watch again right now . . .

Best American Film: *The Palm Beach Story*
Best Foreign Film: *In Which We Serve*
Best Actor: James Cagney, *Yankee Doodle Dandy*
Best Actress: Agnes Moorehead, *The Magnificent Ambersons*
Best Director: Preston Sturges, *The Palm Beach Story*

1943

Okay, name the Best Picture winner of 1943 from this description. An anti-Nazi freedom fighter and his wife escape Germany and find themselves in a neutral city, taking up residence at a popular social spot where many dubious characters of assorted nationalities hang out. As the Nazis close in, the hero shoots the chief threat to their safety, leaving the way clear for the freedom fighter and his wife to continue the fight against Hitler.

Casablanca, obviously—except that I forgot to mention that the neutral city was prewar Washington, D.C., that the hero who shoots the Nazi and the escaping freedom fighter are one and the same, and that the Best Picture award it won was the New York critics', not the Oscar. Amazingly, the two top Oscar contenders of 1943 had almost exactly the same plot—and no one seems to have noticed.

The explanation must be that the tone of the two films is so different that the similarities were irrelevant. *Watch on the Rhine* is propaganda, hot with its mission to change isolationist attitudes; *Casablanca* is the complete opposite, something there wasn't even a word for yet: cool. The paradox, of course, is that the earnest propaganda movie has been half forgotten, while the smart-alecky romance has proven inspirational beyond its makers' wildest dreams. Against any reasonable expectation, the wiseguy, absurdist attitude of *Casablanca* (''Occupation?'' ''Drunkard'') touched something truer in the American character than *Watch on the Rhine*'s preaching about democracy.

Academy Awards

***** *Casablanca* AAW
Oscar atones for *Mrs. Miniver* by picking romance over propaganda this time.

Picture
Casablanca (Warner Bros., Hal B. Wallis)
For Whom the Bell Tolls (Paramount, Sam Wood)
Heaven Can Wait (20th Century–Fox, Ernst Lubitsch)
The Human Comedy (MGM, Clarence Brown)
In Which We Serve (UA, Two Cities, Noël Coward)
Madame Curie (MGM, Sidney Franklin)
The More the Merrier (Columbia, George Stevens)
The Ox-Bow Incident (20th Century–Fox, Lamar Trotti)
The Song of Bernadette (20th Century–Fox, William Perlberg)
Watch on the Rhine (Warner Bros., Hal B. Wallis)

**** Paul Lukas in _Watch on the Rhine_ AAW GLO NYC
Lukas is a bit too old for his part on screen, but it's the role of his life and he gives a forceful and believably lived-in performance.

Actor
Paul Lukas, _Watch on the Rhine_
Humphrey Bogart, _Casablanca_
Gary Cooper, _For Whom the Bell Tolls_
Walter Pidgeon, _Madame Curie_
Mickey Rooney, _The Human Comedy_

** Jennifer Jones in Song of Bernadette AAW GLO
High on the list of Oscar winners this author had managed to avoid seeing until he wrote this book, Darryl F. Zanuck's super-production about the girl who saw the Virgin Mary at Lourdes actually turned out to be one of the more pleasant surprises, an example of Fox's relatively grown-up and realistic approach to stories that other studios would have turned into utter hokum. It won four Oscars, at least one (composer Alfred Newman's) richly deserved, but I can't say that Jennifer Jones' Best Actress Oscar is among them. Bernadette is a simple soul, and Jones gives a simple, one-note performance, all wide eyes and soft speech.

Actress
Jennifer Jones, _The Song of Bernadette_
Jean Arthur, _The More the Merrier_
Ingrid Bergman, _For Whom the Bell Tolls_
Joan Fontaine, _The Constant Nymph_
Greer Garson, _Madame Curie_

Supporting Actor
Charles Coburn, _The More the Merrier_
Charles Bickford, _The Song of Bernadette_
J. Carrol Naish, _Sahara_
Claude Rains, _Casablanca_
Akim Tamiroff, _For Whom the Bell Tolls_

Supporting Actress
Katina Paxinou, _For Whom the Bell Tolls_
Gladys Cooper, _The Song of Bernadette_
Paulette Goddard, _So Proudly We Hail_
Anne Revere, _The Song of Bernadette_
Lucile Watson, _Watch on the Rhine_

Director
Michael Curtiz, _Casablanca_
Clarence Brown, _The Human Comedy_
Henry King, _The Song of Bernadette_
Ernst Lubitsch, _Heaven Can Wait_
George Stevens, _The More the Merrier_

Original Screenplay: Norman Krasna, _Princess O'Rourke_
Adapted Screenplay: Julius J. Epstein, Philip G. Epstein, Howard Koch, _Casablanca_
Original Story: William Saroyan, _The Human Comedy_
Cinematography/B&W: Arthur Miller, _The Song of Bernadette_
Cinematography/Color: Hal Mohr, W. Howard Greene, _The Phantom of the Opera_
Dramatic or Comedy Score: Alfred Newman, _The Song of Bernadette_

Musical Score: Ray Heindorf, *This Is the Army*
Song: "You'll Never Know," *Hello, Frisco, Hello,* m: Harry Warren, 1: Mack Gordon
Interior Decoration/B&W: James Basevi, William Darling, *The Song of Bernadette*
Interior Decoration/Color: Alexander Golitzen, *The Phantom of the Opera*
Editing: *Air Force*
Sound Recording: *This Land Is Mine*
Special Effects: *Crash Dive*
Short/Cartoon: *Yankee Doodle Mouse* (MGM/Hanna-Barbera/ Tom & Jerry)
Short/One-Reel: *Amphibious Fighters* (Paramount)
Short/Two-Reel: *Heavenly Music* (MGM)
Documentary/Feature: *Desert Victory* (British Ministry of Information)
Documentary/Short: *December 7th* (U. S. Navy, directed by John Ford, Gregg Toland)
Irving G. Thalberg Award: Hal B. Wallis
Special Award: George Pal for Puppetoons [stop-motion animation]

Golden Globes
Picture: *The Song of Bernadette*
Actor: Paul Lukas, *Watch on the Rhine*
Actress: Jennifer Jones, *The Song of Bernadette*
Supporting Actor: Akim Tamiroff, *For Whom the Bell Tolls*
Supporting Actress: Katina Paxinou, *For Whom the Bell Tolls*

*** ***Watch on the Rhine*** NYC Quite a good topical thriller . . . but no *Casablanca*. Actually, the two didn't even compete head to head here, since *Casablanca* was a '42 release in New York.

New York Film Critics Circle
Picture: *Watch on the Rhine*
Actor: Paul Lukas, *Watch on the Rhine*
Actress: Ida Lupino, *The Hard Way*
Director: George Stevens, *The More the Merrier*
Special Award: U.S. Army Signal Corps and Lt. Col. Frank Capra for the *Why We Fight* series

National Board of Review
Best English-Language Film:
The Ox-Bow Incident
Watch on the Rhine
Air Force
Holy Matrimony
The Hard Way
Casablanca
Lassie Come Home
Bataan
The Moon Is Down
The Next of Kin
Best Documentaries:
Desert Victory
Battle of Russia [*Why We Fight* series]
Prelude to War [*Why We Fight* series]
Saludos Amigos
The Silent Village

Box Office (Domestic Rentals)

1	*For Whom the Bell Tolls*	$11,000,000*	Par
2	*Song of Bernadette*	7,000,000	Fox
3	*This Is the Army*	6,800,000	WB

*In 1970, *Variety* reported that actual rentals were $7,100,000.

4	*Stage Door Canteen*	5,000,000	UA
5	*Random Harvest*	4,600,000	MGM
6	*Star Spangled Rhythm*	3,850,000	Par
7	*Casablanca*	3,700,000	WB
8	*Coney Island*	3,500,000	Fox
	Madame Curie	3,500,000	MGM
10	*Hello, Frisco, Hello*	3,400,000	Fox
	Sweet Rosie O'Grady	3,400,000	Fox

Other films of note:

	Hitler's Children	3,250,000	RKO
	In Which We Serve	1,800,000	U A
	Cat People	1,200,000	RKO
	Shadow of a Doubt	1,200,000	Uni

Selznick strikes again! Gone With the Wind *meets the Spanish Civil War in* For Whom the Bell Tolls, *and the results were again box office magic, well above what Ingrid Bergman pulled in with* Casablanca *(even once the figures are adjusted for reality). No less than three all-star, not-much-plot wartime musicals managed to make the top ten; and RKO had its most profitable film of all time with a B thriller—not* Cat People, *but* Hitler's Children, *which managed to sneak a titillating "forced breeding" theme past censors under the guise of aiding the war effort.*

Gebert's Golden Armchairs

One reason that so many of us prefer non-romantic genres like gangsters and screwball comedy is that, next to Groucho or Cagney, the average '30s or '40s romantic lead seems so *stupid*—an insipid powderpuff with slicked-back hair and the worst dialogue in the picture. Bogart and co. in *Casablanca* made love and idealism cool again—by making them intellectually respectable.

British ones aside, foreign films rarely made it to the U.S. during the war, so critics and art-house audiences had to wait until after the war to see Soviet filmmaker Sergei Eisenstein's magnificently photographed, stylized-within-an-inch-of-its-life film about the ruthless Russian dictator Stal—er, Ivan.

Best American Film: *Casablanca*
Best Foreign Film: *Ivan the Terrible, Part I*
Best Cast: Humphrey Bogart, Ingrid Bergman, Claude Rains and ensemble, *Casablanca*
Best Director: Michael Curtiz, *Casablanca*

1944

The Oscars, without a doubt, were clean by 1944—because if they hadn't been, Darryl F. Zanuck would have succeeded in fixing them to produce a Best Picture win for his wartime biography of an earlier wartime Democrat president, *Wilson*. He certainly spared no other expense or effort; at a cost of $5.2 million (a million more than *Gone With the Wind*) it was the most expensive movie ever made, and even by the standards of the day, in which every grotty little potboiler was acclaimed as one for the ages, its PR campaign (which even reached the floor of the Senate) was excessive.

Zanuck needed a boost from the critics to carry his prestige picture to Oscar glory, and the reviews were respectful enough—but in the meantime a genuine popular hit had emerged, and the critics, like the public, turned to it with relief. In the New York voting *Going My Way* led from the first ballot, and by the third ballot, when *Going My Way* got its majority and won, *Wilson* had actually fallen to third place behind Preston Sturges' *Hail the Conquering Hero*. With Best Actor and Director also going to Barry Fitzgerald and Leo McCarey, from that point on Zanuck's Selznick-sized Oscar hopes were dashed.

Academy Awards

** *Going My Way* AAW GLO NYC PHO
*** **Bing Crosby** AAW PHO
**** **Barry Fitzgerald** AAW GLO NYC

As the young go-getter priest who rekindles the spark in an old fuddy-duddy pastor, *Going My Way* stars Bing Crosby and Barry Fitzgerald—and if it didn't, you'd never have heard of it, because the script was a thin, overlong retread of *Boys Town* and every other priest movie you'd ever seen. But the interplay betwen easygoing Bing and crusty old Barry is undeniably charming, and there's a surefire tearjerker ending that, for once in the picture, is underplayed to perfection. I suspect you'd have to be three years into a world war to love it the way people in 1944 did, but at least you can still see why they did—and why it made Crosby the most popular and best-loved star of his time. And Fitzgerald, no matter what the *Harvard Lampoon* would later have to say, is great—a collection of doddering quirks adding up to a rich, delightful portrait of old age.

Picture
Going My Way (Paramount, Leo McCarey)
Double Indemnity (Paramount, Joseph Sistrom)
Gaslight (MGM, Arthur Hornblow, Jr.)
Since You Went Away (UA, David O. Selznick)
Wilson (20th Century–Fox, Darryl F. Zanuck)

Actor
Bing Crosby, *Going My Way*
Charles Boyer, *Gaslight*
Barry Fitzgerald, *Going My Way*
Cary Grant, *None But the Lonely Heart*
Alexander Knox, *Wilson*

*** Ingrid Bergman in *Gaslight* AAW GLO
Once-beloved, now rather moldy thriller in which Ingrid Bergman marries villain Charles Boyer (the sort of villain who, when you say something incriminating to him, suddenly pounds the five lowest keys on the piano), only to be kept captive by him while he tries to convince her she's going mad. Bergman gets all the things you need to win an Oscar—mad scenes, fainting scenes, desperation scenes, a boffo revenge finish—but hey, we're talking Ingrid Bergman here, and it's a bit depressing to see her having to descend to such cheap tricks to get our sympathy. Leave those to the lesser mortals who need them. Hitchcock's *Notorious*, made two years later, is practically the same movie except better in every way.

Actress
Ingrid Bergman, *Gaslight*
Claudette Colbert, *Since You Went Away*
Bette Davis, *Mr. Skeffington*
Greer Garson, *Mrs. Parkington*
Barbara Stanwyck, *Double Indemnity*

Supporting Actor
Barry Fitzgerald, *Going My Way*
Hume Cronyn, *The Seventh Cross*
Claude Rains, *Mr. Skeffington*
Clifton Webb, *Laura*
Monty Woolley, *Since You Went Away*

Supporting Actress
Ethel Barrymore, *None But the Lonely Heart*
Jennifer Jones, *Since You Went Away*
Angela Lansbury, *Gaslight*
Aline MacMahon, *Dragon Seed*
Agnes Moorehead, *Mrs. Parkington*

Director
Leo McCarey, *Going My Way*
Alfred Hitchcock, *Lifeboat*
Henry King, *Wilson*
Otto Preminger, *Laura*
Billy Wilder, *Double Indemnity*

Original Screenplay: Lamar Trotti, *Wilson*
Adapted Screenplay: Frank Butler, Frank Cavett, *Going My Way*
Original Story: Leo McCarey, *Going My Way*
Cinematography/B&W: Joseph LaShelle, *Laura*
Cinematography/Color: Leon Shamroy, *Wilson*
Dramatic or Comedy Score: Max Steiner, *Since You Went Away*
Musical Score: Carmen Dragon, Morris Stoloff, *Cover Girl*

Song: "Swinging on a Star,"
Going My Way, m: James Van
Heusen, l: Johnny Burke
Interior Decoration/B&W:
Cedric Gibbons, *Gaslight*
Interior Decoration/Color:
Wiard Ihnen, *Wilson*
Editing: *Wilson*
Sound Recording: *Wilson*
Special Effects: *Thirty Seconds
Over Tokyo*
Short/Cartoon: *Mouse Trouble*
(MGM/Hanna-Barbera/Tom &
Jerry)
Short/One-Reel: *Who's Who in
Animal Land* (Paramount/
Speaking of Animals)
Short/Two-Reel: *I Won't Play*
(Warner Bros. Featurette)
Documentary/Feature: *The
Fighting Lady* (20th
Century–Fox, U.S. Navy)
Documentary/Short: *With the
Marines at Tarawa* (U. S. Marine
Corps)
Irving G. Thalberg Award:
Darryl F. Zanuck
Special Awards: Margaret
O'Brien, outstanding child
actress of 1944
Bob Hope for his many services
to the Academy

Golden Globes
Picture: *Going My Way*
Actor: Alexander Knox, *Wilson*
Actress: Ingrid Bergman,
Gaslight
Supporting Actor: Barry
Fitzgerald, *Going My Way*
Supporting Actress: Agnes
Moorehead, *Mrs. Parkington*

New York Film Critics Circle
Picture: *Going My Way*
Actor: Barry Fitzgerald, *Going
My Way*
Actress: Tallulah Bankhead,
Lifeboat
Director: Leo McCarey, *Going
My Way*

Special Recognition: to the U.S.
Army for its factual films of the
war, with specific commendation
for *Memphis Belle* and *Attack!
The Battle For New Britain*

National Board of Review
Best English-Language Film:
None But the Lonely Heart
Going My Way
The Miracle of Morgan's Creek
Hail the Conquering Hero
The Song of Bernadette
Wilson
Meet Me in St. Louis
Thirty Seconds Over Tokyo
Thunder Rock
Lifeboat
Best Documentaries:
Memphis Belle
Attack! The Battle for New Britain
With the Marines at Tarawa
Battle for the Marianas
Tunisian Victory

Photoplay Gold Medal Awards
Gold Medal: *Going My Way*
Most Popular Male Star: Bing
Crosby
Most Popular Female Star:
Greer Garson

Harvard Lampoon Movie Worsts
Ten worst pictures:
Kismet
A Song to Remember
Frenchman's Creek
Tonight and Every Night
Mr. Skeffington
Hollywood Canteen
Follow the Boys
Till We Meet Again
Thousands Cheer
Winged Victory
Worst Discovery: Maria Montez
in anything; Frank Sinatra and/or
Van Johnson
Worst Scene: The ketchup on the
keys in *A Song to Remember*

Most in Need of Retirement:
Paul Muni
Most Unattractive: The Andrews

Sisters in anything but a total
blackout

Box Office (Domestic Rentals)

1	*Going My Way*	$6,500,000	Par
2	*Meet Me in St. Louis*	5,200,000	MGM
3	*Thirty Seconds Over Tokyo*	4,500,000	MGM
4	*Hollywood Canteen*	4,200,000	WB
5	*A Guy Named Joe*	4,070,000	MGM
6	*The White Cliffs of Dover*	4,050,000	MGM

Going My Way *was the year's runaway hit in a year mainly distinguished by morale-boosting, victory-is-in-sight war films—a look back at our first strike back at the Japanese (Doolittle's 1942 raid on Tokyo, with Spencer Tracy as Doolittle), another all-star musical extravaganza, a sentimental fantasy about a dead soldier named Joe (Spencer Tracy again) who helps the living get on with life, and an Anglo-American soap opera about what good allies we were in the first war.*

Gebert's Golden Armchairs

Given the Academy's general resistance to sordid crime tales, the fact that *Double Indemnity* was even nominated for Best Picture is a tribute to its stature as one of the first and close to the best of the film *noir* cycle; Billy Wilder's cynical, sultry adaptation of James M. Cain's hardboiled thriller starred a sizzling Barbara Stanwyck as destiny in high heels. Given a choice between Bing (who won a real Oscar) and Bob (who won his second honorary one this year), I'd take Bob at his youthful, weaselly best in *The Princess and the Pirate* (one of his few costume pictures where the poshness doesn't dampen down the comedy). And why is there an MGM Spencer Tracy picture in my Foreign Film slot?

This powerful, realistic drama of a concentration camp escapee's trek across Germany was made in large part by emigres from Europe, including director Fred Zinnemann and cinematographer Karl Freund. It stands in for all the movies those refugees would have made in their own countries had war not devastated them.

Best American Film: *Double Indemnity*
Best Foreign Film: *The Seventh Cross*
Best Actor: Bob Hope, *The Princess and the Pirate*
Best Actress: Barbara Stanwyck, *Double Indemnity*
Best Director: Billy Wilder, *Double Indemnity*

1945

The war years are often remembered for escapism—yet look at the nearly unbroken string of awards for *The Lost Weekend* and its star, Ray Milland. There seemed to be an almost insatiable appetite and admiration, in the dying days of the war and the first days of a new world, for this tale of a chronic alcoholic who goes on a bender that nearly drives him to suicide. What could be more grimly realistic?

It seems crazy to say it at first, but in its own way Billy Wilder's alcoholism drama *was* a form of escapism. The setting and clothes are obviously of the present, and there's nothing to indicate that it's prior to Pearl Harbor. Yet the war is never mentioned; and an able-bodied, draft-age male has nothing better to do than attend the opera, work on the Great American Novel, and devote himself most seriously to getting plastered. Bizarre as it sounds, *The Lost Weekend* is some kind of '40s fantasy in which the war has never happened, and free from the global problem of stopping Hitler, people can devote themselves happily to their own ordinary problems—like alcoholism.

Spellbound is the same way—Gregory Peck has nothing more pressing to do than to work on unlocking his childhood neuroses and ski. And Joan Crawford's *Mildred Pierce* is the most obvious case of all, since it takes place over more than a decade—a decade in which, apparently, neither Depression nor war ever occur, and in which Mildred can raise to adulthood an unholy little brat who thinks of nothing more than convincing her way into society. After a five-year hiatus, the high society movie was back in new *noir* clothing—and audiences were ready to put the war behind them, and get back to the brand of misery they loved best.

Academy Awards

** *The Lost Weekend* AAW GLO NYC PHO CAN '46
• **Ray Milland** AAW GLO NYC BOR CAN '46
Oscar always loved a drunk scene, and Billy Wilder's trendsetting slice of realistic filmmaking is drunk with drunk scenes. But 50 years later they just come across like slices of ham with no resemblance to alcoholic reality: Milland, upon receiving each glass of his favorite rotgut, launches into a five-minute soliloquy on the magical transformative powers of liquor, then, having drunk it, clutches his throat as if expecting to turn into Mr.

116

Hyde. If that's the brand of drunken actorly self-indulgence you wish to imbibe, Richard E. Grant delivers it with more wit and bravura in *Withnail & I*.

Picture
The Lost Weekend (Paramount, Charles Brackett)
Anchors Aweigh (MGM, Joe Pasternak)
The Bells of St. Mary's (RKO Radio, Rainbow, Leo McCarey)
Mildred Pierce (Warner Bros., Jerry Wald)
Spellbound (UA, David O. Selznick)

Actor
Ray Milland, *The Lost Weekend*
Bing Crosby, *The Bells of St. Mary's*
Gene Kelly, *Anchors Aweigh*
Gregory Peck, *The Keys of the Kingdom*
Cornel Wilde, *A Song to Remember*

*** Joan Crawford in *Mildred Pierce* AAW BOR
God knows, if you have to see a Best Actress Oscar–winner about social climbing, you could do a lot worse than this one, with its sleek Michael Curtiz direction and sharp characterizations. That doesn't make it one of the great *noirs*, but it's certainly enjoyable, and if Crawford isn't quite honed to the neurotic edge that she has in her best later roles (*Johnny Guitar*, *Sudden Fear*, *Baby Jane*), her first Warner's picture is still the juiciest vehicle she'd had in years and

deservedly made her a star again.

Actress
Joan Crawford, *Mildred Pierce*
Ingrid Bergman, *The Bells of St. Mary's*
Greer Garson, *The Valley of Decision*
Jennifer Jones, *Love Letters*
Gene Tierney, *Leave Her to Heaven*

Supporting Actor
James Dunn, *A Tree Grows in Brooklyn*
Michael Chekhov, *Spellbound*
John Dall, *The Corn Is Green*
Robert Mitchum, *The Story of G. I. Joe*
J. Carrol Naish, *A Medal for Benny*

Supporting Actress
Anne Revere, *National Velvet*
Eve Arden, *Mildred Pierce*
Ann Blyth, *Mildred Pierce*
Angela Lansbury, *The Picture of Dorian Gray*
Joan Lorring, *The Corn Is Green*

Director
Billy Wilder, *The Lost Weekend*
Clarence Brown, *National Velvet*
Alfred Hitchcock, *Spellbound*
Leo McCarey, *The Bells of St. Mary's*
Jean Renoir, *The Southerner*

Original Screenplay: Richard Schweizer, *Marie-Louise* [Switzerland]
Adapted Screenplay: Charles Brackett, Billy Wilder, *The Lost Weekend*
Original Story: Charles G. Booth, *The House on 92nd Street*
Cinematography/B&W: Harry Stradling, *The Picture of Dorian Gray*

Cinematography/Color: Leon Shamroy, *Leave Her to Heaven*
Dramatic or Comedy Score: Miklos Rozsa, *Spellbound*
Musical Score: Georgie Stoll, *Anchors Aweigh*
Song: "It Might As Well Be Spring," *State Fair*, m: Richard Rodgers, l: Oscar Hammerstein II
Interior Decoration/B&W: Wiard Ihnen, *Blood on the Sun*
Interior Decoration/Color: Hans Dreier, Ernst Fegte, *Frenchman's Creek*
Editing: *National Velvet*
Sound Recording: *The Bells of St. Mary's*
Special Effects: *Wonder Man*
Short/Cartoon: *Quiet Please* (MGM/Hanna-Barbera/Tom & Jerry)
Short/One-Reel: *Stairway to Light* (MGM/Passing Parade)
Short/Two-Reel: *A Star in the Night* (Warner Bros. Broadway Brevities, directed by Don Siegel)
Documentary/Feature: *The True Glory* (Governments of U.S.A., Britain; directed by Carol Reed, Garson Kanin)
Documentary/Short: *Hitler Lives?* (Warner Bros., directed by Don Siegel)
Special Awards: Walter Wanger, for his six years of service as President of the Academy
Peggy Ann Garner, outstanding child actress of 1945
The House I Live In, tolerance short subject; produced by Frank Ross and Mervyn LeRoy; directed by LeRoy; screenplay by Albert Maltz; song "The House I Live In," m: Earl Robinson, l: Lewis Allen; starring Frank Sinatra; released by RKO Radio
Republic Studio for the building of an outstanding musical scoring auditorium

Golden Globes

Picture: *The Lost Weekend*
Actor: Ray Milland, *The Lost Weekend*
Actress: Ingrid Bergman, *The Bells of St. Mary's*
Supporting Actor: J. Carrol Naish, *A Medal for Benny*
Supporting Actress: Angela Lansbury, *The Picture of Dorian Gray*
Best Film for Promoting International Good Will: *The House I Live In*

New York Film Critics Circle

Picture: *The Lost Weekend*
Actor: Ray Milland, *The Lost Weekend*
Actress: Ingrid Bergman, *Spellbound*, *The Bells of St. Mary's*
Director: Billy Wilder, *The Lost Weekend*
Special Awards/Factual Filmmaking: *The True Glory* (Garson Kanin, Carol Reed), *The Fighting Lady* (William Wyler)

**** *The True Glory*   AAW NYC BOR

The most-honored documentary of 1945 isn't well-remembered today, but at the time it was admired as a summing-up of both Anglo-American cooperation in the final stages of the war and of the British and American documentary traditions. A British-American team under Carol Reed and Garson Kanin assembled it from some six million feet of footage shot between D-Day and V-E Day, telling the story of the final days of the war. In the end the

British influence—which is to say, the Soviet influence on British editors—seems the strongest: the editing is rapid-fire and amazingly crisp, making you realize how lazy most of the documentaries that play on cable are.

National Board of Review

Best Film: *The True Glory*
The Lost Weekend
The Southerner
The Story of G.I. Joe
The Last Chance
The Life and Death of Colonel Blimp
A Tree Grows in Brooklyn
The Fighting Lady
The Way Ahead
The Clock
Actor: Ray Milland, *The Lost Weekend*
Actress: Joan Crawford, *Mildred Pierce*
Director: Jean Renoir, *The Southerner*

Photoplay Gold Medal Awards

Gold Medal: *The Valley of Decision*
Most Popular Male Star: Bing Crosby
Most Popular Female Star: Greer Garson

Harvard Lampoon Movie Worsts

Ten worst pictures:
Weekend at the Waldorf
Music for Millions
This Love of Ours
The Enchanted Cottage
Where Do We Go from Here?
Spellbound
Anchors Aweigh
Guest Wife
She Wouldn't Say Yes
[The Strange Affair of] Uncle Harry
Worst Performance—Male: Van Johnson, *Thrill of a Romance*
Worst Performance—Female: June Allyson, *Her Highness and the Bellboy*
Most Consistently Bovine Performances: Alexis Smith
Oldest Actress of the Year: Joan Crawford (honorable mention to Joan Bennett)

Box Office (Domestic Rentals)

1	The Valley of Decision	$5,560,000	MGM
2	Anchors Aweigh	4,500,000	MGM
3	The Paleface	4,500,000	Par
4	Thrill of a Romance	4,500,000	MGM
5	Weekend at the Waldorf	4,370,000	MGM
6	National Velvet	4,050,000	MGM
7	State Fair	4,050,000	Fox
8	The Dolly Sisters	4,000,000	Fox

Not a single war film to be had (unless you count the sailors in Anchors Aweigh*)— instead it's escapism of every kind, and at #6 the first starring role of the young woman who would grow into the most consistent female box office attraction of the '50s and '60s, Elizabeth Taylor.*

Gebert's Golden Armchairs

Hands down the best movie of '45 was the French classic *Children of Paradise*, often called the French *Gone With the Wind* (though the French *All About Eve* would be closer to the mark), with the glorious Arletty as the worldly actress-courtesan at the center of a triangle in the Paris theater of the 19th century. In a curiously weak year for American films, Edgar Ulmer's *Detour* stands out for achieving Fritz Langian *noir* atmosphere on an Ed Wood budget, and Boris Karloff has one of his most colorful parts as a dealer in corpses in a B horror film (*somewhat* higher-budgeted than *Detour*) from the *Cat People* people.

Best American Film: *Detour*
Best Foreign Film: *Les Enfants du Paradis/Children of Paradise*
Best Actor: Boris Karloff, *The Body-Snatchers*
Best Actress: Arletty, *Les Enfants du Paradise*
Best Director: Edgar Ulmer, *Detour*

1946

Cannes and Venice both revived their film festivals in 1946, but where Venice was admirably well-managed, Cannes was very nearly a fiasco—the projection of the Russian opening night film, *Berlin*, was interrupted by equipment failures so often that the Soviet delegation decided it was deliberate sabotage and walked out, skipping the 1947 festival entirely. And the first jury, in a fit of diplomatic dullness, decided to award a Grand Prize to the best film from every single country participating—which for some countries may have been the *only* film.

If the jury hadn't copped out, they could have launched Cannes on an unbeatable high note, because they had in their hands the one real discovery of their time: Roberto Rossellini's *Open City*, the first widely seen example of neorealism, the Italian school that went even beyond the documentary realism of a *Lost Weekend* to show plain-looking people acting utterly realistic stories in the real rubble of the war. Neorealism would become the most important influence of the postwar era—it's basically responsible for the trend toward location filming and realistic sets that has lasted to this day—and a host of filmmakers with roots in the movement (including Fellini, who got an Oscar nomination for *Open City*'s script) would be launched into international prominence by the festivals over the next two decades. Even without a Grand Prize, Rossellini summed up the promise that Cannes has held ever since for young filmmakers when he said, "At noon I was a bum, and at two I was an international artist."

Academy Awards

**** *The Best Years of Our Lives* AAW GLO NYC BAA '47
*** Fredric March AAW
America was ready for a movie which told us what the war had meant and dealt seriously with the problem of reintegrating soldiers into society, and *The Best Years of Our Lives* fulfilled these expectations flawlessly, not shirking from such problems as the husband and wife who no longer know each other (or want to), the triviality of ordinary work for men who've been in life-or-death situations for four years, and the problems of handicapped veterans (and it's impossible now to comprehend how startling it was then to use an actual handicapped man in the role). Its triumph is the

121

triumph of the *Grapes of Wrath* faction from six years earlier; from now on, this is what Best Picture–winners were (and are). As for March, though very solid, he's overshadowed by the *other* savings-and-loan officer in a 1946 film, Jimmy Stewart's George Bailey.

Picture
The Best Years of Our Lives (RKO Radio, Samuel Goldwyn)
Henry V (UA, Rank-Two Cities, Laurence Olivier)
It's a Wonderful Life (RKO Radio, Liberty, Frank Capra)
The Razor's Edge (20th Century–Fox, Darryl F. Zanuck)
The Yearling (MGM, Sidney Franklin)

Actor
Fredric March, *The Best Years of Our Lives*
Laurence Olivier, *Henry V*
Larry Parks, *The Jolson Story*
Gregory Peck, *The Yearling*
James Stewart, *It's a Wonderful Life*

Actress
Olivia de Havilland, *To Each His Own*
Celia Johnson, *Brief Encounter*
Jennifer Jones, *Duel in the Sun*
Rosalind Russell, *Sister Kenny*
Jane Wyman, *The Yearling*

Supporting Actor
Harold Russell, *The Best Years of Our Lives*
Charles Coburn, *The Green Years*
William Demarest, *The Jolson Story*
Claude Rains, *Notorious*
Clifton Webb, *The Razor's Edge*

Supporting Actress
Anne Baxter, *The Razor's Edge*
Ethel Barrymore, *The Spiral Staircase*

Lillian Gish, *Duel in the Sun*
Flora Robson, *Saratoga Trunk*
Gale Sondergaard, *Anna and the King of Siam*

Director
William Wyler, *The Best Years of Our Lives*
Clarence Brown, *The Yearling*
Frank Capra, *It's a Wonderful Life*
David Lean, *Brief Encounter*
Robert Siodmak, *The Killers*

Original Screenplay: Muriel Box, Sydney Box, *The Seventh Veil*
Adapted Screenplay: Robert E. Sherwood, *The Best Years of Our Lives*
Original Story: Clemence Dane, *Vacation from Marriage*
Cinematography/B&W: Arthur Miller, *Anna and the King of Siam*
Cinematography/Color: Charles Rosher, Leonard Smith, Arthur Arling, *The Yearling*
Dramatic or Comedy Score: Hugo Friedhofer, *The Best Years of Our Lives*
Musical Score: Morris Stoloff, *The Jolson Story*
Song: "On the Atchison, Topeka and Santa Fe," *The Harvey Girls*, m: Harry Warren, l: Johnny Mercer
Interior Decoration/B&W: Lyle Wheeler, William Darling, *Anna and the King of Siam*
Interior Decoration/Color: Cedric Gibbons, Paul Groesse, *The Yearling*
Editing: *The Best Years of Our Lives*
Sound Recording: *The Jolson Story*
Special Effects: *Blithe Spirit*
Short/Cartoon: *The Cat Concerto* (MGM/Hanna-Barbera/Tom & Jerry)
Short/One-Reel: *Facing Your*

Danger (Warner Bros. Sports
Parade)
Short/Two-Reel: *A Boy and His
Dog* (Warner Bros. Featurettes)
Documentary/Short: *Seeds of
Destiny* (U. S. War Department)
Irving G. Thalberg Award:
Samuel Goldwyn
Special Awards:
Laurence Olivier as actor,
producer and director, *Henry V*
Harold Russell for bringing hope
and courage to his fellow
veterans through his appearance
in *The Best Years of Our Lives*
Ernst Lubitsch for his
distinguished contributions to the
art of the motion picture
Claude Jarman, Jr., outstanding
child actor of 1946

Golden Globes

Picture: *The Best Years of Our
Lives*
Actor: Gregory Peck, *The
Yearling*
Actress: Rosalind Russell, *Sister
Kenny*
Supporting Actor: Clifton Webb,
The Razor's Edge
Supporting Actress: Anne
Baxter, *The Razor's Edge*
Director: Frank Capra, *It's a
Wonderful Life*
**Best Film Promoting
International Understanding:**
The Last Chance (Switzerland)
**Award for Non-Professional
Acting:** Harold Russell, *The
Best Years of Our Lives*

**** Laurence Olivier in
Henry V NYC BOR
Though Kenneth Branagh's
gritty 1989 film has taken
some of the bloom off of it, and
Laurence Olivier's own
subsequent Shakespeare films
(1948's *Hamlet* and 1955's
Richard III) are both better as

movies, Olivier's first film was
easily the best cinematic
adaptation of Shakespeare to
date. What impresses more than
anything is the sheer
confidence with which it was
made (and acted): Britain's
film industry spends most of its
time nervously checking to see
if Hollywood is gaining on it,
and *Henry V* is one of the few
films that seems completely
proud to be English.

**** Celia Johnson in *Brief
Encounter* NYC
The Oscar winner, Olivia de
Havilland in *To Each His
Own*, isn't on video for me to
compare, but I doubt she could
compare to Johnson, the plain-
Jane heart and soul of Noël
Coward's and David Lean's
classic stiff-upper-lip
romance—a performance that
time, imitation, and a million
Carol Burnett parodies have
done nothing to dim.

New York Film Critics Circle

Picture: *The Best Years of Our
Lives*
Foreign Film: *Open City*
Actor: Laurence Olivier, *Henry V*
Actress: Celia Johnson, *Brief
Encounter*
Director: William Wyler, *The
Best Years of Our Lives*

National Board of Review

Best Picture: *Henry V*
Best Foreign-Language Film:
Open City
The Best Years of Our Lives
Brief Encounter
A Walk in the Sun
It Happened at the Inn

My Darling Clementine
The Diary of a Chambermaid
The Killers
Anna and the King of Siam
Actor: Laurence Olivier, *Henry V*
Actress: Anna Magnani, *Open City*
Director: William Wyler, *The Best Years of Our Lives*

Photoplay Gold Medal Awards
Gold Medal: *The Bells of St. Mary's*
Most Popular Male Star: Bing Crosby
Most Popular Female Star: Ingrid Bergman

** ***Open City***   NYC BOR CAN
At the risk of consigning myself to the shallow table at the critics' club, I have to say that I think Rossellini's influence is far greater than his films—for me De Sica, who worked more melodrama into his neorealist films, and Visconti, who worked pure opera into his, still have the power to move audiences in a way that Rossellini's anti-drama dramas don't. *Shoeshine*, *Umberto D.*, and *La Terra Trema* are the masterpieces of neorealism; *Open City* and *Paisan* are only the landmarks.

Cannes Film Festival
Note: In the first festival, a Grand Prize was awarded by the jury to the best film from each of eleven countries in competition.
Czechoslovakia: *Muzi Bez Krídel* (Frantisek Cáp)
Denmark: *The Earth Will Be Red* (Bodil Ipsen, Lau Lauritzen)
France: *La Symphonie Pastorale* (Jean Delannoy)

Great Britain: *Brief Encounter* (David Lean)
India: *Neecha Nagar* (Chetan Anand)
Italy: *Open City* (Roberto Rossellini)
Mexico: *Maria Candelaria* (Emilio Fernandez)
Sweden: *Torment* [*Frenzy*] (Alf Sjöberg)
Switzerland: *The Last Chance* (Léopold Lindtberg)
USA: *The Lost Weekend* (Billy Wilder)
USSR: *The Turning Point* (Friedrich Ermler)
International Jury Prize: *La Bataille du Rail* (René Clément, France)
Actor: Ray Milland, *The Lost Weekend*
Actress: Michéle Morgan, *La Symphonie Pastorale*
Director: René Clément, *La Bataille du Rail*
Director (Filmmakers' Society): Mikhail Romm, *Girl No. 217* (USSR)
Screenplay (Society of Playwrights and Drama Composers): Tschirskov, *Girl No. 217* (USSR)
Photography: Gabriel Figueroa, *Maria Candelaria*, *The Three Musketeers* (Mexico)
Color: *Kamennitsvetok* [*The Stone Flower*] (Alexander Ptushko, USSR)
Score (Society of Writers, Composers and Music Publishers): Georges Auric, *Beauty and the Beast*, *La Symphonie Pastorale* (France)
Documentary: *Berlin* (Yuli Raizman, USSR)
Animated Film: *Make Mine Music* (Walt Disney, USA)
International Peace Prize: *The Last Chance*
C.I.D.A.L.C. Prize: *Epaves* (*Wrecks*) (Jacques-Yves Cousteau, France)

**** *The Southerner* VEN
The only significant result of
Jean Renoir's wartime sojourn in
Hollywood, a lovely, simple
slice of Southern naturalistic
poetry (William Faulkner had
a hand in the script)—part
Grapes of Wrath, part
Sunrise.

Venice Film Festival
Best Film: *The Southerner* (Jean
Renoir, USA)
Special Mention:
*Les Enfants du Paradis/Children
of Paradise* (Marcel Carné,
France)
The Oath (Mikhail Chiaureli,
USSR)
Hangmen Also Die (Fritz Lang,
USA)
Henry V (Laurence Olivier, UK)
The Undaunted (Mark Donskoi,
USSR)
Paisan (Roberto Rossellini, Italy)
Panique (Julien Duvivier, France)
Il Sole Sorge Ancora (Aldo
Vergano, Italy)
Documentary: *In the Sands of
Central Asia* (Alexander
Zguridi, USSR)

Animated Film: *Le Voleur de
Paratonnères* (Paul Grimault,
France)

Harvard Lampoon Movie Worsts
Twelve worst pictures:
Night and Day
I've Always Loved You
Leave Her to Heaven
Margie
Adventure
Make Mine Music
The Searching Wind
No Leave, No Love
The Road to Utopia
Of Human Bondage
Scarlet Streets
The Harvey Girls
Worst Performance—Male:
Orson Welles, *The Stranger*
Worst Performance—Female:
Alexis Smith, *Night and Day*
**Most Outrageous
Misrepresentation of Fact:**
Cornel Wilde as a former
Lampoon editor in *Leave Her to
Heaven*
Least Talented New Finds:
Glenn Ford and Catherine
MacLeod
**Actress with Most Toes in the
Grave:** Joan Crawford

Box Office (Domestic Rentals)

1	The Bells of St. Mary's	$8,000,000	RKO
2	Leave Her to Heaven	5,750,000	Fox
3	Blue Skies	5,000,000	Par
	The Road to Utopia	5,000,000	Par
	Spellbound	5,000,000	U A
6	The Green Years	4,750,000	MGM
7	Adventure	4,500,000	MGM
	Easy to Wed	4,500,000	MGM
	Notorious	4,500,000	RKO
10	Two Years Before the Mast	4,400,000	Par
Other films of note			
11	The Lost Weekend	4,300,000	Par
14	The Postman Always Rings Twice	4,000,000	MGM

| 20 | *Gilda* | 3,750,000 | Col |
| 34 | *The Big Sleep* | 3,000,000 | WB |

Bing in a collar again proved to be box office magic, but then so did Bing with Fred in Blue Skies *and Bing with Bob in* Utopia. *Film noir, at least the glossier, big-star brand, seemed to be catching on with two noirish Hitchcock films in the top ten and healthy revenues from* The Lost Weekend, Gilda, *etc.— though the most successful "noir" was the one in Technicolor,* Leave Her to Heaven.

Gebert's Golden Armchairs

The Best Years of Our Lives captured the postwar world's acknowledged problems; Frank Capra's masterpiece captured its hidden fears, and 50 years later it's the one that affects us the most. Cary Grant, walking the fine line between charming and bastard, gave his best dramatic performance in one of Hitch's more underrated films, and Lauren Bacall was the smart, saucy gal that Bogie's characters had always been looking for, and deserved—on screen and off.

Best American Film: *It's a Wonderful Life*
Best Foreign Film: *Henry V*
Best Actor: Cary Grant, *Notorious*
Best Actress: Lauren Bacall, *The Big Sleep*
Best Director: Frank Capra, *It's a Wonderful Life*

1947

After the Holocaust, many of Hollywood's younger figures felt the need to tackle anti-Semitism on screen—despite the intense resistance of the older moguls, who feared an anti-Semitic backlash if Hollywood tried to advance Jewish causes, or even culture. (Judging purely by what was on screen, you'd have guessed that Hollywood *was* dominated by one religious group—Irish priests.) So ironically enough, it was two Gentile producers—Fox chief Darryl Zanuck and RKO producer Adrian Scott—who finally introduced the subject, almost simultaneously, with Elia Kazan's *Gentleman's Agreement* and Edward Dmytryk's *Crossfire*.

Both films enjoyed considerable success: Kazan's film won the Best Picture Oscar (Zanuck, accepting, grumbled again about *Wilson*), while *Crossfire* became the only B movie film *noir* to gain a Best Picture nomination. A cycle of other socially concerned movies followed—but the older moguls may not have been wrong to fear a backlash. Within months, the House Committee on Un-American Activities, fueled in part by a barely hidden anti-Semitism, would begin its anti-Communist witch-hunt in Hollywood. Many of the progressive figures involved in these films—including Scott, Kazan, and Dmytryk—would find themselves forced to testify or go to jail.

Academy Awards

• Gentleman's Agreement
AAW GLO NYC BOR
This story of a reporter going "undercover" in order to expose anti-Semitism at "restricted" hotels (ones that didn't allow Jews) provoked an orgy of self-congratulation for its daring in taking on such a subject. In retrospect, rarely has so much praise been lavished on such an inconsequential film. I don't doubt that "restricted" policies were hurtful and demeaning, but they're not especially dramatic—for Pete's sake, this is a movie about Gregory Peck *having trouble checking into hotels.* ("Would it matter if my name was . . . Greenberg?" "I'm sorry, Mr. Green, we seem to have just burned down." There, that's the whole movie.) Coming on the heels of the Holocaust, it seems almost obscene (not to mention potentially counterproductive) to lavish so much attention on such a minor, upper-class aspect of anti-Semitism—even if it *was* the aspect that movie moguls could most relate to.

Picture
Gentleman's Agreement (20th
Century–Fox, Darryl F. Zanuck)
The Bishop's Wife (RKO Radio,
Samuel Goldwyn)
Crossfire (RKO Radio, Adrian
Scott)
Great Expectations (Universal,
Rank-Cineguild, Ronald
Neame)
Miracle on 34th Street (20th
Century–Fox, William
Perlberg)

• **Ronald Colman in A** *Double*
Life AAW GLO
Just before the triumphs of *Born
Yesterday* and *Adam's Rib*, the
team of Garson Kanin, Ruth
Gordon, and director George
Cukor somehow produced this
dreadful stinker, which earns
Colman the unenviable
distinction of giving the worst
performance to win a Best Actor
Oscar. Colman plays a great
actor so immersed in the role of
Othello that he starts to
become Othello—to his wife's
increasing concern. The first
problem with the film is
miscasting: it's a satire on the
Method idea of putting your
deepest inner torment into
your role, starring the actor who
was the epitome of surface
charm. This isn't an Othello
tormented by jealousy—this
is an Othello who can't
remember if his wife's
handkerchief was in his suit
when it went to the cleaners. But
Colman's performance as the
actor himself is no better; his
windy speeches about the
glorious theatah fall flat, and
when he starts to go crazy, eyes

a-rollin', he might as well be
in *Carry On Up Your Iago*.
Colman campaigned hard to
finally win an Oscar on
sentimental grounds—and the
Academy, by giving in, gave the
second most disgraceful
performance of the year.

Actor
Ronald Colman, *A Double Life*
John Garfield, *Body and Soul*
Gregory Peck, *Gentleman's
Agreement*
William Powell, *Life with Father*
Michael Redgrave, *Mourning
Becomes Electra*

Actress
**Loretta Young, *The Farmer's
Daughter***
Joan Crawford, *Possessed*
Susan Hayward, *Smash Up—The
Story of a Woman*
Dorothy McGuire, *Gentleman's
Agreement*
Rosalind Russell, *Mourning
Becomes Electra*

Supporting Actor
**Edmund Gwenn, *Miracle on
34th Street***
Charles Bickford, *The Farmer's
Daughter*
Thomas Gomez, *Ride the Pink
Horse*
Robert Ryan, *Crossfire*
Richard Widmark, *Kiss of Death*

Supporting Actress
**Celeste Holm, *Gentleman's
Agreement***
Ethel Barrymore, *The Paradine
Case*
Gloria Grahame, *Crossfire*
Marjorie Main, *The Egg and I*
Anne Revere, *Gentleman's
Agreement*

Director
**Elia Kazan, *Gentleman's
Agreement***

George Cukor, *A Double Life*
Edward Dmytryk, *Crossfire*
Henry Koster, *The Bishop's Wife*
David Lean, *Great Expectations*

Original Screenplay: Sidney
Sheldon, *The Bachelor and the
Bobby-Soxer*
Adapted Screenplay: George
Seaton, *Miracle on 34th Street*
Original Story: Valentine
Davies, *Miracle on 34th Street*
Cinematography/B&W: Guy
Green, *Great Expectations*
Cinematography/Color: Jack
Cardiff, *Black Narcissus*
Song: "Zip-A-Dee-Doo-Dah,"
Song of the South, m: Allie
Wrubel, l: Ray Gilbert
Dramatic or Comedy Score:
Miklos Rozsa, *A Double Life*
Musical Score: Alfred Newman,
Mother Wore Tights
Art Direction/B&W: John
Bryan, *Great Expectations*
Art Direction/Color: Alfred
Junge, *Black Narcissus*
Editing: *Body and Soul*
Sound Recording: *The Bishop's
Wife*
Special Effects: *Green Dolphin
Street*
Short/Cartoon: *Tweetie Pie*
(Warner/Friz Freleng/Tweety &
Sylvester) [NOTE: first Warner
cartoon winner]
Short/One-Reel: *Goodbye Miss
Turlock* (MGM/Passing Parade)
Short/Two-Reel: *Climbing the
Matterhorn* (Monogram Color,
Irving Allen) [NOTE: the only
Oscar to this studio]
Documentary/Feature: *Design
for Death* (RKO Radio)
Documentary/Short: *First Steps*
(United Nations Division of Films
and Visual Education)
Special Awards: James Baskette
as Uncle Remus, friend and
storyteller to the children of the
world

Bill and Coo [live-action animal
film]
Shoeshine (Italy)—outstanding
foreign-language film
Colonel William N. Selig, Albert
E. Smith, Thomas Armat, and
George K. Spoor [early film
pioneers]

***** *Shoeshine* AAW**
De Sica was the supreme
tearjerker of neorealism, and
if this doesn't jerk quite as many
tears as *Umberto D.* (which
has the unfair advantage of a pet
dog), the heartrending tale of
two best-friend shoeshine boys
who wind up betraying each
other in reform school is like
Boys Town crossed with *The
Postman Always Rings Twice*.

Golden Globes
Picture: *Gentleman's Agreement*
Actor: Ronald Colman, *A Double
Life*
Actress: Rosalind Russell,
Mourning Becomes Electra
Supporting Actor: Edmund
Gwenn, *Miracle on 34th Street*
Supporting Actress: Celeste
Holm, *Gentleman's Agreement*
Director: Elia Kazan,
Gentleman's Agreement
Screenplay: George Seaton,
Miracle on 34th Street
Cinematography: Jack Cardiff,
Black Narcissus
Score: Max Steiner, *Life With
Father*
**Most Promising Newcomer
(Male):** Richard Widmark, *Kiss
of Death*
**Most Promising Newcomer
(Female):** Lois Maxwell, *That
Hagen Girl*
**Special Award to Best Juvenile
Actor:** Dean Stockwell,
Gentleman's Agreement
Special Award for Furthering

the Influence of the Screen:
Walt Disney, for the Hindustani
version of *Bambi*

New York Film Critics Circle
Picture: *Gentleman's Agreement*
Foreign Film: *To Live in Peace*
Actor: William Powell, *Life With
Father, The Senator Was
Indiscreet*
Actress: Deborah Kerr, *Black
Narcissus, The Adventuress*
Director: Elia Kazan,
*Gentleman's Agreement,
Boomerang!*

National Board of Review
Best Film: *Monsieur Verdoux
Great Expectations
Shoeshine
Crossfire
Boomerang!
Odd Man Out
Gentleman's Agreement
To Live in Peace
It's a Wonderful Life
The Overlanders*
Actor: Michael Redgrave,
Mourning Becomes Electra
Actress: Celia Johnson, *This
Happy Breed*
Director: Elia Kazan,
*Boomerang!, Gentleman's
Agreement*

Photoplay Gold Medal Awards
Gold Medal: *The Jolson Story*
Most Popular Male Star: Bing
Crosby
Most Popular Female Star:
Ingrid Bergman

British Academy Awards
Film: *The Best Years of Our Lives*
British Film: *Odd Man Out*

Cannes Film Festival
**Romantic and Psychological
Film:** *Antoine et Antoinette*
(Jacques Becker, France)

Adventure and Thriller Film:
Les Maudits (René Clément,
France)
Socially Minded Film: *Crossfire*
(Edward Dmytryk, USA)
Musical Comedy: *The Ziegfeld
Follies* (Vincente Minnelli,
USA)
Documentary Short: *Floods in
Poland* (Poland)
Animated Film: *Dumbo* (Walt
Disney, USA)
Special Mention: *Mine Own
Executioner* (Anthony
Kimmins, UK); *A Ship to India/
Frustration* (Ingmar Bergman,
Sweden)

Venice Film Festival
International Grand Prize:
Sirena (Karel Stekely,
Czechoslovakia)
Actor: Pierre Fresnay, *Monsieur
Vincent* (France)
Actress: Anna Magnani,
Honorable Angelina (Italy)
Director: Henri-Georges
Clouzot, *Quai des Orfèvres*
(France)
Most Original Story: *Vesna*
(Grigori V. Alexandrov, USSR)
Cinematography: Gabriel
Figueroa, *The Pearl* (Mexico)
Score: E. F. Burian, *Sirena*
**Best Original Contribution to
Film Progress:** *The Pearl*
(Emilio Fernandez, Mexico),
Dreams That Money Can Buy
(Hans Richter, et al., USA)
Documentary Feature: *On the
Trail of the Animals* (Boris
Dolin, USSR)
Documentary Short: *Piazza San
Marco* (Francesco Pasinetti,
Italy)
Best Italian Film: *Caccia tragica*
(Giuseppe De Santis)
Special Homage: Carl Dreyer,
Day of Wrath (Denmark)

Box Office (Domestic Rentals)

1	*The Best Years of Our Lives*	$11,500,000	RKO
2	*Duel in the Sun*	10,750,000	Selznick
3	*The Jolson Story*	8,000,000	Col
	Forever Amber	8,000,000	Fox
5	*Unconquered*	7,500,000	Par
6	*Life with Father*	6,250,000	WB
7	*Welcome Stranger*	6,100,000	Par
8	*The Egg and I*	5,750,000	Uni
9	*The Yearling*	5,250,000	MGM
10	*Green Dolphin Street*	5,000,000	MGM
	The Razor's Edge	5,000,000	Fox
Other films of note:			
23	*Song of the South*	3,400,000	Disney/RKO
26	*It's a Wonderful Life*	3,300,000	RKO
45	*Miracle on 34th Street*	2,650,000	Fox
50	*Crossfire*	2,500,000	RKO
68	*Great Expectations*	2,000,000	Uni

The Best Years of Our Lives, *capturing its moment perfectly, became the biggest hit since* Gone With the Wind, *even beating out David O. Selznick's most spectacular attempt at duplicating that earlier success. The story that* It's a Wonderful Life *was a flop upon release is refuted by its more-than-respectable $3.3 million rental; it was its lukewarm critical reaction that led to its being forgotten—and thus, to its being in a position to be rediscovered in the '70s.*

Gebert's Golden Armchairs

A braver and tougher-minded film than *Gentleman's Agreement* in every way, the film *noir Crossfire* was a mystery in which anti-Semitism was the m.o. Robert Ryan gives a dismayingly believable performance as a bullying, bigoted soldier who meets a Jewish businessman in a bar and winds up killing him out of drunken hatred. The most respectable Technicolor drama produced by the increasingly florid Powell and Pressburger, *Black Narcissus* is a superb grown-up drama about nuns who start a convent in the Himalayas, not realizing that Western rationalism and *Sound of Music* nunly confidence are no match for the mystery and Zen emptiness of the Orient. A dazzling precursor to East-beats-West dramas like *Lawrence of Arabia*—doubly amazing when you know that the Himalayas are all Scottish locations and papier-mâché models.

Best American Film: *Crossfire*
Best Foreign Film: *Black Narcissus*
Best Actor: Robert Ryan, *Crossfire*
Best Actress: Deborah Kerr, *Black Narcissus*
Best Director: Michael Powell, Emeric Pressburger, *Black Narcissus*

1948

Laurence Olivier's *Hamlet* was a success almost everywhere it competed, but at Venice it might have had some truly interesting competition for the Grand Prize it ultimately took home—Orson Welles' own more radically cinematic Shakespeare adaptation, *Macbeth*.

The screening of Welles' film enjoyed—according to Elsa Maxwell—"the largest enthusiastic audience of the entire festival." Unfortunately, Welles then withdrew it from competition, citing the personal hostility of the Italian press and public. "I know they will say that I was afraid to compete with *Hamlet*," Welles said. "They don't like me in Italy and my love affair with this beautiful country is unrequited . . . Why risk my picture, which will never be shown in Italy, because you cannot dub Shakespeare, and *Macbeth* is only intended for an English-speaking audience? I prefer *Macbeth* be judged by a public that is intelligent."

Intelligent or not, Venice would go on to give prizes to *Romeo and Juliet*, a Russian *Hamlet* and *Rosencrantz and Guildenstern Are Dead*; but a duel between the two most famous actor-directors of Shakespeare was never to be.

Academy Awards

**** *Hamlet* AAW GLO BOR BAA VEN
**** Laurence Olivier AAW GLO NYC
How to do Shakespeare with impeccable taste and intelligence (if not quite genius)—strip a four-hour play down to 153 sleek minutes, give it a chilly film *noir* look, play Hamlet nimbly and energetically—and think the soliloquies as voiceovers, rather than speaking them out loud to an empty room.

Picture
Hamlet (Universal, Rank/Two Cities, Laurence Olivier)

Johnny Belinda (Warner Bros., Jerry Wald)
The Red Shoes (Eagle-Lion, Rank-Archers, Michael Powell, Emeric Pressburger)
The Snake Pit (20th Century–Fox, Anatole Litvak, Robert Bassler)
The Treasure of the Sierra Madre (Warner Bros., Henry Blanke)

Actor
Laurence Olivier, *Hamlet*
Lew Ayres, *Johnny Belinda*
Montgomery Clift, *The Search*
Dan Dailey, *When My Baby Smiles at Me*
Clifton Webb, *Sitting Pretty*

** Jane Wyman in *Johnny Belinda* AAW GLO PHO '49
The role and player who started Oscar's trend toward honoring handicapped roles was, of

course, real-life amputee Harold Russell in *The Best Years of Our Lives*; but 1948 was the year that playing a handicapped person became an Oscar standby, with no less than three actresses nominated for such parts—Olivia de Havilland as *The Snake Pit*'s mental case, Barbara Stanwyck as the crippled woman who overhears a murder plot in *Sorry, Wrong Number*, and the winner, Jane Wyman as the deaf-mute in *Johnny Belinda*. (Maybe four, depending on how clinical a view you take of Joan of Arc's voices.) Much as I'd like to praise any woman who gave up the chance to be First Lady because it would have entailed remaining married to Ronald Reagan, Wyman's performance (one of the first to rely on study of actual handicapped people and not just theatrical tricks) is never-theless fairly ordinary, and the movie itself is a trashy melodrama that counts on its inspirational qualities to lift it out of the muck.

Actress
Jane Wyman, *Johnny Belinda*
Ingrid Bergman, *Joan of Arc*
Olivia de Havilland, *The Snake Pit*
Irene Dunne, *I Remember Mama*
Barbara Stanwyck, *Sorry, Wrong Number*

Supporting Actor
Walter Huston, *The Treasure of the Sierra Madre*
Charles Bickford, *Johnny Belinda*
José Ferrer, *Joan of Arc*
Oscar Homolka, *I Remember Mama*

Cecil Kellaway, *The Luck of the Irish*

Supporting Actress
Claire Trevor, *Key Largo*
Barbara Bel Geddes, *I Remember Mama*
Ellen Corby, *I Remember Mama*
Agnes Moorehead, *Johnny Belinda*
Jean Simmons, *Hamlet*

Director
John Huston, *The Treasure of the Sierra Madre*
Anatole Litvak, *The Snake Pit*
Jean Negulesco, *Johnny Belinda*
Laurence Olivier, *Hamlet*
Fred Zinnemann, *The Search*

Screenplay: John Huston, *The Treasure of the Sierra Madre*
Original Story: Richard Schweizer, David Wechsler, *The Search*
Cinematography/B&W: William Daniels, *The Naked City*
Cinematography/Color: Joseph Valentine, William V. Skall, Winton Hoch, *Joan of Arc*
Dramatic or Comedy Score: Brian Easdale, *The Red Shoes*
Musical Score: Johnny Green, Roger Edens, *Easter Parade*
Song: "Buttons and Bows," *The Paleface*, ml: Jay Livingston, Ray Evans
Art Direction/B&W: Roger K. Furse, *Hamlet*
Art Direction/Color: Hein Heckroth, *The Red Shoes*
Costumes/B&W: Roger K. Furse, *Hamlet*
Costumes/Color: Dorothy Jeakins, Karinska, *Joan of Arc*
Editing: *The Naked City*
Sound Recording: *The Snake Pit*
Special Effects: *Portrait of Jennie*
Short/Cartoon: *The Little*

Orphan (MGM/Hanna-Barbera/ Tom & Jerry)
Short/One-Reel: *Symphony of a City* (Movietone Specialty)
Short/Two-Reel: *Seal Island* (Walt Disney's True Life Adventures)
Documentary/Feature: *The Secret Land* (U. S. Navy, MGM)
Documentary/Short: *Toward Independence* (U. S. Army)
Irving G. Thalberg Award: Jerry Wald
Special Awards:
Monsieur Vincent (France)— outstanding foreign-language film
Ivan Jandl, outstanding juvenile performance of 1948, *The Search*
Sid Grauman, master showman
Adolph Zukor, for his services to the industry over a period of 40 years
Walter Wanger, for distinguished service to the industry in adding to its moral stature in the world community by his production of the picture *Joan of Arc*

*** ***The Treasure of the Sierra Madre*** GLO NYC
***** **Walter Huston** AAW GLO BOR
A little too self-consciously designed to be a great film with a great theme (how a group of men fall apart through greed); director John Huston's subsequent *Asphalt Jungle* is better because it doesn't have such a pat answer for why its characters destroy themselves. Still, A for effort, and Huston's dad, always terrific, is especially so here.

Golden Globes
Picture: *The Treasure of the Sierra Madre*, *Johnny Belinda* (tie)
Foreign Film: *Hamlet*
Actor: Laurence Olivier, *Hamlet*
Actress: Jane Wyman, *Johnny Belinda*
Supporting Actor: Walter Huston, *The Treasure of the Sierra Madre*
Supporting Actress: Ellen Corby, *I Remember Mama*
Director: John Huston, *The Treasure of the Sierra Madre*
Screenplay: Richard Schweizer, *The Search*
Cinematography: Gabriel Figueroa, *The Pearl* (Mexico)
Score: Brian Easdale, *The Red Shoes*
Best Film Promoting International Understanding: *The Search*
Special Award to Best Juvenile Actor: Ivan Jandl, *The Search*

Directors Guild of America
Quarterly Awards, 1948–49:
Fred Zinnemann, *The Search*
Howard Hawks, *Red River*
Anatole Litvak, *The Snake Pit*
Joseph L. Mankiewicz, *A Letter to Three Wives*
Annual Award: Joseph L. Mankiewicz
Honorary Lifetime Member: Rex Ingram [director, not the actor]

** *Paisan* NYC BOR
Roberto Rossellini's follow-up to *Open City*: six tales of ordinary life in the rubble of Sicily following the Allied invasion. Fresh then, ordinary now.

*** **Olivia de Havilland in *The Snake Pit* NYC BOR VEN '49**

Honorable for its time, if not especially revealing study of mental problems; the few moments of *Cuckoo's Nest*–absurdism (the rug no one is allowed to walk on) only make you wish for more such flashes of imagination. Olivia is careful never to go over the top, but Oscar was right to hold her off until next year.

New York Film Critics Circle
Picture: *The Treasure of the Sierra Madre*
Foreign Film: *Paisan*
Actor: Laurence Olivier, *Hamlet*
Actress: Olivia de Havilland, *The Snake Pit*
Director: John Huston, *The Treasure of the Sierra Madre*

National Board of Review
Best Film: *Paisan*
Day of Wrath
The Search
The Treasure of the Sierra Madre
Louisiana Story
Hamlet
The Snake Pit
Johnny Belinda
Joan of Arc
The Red Shoes
Actor: Walter Huston, *The Treasure of the Sierra Madre*
Actress: Olivia de Havilland, *The Snake Pit*
Director: Roberto Rossellini, *Paisan*
Screenplay: John Huston, *The Treasure of the Sierra Madre*

Photoplay Gold Medal Awards
Gold Medal: *Sitting Pretty*
Most Popular Male Star: Bing Crosby
Most Popular Female Star: Ingrid Bergman

British Academy Awards
Film: *Hamlet*
British Film: *The Fallen Idol*
Documentary: *Louisiana Story*

Venice Film Festival
International Grand Prize: *Hamlet* (Laurence Olivier, UK)
Actor: Ernst Deutsch, *Der Prozess/The Trial* (G. W. Pabst, Austria)
Actress: Jean Simmons, *Hamlet*
Director: G.W. Pabst, *Der Prozess/The Trial*
Story and Screenplay: Graham Greene, *The Fallen Idol* (UK)
Cinematography: Desmond Dickinson, *Hamlet*
Score: Max Steiner, *The Treasure of the Sierra Madre* (USA)
Scenography [Set Design]: John Bryan, *Oliver Twist* (UK)
Documentary: *Goémons* (Yannick Bellon, France)
Animated Film: *Melody Time* (Walt Disney, USA); *Le Petit Soldat* (Paul Grimault, France)
Best Italian Film: *Under the Sun of Rome* (Renato Castellani)
International Prizes:
John Ford, *The Fugitive* (USA), for its drama
Robert Flaherty, *Louisiana Story* (USA), for its lyrical beauty
Luchino Visconti, *La Terra Trema* (Italy), for its choral qualities and style
Italian Film Critics Prize: *Hamlet*

Harvard Lampoon Movie Worsts
Ten worst pictures:
Winter Meeting
Homecoming
The Emperor Waltz
Miracle of the Bells
Beyond Glory
On an Island With You
The Paradine Case
The Three Musketeers
Arch of Triumph
Sorry, Wrong Number

Worst Performances:
Lana Turner, *The Three
Musketeers*
Burt Lancaster, *I Walk Alone*
Shirley Temple, *Fort Apache*
Worst Deception: Joan Fontaine
as a 16-year-old girl in *Letter
from an Unknown Woman*
Worst Reincarnation: Jeanette

MacDonald, *Three Daring
Daughters*
**Actress Most Likely to Drag
Down Her Husband's Dubious
Rep. as an Actor:** Mrs. Agar
[Shirley Temple]
All-Time Worst Hoyden: Mrs.
Agar
Most Nauseating Screen Voice:
Mrs. Agar

Box Office (Domestic Rentals)

1	*The Road to Rio*	$4,500,000	Par
2	*Easter Parade*	4,200,000	MGM
3	*Red River*	4,150,000	UA
4	*The Three Musketeers*	4,100,000	MGM
	Johnny Belinda	4,100,000	WB
6	*Cass Timberlane*	4,050,000	MGM
7	*The Emperor Waltz*	4,000,000	Par
8	*Gentleman's Agreement*	3,900,000	Fox
9	*A Date with Judy*	3,700,000	MGM
10	*Captain from Castile*	3,650,000	Fox
Other films of note:			
12	*Sitting Pretty*	3,550,000	Fox
13	*The Paleface*	3,500,000	Par
17	*Hamlet*	3,250,000	Uni
	Key Largo	3,250,000	WB
21	*Fort Apache*	3,000,000	RKO
50	*The Treasure of the Sierra Madre*	2,300,000	WB
51	*Abbott & Costello Meet Frankenstein*	2,250,000	Uni
55	*The Red Shoes*	2,200,000	Eagle-Lion
	[eventual total rentals:	5,000,000]	

*In a fairly weak year (there was some new gadget called television that everyone
was talking about), Hope & Crosby beat Garland & Astaire as a musical duo—
though the eventual winner was the British ballet film* The Red Shoes, *which would
remain a staple of art houses for the next couple of decades. Another art-house hit
was Olivier's* Hamlet, *at #17. And Universal's attempt to salvage its two franchises—
Abbott & Costello, and its monsters—by combining them in one movie produced
decent box office, but hastened the demise of the latter.*

Gebert's Golden Armchairs

The greatest three-hankie matinee in movie history is Max Ophüls' magnificently old-world, sadder-but-wiser tale of the Viennese cad who never knew the girl who loved him until it was too late, *Letter from an Unknown Woman*. The kind of movie they don't make any more—and even then, they already didn't, which is why it was patronized then but is treasured now. The best British film of '48 isn't black-and-white *Hamlet* but Powell and Pressburger's wildly colored ballet classic *The Red Shoes*; every edge *Hamlet* skirts, *The Red Shoes* leaps blindly over.

Best American Film: *Letter from an Unknown Woman*
Best Foreign Film: *The Red Shoes*
Best Actor: Walter Huston, *The Treasure of the Sierra Madre*
Best Actress: Joan Fontaine, *Letter from an Unknown Woman*
Best Director: Max Ophüls, *Letter from an Unknown Woman*

1949

1949 may not look like it, but it was one of the movies' watershed years, with a host of serious films—*All the King's Men, The Heiress, Twelve O'Clock High, Intruder in the Dust, Champion,* even the apparent comedy *A Letter to Three Wives*—that, unlike the cut-and-dried social problem films of the immediate postwar years, raised difficult questions and didn't answer them in ways that were very comfortable. Or, indeed, answer them at all.

At the same time, however, this new school of filmmaking was on a collision course with the blacklist, which would chill efforts to deal with American realities honestly. And while large parts of Hollywood would still attempt to explore serious themes and reward pictures like *A Streetcar Named Desire, From Here to Eternity,* and *On the Waterfront* with Oscars, other parts of Hollywood would be perfectly happy to make big, silly escapist fare like *The Greatest Show on Earth* and *Around the World in 80 Days*—and reward *them* with Oscars. The 1950s, which seemed from 1949's vantage point to promise a new maturity in filmmaking, would prove to be the most schizophrenic decade in Hollywood history.

Academy Awards

**** *All the King's Men* AAW GLO DGA NYC
**** Broderick Crawford AAW GLO NYC
Based on the Robert Penn Warren novel about a Southern demagogue, as obviously based on Huey Long as *Citizen Kane* was on Hearst, Robert Rossen's film was the most serious film about American politics since *Kane*. It boasted a dynamic performance by Broderick Crawford as the bullying good ol' boy who rises in Louisiana politics the way Little Caesar rose in the rackets—and a harsh, bitter supporting performance by Mercedes McCambridge as

his homely, sexually frustrated speechwriter.

Picture
All the King's Men (Columbia, Robert Rossen)
Battleground (MGM, Dore Schary)
The Heiress (Paramount, William Wyler)
A Letter to Three Wives (20th Century–Fox, Sol C. Siegel)
Twelve O'Clock High (20th Century–Fox, Darryl F. Zanuck)

Actor
Broderick Crawford, *All the King's Men*
Kirk Douglas, *Champion*
Gregory Peck, *Twelve O'Clock High*
Richard Todd, *The Hasty Heart*
John Wayne, *Sands of Iwo Jima*

***** **Olivia de Havilland in**
The Heiress AAW GLO
NYC
Only the second American
sound film to be based on
Henry James—an author who
had so far proven too clinical
and cynical for costume-movie
adaptation—*The Heiress* is
one of the most chilling and
anti-romantic romances ever put
on screen, closer in tone to a
Vincent Price Edgar Allan Poe
thriller than Wyler's romantic
costume hit of a decade earlier,
Wuthering Heights. De
Havilland ignores the traditional
affectations and material
comforts of a Hollywood
costume role to concentrate on
the heartrendingly plain and
needy character underneath.

Actress
Olivia de Havilland, *The Heiress*
Jeanne Crain, *Pinky*
Susan Hayward, *My Foolish Heart*
Deborah Kerr, *Edward, My Son*
Loretta Young, *Come to the Stable*

Supporting Actor
Dean Jagger, *Twelve O'Clock High*
John Ireland, *All the King's Men*
Arthur Kennedy, *Champion*
Ralph Richardson, *The Heiress*
James Whitmore, *Battleground*

Supporting Actress
Mercedes McCambridge, *All the King's Men*
Ethel Barrymore, *Pinky*
Celeste Holm, *Come to the Stable*
Elsa Lanchester, *Come to the Stable*
Ethel Waters, *Pinky*

Director
Joseph L. Mankiewicz, *A Letter to Three Wives*
Carol Reed, *The Fallen Idol*
Robert Rossen, *All the King's Men*
William A. Wellman, *Battleground*
William Wyler, *The Heiress*

Screenplay: Joseph L. Mankiewicz, *A Letter to Three Wives*
Story and Screenplay: Robert Pirosh, *Battleground*
Original Story: Douglas Morrow, *The Stratton Story*
Cinematography/B&W: Paul C. Vogel, *Battleground*
Cinematography/Color: Winton Hoch, *She Wore a Yellow Ribbon*
Dramatic or Comedy Score: Aaron Copland, *The Heiress*
Musical Score: Roger Edens, Lennie Hayton, *On the Town*
Song: "Baby, It's Cold Outside," *Neptune's Daughter*, ml: Frank Loesser
Art Direction/B&W: John Meehan, Harry Horner, *The Heiress*
Art Direction/Color: Cedric Gibbons, Paul Groesse, *Little Women*
Costumes/B&W: Edith Head, *The Heiress*
Costumes/Color: *Adventures of Don Juan*
Editing: *Champion*
Sound Recording: *Twelve O'Clock High*
Special Effects: *Mighty Joe Young* [Willis O'Brien, Ray Harryhausen]
Short/Cartoon: *For Scent-imental Reasons* (Warner/Chuck Jones/Pepe LePew)
Short/One-Reel: *Aquatic House-Party* (Grantland Rice Sportlights)
Short/Two-Reel: *Van Gogh*
Documentary/Feature: *Daybreak in Udi* (British Information Services)

Documentary/Short: *A Chance to Live* (March of Time); *So Much for So Little* (Public Health Service and Warner Bros. cartoon unit)
Special Awards:
The Bicycle Thief (Italy)—outstanding foreign-language film
Bobby Driscoll, outstanding juvenile actor of 1949
Fred Astaire
Cecil B. DeMille
Jean Hersholt, for service to the industry

Golden Globes
Picture: *All the King's Men*
Foreign Film: *The Bicycle Thief*
Actor: Broderick Crawford, *All the King's Men*
Actress: Olivia de Havilland, *The Heiress*
Supporting Actor: James Whitmore, *Battleground*
Supporting Actress: Mercedes McCambridge, *All the King's Men*
Director: Robert Rossen, *All the King's Men*
Screenplay: Robert Pirosh, *Battleground*
Cinematography/Color: Walt Disney Studios, *Ichabod & Mr. Toad*
Cinematography/B&W: Frank Planer, *Champion*
Score: Johnny Green, *The Inspector General*
Most Promising Newcomer (Male): Richard Todd, *The Hasty Heart*
Most Promising Newcomer (Female): Mercedes McCambridge, *All the King's Men*
Best Film Promoting International Understanding: *The Hasty Heart*

Directors Guild of America
Quarterly Awards, 1949–50: Mark Robson, *Champion*

Alfred L. Werker, *Lost Boundaries*
Robert Rossen, *All the King's Men*
Carol Reed, *The Third Man*
Annual Award: Robert Rossen, *All the King's Men*

*** *The Bicycle Thief* AAW GLO NYC BOR BAA
Perhaps the most acclaimed of all Italian neorealist films—certainly a unanimous choice anywhere it competed. De Sica's drama is about a sign poster whose bicycle, essential to keeping his job, is stolen, sending him and his son on a desperate search. It has an admirable simplicity of storyline (dare one say "high concept"?)—but I feel that it's not until the ice-cream scene halfway through that the father and son stop being mere symbols of humanity and become characters.

New York Film Critics Circle
Picture: *All the King's Men*
Foreign Film: *The Bicycle Thief*
Actor: Broderick Crawford, *All the King's Men*
Actress: Olivia de Havilland, *The Heiress*
Director: Carol Reed, *The Fallen Idol*

National Board of Review
Best Picture: *The Bicycle Thief*
The Quiet One
Intruder in the Dust
The Heiress
Devil in the Flesh
Quartet
Germany Year Zero
Home of the Brave
A Letter to Three Wives
The Fallen Idol

Actor: Ralph Richardson, *The Heiress*, *The Fallen Idol*
Actress: none
Director: Vittorio De Sica, *The Bicycle Thief*
Screenplay: Graham Greene, *The Fallen Idol* [NOTE: Lesley Storm and William Templeton also receive on-screen credit]

Photoplay Gold Medal Awards
Gold Medal: *The Stratton Story*
Most Popular Male Star: James Stewart, *The Stratton Story*
Most Popular Female Star: Jane Wyman, *Johnny Belinda*

British Academy Awards
Film: *The Bicycle Thief*
British Film: *The Third Man*
Documentary: *Daybreak in Udi*

***** *The Third Man* CAN
Graham Greene never liked Hitchcock, feeling there was a lack of moral seriousness in his work. Carol Reed's second film from a Greene script (after *The Fallen Idol*) puts David Selznick's money where Greene's mouth is, using a thriller plot as brilliantly executed as any of Hitch's to probe moral issues—most daringly of all, by making one American character a stand-in for Nazi evil and another his naive dupe.

Cannes Film Festival
Grand Prize: *The Third Man* (Carol Reed, UK)
Actor: Edward G. Robinson, *House of Strangers* (USA)
Actress: Isa Miranda, *The Walls of Malapaga* (René Clément, Italy)

Director: René Clément, *The Walls of Malapaga*
Screenplay: Virginia Shaler, Eugene Ling, *Lost Boundaries* (USA)
Photography: Milton Krasner, *The Set-Up* (USA)
Score: *Pueblerina* [Mexico, directed by Emilio Fernandez]
Set Design: *Occupe-Toi d'Amélie* (Claude Autant-Lara, France)
[Short film prizes included Best Editing to *Pacific 231* by Jean Mitry (France), Best Film Reporting to *Seal Island*, Walt Disney (USA)]

Venice Film Festival
International Grand Prize: *Manon* (Henri-Georges Clouzot, France)
Actor: Joseph Cotten, *Portrait of Jennie* (USA)
Actress: Olivia de Havilland, *The Snake Pit* (USA)
Director: Augusto Genina, *Cielo sulla Palude* (Italy)
Screenplay: Jacques Tati, *Jour de Fete* (France)
Cinematography: Gabriel Figueroa, *La Malquerida* (Mexico)
Score: John Greenwood, *The Last Days of Dolwyn* (UK)
Scenography [Set Design]: William Kellner, *Kind Hearts and Coronets* (UK)
Documentary: *L'Equateur aux Cent Visages* (Andre Cauvin, Belgium)
Best Italian Film: *Cielo sulla Palude*
International Prizes:
Sidney Meyers, *The Quiet One* (USA)
Anatole Litvak, *The Snake Pit* (USA)
Robert A. Stemmle, *Berliner Ballade* (W. Germany)
Italian Film Critics' Prize: *The Quiet One* (Sidney Meyers, USA)

Harvard Lampoon Movie Worsts

Ten worst pictures:
Special Award: Worst Picture of the Century: *Joan of Arc*
The Great Gatsby
The Night Has a Thousand Eyes
Flamingo Road
Look for the Silver Lining
Top o' the Morning
The Fountainhead
The Fan
That Midnight Kiss
A Connecticut Yankee in King Arthur's Court
Worst Single Performance—
Male: Gregory Peck, *The Great Sinner*
Worst Single Performance—
Female: Shirley Temple, *Mr. Belvedere Goes to College*
Least Likely to Warm Cockles of Heart: Barry Fitzgerald
Least Likely to Warm Anything: Barry Fitzgerald
Least Deserving But Most Due for a Pension: Barry Fitzgerald
Finest Example for Cleancut American Youth: Mrs. Aly Khan [Rita Hayworth]
Best-Known Wife of Racehorse Owner: Mrs. Aly Khan
Meatball: Mrs. Aly Khan

Box Office (Domestic Rentals)

1	*Jolson Sings Again*	$5,500,000	Col
2	*Pinky*	4,200,000	Fox
3	*I Was a Male War Bride*	4,100,000	Fox
	The Snake Pit	4,100,000	Fox
	Joan of Arc	4,100,000	RKO
6	*The Stratton Story*	3,700,000	MGM
7	*Mr. Belvedere Goes to College*	3,650,000	Fox
8	*Little Women*	3,600,000	MGM
9	*Words and Music*	3,500,000	MGM
10	*Neptune's Daughter*	3,450,000	MGM
Other films of note:			
11	*In the Good Old Summertime*	3,400,000	MGM
16	*Adam's Rib*	3,000,000	MGM
	[total 1949–50 rentals:	5,750,000]	
21	*My Friend Irma*	2,800,000	Par
31	*Ma and Pa Kettle*	2,300,000	Uni
51	*Mighty Joe Young*	1,950,000	RKO
54	*White Heat*	1,900,000	WB

Jolson rings the register again, and Esther Williams (#10) passed Judy Garland (#11) as MGM's top female musical star. But Walter Wanger's Joan of Arc, which broke Duel in the Sun's $6 million cost record by nearly $3 million more, turned out to be a snooze and something of a running joke. At #21 Paramount did surprisingly well with the movie debut of a Borscht Belt duo named Martin & Lewis, and Universal had an even more surprising success with a low-budget, lowbrow comedy starring Ma and Pa Kettle, supporting characters from The Egg and I.

Gebert's Golden Armchairs

Going against the grain of every morale-builder made during the war, the bomber-squadron movie *Twelve O'Clock High* suggested that officers and men were fundamentally different creatures after all (by job if not by nature), that the individuality we were fighting to preserve was the one luxury we could not afford during wartime—and that the price of victory was a commanding officer's soul. All of which are more original and daring things to say than that some politicians are crooks, the message of *All the King's Men*.

The writing-directing team of Graham Greene and Carol Reed screened *The Third Man* at Cannes in late 1949, but their most widely seen work at this point was their previous film, *The Fallen Idol*, a superb screw-turning thriller about a butler who is implicated in a suspected murder by the innocent actions of the young boy of the house. Ralph Richardson's portrait of rising desperation is, in its own way, every bit as impressive as his more widely acclaimed performance as the heartless father in *The Heiress*.

Best American Film: *Twelve O'Clock High*
Best Foreign Film: *The Fallen Idol*
Best Actor: Ralph Richardson, *The Fallen Idol*
Best Actress: Olivia de Havilland, *The Heiress*
Best Director: Carol Reed, *The Fallen Idol*

1950

1950 has to be the only time a film ever competed against part of *itself* for an award. Roberto Rossellini's *L'Amore* had two parts—one of them a tale called *The Miracle*, written by and co-starring Fellini, about a peasant woman (Anna Magnani) who believes she's pregnant with the Messiah. An American distributor took *The Miracle*, combined it with two other featurettes—Marcel Pagnol's 1934 *Jofroi* and Jean Renoir's unfinished 1936 *A Day in the Country*—and called the resulting compilation *Ways of Love*. Then the Legion of Decency attacked *The Miracle* as blasphemous, and the New York License Commissioner decided to ban it (eventually resulting in an important Supreme Court decision that movies were protected speech like books or plays, not just articles of commerce like soap). Some critics wanted to support *The Miracle* and free speech by promoting *Ways of Love* for the critics' foreign film prize—while others, opposing it and hoping to divide *Ways of Love*'s fans, campaigned for *Jofroi* on its own for Best Foreign-Language Film. In fact, it was the Renoir film that was the masterpiece in the bundle. But in the end, *Ways of Love*'s whole defeated one of its parts, 9–4.

Academy Awards

***** *All About Eve* AAW DGA NYC BAA CAN '51
We admire Quentin Tarantino, rightly, for writing the juiciest parts today's movies have to offer, but he writes dialogue so strong and distinctive that *anybody* could deliver it well—as *Pulp Fiction* proved, since John Travolta, Uma Thurman, and Bruce Willis would not normally be anyone's idea of the cast of the year. There's an exchange in *All About Eve* in a party scene that runs, "I can't see why she hasn't given Addison heartburn." "No heart to burn." To which Bette Davis tipsily replies, "*Everybody* has a heart. Except *some* people." On the page it seems like nonsense, even ineffectual writing—in a movie full of perfect little bon mots, it's the one time someone simply babbles. But somehow Joe Mankiewicz understood acting well enough, and he understood Bette Davis (whom he'd never directed before) well enough, that he could write a line like that knowing that she could deliver it so it would not only make sense, it would reveal something tender and vulnerable about her character that wasn't even in the words themselves. I don't even know *how* you learn to write like

that—except that just watching movies *isn't* it.

Picture
All About Eve (20th Century–Fox, Darryl F. Zanuck)
Born Yesterday (Columbia, S. Sylvan Simon)
Father of the Bride (MGM, Pandro S. Berman)
King Solomon's Mines (MGM, Sam Zimbalist)
Sunset Boulevard (Paramount, Charles Brackett)

**** José Ferrer in *Cyrano*
AAW GLO
Gérard Depardieu's 1989 film has replaced this as the definitive screen version, but Ferrer brings tremendous virtuosity and that voice like 100-year-old port to the part, and it's easy to see why he bowled over a post-*Hamlet* Hollywood.

Actor
José Ferrer, *Cyrano de Bergerac*
Louis Calhern, *The Magnificent Yankee*
William Holden, *Sunset Boulevard*
James Stewart, *Harvey*
Spencer Tracy, *Father of the Bride*

*** Judy Holliday in *Born Yesterday* AAW GLO
The Oscar upset of all time is that Holliday's endearing comic dumb-blonde part in this imitation-Capra comedy (which, at its clunkiest, could have been written by Barton Fink) somehow stole the Oscar from two of the juiciest roles ever written for two great actresses. Ordinarily the injustice

works the other way—Oscar favoring bad drama over great comedy.

Actress
Judy Holliday, *Born Yesterday*
Anne Baxter, *All About Eve*
Bette Davis, *All About Eve*
Eleanor Parker, *Caged*
Gloria Swanson, *Sunset Boulevard*

Supporting Actor
George Sanders, *All About Eve*
Jeff Chandler, *Broken Arrow*
Edmund Gwenn, *Mister 880*
Sam Jaffe, *The Asphalt Jungle*
Erich von Stroheim, *Sunset Boulevard*

Supporting Actress
Josephine Hull, *Harvey*
Hope Emerson, *Caged*
Celeste Holm, *All About Eve*
Nancy Olson, *Sunset Boulevard*
Thelma Ritter, *All About Eve*

Director
Joseph L. Mankiewicz, *All About Eve*
George Cukor, *Born Yesterday*
John Huston, *The Asphalt Jungle*
Carol Reed, *The Third Man*
Billy Wilder, *Sunset Boulevard*

Screenplay: Joseph L. Mankiewicz, *All About Eve*
Story and Screenplay: Charles Brackett, Billy Wilder, D. M. Marshman, Jr., *Sunset Boulevard*
Original Story: Edward Anhalt, Edna Anhalt, *Panic in the Streets*
Cinematography/B&W: Robert Krasker, *The Third Man*
Cinematography/Color: Robert Surtees, *King Solomon's Mines*
Dramatic or Comedy Score: Franz Waxman, *Sunset Boulevard*
Musical Score: Adolph Deutsch,

Roger Edens, *Annie Get Your Gun*
Song: "Mona Lisa," *Captain Carey*, ml: Ray Evans, Jay Livingston
Art Direction/B&W: Hans Dreier, John Meehan, *Sunset Boulevard*
Art Direction/Color: Hans Dreier, *Samson and Delilah*
Costumes/B&W: Edith Head, *All About Eve*
Costumes/Color: Edith Head, *Samson and Delilah*
Editing: *King Solomon's Mines*
Sound Recording: *All About Eve*
Special Effects: *Destination Moon*
Short/Cartoon: *Gerald McBoing-Boing* (UPA/Robert Cannon)
Short/One-Reel: *Granddad of Races* (Warner Bros. Sports Parade)
Short/Two-Reel: *In Beaver Valley* (Disney True-Life Adventures)
Documentary/Feature: *The Titan—The Story of Michelangelo* (Robert Snyder)
Documentary/Short: *Why Korea?* (Fox Movietone)
Irving G. Thalberg Award: Darryl F. Zanuck
Special Awards:
George Murphy
Louis B. Mayer
The Walls of Malapaga (France-Italy)—outstanding foreign-language film

**** *Sunset Boulevard* GLO BOR
***** **Gloria Swanson** GLO BOR
How would a silent actress talk if silent movies had had dialogue which was like the way they acted? That was the question Billy Wilder & co. had to solve in writing the great Hollywood gothic; Swanson got it, and gives a dazzlingly over-the-top performance with one foot in the '20s and the other in film *noir*.

Golden Globes
Picture: *Sunset Boulevard*
Actor (Drama): José Ferrer, *Cyrano de Bergerac*
Actor (Comedy/Musical): Fred Astaire, *Three Little Words*
Actress (Drama): Gloria Swanson, *Sunset Boulevard*
Actress (Comedy/Musical): Judy Holliday, *Born Yesterday*
Supporting Actor: Edmund Gwenn, *Mister 880*
Supporting Actress: Josephine Hull, *Harvey*
Director: Billy Wilder, *Sunset Boulevard*
Screenplay: Joseph L. Mankiewicz, *All About Eve*
Cinematography/Color: Robert Surtees, *King Solomon's Mines*
Cinematography/B&W: Frank Planer, *Cyrano de Bergerac*
Score: Franz Waxman, *Sunset Boulevard*
Most Promising Newcomer: Gene Nelson, *Tea for Two*
World Film Favorite (Male): Gregory Peck
World Film Favorite (Female): Jane Wyman
Best Film Promoting International Understanding: *Broken Arrow*

Directors Guild of America
Quarterly Awards, 1950–51:
Billy Wilder, *Sunset Boulevard*
John Huston, *The Asphalt Jungle*
Joseph L. Mankiewicz, *All About Eve*
Vincente Minnelli, *Father's Little Dividend*
Annual Award: Joseph L. Mankiewicz, *All About Eve*

Honorary Lifetime Member:
J. P. McGowan

***** **Bette Davis** NYC CAN
'51
Davis' narrow win in New York
foreshadowed her eventual
Oscar loss to Holliday—they
tied 7–7 on the first ballot, and
Holliday actually pulled ahead
by one on the second until
Davis picked up Gloria
Swanson's votes (and, apparently,
some lukewarm Holliday fans)
and won 10–6. I can only think
Davis' familiarity was
responsible for this cavalier
treatment—oh, look, it's one of
the greatest actresses alive, with
a dazzling performance
promising that her middle age will
be as rich as everything that
came before it. *Let's vote for
the blonde.*

New York Film Critics Circle
Picture: *All About Eve*
Foreign Film: *Ways of Love*
Actor: Gregory Peck, *Twelve
O'Clock High*
Actress: Bette Davis, *All About
Eve*
Director: Joseph L. Mankiewicz,
All About Eve

National Board of Review
Best American Film: *Sunset
Boulevard*
All About Eve
The Asphalt Jungle
The Men
Edge of Doom
Twelve O'Clock High
Panic in the Streets
Cyrano de Bergerac
No Way Out
Stage Fright

Best Foreign Film: *The Titan—
The Story of Michelangelo*
Tight Little Island [*Whiskey
Galore*]
The Third Man
Kind Hearts and Coronets
Paris 1900
Actor: Alec Guinness, *Kind
Hearts and Coronets*
Actress: Gloria Swanson, *Sunset
Boulevard*
Director: John Huston, *The
Asphalt Jungle*

Photoplay Gold Medal Awards
Gold Medal: *Battleground*
Most Popular Male Star: John
Wayne, *Sands of Iwo Jima*
Most Popular Female Star:
Betty Hutton, *Annie Get Your
Gun*

British Academy Awards
Film: *All About Eve*
British Film: *The Blue Lamp*

Venice Film Festival
Golden Lion: *Justice Is Done*
(André Cayatte, France)
Special Jury Prize: Walt Disney,
Cinderella, Beaver Valley
(USA)
Actor: Sam Jaffe, *The Asphalt
Jungle* (USA)
Actress: Eleanor Parker, *Caged*
(USA)
Screenplay: Jacques Natanson,
Max Ophüls, *La Ronde* (France)
Cinematography: Martin Bodin,
Bara en mor (Sweden)
Score: Brian Easdale, *Gone to
Earth* (UK)
Scenography [Set Design]: Jean
d'Eaubonne, *La Ronde*
Documentary: *Visite á Picasso*
(Paul Haesaert, Belgium)
Best Italian Film: *Domani é
troppo tardi* (Léonide Moguy)
International Prizes:
Elia Kazan, *Panic in the Streets*
(USA)

Jean Delannoy, *Dieu a Besoin des Hommes* [*Isle of Sinners/God Needs Men*] (France)

Alessandro Blasetti, *Prima Comunione* (Italy)

Harvard Lampoon Movie Worsts

Ten worst pictures:
Our Very Own
Samson and Delilah
Three Came Home
The Next Voice You Hear
An American Guerilla in the Philippines
Cheaper By the Dozen
Stromboli
The Flame and the Arrow
The Conspirators

The Duchess of Idaho
Worst Actor: Clifton Webb, *Cheaper By the Dozen*
Worst Actress: Elizabeth Taylor, *The Conspirators*
Most Unnecessary Contribution to the American Way of Life: Bing Crosby
Worst Insult to the American Fighting Man: John Wayne
Greatest Travesty of the Holy Year: *Samson and Delilah*
Happiest Event of the Year: Shirley Temple's announced retirement
The Roscoe Award: Elizabeth Taylor for so gallantly persisting in her career despite a total inability to act

Box Office (Domestic Rentals)

1	*Samson and Delilah*	$11,000,000	Par
2	*Battleground*	4,550,000	MGM
3	*King Solomon's Mines*	4,400,000	MGM
4	*Cheaper By the Dozen*	4,325,000	Fox
5	*Annie Get Your Gun*	4,200,000	MGM
6	*Cinderella*	4,150,000	RKO
	Father of the Bride	4,150,000	MGM
8	*Sands of Iwo Jima*	3,900,000	Republic
9	*Broken Arrow*	3,550,000	Fox
10	*Twelve O'Clock High*	3,225,000	Fox
Other films of note:			
11	*All About Eve*	2,900,000	Fox
	Francis	2,900,000	Uni
	On the Town	2,900,000	MGM
28	*Sunset Boulevard*	2,350,000	Par
33	*Winchester '73*	2,250,000	Uni
40	*Ma and Pa Kettle Go to Town*	2,175,000	Uni
41	*The Third Man*	2,150,000	Selznick
88	*Destination Moon*	1,300,000	Eagle-Lion
92	*Abbott & Costello in the Foreign Legion*	1,275,000	Uni

The first big biblical epic of the postwar era set the pace for the genre, outgrossing any film since The Best Years of Our Lives; *much less impressive, though still a good moneymaker for its studio, was the performance of the first major sci-fi film of the postwar era,* Destination Moon. *(Eagle-Lion was the result of a takeover of small*

Poverty Row studios by J. Arthur Rank's British Lion; it later became part of United Artists.) Cinderella was Disney's first big hit since Snow White, and as Abbott & Costello faded from the scene, Universal found salvation in cornball comedy—Francis the Talking Mule joined Ma and Pa Kettle as the studio's meal tickets.

Gebert's Golden Armchairs

Hey, Oscar's had two acting ties, I'm entitled to one.

Best American Film: *All About Eve*

Best Foreign Film: *The Third Man*

Best Actor: George Sanders, *All About Eve*

Best Actress: Bette Davis, *All About Eve*; Gloria Swanson, *Sunset Boulevard* (tie)

Best Director: Joseph L. Mankiewicz, *All About Eve*

1951

The 1950s were the glory years of the film festivals, the decade in which they introduced one major filmmaker or national school after another to the world; and 1951 was arguably the year in which both Cannes and Venice made their most important and valuable discoveries. Venice gave its top prize to Akira Kurosawa's *Rashomon* (or as it was billed, *Rasciomon*), opening the West to the incredible richness of Japanese cinema. Cannes began with a political brouhaha—the Soviets insisted on the removal of the Berlin winner *Four in a Jeep*, which satirized the Four Powers' occupation of Austria. But the festival redeemed itself with the screening of Luis Buñuel's *Los Olvidados*, a drama of Mexican slum children that was like *Shoeshine* crossed with Goya. The Spanish-born avant-garde filmmaker of the early '30s had been forgotten for 20 years, but his Best Direction award relaunched him as one of the postwar cinema's masters (and paved the way for a delicious scandal a decade later, when his *Viridiana* won the Palme d'Or).

At home the obvious highlight of the year was Marlon Brando's Stanley Kowalski in *A Streetcar Named Desire*—the most important performance of the century, the dividing line between the clipped diction of the '30s and '40s and the smoldering, half-withdrawn inarticulateness of every male sex symbol since. He was so new and impactful, in fact, that not a *single* award group honored him—even in New York, where they'd seen him on stage, Brando lost 10–5 to Arthur Kennedy as a blind vet. Brando spent most of the decade picking up awards, for *Viva Zapata!* or *On the Waterfront*, that were really atonement for what happened to *Streetcar*.

Academy Awards

*** An American in Paris
AAW GLO
A surprise winner over *A Place in the Sun* and *Streetcar*, Gene Kelly's attempt to outdo *The Red Shoes* in the arty-musical sweepstakes looks fantastic, but lacks the exuberance of *Singin' in the Rain*. Still, nice try.

Picture
An American in Paris (MGM, Arthur Freed)
Decision Before Dawn (20th Century–Fox, Anatole Litvak, Frank McCarthy)
A Place in the Sun (Paramount, George Stevens)
Quo Vadis? (MGM, Sam Zimbalist)
A Streetcar Named Desire (Warner Bros., Charles K. Feldman)

150

*** Humphrey Bogart in *The African Queen* AAW
Oscar's sentimental pick of Bogie for his self-parodic change of pace was as good an anybody-but-Brando choice as any.

Actor
Humphrey Bogart, *The African Queen*
Marlon Brando, *A Streetcar Named Desire*
Montgomery Clift, *A Place in the Sun*
Arthur Kennedy, *Bright Victory*
Fredric March, *Death of a Salesman*

***** Vivien Leigh in *A Streetcar Named Desire*
AAW NYC VEN BAA '52
A spooky performance of quavering grandiosity.

Actress
Vivien Leigh, *A Streetcar Named Desire*
Katharine Hepburn, *The African Queen*
Eleanor Parker, *Detective Story*
Shelley Winters, *A Place in the Sun*
Jane Wyman, *The Blue Veil*

Supporting Actor
Karl Malden, *A Streetcar Named Desire*
Leo Genn, *Quo Vadis?*
Kevin McCarthy, *Death of a Salesman*
Peter Ustinov, *Quo Vadis?*
Gig Young, *Come Fill the Cup*

Supporting Actress
Kim Hunter, *A Streetcar Named Desire*
Joan Blondell, *The Blue Veil*
Mildred Dunnock, *Death of a Salesman*

Lee Grant, *Detective Story*
Thelma Ritter, *The Mating Season*

Director
George Stevens, *A Place in the Sun*
John Huston, *The African Queen*
Elia Kazan, *A Streetcar Named Desire*
Vincente Minnelli, *An American in Paris*
William Wyler, *Detective Story*

Screenplay: Michael Wilson, Harry Brown, *A Place in the Sun*
Story and Screenplay: Alan Jay Lerner, *An American in Paris*
Original Story: Paul Dehn, James Bernard, *Seven Days to Noon*
Cinematography/B&W: William C. Mellor, *A Place in the Sun*
Cinematography/Color: Alfred Gilks, John Alton, *An American in Paris*
Dramatic or Comedy Score: Franz Waxman, *A Place in the Sun*
Musical Score: Johnny Green, Saul Chaplin, *An American in Paris*
Song: "In the Cool, Cool, Cool of the Evening," *Here Comes the Groom*, m: Hoagy Carmichael, l: Johnny Mercer
Art Direction/B&W: Richard Day, *A Streetcar Named Desire*
Art Direction/Color: Cedric Gibbons, Preston Ames, *An American in Paris*
Costumes/B&W: Edith Head, *A Place in the Sun*
Costumes/Color: Walter Plunkett, Irene Sharaff, *An American in Paris*
Editing: *A Place in the Sun*
Sound Recording: *The Great Caruso*
Special Effects: *When Worlds Collide*
Short/Cartoon: *Two*

Mouseketeers (MGM/Hanna-Barbera/Tom & Jerry)
Short/One-Reel: *World of Kids* (Vitaphone Novelties, Robert Youngson)
Short/Two-Reel: *Nature's Half Acre* (Disney True-Life Adventures)
Documentary/Feature: *Kon-Tiki* [Norway]
Documentary/Short: *Benjy* (Fred Zinnemann, Los Angeles Orthopædic Hospital)
Irving G. Thalberg Award: Arthur Freed
Special Awards:
Gene Kelly, in appreciation of his versatility and specifically for his brilliant achievements in choreography on film
Rashomon (Japan)—outstanding foreign-language film

** *A Place in the Sun* GLO DGA BOR
George Stevens' bid to make The Great American Movie out of a great American novel (Dreiser's *An American Tragedy*). Since Dreiser's plot—worker (Monty Clift) hopes to marry local gentry (Liz Taylor) but is undone by his past—sounds in outline like a film *noir*, you only have to compare this with a first-rate film *noir* (*Out of the Past*, say, or *They Won't Believe Me*) to see precisely where it fails by comparison. It spells every motivation out, it doesn't capture a real sense of its time and place (New England, 1920s), it goes sentimental when it needs to be toughest and—most of all—it runs two hours when it ought to zip by in 80 minutes.

Golden Globes
Picture (Drama): *A Place in the Sun*
Picture (Comedy/Musical): *An American in Paris*
Actor (Drama): Fredric March, *Death of a Salesman*
Actor (Comedy/Musical): Danny Kaye, *On the Riviera*
Actress (Drama): Jane Wyman, *The Blue Veil*
Actress (Comedy/Musical): June Allyson, *Too Young to Kiss*
Supporting Actor: Peter Ustinov, *Quo Vadis?*
Supporting Actress: Kim Hunter, *A Streetcar Named Desire*
Director: Laslo Benedek, *Death of a Salesman*
Screenplay: Robert Buckner, *Bright Victory*
Cinematography/Color: Robert Surtees, William V. Skall, *Quo Vadis?*
Cinematography/B&W: Frank Planer, *Death of a Salesman*
Score: Victor Young, *September Affair*
Most Promising Newcomer (Male): Kevin McCarthy, *Death of a Salesman*
Most Promising Newcomer (Female): Pier Angeli, *Teresa*
Best Film Promoting International Understanding: *The Day the Earth Stood Still*
Cecil B. DeMille Award: Cecil B. DeMille

Directors Guild of America
Quarterly Awards [only three given, due to award period changing to calendar year]:
Alfred Hitchcock, *Strangers on a Train*
George Stevens, *A Place in the Sun*
Vincente Minnelli, *Father's Little Dividend*
Annual Award: George Stevens, *A Place in the Sun*

Honorary Lifetime Member:
Louis B. Mayer

****** *A Streetcar Named
Desire* NYC VEN**
Howard Hawks complained that
Streetcar reintroduced into
screen acting every bad habit
he'd spent his career
eliminating. You can see his
point; there's really no excuse
for it—*Streetcar* is a
masterpiece of overheated
artificiality, of overemphasis, of
everything borrowed from the
theater that the movies shouldn't
do. We'd have our
punishment, soon enough, in
more overblown, unnaturally
"naturalistic" Tennessee
Williams movies than we
could stomach—but this one
achieves a sort of luminous
perfection.

**New York Film Critics
Circle**
Picture: *A Streetcar Named
Desire*
Foreign Film: *Miracle in Milan*
Actor: Arthur Kennedy, *Bright
Victory*
Actress: Vivien Leigh, *A
Streetcar Named Desire*
Director: Elia Kazan, *A Streetcar
Named Desire*

National Board of Review
Best American Film: *A Place in
the Sun*
The Red Badge of Courage
An American in Paris
Death of a Salesman
Detective Story
A Streetcar Named Desire
Decision Before Dawn
Strangers on a Train
Quo Vadis?
Fourteen Hours

Best Foreign Film: *Rashomon*
The River
Miracle in Milan
Kon-Tiki
The Browning Version
Actor: Richard Basehart,
Fourteen Hours
Actress: Jan Sterling, *The Big
Carnival* [*Ace in the Hole*]
Director: Akira Kurosawa,
Rashomon
Screenplay: T. E. B. Clarke, *The
Lavender Hill Mob*

**Photoplay Gold Medal
Awards**
Gold Medal: *Show Boat*
Most Popular Male Star: Mario
Lanza, *The Great Caruso*
Most Popular Female Star:
Doris Day, *Lullaby of Broadway*

British Academy Awards
Film: *La Ronde*
British Film: *The Lavender Hill
Mob*
Documentary: *Beaver Valley*
(Walt Disney, USA)
Specialized Film: *Gerald
McBoing-Boing* (Robert
Cannon, USA)

***** *Miracle in Milan* NYC
CAN**
A sweet, whimsical fable about
a shantytown with oil
underneath it, inspired by René
Clair's films of the early '30s.
De Sica's only Cannes winner
(which also beat *Rashomon*
10–5 in the New York critics'
voting) marks the shift in the
Italian neorealism movement
from social concern to the
fantasy that Fellini, in
particular, would make his stock-
in-trade.

**** *Miss Julie* CAN
A powerful film version of
Strindberg's merciless play,

directed with *Kane*-like
flashbacks and Expressionist
lighting by one of Ingmar
Bergman's mentors, Alf
Sjöberg—and shot,
interestingly, by Strindberg's
grandson.

Cannes Film Festival
Grand Prize: *Miracle in Milan*
(Italy, Vittorio De Sica), *Miss
Julie* (Sweden, Alf Sjöberg)
Special Jury Prize: *All About Eve*
(Joseph L. Mankiewicz, USA)
Actor: Michael Redgrave, *The
Browning Version* (UK)
Actress: Bette Davis, *All About
Eve*
Director: Luis Buñuel, *Los
Olvidados* (Mexico)
Screenplay: Terence Rattigan,
The Browning Version
Cinematography: Luis-Maria
Beltran, *La Balandra Isabel
Llego Esta Tarde* (Venezuela)
Score: Joseph Kosma, *Juliette or
the Key of Dreams* (France)
Sets: Suvorov A. Veksler,
Moussorgsky (USSR)
Exceptional Prize: *The Tales of
Hoffmann*, Michael Powell and
Emeric Pressburger, Great
Britain, for the originality of the
transposition into film of a musical
work
Special Citation: to Italy for the
best national selection
International Critics Prize:
Miracle in Milan; career citation
to Luis Buñuel

**** *Rashomon*   AAW BOR
VEN
A bandit meets a husband and
wife in the forest; the husband
is killed, but what *really*
happened? The first Japanese
film to attract worldwide
attention announced the
arrival of a filmmaker, Akira
Kurosawa, with a classical
mastery of action, character, and
visuals. Part of what made it
so admired was the conceit of
having the same event told by
four different observers with
four different perspectives—
but that's more a literary conceit
than a cinematic one, and there
were even better things to come
from one of the most
cinematic of directors.

Venice Film Festival
Golden Lion: *Rashomon* (Akira
Kurosawa, Japan)
Special Jury Prize: *A Streetcar
Named Desire* (Elia Kazan, USA)
International Prizes:
Robert Bresson, *Diary of a
Country Priest* (France)
Billy Wilder, *The Big Carnival
[Ace in the Hole]* (USA)
Jean Renoir, *The River* (India)
Actor: Jean Gabin, *La Nuit est
Mon Royaume* (France)
Actress: Vivien Leigh, *A
Streetcar Named Desire* (USA)
Screenplay: T. E. B. Clarke, *The
Lavender Hill Mob* (UK)
Cinematography: L.-H. Burel,
Diary of a Country Priest
Score: Hugo Friedhofer, *The Big
Carnival* (USA)
Documentary: *Nature's Half
Acre* (Walt Disney, USA)
Best Italian Film: *La Città si
difende* (Pietro Germi)
**Italian Critics Prize for Best
Foreign Film:** *Rashomon*;
Diary of a Country Priest

Berlin Film Festival
An all-German Jury awarded
Golden, Silver, and Bronze
Bears in each of the following
categories:

Dramatic Films
Gold: *Four in a Jeep* (Leopold Lindtberg, Switzerland)
Silver: *The Way of Hope* (Pietro Germi, Italy)
Bronze: *The Browning Version* (Anthony Asquith, UK)
Comedy
Gold: *Sans Lasser d'Advance/No Address Given* (Jean-Paul Le Chanois, France)
Silver: *Leva Pa "Hoppet"* (Göran Gentele, Sweden)
Bronze: *The Mating Season* (Mitchell Leisen, USA)
Crime and Adventure
Gold: *Justice Is Done* (André Cayatte, France)
Silver: not awarded
Bronze: *Destination Moon* (Irving Pichel, USA)
Musical
Gold: *Cinderella* (Walt Disney, USA)
Silver: *The Tales of Hoffmann* (Michael Powell, Emeric Pressburger, UK)
Bronze: not awarded
Documentary
Gold: *Beaver Valley* (Walt Disney, USA)
Silver: not awarded
Bronze: *The Undefeated* (UK)
Cultural Documentary
Gold: *Little Night Ghosts* (West Germany)
Silver: *Begone Dull Care* (Norman McLaren, Canada)
Bronze: *Yellow Dome* (West Germany)
Special Prizes of the City of Berlin: *Dieu a Besoin des Hommes* [*Isle of Sinners/God Needs Men*] (Jean Delannoy, France); *Il Christo Proibito* (Curzio Malaparte, Italy); Best German Film: *Dr. Holl* (Rolf Hansen, West Germany)
Audience Awards
Large Bronze Plate: *Cinderella*
Small Bronze Plate: *The Browning Version*

Harvard Lampoon Movie Worsts

Ten worst pictures:
Tales of Hoffmann
Valentino
Alice in Wonderland
That's My Boy
Texas Carnival
Take Care of My Little Girl
The Flame of Araby
Here Comes the Groom
David and Bathsheba
I Want You
Worst Actor: Robert Taylor, *Quo Vadis?*
Worst Actress: Corinne Calvet, *On the Riviera*
Biggest Argument for Stricter Immigration Laws: Mario Lanza
Finest Example of Idyllic Young Love: Ava Gardner and Frank Sinatra
Most Noteworthy Examples of Physical Fitness: Franchot Tone kicking Miss Florabella Muri [*Here Comes the Groom*] Humphrey Bogart felling unidentified girl in El Morocco [nightclub]
Worst Comic Duo: Martin and Lewis in anything [NOTE: this item reportedly inspired the most angry mail of any *Lampoon* award in history]

Box Office (Domestic Rentals)

1	*David and Bathsheba*	$7,000,000	Fox
2	*Show Boat*	5,200,000	MGM
3	*An American in Paris*	4,500,000	MGM

	Title		
	The Great Caruso	4,500,000	MGM
5	*A Streetcar Named Desire*	4,250,000	WB
6	*Born Yesterday*	4,150,000	Col
7	*That's My Boy*	3,800,000	Par
8	*A Place in the Sun*	3,500,000	Par
9	*At War with the Army*	3,350,000	Par
10	*Father's Little Dividend*	3,100,000	MGM
Other films of note:			
17	*Royal Wedding*	2,600,000	MGM
20	*On the Riviera*	2,500,000	Fox
27	*Francis Goes to the Races*	2,300,000	Uni
	The Lemon Drop Kid	2,300,000	Uni
46	*The Thing*	1,950,000	RKO
52	*The Day the Earth Stood Still*	1,850,000	Fox
69	*When Worlds Collide*	1,600,000	Par
95	*I Was a Communist For the FBI*	1,300,000	WB
109	*Bedtime for Bonzo*	1,200,000	Uni

Three MGM musicals placed in the top four—and who would have guessed that the most popular male musical stars, in order, would be Howard Keel, Gene Kelly, Mario Lanza—and Fred Astaire, way down at #17? Meanwhile, the notion persists, even in a world in which Jim Carrey is a huge star, that Jerry Lewis was only ever popular among the French; as the chart shows, in 1951 Martin & Lewis landed two pictures, That's My Boy *and* At War with the Army, *in the top 10 (yes, that's the American top 10), far ahead of comic rivals like Danny Kaye in* On the Riviera *or Bob Hope in* The Lemon Drop Kid. *Sci-fi, though gaining in popularity, still didn't have the lift-off power to pass $2 mil.*

Gebert's Golden Armchairs

With its tightly wound plot and rich psychological underpinnings, *Strangers on a Train* might be Hitchcock's best film, and in any year but the year Brando revolutionized screen acting, Robert Walker's brainy-cuckoo Bruno Anthony would be the performance of the year.

Best American Film: *Strangers on a Train*
Best Foreign Film: *Miss Julie*
Best Actor: Marlon Brando, *A Streetcar Named Desire*
Best Actress: Vivien Leigh, *A Streetcar Named Desire*
Best Director: Alfred Hitchcock, *Strangers on a Train*

1952

Okay, let's get it out of the way right now. *The Greatest Show on Earth* is the most boneheaded Best Picture Oscar–winner since *Cavalcade* beat *King Kong*; it shoulda been *Singin' in the Rain* (well, it woulda been *High Noon*), blah blah blah—are you done? Admittedly, Cecil B. DeMille's circus epic is utterly cornball—a tribute by one splashy, vulgar art form for five-year-olds to another. But corny as it is—as close as it comes to being its own Zucker Bros. parody ("You're not a man, you've got sawdust in your veins!")—it works; DeMille *always* worked, and he deserved, once in his life, the full honors of the Academy. Here was a man who had stayed on top of the box office charts from *The Cheat* in 1915 to *The Ten Commandments* in the late 1950s. And not just *on* top—he *set* the top, his movies consistently doing twice the business of the next picture below them; if Steven Spielberg's box office dominance lasts twice as long as it has so far, he'll just begin to rival DeMille. This was an Oscar for bread and butter.

Academy Awards

*** *The Greatest Show on Earth* AAW GLO
A Best Picture–winner for anyone who thought there hadn't been a really good one since *The Great Ziegfeld*.

Picture
The Greatest Show on Earth (Paramount, Cecil B. DeMille)
High Noon (UA, Stanley Kramer)
Ivanhoe (MGM, Pandro S. Berman)
Moulin Rouge (UA, Romulus, John Huston)
The Quiet Man (Republic, Argosy, John Ford, Merian C. Cooper)

**** **Gary Cooper in *High Noon*** AAW GLO PHO
Cooper is rock-solid, and the note of middle-aged desperation that crept into his later performances serves him especially well here (a little Jack Lemmon with your John Wayne, sir?).

Actor
Gary Cooper, *High Noon*
Marlon Brando, *Viva Zapata!*
Kirk Douglas, *The Bad and the Beautiful*
José Ferrer, *Moulin Rouge*
Alec Guinness, *The Lavender Hill Mob*

• **Shirley Booth in *Come Back, Little Sheba*** AAW GLO NYC BOR CAN '53
Anyone writing a book like this should be allowed one instance in which he simply reacts irrationally to a performance that makes his teeth ache, and Booth's whiny, childlike housewife is mine.

Actress
Shirley Booth, *Come Back, Little Sheba*

157

Joan Crawford, *Sudden Fear*
Bette Davis, *The Star*
Julie Harris, *The Member of the Wedding*
Susan Hayward, *With a Song in My Heart*

Supporting Actor
Anthony Quinn, *Viva Zapata!*
Richard Burton, *My Cousin Rachel*
Arthur Hunnicutt, *The Big Sky*
Victor McLaglen, *The Quiet Man*
Jack Palance, *Sudden Fear*

Supporting Actress
Gloria Grahame, *The Bad and the Beautiful*
Jean Hagen, *Singin' in the Rain*
Colette Marchand, *Moulin Rouge*
Terry Moore, *Come Back, Little Sheba*
Thelma Ritter, *With a Song in My Heart*

Director
John Ford, *The Quiet Man*
Cecil B. DeMille, *The Greatest Show on Earth*
John Huston, *Moulin Rouge*
Joseph L. Mankiewicz, *Five Fingers*
Fred Zinnemann, *High Noon*

Screenplay: Charles Schnee, *The Bad and the Beautiful*
Story and Screenplay: T. E. B. Clarke, *The Lavender Hill Mob*
Original Story: Frederic M. Frank, Theodore St. John, Frank Cavett, *The Greatest Show on Earth*
Cinematography/B&W: Robert Surtees, *The Bad and the Beautiful*
Cinematography/Color: Winton C. Hoch, Archie Stout, *The Quiet Man*
Dramatic or Comedy Score: Dimitri Tiomkin, *High Noon*
Musical Score: Alfred Newman, *With a Song in My Heart*
Song: "High Noon (Do Not Forsake Me, Oh My Darlin')," *High Noon*, m: Dimitri Tiomkin, l: Ned Washington
Art Direction/B&W: Cedric Gibbons, *The Bad and the Beautiful*
Art Direction/Color: Paul Sheriff, Marcel Vertes, *Moulin Rouge*
Costumes/B&W: Helen Rose, *The Bad and the Beautiful*
Costumes/Color: Marcel Vertes, *Moulin Rouge*
Editing: *High Noon*
Sound Recording: *Breaking the Sound Barrier*
Special Effects: *Plymouth Adventure*, MGM
Short/Cartoon: *Johann Mouse* (MGM/Hanna-Barbera/Tom & Jerry)
Short/One-Reel: *Light in the Window*
Short/Two-Reel: *Water Birds* (Disney True-Life Adventures)
Documentary/Feature: *The Sea Around Us* (RKO Radio, Irwin Allen)
Documentary/Short: *Neighbours* (National Film Board of Canada, Norman McLaren)
Irving G. Thalberg Award: Cecil B. DeMille
Special Awards:
George Alfred Mitchell for the design and development of the camera which bears his name
Joseph M. Schenck
Merian C. Cooper
Harold Lloyd, master comedian and good citizen [NOTE: same year that Charlie Chaplin had his citizenship troubles]
Bob Hope for his contribution to the laughter of the world, his service to the motion picture industry, and his devotion to the American premise
Forbidden Games (France)— outstanding foreign-language film

Golden Globes

Picture (Drama): *The Greatest Show on Earth*
Picture (Comedy/Musical): *With a Song in My Heart*
Actor (Drama): Gary Cooper, *High Noon*
Actor (Comedy/Musical): Donald O'Connor, *Singin' in the Rain*
Actress (Drama): Shirley Booth, *Come Back, Little Sheba*
Actress (Comedy/Musical): Susan Hayward, *With a Song in My Heart*
Supporting Actor: Millard Mitchell, *My Six Convicts*
Supporting Actress: Katy Jurado, *High Noon*
Director: Cecil B. DeMille, *The Greatest Show on Earth*
Screenplay: Michael Wilson, *Five Fingers*
Cinematography/Color: George Barnes, J. Peverell Marley, *The Greatest Show on Earth*
Cinematography/B&W: Floyd Crosby, *High Noon*
Score: Dimitri Tiomkin, *High Noon*
Most Promising Newcomer (Male): Richard Burton, *My Cousin Rachel*
Most Promising Newcomer (Female): Colette Marchand, *Moulin Rouge*
World Film Favorite (Male): John Wayne
World Film Favorite (Female): Susan Hayward
Best Film Promoting International Understanding: *Anything Can Happen*
Cecil B. DeMille Award: Walt Disney
Special Award to Best Juvenile Actors: Brandon de Wilde, *The Member of the Wedding*; Francis Kee Teller, *Navajo*

Directors Guild of America

Quarterly Awards:
Charles Crichton, *The Lavender Hill Mob*
Joseph L. Mankiewicz, *Five Fingers*
Fred Zinnemann, *High Noon*
John Ford, *The Quiet Man*
Annual Award: John Ford, *The Quiet Man*
D. W. Griffith Award: Cecil B. DeMille

*** *High Noon* NYC BOR
Cooper deserved his Oscar on equal parts artistic and sentimental grounds, but the movie has been wildly overrated—*Bad Day at Black Rock* beats it all to hell as both a western-with-a-message (for one thing, its message about the treatment of the Japanese is a lot clearer than *High Noon*'s vague parallels to McCarthyism) and as a tightly focused, almost-real-time thriller.

*** Ralph Richardson in *Breaking the Sound Barrier* NYC BOR BAA
David Lean's oddest film—a perfectly standard and exciting Jimmy Stewart flying picture, except it's all high-class Brit actors instead (Ralph Richardson as the big-brain airplane designer, Denholm Elliott as the weak son who has Flaming Debris written all over him) . . . which is no doubt why it enjoyed respect from critical groups its American inspiration could only dream of.

New York Film Critics Circle

Picture: *High Noon*
Foreign Film: *Forbidden Games*
Actor: Ralph Richardson, *Breaking the Sound Barrier*

Actress: Shirley Booth, *Come Back, Little Sheba*
Director: Fred Zinnemann, *High Noon*

National Board of Review
Best American Film: *The Quiet Man*
High Noon
Limelight
Five Fingers
The Snows of Kilimanjaro
The Thief
The Bad and the Beautiful
Singin' in the Rain
Above and Beyond
My Son John
Best Foreign Film: *Breaking the Sound Barrier*
The Man in the White Suit
Forbidden Games
Beauty and the Devil
Ivory Hunter
Actor: Ralph Richardson, *Breaking the Sound Barrier*
Actress: Shirley Booth, *Come Back, Little Sheba*
Director: David Lean, *Breaking the Sound Barrier*

Photoplay Gold Medal Awards
Gold Medal: *With a Song in My Heart*
Most Popular Male Star: Gary Cooper, *High Noon*
Most Popular Female Star: Susan Hayward, *With a Song in My Heart*
Special Awards: Marilyn Monroe, Martin and Lewis

British Academy Awards
Film: *Breaking the Sound Barrier*
British Film: *Breaking the Sound Barrier*
Actor (British): Ralph Richardson, *Breaking the Sound Barrier*
Actor (Foreign): Marlon Brando, *Viva Zapata!*
Actress (British): Vivien Leigh, *A Streetcar Named Desire*
Actress (Foreign): Simone Signoret, *Casque d'Or*

*** *Othello* CAN
Orson Welles' second Shakespeare film went straight from its Palme d'Or to distribution limbo, and it's only recently that we can see it to evaluate it again: stylish and ingenious but also clearly hampered by its production problems, it seems to have won more as a vote of encouragement to Welles than because it is really on a par with *Kane* or *Touch of Evil.*

Cannes Film Festival
Grand Prize: *Othello* (Orson Welles, Morocco), *Two Cents Worth of Hope* (Italy, Renato Castellani)
Special Jury Prize: *We Are All Murderers* (France, André Cayatte)
Actor: Marlon Brando, *Viva Zapata!* (USA)
Actress: Lee Grant, *Detective Story* (USA)
Director: Christian-Jaque, *Fanfan the Tulip* (France)
Screenplay: Piero Fellini, *Cops and Robbers* (Italy)
Photography and Plastic Composition: Kohei Sugiyama, *Tales of Genji* (Japan)
Score: Sven Skold, *One Summer of Happiness* (Sweden)
Best Operatic Film: *The Medium* (Gian Carlo Menotti, USA)
Special Citation: to Italy for the best national selection
Special Tribute: to the Netherlands for its documentary short films
To young director Alexander

Astruc, *The Crimson Curtain*
(France)
International Critics Prize: for
avant-garde film, *Mexican Bus
Ride* (Luis Buñuel, Mexico)

***** *Forbidden Games* AAW
NYC VEN BAA '53**
Just as Oscar is a sucker for
handicapped and accent parts, the
film festivals have their favorite
minigenres, too. Number one is
what might be called the UNICEF
film, tales of plucky children in
trying historical/cultural
situations, such as *Pather Panchali,
The 400 Blows, Cria!, When
Father Was Away on Business,
Freeze—Die—Come to Life,
Pelle the Conqueror*—and this
René Clément Grand
Prize–winner, the prototype for
them all. Brigitte Fossey is a
French war orphan, taken in by
a peasant family, obsessed with
properly burying any animal
that dies on the farm as a way of
dealing with her parents' death.
Not as morbid as it sounds—but
also not the instant humanist
classic it was thought to be in '52;
the sensitive handling of Fossey
and fellow child actor Georges
Poujouly remains the best thing
about it.

Venice Film Festival
Golden Lion: *Forbidden Games*
(France, René Clément)
Special Jury Prize: *Mandy*
[*Crash of Silence*] (Alexander
Mackendrick, UK)
International Prizes:
John Ford, *The Quiet Man* (USA)
Roberto Rossellini, *Europa 51*
(Italy)
Kenji Mizoguchi, *The Life of
Oharu* (Japan)

Actor: Fredric March, *Death of a
Salesman* (USA)
Screenplay: Nunnally Johnson,
Phone Call from a Stranger (USA)
Music: Georges Auric, *The
Respectful Prostitute* (France)
Décor: Carmen Dillon, *The
Importance of Being Earnest* (UK)
Best National Entry: USA
International Critics Prize: *Les
Belles de Nuit* (René Clair, France)

Berlin Film Festival
Audience Awards
Golden Bear: *One Summer of
Happiness* (Arne Mattson,
Sweden)
Silver Bear: *Fanfan the Tulip*
(Christian-Jacque, France)
Bronze Bear: *The Overcoat*
(Alberto Lattuada, Italy)

***Harvard Lampoon* Movie
Worsts**
Ten worst pictures:
*Jumping Jacks
The Snows of Kilimanjaro
Quo Vadis?
Son of Paleface
Million Dollar Mermaid
Bloodhounds of Broadway
Niagara
Because You're Mine
An Affair in Trinidad
The Merry Widow*
Worst Male Performance: Jerry
Lewis, *Sailor Beware, Jumping
Jacks*, etc.
**Worst Supporting Male
Performance:** Dean Martin,
Sailor Beware, Jumping Jacks, etc.
Worst Female Performance:
Marilyn Monroe, *Niagara*
**Strongest Indictment of
Academic Freedom:** *Bonzo
Goes to College*
**Most Inspiring Example of
American Virility:** Jerry Lewis
**Most Embarassing Infatuation
with One's Own Folksiness:**
Barry Fitzgerald, Edmund Gwenn
Most Miscast: Entire personnel

of *Plymouth Adventure* as New England Puritans
Most Noteworthy Pre-Pubic Flop: Tab "Sigh-Guy" Hunter
The Roscoe Award: Jerry Lewis, who, by dint of incessant struggle, has unquestionably established himself as The Worst Comedian of All Time

Box Office (Domestic Rentals)

1	*The Greatest Show on Earth*	$12,000,000	Par
2	*Quo Vadis?*	10,500,000	MGM
3	*Ivanhoe*	7,000,000	MGM
4	*The Snows of Kilimanjaro*	6,500,000	Fox
5	*Sailor Beware*	4,300,000	Par
6	*The African Queen*	4,000,000	UA
	Jumping Jacks	4,000,000	Par
8	*High Noon*	3,400,000	UA
	Son of Paleface	3,400,000	Par
10	*Singin' in the Rain*	3,300,000	MGM
Other films of note:			
11	*With a Song in My Heart*	3,250,000	Fox
12	*The Quiet Man*	3,200,000	Republic
13	*Bend of the River*	3,000,000	Uni
21	*Million Dollar Mermaid*	2,750,000	Uni
	Scaramouche	2,750,000	MGM
27	*My Favorite Spy*	2,600,000	Par

Cecil B. DeMille once again proved his uncanny ability to manufacture must-see movie events, and Bob Hope reversed his slump with a comedy at #8 that came close to the levels achieved by Martin & Lewis (again with two in the top 10). But the most interesting item is #13, a western with Jimmy Stewart—one of the first films in which the star received a piece of the profits instead of a salary. As you can see, it was a wise move, and started a trend in that direction—a trend that Stewart's agent, Lew Wasserman, would have reason to regret having negotiated, once he became head of the very same studio he'd made the deal with.

Gebert's Golden Armchairs

No one ranked *Singin' in the Rain* among 1952's best films; maybe it took MGM's decline and fall before anyone could see it as the most perfect and joyful of all musicals. *El* is Luis Buñuel's best film, a devastating psychological portrait of *homo españa-bourgeois-catholicus.* Alec Guinness gives a comic performance of little miracles as the mousy bank employee who decides to commit the perfect crime in Ealing Studios' masterpiece, *The Lavender Hill Mob.* And the *other* western about McCarthyism, *Johnny Guitar,* also manages to tackle sexual politics as well in pairing bad girl Joan Crawford against lynch-mob mobilizer Mercedes McCambridge—plus it has *style.*

Best American Film: *Singin' in the Rain*
Best Foreign Film: *El*

Best Actor: Alec Guinness, *The
Lavender Hill Mob*
Best Actress: Jean Hagen, *Singin'
in the Rain*

Best Director: Nicholas Ray,
Johnny Guitar

The *Sight & Sound* International Critics Surveys

What are the 10 greatest movies ever made?

The longest-running and best-publicized attempt to play that
perennial parlor game began in 1952, when the
Cinémathèque Belgique posed the question to 100 filmmakers.
63 from nine countries responded, ranging from Luis Buñuel
and Vittorio De Sica to Billy Wilder, Orson Welles, and Cecil
B. DeMille—who voted for no less than four of his own
films. After the results of the Belgian survey were announced,
the British magazine *Sight & Sound* decided to see what
would happen when the same question was put to such leading
film critics and academics as André Bazin, Henri Langlois,
Paul Rotha, and Dr. Siegfried Kracauer.

You might expect the academics and the working filmmakers
to display radically different notions of what constituted the best
movies ever made—*Caligari* on one list and *Casablanca* on
the other. In fact the lists matched eight out of 12 times
(with ties). Both groups followed the line of influential film
histories, such as Rotha's *The Film Till Now*, in regarding
the highest cinematic art as being whatever *wasn't* conventional
Hollywood entertainment: landmark silents like *Intolerance*
and *Potemkin*, documentaries like Flaherty's *Man of Aran*,
intellectual French dramas like *Grand Illusion* or neorealist Italian
ones like *The Bicycle Thief*. The sole concession to popular
taste was the one Hollywood figure universally recognized
as a genius for the ages—Chaplin.

If 1952 established the canon of old masters, when *Sight & Sound*
again posed the question in 1962, a revolution had tumbled many
of them from their spots. The list showed instead the rapid rise of a
generation of new masters in tune with the modern malaises of the
postwar world—Fellini, Godard, and Antonioni, whose
L'Avventura reached the #2 spot just two years after it was made.
The same year the #1 spot was claimed by an older but certainly
kindred film, *Citizen Kane*, the inspiration for every young
filmmaker who burned to show what he could do with a camera.
It's held the top spot in every survey since.

1972 largely echoed 1962, with the addition of Ingmar Bergman
(placing two out of 11). But buried in the runners-up were
harbingers of things to come: a Hitchcock thriller, *Vertigo*, and a
John Wayne western, *The Searchers*, which by 1982 would

join *Kane* as the critical trinity of Hollywood moviemaking—
ironically, thanks in large part to the critic-filmmakers of the
French New Wave, who had changed American thinking about
what our best films were. Indeed, in 1982 the list was more
than half American, for the first (and thus far only) time.

Multiculturalism being a hot issue at the moment, for the most
recent survey in 1992, *Sight & Sound* made a special effort
to include more critics from Asian and Third World countries.
The result, surprisingly, wasn't a radically innovative list, but
the most conservative one in decades—not only were there no
new films on the list, but even the '60s were virtually wiped
out. Part of that is undoubtedly the result of casting a broader
net—American and Bengali critics are more likely to agree
on their distant shared heritage than on the films of the '80s, or
even the '60s—but it also points to the fact that there aren't,
by and large, moviemakers today who are as exciting and
revelatory as Bergman or Fellini or Kubrick were in their
heyday.

Perhaps sensing that the list was beginning to fossilize, in
1992 *Sight & Sound* returned to the poll's origins and
surveyed international filmmakers, ranging from Martin
Scorsese and Federico Fellini to Terry Gilliam, Wes Craven,
and John Woo. The filmmakers give much higher place to such
recent classics as *Raging Bull* and the *Godfather* films, and
they show more regard than the critics for Fellini, Kurosawa,
The Conformist and *Lawrence of Arabia* (not surprisingly,
given the number of contemporary directors who've borrowed
from each of them). Yet in the end their list still isn't all
that different from the critics': *Kane* is again #1, and *The
Searchers*, *Vertigo*, *L'Atalante*, and *The Passion of Joan of
Arc* all place on both lists.

That is the film till now; and we will have to wait, in 2002
or 2012, for the next revolution which will tumble those
exalted names from their perches, and replace them with
something that would seem as unlikely to us as, well, a John
Wayne western would have seemed to Dr. Siegfried Kracauer.

Films that tied are listed alphabetically under their rank in
the voting. The first appearance of a film on any of the polls
is accompanied by its director, country of origin, and date.

_____

1952 Cinémathèque Belgique Filmmakers Survey

1   *The Battleship Potemkin* (Eisenstein, USSR/1925)
2   *The Gold Rush* (Chaplin, USA/1925)
3   *The Bicycle Thief* (De Sica, Italy/1949)
4   *City Lights* (Chaplin, USA/1931)

    Grand Illusion (Renoir, France/1937)
    Le Million (Clair, France/1931)
7   *Greed* (Von Stroheim, USA/1924)
8   *Hallelujah!* (Vidor, USA/1929)
9   *Brief Encounter* (Lean, UK/1945)
    Intolerance (Griffith, USA/1916)
    Man of Aran (Flaherty, UK/1934)
    The Threepenny Opera (Pabst, Germany/1931)
13 *The Passion of Joan of Arc* (Dreyer, France/1928)
14 *Les Enfants du Paradis/Children of Paradise* (Carné, France/1945)
    Foolish Wives (Von Stroheim, USA/1921)
    Storm Over Asia (Pudovkin, USSR/1928)
17 *L'Age d'Or* (Buñuel, France/1930)
    Birth of a Nation (Griffith, USA/1915)
    Broken Blossoms (Griffith, USA/1919)
    The Devil in the Flesh (Autant-Lara, France/1946)

1952 *Sight & Sound* Critics Survey

1   *The Bicycle Thief*
2   *City Lights*
    The Gold Rush
4   *The Battleship Potemkin*
5   *Louisiana Story* (Flaherty, USA/1947)
    Intolerance
7   *Greed*
    Le Jour se Lève (Carné, France/1939)
    The Passion of Joan of Arc
10 *Brief Encounter*
    Le Million
    The Rules of the Game (Renoir, France/1939)
13 *Citizen Kane* (Welles, USA/1941)
    Grand Illusion
    The Grapes of Wrath (Ford, USA/1940)
16 *The Childhood of Maxim Gorki* (Donskoi, USSR/1938)
    Monsieur Verdoux (Chaplin, USA/1947)
    Que Viva Mexico (Eisenstein, Mexico/1931)
19 *Earth* (Dovzhenko, USSR/1930)
    Zero for Conduct (Vigo, France/1933)

1962 *Sight & Sound* Critics Survey

1   *Citizen Kane*
2   *L'Avventura* (Antonioni, Italy/1960)
3   *The Rules of the Game*
4   *Greed*
    Ugetsu (Mizoguchi, Japan/1953)
6   *The Battleship Potemkin*
    The Bicycle Thief
    Ivan the Terrible (Eisenstein, USSR/1943–6)
9   *La Terra Trema* (Visconti, Italy/1948)
10 *L'Atalante* (Vigo, France/1934)

11   *Hiroshima, Mon Amour* (Resnais, France/1959)
     Pather Panchali (Ray, India/1955)
     Zero for Conduct
14   *City Lights*
     The Childhood of Maxim Gorki
     The Gold Rush
17   *Sunrise* (Murnau, USA/1927)
18   *Earth*
     Monsieur Verdoux

1972 *Sight & Sound* Critics Survey

1   *Citizen Kane*
2   *The Rules of the Game*
3   *The Battleship Potemkin*
4   *8½* (Fellini, Italy/1963)
5   *L'Avventura*
     Persona (Bergman, Sweden/1967)
7   *The Passion of Joan of Arc*
8   *The General* (Keaton, USA/1927)
     The Magnificent Ambersons (Welles, USA/1942)
10   *Ugetsu*
     Wild Strawberries (Bergman, Sweden/1957)
12   *The Gold Rush*
     Hiroshima, Mon Amour
     Ikiru (Kurosawa, Japan/1952)
     Ivan the Terrible
     Pierrot le Fou (Godard, France/1965)
     Vertigo (Hitchcock, USA/1958)
18   *Grand Illusion*
     Mouchette (Bresson, France/1966)
     The Searchers (Ford, USA/1956)
     Sunrise
     2001: A Space Odyssey (Kubrick, USA/1968)
     Viridiana (Buñuel, Spain/1960)

1982 *Sight & Sound* Critics Survey

1   *Citizen Kane*
2   *The Rules of the Game*
3   *Seven Samurai* (Kurosawa, Japan/1954)
     Singin' in the Rain (Donen/Kelly, 1952)
5   *8½*
6   *The Battleship Potemkin*
7   *L'Avventura*
     The Magnificent Ambersons
     Vertigo
9   *The General*
     The Searchers
11   *2001: A Space Odyssey*
     Andrei Rublev (Tarkovsky, USSR/1966)
13   *Greed*

   Jules and Jim (Truffaut, France/1961)
   The Third Man (Reed, UK/1950)
16 *The Godfather* (Coppola, USA/1972)*
   The Passion of Joan of Arc
   Sunrise
   Touch of Evil (Welles, USA/1958)

*Includes two votes for *Godfather I* and *II* as a single work

1992 *Sight & Sound* Critics Survey

1 *Citizen Kane*
2 *Rules of the Game*
3 *Tokyo Story* (Ozu, Japan/1953)
4 *Vertigo*
5 *The Searchers*
6 *L'Atalante*
   The Passion of Joan of Arc
   Pather Panchali
   The Battleship Potemkin
10 *2001: A Space Odyssey*
11 *The Bicycle Thief*
   8½
   Seven Samurai
   Singin' in the Rain
   Sunrise
16 *L'Avventura*
   The General

1992 *Sight & Sound* Filmmakers Survey

1 *Citizen Kane*
2 *8½*
   Raging Bull (Scorsese, USA/1980)
4 *La Strada* (Fellini, Italy/1954)
5 *L'Atalante*
6 *The Godfather*
   Modern Times (Chaplin, USA/1936)
   Vertigo
9 *The Godfather, Part II* (Coppola, USA/1974)
   The Passion of Joan of Arc
   Rashomon (Kurosawa, Japan/1950)
   Seven Samurai
13 *2001: A Space Odyssey*
14 *The Battleship Potemkin*
   La Dolce Vita (Fellini, Italy/1960)
   Lawrence of Arabia (Lean, UK/1962)
   The Rules of the Game
   Tokyo Story
   The Wizard of Oz (Fleming, USA/1939)

1953

"Red-Tainted French Film seen as Cannes Film Fest Winner," read the headline in *Variety*. The offending film, improbable as it seems now, was the French thriller *The Wages of Fear*, which was branded as Communist propaganda by the American press for making even the suggestion that American oil companies might be less than totally benevolent toward their South American employees. McCarthyism was snaking its way into the European film milieu in other ways: certain American stars threatened to exit the festival if that known Commie Charlie Chaplin attended the festival (he didn't, and they should be ashamed), and after Zsa Zsa Gabor was pressured to quit a French film directed by blacklistee Jules Dassin, an anti-blacklist manifesto signed by French directors circulated at the festival. In response, a mostly French jury led by Jean Cocteau pointedly gave *Wages of Fear* the Palme d'Or, but even so, by the time it reached the U.S., 50 minutes had been cut.

No one could accuse Sam Fuller's B movie *Pickup on South Street* of being anywhere to the left of John Wayne—but Francis Koval in *Films in Review* couldn't understand "why such a slick spy melodrama was chosen by the Selection Committee" at Venice, Gavin Lambert in *Sight & Sound* called its selection "indecent" and "a bitter farce" (in part because the more obvious Red-baiting speeches were bleeped in deference to Soviet guests), and its Bronze Lion was accompanied by boos. It would be another decade before the European taste for American genre films, the grungier the better, would be widely spread (or even comprehended). At least it didn't win the Leone d'Oro; nothing did. For the first time, a festival jury had found nothing worthy of its top prize—even though at least two of the competing films, Fellini's *I Vitelloni* and Kenji Mizoguchi's *Ugetsu*, would have won hands down at many a later festival.

Academy Awards

**** *From Here to Eternity* AAW DGA NYC PHO Fred Zinnemann's film of the James Jones novel about peacetime soldiers in the months before Pearl Harbor is the most intelligent soap opera ever made, and occasionally more than that—especially whenever Montgomery Clift's achingly vulnerable, eternal misfit Private Pruitt is on screen.

Picture
From Here to Eternity
(Columbia, Buddy Adler)
Julius Caesar (MGM, John
Houseman)
The Robe (20th Century–Fox,
Frank Ross)
Roman Holiday (Paramount,
William Wyler)
Shane (Paramount, George
Stevens)

****** William Holden in *Stalag
17* AAW**
Billy Wilder's P.O.W. drama
was a stage play first, and
some of the comic supporting
characters have obviously done
their business a thousand times
already. But Holden's cynical
operator is his quintessential
screen performance—a
reverse Mr. Deeds, fighting the
dumb mob for what his own
smarts tell him.

Actor
William Holden, *Stalag 17*
Marlon Brando, *Julius Caesar*
Richard Burton, *The Robe*
Montgomery Clift, *From Here to
Eternity*
Burt Lancaster, *From Here to
Eternity*

***** Audrey Hepburn in
Roman Holiday AAW GLO
NYC BAA**
The whole world fell in love
with Audrey Hepburn from the
moment she made her starring
debut here as the princess who
goes on the lam in Rome and
meets reporter Gregory Peck.
Class, delicacy, and romance
personified, she was the anti-
Marilyn. William Wyler, not

exactly Mr. Light Comedy, lets
it run on too long, and the next
year's *Sabrina* is better—but it's
still charming.

Actress
**Audrey Hepburn, *Roman
Holiday***
Leslie Caron, *Lili*
Ava Gardner, *Mogambo*
Deborah Kerr, *From Here to
Eternity*
Maggie McNamara, *The Moon Is
Blue*

Supporting Actor
**Frank Sinatra, *From Here to
Eternity***
Eddie Albert, *Roman Holiday*
Brandon de Wilde, *Shane*
Jack Palance, *Shane*
Robert Strauss, *Stalag 17*

Supporting Actress
**Donna Reed, *From Here to
Eternity***
Grace Kelly, *Mogambo*
Geraldine Page, *Hondo*
Marjorie Rambeau, *Torch Song*
Thelma Ritter, *Pickup on South
Street*

Director
**Fred Zinnemann, *From Here to
Eternity***
George Stevens, *Shane*
Charles Walters, *Lili*
Billy Wilder, *Stalag 17*
William Wyler, *Roman Holiday*

Screenplay: Daniel Taradash,
From Here to Eternity
Story and Screenplay: Charles
Brackett, Walter Reisch,
Richard Breen, *Titanic*
Original Story: Ian McLellan
Hunter, *Roman Holiday*
[Note: Hunter was a front for
blacklistee Dalton Trumbo,
later awarded the Oscar
posthumously]

Cinematography/B&W: Burnett Guffey, *From Here to Eternity*
Cinematography/Color: Loyal Griggs, *Shane*
Dramatic or Comedy Score: Bronislau Kaper, *Lili*
Musical Score: Alfred Newman, *Call Me Madam*
Song: "Secret Love," *Calamity Jane*, m: Sammy Fain, l: Paul Francis Webster
Art Direction/B&W: Cedric Gibbons, *Julius Caesar*
Art Direction/Color: Lyle Wheeler, George W. Davis, *The Robe*
Costumes/B&W: Edith Head, *Roman Holiday*
Costumes/Color: Charles LeMaire, Emile Santiago, *The Robe*
Editing: *From Here to Eternity*
Sound Recording: *From Here to Eternity*
Special Effects: *War of the Worlds*
Short/Cartoon: *Toot, Whistle, Plunk and Boom* (Walt Disney)
Short/One-Reel: *The Merry Wives of Windsor Overture* (MGM Overture Series)
Short/Two-Reel: *Bear Country* (Disney True-Life Adventures)
Documentary/Feature: *The Living Desert* (Disney True-Life Adventures)
Documentary/Short: *The Alaskan Eskimo* (Disney True-Life Adventures)
Irving G. Thalberg Award: George Stevens
Special Awards:
Pete Smith for his witty and pungent observations on the American scene in his "Pete Smith Specialties"
20th Century–Fox, for CinemaScope
Joseph I. Breen, for his conscientious, open-minded, and dignified management of the Motion Picture Production Code

[Note: same year as *The Moon Is Blue*'s challenge to the Code]
Bell and Howell Company

Golden Globes
Picture: *The Robe*
Actor (Drama): Spencer Tracy, *The Actress*
Actor (Comedy/Musical): David Niven, *The Moon Is Blue*
Actress (Drama): Audrey Hepburn, *Roman Holiday*
Actress (Comedy/Musical): Ethel Merman, *Call Me Madam*
Supporting Actor: Frank Sinatra, *From Here to Eternity*
Supporting Actress: Grace Kelly, *Mogambo*
Director: Fred Zinnemann, *From Here to Eternity*
Screenplay: Helen Deutsch, *Lili*
Best Documentary of Historical Interest: *A Queen Is Crowned*
Most Promising Newcomers (Male): Hugh O'Brian, Steve Forrest, Richard Egan
Most Promising Newcomers (Female): Pat Crowley, Bella Darvi, Barbara Rush
World Film Favorite (Male): Robert Taylor, Alan Ladd
World Film Favorite (Female): Marilyn Monroe
Best Western Star: Guy Madison
Best Film Promoting International Understanding: *Little Boy Lost*
Cecil B. DeMille Award: Darryl F. Zanuck
Special Award: James Algar, Walt Disney, for *The Living Desert*
Honor Award: Jack Cummings, MGM producer

Directors Guild of America
Most Outstanding Directorial Achievement: Fred Zinnemann, *From Here to Eternity*
Outstanding Directorial Achievement:

Charles Walters, *Lili*
William Wyler, *Roman Holiday*
George Stevens, *Shane*
Billy Wilder, *Stalag 17*
D. W. Griffith Award: John Ford
Critic Award: Bosley Crowther,
The New York Times

New York Film Critics Circle
Picture: *From Here to Eternity*
Foreign Film: *Justice Is Done*
Actor: Burt Lancaster, *From Here to Eternity*
Actress: Audrey Hepburn, *Roman Holiday*
Director: Fred Zinnemann, *From Here to Eternity*
Special Awards: *A Queen Is Crowned*, *The Conquest of Everest*

National Board of Review
Best American Film: *Julius Caesar*
Shane
From Here to Eternity
Martin Luther
Lili
Roman Holiday
Stalag 17
The Little Fugitive
Mogambo
The Robe
Best Foreign Film: *A Queen Is Crowned*
Moulin Rouge
The Little World of Dan Camillo
Strange Deception
The Conquest of Everest
Actor: James Mason, *Face to Face, The Desert Rats, The Man Between, Julius Caesar*
Actress: Jean Simmons, *Young Bess, The Robe, The Actress*
Director: George Stevens, *Shane*

Photoplay Gold Medal Awards
Gold Medal: *From Here to Eternity*

Most Popular Male Star: Alan Ladd
Most Popular Female Star: Marilyn Monroe

British Academy Awards
Film: *Forbidden Games*
British Film: *Genevieve*
Actor (British): John Gielgud, *Julius Caesar*
Actor (Foreign): Marlon Brando, *Julius Caesar*
Actress (British): Audrey Hepburn, *Roman Holiday*
Actress (Foreign): Leslie Caron, *Lili*

**** *The Wages of Fear* CAN BER BAA '54
A brilliantly engineered thriller about four losers driving highly combustible nitroglycerin on the worst roads in South America to put out an oil company fire. Some hints of existentialism and deeper meanings, but at its heart, mainly an edge-of-your-seat adventure film that'd give *Speed* a run for its money.

Cannes Film Festival
[NOTE: The Jury paid tribute to Walt Disney and placed him out of competition; Disney also received the Legion of Honor from the French government while at the Festival]
Grand Prize: *The Wages of Fear* (Henri Georges Clouzot, France)
Actor: Charles Vanel, *The Wages of Fear*
Actress: Shirley Booth, *Come Back, Little Sheba* (USA)
International Prizes:
Dramatic Film: *Come Back, Little Sheba* (Daniel Mann, USA)
Adventure Film: *O Cangaceiro*

[*The Outlaw*] (Lima Barreto,
Brazil), mention for music
Fairy-Tale Film: *The White
Reindeer* (Erik Blomberg,
Finland)
Exploration [Documentary]: *The
Green Secret* (Gian Gaspare
Napolitano, Italy), mention for
color
Film Told Through Images: *La
Red* [*Rosanna*] (Emilio
Fernandez, Mexico)
Good-Mood Film: *Bienvenido,
Mr. Marshall* [*Welcome, Mr.
Marshall*] (Luis Garcia Berlanga,
Spain), mention for screenplay
Entertainment Film: *Lili*
(Charles Walters, USA), mention
for the charm of its performances
Special Award: *Flamenco* (Edgar
Neville, Spain), for illustrating
the beauty of Spanish dance
International Critics Prize: *Mr.
Hulot's Holiday* (Jacques Tati,
France)

Venice Film Festival
Golden Lion: not awarded
Silver Lions:
Ugetsu (Kenji Mizoguchi, Japan)
I Vitelloni (Federico Fellini, Italy)
The Little Fugitive (Ray Ashley,
Morris Engel, Ruth Orkin, USA)
Moulin Rouge (John Huston, UK)
Sadko (Alexander Ptushko,
USSR)
Thérèse Raquin (Marcel Carné
France)
Bronze Prize Winners:
War of God (Rafael Gil, Spain)
Les Orgueilleux [*The Proud Ones/
The Proud and the Beautiful*]
(Yves Allégret, France)
Pickup on South Street (Samuel
Fuller, USA)
Sinha Moca (Tom Payne, Brazil)
Actor: Henri Vilbert, *Absolution
Without Confession* (France)
Actress: Lilli Palmer, *The
Fourposter* (USA)

Berlin Film Festival Audience Awards
Golden Bear: *The Wages of Fear*
(Henri-Georges Clouzot,
France)
Silver Bear: *The Green Secret*
(Gian Gaspare Napolitano,
Italy)
Bronze Bear: *Pestalozzi Village*
(Leopold Lindtberg,
Switzerland)
**International Delegate-Jury
Prize of the Berlin Senate:** *Man
on a Tightrope* (Elia Kazan,
USA)
City on Trial (Luigi Zampa, Italy)
Where Chimneys Are Seen
(Heinosuke Gosho, Japan)

Harvard Lampoon Movie Worsts
Ten worst pictures:
The Robe
Salome
Beneath the 12-Mile Reef
Hondo
Torch Song
Call Me Madam
How to Marry a Millionaire
Easy to Love
I, the Jury
Gentlemen Prefer Blondes
Worst Actor: Victor Mature, *The
Robe*
Worst Actress: Terry Moore,
Beneath the 12-Mile Reef
Worst Supporting Actor:
Brandon de Wilde, *Shane*
Worst Supporting Actress: Zsa
Zsa Gabor, *Moulin Rouge*
**Greatest Setback to Christianity
Since Nero:** *The Robe*
Most Degrading Moment:
Charles Laughton being hit over
the head with a shovel by Lou
Costello in *Abbott and Costello
Meet Captain Kidd*
The Roscoe Award: Miss Terry
Moore, the worst ingenue of 1953

Box Office (Domestic Rentals)

1	*The Robe*	$20,000,000	Fox
2	*From Here to Eternity*	12,000,000	Col
3	*Shane*	8,000,000	Par
4	*How to Marry a Millionaire*	7,500,000	Fox
5	*Peter Pan*	7,000,000	Disney
6	*Hans Christian Andersen*	6,000,000	RKO
7	*House of Wax [3-D]*	5,500,000	WB
	Mogambo	5,500,000	WB
9	*Gentlemen Prefer Blondes*	5,100,000	Fox
10	*Moulin Rouge*	5,000,000	UA

Other films of note:

12	*Charge at Feather River [3-D]*	3,650,000	WB
13	*The Moon Is Blue*	3,500,000	UA
	Scared Stiff	3,500,000	Par
19	*The Road to Bali*	3,000,000	Par
26	*Bwana Devil [3-D]*	2,700,000	UA
29	*Kiss Me Kate [3-D/flat]*	2,500,000	MGM
	[total 1953–54:	4,500,000]	
38	*Niagara*	2,350,000	Fox
49	*War of the Worlds*	2,000,000	Par
75	*It Came From Outer Space [3-D]*	1,600,000	Uni

1953 shows Hollywood reacting to the threat of television by introducing new screen formats. Widescreen CinemaScope was the drawing card for the phenomenally successful The Robe, *and it also lifted* How to Marry a Millionaire, *the first 'Scope movie in modern dress, above co-star Marilyn Monroe's other 1953 vehicles,* Gentlemen Prefer Blondes *and* Niagara. *3-D, on the other hand, was merely a fad whose entire rise and fall is captured in this chart—from the first 3-D hit,* Bwana Devil, *in anaglyphic (red and green) 3-D, to the biggest 3-D hit,* House of Wax *(in polarized color 3-D), to* Kiss Me Kate—*which was mainly released "flat," the novelty by then having worn off. Meanwhile,* The Moon Is Blue *reached #13 by boasting something else you couldn't get on television—the heretofore-banned word "virgin" in its dialogue. Its success would start Otto Preminger on his career as the decade's most dedicated taboo-breaker.*

Gebert's Golden Armchairs

The Naked Spur is arguably the best of the westerns Jimmy Stewart and director Anthony Mann made in the early '50s— spare, tough-minded little morality plays with a keen yet unshowy feel for the western landscape (comparison with the self-important *Shane* is encouraged here). Character actress Thelma Ritter was the screen's great world-weary, streetwise middle-aged woman, earning Sam Fuller's low-budget B thriller *Pickup on South Street* an unexpected Oscar nomination (perhaps as a result of its Venice attention).

Best American Film: *The Naked Spur*

Best Foreign Film: *The Wages of Fear*

Best Actor: Montgomery Clift, *From Here to Eternity*

Best Actress: Thelma Ritter, *Pickup on South Street*

Best Director: Anthony Mann, *The Naked Spur*

1954

1953's tiff between Cannes and American producers continued, with a jury again led by Jean Cocteau (and including André Bazin and Luis Buñuel) deciding to remove *From Here to Eternity* from competition because they didn't feel Cannes needed to add to its endless string of awards. "The Commies on the Festival jury ran Cocteau and his weak sisters ragged," was the explanation given by one American observer (impressively managing to both red-bait Buñuel and gay-bait Cocteau in a single slur).

Venice, which continued to demonstrate a first-rate eye for B movies by showcasing Don Siegel's *Riot in Cell Block 11* right next to glossy things like *Executive Suite*, also settled forever the question of whether the festival atmosphere affects a jury's judgment. The public reception for a moderately well-made but colorful and star-laden British-Italian film of *Romeo and Juliet* was so enthusiastic after its evening premiere that the jury voted it the Golden Lion—leaving mere pikers like *On the Waterfront*, *Seven Samurai*, *Sansho the Bailiff*, and *La Strada* to settle for runner-up status. (Of course, *Romeo and Juliet* premiered at a reasonable hour, and both of the Japanese masterpieces ran past midnight. . . .)

Academy Awards

**** *On the Waterfront* AAW GLO DGA NYC BOR BAA VEN
***** Marlon Brando AAW GLO
Its origins are a bit dubious—Elia Kazan, wanting to justify his naming names to HUAC, did so with a drama about someone who informs on something considerably more serious than Communism in Hollywood. But set that aside and it's one of Hollywood's best realistic dramas, gritty and charged with powerful performances; the Academy, which had snubbed Brando in '51, finally agreed that his mumbling and scratching was great acting after all.

Picture
On the Waterfront (Columbia, Sam Spiegel)
The Caine Mutiny (Columbia, Stanley Kramer)
The Country Girl (Paramount, William Perlberg)
Seven Brides for Seven Brothers (MGM, Jack Cummings)
Three Coins in the Fountain (20th Century–Fox, Sol C. Siegel)

Actor
Marlon Brando, *On the Waterfront*
Humphrey Bogart, *The Caine Mutiny*
Bing Crosby, *The Country Girl*
James Mason, *A Star Is Born*

Dan O'Herlihy, *Adventures of Robinson Crusoe*

Actress
Grace Kelly, *The Country Girl*
Dorothy Dandridge, *Carmen Jones*
Judy Garland, *A Star Is Born*
Audrey Hepburn, *Sabrina*
Jane Wyman, *Magnificent Obsession*

Supporting Actor
Edmond O'Brien, *The Barefoot Contessa*
Lee J. Cobb, *On the Waterfront*
Karl Malden, *On the Waterfront*
Rod Steiger, *On the Waterfront*
Tom Tully, *The Caine Mutiny*

Supporting Actress
Eva Marie Saint, *On the Waterfront*
Nina Foch, *Executive Suite*
Katy Jurado, *Broken Lance*
Jan Sterling, *The High and the Mighty*
Claire Trevor, *The High and the Mighty*

Director
Elia Kazan, *On the Waterfront*
Alfred Hitchcock, *Rear Window*
George Seaton, *The Country Girl*
William Wellman, *The High and the Mighty*
Billy Wilder, *Sabrina*

Screenplay: George Seaton, *The Country Girl*
Story and Screenplay: Budd Schulberg, *On the Waterfront*
Original Story: Philip Yordan, *Broken Lance*
Cinematography/B&W: Boris Kaufman, *On the Waterfront*
Cinematography/Color: Milton Krasner, *Three Coins in the Fountain*
Dramatic or Comedy Score: Dimitri Tiomkin, *The High and the Mighty*

Musical Score: Adolph Deutsch, Saul Chaplin, *Seven Brides for Seven Brothers*
Song: "Three Coins in the Fountain," *Three Coins in the Fountain*, m: Jule Styne, l: Sammy Cahn
Art Direction/B&W: Richard Day, *On the Waterfront*
Art Direction/Color: John Meehan, *20,000 Leagues Under the Sea*
Costumes/B&W: Edith Head, *Sabrina*
Costumes/Color: Sanzo Wada, *Gate of Hell*
Editing: *On the Waterfront*
Sound Recording: *The Glenn Miller Story*
Special Effects: *20,000 Leagues Under the Sea*
Short/Cartoon: *When Magoo Flew* (UPA/Mr. Magoo/Pete Burness)
Short/One-Reel: *This Mechanical Age* (Warner Bros., Robert Youngson)
Short/Two-Reel: *A Time Out of War* (Carnival Prods.)
Documentary/Feature: *The Vanishing Prairie* (Disney True-Life Adventures)
Documentary/Short: *Thursday's Children* (British Information Services)
Special Awards:
Bausch & Lomb Optical Company
Kemp R. Niver, for the development of the Renovare Process which has made possible the restoration of the Library of Congress Paper Film Collection
Greta Garbo
Danny Kaye
Jon Whiteley, Vincent Winter, outstanding juvenile performances, *The Little Kidnappers*
Gate of Hell (Japan)—best foreign-language film

***** **Judy Garland in** *A Star Is Born* GLO BAA

Grace Kelly's multi–award-winning performance in the booze drama *The Country Girl* (which I last saw on the Cash Calls Movie when I was ten) has proven impossible to find on video—but I doubt it would really stand above her subtly sexy turn in *Rear Window*, anyway. The year's knockout performance was Judy Garland's—even for a star whose whole appeal was built on always pouring her heart into a role, she *really* pours her heart into the role of the star whose rise coincides with her husband's fall. Another example, like that of Crawford in *Mildred Pierce*, of a longtime MGM star only finding the dramatic meat she needed at Warner's—though unlike in '45, the contract system was dead and Warner's didn't feel the need to build up a one-shot star for an Oscar.

Golden Globes

Picture (Drama): *On the Waterfront*
Picture (Comedy/Musical): *Carmen Jones*
Foreign Films: *Genevieve* (UK), *No Way Back* (West Germany), *Twenty-four Eyes* (Japan), *La Mujer de las Camelias* (Argentina)
Actor (Drama): Marlon Brando, *On the Waterfront*
Actor (Comedy/Musical): James Mason, *A Star Is Born*
Actress (Drama): Grace Kelly, *The Country Girl*
Actress (Comedy/Musical): Judy Garland, *A Star Is Born*
Supporting Actor: Edmond O'Brien, *The Barefoot Contessa*
Supporting Actress: Jan Sterling, *The High and the Mighty*
Director: Elia Kazan, *On the Waterfront*
Screenplay: Billy Wilder, Samuel Taylor, Ernest Lehman, *Sabrina*
Cinematography/Color: Joseph Ruttenberg, *Brigadoon*
Cinematography/B&W: Boris Kaufman, *On the Waterfront*
Most Promising Newcomers (Male): Joe Adams, George Nader, Jeff Richards
Most Promising Newcomers (Female): Shirley MacLaine, Kim Novak, Karen Sharpe
World Film Favorite (Male): Gregory Peck
World Film Favorite (Female): Audrey Hepburn
Best Film Promoting International Understanding: *Broken Lance*
Cecil B. DeMille Award: Jean Hersholt
Special Award for Creative Musical Contribution: Dimitri Tiomkin
Special Award for Experimental Film: *Anywhere in Our Time* (W. Germany)
Pioneer Award: John Ford
Pioneer Award for Color: Dr. Herbert Kalmus [Technicolor inventor]

Directors Guild of America

Most Outstanding Directorial Achievement: Elia Kazan, *On The Waterfront*
Outstanding Directorial Achievement:
George Seaton, *The Country Girl*
Alfred Hitchcock, *Rear Window*
Billy Wilder, *Sabrina*
William Wellman, *The High and the Mighty*
Honorary Lifetime Member: Walt Disney

Critic Award: Harold V. Cohen, *Pittsburgh Post-Gazette*

New York Film Critics Circle
Picture: *On the Waterfront*
Foreign Film: *Gate of Hell*
Actor: Marlon Brando, *On the Waterfront*
Actress: Grace Kelly, *The Country Girl, Rear Window, Dial M for Murder*
Director: Elia Kazan, *On the Waterfront*

National Board of Review
Best American Film: *On the Waterfront*
Seven Brides for Seven Brothers
The Country Girl
A Star Is Born
Executive Suite
The Vanishing Prairie
Sabrina
20,000 Leagues Under the Sea
The Unconquered
Beat the Devil
Best Foreign Film: *Romeo and Juliet*
The Heart of the Matter
Gate of Hell
Diary of a Country Priest
The Little Kidnappers
Genevieve
Beauties of the Night
Mr. Hulot's Holiday
The Detective
Bread, Love and Dreams
Actor: Bing Crosby, *The Country Girl*
Actress: Grace Kelly, *The Country Girl, Dial M For Murder, Rear Window*
Supporting Actor: John Williams, *Sabrina, Dial M for Murder*
Supporting Actress: Nina Foch, *Executive Suite*
Director: Renato Castellani, *Romeo and Juliet*
Special Awards:
For the choreography of Michael Kidd in *Seven Brides for Seven Brothers*
For the modernization of traditional Japanese acting by Machiko Kyo in *Ugetsu* and *Gate of Hell*
For the new methods of moving puppets in *Hansel and Gretel*

Photoplay Gold Medal Awards
Gold Medal: *Magnificent Obsession*
Most Popular Male Star: William Holden
Most Popular Female Star: June Allyson

British Academy Awards
Film: *The Wages of Fear*
British Film: *Hobson's Choice*
Actor (British): Kenneth More, *Doctor in the House*
Actor (Foreign): Marlon Brando, *On the Waterfront*
Actress (British): Yvonne Mitchell, *The Divided Heart*
Actress (Foreign): Cornell Borchers, *The Divided Heart*
Screenplay: George Tabori, Robin Estridge, *The Young Lovers* [*Chance Meeting*]

** *Gate of Hell*   AAW NYC BOR CAN
One of the first Japanese films to be an art-house success in the West, this tale of a samurai who loses his heart to his lord's lady was especially admired for its color cinematography, and proved to be a film society staple for decades. But André Bazin guessed correctly that we'd be less impressed with it the more Japanese films we saw. It's a little arthritic next to Kurosawa,

and doesn't have Mizoguchi's depth of feeling.

Cannes Film Festival
[NOTE: *From Here to Eternity* given "special recognition" and placed "out of competition" because of its many other awards]
Grand Prize: *Gate of Hell* (Teinosuke Kinugasa, Japan)
Special Jury Prize: *Monsieur Ripois/Knave of Hearts* (René Clément, France)
International Prizes:
Austria: *The Last Bridge* (Helmut Kautner), mention to Maria Schell [actress]
France: *Avant le Déluge* (André Cayatte), mention to Cayatte and co-writer Charles Spaak
India: *Do Binghazamin* [*Two Acres of Land*] (Bimal Roy)
Italy: *Neapolitan Carousel* (Ettore Giannini); *Cronache di poveri Amanti* (Carlo Lizzani)
Poland: *Five Boys from Barska Street* (Aleksander Ford)
Switzerland: *The Great Adventure* (Arne Sucksdorff)
USA: *The Living Desert*, Walt Disney, mention to its camera crews
USSR: *The Great Warrior/ Skanderbeg* (Sergei Yutkevich)
Best Selection: The Netherlands [Short-film prizes include *Toot, Whistle, Plunk and Boom* (Walt Disney, USA), *The Pleasure Garden* (James Broughton, USA)]
International Critics Prize: *Avant le Déluge*

Venice Film Festival
Golden Lion: *Romeo and Juliet* (Renato Castellani, Italy- UK)
Silver Prize Winners:
On the Waterfront (Elia Kazan, USA)
Seven Samurai (Akira Kurosawa, Japan)

La Strada (Federico Fellini, Italy)
Sansho the Bailiff (Kenji Mizoguchi, Japan)
Actor: Jean Gabin, *Touchez pas au Grisbi*, *The Air of Paris* (France)
Special Jury Prize for Ensemble Acting: *Executive Suite* (USA)
Italian Critics Prize: *On the Waterfront*

Berlin Film Festival
Audience Awards
Golden Bear: *Hobson's Choice* (David Lean, UK)
Silver Bear: *Bread, Love and Dreams* (Luigi Comencini, Italy)
Bronze Bear: *Le Défroqué* (Léo Joannon, France)
Documentary/Gold: *The Living Desert* (Walt Disney, USA)
International Delegate-Jury Prize of the Berlin Senate: *La Grande Speranza* (Duilio Coletti, Italy)
Sinha Moca (Tom Payne, Brazil)
Ikiru (Akira Kurosawa, Japan)
Special Prize: Walt Disney, for supporting the festival with his films

Harvard Lampoon Movie Worsts
Ten worst pictures:
Haaji Baba
There's No Business Like Show Business
The Egyptian
The High and the Mighty
Magnificent Obsession
Beau Brummel
The Student Prince
Knights of the Round Table
Demetrius and the Gladiators
White Christmas
Best Reasons for Healthy Paganism: *Demetrius and the Gladiators*, *The Silver Chalice*
Best Excuse for Another Thugee Rebellion in India: *The Bengal Brigade*

Best Argument Against N.R.O.T.C.: *The Caine Mutiny*
Saddest Evidence of Rapid Aging: Jimmy Stewart impassively receiving a massage from Grace Kelly in *Rear Window*

The Roscoe Award: Tony Curtis, whose marcelled and Mobil-greased locks have titillated scores of bobby-soxers, and Grace Kelly, who easily earns the title "Ironclad Virgin of 1954"

Box Office (Domestic Rentals)

1	*White Christmas*	$12,000,000	Par
2	*The Caine Mutiny*	8,700,000	Col
3	*The Glenn Miller Story*	7,000,000	Uni
4	*The Egyptian**	6,000,000	Fox
5	*Rear Window*	5,300,000	Par
6	*The High and the Mighty**	5,200,000	WB
7	*Magnificent Obsession*	5,000,000	Uni
	*Three Coins in the Fountain**	5,000,000	WB
9	*Seven Brides for Seven Brothers**	4,750,000	MGM
10	*Desiree**	4,500,000	Fox
Other films of note:			
11	*Knights of the Round Table**	4,400,000	MGM
12	*Dragnet*	4,300,000	WB
13	*Demetrius and the Gladiators**	4,250,000	Fox
14	*Living It Up*	4,250,000	Par
15	*On the Waterfront*	4,200,000	Col
17	*The Long, Long Trailer*	4,000,000	MGM
25	*Beneath the 12-Mile Reef**	3,600,000	Fox
51	*Them!*	2,000,000	WB
73	*Casanova's Big Night*	1,600,000	Par

*CinemaScope

*CinemaScope + ancient Egypt, CinemaScope + modern Rome (*Three Coins in the Fountain*), CinemaScope + Arthurian England, and a cheesy 'Scope sequel to* The Robe *all produced hits, but it was VistaVision (a not-so-widescreen process of exceptional image quality) plus Bing Crosby and Danny Kaye that provided the biggest hit of the year. Crosby's pal Hope wasn't nearly so fortunate; his big comedy for 1954 went no higher than #73, just below* The Kettles at Home. *Meanwhile, TV struck back by offering a more violent color movie version of its most distinctive cop show, as well as the first co-starring vehicle of a minor movie star who'd become a major TV star, Lucille Ball, and her husband Desi. Both* Dragnet *and* The Long, Long Trailer *proved to be big hits—and suggested that maybe movies and TV weren't mortal enemies after all.*

Gebert's Golden Armchairs

Rear Window comes about as close to perfection as any of perfectionist Hitch's films—a puppet show about people watching other puppet shows and playing with the strings themselves. Nothing against Brando's performance in *Waterfront*, clearly the best of Oscar's choices, but the performance of the year was the Japanese Brando's—Toshiro Mifune, breaking down the gentility of Japanese acting as a ferocious, impetuous young samurai wannabe in Akira Kurosawa's *Seven Samurai*. *Seven Samurai* is one of the greatest Japanese films, but 1954 brought an even greater one yet—Kenji Mizoguchi's heartbreaking *Sansho the Bailiff*, about the travails of a mother and daughter during a period of war, one of the films that has earned Mizoguchi a rare place as a feminist hero among filmmakers of his time.

Best American Film: *Rear Window*
Best Foreign Film: *Sansho the Bailiff*
Best Actor: Toshiro Mifune, *Seven Samurai*
Best Actress: Judy Garland, *A Star Is Born*
Best Director: Alfred Hitchcock, *Rear Window*

1955

With the realization growing that fighting with Hollywood was bad for Cannes' booming business, a Cannes jury led by Marcel Pagnol attempted to atone for the festival's treatment of *From Here to Eternity* the year before by honoring *Marty*—which still fed Hollywood grumbling that the festivals only went for pictures that showed the grimy side of American life, and wouldn't take the big splashy commercial pictures that Hollywood producers wanted to shove down their throats. *Realpolitik* intruded in other ways, too, with an almost equal split of awards between the U.S. and the U.S.S.R.

Cannes wasn't alone in going for *Marty*'s naturalism, though—the New York critics picked it 12 to 4 over *Mister Roberts*, also picking Borgnine (in a tight race with Sinatra in *The Man With the Golden Arm*) and Anna Magnani in *The Rose Tattoo*. The second year in a row and only the third time ever that the critics and Oscar had agreed on the big three, 1955 demonstrated the Critics Circle's influence in making Hollywood knuckle under to its taste for naturalistic, little black-and-white films. A backlash would soon come in the Best Picture category, but both *Marty* and *The Rose Tattoo* would serve to establish no-makeup, ordinary-Joe-and-Jane roles as surefire Oscar-getters in the years to come.

Academy Awards

*** **Marty** AAW DGA NYC BOR BAA CAN
*** **Ernest Borgnine** AAW GLO NYC BOR BAA CAN
Paddy Chayefsky's earnest TV drama of an ordinary guy who meets an ordinary gal—a Bronx butcher's shop *Brief Encounter*—is still a sweet little piece. But by casting Borgnine instead of Rod Steiger, whose plain, colorless Marty really did seem like the guy no one would look twice at, Hollywood *was* hedging its bets with a little hidden star appeal in this supposed ultrarealistic drama—

Borgnine is a meatball Barry Fitzgerald, a warthog with a twinkle in his eye. Incidentally, the only film ever to win both a Palme d'Or and a Best Picture Oscar.

Picture
Marty (UA, Hecht-Lancaster)
Love Is a Many-Splendored Thing (20th Century–Fox, Buddy Adler)
Mister Roberts (Warner Bros., Leland Hayward)
Picnic (Columbia, Fred Kohlmar)
The Rose Tattoo (Paramount, Hal Wallis)

Actor
Ernest Borgnine, *Marty*
James Cagney, *Love Me or Leave Me*

James Dean, *East of Eden*
Frank Sinatra, *The Man With the Golden Arm*
Spencer Tracy, *Bad Day at Black Rock*

** **Anna Magnani in *The Rose Tattoo*** AAW GLO NYC BOR BAA '56
Magnani, the star of Rossellini's *Open City*, was one of the great natural actresses, but Tennessee Williams must have written this after getting drunk during a screening of *Miracle in Milan*—it's about-a da Italian mama an-a da truck driver who's-a not too smart but has-a-da muscles that drive her *pastafazoola*. The worst, or at least the silliest, of '50s Williams films (though worse was to come in the '60s).

Actress
Anna Magnani, *The Rose Tattoo*
Susan Hayward, *I'll Cry Tomorrow*
Katharine Hepburn, *Summertime*
Jennifer Jones, *Love Is a Many-Splendored Thing*
Eleanor Parker, *Interrupted Melody*

Supporting Actor
Jack Lemmon, *Mister Roberts*
Arthur Kennedy, *Trial*
Joe Mantell, *Marty*
Sal Mineo, *Rebel Without a Cause*
Arthur O'Connell, *Picnic*

Supporting Actress
Jo Van Fleet, *East of Eden*
Betsy Blair, *Marty*
Peggy Lee, *Pete Kelly's Blues*
Marisa Pavan, *The Rose Tattoo*
Natalie Wood, *Rebel Without a Cause*

Director
Delbert Mann, *Marty*
Elia Kazan, *East of Eden*
David Lean, *Summertime*
Joshua Logan, *Picnic*
John Sturges, *Bad Day at Black Rock*

Screenplay: Paddy Chayefsky, *Marty*
Story and Screenplay: William Ludwig, Sonya Levien, *Interrupted Melody*
Original Story: Daniel Fuchs, *Love Me or Leave Me*
Cinematography/B&W: James Wong Howe, *The Rose Tattoo*
Cinematography/Color: Robert Burks, *To Catch a Thief*
Dramatic or Comedy Score: Alfred Newman, *Love Is a Many-Splendored Thing*
Musical Score: Robert Russell Bennett, Jay Blackton, Adolph Deutsch, *Oklahoma!*
Song: "Love Is a Many-Splendored Thing," *Love Is a Many-Splendored Thing*, m: Sammy Fain, l: Paul Francis Webster
Art Direction/B&W: Hal Pereira, Tambi Larsen, *The Rose Tattoo*
Art Direction/Color: William Flannery, *Picnic*
Costumes/B&W: Helen Rose, *I'll Cry Tomorrow*
Costumes/Color: Charles LeMaire, *Love Is a Many-Splendored Thing*
Editing: *Picnic*
Sound Recording: *Oklahoma!*
Special Effects: *The Bridges at Toko-Ri*
Short/Cartoon: *Speedy Gonzales* (Warner Bros./Friz Freleng)
Short/One-Reel: *Survival City*
Short/Two-Reel: *The Face of Lincoln* (University of Southern California)
Documentary/Short: *Men Against the Arctic* (Walt Disney)

Documentary/Feature: *Helen Keller in Her Story*
Special Award: *Samurai, The Legend of Musashi* (Japan—outstanding foreign-language film

Golden Globes
Picture (Drama): *East of Eden*
Picture (Comedy/Musical): *Guys and Dolls*
Foreign Films: *Ordet* (Denmark), *Stella* (Greece), *Eyes of Children* (Japan), *Sons, Mothers, and a General* (West Germany), *Dangerous Curves* (Brazil)
Best Outdoor Drama: *Wichita*
Actor (Drama): Ernest Borgnine, *Marty*
Actor (Comedy/Musical): Tom Ewell, *The Seven Year Itch*
Actress (Drama): Anna Magnani, *The Rose Tattoo*
Actress (Comedy/Musical): Jean Simmons, *Guys and Dolls*
Supporting Actor: Arthur Kennedy, *Trial*
Supporting Actress: Marisa Pavan, *The Rose Tattoo*
Director: Joshua Logan, *Picnic*
Most Promising Newcomers (Male): Ray Danton, Russ Tamblyn
Most Promising Newcomers (Female): Anita Ekberg, Virginia Shaw, Dana Wynter
World Film Favorite (Male): Marlon Brando
World Film Favorite (Female): Grace Kelly
Best Film Promoting International Understanding: *Love Is a Many-Splendored Thing*
Cecil B. DeMille Award: Jack Warner
Hollywood Citizenship Award: Esther Williams
Posthumous Award for Best Dramatic Actor: James Dean

Directors Guild of America
Most Outstanding Directorial Achievement: Delbert Mann, *Marty*

Outstanding Directorial Achievement:
John Sturges, *Bad Day at Black Rock*
John Ford and Mervyn LeRoy, *Mister Roberts*
Elia Kazan, *East of Eden*
Joshua Logan, *Picnic*
D. W. Griffith Award: Henry King
Honorary Lifetime Member: Donald Crisp
Critic Award: John Rosenfield, *Dallas Morning-Evening Star*

New York Film Critics Circle
Picture: *Marty*
Foreign Film: *Umberto D.*, *Diabolique* (tie)
Actor: Ernest Borgnine, *Marty*
Actress: Anna Magnani, *The Rose Tattoo*
Director: David Lean, *Summertime*

National Board of Review
Best American Film: *Marty*
East of Eden
Mister Roberts
Bad Day at Black Rock
Summertime
The Rose Tattoo
A Man Called Peter
Not as a Stranger
Picnic
The African Lion
Best Foreign Film: *The Prisoner*
The Great Adventure
The Divided Heart
Diabolique
The End of the Affair
Actor: Ernest Borgnine, *Marty*
Actress: Anna Magnani, *The Rose Tattoo*
Supporting Actor: Charles Bickford, *Not as a Stranger*
Supporting Actress: Marjorie Rambeau, *A Man Called Peter*, *The View from Pompey's Head*
Director: William Wyler, *The Desperate Hours*

Special Citation: For aerial
photography in *Strategic Air
Command*

Photoplay Gold Medal Awards

Gold Medal: *Love Is a Many-
Splendored Thing*
Most Popular Male Star:
William Holden
Most Popular Female Star:
Jennifer Jones

British Academy Awards

Film: *Richard III*
British Film: *Richard III*
Actor (British): Laurence
Olivier, *Richard III*
Actor (Foreign): Ernest
Borgnine, *Marty*
Actress (British): Katie Johnson,
The Ladykillers
Actress (Foreign): Betsy Blair,
Marty
Screenplay: William Rose, *The
Ladykillers*
Documentary: *The Vanishing
Prairie* (Walt Disney, USA)
Short Animated Film: *Blinkity
Blank* (Norman McLaren, Canada)

Cannes Film Festival

Palme d'Or: *Marty* (USA), with
particular praise for the
screenplay by Paddy Chayefsky,
the direction by Delbert Mann,
and the performances by Ernest
Borgnine, Betsy Blair
Special Jury Prize: *The Lost
Continent* (Leonardo Bonzi, et
al., Italy)
Best Performances: Spencer
Tracy, *Bad Day at Black Rock*
(USA), and the cast of *The Big
Family*, Josef Heifitz (USSR)
Director: Sergei Vasiliev, *Heroes
of Shipka* (USSR), Jules Dassin,
Rififi (France)
Dramatic Film: *East of Eden*
(Elia Kazan, USA)
Lyrical Film: *Romeo and Juliet*
(Lev Arnshtam, Leonid

Lavrovsky, USSR) [NOTE: Soviet
ballet film—not the '54
Castellani version], and for the
performance by Galina Ulanova
Mention: Baby Naaz, *Boot Polish*
(India), Pablito Calvo,
Marcelino (Spain) [child actors]
Homage: Haya Harareet, *Hill 24
Doesn't Answer* (Israel) [actress]
Palme d'Or/Short Film: *Blinkity
Blank* (Norman McLaren,
Canada)
International Critics Prize:
Raisces [Roots] (Benito
Alazraki, Mexico), *Death of a
Cyclist* (Juan Antonio Bardem,
Spain)

***** *Ordet*   GLO VEN BOR '57

An eerily out-of-time
masterpiece about the power
of faith, filmed in blinding white
Mediev-O-Vision by the
director of *The Passion of Joan
of Arc*, Carl Dreyer—though
interestingly, the film of his that
it actually has the most
resemblance to, in its dreamy,
waterlogged style and its
matter-of-fact acceptance of the
supernatural, is *Vampyr*.
(There's a nice Ph.D thesis to
be written on the subject of
why horror films hint more
effectively at the mystery of
faith than Hollywood's
lumbering Bible soaps . . .
why Peter Cushing's faith is so
much more convincing than
Charlton Heston's.) Bonus: the
answer to the trivia question,
What do Carl Dreyer and Pia
Zadora have in common? (A
Golden Globe). . . .

Venice Film Festival

Golden Lion: *Ordet* (Carl Dreyer,
Denmark)

Silver Prize Winners:
The Gadfly [*The Grasshopper/The Cricket*] (Samson Samsonov, USSR)
The Big Knife (Robert Aldrich, USA)
Le Amiche (Michelangelo Antonioni, Italy)
Ciske de Rat (Wolfgang Staudte, Holland)
Actor: Kenneth More, *The Deep Blue Sea* (UK); Curt Jurgens, *The Devil's General* (West Germany); *Les Héros sont Fatigués* (France)
Most Promising New Directors: Alexandre Astruc (France), Vaclav Kraka (Czechoslovakia), William Fairchild (UK), Francesco Maselli (Italy), Andrzej Munk (Poland)
Italian Critics Prize: *The Gadfly*

Berlin Film Festival
Audience Awards
Golden Bear: *The Rats* (Robert Siodmak, West Germany)
Silver Bear: *Marcellino, Pan y Vino* (Ladislas Vajda, Spain)
Bronze Bear: *Carmen Jones* (Otto Preminger, USA)
Documentary: Gold: *The Vanishing Prairie* (Walt Disney, USA)
International Critics Prize: Anthony Asquith, for the high moral standards and humanitarian lessons of *The Young Lovers*
German Critics Prize: Helmut Kautner [actor]

Harvard Lampoon Movie Worsts
Ten worst pictures:
Not As a Stranger
Ulysses
The Prodigal
Hit the Deck
The Tall Men
The Rains of Ranchipur [remake of very first Worst Film, *The Rains Came*]
Battle Cry
The Last Time I Saw Paris
The Long Grey Line
Underwater
Worst Actor: Kirk Douglas, *Ulysses, Indian Fighter*
Worst Actress: Debbie Reynolds, *Hit the Deck, Susan Slept Here*
First Annual Award for Crude Symbolism: The fireworks in mounting crescendo as a backdrop for Grace Kelly and Cary Grant in their big scene in *To Catch a Thief*
Most Pathetic Remnant of a Vanishing Race: Victor Mature as Chief Crazy Horse in the movie of the same title
The Bosco Award (in recognition of the advances recently made in the science of geriatrics): June Allyson, who with eternally girlish hominess, an aura of fresh-baked deep-dish apple pie like Mother used to make, and an endless supply of tears, bravely but vainly attempts to resist the onslaught of the passing years

Box Office (Domestic Rentals)

1	*Cinerama Holiday*	$10,000,000	Cinerama
2	*Mister Roberts*	8,500,000	WB
3	*Battle Cry*	8,000,000	WB
	20,000 Leagues Under the Sea	8,000,000	Disney
5	*Not as a Stranger*	7,100,000	UA
6	*The Country Girl*	6,900,000	Par
7	*The Lady and the Tramp*	6,500,000	Disney
	Strategic Air Command	6,500,000	Par

9	*To Hell and Back*	6,000,000	Uni
	Sea Chase	6,000,000	WB
	A Star Is Born	6,000,000	WB
Other films of note:			
12	*Blackboard Jungle*	5,200,000	MGM
13	*The Seven Year Itch*	5,000,000	Fox
29	*The Man from Laramie*	3,300,000	Col
53	*Davy Crockett, King of the Wild Frontier*	2,150,000	Disney
56	*Marty*	2,000,000	UA
74	*It Came from Beneath the Sea*	1,700,000	Col
	This Island Earth	1,700,000	Uni
77	*Jupiter's Darling*	1,600,000	MGM

Cinerama offered the widest screen of all—it was actually three regular (1.33:1) images projected side by side—and a Cinerama travelogue at raised prices attracted more curiosity than any other film of the year. Meanwhile, after years as a mere cartoon studio, Disney established itself as a full-fledged Hollywood player with simultaneous animated and live-action hits in Lady and the Tramp *and* 20,000 Leagues Under the Sea, *as well as a TV sensation in its Davy Crockett series, re-edited into a feature film. Rock 'n' roll made its first entry onto the Hollywood scene when* Blackboard Jungle *made a Top 40 hit out of its two-year-old theme song, "Rock Around the Clock," while at #77, Esther Williams was—ahem—washed up.*

Gebert's Golden Armchairs

If Cannes mostly rejected big-budget offerings, one of 1955's splashy commercial pictures *would* eventually become a European favorite (even being loosely remade by Rainer Werner Fassbinder): Douglas Sirk's *All That Heaven Allows*, with Jane Wyman as a middle-aged widow who flouts society by dating a younger, lower-class man (Rock Hudson)—a far more radical soap opera than anything the neo-'50s '80s ever gave us, saying that suburban moms should quit worrying about maintaining the perfect home and follow their hearts. Another American film which the French got before we did was Robert Aldrich's jazzy, rude-attitude Mickey Spillane self-parody, *Kiss Me Deadly*—though the guys who did the James Bond series obviously paid attention, so did Stanley Kubrick in *Dr. Strangelove* . . . and a Mr. Tarantino borrowed its glowing suitcase. David Lean captured a beautiful quavering frailty in Katharine Hepburn in his Venetian romance, *Summertime*, and James Dean reinforced his troubled-teen archetype in his best role, *East of Eden*.

Best American Film: *All That Heaven Allows*
Best Foreign Film: *Ordet*
Best Actor: James Dean, *East of Eden*
Best Actress: Katharine Hepburn, *Summertime*
Best Director: Robert Aldrich, *Kiss Me Deadly*

1956

Cannes made another of its legendary discoveries this year with *Pather Panchali*, a low-budget film by an Indian, Satyajit Ray. With the first part of his Apu trilogy (followed by *Aparajito* and *The World of Apu*), Ray showed that the Italian neorealist approach could be applied to ordinary life in radically different cultures—and in fact Ray's majestically simple and pure films fulfill neorealism's aim better than any Italian filmmaker did. It was a rare highlight in a festival marred by one politically motivated cancellation after another. *A Town Like Alice* offended the Japanese for depicting the occupation of Malaya; the Finnish *Unknown Soldier* offended the Soviets; Alain Resnais's Holocaust documentary *Night and Fog* allegedly offended the German ambassador—though the real reason for its withdrawal, many felt, was that in one shot a French soldier's *kepi* was visible among German caps, and that hint, however slight, of French collaboration during the war was enough to get it yanked. To its great credit, the Berlin Senate then invited the film to the Berlin Filmfestspiele, where it was shown to general acclaim. The lesson, alas, didn't take hold: a few months later American ambassador Claire Boothe Luce had *Blackboard Jungle* yanked from Venice, for giving the wrong picture of American life.

Academy Awards

*** Around the World in 80 Days AAW GLO NYC BOR
Oscar, atoning for picking small black-and-white dramas of late, held a four-way competition for Biggest Film of the Year, and Mike Todd's star-studded extravaganza won. It certainly had plenty of spectacle for the money (even at Todd's jacked-up prices), but it hasn't got *The Ten Commandments*' unstoppable narrative drive, and you'll be hard-pressed not to check your watch at some point—hasn't it been eighty days yet?

Picture
Around the World in 80 Days (UA, Michael Todd)
Friendly Persuasion (Allied Artists, William Wyler)
Giant (Warner Bros., George Stevens, Henry Ginsberg)
The King and I (20th Century–Fox, Charles Brackett)
The Ten Commandments (Paramount, Cecil B. DeMille)

**** Yul Brynner in *The King and I* AAW BOR
Brynner (who only got the part in the movie after Marlon Brando turned it down) transfers his performance from stage to screen without toning it down in the least—apparently what people wanted in a film of a

Rodgers & Hammerstein stage hit. All the same, his identification with the role is deserved; his progressive-minded child-man of a king is an original and charming creation that breaks with the slinky yellow devil-lovers and fortune-cookie wise men of earlier Asian romances.

Actor
Yul Brynner, *The King and I*
James Dean, *Giant*
Kirk Douglas, *Lust for Life*
Rock Hudson, *Giant*
Laurence Olivier, *Richard III*

*** Ingrid Bergman in *Anastasia* AAW GLO NYC
Ingrid, you're back, all is forgiven. This melodrama about the woman who might or might not have been a Romanov is so lavishly produced that the cast seems to be shouting to drown out the roar of the decor; Bergman, alone among them, manages subtlety—but hers was a face made for dreamy black-and-white closeups in which she alone fills the frame, not the candy-box rectangles of a Technicolor CinemaScope super-production.

Actress
Ingrid Bergman, *Anastasia*
Carroll Baker, *Baby Doll*
Katharine Hepburn, *The Rainmaker*
Nancy Kelly, *The Bad Seed*
Deborah Kerr, *The King and I*

Supporting Actor
Anthony Quinn, *Lust for Life*
Don Murray, *Bus Stop*

Anthony Perkins, *Friendly Persuasion*
Mickey Rooney, *The Bold and the Brave*
Robert Stack, *Written on the Wind*

Supporting Actress
Dorothy Malone, *Written on the Wind*
Mildred Dunnock, *Baby Doll*
Eileen Heckart, *The Bad Seed*
Mercedes McCambridge, *Giant*
Patty McCormack, *The Bad Seed*

Director
George Stevens, *Giant*
Michael Anderson, *Around the World in 80 Days*
Walter Lang, *The King and I*
King Vidor, *War and Peace*
William Wyler, *Friendly Persuasion*

Original Screenplay: Albert Lamorisse, *The Red Balloon*
Adapted Screenplay: James Poe, John Farrow, S. J. Perelman, *Around the World in 80 Days*
Original Story: "Robert Rich," *The Brave One* [NOTE: pseudonym for blacklistee Dalton Trumbo]
Cinematography/B&W: Joseph Ruttenberg, *Somebody Up There Likes Me*
Cinematography/Color: Lionel Lindon, *Around the World in 80 Days*
Dramatic or Comedy Score: Victor Young, *Around the World in 80 Days*
Musical Score: Alfred Newman, Ken Darby, *The King and I*
Song: "Whatever Will Be, Will Be (Que Será, Será)," *The Man Who Knew Too Much,* ml: Jay Livingston, Ray Evans
Art Direction/B&W: Cedric Gibbons, *Somebody Up There Likes Me*
Art Direction/Color: Lyle Wheeler, *The King and I*

Costumes/B&W: Jean Louis, *The Solid Gold Cadillac*
Costumes/Color: Irene Sharaff, *The King and I*
Editing: *Around the World in 80 Days*
Sound Recording: *The King and I*
Special Effects: *The Ten Commandments*
Short/Cartoon: *Mister Magoo's Puddle Jumper* (UPA/Pete Burness)
Short/One-Reel: *Crashing the Water Barrier* (Warner Bros.)
Short/Two-Reel: *The Bespoke Overcoat* (Romulus Films, directed by Jack Clayton)
Documentary/Feature: *The Silent World* (Jacques-Yves Cousteau)
Documentary/Short: *The True Story of the Civil War*
Foreign Language Film: *La Strada* (Italy)
Irving G. Thalberg Award: Buddy Adler
Jean Hersholt Humanitarian Award: Y. Frank Freeman
Special Award: Eddie Cantor

Golden Globes
Picture (Drama): *Around the World in 80 Days*
Picture (Comedy/Musical): *The King and I*
English-Language Foreign Film: *Richard III*
Foreign-Language Films: *The White Reindeer* (Finland), *Before Sundown* (West Germany), *A Girl in Black* (Greece), *The Rose on His Arm* (Japan), *War and Peace* (Italy-USA)
Actor (Drama): Kirk Douglas, *Lust For Life*
Actor (Comedy/Musical): Cantínflas, *Around the World in 80 Days*
Actress (Drama): Ingrid Bergman, *Anastasia*
Actress (Comedy/Musical): Deborah Kerr, *The King and I*

Supporting Actor: Earl Holliman, *The Rainmaker*
Supporting Actress: Eileen Heckart, *The Bad Seed*
Director: Elia Kazan, *Baby Doll*
Most Promising Newcomers (Male): John Kerr, Paul Newman, Anthony Perkins; foreign: Jacques Bergerac (France)
Most Promising Newcomers (Female): Carroll Baker, Jayne Mansfield, Natalie Wood; foreign: Taina Elg (Finland)
World Film Favorite (Male): James Dean
World Film Favorite (Female): Kim Novak
Best Film Promoting International Understanding: *Battle Hymn*
Cecil B. DeMille Award: Mervyn LeRoy
Hollywood Citizenship Award: Ronald Reagan
Special Award for Advancing Film Industry: Edwin Schallert
Special Award for Consistent Performance: Elizabeth Taylor

Directors Guild of America
Most Outstanding Directorial Achievement: George Stevens, *Giant*
Outstanding Directorial Achievement: Michael Anderson, *Around the World in 80 Days*
William Wyler, *Friendly Persuasion*
King Vidor, *War and Peace*
Walter Lang, *The King and I*
D. W. Griffith Award: King Vidor
Honorary Lifetime Member: Donald Crisp
Critic Award: Francis J. Carmody, *Washington News*

**** *La Strada* VEN '55, AAW NYC

Fellini's breakthrough film was one of the biggest art-house hits of its time (and probably had something to do with Anthony Quinn winning a supporting Oscar that year for his small role as Gauguin in *Lust for Life*). It also marked the final break between Italian neorealism and reality—this is neorealism as a mere background for a fable-like universe straight out of Commedia dell'Arte (or Chaplin). A lovely, if ever-so-faintly precious, drama about a simple soul (Giulietta Masina, Mrs. Fellini) married to a brutish circus strongman (Quinn).

**** **Kirk Douglas in** *Lust for Life* GLO NYC

Along with *Detective Story*, Douglas' best performance is, of all things, as a driven, sympathetically needy Vincent van Gogh in a brilliantly colorful drama which almost completely avoids kitsch.

New York Film Critics Circle

Picture: *Around the World in 80 Days*
Foreign Film: *La Strada*
Actor: Kirk Douglas, *Lust for Life*
Actress: Ingrid Bergman, *Anastasia*
Director: John Huston, *Moby Dick*
Screenplay: S. J. Perelman, *Around the World in 80 Days*

National Board of Review

Best American Film: *Around the World in 80 Days*
Moby Dick
The King and I
Lust For Life
Friendly Persuasion
Somebody Up There Likes Me
The Catered Affair
Anastasia
The Man Who Never Was
Bus Stop
Best Foreign Film: *The Silent World*
War and Peace
Richard III
La Strada
Rififi
Actor: Yul Brynner, *The King and I, Anastasia, The Ten Commandments*
Actress: Dorothy McGuire, *Friendly Persuasion*
Supporting Actor: Richard Basehart, *Moby Dick*
Supporting Actress: Debbie Reynolds, *The Catered Affair*
Director: John Huston, *Moby Dick*

Photoplay Gold Medal Awards

Gold Medal: *Giant*
Most Popular Male Star: Rock Hudson
Most Popular Female Star: Kim Novak

British Academy Awards

Film: *Gervaise*
British Film: *Reach For the Sky*
Actor (British): Peter Finch, *A Town Like Alice* [*Rape of Malaya*]
Actor (Foreign): François Périer, *Gervaise*
Actress (British): Virginia McKenna, *A Town Like Alice*
Actress (Foreign): Anna Magnani, *The Rose Tattoo*
Screenplay: Nigel Balchin, *The Man Who Never Was*

Documentary: *On the Bowery* (Lionel Rogosin, USA)
Short Animated Film: *Gerald McBoing Boing on Planet Moo* (Robert Cannon, USA)
Specialized Film: *The Red Balloon* (Albert Lamorisse, France)

Cannes Film Festival
Palme d'Or: *The Silent World* (Louis Malle, Jacques Cousteau, France)
Special Jury Prize: *The Mystery of Picasso* (Henri-Georges Clouzot, France)
Best Performance: Susan Hayward, *I'll Cry Tomorrow* (USA)
Director: Sergei Yutkevich, *Othello* (USSR)
Poetic Humor Prize: *Smiles of a Summer Night* (Ingmar Bergman, Sweden)
Best Human Document: *Pather Panchali* (Satyajit Ray, India)
Palme d'Or/Short Film: *The Red Balloon* (Albert Lamorisse, France) [prize seconded by the feature film jury]
Special Mention: The marionette films of Jiri Trnka (Czechoslovakia)

Venice Film Festival
Golden Lion: not awarded
Actor: Bournvil, *La Traverse de Paris* (France)
Actress: Maria Schell, *Gervaise* (France)
International Critics Prize: *Gervaise* (René Clément, France); *Calle Mayor* [*The Love Maker*] (Juan Antonio Bardem, Spain)
Italian Critics Award: *Attack!* (Robert Aldrich, USA)

Berlin Film Festival
Golden Bear: *Invitation to the Dance* (Gene Kelly, USA)
Silver Bear: *Richard III* (Laurence Olivier, UK)

Honorable Mentions: *The Long Arm* [*The Third Key*] (Charles Frend, UK); *The Sorceress* (André Michel, France)
Actor: Burt Lancaster, *Trapeze* (USA)
Actress: Elsa Martinelli, *Donatella* (Italy)
Director: Robert Aldrich, *Autumn Leaves* (USA); award of merit, Alfonso Corona Blake, *The Road to Life* (Mexico)
Mention for Color: *The White Snake Enchantress* (Taiji Yabushita, Kazuhiko Okabe, Japan)
Comedy: *Bread, Love and Jealousy* (Luigi Comencini, Italy)
Documentary: Silver: *The African Lion* (Walt Disney, USA)
Audience Awards: *Before Sunset* (Gottfried Reinhardt, West Germany)
Mi Tío Jacinto (Ladislao Vajda, Spain)
Trapeze (Carol Reed, USA)

Harvard Lampoon Movie Worsts
Ten worst pictures:
The Ten Commandments
Alexander the Great
Trapeze
The Benny Goodman Story
Gaby
Serenade
Bhowani Junction
Miracle in the Rain
The Vagabond King
The Proud and the Profane
Worst Actor: Gregory Peck, *Moby Dick*
Worst Actress: Jennifer Jones, *The Man in the Grey Flannel Suit*
Worst Supporting Actor: Elvis Presley, *Love Me Tender*
Worst Supporting Actress: Anne Baxter, *The Ten Commandments*
Life-Begins-at-Fifty Award: A passionate Joan Crawford in the

throes of senilescence culminating
her *Autumn Leaves* love affair
by tossing about in the waves with
Cliff Robertson
**Most Thoroughly Unsatisfying
Ending:** Rock Hudson's

recovery in *All That Heaven
Allows*
Hypocrisy-of-the-Year Award
(Big-as-Texas Variety): The five
million dollars spent on the theme
of antimaterialism in *Giant*

Box Office (Domestic Rentals)

1	*Guys and Dolls*	$9,000,000	Goldwyn
2	*The King and I*	8,500,000	Fox
3	*Trapeze*	7,500,000	UA
4	*High Society*	6,500,000	MGM
	I'll Cry Tomorrow	6,500,000	UA
6	*Picnic*	6,300,000	Col
7	*War and Peace*	6,250,000	Par
8	*The Eddy Duchin Story*	5,300,000	Col
9	*Moby Dick*	5,200,000	WB
10	*The Searchers*	4,800,000	WB

Other films of note:

11	*The Conqueror*	4,500,000	RKO
	Rebel Without a Cause	4,500,000	WB
13	*The Man With the Golden Arm*	4,350,000	UA
17	*The Man Who Knew Too Much*	4,100,000	Par
22	*Love Me Tender*	3,750,000	Fox
27	*All That Heaven Allows*	3,100,000	Uni
61	*Forbidden Planet*	1,600,000	MGM
89	*Invasion of the Body Snatchers*	1,200,000	Allied Artists
95	*Rock Around the Clock*	1,100,000	Col
	Tarantula	1,100,000	Uni

Elvis Presley may have made his movie debut that year in Love Me Tender, *but
traditional Broadway musicals dominated the box office and it was Ol' Blue Eyes,
not the Pelvis, who had two Top Ten hits. Still, the fact that Presley's debut did exactly
as well as* Carousel—*at a fraction of the cost—was a lesson not lost on Hollywood,
which started cranking out ultra-cheapies like* Rock Around the Clock. *John Wayne
managed to prove that he could pack 'em in for anything from the sublime (*The
Searchers) *to the ridiculous (*The Conqueror, *Howard Hughes' epic in which the Duke
played Genghis Khan—and, along with the rest of the cast, received significant
exposure to A-bomb test fallout while on location in Utah). Despite, or perhaps
because of, the reality of such atomic-age horrors, sci-fi continued to be only a minor
box office genre until the late '60s—and the one big-budget attempt at the genre,
MGM's million-dollar* Forbidden Planet, *was an underachiever.*

Gebert's Golden Armchairs

If *Red River* was "Mutiny on the Range," John Ford's *The Searchers* is "Moby Dick Goes West"—a raging, haunting drama of obsession, with John Wayne as the scout whose search for his niece, kidnapped by Indians, turns into the determination to expunge her defilement with her blood. No movie has ever peered deeper into the dark recesses of American attitudes toward race—and anybody who ever thought John Wayne wasn't a good (let alone great) actor is referred to the scene where he reveals that he'd found the niece's older sister, and is asked what happened to her . . . As a great middle-aged actress, Eva Dahlbeck is the wisest of the worldly-wise females in Bergman's *Smiles of a Summer Night*, the most serious sex comedy ever made. And Robert Bresson's amazingly concentrated *A Man Escaped*, based on a true story of a prisoner's escape from a Vichy prison, weaves a heart-pounding suspense film out of its few simple materials the way its protagonist makes an arsenal of escape tools out of the few things in his bare cell.

Best American Film: *The Searchers*
Best Foreign Film: *A Man Escaped*
Best Actor: John Wayne, *The Searchers*
Best Actress: Eva Dahlbeck, *Smiles of a Summer Night*
Best Director: Robert Bresson, *A Man Escaped*

1957

"A few highbrows in all countries will hail it as a masterpiece, but the average moviegoer will find it incoherent," wrote Francis Koval in *Films in Review* of the Cannes premiere of Ingmar Bergman's *The Seventh Seal*. Jeers greeted the announcement that it would share the Special Jury Prize with Andrzej Wajda's much better-received *Kanal*. A surprisingly conservative Cannes jury including Cocteau, Michael Powell, and George Stevens, seeking again to make peace with Hollywood, picked another "small" film, William Wyler's old-fashioned *Friendly Persuasion*, for the Palme d'Or over a field that included *A Man Escapes*, Fellini's *Nights of Cabiria*, Jules Dassin's *He Who Must Die,* and the Bergman film. Incoherent or not, *The Seventh Seal* went on to become a classic, the epitome of the art movie for a generation of Americans—and still capable of spawning parodies as late as *Bill and Ted's Bogus Journey* and *The Last Action Hero* three decades later.

Academy Awards

**** *The Bridge on the River Kwai* AAW GLO DGA NYC BOR BAA
**** Alec Guinness AAW GLO NYC BOR BAA
David Lean's war epic was probably the best movie made for this much money to date—high artistic ambitions were rare enough in films of this sort, and actually managing to keep characterization on an equal footing with spectacle is even rarer (actually, just about unique to Lean's work). Playing a Brit P.O.W. whose stubborn determination blocks out the bigger picture about what the bridge he's building is for, Alec Guinness' performance has the same sort of stubborn determination—the dense muddleheadedness of his character never cracks, which is both to Guinness' credit as an actor, and why I wouldn't consider it his most insightful performance.

Picture
The Bridge on the River Kwai (Columbia, Sam Spiegel)
Peyton Place (20th Century–Fox, Jerry Wald)
Sayonara (Warner Bros., William Goetz)
12 Angry Men (UA, Orion-Nova, Henry Fonda)
Witness for the Prosecution (UA, Arthur Hornblow, Jr.)

Actor
Alec Guinness, *The Bridge on the River Kwai*
Marlon Brando, *Sayonara*
Anthony Franciosa, *A Hatful of Rain*
Charles Laughton, *Witness for the Prosecution*
Anthony Quinn, *Wild Is the Wind*

** **Joanne Woodward in** *The Three Faces of Eve* AAW GLO BOR
Getting to play multiple characters—two of them labeled Eve White and Eve Black (why not Eve Madonna and Eve Whore, to make it really obvious?)—is an absolute invitation to overact, and to Woodward's credit, she only partly accepts the invitation (and even has some fun with it). Still, a cornball view of psychology, a couple of steps backward from even *The Snake Pit*, and she's better in lots of other things.

Actress
Joanne Woodward, *The Three Faces of Eve*
Deborah Kerr, *Heaven Knows, Mr. Allison*
Anna Magnani, *Wild Is the Wind*
Elizabeth Taylor, *Raintree County*
Lana Turner, *Peyton Place*

Supporting Actor
Red Buttons, *Sayonara*
Vittorio de Sica, *A Farewell to Arms*
Sessue Hayakawa, *The Bridge on the River Kwai*
Arthur Kennedy, *Peyton Place*
Russ Tamblyn, *Peyton Place*

Supporting Actress
Miyoshi Umeki, *Sayonara*
Carolyn Jones, *The Bachelor Party*
Elsa Lanchester, *Witness for the Prosecution*
Hope Lange, *Peyton Place*
Diane Varsi, *Peyton Place*

Director
David Lean, *The Bridge on the River Kwai*

Joshua Logan, *Sayonara*
Sidney Lumet, *12 Angry Men*
Mark Robson, *Peyton Place*
Billy Wilder, *Witness for the Prosecution*

Original Screenplay: George Wells, *Designing Woman*
Adapted Screenplay: Pierre Boulle, *The Bridge on the River Kwai* [NOTE: Boulle, author of the original novel, was front for blacklistees Carl Foreman and Michael Wilson]
Cinematography: Jack Hildyard, *The Bridge on the River Kwai*
Score: Malcolm Arnold, *The Bridge on the River Kwai*
Song: "All the Way," *The Joker Is Wild*, m: James Van Heusen, l: Sammy Cahn
Art Direction: Ted Haworth, *Sayonara*
Costume Design: Orry-Kelly, *Les Girls*
Editing: *The Bridge on the River Kwai*
Sound: *Sayonara*
Special Effects: *The Enemy Below*
Short/Cartoon: *Birds Anonymous* (Warner Bros./Friz Freleng/Sylvester & Tweety)
Short/Live Action: *The Wetback Hound* (Walt Disney)
Documentary/Feature: *Albert Schweitzer*
Foreign-Language Film: *Nights of Cabiria* (Italy)
Jean Hersholt Humanitarian Award: Samuel Goldwyn
Special Awards:
Charles Brackett
B. B. Kahane
Gilbert M. ("Broncho Billy") Anderson, motion picture pioneer
The Society of Motion Picture and Television Engineers

Golden Globes
Picture (Drama): *The Bridge on the River Kwai*

Picture (Comedy/Musical): *Les Girls*

English-Language Foreign Film: *Woman in a Dressing Gown*

Foreign-Language Films: *The Confessions of Felix Krull* (West Germany), *Yellow Crow* (Japan), *Tizoc* (Mexico)

Actor (Drama): Alec Guinness, *The Bridge on the River Kwai*

Actor (Comedy/Musical): Frank Sinatra, *Pal Joey*

Actress (Drama): Joanne Woodward, *The Three Faces of Eve*

Actress (Comedy/Musical): Kay Kendall, *Les Girls*

Supporting Actor: Red Buttons, *Sayonara*

Supporting Actress: Elsa Lanchester, *Witness for the Prosecution*

Director: David Lean, *The Bridge on the River Kwai*

Special Award for Choreography: LeRoy Prinz

Most Promising Newcomers (Male): James Garner, John Saxon, Patrick Wayne

Most Promising Newcomers (Female): Sandra Dee, Carolyn Jones, Diane Varsi

World Film Favorite (Male): Tony Curtis

World Film Favorite (Female): Doris Day

Most Versatile Actress: Jean Simmons

Most Glamorous Actress: Zsa Zsa Gabor

Best World Entertainment Through Musical Films: George Sidney

Best Film Promoting International Understanding: *The Happy Road*

Cecil B. DeMille Award: Buddy Adler

Special Award for Bettering the Standard of Motion Picture Music: Hugo Friedhofer

Ambassador of Good Will: Bob Hope

Directors Guild of America

Most Outstanding Directorial Achievement: David Lean, *The Bridge on the River Kwai*

Outstanding Directorial Achievement:
Joshua Logan, *Sayonara*
Sidney Lumet, *12 Angry Men*
Mark Robson, *Peyton Place*
Billy Wilder, *Witness for the Prosecution*

Critic Award: Hollis Alpert and Arthur Knight, *Saturday Review*

New York Film Critics Circle

Picture: *The Bridge on the River Kwai*

Foreign Film: *Gervaise*

Actor: Alec Guinness, *The Bridge on the River Kwai*

Actress: Deborah Kerr, *Heaven Knows, Mr. Allison*

Director: David Lean, *The Bridge on the River Kwai*

National Board of Review

Best American Film: *The Bridge on the River Kwai*
12 Angry Men
The Spirit of St. Louis
The Rising of the Moon
Albert Schweitzer
Funny Face
The Bachelor Party
The Enemy Below
A Hatful of Rain
A Farewell to Arms

Best Foreign Film: *Ordet*
Gervaise
Torero!
The Red Balloon
A Man Escaped

Actor: Alec Guinness, *The Bridge on the River Kwai*

Actress: Joanne Woodward, *The Three Faces of Eve*, *No Down Payment*

Supporting Actor: Sessue

Hayakawa, *The Bridge on the River Kwai*
Supporting Actress: Dame Sybil Thorndike, *The Princess and the Showgirl*
Director: David Lean, *The Bridge on the River Kwai*
Special Citation: For the photographic innovations in *Funny Face*

Photoplay Gold Medal Awards
Gold Medal: *An Affair To Remember*
Most Popular Male Star: Rock Hudson
Most Popular Female Star: Deborah Kerr

British Academy Awards
Film: *The Bridge on the River Kwai*
British Film: *The Bridge on the River Kwai*
Actor (British): Alec Guinness, *The Bridge on the River Kwai*
Actor (Foreign): Henry Fonda, *12 Angry Men*
Actress (British): Heather Sears, *The Story of Esther Costello*
Actress (Foreign): Simone Signoret, *The Witches of Salem* [*The Crucible*]
Screenplay: Pierre Boulle, *The Bridge on the River Kwai*
Specialized Film: *A Chairy Tale* (Norman McLaren, Canada)

Cannes Film Festival
Palme d'Or: *Friendly Persuasion* (William Wyler, USA)
Special Jury Prize: *The Seventh Seal* (Ingmar Bergman, Sweden), *Kanal* (Andrzej Wajda, Poland)
Actor: John Kitzmiller, *Valley of Peace* (Yugoslavia)
Actress: Giulietta Masina, *Nights of Cabiria* (Italy)
Director: Robert Bresson, *A Man Escaped* (France)

Screenplay: *The 41st* (Grigori Chukhrai, USSR)
Romantic Documentary Prize: *Shiroi Sammyaku* (Sadao Imamura, Japan), *Qivitoq* (Erik Balling, Denmark)
Exceptional Mention: *Gautama the Buddha* (Rajbans Khanna, India)
Best Selection: France, including *He Who Must Die* (Jules Dassin), *A Man Escaped*

*** *Aparajito*   VEN '59
The middle part of Ray's *Apu Trilogy*, in which Apu grows up and goes to school, is equally impressive in its pure and delicate handling—but not as affecting as the magnificent first, *Pather Panchali*, with its magical portrait of childhood. The award was no doubt really intended for that film.

Venice Film Festival
Golden Lion: *Aparajito* (Satyajit Ray, India)
Silver Lion: *White Nights* (Luchino Visconti, Italy)
Actor: Anthony Franciosa, *A Hatful of Rain* (USA)
Actress: Dzidra Ritenberg, *Malva* (USSR)
International Critics Prize: *A Hatful of Rain* (Fred Zinnemann, USA)
Most Cooperative Performer at the Festival: Esther Williams

**** *12 Angry Men*   DGA BER
The case they discuss is a little contrived, but the dramatic situation—one star and eleven great character actors as members of a jury, dividing as neatly into types as any WWII bomber crew—could hardly be

improved upon. Rightly remembered as one of the best "little" black-and-white dramas of its time (as well as one of the classics of bleeding-heart liberal cinema)—and what a cast: Henry Fonda, Ed Begley, E. G. Marshall, Jack Warden, John Fiedler, etc., etc.

Berlin Film Festival
Golden Bear: *12 Angry Men* (Sidney Lumet, USA)
Silver Bear: *Whom God Forgives* (José Maria Forqué, Spain)
Actor: Pedro Infante, *Tizoc* (Mexico)
Actress: Yvonne Mitchell, *Woman in a Dressing Gown* (UK)
Director: Mario Monicelli, *Fathers and Sons* (Italy)
Music: Ravi Shankar, *Kabuliwala* (India)
Documentary: Gold: *Secrets of Life* (Walt Disney, USA)
International Critics Prize: *Woman in a Dressing Gown* (J. Lee Thompson, UK)

Harvard Lampoon Movie Worsts
Ten worst pictures:
Raintree County
The Pride and the Passion
Peyton Place
Island in the Sun
Jeanne Eagels
Funny Face
The Hunchback of Notre Dame
The Sun Also Rises
Pal Joey
April Love
The Worst-Film-of-the-Century Award: This award, given once every hundred years, is presented for the century 1857–1957 to Otto Preminger's *Saint Joan*
Worst Actor: Rock Hudson, *A Farewell to Arms*
Worst Actress: Kim Novak, *Jeanne Eagels, Pal Joey*
Worst Supporting Actor: McGeorge Bundy, *To the Age That Is Waiting*
Worst Supporting Actress: Joan Collins, *Island in the Sun*
The "Any Connection?" Prize: Given jointly to Rita Hayworth, *Fire Down Below*, and Bing Crosby, *Man on Fire*
The Suzy Parker Award for the most inauspicious male debut: Pat Boone, *Bernadine*
The Pat Boone Award for the most inauspicious female debut: Suzy Parker, *Kiss Them for Me*

Box Office (Domestic Rentals

1	*The Ten Commandments [1957 only]*	$18,500,000	Par
	[approximate first-run total:	34,200,000]	
2	*Around the World in 80 Days*		UA
	[1957 only]	16,200,000	
	[approximate first-run total:	22,000,000]	
3	*Giant*	12,000,000	WB
4	*Oklahoma! [total through 1964:*	7,100,000]	Magna
5	*Pal Joey*	6,700,000	Col
6	*Seven Wonders of the World*	6,500,000	Cinerama
7	*The Teahouse of the August Moon*	5,600,000	MGM
8	*The Pride and the Passion*	6,250,000	Par
9	*Anastasia*	5,000,000	Fox
	Island in the Sun	5,000,000	Fox

Other films of note:

12	*Written on the Wind*	4,400,000	Uni
15	*Jailhouse Rock*	4,000,000	MGM
19	*Loving You*	3,700,000	Par
22	*The Sad Sack*	3,500,000	Par
38	*The Sweet Smell of Success*	2,250,000	UA
85	*Don't Knock the Rock*	1,200,000	Col

By playing in what Paramount called "booking waves" of first-run engagements for some six years straight, Cecil B. DeMille's The Ten Commandments *finally managed to break* Gone With the Wind*'s first-run box office record of $22.6 million. Even so, constant re-release kept GWTW ahead as the all-time box office champ. Mike Todd's* Around the World in 80 Days *also came within a hair's breadth of GWTW's record through novel methods of showmanship—Todd limited theaters to two shows a day and sold reserved seats at a premium price, just like a stage play (check your grandparents' attic and there's a good chance you'll find the program for it tucked away somewhere). At the other end of the stylistic scale, film noir has a reputation for being box office poison, and* The Sweet Smell of Success *is remembered as a flop (by the 1957 box office standards of very reliable Burt Lancaster and white-hot Tony Curtis), but it actually returned a respectable two million.*

Gebert's Golden Armchairs

For sheer filmmaking virtuosity, no 1957 feature can top Chuck Jones' reduction of the Wagner Ring cycle into eight deeply bathetic minutes, the greatest cartoon ever made: *What's Opera, Doc?* (You know it—"Kill the wabbit, kill the wabbit, kill the waaaaa-a-a-bbit!") If you must have a feature, it would be *The Sweet Smell of Success*, a dazzlingly shot, wonderfully quotable underbelly-of-showbiz noir with Tony Curtis giving a revelatory performance as a self-loathing publicity agent under the thumb of corrupt Winchell-like columnist Burt Lancaster.

And Giulietta Masina is charming as a happy-sad prostitute in another no-relation-to-reality neorealist fable from Fellini—about the last time that worked, for him or anybody else.

Best American Film: *What's Opera, Doc?*
Best Foreign Film: *Nights of Cabiria*
Best Actor: Tony Curtis, *The Sweet Smell of Success*
Best Actress: Giulietta Masina, *Nights of Cabiria*
Best Director: Alexander Mackendrick, *The Sweet Smell of Success*

1958

Nothing was more topsy-turvy about Cannes in its early years than the respective behavior of the American and Soviet delegations. The Cossacks from Hollywood would send only minor celebrities, spend almost nothing on promotion, and demand prizes just for honoring Cannes with their presence. While the Soviets threw lavish parties (legendary enough to rate parody in Powell and Pressburger's *Oh . . . Rosalinda!!*, and responsible for at least one scandal in 1955 when the jurors were too crocked to watch a major award contender), they took years of anti-Red hostility with good grace, and in general were the picture of aristocratic hospitality and breeding.

Good manners finally paid off in 1958 with the Soviet Union's only Palme d'Or, to Mikhail Kalotozov's *The Cranes Are Flying*. A likable, energetically filmed and relatively undoctrinaire wartime romance, it went on from Cannes to be released in the U.S. as part of a cultural exchange program—providing the first exposure to ordinary Russian life (and movies) for a fair part of the Cold War–era moviegoing public.

Academy Awards

• *Gigi* AAW GLO DGA PHO
One of the last really big MGM musicals didn't catch on with the public until it won an Oscar—its Fabergé-egg look and sub-Lubitsch cartoon of Gallic sophistication must have seemed pretty irrelevant and dated even in 1958, when *West Side Story* was the biggest hit on Broadway. Today it has another problem: the idea of young schoolgirl Gigi (Leslie Caron) being coached in how to be a courtesan by all her decadent older relatives seems distinctly distasteful (no matter that we know she'll end up turning Louis Jourdan into a proper bourgeois). It's like a musical version of *The Story of O*.

Picture
Gigi (MGM, Arthur Freed)
Auntie Mame (Warner Bros., Jack L. Warner)
Cat on a Hot Tin Roof (MGM, Avon, Lawrence Weingarten)
The Defiant Ones (UA, Stanley Kramer)
Separate Tables (UA, Hecht-Hill-Lancaster)

** David Niven, *Separate Tables* AAW GLO NYC
Niven, like Ronald Colman before him (and Hugh Grant after), was the epitome of a certain rightly beloved movie type—the urbane light-comedy English gent. But charm only wins hearts, not Oscars—and so like Colman before him, Niven had to take on a serious

part (pathetic military fraud and sex deviate) and do it roughly half as well as any 50 other British character actors could have done to win one. Bit of a sticky wicket, really, old man, but it's what a chap's got to do to get the blighted thing. No doubt we'll have to sit through Hugh Grant in the remake someday.

Actor
David Niven, *Separate Tables*
Tony Curtis, *The Defiant Ones*
Paul Newman, *Cat on a Hot Tin Roof*
Sidney Poitier, *The Defiant Ones*
Spencer Tracy, *The Old Man and the Sea*

** **Susan Hayward in *I Want To Live!*** AAW GLO NYC
Could this be that rarity—a film *noir* that won an award? No, it's just Oscar's old favorite, the maternal-tragedy yarn, dressed up in jazzy new trappings. Susan Hayward plays Barbara Graham, a good-time-gal turned struggling mother sentenced to Death Row (unjustly, according to the film). Early in her career, Hayward had played these kinds of juke-girl parts as if to the manor born (e.g., *They Won't Believe Me*), but by now she's a star—and she makes sure we know that she is Susan Hayward, Respected Thespian Playing Someone Beneath Her.

Actress
Susan Hayward, *I Want to Live!*
Deborah Kerr, *Separate Tables*
Shirley MacLaine, *Some Came Running*
Rosalind Russell, *Auntie Mame*
Elizabeth Taylor, *Cat on a Hot Tin Roof*

Supporting Actor
Burl Ives, *The Big Country*
Theodore Bikel, *The Defiant Ones*
Lee J. Cobb, *The Brothers Karamazov*
Arthur Kennedy, *Some Came Running*
Gig Young, *Teacher's Pet*

Supporting Actress
Wendy Hiller, *Separate Tables*
Peggy Cass, *Auntie Mame*
Martha Hyer, *Some Came Running*
Maureen Stapleton, *Lonelyhearts*
Cara Williams, *The Defiant Ones*

Director
Vincente Minnelli, *Gigi*
Richard Brooks, *Cat on a Hot Tin Roof*
Stanley Kramer, *The Defiant Ones*
Mark Robson, *The Inn of the Sixth Happiness*
Robert Wise, *I Want to Live!*

Original Screenplay: Nathan E. Douglas, Harold Jacob Smith, *The Defiant Ones*
Adapted Screenplay: Alan Jay Lerner, *Gigi*
Cinematography/B&W: Sam Leavitt, *The Defiant Ones*
Cinematography/Color: Joseph Ruttenberg, *Gigi*
Dramatic or Comedy Score: Dimitri Tiomkin, *The Old Man and the Sea*
Musical Score: André Previn, *Gigi*
Song: "Gigi," *Gigi*, m: Frederick Loewe, 1: Alan Jay Lerner
Art Direction: William A. Horning, Preston Ames, *Gigi*
Costume Design: Cecil Beaton, *Gigi*

Editing: *Gigi*
Sound: *South Pacific*
Special Effects: *tom thumb*
Short/Cartoon: *Knighty Knight Bugs* (Warner Bros./Friz Freleng/Bugs Bunny)
Short/Live Action: *Grand Canyon* (Walt Disney)
Documentary/Feature: *White Wilderness* (Walt Disney)
Documentary/Short: *AMA Girls* (Walt Disney)
Foreign-Language Film: *My Uncle [Mon Oncle]* (France)
Irving G. Thalberg Award: Jack L. Warner
Special Award: Maurice Chevalier

*** *The Defiant Ones* GLO NYC
Big-Theme-Tackler Stanley Kramer's tackling of the race problem is one of his better efforts, thanks to the fact that it has a solid thriller underpinning (black and white convicts chained together and on the lam) and hardbitten performances from Sidney Poitier and Tony Curtis.

Golden Globes
Picture (Drama): *The Defiant Ones*
Picture (Comedy): *Auntie Mame*
Picture (Musical): *Gigi*
English-Language Foreign Film: *A Night to Remember*
Foreign-Language Films: *The Road a Year Long* (Yugoslavia), *The Girl and the River* (France), *The Girl Rosemarie* (W. Germany)
Actor (Drama): David Niven, *Separate Tables*
Actor (Comedy/Musical): Danny Kaye, *Me and the Colonel*

Actress (Drama): Susan Hayward, *I Want to Live!*
Actress (Comedy/Musical): Rosalind Russell, *Auntie Mame*
Supporting Actor: Burl Ives, *The Big Country*
Supporting Actress: Hermione Gingold, *Gigi*
Director: Vincente Minnelli, *Gigi*
Most Promising Newcomers (Male): Bradford Dillman, John Gavin, Efrem Zimbalist, Jr.
Most Promising Newcomers (Female): Linda Cristal, Susan Kohner, Tina Louise
World Film Favorite (Male): Rock Hudson
World Film Favorite (Female): Deborah Kerr
Most Versatile Actress: Shirley MacLaine
Best Film Promoting International Understanding: *The Inn of the Sixth Happiness*
Cecil B. DeMille Award: Maurice Chevalier
Samuel Goldwyn Award: *Two Eyes, Twelve Hands* (Italy)
Special Award to Best Juvenile: David Ladd

Directors Guild of America
Grand Award For Direction: Vincente Minnelli, *Gigi*
Best-Directed Non-English Film: René Clair, *Gates of Paris*
D.W. Griffith Award: Frank Capra
Honorary Lifetime Member: George Sidney
Critic Award: Philip K. Scheuer, *Los Angeles Times*
Special Award: Louella Parsons

• *Mon Oncle* AAW NYC BOR CAN
Since I already used up my irrational-reaction allotment, let me just say that there were many people who found Jacques Tati's modernist

throwback to silent comedy—
about a family in an unlivably
modern suburban house and
their uncle who lives in
rundown old Paris—charming
and original. And who did not
want to scream the five-
hundredth time the gate on the
modern house squeaked.

New York Film Critics Circle

Picture: *The Defiant Ones*
Foreign Film: *Mon Oncle*
Actor: David Niven, *Separate Tables*
Actress: Susan Hayward, *I Want to Live!*
Director: Stanley Kramer, *The Defiant Ones*
Screenplay: Nathan E. Douglas, Harold Jacob Smith, *The Defiant Ones*

National Board of Review

Best American Film: *The Old Man and the Sea*
Separate Tables
The Last Hurrah
The Long Hot Summer
Windjammer
Cat on a Hot Tin Roof
The Goddess
The Brothers Karamazov
Me and the Colonel
Gigi
Best Foreign Film: *Pather Panchali*
Rouge et Noir
The Horse's Mouth
Mon Oncle
A Night to Remember
Actor: Spencer Tracy, *The Old Man and the Sea, The Last Hurrah*
Actress: Ingrid Bergman, *The Inn of the Sixth Happiness*
Supporting Actor: Albert Salmi, *The Brothers Karamazov, The Bravados*

Supporting Actress: Kay Walsh, *The Horse's Mouth*
Director: John Ford, *The Last Hurrah*
Special Citation: For the valor of Robert Donat's last performance in *The Inn of the Sixth Happiness*

Photoplay Gold Medal Awards

Gold Medal: *Gigi*
Most Popular Male Star: Tony Curtis
Most Popular Female Star: Debbie Reynolds

British Academy Awards

Film: *Room At the Top*
British Film: *Room At the Top*
Actor (British): Trevor Howard, *The Key*
Actor (Foreign): Sidney Poitier, *The Defiant Ones*
Actress (British): Irene Worth, *Orders to Kill*
Actress (Foreign): Simone Signoret, *Room At the Top*
Screenplay: Paul Dehn, *Orders to Kill*
Documentary: *Glass* (Bert Haanstra, Holland)

*** *The Cranes Are Flying* CAN

A Moscow boy goes off to fight
in World War II, leaving his girl
at home, where she marries his
decadent concert-pianist
cousin and lives to regret it.
Kalatozov's film could hardly
have been better suited for its
job as a Cold War icebreaker,
since it combined echoes of '20s
Soviet cinematic invention
(very welcome in those stolid
pre–French New Wave days)
with a plot straight out of a first-
class '40s Hollywood soaper
like *Since You Went Away*. And

it has at least one moment of high Hollywood camp—when the girl first repulses, then relents to the cousin's advances, to the accompaniment of crashing bombs and thundering Tschaikovsky.

Cannes Film Festival
Palme d'Or: *The Cranes Are Flying* (Mikhail Kalatozov, USSR); mention for performance of Tatiana Samoilova
Special Jury Prize: *Mon Oncle* (Jacques Tati, France)
Actor: Paul Newman, *The Long Hot Summer* (USA)
Actress: collectively to Eva Dahlbeck, Ingrid Thulin, Bibi Andersson, Barbro Hiort af Ornäs, *Brink of Life* (Sweden)
Director: Ingmar Bergman, *Brink of Life*
Documentary: *Goha* (Jacques Baratier, Tunisia), *Visages de Bronze* (Bernard Taisant, Switzerland)
[Short Film Palme d'Or co-won by *La Seine a Réncontré Paris*, Joris Ivens *(France)*]
International Critics Prize: *Vengeance* (Juan Antonio Bardem, Spain)

Venice Film Festival
Golden Lion: *Rickshaw Man* (Hiroshi Inagaki, Japan)
Silver Lion: *Les Amants/The Lovers* (Louis Malle, France), *La Sfida [The Challenge]* (Francesco Rosi, Italy)
Actor: Alec Guinness, *The Horse's Mouth* (UK)
Actress: Sophia Loren, *The Black Orchid* (USA)
Documentary: *The Last Day of Summer* (Tadeusz Konwicki, Jan Laskowski, Poland)
International Critics Prize: *The Wolf Trap* (Jiri Weiss, Czechoslovakia)

Italian Film Critics Prize: in competition, *The Girl Rosemarie* (Rolf Thiele, West Germany); out of competition, *Wild Strawberries* (Ingmar Bergman, Sweden), *Weddings and Babies* (Morris Engel, USA)

*****Wild Strawberries** BER '59, GLO BOR
As the philosophical chatter of Bergman's '50s work begins to sound less convincing (e.g., *The Seventh Seal*), the emotional impact of this drama—a tearjerker for intellectuals—looks better all the time. Victor Sjöström, the greatest director of Sweden's silent era, plays an aged professor remembering— with some regret—his life.

Berlin Film Festival
Golden Bear: *Wild Strawberries* (Ingmar Bergman, Sweden)
Silver Bear: *Two Eyes, Twelve Hands* (V. Shantaram, India)
Actor: Sidney Poitier, *The Defiant Ones* (USA)
Actress: Anna Magnani, *Wild Is the Wind* (USA)
Director: Tadashi Imai, *Story of True Love* (Japan)
Documentary: Gold: *Perri* (Walt Disney, USA)
International Critics Prize: *Ice Cold in Alex* (J. Lee Thompson, UK); special prize to Victor Sjöström for his performance in *Wild Strawberries* and his life's work

Harvard Lampoon Movie Worsts
Ten worst pictures:
South Pacific
The Vikings
The Roots of Heaven
The Last Hurrah

Marjorie Morningstar
The Buccaneers
The Big Country
The Old Man and the Sea
A Certain Smile
Windjammer
Worst Actor: Kirk Douglas, *The Vikings* (the trophy will be retired, Mr. Douglas having won it for the third time)
Worst Actress: Rita Hayworth, *Separate Tables*
Worst Supporting Actor: Errol Flynn, *The Roots of Heaven*

Worst Supporting Actress: Christine Carrere, *A Certain Smile*
The Fauntleroy Bequest (a stipend set up in the will of the late Lord Fauntleroy to send a young lad to acting school): Awarded to James (*A Light in the Forest*) MacArthur, with all dispatch
Most Unreasonable Request: Susan Hayward in *I Wanna Live!*

Box Office (Domestic Rentals)

1	*The Bridge on the River Kwai*	$18,000,000	Col
2	*Peyton Place*	12,000,000	Fox
3	*Sayonara*	10,500,000	WB
4	*No Time for Sergeants*	7,200,000	WB
5	*The Vikings*	7,000,000	UA
6	*The Search for Paradise*	6,500,000	Cinerama
7	*South Pacific*	6,400,000	Magna
8	*Cat on a Hot Tin Roof*	6,100,000	Fox
9	*Raintree County*	6,000,000	MGM
10	*Old Yeller*	5,900,000	Disney
Other films of note:			
17	*The Long Hot Summer*	3,500,000	Fox
21	*Vertigo*	3,200,000	Par
28	*Les Girls*	2,750,000	MGM
38	*Gigi*	2,400,000	MGM
	[through 1964:	6,750,000]	
53	*The Fly*	1,700,000	Fox
72	*Horror of Dracula*	1,000,000	Uni
	Thunder Road	1,000,000	UA

Its blend of splashy action, top-drawer acting, literate writing, and location photography made The Bridge on the River Kwai *a huge hit and spawned a new minigenre, the international action epic. Also launching its own minigenre—the color gore-horror film—was the British Hammer studio's* Horror of Dracula, *the first in that company's series of Peter Cushing–Christopher Lee vehicles. At the end of 1958* Variety *estimated that its net would amount to only about a million; in fact it probably made at least twice that (as did the last film on the list, Robert Mitchum's moonshiner melodrama* Thunder Road, *which would be a staple of Southern drive-ins for decades). Meanwhile, the genre that was clearly beginning to fade by this point was the MGM musical, though a Best Picture Oscar eventually boosted* Gigi *a bit.*

Gebert's Golden Armchairs

Wild Strawberries and Orson Welles' last masterpiece, *Touch of Evil*, make an interesting pair on the subject of old-age regret (though there's certainly little else in common between Bergman's family drama, which finds a little cold comfort in old age, and Welles' dazzling bordertown thriller, pure ice). *Auntie Mame* is the essence of '50s vulgarity, garish and shouted to the third balcony, but even if Russell is a shadow of her *His Girl Friday* comic self, freethinking Mame wins just for being the antidote to all those weak-as-dishwater 1950s gals (Sandra Dee, Doris Day, even Deborah Kerr this year in *Separate Tables*). And lastly, there are many years in which Jimmy Stewart might have rated the Best Actor award—I've saved it for Hitchcock's indelible portrait of obsession, *Vertigo*.

Best American Film: *Touch of Evil*
Best Foreign Film: *Wild Strawberries*
Best Actor: James Stewart, *Vertigo*
Best Actress: Rosalind Russell, *Auntie Mame*
Best Director: Orson Welles, *Touch of Evil*

1959

The last of the great festival discoveries of the '50s was right out of Cannes' backyard—the *nouvelle vague* or French new wave, represented at Cannes by Alain Resnais' *Hiroshima, Mon Amour* (a breakthrough in 1959 for its novel use of flashbacks, but exasperating today), and Francois Truffaut's *The 400 Blows*. Resnais' success after the *Night and Fog* fiasco in 1956 was sweet, though at first it seemed like a repeat was in the works—*Hiroshima* featured a French woman who had been the lover of an occupying German soldier, and that was enough to have it pulled from competition and, it seemed, barred from the festival until Minister of Culture André Malraux personally intervened to have the film shown on Closing Night.

But Truffaut's victory (even if it probably came about only because the Resnais film was yanked) was equally delicious—the previous year, as a mere critic (and a famously vicious one), he'd been forcibly evicted from the festival for insulting it publicly. (He'd said something about it being a commercial success and an artistic failure. Imagine.)

Academy Awards

• *Ben-Hur* AAW GLO DGA NYC BAA
*** **Charlton Heston** AAW
The award groups dutifully lined up to honor the expensive, self-important *Ben-Hur*, but apart from Oscar they drew the line at calling Heston the year's best actor. They all got it backwards. The movie is more respectable at any given moment than any previous biblical epic—but at 3½ hours, the final result is simply deadly (Dwight MacDonald compared it to watching a train go by). Heston's slow-burning intensity and a few of the supporting performances are the only signs of life, at least in anything the *first* unit directed. Yet even the chariot race, when it finally comes, is little enough reward for the hours of waiting—or counting cars.

Picture
Ben-Hur (MGM, Sam Zimbalist)
Anatomy of a Murder (Columbia, Otto Preminger)
The Diary of Anne Frank (20th Century–Fox, George Stevens)
The Nun's Story (Warner Bros., Henry Blanke)
Room at the Top (Romulus, Continental, John and James Woolf)

Actor
Charlton Heston, *Ben-Hur*
Laurence Harvey, *Room at the Top*
Jack Lemmon, *Some Like It Hot*
Paul Muni, *The Last Angry Man*
James Stewart, *Anatomy of a Murder*

*** **Simone Signoret in *Room at the Top*** BAA '58 AAW BOR CAN

Out of all the British kitchen-sink films, why did this one alone get Oscar attention? Because for all its gritty realism, it was basically *Kitty Foyle* in reverse—working-class climber Laurence Harvey keeps his options open between the mill owner's daughter and the older woman who really loves him (Signoret). Signoret is pretty good and certainly sultry, but it's a sob sister part with less complexity to it than Harvey's role, which really smolders.

Actress
Simone Signoret, *Room at the Top*
Doris Day, *Pillow Talk*
Audrey Hepburn, *The Nun's Story*
Katharine Hepburn, *Suddenly, Last Summer*
Elizabeth Taylor, *Suddenly, Last Summer*

Supporting Actor
Hugh Griffith, *Ben-Hur*
Arthur O'Connell, *Anatomy of a Murder*
George C. Scott, *Anatomy of a Murder*
Robert Vaughn, *The Young Philadelphians*
Ed Wynn, *The Diary of Anne Frank*

Supporting Actress
Shelley Winters, *The Diary of Anne Frank*
Hermione Baddeley, *Room at the Top*
Susan Kohner, *Imitation of Life*
Juanita Moore, *Imitation of Life*
Thelma Ritter, *Pillow Talk*

Director
William Wyler, *Ben-Hur*
Jack Clayton, *Room at the Top*
George Stevens, *The Diary of Anne Frank*
Billy Wilder, *Some Like It Hot*
Fred Zinnemann, *The Nun's Story*

Original Screenplay: Russell Rouse, Clarence Green, Stanley Shapiro, Maurice Richlin, *Pillow Talk*
Adapted Screenplay: Neil Paterson, *Room at the Top*
Cinematography/B&W: William C. Mellor, *The Diary of Anne Frank*
Cinematography/Color: Robert L. Surtees, *Ben-Hur*
Dramatic or Comedy Score: Miklos Rozsa, *Ben-Hur*
Musical Score: André Previn, Ken Darby, *Porgy and Bess*
Song: "High Hopes," *A Hole in the Head*, m: James Van Heusen, l: Sammy Cahn
Art Direction/B&W: Lyle R. Wheeler, George W. Davis, *The Diary of Anne Frank*
Art Direction/Color: William A. Horning, *Ben-Hur*
Costumes/B&W: Orry-Kelly, *Some Like It Hot*
Costumes/Color: Elizabeth Haffenden, *Ben-Hur*
Editing: *Ben-Hur*
Sound: *Ben-Hur*
Special Effects: *Ben-Hur*
Short/Cartoon: *Moonbird* (John Hubley)
Short/Live Action: *The Golden Fish* (Jacques-Yves Cousteau)
Documentary/Short: *Glass* (Bert Haanstra, Holland)
Documentary/Feature: *Serengeti Shall Not Die* (Germany)
Foreign-Language Film: *Black Orpheus* (France)
Jean Hersholt Humanitarian Award: Bob Hope
Special Awards: Lee de Forest,

for his pioneering inventions which brought sound to the motion picture
Buster Keaton

Golden Globes
Picture (Drama): *Ben-Hur*
Picture (Comedy): *Some Like It Hot*
Picture (Musical): *Porgy and Bess*
Foreign-Language Films: *Black Orpheus* (France), *Odd Obsession* (Japan), *The Bridge* (West Germany), *Wild Strawberries* (Sweden), *Aren't We Wonderful?* (West Germany)
Outstanding Merit: *The Nun's Story*
Actor (Drama): Anthony Franciosa, *Career*
Actor (Comedy/Musical): Jack Lemmon, *Some Like It Hot*
Actress (Drama): Elizabeth Taylor, *Suddenly, Last Summer*
Actress (Comedy/Musical): Marilyn Monroe, *Some Like It Hot*
Supporting Actor: Stephen Boyd, *Ben-Hur*
Supporting Actress: Susan Kohner, *Imitation of Life*
Director: William Wyler, *Ben-Hur*
Score: Ernest Gold, *On the Beach*
Most Promising Newcomers (Male): James Shigeta, Barry Coe, Troy Donahue, George Hamilton
Most Promising Newcomers (Female): Tuesday Weld, Angie Dickinson, Janet Munro, Stella Stevens
World Film Favorite (Male): Rock Hudson
World Film Favorite (Female): Doris Day
Best Film Promoting International Understanding: *The Diary of Anne Frank*
Cecil B. DeMille Award: Bing Crosby

Samuel Goldwyn Award: *Room at the Top*
Journalistic Merit: Hedda Hopper, Louella Parsons
Special Award for Directing the Chariot Race in *Ben-Hur*: Andrew Marton
Special Awards to Famous Silent Film Stars: Francis X. Bushman, Ramon Novarro [stars of 1926 *Ben-Hur*]

Directors Guild of America
Direction: William Wyler, *Ben-Hur*
D. W. Griffith Award: George Stevens
Critic Award: John E. Fitzgerald, *Our Sunday Visitor*

***** *The 400 Blows*   NYC CAN
Truffaut's feature debut was an enormously sympathetic (and largely autobiographical) portrait of a misunderstood juvenile delinquent—and with all that was to come, it remained his best film.

**** James Stewart, *Anatomy of a Murder*   NYC VEN
A characteristically sharp, canny performance in Otto Preminger's *Basic Instinct of 1959* that probably would have had the Oscar if MGM hadn't campaigned so hard for a *Ben-Hur* sweep.

New York Film Critics Circle
Picture: *Ben-Hur*
Foreign Film: *The 400 Blows*
Actor: James Stewart, *Anatomy of a Murder*
Actress: Audrey Hepburn, *The Nun's Story*

Director: Fred Zinnemann, *The Nun's Story*
Screenplay: Wendell Mayes, *Anatomy of a Murder*

National Board of Review
Best American Film: *The Nun's Story*
Ben-Hur
Anatomy of a Murder
The Diary of Anne Frank
Middle of the Night
The Man Who Understood Women
Some Like It Hot
Suddenly, Last Summer
On the Beach
North by Northwest
Best Foreign Film: *Wild Strawberries*
Room at the Top
Aparajito
The Roof
Look Back in Anger
Actor: Victor Seastrom [Sjöström], *Wild Strawberries*
Actress: Simone Signoret, *Room at the Top*
Supporting Actor: Hugh Griffith, *Ben-Hur*
Supporting Actress: Dame Edith Evans, *The Nun's Story*
Director: Fred Zinnemann, *The Nun's Story*
Special Citation: To Ingmar Bergman, for the body of his work
To Andrew Marton and Yakima Canutt, for their direction of the chariot race in *Ben-Hur*

Photoplay Gold Medal Awards
Gold Medal: *Pillow Talk*
Most Popular Male Star: Rock Hudson
Most Popular Female Star: Doris Day

British Academy Awards
Film: *Ben-Hur*
British Film: *Sapphire*
Actor (British): Peter Sellers, *I'm All Right Jack*
Actor (Foreign): Jack Lemmon, *Some Like It Hot*
Actress (British): Audrey Hepburn, *The Nun's Story*
Actress (Foreign): Shirley MacLaine, *Ask Any Girl*
Screenplay: Frank Harvey, John Boulting, Alan Hackney, *I'm All Right Jack*
Robert Flaherty Documentary Award: *The Savage Eye* (Ben Maddow, Sidney Meyers, Joseph Strick, USA)

**** *Black Orpheus* AAW GLO CAN
The legend of Orpheus retold in Rio during Carnival, with Orpheus a streetcar driver who has to take his tram into the Underworld to rescue Eurydice. The quintessential film of the United Nations era, a bit naive and traveloguish in its view of South American life (or in its notion that what a story of New World life most needs is an underpinning in Old World myth), but filled with color, music, and good humor—and perfectly delightful. It deservedly made composer Antonio Carlos Jobim world-famous and sparked a Brazilian music craze.

Cannes Film Festival
Palme d'Or: *Black Orpheus* (Marcel Camus, France-Brazil)
Special Jury Prize: *Stars* (Konrad Wolf, Bulgaria–East Germany)
International Prize: Luis Buñuel, *Nazarin* (Mexico), and for his body of work
Comedy Prize: *Policarpo dei Tappeti* (Mario Soldati, Italy)
Actor: collectively to Dean Stockwell, Bradford Dillman, Orson Welles, *Compulsion* (USA)

Actress: Simone Signoret, *Room at the Top* (UK)
Director: François Truffaut, *The 400 Blows* (France)
Best Selection: Czechoslovakia
Mention: *Shirasagi* [*The White Heron*] (Teinosuke Kinugasa, Japan)
Tribute: In memoriam, Alain Kaminker, who disappeared in the sea during production of *La Mer et les Jours*
International Critics Prize: *Hiroshima, Mon Amour* (Alain Resnais, France), *Araya* (Margot Benacerraf, Venezuela)

*** *General Della Rovere*
VEN
Rossellini and De Sica, together again—as director and actor respectively, for a nice old-fashioned neorealist tale about a small-time crook posing as a big-time Resistance leader (just call it *A Tale of Two Open Cities.* . . .)

Venice Film Festival
Golden Lion: *General Della Rovere* (Roberto Rossellini, Italy), *The Great War* (Mario Monicelli, Italy)
Actor: James Stewart, *Anatomy of a Murder* (USA)
Actress: Madeline Robinson, *Double Tour* (France)
Special Jury Prize: Ingmar Bergman, *The Magician* (Sweden)
International Critics Prize: *Ashes and Diamonds* (Andrzej Wajda, Poland)

*** *Les Cousins*   BER
Largely forgotten now among the first wave of the French new wave, Claude Chabrol's second film deserves rediscovery—it's great nasty fun. The story of two Parisian college students more interested in drinking and seduction than their studies, it's like a Parisian boulevardier's version of *Animal House*, though more quaint than shocking today— no matter what terrible things they do, they always do them in a suit and tie, and usually with Wagner blasting on the hi-fi.

Berlin Film Festival
Golden Bear: *Les Cousins* (Claude Chabrol, France)
Actor: Jean Gabin, *Archiméde le Clochard* [*The Magnificent Tramp*] (France)
Actress: Shirley MacLaine, *Ask Any Girl* (USA)
Outstanding Single Performance: Hayley Mills, *Tiger Bay* (UK)
Director: Akira Kurosawa, *The Hidden Fortress* (Japan)
Documentary: Gold: *White Wilderness* (Walt Disney, USA)
International Critics Prize: *The Hidden Fortress*

Harvard Lampoon Movie Worsts
Ten worst pictures:
The Best of Everything
The Miracle
Career
Never So Few
Solomon and Sheba
The Tempest
A Summer Place
They Came to Cordura
Say One for Me
Hercules
Worst Actor: Sal Mineo, *Tonka*
Worst Actress: Lana Turner, *Imitation of Life*
Worst Supporting Actor: Dick Nixon, *The Best of Benson*
Worst Supporting Actress: Sandra Dee, *A Summer Place*
The Bratwurst Award (to the worst child actor of the year,

presented by the Delicatessen
Owners' Assn.): Eddie Hodges,
A Hole in the Head

The Wish-It-Were-True Award:
Bing Crosby as a celibate priest
in *Say One for Me*

Box Office (Domestic Rentals)

1	*Auntie Mame*	$9,000,000	WB
2	*The Shaggy Dog*	8,100,000	Disney
3	*Some Like It Hot*	7,200,000	UA
4	*Pillow Talk*	7,000,000	Uni
5	*Imitation of Life*	6,400,000	Uni
6	*The Nun's Story*	6,300,000	WB
7	*Anatomy of a Murder*	5,500,000	Col
	North by Northwest	5,500,000	MGM
9	*Sleeping Beauty*	5,300,000	Disney
10	*Rio Bravo*	5,200,000	WB
Other films of note:			
12	*Hercules*	4,700,000	Embassy
	The Horse Soldiers	4,700,000	UA
21	*Geisha Boy*	3,200,000	Par
	The Seventh Voyage of Sinbad	3,200,000	Col
57	*Gidget*	1,500,000	Col

*1959 looks like a normal Hollywood year, with hits from Rock and Doris, Otto
and Hitch, Walt and the Duke. But there's a harbinger of things to come at #12 with
Hercules, a run-of-the-mill Italian-made muscleman picture which Joseph E. Levine,
the American distributor of Godzilla, hyped into a hit through the first modern
marketing campaign—advertising it on TV and in newspapers, then opening it in
hundreds of theaters at once before word could get out about how bad it was. Levine
atoned by using his profits to become a class producer of international successes like
8½, The Graduate, and The Lion in Winter, even enabling Jean-Luc Godard and
Jack Palance to caricature him with his own money in Contempt.*

Gebert's Golden Armchairs

Howard Hawks' western *Rio
Bravo* returns to the
preoccupations of his *Only Angels
Have Wings* (to the point that
you can match up the major
characters in each), exploring the
nature of masculinity—what it is,
how to get it back if you lost it,
can you be one of the boys if
you're Angie Dickinson (the
answer to the last, this being
Hawks rather than real life, a
resounding yes). As a laugh
machine I think *Some Like It Hot*
is overrated, but Monroe was
never more fetching or vulnerable,
and Lemmon's neurotic
spinelessness is taken to its most
emasculated extreme.

Best American Film: *Rio Bravo*
Best Foreign Film: *The 400 Blows*
Best Actor: Jack Lemmon, *Some
Like It Hot*
Best Actress: Marilyn Monroe,
Some Like It Hot
Best Director: Howard Hawks,
Rio Bravo

1960

"New Wave: Dead Champagne" declared *Variety*, echoing French producers at Cannes who hoped that the wave of French youth films started by Truffaut, Godard, Chabrol, and Resnais was over and that they would be back to Fernandel comedies and Bardot sex films as soon as possible. It was a strange Cannes, with *Ben-Hur* (unenthusiastically received) showing next to *La Dolce Vita* and *L'Avventura*—which, unlike the great discoveries of the 1950s, were poorly received by the attending public and by mainstream critics. The audience at *L'Avventura* was so hostile that both director Michelangelo Antonioni and star Lea Massari left the screening in tears, and *Films in Review* wrote that "presenting [*L'Avventura*] at Cannes is an insult to intelligent cinema . . . the film needs to be cut—right down the middle."

At the awards ceremony, a mixture of boos and cheers greeted *La Dolce Vita*'s Palme d'Or—but outright derision greeted the Antonioni film's Special Jury Prize. Within two years *La Dolce Vita* would be the most successful foreign film ever released in the U.S., and *L'Avventura* would be voted the second best film of all time in the *Sight & Sound* international critics poll.

Academy Awards

**** *The Apartment* AAW GLO DGA NYC BAA
Billy Wilder's satirical comedy about the the employee (Jack Lemmon) and the mistress (Shirley MacLaine) of the boss who's using them both (Fred MacMurray) was several steps more cynical than any big Hollywood movie before it—even though, if you dig hard enough, you can find the candy center of the poison pill. In any case, that doesn't detract from MacLaine's quirky, immensely likable comic performance.

Picture
The Apartment (UA, Mirisch, Billy Wilder)
The Alamo (UA, Batjac, John Wayne)
Elmer Gantry (UA, Lancaster-Brooks)
Sons and Lovers (20th Century–Fox, Jerry Wald)
The Sundowners (Warner Bros., Fred Zinnemann)

*** Burt Lancaster in *Elmer Gantry* AAW GLO NYC BAA
As Sinclair Lewis' traveling salesman turned evangelist, Lancaster is a powerhouse—though he doesn't leave you in much doubt that Gantry's a phony. And the movie leaves itself an out by making the Aimee Semple Macpherson character (Jean Simmons) his dupe—hardly the case in real life.

Actor
Burt Lancaster, *Elmer Gantry*
Trevor Howard, *Sons and Lovers*
Jack Lemmon, *The Apartment*
Laurence Olivier, *The Entertainer*
Spencer Tracy, *Inherit the Wind*

• **Elizabeth Taylor in**
Butterfield 8 AAW
Taylor wakes up in a strange
apartment, wanders around,
spritzes perfume, takes a drink,
scratches herself, examines
the furs in a closet, writes a note
in lipstick, lights a cigarette,
and throws an ashtray at a mirror
before stalking out to find a
cab. With its fetishistically
precise depiction of the fleshy,
frowzy Taylor's morning rituals,
every moment lovingly
recorded in queasily bright
Metrocolor, the first ten
minutes of *Butterfield 8*
establish it as the missing link
between MGM's glamorizing of
the divine Garbo and Andy
Warhol's real-time films of
strung-out drag queens (who
were probably *Butterfield 8*'s
most receptive audience,
anyway). The rest is just a trashy
rehash of *Room at the Top*
(complete with Laurence
Harvey and car crash), in
which Taylor is several notches
better than the movie—but
who could care?

Actress
Elizabeth Taylor, *Butterfield 8*
Greer Garson, *Sunrise at
Campobello*
Deborah Kerr, *The Sundowners*
Shirley MacLaine, *The Apartment*
Melina Mercouri, *Never on
Sunday*

Supporting Actor
Peter Ustinov, *Spartacus*
Peter Falk, *Murder, Inc.*
Jack Kruschen, *The Apartment*
Sal Mineo, *Exodus*
Chill Wills, *The Alamo*

Supporting Actress
Shirley Jones, *Elmer Gantry*
Glynis Johns, *The Sundowners*
Shirley Knight, *The Dark at the
Top of the Stairs*
Janet Leigh, *Psycho*
Mary Ure, *Sons and Lovers*

Director
Billy Wilder, *The Apartment*
Jack Cardiff, *Sons and Lovers*
Jules Dassin, *Never on Sunday*
Alfred Hitchcock, *Psycho*
Fred Zinnemann, *The Sundowners*

Original Screenplay: Billy
Wilder, I.A.L. Diamond, *The
Apartment*
Adapted Screenplay: Richard
Brooks, *Elmer Gantry*
Cinematography/B&W: Freddie
Francis, *Sons and Lovers*
Cinematography/Color: Russell
Metty, *Spartacus*
Dramatic or Comedy Score:
Ernest Gold, *Exodus*
Musical Score: Morris Stoloff,
Harry Sukman, *Song Without
End*
Song: "Never on Sunday," *Never
on Sunday,* ml: Manos
Hadjidakis
Art Direction/B&W: Alexander
Trauner, *The Apartment*
Art Direction/Color: Alexander
Golitzen, *Spartacus*
Costume Design/B&W: Edith
Head, *The Facts of Life*
Costume Design/Color: Valles
and Bill Thomas, *Spartacus*
Editing: *The Apartment*
Sound: *The Alamo*
Special Effects: *The Time
Machine*

Short/Cartoon: *Munro* (William L. Snyder)
Short/Live Action: *Day of the Painter* (Little Movies, Ezra R. Baker)
Documentary/Feature: *The Horse with the Flying Tail* (Walt Disney)
Documentary/Short: *Giuseppina* (James Hill)
Foreign-Language Film: *The Virgin Spring* (Sweden)
Jean Hersholt Humanitarian Award: Sol Lesser
Special Awards:
Gary Cooper
Stan Laurel
Hayley Mills, for *Pollyanna*, outstanding juvenile performance

Golden Globes

Picture (Drama): *Spartacus*
Picture (Comedy): *The Apartment*
Picture (Musical): *Song Without End*
English-Language Foreign Film: *The Man With the Green Carnation* [*The Trials of Oscar Wilde*]
Foreign-Language Films: *La Vérité* (France), *The Virgin Spring* (Sweden)
Merit Award: *The Sundowners*
Actor (Drama): Burt Lancaster, *Elmer Gantry*
Actor (Comedy/Musical): Jack Lemmon, *The Apartment*
Actress (Drama): Greer Garson, *Sunrise at Campobello*
Actress (Comedy/Musical): Shirley MacLaine, *The Apartment*
Supporting Actor: Sal Mineo, *Exodus*
Supporting Actress: Janet Leigh, *Psycho*
Director: Jack Cardiff, *Sons and Lovers*
Score: Dimitri Tiomkin, *The Alamo*

Most Promising Newcomers (Male): Michael Callan, Mark Damon, Brett Halsey
Most Promising Newcomers (Female): Ina Balin, Nancy Kwan, Hayley Mills
World Film Favorite (Male): Rock Hudson, Tony Curtis
World Film Favorite (Female): Gina Lollobrigida
Best Film Promoting International Understanding: *Hand in Hand* (UK)
Cecil B. DeMille Award: Fred Astaire
Samuel Goldwyn Award: *Never on Sunday* (Greece)
Special Award for Artistic Integrity: Stanley Kramer
Special Awards for Comedy: Cantínflas

Directors Guild of America

Direction: Billy Wilder, *The Apartment*
D. W. Griffith Award: Frank Borzage
Honorary Lifetime Member: Y. Frank Freeman
Critic Award: Paul Beckley, *New York Herald Tribune*

New York Film Critics Circle

Picture: *The Apartment, Sons and Lovers* (tie)
Foreign Film: *Hiroshima, Mon Amour*
Actor: Burt Lancaster, *Elmer Gantry*
Actress: Deborah Kerr, *The Sundowners*
Director: Billy Wilder, *The Apartment*; Jack Cardiff, *Sons and Lovers* (tie)
Screenplay: Billy Wilder, I.A.L. Diamond, *The Apartment*

National Board of Review

Best Film: *Sons and Lovers*
The Alamo
The Sundowners

Inherit the Wind
Sunrise at Campobello
Elmer Gantry
Home from the Hill
The Apartment
Wild River
The Dark at the Top of the Stairs
Best Foreign Film: *The World of Apu*
General Della Rovere
The Angry Silence
I'm All Right Jack
Hiroshima, Mon Amour
Actor: Robert Mitchum, *The Sundowners, Home From the Hill*
Actress: Greer Garson, *Sunrise at Campobello*
Supporting Actor: George Peppard, *Home from the Hill*
Supporting Actress: Shirley Jones, *Elmer Gantry*
Director: Jack Cardiff, *Sons and Lovers*

British Academy Awards
Film: *The Apartment*
British Film: *Saturday Night and Sunday Morning*
Actor (British): Peter Finch, *The Trials of Oscar Wilde* [*The Man With the Green Carnation*]
Actor (Foreign): Jack Lemmon, *The Apartment*
Actress (British): Rachel Roberts, *Saturday Night and Sunday Morning*
Actress (Foreign): Shirley MacLaine, *The Apartment*
Screenplay: Bryan Forbes, *The Angry Silence*

***** *La Dolce Vita*
CAN NYC '61
Fellini's panoramic view of life in a decadent, spiritually empty Rome probably has as much to say about modern life as *L'Avventura*—but *La Dolce Vita* depicts emptiness and ennui by being fast-paced and full of life (and, unlike *8½* three years later, by believing that it matters).

** *L'Avventura* CAN
Michelangelo Antonioni's film about a socialite who mysteriously vanishes on an island, and the subsequent search, which turns into a sort of *Hunting for Godot*. I grant that Antonioni's depiction of modern man's existential condition brought the movies forward about ten years in one jolt (that is, to where art and literature already were), and that his eye for images, ear for natural sounds, and sense of how events unfold in real time are all superb—and influential on everyone from Kubrick and Polanski to Bergman and Tarkovsky. But thirty minutes into it, when they start wandering around looking under rocks for a 5' 7" female—which is *all* they will do for the next two hours—I suddenly develop a deep spiritual hunger to see what else is on TV. As dissections of the bourgeoisie go, give me Buñuel's discreet charm over Antonioni's existential ennui any day.

Cannes Film Festival
[NOTE: The Jury decided to place the masterpieces *The Virgin Spring* (Ingmar Bergman, Sweden) and *The Young One* (Luis Buñuel, Mexico) out of competition]
Palme d'Or: *La Dolce Vita* (Federico Fellini, Italy)
Jury Prize: *L'Avventura* (Michelangelo Antonioni, Italy),

Odd Obsession (Kon Ichikawa, Japan)
Actor: none awarded
Actress: Melina Mercouri, *Never on Sunday* (Greece), Jeanne Moreau, *Moderato Cantabile* (France)
Best Selection: USSR, for *Ballad of a Soldier* (Grigori Chukhrai), *Lady With a Dog* (Josef Heifitz)

Venice Film Festival
Golden Lion: *La Passage du Rhine* (André Cayatte, France)
Special Prize: *Rocco and His Brothers* (Luchino Visconti, Italy)
Actor: John Mills, *Tunes of Glory* (UK)
Actress: Shirley MacLaine, *The Apartment* (USA)
Best First Feature: Florestano Vancini, *That Long Night in '43* (Italy)
International Critics Prize: *The Motorcart* (Marco Ferreri, Italy), *Rocco and His Brothers*

Berlin Film Festival
Golden Bear: *Lazarillo de Tormes* (Cesar Ardavin, Spain)
Silver Bear/Comedy: *The Love Game* (Philippe de Broca, France)
Actor: Fredric March, *Inherit the Wind* (USA)
Actress: Juliette Mayniel, *Country Fair* (France)
Director: Jean-Luc Godard, *Breathless* (France)

Documentary: *Faja Lobbi* (The Netherlands)
International Critics Prize: *The Angry Silence* (Guy Green, UK)

Harvard Lampoon Movie Worsts
Ten worst pictures:
Butterfield 8
Strangers When We Meet
The Gazebo
Ice Palace
Exodus
It Started in Naples
Pepe
Pollyanna
Because They're Young
High Time
Worst Actor: Frank Sinatra, *Can-Can*
Worst Actress: Eva Marie Saint, *Exodus*
Worst Supporting Actor: Eddie Fisher, *Butterfield 8*
Worst Supporting Actress: Annette Funicello, *The Horse Masters*
The Bratwurst Award (to the most obnoxious child star of the year): David Ladd, *A Dog of Flanders*
The Merino Award (to that motion picture personality who, in the opinion of the officers, editors, and staff of the *Harvard Lampoon*, has, during the past year, done the most to enhance the fame and glory of the merino [sheep]): Maureen O'Hara

Box Office (Domestic Rentals)

1	*Ben-Hur*	$17,300,000	MGM
	[through 1964:	38,000,000]	
2	*Can-Can*	10,000,000	Fox
3	*Psycho*	9,200,000	Par
4	*Operation Petticoat*	7,000,000	Uni
5	*Suddenly, Last Summer*	6,875,000	Col
6	*The Apartment*	6,850,000	UA
7	*Solomon and Sheba*	6,500,000	UA
8	*On the Beach*	6,200,000	UA

9	*Butterfield 8*	6,000,000	MGM
10	*From the Terrace*	6,000,000	Fox
Other films of note:			
13	*Elmer Gantry*	5,200,000	UA
14	*Journey to the Center of the Earth*	5,000,000	Fox
15	*G.I. Blues*	4,300,000	Par
34	*Hercules Unchained*	2,500,000	Embassy
39	*The Magnificent Seven*	2,250,000	UA
49	*I Passed for White*	1,700,000	Allied Artists
54	*Goliath and the Barbarians*	1,600,000	American Int'l
56	*13 Ghosts*	1,500,000	Col
64	*The Fall of the House of Usher*	1,450,000	American Int'l

Take that, Hercules*! MGM's Oscar-winning beefcake epic far outgrosses a* Hercules *sequel and an attempt by* Goliath *to cash in on his fellow mythological figure's success—among numerous muscleman pictures suddenly flooding these shores. Elsewhere in the exploitation sweepstakes,* I Passed for White *passed for an imitation of* Imitation of Life, *and William Castle made decent money with the gimmick of Illusion-O (if you were brave, you could look through the red side of what looked suspiciously like a leftover pair of 3-D glasses, and see the* 13 Ghosts; *if you weren't brave enough, you could look through the blue side and they would be invisible). At the bottom is the one drive-in flick that everyone would actually remember years later—the first of Roger Corman's Edgar Allan Poe series.*

Gebert's Golden Armchairs

Good as Burt Lancaster is, it isn't just Hitchcock's clever plot that makes Norman Bates the most memorable and disquieting character of the year.

Best American Film: *The Apartment*

Best Foreign Film: *La Dolce Vita*
Best Actor: Anthony Perkins, *Psycho*
Best Actress: Shirley MacLaine, *The Apartment*
Best Director: Federico Fellini, *La Dolce Vita*

1961

The year before the New York newspaper strike shows the apogee of the New York Critics Circle's influence on Oscar. They agree on the top three for only the fourth time in 25 years, all of them the kinds of things New York championed—a Broadway musical, an oh-so-serious drama, and even Oscar's lone foreign-language film acting prize.

Academy Awards

**** *West Side Story* AAW GLO DGA NYC
More musicals won the Best Picture Oscar in the '60s than any other decade, and of the four this is far and away the best—both innovative and surefire entertainment. The further it gets from juvenile-delinquent reality, the less its flaws (Wood and Beymer as Noo Yawk street kids?) matter, and the more it seems to inhabit the same kind of stylized fantasy world as *Top Hat* or *An American in Paris*.

Picture
West Side Story (UA, Mirisch–B&P Enterprises)
Fanny (Warner Bros., Joshua Logan)
The Guns of Navarone (Columbia, Carl Foreman)
The Hustler (20th Century–Fox, Robert Rossen)
Judgment at Nuremberg (UA, Stanley Kramer)

*** **Maximilian Schell in *Judgment at Nuremberg*** AAW GLO NYC
The central dramatic conflict in Stanley Kramer and Abby Mann's Holocaust trial drama—between Nazi judge Burt Lancaster, who finally accepts his guilt, and defense attorney Maximilian Schell, arguing the Nuremberg defense—focuses on the most universal and also least interesting aspect of Nazi crime. The real Nazi question isn't individual responsibility—it's man's capacity for evil, period, and (in Hannah Arendt's overworked phrase) the banality of same; in reality the Lancaster character would have sat in the box without saying a word or acknowledging a thing, like Eichmann—whom Schell later played in *The Man in the Glass Booth*. Anyway, to talk about the performance, Schell is forceful and uses his deep voice to good effect, but the catharsis of seeing him get told what's what by Lancaster is pretty small stuff given the enormity of the subject.

Actor
Maximilian Schell, *Judgment at Nuremberg*
Charles Boyer, *Fanny*
Paul Newman, *The Hustler*
Spencer Tracy, *Judgment at Nuremberg*
Stuart Whitman, *The Mark*

*** **Sophia Loren in** *Two Women*   AAW NYC BAA CAN

Vittorio De Sica's return to neorealism stars Sophia Loren as a gutsy mother hauling herself and her daughter around the Italian countryside during the dying days of World War II. A well-made and moving piece—though it would figure that the only foreign-language film performance to win an Oscar would go to a character type Oscar could feel very comfortable with, the strong, self-sacrificing mother. (Trivia: though the only foreign-language *film* performance, it's not the only foreign-*language* performance to win an Oscar—De Niro speaks only Italian in *Godfather II*.)

Actress
Sophia Loren, *Two Women*
Audrey Hepburn, *Breakfast at Tiffany's*
Piper Laurie, *The Hustler*
Geraldine Page, *Summer and Smoke*
Natalie Wood, *Splendor in the Grass*

Supporting Actor
George Chakiris, *West Side Story*
Montgomery Clift, *Judgment at Nuremberg*
Peter Falk, *Pocketful of Miracles*
Jackie Gleason, *The Hustler*
George C. Scott, *The Hustler*

Supporting Actress
Rita Moreno, *West Side Story*
Fay Bainter, *The Children's Hour*
Judy Garland, *Judgment at Nuremberg*
Lotte Lenya, *The Roman Spring of Mrs. Stone*
Una Merkel, *Summer and Smoke*

Director
Robert Wise, Jerome Robbins, *West Side Story*
Federico Fellini, *La Dolce Vita*
Stanley Kramer, *Judgment at Nuremberg*
Robert Rossen, *The Hustler*
J. Lee Thompson, *The Guns of Navarone*

Original Screenplay: William Inge, *Splendor in the Grass*
Adapted Screenplay: Abby Mann, *Judgment at Nuremberg*
Cinematography/B&W: Eugene Shuftan, *The Hustler*
Cinematography/Color: Daniel L. Fapp, *West Side Story*
Dramatic or Comedy Score: Henry Mancini, *Breakfast at Tiffany's*
Musical Score: Saul Chaplin, Johnny Green, Sid Ramin, Irwin Kostal, *West Side Story*
Song: "Moon River," *Breakfast at Tiffany's*, m: Henry Mancini, l: Johnny Mercer
Art Direction/B&W: Harry Horner, *The Hustler*
Art Direction/Color: Boris Leven, *West Side Story*
Costume Design/B&W: Piero Gherardi, *La Dolce Vita*
Costume Design/Color: Irene Sharaff, *West Side Story*
Editing: *West Side Story*
Sound: *West Side Story*
Special Effects: *The Guns of Navarone*
Short/Cartoon: *Ersatz* [*The Substitute*] (Zagreb Film, Dusan Vukotic, Czechoslovakia)
Short/Live Action: *Seawards the Great Ships*
Documentary/Feature: *Le Ciel et La Boue* [*The Sky Above, The Mud Below*] (Pierre-Dominique Gaisseau, France)
Documentary/Short: *Project Hope*
Foreign-Language Film:

Through a Glass Darkly
(Sweden)
Irving G. Thalberg Award:
Stanley Kramer
Jean Hersholt Humanitarian Award: George Seaton
Special Awards:
William Hendricks, for his outstanding patriotic service in the production of the Marine Corps film, *A Force in Readiness*
Fred L. Metzler
Jerome Robbins, for his brilliant achievements in choreography on film

Golden Globes
Picture (Drama): *The Guns of Navarone*
Picture (Comedy): *A Majority of One*
Picture (Musical): *West Side Story*
Foreign-Language Films:
Golden Globe: *Two Women* (Italy); **Silver Globes:** *The Important Man* (Mexico), *The Good Soldier Schweik* (West Germany)
Actor (Drama): Maximilian Schell, *Judgment at Nuremberg*
Actor (Comedy/Musical): Glenn Ford, *Pocketful of Miracles*
Actress (Drama): Geraldine Page, *Summer and Smoke*
Actress (Comedy/Musical): Rosalind Russell, *A Majority of One*
Supporting Actor: George Chakiris, *West Side Story*
Supporting Actress: Rita Moreno, *West Side Story*
Director: Stanley Kramer, *Judgment at Nuremberg*
Score: Dimitri Tiomkin, *Judgment at Nuremberg*
Song: "Town Without Pity," *Town Without Pity*, m: Dimitri Tiomkin, l: Ned Washington
Most Promising Newcomers (Male): Richard Beymer, Bobby Darin, Warren Beatty

Most Promising Newcomers (Female): Christine Kaufman, Ann-Margret, Jane Fonda
World Film Favorite (Male): Charlton Heston
World Film Favorite (Female): Marilyn Monroe
Best Film Promoting International Understanding: *A Majority of One*
Cecil B. DeMille Award: Judy Garland
Samuel Goldwyn Award for Best English Film: *The Mark*
Special Merit Award: Samuel Bronston, *El Cid* [producer]
Special Journalistic Merit Awards: Army Archerd, *Daily Variety*; Mike Connolly, *The Hollywood Reporter*

Directors Guild of America
Director: Robert Wise and Jerome Robbins, *West Side Story*
Honorary Lifetime Member: Hobe Morrison
Critic Award: John Beaufort, *Christian Science Monitor*

New York Film Critics Circle
Picture: *West Side Story*
Foreign Film: *La Dolce Vita*
Actor: Maximilian Schell, *Judgment at Nuremberg*
Actress: Sophia Loren, *Two Women*
Director: Robert Rossen, *The Hustler*
Screenplay: Abby Mann, *Judgment at Nuremberg*

National Board of Review
Best American Film: *Question 7*
The Hustler
West Side Story
The Innocents
The Hoodlum Priest
Summer and Smoke
The Young Doctors
Judgment at Nuremberg
One, Two, Three

Fanny
Best Foreign Film: *The Bridge*
La Dolce Vita
Two Women
*Saturday Night and Sunday
    Morning*
A Summer to Remember
Actor: Albert Finney, *Saturday
Night and Sunday Morning*
Actress: Geraldine Page, *Summer
and Smoke*
Supporting Actor: Jackie
Gleason, *The Hustler*
Supporting Actress: Ruby Dee,
A Raisin in the Sun
Director: Jack Clayton, *The
Innocents*

Photoplay **Gold Medal
Awards**
Gold Medal: *Splendor in the
Grass*
Most Popular Male Star: Troy
Donahue
Most Popular Female Star:
Connie Stevens

British Academy Awards
Film: *Ballad of a Soldier*, *The
Hustler*
British Film: *A Taste of Honey*
Actor (British): Peter Finch, *No
Love for Johnny*
Actor (Foreign): Paul Newman,
The Hustler
Actress (British): Dora Bryan, *A
Taste of Honey*
Actress (Foreign): Sophia Loren,
Two Women
Screenplay: Val Guest, Wolf
Mankowitz, *The Day the Earth
Caught Fire*; Shelagh
Delaney, Tony Richardson, *A
Taste of Honey*
Short Film: *Terminus* (John
Schlesinger, UK)
Animated Film: *101 Dalmatians*
(Walt Disney, USA)

*** *Viridiana* CAN
Luis Buñuel's *Nazarin*, about an
idealistic priest who finds it
impossible to live up to true
Christian ideals, had been
ambiguous enough to win a
prize from a Catholic group
and get the great Surrealist
invited back to Franco's Spain.
The result was a good film and
a great scandal: *Viridiana*,
about a young nun (actually,
novice) and her inevitable
corruption by the real world.
Somehow the script was
approved, and Buñuel just
finished it as Cannes opened,
rushing it to the festival without
the censors having fully
realized what they had allowed.
It won the Palme d'Or; then a
reporter for the Vatican
L'Osservatore Romano
denounced it as immoral—and
an international scandal
ensued, to the intense
embarrassment of the Franco
regime, which found itself
having deeply offended the
church.

*** *Such a Long Absence*
CAN
A Parisian bar owner (Alida
Valli) believes an amnesiac
derelict (Georges Wilson) to be
the husband who disappeared
in a Vichy jail during the war,
and tries to revive his lost
memories of their life together.
A sensitive tragedy, with an
unadorned style, regard for the
quiet details of ordinary life
and faultlessly observed
performances. If it seems
remarkable that a first-time
director should have managed
to win a Palme d'Or alongside
Buñuel with a film largely

forgotten today, the real story is that the award was given (by a jury including Francois Truffaut) to make up for *Hiroshima, Mon Amour*'s shabby treatment two years earlier—director Henri Colpi and co-writer Marguerite Duras had been editor and writer respectively of that trendsetting film.

Cannes Film Festival
Palme d'Or: *Viridiana* (Luis Buñuel, Spain), *Such a Long Absence* (Henri Colpi, France)
Special Jury Prize: *Mother Joan of the Angels* (Jerzy Kawalerowicz, Poland)
Actor: Anthony Perkins, *Goodbye Again* (USA)
Actress: Sophia Loren, *Two Women* (Italy)
Direction: Yulia Solntseva, for continuing the work of Alexander Dovzhenko, *Story of the Flaming Years* (USSR)
Best Selection: Italy
Gary Cooper Award: *A Raisin in the Sun* (Daniel Petrie, USA) [NOTE: award was created to recognize "the human valor of the films' content and treatment." Given only in 1961 and 1963.]
International Critics Prize: *The Hand in the Trap* (Leopoldo Torre Nilsson, Argentina)

** *Last Year at Marienbad* VEN
Alain Resnais' second feature—a cryptic, baroquely photographed drama about a man and a woman who seem to have met before—was acclaimed as a masterpiece at Venice by some, denounced as a put-on by others. Both have a point, in that it's basically a game played on the viewer, intentionally indecipherable, stylish as can be—and tiresome once you've figured it out. Think of it as a phase the cinema had to go through.

Venice Film Festival
Golden Lion: *Last Year at Marienbad* (Alain Resnais, France)
Silver Lion: *Peace to All Who Enter Here* (Alexander Alov, USSR)
Actor: Toshiro Mifune, *Yojimbo* (Japan)
Actress: Suzanne Flon, *Thou Shalt Not Kill* (Yugoslavia-France)
First Film: *The Bandits at Orgosolo* (Vittorio de Seta, Italy)
International Critics Prize: *Il Brigante* (Renato Castellani, Italy)
Italian Critics Prize: *Il Posto* [*The Sound of Trumpets*] (Ermanno Olmi, Italy)

*** *La Notte* BER
Michelangelo Antonioni's follow-up to *L'Avventura* is usually considered a weak successor, but with its urban-*noir* setting (exquisitely shot as ever) and lively performers like Marcello Mastroianni and Jeanne Moreau joining his usual alienation-poster-child Monica Vitti, it's kind of cool on a purely superficial '60s-hipster level. Wear a skinny tie and have an espresso afterwards.

Berlin Film Festival
Golden Bear: *La Notte* (Michelangelo Antonioni, Italy)
Silver Bear: *A Woman Is a Woman*

(Jean-Luc Godard, France), *Mabu* (Dae Jin-Kang, South Korea), *When It Does Not Come from the Heart* (Fons Rademakers, Netherlands)
Actor: Peter Finch, *No Love for Johnny* (UK)
Actress: Anna Karina, *A Woman Is a Woman*
Director: Bernhard Wicki, *The Miracle of Father Malachias* (West Germany)
Documentary: Gold: *Description of a Struggle* (Chris Marker, Israel)
International Critics Prize: Michelangelo Antonioni, for his body of work

Harvard Lampoon **Movie Worsts**
Ten worst pictures:
King of Kings and *Parrish* (tie)
By Love Possessed
The Devil at 4 O'Clock
The Last Sunset
The Young Doctors
Ada
Flower Drum Song
Babes in Toyland
Sergeants Three
The Kirk Douglas Award to the Worst Actor: Richard Beymer, *West Side Story*
Worst Actress: Susan Hayward, *Ada*, *Back Street*
The Cellophane Figleaf (for false modesty): to Warren Beatty, most of whose publicity has been based on his constant statements that he wants no publicity from the fact that he is Shirley MacLaine's younger brother
The Arrested Development Oblation (to that adult actor who has displayed the lowest level of maturity, always awarded to Jerry Lewis): Jerry Lewis [Lewis has indeed won this every year it has been given]
The Merino Award: To Rita Moreno, for saving *West Side Story* from Richard Beymer and Natalie Wood
The Roscoe Award: to Natalie Wood, for so gallantly persisting in her career despite a total inability to act

Box Office (Domestic Rentals)

1	The Guns of Navarone	$12,500,000	Col
2	Exodus	10,000,000	UA
3	The Parent Trap	9,300,000	Disney
4	The Absent-Minded Professor	9,100,000	Disney
5	The Alamo	8,000,000	UA
6	Swiss Family Robinson	7,900,000	Disney
7	Come September	7,500,000	Uni
8	The World of Suzie Wong	7,300,000	Par
9	Gone With the Wind [reissue]	6,700,000	MGM
10	101 Dalmatians	6,400,000	Disney
Other films of note:			
11	La Dolce Vita	6,000,000	Astor
13	North to Alaska	5,000,000	Fox
15	Return to Peyton Place	4,500,000	Par
20	The Misfits	4,100,000	UA
21	Never on Sunday	4,000,000	Lopert
26	Where the Boys Are	3,500,000	MGM
	Breakfast at Tiffany's	3,500,000	Par

| 42 | *Voyage to the Bottom of the Sea* | 2,300,000 | Fox |
| 47 | *Pit and the Pendulum* | 2,000,000 | American Int'l |

Disney dominated the box office—maybe because adults were all out catching the racy art-house sensation of the year, Fellini's La Dolce Vita, *still the foreign film that has sold more tickets than any other. Another art-house hit was blacklisted American director Jules Dassin's Greek-made* Never on Sunday, *about a prostitute with a six-day work-week (played by his wife, Melina Mercouri). Anything to avoid seeing John Wayne's $12 million* The Alamo—*hell, people even sat through* Gone With the Wind *again (in its Civil War Centenary Reissue—shortly to be followed by its Robert E. Lee's 150th Birthday Reissue, its 200th Anniversary of the Invention of the Hoop Skirt Reissue, and its We're Going to Beat* The Sound of Music *If Lee Has to Invade Austria Reissue).*

Gebert's Golden Armchairs

Being more of a film *noir* than a musical fan, I'd pick Robert Rossen's bleak, unsentimental character study of pool shark Paul Newman over *West Side Story*'s hoofer hoodlums, but that's not to say Oscar was wrong. *Breakfast at Tiffany's* probably ruined more young lives than any other film in the '60s—sending a generation of girls to New York to live like Holly Golightly, the kooky call girl whose life is a round of wild parties, great hats, and self-evasion. Some critics complained about the winsome Hepburn having taken the bite out of Truman Capote's character, but she's so lovely and vulnerable as the self-invented fantasy Holly that only the most coldblooded cynic could resist her. (We'd have *Midnight Cowboy* soon enough.) And like a crumbling one-man fortress of ham against the tide of Brandoesque naturalistic acting, Vincent Price moaned and went mad in glorious form in this, one of the best of Roger Corman's Poe chillers.

Best American Film: *The Hustler*
Best Foreign Film: *Such a Long Absence*
Best Actor: Vincent Price, *Pit and the Pendulum*
Best Actress: Audrey Hepburn, *Breakfast at Tiffany's*
Best Director: Robert Rossen, *The Hustler*

1962

Both a popular and a critical success, *Lawrence of Arabia* seems like an obvious Oscar choice. But would it have won the Oscar if the New York Film Critics Circle hadn't been put out of commission by the newspaper strike? Bosley Crowther didn't put it on his ten-best list, and later wrote that he would have campaigned for *A Taste of Honey*. But the "lady-reviewer" fiction would have turned up their noses at that tawdry British drama—and might have done so at *Lawrence*, with its hints of homosexuality, S&M, and European art filmmaking.

There was another candidate on Crowther's list that was expensive, star-studded, and conventional enough for both Oscar and the bluenoses among the critics, and it was on a true-blue subject that—with the critics' backing—Oscar could easily have found irresistible. (The National Board of Review did.) It's entirely possible that if the Circle *had* met, we might be talking instead about how *The Longest Day* robbed the obviously superior *Lawrence* of Best Picture.

Academy Awards

***** *Lawrence of Arabia*
AAW GLO DGA BAA
One of the first English-language films in which visual storytelling and atmosphere is more important than dialogue (which makes it the father of everything from *2001* to *Natural Born Killers*); one of the first to present a protagonist whom the audience is supposed to stand apart from and analyze rather than identify with and cheer on (which makes it the father of everything from *The Godfather* to *The Last Emperor*); one of the dividing lines between old movies and modern ones, which makes it a father of everything since.

Picture
Lawrence of Arabia (Columbia, Sam Spiegel)
The Longest Day (20th Century–Fox, Darryl F. Zanuck)
The Music Man (Warner Bros., Morton Da Costa)
Mutiny on the Bounty (MGM, Arcola, Aaron Rosenberg)
To Kill a Mockingbird (Universal, Pakula-Mulligan-Brentwood)

**** **Gregory Peck in *To Kill a Mockingbird*** AAW GLO
Twelve O'Clock High is probably the movie that makes the best use of Peck's ramrod-stiffness, *The Gunfighter* the one in which he gives the best performance. But this is the movie for which he'll be remembered, one of the great Hollywood liberals in one of the great Hollywood liberal movies, full of Kennedy-era confidence and firmness about

what is wrong (race prejudice) and what is right (standing against the mob), plus, as a bonus, an unusually sensitive picture of childhood, as much *The 400 Blows* as *The Yearling*. Stand up, child, your father is going by.

Actor
Gregory Peck, *To Kill a Mockingbird*
Burt Lancaster, *Birdman of Alcatraz*
Jack Lemmon, *Days of Wine and Roses*
Marcello Mastroianni, *Divorce—Italian Style*
Peter O'Toole, *Lawrence of Arabia*

*** Anne Bancroft in *The Miracle Worker* AAW BOR BAA
The movie is the best of all the Oscar-winners about people with disabilities—a spare, unsentimental, and authentic-feeling account of the blind-deaf child Helen Keller's (Patty Duke) transformation from an uncontrollable vegetable to a member of the human community in the hands of teacher Annie Sullivan (Bancroft). That said, Bancroft's part is still just an inspirational one at heart, and she did better elsewhere—especially, of course, in *The Graduate*.

Actress
Anne Bancroft, *The Miracle Worker*
Bette Davis, *What Ever Happened to Baby Jane?*
Katharine Hepburn, *Long Day's Journey into Night*
Geraldine Page, *Sweet Bird of Youth*
Lee Remick, *Days of Wine and Roses*

Supporting Actor
Ed Begley, *Sweet Bird of Youth*
Victor Buono, *What Ever Happened to Baby Jane?*
Telly Savalas, *Birdman of Alcatraz*
Omar Sharif, *Lawrence of Arabia*
Terence Stamp, *Billy Budd*

Supporting Actress
Patty Duke, *The Miracle Worker*
Mary Badham, *To Kill a Mockingbird*
Shirley Knight, *Sweet Bird of Youth*
Angela Lansbury, *The Manchurian Candidate*
Thelma Ritter, *Birdman of Alcatraz*

Director
David Lean, *Lawrence of Arabia*
Pietro Germi, *Divorce—Italian Style*
Robert Mulligan, *To Kill a Mockingbird*
Arthur Penn, *The Miracle Worker*
Frank Perry, *David and Lisa*

Original Screenplay: Ennio de Concini, Alfredo Giannetti, Pietro Germi, *Divorce—Italian Style*
Adapted Screenplay: Horton Foote, *To Kill a Mockingbird*
Cinematography/B&W: Jean Bourgoin, Walter Wottitz, *The Longest Day*
Cinematography/Color: Freddie Young, *Lawrence of Arabia*
Original Score: Maurice Jarre, *Lawrence of Arabia*
Adapted Score: Ray Heindorf, *The Music Man*
Song: "Days of Wine and Roses,"

Days of Wine and Roses,
m: Henry Mancini, l: Johnny
Mercer
Art Direction/B&W: Alexander
Golitzen, Henry Bumstead, *To
Kill a Mockingbird*
Art Direction/Color: John Box,
Lawrence of Arabia
Costume Design/B&W: Norma
Koch, *What Ever Happened to
Baby Jane?*
Costume Design/Color: Mary
Wills, *The Wonderful World of
the Brothers Grimm*
Editing: *Lawrence of Arabia*
Sound: *Lawrence of Arabia*
Special Effects: *The Longest Day*
Short/Cartoon: *The Hole* (John
and Faith Hubley)
Short/Live Action: *Heureux
Anniversaire* [*Happy
Anniversary*] (Pierre Etaix)
Documentary/Feature: *Black
Fox*
Documentary/Short: *Dylan
Thomas*
Foreign-Language Film:
Sundays and Cybéle (France)
**Jean Hersholt Humanitarian
Award:** Steve Broidy

**** *Divorce—Italian Style*
AAW GLO CAN
Thirty years of bad Italian sex
comedies had to begin with
one good one, and this is it—a
sly, often hilarious black
comedy about a middle-aged
aristocrat (Marcello Mastroianni)
wanting to get rid of his wife so
he can marry the luscious
young thing he has the hots for.

Golden Globes
Picture (Drama): *Lawrence of
Arabia*
Picture (Comedy): *That Touch of
Mink*
Picture (Musical): *The Music
Man*

Foreign-Language Films:
Divorce—Italian Style; *Best of
Enemies* (both Italy)
Actor (Drama): Gregory Peck,
To Kill a Mockingbird
Actor (Comedy/Musical):
Marcello Mastroianni,
Divorce—Italian Style
Actress (Drama): Geraldine
Page, *Sweet Bird of Youth*
Actress (Comedy/Musical):
Rosalind Russell, *Gypsy*
Supporting Actor: Omar Sharif,
Lawrence of Arabia
Supporting Actress: Angela
Lansbury, *The Manchurian
Candidate*
Director: David Lean, *Lawrence
of Arabia*
Cinematography (Color):
Freddie Young, *Lawrence of
Arabia*
Cinematography (B&W): Henri
Persin, Walter Wottitz, Jean
Bourgoin, *The Longest Day*
Original Score: Elmer Bernstein,
To Kill a Mockingbird
**Most Promising Newcomers
(Male):** Keir Dullea, Omar
Sharif, Terence Stamp
**Most Promising Newcomers
(Female):** Patty Duke, Sue
Lyon, Rita Tushingham
World Film Favorite (Male):
Rock Hudson
World Film Favorite (Female):
Doris Day
**Best Film Promoting
International Understanding:**
To Kill a Mockingbird
Cecil B. DeMille Award: Bob
Hope
Samuel Goldwyn Award:
Sundays and Cybéle (France)

Directors Guild of America
Director: David Lean, *Lawrence
of Arabia*

National Board of Review
Best English-Language Film:
The Longest Day

Billy Budd
The Miracle Worker
Lawrence of Arabia
Long Day's Journey into Night
Whistle Down the Wind
Requiem for a Heavyweight
A Taste of Honey
Birdman of Alcatraz
War Hunt
Best Foreign-Language Film:
Sundays and Cybéle
Barabbas
Divorce—Italian Style
The Island
Through a Glass Darkly
Actor: Jason Robards, *Long
Day's Journey into Night, Tender Is
the Night*
Actress: Anne Bancroft, *The
Miracle Worker*
Supporting Actor: Burgess
Meredith, *Advise and Consent*
Supporting Actress: Angela
Lansbury, *The Manchurian
Candidate, All Fall Down*
Director: David Lean, *Lawrence
of Arabia*

Photoplay Gold Medal Awards
Gold Medal: *The Miracle Worker*
Most Popular Male Star:
Richard Chamberlain
Most Popular Female Star:
Bette Davis

British Academy Awards
Film: *Lawrence of Arabia*
British Film: *Lawrence of Arabia*
Actor (British): Peter O'Toole,
Lawrence of Arabia
Actor (Foreign): Burt Lancaster,
Birdman of Alcatraz
Actress (British): Leslie Caron,
The L-Shaped Room
Actress (Foreign): Anne
Bancroft, *The Miracle Worker*
Screenplay: Robert Bolt,
Lawrence of Arabia
Short Film: *An Occurrence at
Owl Creek Bridge* (Robert
Enrico, France)

Short Animated Film: *The Apple*
(George Dunning, UK)

Cannes Film Festival
Palme d'Or: *The Given Word*
(Anselmo Duarte, Brazil)
Special Jury Prize: *The Trial of
Joan of Arc* (Robert Bresson,
France), *The Eclipse*
(Michelangelo Antonioni, Italy)
Collective Acting Awards: to
Katharine Hepburn, Ralph
Richardson, Jason Robards, Jr.,
Dean Stockwell, *Long Day's
Journey into Night* (USA); and to
Rita Tushingham, Murray
Melvin, *A Taste of Honey* (UK)
Best Adaptation of Stage Play:
Elektra (Michael Cacoyannis,
Greece)
Best Comedy: *Divorce—Italian
Style* (Pietro Germi, Italy)
Short Film Palme d'Or: *An
Occurrence at Owl Creek
Bridge* (Robert Enrico, France)
International Critics Prize: *The
Exterminating Angel* (Luis
Buñuel, Spain)

*** *My Name Is Ivan*   VEN
The life of an old-before-his-
time boy employed as a
courier by a Soviet platoon
during the dying days of the
Nazi invasion of Russia. Andrei
Tarkovsky's first film looks at
first glance like a typical
humanist '50s film, but it's
considerably more tough-
minded, and the character of
the boy is surprisingly
hardbitten—closer to *The Tin
Drum* than *Forbidden Games*.
The first debut film ever to win
the top prize at Venice,
impressively controlled and
with many of the qualities of
Andrei Roublev, Tarkovsky's
second film and masterpiece.

Venice Film Festival
Golden Lion: *My Name Is Ivan/ Ivan's Childhood* (Andrei Tarkovsky, USSR), *Family Diary* (Valerio Zurlini, Italy)
Special Jury Prize: *Vivre Sa Vie* [*My Life To Live*] (Jean-Luc Godard, France)
Actor: Burt Lancaster, *Birdman of Alcatraz* (USA)
Actress: Emmanuelle Riva, *Thérèse Desqueyroux* (France)
Best First Film: *David and Lisa* (Frank Perry, USA), *Los Innudados* (Fernando Birri, Argentina)
International Critics Prize: *Knife in the Water* (Roman Polanski, Poland)
Italian Critics Prize: *A Man for Burning* (Paolo and Vittorio Taviani, Valentino Orsina, Italy)
Pasinetti Italian Critics Prize: *Vivre Sa Vie* [*My Life to Live*]

Berlin Film Festival
Golden Bear: *A Kind of Loving* (John Schlesinger, Britain)
Actor: James Stewart, *Mr. Hobbs Takes a Vacation* (USA)
Actress: Rita Gam, Viveca Lindfors, *No Exit* (Argentina-UK-USA)
Director: Francesco Rosi, *Salvatore Giuliano* (Italy)
Documentary: *Galapagos* (Heinz Sielmann, West Germany)
First Film: Jon Yung Sun, *To the Last Day* (South Korea)
International Critics Prize: *Zoo* (Bert Haanstra, The Netherlands)

Harvard Lampoon Movie Worsts
Ten worst pictures:
The Chapman Report
If a Man Answers
Hemingway's Adventures of a Young Man
Diamond Head
The Wonderful World of the Brothers Grimm
White Slave Ship
Mutiny on the Bounty
Taras Bulba
Barabbas
The Mongols or *The Tartars* or *The Huns*
The Kirk Douglas Award to the Worst Actor: Charlton Heston, *Diamond Head*, *The Pigeon That Took Rome*
Worst Actress: Jane Fonda, *The Chapman Report*
The Please-Don't-Put-Us-Through-DeMille-Again Award (presented to that religious movie of the past year which best embodies the pretentious extravagance and blundering ineffectiveness of the traditional Christian Screen Spectacular): *Barabbas* and *Sodom and Gomorrah*
The Great Ceremonial Hot Dog (for the worst scenes of the past cinema season): The Naming of the Fairy Tale Characters in *The Wonderful World of the Brothers Grimm*, and The Polish Army Hurtling Over the Cliff in *Taras Bulba*
The Merino Award: Maureen O'Sullivan

Box Office (Domestic Rentals)
1	*West Side Story*	$19,000,000	UA
2	*Spartacus*	14,000,000	Uni
3	*El Cid*	11,500,000	Allied Artists
4	*Lover Come Back*	8,500,000	Uni
	That Touch of Mink	8,500,000	Uni
6	*King of Kings*	8,000,000	MGM

	The Music Man	8,000,000	War
8	*Hatari!*	7,000,000	Par
9	*Bon Voyage*	5,500,000	Disney
10	*Flower Drum Song*	5,000,000	Uni
	The Interns	5,000,000	Col
	Judgment at Nuremberg	5,000,000	UA
	What Ever Happened to Baby Jane?	5,000,000	WB

Other films of note:

16	*Lolita*	4,500,000	MGM
22	*Splendor in the Grass*	3,500,000	WB
25	*The Manchurian Candidate*	3,300,000	UA
26	*The Man Who Shot Liberty Valance*	3,200,000	Par
28	*Two Women*	3,000,000	Embassy
34	*The Road to Hong Kong*	2,600,000	UA
47	*Cape Fear*	1,900,000	Uni
49	*Tales of Terror*	1,750,000	American Int'l

Hollywood died on a bright smoggy day in 1962, when What Ever Happened to Baby Jane? *presented two legendary stars, every wrinkle visible, acting like the drag queens and junkies in an Andy Warhol picture. It was survived by Doris Day in* Lover Come Back *and* That Touch of Mink, *and by three European-shot historical epics— Stanley Kubrick's* Spartacus, *and* King of Kings *and* El Cid. *The latter were both products of the short-lived moviemaking empire of former MGM sales rep Samuel Bronston, who built a studio in Spain, had these two hits, then went bust on* 55 Days at Peking *and* The Fall of the Roman Empire.

Gebert's Golden Armchairs

For coming at the death of the studio era, 1962 is a surprisingly strong year, with a good six pictures—*Lawrence, Mockingbird,* Kubrick's *Lolita, The Manchurian Candidate,* John Ford's *The Man Who Shot Liberty Valance,* and Sam Peckinpah's *Ride the High Country*—that might rank as the best film in a weaker year . . . like 1963. Nevertheless, *Lawrence* stands head and shoulders above the rest as a seamless combination of intelligent, insightful writing and post–*L'Avventura* visual storytelling.

Writing just as the long-feared remake of *Lolita* goes into production, I am happy to pay tribute to Sellers' spectral, sublimely weird Clare Quilty, and especially to Shelley Winters' brilliantly comic-pathetic suburban mom, Charlotte the Haze cow, mother of luscious Lo.

Best American Film: *Lawrence of Arabia*
Best Foreign Film: *Divorce— Italian Style*
Best Actor: Peter Sellers, *Lolita*
Best Actress: Shelley Winters, *Lolita*
Best Director: David Lean, *Lawrence of Arabia*

1963

Paul Newman shouldn't have been one of Oscar's perennial losers until finally winning on his seventh nomination in 1986. In fact, it took hard work by a lot of people to screw up his surefire chances 23 years earlier, for *Hud*.

Hud entered Oscar season as the favorite, but in the meantime United Artists had picked up a British film called *Tom Jones*, and cannily screened it for the only people in America to whom star Albert Finney and director Tony Richardson were familiar—the New York critics. It worked; Bosley Crowther (who had said he would have voted for Richardson's *A Taste of Honey* in the strike year of 1962) and the other critics narrowly picked both *Tom Jones* and Finney, in an upset that helped propel both film and star to fame.

The impending success of a British film brought out Hedda Hopper and the other reactionaries who had blasted Oscar for liking *Hamlet* 15 years earlier. But this time they were cannier about it, hoping to split the art-house crowd by playing up the chances of a little independent film that had won Sidney Poitier a prize at Berlin the previous July—*Lilies of the Field*. In the end the strategy didn't exactly work; the genuinely popular *Tom Jones* still beat the downbeat *Hud* for Best Picture. But the anti-British faction had managed to turn an easy two-way race for Best Actor—which the better-known Newman would likely have won—into a three-way race with *two* well-liked Americans in it. The result, no doubt to the intense chagrin of some of the reactionaries, was a milestone for minorities in the movie business: the first leading player Oscar to go to an African-American.

Academy Awards

*** *Tom Jones* AAW GLO DGA NYC BOR BAA
Tony Richardson's rollicking, tongue-in-cheek costume picture was precisely the breath of fresh air that that genre needed in '63. Unfortunately, we're at precisely the point where its '60s-era innovations look the stalest, like a *Monkees* episode set in the 18th century (characters looking into the camera, sped-up action like a silent film—yeah, yeah, yeah, get on with it). In another 10 or 20 years, as it gets so far from the cutting edge that it begins to look downright classical, it will probably look very pleasing again.

Picture
Tom Jones (UA-Lopert, Woodfall)

233

America, America (Warner Bros., Athena)
Cleopatra (20th Century–Fox, Walter Wanger)
How the West Was Won (MGM, Cinerama, Bernard Smith)
Lilies of the Field (UA, Rainbow, Ralph Nelson)

*** Sidney Poitier in *Lilies of the Field* AAW GLO BER
A black handyman driving around rural California runs across a mission full of East German nuns, and is conned into building them a church. An indie production that became a sleeper hit in '63—a time, one should remember, when black Freedom Riders driving around the rural South tended to run into people with pointy hats who *weren't* nuns. In other words, it's precisely the fantasy of happy race relations that a troubled time wanted. But it's pleasant enough as a family film, and Poitier, who's the whole show, radiates old-fashioned movie star charisma.

Actor
Sidney Poitier, *Lilies of the Field*
Albert Finney, *Tom Jones*
Richard Harris, *This Sporting Life*
Rex Harrison, *Cleopatra*
Paul Newman, *Hud*

**** Patricia Neal in *Hud*
AAW NYC BOR BAA
About the best of the look-plain-and-win-an-Oscar actress winners, Neal's turn as the down-to-earth, decent housekeeper who has Hud's number (but falls for him anyway) has a lanky

believability that adds a lot to the credibility of Larry McMurtry's *Last Picture Show*–with-a-Message.

Actress
Patricia Neal, *Hud*
Leslie Caron, *The L-Shaped Room*
Shirley MacLaine, *Irma La Douce*
Rachel Roberts, *This Sporting Life*
Natalie Wood, *Love with the Proper Stranger*

Supporting Actor
Melvyn Douglas, *Hud*
Nick Adams, *Twilight of Honor*
Bobby Darin, *Captain Newman, M.D.*
Hugh Griffith, *Tom Jones*
John Huston, *The Cardinal*

Supporting Actress
Margaret Rutherford, *The V.I.P.s*
Diane Cilento, *Tom Jones*
Dame Edith Evans, *Tom Jones*
Joyce Redman, *Tom Jones*
Lilia Skala, *Lilies of the Field*

Director
Tony Richardson, *Tom Jones*
Federico Fellini, *Federico Fellini's 8½*
Elia Kazan, *America, America*
Otto Preminger, *The Cardinal*
Martin Ritt, *Hud*

Original Screenplay: James R. Webb, *How the West Was Won*
Adapted Screenplay: John Osborne, *Tom Jones*
Cinematography/B&W: James Wong Howe, *Hud*
Cinematography/Color: Leon Shamroy, *Cleopatra*
Original Score: John Addison, *Tom Jones*
Adapted Score: André Previn, *Irma La Douce*
Song: "Call Me Irresponsible," *Papa's Delicate Condition*, m:

James Van Heusen, l: Sammy
Cahn
Art Direction/B&W: Gene
Callahan, *America, America*
Art Direction/Color: John
DeCuir [and nine others],
Cleopatra
Costume Design/B&W: Piero
Gherardi, *Federico Fellini's 8½*
Costume Design/Color: Irene
Sharaff, Vittorio Nino Novarese,
Renie, *Cleopatra*
Editing: *How the West Was Won*
Sound: *How the West Was Won*
Special Visual Effects: *Cleopatra*
Sound Effects: *It's a Mad, Mad,
Mad, Mad World*
Short/Cartoon: *The Critic*
(Ernest Pintoff/Mel Brooks)
Short/Live Action: *An
Occurrence at Owl Creek Bridge*
(Robert Enrico)
Documentary/Feature: *Robert
Frost: A Lover's Quarrel With
the World* (WGBH Educational
Foundation)
Documentary/Short: *Chagall*
Foreign-Language Film:
Federico Fellini's 8½ (Italy)
Irving G. Thalberg Award: Sam
Spiegel

Golden Globes
Picture (Drama): *The Cardinal*
Picture (Comedy/Musical): *Tom
Jones*
**English-Language Foreign
Film:** *Tom Jones*
Foreign-Language Film: *Any
Number Can Win* (France)
Actor (Drama): Sidney Poitier,
Lilies of the Field
Actor (Comedy/Musical):
Alberto Sordi, *To Bed or Not to
Bed*
Actress (Drama): Leslie Caron,
The L-Shaped Room
Actress (Comedy/Musical):
Shirley MacLaine, *Irma La
Douce*
Supporting Actor: John Huston,
The Cardinal

Supporting Actress: Margaret
Rutherford, *The V.I.P.s*
Director: Elia Kazan, *America,
America*
**Most Promising Newcomers
(Male):** Albert Finney, Robert
Walker, Stathis Giallelis
**Most Promising Newcomers
(Female):** Ursula Andress,
Tippi Hedren, Elke Sommer
World Film Favorite (Male):
Paul Newman
World Film Favorite (Female):
Sophia Loren
**Best Film Promoting
International Understanding:**
Lilies of the Field
Cecil B. DeMille Award: Joseph
E. Levine
**Samuel Goldwyn International
Award:** *Yesterday, Today and
Tomorrow* (Italy)

Directors Guild of America
Director: Tony Richardson, *Tom
Jones*
Honorary Lifetime Member:
Joseph C. Youngerman
Critic Award: Paine
Knickerbocker, *San Francisco
Chronicle*

*** *8½* AAW NYC BOR
The absolute height of personal,
director-talking-right-to-the-
audience filmmaking in 1963,
Fellini's film was three hours
of vamping about how he has
nothing to say—a dazzlingly
original conceit then, somewhat
less so today now that
everyone from Paul Mazursky
to Woody Allen has imitated
it—and since Fellini turned out
not to be kidding.

New York Film Critics
Circle
Picture: *Tom Jones*
Foreign Film: *8½*

Actor: Albert Finney, *Tom Jones*
Actress: Patricia Neal, *Hud*
Director: Tony Richardson, *Tom Jones*
Screenplay: Irving Ravetch, Harriet Frank, *Hud*

National Board of Review
Best English-Language Film:
Tom Jones
Lilies of the Field
All the Way Home
Hud
This Sporting Life
Lord of the Flies
The L-Shaped Room
The Great Escape
How the West Was Won
The Cardinal
Best Foreign-Language Film:
8½
The Four Days of Naples
Winter Light
The Leopard
Any Number Can Win
Actor: Rex Harrison, *Cleopatra*
Actress: Patricia Neal, *Hud*
Supporting Actor: Melvyn Douglas, *Hud*
Supporting Actress: Margaret Rutherford, *The V.I.P.s*
Director: Tony Richardson, *Tom Jones*

Photoplay Gold Medal Awards
Gold Medal: *How the West Was Won*
Most Popular Male Star: Richard Chamberlain
Most Popular Female Star: Connie Stevens

British Academy Awards
Film: *Tom Jones*
British Film: *Tom Jones*
Actor (British): Dirk Bogarde, *The Servant*
Actor (Foreign): Marcello Mastroianni, *Divorce—Italian Style*

Actress (British): Rachel Roberts, *This Sporting Life*
Actress (Foreign): Patricia Neal, *Hud*
Screenplay: John Osborne, *Tom Jones*
Short Film: *Happy Anniversary* (France, Pierre Etaix)
Short Animated Film: *Automania 2000* (John Halas, UK); *The Critic* (Ernest Pintoff/ Mel Brooks, USA)

**** *The Leopard* CAN
Luchino Visconti, once one of neorealism's founders, returns to his classical roots with a handsome Italian soap opera that's the last word in aristocratic posh. Burt Lancaster plays the leonine paterfamilias, Alain Delon the dashing young nephew (he looks *marvelous* rushing to the barricades in the *risorgimento*). Paradoxically, this highly satisfying but admittedly skin-deep epic is the rare film that has inspired imitations with *more* depth than the original— including *The Godfather*, *1900*, and *The Deer Hunter*, among others.

Cannes Film Festival
Palme d'Or: *The Leopard* (Luchino Visconti, Italy)
Special Jury Prize: *Seppuku* [*Harakiri*] (Masaki Kobayashi, Japan), *One Day, a Cat* [*Cassandra Cat*] (Wojtech Jasny, Czechoslovakia)
Actor: Richard Harris, *This Sporting Life* (UK)
Actress: Marina Vlady, *The Conjugal Bed/Queen Bee* (Italy)
Screenplay: *Codine*, written by Yves Jamiaque, Dimitriu Carabat, Henri Colpi (France-Romania)

Best Evocation of a Revolutionary Epic: *The Optimistic Tragedy* (Samson Samsonov, USSR)
Gary Cooper Award: *To Kill a Mockingbird* (USA), a film that exults human solidarity
International Critics Prize: *This Sporting Life, Les Abysses* (Nico Papatakis, France), *Le Joli Mai* (Chris Marker, France)
[Short-film prizes include Special Mention to *You*, directed by 25-year-old István Szábo (Hungary)]

Venice Film Festival
Golden Lion: *Hands Over the City* (Francesco Rosi, Italy)
Special Jury Prize: *Le Feu Follet/The Fire Within* (Louis Malle, France), *Introduction to Life* (Igor Talankin, USSR)
Actor: Albert Finney, *Tom Jones* (UK)
Actress: Delphine Seyrig, *Muriel* (France)
First Film: *A Sunday in September* (Jörn Donner, Sweden), *Le Joli Mai* (Chris Marker, France)
International Critics Prize: *The Hangman* (Luis Garcia Berlanga, Spain)
Italian Critics Prize: *Le Feu Follet, Il Terrorista* (Gianfranco de Bosio, Italy)

Berlin Film Festival
Golden Bear: *Bushido: Samurai Saga* [*Oath of Obedience*] (Tadashi Imai, Japan), *Il Diavolo* [*To Bed or Not to Bed*] (Gian Luigi Polidoro, Italy)
Special Jury Prize: *The Caretaker* (Clive Donner, UK)
Actor: Sidney Poitier, *Lilies of the Field* (USA)
Actress: Bibi Andersson, *The Swedish Mistress* (Sweden)
Director: Nikos Koundouros, *Little Aphrodite* (Greece)

Documentary: *The Great Atlantic* (Peter Baylis, West Germany)
International Critics Prize: *Little Aphrodite, The Reunion* (Damiano Damiani, Italy)

Harvard Lampoon Movie Worsts
Ten worst pictures:
Cleopatra
The V.I.P.s
The Prize
It's a Mad, Mad, Mad, Mad World
How the West Was Won
Heavens Above!
55 Days at Peking
Act One
The Birds and *Bye Bye Birdie* (tied)
Gidget Goes to Rome and *Tammy and the Doctor* (tied)
Worst Film of the Century Award: For the century 1863–1963 to *Cleopatra*
The Kirk Douglas Award to the Worst Actor: Burt Lancaster, *The Leopard, Seven Days in May*
Worst Actress: Debbie Reynolds, *How the West Was Won, Mary, Mary*
Worst Supporting Actor: Roy Cohn, *Point of Order*
Worst Supporting Actress: Carol Burnett, *Who's Been Sleeping in My Bed?*
The Timothy Cratchit Memorial Crutch (to that Hollywood personality who offers the lamest excuse for unsavory behavior): Elizabeth Taylor, for divorcing Eddie Fisher on the grounds of abandonment
The Ayn Rand Award (to the author whose bad books made worse movies): Irving Wallace, *The Chapman Report, The Prize*
The Merino Award: to the Marine standing sentry dutry outside the American Embassy in *Charade*

Box Office (Domestic Rentals)

1	*How the West Was Won*	$17,000,000	Cinerama-MGM
	[through 1964:	20,000,000]	
2	*Cleopatra*	15,700,000	Fox
	[through 1964:	21,200,000]	
3	*The Longest Day*	15,250,000	Fox
4	*Lawrence of Arabia*	15,000,000	Col
5	*Irma La Douce*	11,000,000	UA
6	*Mutiny on the Bounty*	9,800,000	MGM
7	*The V.I.P.s*	7,500,000	MGM
8	*To Kill a Mockingbird*	7,500,000	Uni
9	*Son of Flubber*	7,400,000	Disney
10	*McLintock!*	7,250,000	UA

Other films of note:

12	*Bye Bye Birdie*	6,000,000	Col
16	*The Great Escape*	5,100,000	UA
17	*The Birds*	5,000,000	Uni
24	*Hud*	4,000,000	Par
26	*The Nutty Professor*	3,500,000	Par
	8 1/2	3,500,000	Embassy
44	*Dr. No*	2,400,000	UA
45	*David and Lisa*	2,300,000	Walter Reade
	Beach Party	2,300,000	American Int'l

The $40 million Cleopatra *had guaranteed bookings of $15.7 million;* Variety *declined to even guess what its actual final gross would be, perhaps because it knew that a truthful answer could send 20th Century–Fox's stock tumbling. By 1964's all-time-champs list the truth was out:* Cleopatra, *the fifth highest-grossing film in history, had lost half of its investment. The débâcle had led to the removal of studio head Spyros Skouras and the reinstatement of founder Darryl F. Zanuck, who kept the studio afloat with his own epic,* The Longest Day—*and, two years later,* The Sound of Music. *Skouras would have been better off making the Burtons' other picture of the year,* The V.I.P.s—*not to mention the first James Bond film, the first beach movie, or even the art-house indie hit* David and Lisa.

Gebert's Golden Armchairs

Considering that a remake is on its way as I write, and a semi-ripoff—*The Mask*—was a huge hit, *The Nutty Professor* looks more like one of the key films of the 1960s all the time. And in terms of how far it probed into the dark side of a comic's personality, *The Mask* is a mere *Interiors* next to *The Nutty Professor*'s *Persona*—as proven by the fact that Lewis basically turned into this Jekyll-and-Hyde story's Hyde character, the lounge act–lizard Buddy Love. Another mild-diversion-of-1963 that turned out to be a major influence on things to come was the Japanese action film *An Actor's Revenge*—its wild stunts and comic-book–like panels of color and blackness have been a big inspiration to the current generation of Hong Kong filmmakers. Last, inside every fat three-hour comedy there's a thin 85-minute one struggling to get out, and part of the one inside *It's a Mad*, etc. is Ethel Merman's spectacular battle-ax of a mother-in-law.

Best American Film: *The Nutty Professor*

Best Foreign Film: *An Actor's Revenge*
Best Actor: Jerry Lewis, *The Nutty Professor*
Best Actress: Ethel Merman, *It's a Mad, Mad, Mad, Mad World*
Best Director: Kon Ichikawa, *An Actor's Revenge*

1964

"An allegory in miniature of the Sixties" is how *Film Comment* recently described the New York Film Critics Circle's most heated battle in years—between *My Fair Lady*, Jack Warner's tribute to the MGM musical, and *Dr. Strangelove*, Stanley Kubrick's blast from the future. The first vote drew the lines clearly: *My Fair Lady* started with seven votes, while *Strangelove* had three and the rest were scattered over an assortment of art-house choices like *The Servant*, *Zorba the Greek*, and *Becket*. Bosley Crowther gathered the highbrow end of the group behind the satire, and it actually pulled ahead on the second ballot, 6–5. But the lady reviewers lured the two holdouts over to the *Lady* side, and the final vote went 8 to 5 for Lerner and Loewe.

The acting race was even more of a rout: Sterling Hayden and George C. Scott were both eliminated after the first ballot (Sellers didn't even appear), and Rex Harrison's only competition was another Brit, *The Servant*'s Dirk Bogarde. Whatever temptation Oscar might have had to take a chance on *Strangelove*—and start the movie revolution of the '60s a few years early—was nuked in New York by the right wing of the Critics Circle.

Academy Awards

** *My Fair Lady* AAW GLO DGA NYC BAA '65
*** **Rex Harrison** AAW GLO NYC
All the skill of Forest Lawn has gone into making the embalming job seem as lifelike as possible, with the result that the hit Broadway musical is transferred to the screen in an amazing simulation of the revival tour 20 years later, when everybody would be too old and bored for their parts.

Picture
My Fair Lady (Warner Bros., Jack L. Warner)
Becket (Paramount, Hal B. Wallis)
Dr. Strangelove or: How I Learned to Stop Worrying and Love the Bomb (Columbia, Hawk Films, Stanley Kubrick)
Mary Poppins (Walt Disney, Bill Walsh)
Zorba the Greek (International Classics/20th Century–Fox, Michael Cacoyannis)

Actor
Rex Harrison, *My Fair Lady*
Richard Burton, *Becket*
Peter O'Toole, *Becket*
Anthony Quinn, *Zorba the Greek*
Peter Sellers, *Dr. Strangelove*

**** **Julie Andrews in *Mary Poppins*** AAW
Andrews won the Oscar mainly as a rebuke to Jack Warner for

cheating her out of the Hepburn part in *My Fair Lady*. Actually the old mogul's instincts were dead on, and we got the best of both worlds. Andrews could get away with Eliza Doolittle on stage, but the camera would have revealed her shamming trying to play Rex Harrison's social and intellectual inferior—she's about as socially insecure as a Sherman tank. Winsome, vulnerable Hepburn was just right for the movie— and the imperturbable Poppins was just right for Andrews' debut.

Actress
Julie Andrews, *Mary Poppins*
Anne Bancroft, *The Pumpkin Eater*
Sophia Loren, *Marriage Italian Style*
Debbie Reynolds, *The Unsinkable Molly Brown*
Kim Stanley, *Séance on a Wet Afternoon*

Supporting Actor
Peter Ustinov, *Topkapi*
John Gielgud, *Becket*
Stanley Holloway, *My Fair Lady*
Edmond O'Brien, *Seven Days in May*
Lee Tracy, *The Best Man*

Supporting Actress
Lila Kedrova, *Zorba the Greek*
Gladys Cooper, *My Fair Lady*
Dame Edith Evans, *The Chalk Garden*
Grayson Hall, *The Night of the Iguana*
Agnes Moorehead, *Hush . . . Hush, Sweet Charlotte*

Director
George Cukor, *My Fair Lady*
Michael Cacoyannis, *Zorba the Greek*
Peter Glenville, *Becket*
Stanley Kubrick, *Dr. Strangelove*
Robert Stevenson, *Mary Poppins*

Original Screenplay: S. H. Barnett, Peter Stone, Frank Tarloff, *Father Goose*
Adapted Screenplay: Edward Anhalt, *Becket*
Cinematography/B&W: Walter Lassally, *Zorba the Greek*
Cinematography/Color: Harry Stradling, *My Fair Lady*
Original Score: Richard M. Sherman, Robert B. Sherman, *Mary Poppins*
Adapted Score: André Previn, *My Fair Lady*
Song: "Chim Chim Cher-ee," *Mary Poppins*, ml: Richard M. Sherman, Robert B. Sherman
Art Direction/B&W: Vassilis Fotopoulos, *Zorba the Greek*
Art Direction/Color: Gene Allen, Cecil Beaton, *My Fair Lady*
Costume Design/B&W: Dorothy Jeakins, *The Night of the Iguana*
Costume Design/Color: Cecil Beaton, *My Fair Lady*
Editing: *Mary Poppins*
Sound: *My Fair Lady*
Special Visual Effects: *Mary Poppins*
Sound Effects: *Goldfinger*
Short/Cartoon: *The Pink Phink* (Friz Freleng/Pink Panther)
Short/Live Action: *Casals Conducts: 1964*
Documentary/Feature: *Jacques-Yves Cousteau's World Without Sun*
Documentary/Short: *Nine from Little Rock* (U.S. Information Agency)
Foreign-Language Film:

Yesterday, Today and Tomorrow
(Italy)
Special Award: William Tuttle,
make-up, *The 7 Faces of Dr. Lao*

**** *Becket*   GLO BOR
Any group that picked it was
chickening out of picking
Strangelove, but the first of the
two films in which Peter O'Toole
played King Henry II is
certainly the better one, an
absorbing, literate historical
drama with restrained and
serious performances by two
hard-drinking hams (Burton as
Becket being the other).

Golden Globes
Picture (Drama): *Becket*
Picture (Comedy/Musical): *My
Fair Lady*
**English-Language Foreign
Film:** *The Girl with Green Eyes*
Foreign-Language Films:
Marriage Italian Style (Italy),
Sallah (Israel)
Actor (Drama): Peter O'Toole,
Becket
Actor (Comedy/Musical): Rex
Harrison, *My Fair Lady*
Actress (Drama): Anne Bancroft,
The Pumpkin Eater
Actress (Comedy/Musical):
Julie Andrews, *Mary Poppins*
Supporting Actor: Edmond
O'Brien, *Seven Days in May*
Supporting Actress: Agnes
Moorehead, *Hush . . . Hush, Sweet
Charlotte*
Director: George Cukor, *My Fair
Lady*
Original Score: Dimitri Tiomkin,
The Fall of the Roman Empire
Song: "Circus World," *Circus
World*, m: Dimitri Tiomkin
l: Ned Washington
**Most Promising Newcomers
(Male):** Harv Presnell, George
Segal, Chaim Topol

**Most Promising Newcomers
(Female):** Mia Farrow, Celia
Kaye, Mary Ann Mobley
World Film Favorite (Male):
Marcello Mastroianni
World Film Favorite (Female):
Sophia Loren

Directors Guild of America
Director: George Cukor, *My Fair
Lady*
Honorary Lifetime Member:
Jack L. Warner
Critic Award: James Meade, *San
Diego Union*

***** Kim Stanley in *Séance on
a Wet Afternoon*   NYC BOR**
A fine little English thriller/
character study, about a pathetic
married couple who plan to
kidnap a child—less for the
money, it turns out, than to fill
the gap in their lives. Terrific
unhealthy atmosphere in a film
which compares favorably
with the thematically similar
*Who's Afraid of Virginia
Woolf?* Interestingly, though,
while the attention in '64 was
on stage actress Kim Stanley as
the neurotic wife, her
performance now seems
mannered and a touch
overblown, while it's Richard
Attenborough, as the docile,
defeated husband, who is by far
the better of the two.

New York Film Critics Circle
Picture: *My Fair Lady*
Foreign Film: *That Man from Rio*
Actor: Rex Harrison, *My Fair
Lady*
Actress: Kim Stanley, *Séance on
a Wet Afternoon*
Director: Stanley Kubrick, *Dr.
Strangelove*

Screenplay: Harold Pinter, *The Servant*
Special Citation: *To Be Alive!* [New York World's Fair film, sponsored by Johnson Wax]

National Board of Review
Best English-Language Film:
Becket
My Fair Lady
The Girl with Green Eyes
The World of Henry Orient
Zorba the Greek
Topkapi
The Chalk Garden
The Finest Hours
Four Days in November
Séance on a Wet Afternoon
Best Foreign-Language Film:
World Without Sun
The Organizer
Anatomy of a Marriage
Seduced and Abandoned
Yesterday, Today and Tomorrow
Actor: Anthony Quinn, *Zorba the Greek*
Actress: Kim Stanley, *Séance on a Wet Afternoon*
Supporting Actor: Martin Balsam, *The Carpetbaggers*
Supporting Actress: Edith Evans, *The Chalk Garden*
Director: Desmond Davis, *The Girl With Green Eyes*

Photoplay Gold Medal Awards
Gold Medal: *The Unsinkable Molly Brown*
Most Popular Male Star: Richard Chamberlain
Most Popular Female Star: Ann-Margret

British Academy Awards
Film: *Dr. Strangelove*
British Film: *Dr. Strangelove*
Actor (British): Richard Attenborough, *Guns at Batasi*, *Séance on a Wet Afternoon*
Actor (Foreign): Marcello Mastroianni, *Yesterday, Today and Tomorrow*
Actress (British): Audrey Hepburn, *Charade*
Actress (Foreign): Anne Bancroft, *The Pumpkin Eater*
Screenplay: Harold Pinter, *The Pumpkin Eater*

**** *The Umbrellas of Cherbourg* CAN
Among French new wave directors, Jacques Demy has been comparatively forgotten—probably because unlike crime-movie fans Godard and Chabrol, he admired a Hollywood genre that is out of fashion, the musical. *The Umbrellas of Cherbourg* sets a sweet, deliberately ordinary little love story to music—*all* of it. Every line of dialogue is sung in a sort of jazzy recitative (you'll recognize many of Michel Legrand's melodies from elevators), and Demy delights in musicalizing the most absurdly mundane incidents—as when, in the middle of a scene, a man (Demy, actually) opens the door to the umbrella shop and sings for directions to the barber's. In English it would probably be unbearably coy; in French, though, it's sweetly, knowingly preposterous and *très charmant*.

Cannes Film Festival
Palme d'Or: *The Umbrellas of Cherbourg* (Jacques Demy, France)
Special Jury Prize: *Woman in the Dunes* (Hiroshi Teshigahara, Japan)
Actor: Antel Pager, *The Lark*

(Hungary), Saro Urzi, *Seduced and Abandoned* (Italy) (shared)
Actress: Anne Bancroft, *The Pumpkin Eater* (UK), Barbara Barrie, *One Potato, Two Potato* (USA) (shared)
Tribute: to *The Passenger*, unfinished film by the late Andrzej Munk (Poland) [completed by his assistant]
Mention: Young directors of promise Jaromil Jires, *The Cry* (Czechoslovakia), Georgui Danelia, *Romance in Moscow* (USSR), Manuel Summers, *La Niña de Luto* (Spain)
International Critics Prize: *The Passenger*

** *Red Desert*   VEN
The epitome of what Pauline Kael derisively called "come dressed as the sick soul of Europe parties"—Monica Vitti is the depressed, alienated housewife wandering through the gloomy, diseased-looking industrial landscape of Michelangelo Antonioni's first color film. Antonioni's eye and ear manage some striking effects, but it's tough to imagine who'd want to sit through it now; I don't think it's philistine to prefer, say, Bertolucci's flamboyant, occasionally kitschy splashing about of color to Antonioni's stingy doling out of impeccably tasteful compositions.

Venice Film Festival
Golden Lion: *Red Desert* (Michelangelo Antonioni, Italy)
Special Jury Prize: *Hamlet* (Grigori Koszintsev, USSR), *The Gospel According to St. Matthew* (Pier Paolo Pasolini, Italy)

Actor: Tom Courtenay, *King and Country* (UK)
Actress: Harriet Andersson, *To Love* (Sweden)
Best First Film: *La Vie à l'Envers* [*Life Upside Down*] (Alain Jessua, France)
International Critics Prize: *Red Desert*
Italian Critics Prize: *The Passenger* (Andrzej Munk, Poland), *La Vie à l'Envers* [*Life Upside Down*]

Berlin Film Festival
Golden Bear: *Dry Summer* (Ismail Metin, Turkey)
Silver Bear: *Os Fuzis* (Ruy Guerra, Brazil)
Actor: Rod Steiger, *The Pawnbroker* (USA)
Actress: Sachiko Hidari, *The Insect Woman* (Shohei Imamura, Japan), *She and He* (Susumu Hani, Japan)
Director: Satyajit Ray, *Mahanagar* [*The Big City*] (India)
Documentary: *Alleman* (Bert Haanstra, The Netherlands)
International Critics Prize: *La Visita* (Antonio Pietrangeli, Italy), *Stag Party* (Wolfgang Staudte, West Germany)

Harvard Lampoon **Movie Worsts**
Ten worst pictures:
The Greatest Story Ever Told, *The Carpetbaggers*, *Sylvia*, *Cheyenne Autumn*, *Station Six–Sahara*, *Kiss Me, Stupid* (tied)
The Outrage
The Fall of the Roman Empire
One Potato, Two Potato
Youngblood Hawke
Kisses for My President
Goodbye Charlie
The Unsinkable Molly Brown
Muscle Beach Party
The Kirk Douglas Award to the

Worst Actor: James Franciscus, *Youngblood Hawke*
Worst Actress: Carroll Baker, *The Greatest Story Ever Told, The Carpetbaggers, Sylvia, Cheyenne Autumn, Station Six–Sahara*
Worst Supporting Actor: Laurence Harvey, *The Outrage*
Worst Supporting Actress: Honor Blackman as Pussy Galore, *Goldfinger*
Worst Performance by a Cast in Toto: The entire population of Western Europe for its performance in *The Fall of the Roman Empire*
The Please-Don't-Put-Us-Through-DeMille-Again Award: *The Greatest Story Ever Told*
The Ayn Rand Award (to the author whose bad books made worse movies): Matthew, Mark, Luke, and John, *The Greatest Story Ever Told*
The Merino Award: to marinophile Jacques Cousteau for his underwater documentary *World Without Sun*

Box Office (Domestic Rentals)

1	*Tom Jones*	$16,000,000	UA
2	*The Carpetbaggers*	13,000,000	Par
3	*It's a Mad, Mad, Mad, Mad World*	10,000,000	UA
	[through 1965:	17,500,000]	
4	*The Unsinkable Molly Brown*	7,500,000	MGM
5	*The Greatest Story Ever Told*		UA
	[through 1973:	7,000,000]	
6	*Charade*	6,150,000	Uni
7	*The Cardinal*	5,275,000	Col
8	*Move Over, Darling*	5,100,000	Fox
9	*My Fair Lady*	5,000,000	WB
	[through 1965:	19,000,000]	
10	*What a Way to Go!*	5,000,000	Fox
Other films of note:			
12	*The Pink Panther*	4,853,000	UA
13	*Viva Las Vegas*	4,675,000	MGM
15	*A Hard Day's Night*	4,473,000	Uni
16	*Dr. Strangelove*	4,148,000	Col
19	*From Russia With Love*	3,849,000	UA
24	*Hamlet*	3,100,000	WB
26	*Becket*	3,000,000	Par
	[through 1967:	5,000,000]	
66	*Hey There, It's Yogi Bear*	870,000	Col
71	*Fail-Safe*	590,000	Col
	[anticipated total:	1,800,000]	

Were the Beatles really bigger than Jesus Christ? Well, The Greatest Story Ever Told *made $7 million, and* A Hard Day's Night *only did four and a half, so draw your own conclusions. Other people that the Beatles were not yet bigger than included that other king of kings, Elvis; and their rival songsmiths Lerner & Loewe. Among the more surprising hits, Richard Burton doing* Hamlet *on video (an early video-to-*

film process called Electronovision) at reserved-seat prices in two-day-only engagements did almost as well as Burton playing Becket the normal way; and as approaches to nuclear armageddon went, Strangelove*'s ahead-of-its-time satiric approach easily bested the deadly serious* Fail-Safe.

Gebert's Golden Armchairs

With its Beat/sick humor sensibility—new to the movies, if not the culture—*Strangelove* is obviously the key movie of 1964. But the most impressive performance in it to me isn't Sellers' trio of parts; except for the American president, they're basically Goon Show caricatures given greater weight by the subject matter. George C. Scott's scary, too-enthusiastic American general, the one who sees nuclear war as the big game and he's got tickets on the 50-yard-line—now *that's* the character who keeps me up nights. Sergei Paradjanov's *Shadows of Forgotten Ancestors* is a beguilingly exotic Soviet color film, a sort of Georgian-peasant *Romeo and Juliet* and the first hint attentive viewers might have had that nationalism was alive and well within the USSR. (The KGB took the hint; Paradjanov spent a major portion of the Brezhnev era in jail.) *Strait-Jacket* is a tawdry *Baby Jane* imitation from exploitation king William Castle, but Joan Crawford—as an ax murderess, no less—senses that it's up to her to bring some dignity to the proceedings, and demonstrates what being a star is by underplaying the part (well, by *her* standards, anyway).

Best American Film: *Dr. Strangelove*
Best Foreign Film: *Shadows of Forgotten Ancestors*
Best Actor: George C. Scott, *Dr. Strangelove*
Best Actress: Joan Crawford, *Strait-Jacket*
Best Director: Stanley Kubrick, *Dr. Strangelove*

1965

"Wasn't there perhaps one little Von Trapp who didn't want to sing his head off, or who screamed that he wouldn't act out little glockenspiel routines for Papa's party guests, or who got nervous and threw up if he had to get on a stage?" ranted Pauline Kael, somewhere near the climax of her splendidly intemperate review of the year's best-loved movie, *The Sound of Music*. Reader response was so outraged that it got her fired from *McCall's*, and members of the reviewing establishment sighed that she got what she deserved for daring to express an honest opinion about a big-budget blockbuster in a mainstream magazine—"If it was naive of *McCall's* to hire her, it was equally naive of her to act as if it were *Film Quarterly* she was exploding in," *Variety* wrote.

Whatever the excesses of Kael's years as the power broker of both critics' groups, let us remember the state of movie reviewing in America as she found it, and give thanks for the verbal carpet-bombing she laid down to make it safe for the infantry of Altman, Coppola, Penn, et al. to go in and create a new American cinema.

Academy Awards

*** *The Sound of Music* AAW GLO DGA
The *Ten Commandments* of musicals—enormous, cute as a button, and a surefire, utterly shameless manipulator (the nuns pulled the battery cable! Isn't that *adorable*! Shoot them with our tiniest guns).

Picture
The Sound of Music (20th Century–Fox, Argyle, Robert Wise)
Darling (Embassy, Anglo-Amalgamated)
Doctor Zhivago (MGM, Carlo Ponti)
Ship of Fools (Columbia, Stanley Kramer)
A Thousand Clowns (UA, Fred Coe)

** **Lee Marvin in *Cat Ballou***
AAW GLO BOR BER
John Wayne's Oscar for *True Grit* I can understand, but it's hard to see what bowled over the Academy (and the other groups—including Berlin!) about *this* broad, audience-pandering spoof-western—or Lee Marvin's pair of slack-jawed performances as the good and the bad gunslinger. Maybe just a desperate desire to flee from the seriousness of the other nominees in the category (two Holocaust films, a grim Cold War yarn, and Shakespeare)?

Actor
Lee Marvin, *Cat Ballou*
Richard Burton, *The Spy Who Came in from the Cold*

Laurence Olivier, *Othello*
Rod Steiger, *The Pawnbroker*
Oskar Werner, *Ship of Fools*

Joyce Redman, *Othello*
Maggie Smith, *Othello*
Peggy Wood, *The Sound of Music*

** Julie Christie in *Darling*
AAW NYC BOR BAA

John Schlesinger and writer Frederic Raphael's story of a fashion model sleeping her way to the top of "Swinging London" was the epitome of smart, trendy filmmaking in its day—and highly influential (*Blowup*, *Nothing But the Best*, etc.). But it hasn't aged well. The problem isn't so much that its satire is snide—the same is true of Raphael's *Two for the Road*, which looks better all the time. But Christie's character is a caricature, more like a '50s kewpie-doll sexpot than the New Woman she seemed to be in '65—and if truth be told, she just isn't *interesting* enough to carry the picture.

Actress
Julie Christie, *Darling*
Julie Andrews, *The Sound of Music*
Samantha Eggar, *The Collector*
Elizabeth Hartman, *A Patch of Blue*
Simone Signoret, *Ship of Fools*

Supporting Actor
Martin Balsam, *A Thousand Clowns*
Ian Bannen, *The Flight of the Phoenix*
Tom Courtenay, *Doctor Zhivago*
Michael Dunn, *Ship of Fools*
Frank Finlay, *Othello*

Supporting Actress
Shelley Winters, *A Patch of Blue*
Ruth Gordon, *Inside Daisy Clover*

Director
Robert Wise, *The Sound of Music*
David Lean, *Doctor Zhivago*
John Schlesinger, *Darling*
Hiroshi Teshigahara, *Woman in the Dunes*
William Wyler, *The Collector*

Original Screenplay: Frederic Raphael, *Darling*
Adapted Screenplay: Robert Bolt, *Doctor Zhivago*
Cinematography/B&W: Ernest Laszlo, *Ship of Fools*
Cinematography/Color: Freddie Young, *Doctor Zhivago*
Original Score: Maurice Jarre, *Doctor Zhivago*
Adapted Score: Irwin Kostal, *The Sound of Music*
Song: "The Shadow of Your Smile," *The Sandpiper*, m: Johnny Mandel, l: Paul Francis Webster
Art Direction/B&W: Robert Clatworthy, *Ship of Fools*
Art Direction/Color: John Box, Terry Marsh, *Doctor Zhivago*
Costume Design/B&W: Julie Harris, *Darling*
Costume Design/Color: Phyllis Dalton, *Doctor Zhivago*
Editing: William Reynolds, *The Sound of Music*
Sound: *The Sound of Music*
Special Visual Effects: *Thunderball*
Sound Effects: *The Great Race*
Short/Cartoon: *The Dot and the Line* (MGM/Chuck Jones)
Short/Live Action: *The Chicken* [*Le Poulet*] (Claude Berri, France)
Documentary/Feature: *The Eleanor Roosevelt Story*
Documentary/Short: *To Be*

Alive! (Johnson Wax Co., for New York World's Fair)
Foreign-Language Film: *The Shop on Main Street* (Czechoslovakia)
Irving G. Thalberg Award: William Wyler
Jean Hersholt Humanitarian Award: Edmond L. DePatie
Special Award: Bob Hope

***** *The Shop on Main Street* AAW CAN NYC '66 During the Nazi occupation, a Czech schnook is made the "Aryan overseer" (that is, recipient of the profits) of an elderly Jewish woman's button shop, only to find that she's really a charity case supported by the other Jews—and she assumes he's been hired as her helper. Then the roundup of the Jews is announced, and he can't quite stand by and let them take her. . . . A powerful and beautifully made film which puts responsibility for the Holocaust in brilliantly personal terms; the only oddity is that Hollywood nominated the old woman, Ida Kaminska, for a supporting Oscar—when the whole movie is carried by Jozef Kroner as the venal, lazy, drunken, and finally tragic-heroic Everyman.

Golden Globes
Picture (Drama): *Doctor Zhivago*
Picture (Comedy/Musical): *The Sound of Music*
English-Language Foreign Film: *Darling*
Foreign-Language Film: *Juliet of the Spirits* (Italy)
Actor (Drama): Omar Sharif, *Doctor Zhivago*

Actor (Comedy/Musical): Lee Marvin, *Cat Ballou*
Actress (Drama): Samantha Eggar, *The Collector*
Actress (Comedy/Musical): Julie Andrews, *The Sound of Music*
Supporting Actor: Oskar Werner, *The Spy Who Came in from the Cold*
Supporting Actress: Ruth Gordon, *Inside Daisy Clover*
Director: David Lean, *Doctor Zhivago*
Screenplay: Robert Bolt, *Doctor Zhivago*
Original Score: Maurice Jarre, *Doctor Zhivago*
Original Song: "Forget Domani," *The Yellow Rolls-Royce*, m: Riz Ortolani, l: Norman Newell
Most Promising Newcomer (Male): Robert Redford, *Inside Daisy Clover*
Most Promising Newcomer (Female): Elizabeth Hartman, *A Patch of Blue*
World Film Favorite (Male): Paul Newman
World Film Favorite (Female): Natalie Wood
Cecil B. DeMille Award: John Wayne

Directors Guild of America
Director: Robert Wise, *The Sound of Music*
Critic Award: Sam Lesner, *Chicago Daily News*
D. W. Griffith Award: William Wyler

New York Film Critics Circle
Picture: *Darling*
Foreign Film: *Juliet of the Spirits*
Actor: Oskar Werner, *Ship of Fools*
Actress: Julie Christie, *Darling*
Director: John Schlesinger, *Darling*

National Board of Review
Best English-Language Film:
The Eleanor Roosevelt Story
The Agony and the Ecstasy
Doctor Zhivago
Ship of Fools
The Spy Who Came in from the Cold
Darling
The Greatest Story Ever Told
A Thousand Clowns
The Train
The Sound of Music
Best Foreign-Language Film:
Juliet of the Spirits
The Overcoat
La Bohème
La Tia Tula
Gertrud
Actor: Lee Marvin, *Cat Ballou,*
Ship of Fools
Actress: Julie Christie, *Darling,*
Doctor Zhivago
Supporting Actor: Harry
Andrews, *The Agony and the
Ecstasy, The Hill*
Supporting Actress: Joan
Blondell, *The Cincinnati Kid*
Director: John Schlesinger,
Darling

Photoplay Gold Medal Awards
Gold Medal: *The Sound of Music*
Most Popular Male Star: Robert
Vaughn
Most Popular Female Star:
Dorothy Malone

British Academy Awards
Film: *My Fair Lady*
British Film: *The Ipcress File*
Actor (British): Dirk Bogarde,
Darling
Actor (Foreign): Lee Marvin,
The Killers, Cat Ballou
Actress (British): Julie Christie,
Darling
Actress (Foreign): Patricia Neal,
In Harm's Way
Screenplay: Frederic Raphael,
Darling

**Robert Flaherty Documentary
Award:** *Tokyo Olympiad* (Kon
Ichikawa, Japan)

• *The Knack . . . And How to Get It* CAN
Richard Lester's first post-
Beatles film is based on a
Swinging London-era play
about one chap teaching 'is mate
(Michael Crawford, ick) how to
pick up birds. However fresh
this sort of youth film looked
then, it was clearly never much
of a play to begin with, and
Lester's by-now-annoying
cinematic tricks no longer hide
the fact.

Cannes Film Festival
Grand Prize: *The Knack . . . And
How to Get It* (Richard Lester,
UK)
Special Jury Prize: *Kwaidan*
(Masahi Kobayashi, Japan)
Actor: Terence Stamp, *The
Collector* (USA)
Actress: Samantha Eggar, *The
Collector*
Director: *The Forest of Hanged
Men* (Liviu Ciulei, Romania)
Screenplay: *The Hill* [written by
Ray Rigby] (Sidney Lumet,
UK), *Le 317éme Section [Platoon
317]* (Pierre Schöndörffer,
France)
Special Mention to Actors: Jozef
Kroner, Ida Kaminska, *The Shop
on Main Street* (Czechoslovakia),
Vera Kuznetsova, *There Was an
Old Man and an Old Woman*
(USSR)
International Critics Prize:
Tarahumara (Luis Alcoriza,
Mexico)

Venice Film Festival
Golden Lion: *Vaghe Stelle
dell'Orsa [Sandra/Of a*

Thousand Delights] (Luchino Visconti, Italy)
Special Jury Prize: *Simon of the Desert* (Luis Buñuel, Mexico), *I Am Twenty* (Marlen Kouziev, USSR)
Actor: Toshiro Mifune, *Red Beard* (Japan)
Actress: Annie Girardot, *Trois chambres à Manhattan* (France)
Best First Film: *Faithfulness* [*Loyalty*] (Pyotr Toderovsky, USSR)
International Critics Prize: *Simon of the Desert*, *Gertrud* (Carl Dreyer, Denmark)
San Michele Prize: *Che Cosa, Che Cosa . . . Scusi Signorina* [*The Wacky Mixed-Up Carabiniers*] (Felix G. Palmer, West Germany–Italy)

*** *Alphaville* BER
Even if, like he does me, Godard mostly drives you up a wall these days (he was exciting and eye-opening when either you or the whole world was 20), this one is faithful enough to its genre roots to have a sort of cracked charm—it's the all-goof/no-plot film *noir* that *Pulp Fiction* dreamt of being. In a sort of *Dirty Harry in Wonderland*, the slab-faced tough guy Eddie Constantine plays his usual character, Lemmy Caution, but he's on a surreal mission to go to the planet Alphaville (reached by expressway from Paris) and find the missing computer genius Dr. Leonard Nosferatu.

Berlin Film Festival
Golden Bear: *Alphaville* (Jean-Luc Godard, France)
Silver Bear: *Le Bonheur* [*Happiness*] (Agnès Varda, France), *Repulsion* (Roman Polanski, UK)
Actor: Lee Marvin, *Cat Ballou* (USA)
Actress: Madhur Jaffrey, *Shakespeare Wallah* (India)
Director: Satyajit Ray, *Charulata* (India)
Special Mention: Walter Newman, Frank Pierson, screenwriters of *Cat Ballou*
International Critics Prize: *Repulsion*, *Karlek 65* (Bo Widerberg, Sweden)

Harvard Lampoon Movie Worsts
Ten worst pictures:
The Sandpiper
The Hallelujah Trail
Lord Jim
What's New, Pussycat?
The Agony and the Ecstasy
Shenandoah
Genghis Khan
Thunderball
The Great Race
The Yellow Rolls-Royce
The Merino Award: Merino Mercouri

Box Office (Domestic Rentals)

1	*Mary Poppins*	$28,500,000	Disney
	[*through 1967:*	31,000,000]	
2	*The Sound of Music*	20,000,000	Fox
	[*through 1967:*	42,500,000]	
3	*Goldfinger*	19,700,000	UA
4	*My Fair Lady*	19,000,000	WB
5	*What's New, Pussycat?*	7,150,000	UA
6	*Shenandoah*	7,000,000	Uni

7	*The Sandpiper*	6,400,000	MGM
8	*Father Goose*	6,000,000	Uni
9	*Von Ryan's Express*	5,600,000	Fox
10	*The Yellow Rolls-Royce*	5,400,000	MGM
Other films of note:			
12	*Cat Ballou*	5,150,000	Col
14	*Help!*	4,140,000	UA
19	*The Train*	3,450,000	UA
22	*Hush . . . Hush, Sweet Charlotte*	3,300,000	Fox
24	*Zorba the Greek*	3,200,000	Fox
27	*Those Magnificent Men in Their Flying Machines*	3,000,000	Fox
	[through 1967:	12,000,000]	
47	*The Ipcress File*	1,750,000	Uni

Not since the heyday of Bing Crosby had a musical star—or any star—so dominated the box office; Mary Poppins *still had plenty of life in it when Julie Andrews' second picture,* The Sound of Music, *started zooming toward* Gone With the Wind's *box office record. It actually passed it in 1966—if only briefly, since GWTW was promptly reissued, of course. Now admit it: if you were a studio executive, wouldn't you have greenlighted Andrews in* Star! *or* Darling Lili? *Of course you would have, and in the meantime, you'd have launched your own spy movie series to rival* Goldfinger, *and made a big-budget all-star comedy called* Those Lovable Prussians in Their Furshlugginer Zeppelins. *And just like all the other studio executives, you'd have been fired by 1970, too.*

Gebert's Golden Armchairs

Singing nuns aside, it was a terrible year in Hollywood—the old Hollywood dead, the new one afraid to be born. The only thing I like much is Tony Richardson's gleefully bad-taste satire on the California funeral business, *The Loved One*, the closest '60s Hollywood ever came to a John Waters film. As Mr. Joyboy, *The Loved One*'s mama's-boy mortician, and as the burned-out Holocaust survivor in the pretentious but powerful *The Pawnbroker*, Rod Steiger certainly won 1965's versatility prize; and Barbara Harris' comic turn as a not-too-sure-of-herself social worker in *A Thousand Clowns* captures womanhood in the post-bimbo/pre-feminism era better than *Darling* did.

But the best and most influential film of 1965 was one of those short experimental films you had to find the right basement 16mm film society to see: painter-filmmaker Bruce Conner's *Report*. Conner's recutting of old educational and government films for surreal comic effect (as in this film on the Kennedy assassination) not only spawned *The Atomic Cafe* and a million music videos, but shattered the mystique of Civil Defense–era authority with ridicule the way Lytton Strachey's *Eminent Victorians* broke the spell of Victorian morality in the 1920s.

Best American Film: *Report*
Best Foreign Film: *The Shop on Main Street*

Best Actor: Rod Steiger, *The Pawnbroker*, *The Loved One*

Best Actress: Barbara Harris, *A Thousand Clowns*
Best Director: Bruce Conner, *Report*

1966

A new film world was being born, and many of the old hands wanted nothing to do with it. In New York, Bosley Crowther decried his fellow critics for going 10–3 for *A Man for All Seasons* over *Who's Afraid of Virginia Woolf?*—but even the foulmouthed Albee play was too conservative for the new National Society of Film Critics, which showed no interest in Hollywood whatsoever. Venice found itself risking prosecution from its own government with Mai Zetterling's Swedish sex film *Night Games*, and its showing of Roger Corman's biker exploitation pic *The Wild Angels*—the *only* American film invited that year—provoked outrage from the relatively few Hollywood visitors, though some of the critics were more ready to acknowledge Corman as the '60s answer to Hawks and Walsh. The political and cultural skew of the festival had gone so far to the left that Count Volpi, the festival's patron and son of its founder, declined for the first time to personally present the acting prizes that bore his family's name.

Academy Awards

**** *A Man for All Seasons*
AAW GLO DGA NYC BOR
BAA '67
**** **Paul Scofield** AAW GLO
NYC BOR BAA '67
An admirably intelligent historical film, with very little flab—either dramatically or rhetorically—and for once, an authentic feel for the Elizabethan period (those long, bare and cold halls, London as a series of manors along the Thames separated by untamed forest). Scofield's sonorous brandy-voice is just what Robert Bolt's snappy speeches wanted, but compared to his marvelously observed turn as head-in-the-clouds intellectual Mark Van Doren in *Quiz Show*, he can be seen coasting on it just a little bit.

Picture
A Man for All Seasons
(Columbia, Fred Zinnemann)
Alfie (Paramount, Lewis Gilbert)
The Russians Are Coming, The Russians Are Coming (UA, Mirisch, Norman Jewison)
The Sand Pebbles (20th Century-Fox, Robert Wise)
Who's Afraid of Virginia Woolf? (Warner Bros., Ernest Lehman)

Actor
Paul Scofield, *A Man for All Seasons*
Alan Arkin, *The Russians Are Coming, The Russians Are Coming*
Richard Burton, *Who's Afraid of Virginia Woolf?*
Michael Caine, *Alfie*
Steve McQueen, *The Sand Pebbles*

**** Elizabeth Taylor in
Who's Afraid of Virginia Woolf?   AAW NYC BOR BAA
Putting Burton and Taylor in Edward Albee's intimate little marital slugfest is sort of like training a Howitzer on a doll house; even given that George and Martha are supposed to have practiced their bitchy-backbiting act in front of audiences like the nice young couple (George Segal and Sandy Dennis) for years, the Burtons come off like the Royal Shakespeare Company of bad marriages. But Albee's play is only superficially realistic, anyway. It's more like a title bout between the two most famous actors on earth; Taylor comes out slugging, Burton tries to wear her down by feinting for the first couple of rounds and scores some points with the judges, but in the end she's the one at her peak and wins on a decision. Apparently they were actually very happy at the time.

Actress
Elizabeth Taylor, *Who's Afraid of Virginia Woolf?*
Anouk Aimée, *A Man and a Woman*
Ida Kaminska, *The Shop on Main Street*
Lynn Redgrave, *Georgy Girl*
Vanessa Redgrave, *Morgan!—A Suitable Case for Treatment*

Supporting Actor
Walter Matthau, *The Fortune Cookie*
Mako, *The Sand Pebbles*
James Mason, *Georgy Girl*

George Segal, *Who's Afraid of Virginia Woolf?*
Robert Shaw, *A Man for All Seasons*

Supporting Actress
Sandy Dennis, *Who's Afraid of Virginia Woolf?*
Wendy Hiller, *A Man for All Seasons*
Jocelyn Lagarde, *Hawaii*
Vivien Merchant, *Alfie*
Geraldine Page, *You're a Big Boy Now*

Director
Fred Zinnemann, *A Man for All Seasons*
Michelangelo Antonioni, *Blowup*
Richard Brooks, *The Professionals*
Claude Lelouch, *A Man and a Woman*
Mike Nichols, *Who's Afraid of Virginia Woolf?*

Original Screenplay: Claude Lelouch, Pierre Uytterhoeven, *A Man and a Woman*
Adapted Screenplay: Robert Bolt, *A Man for All Seasons*
Cinematography/B&W: Haskell Wexler, *Who's Afraid of Virginia Woolf?*
Cinematography/Color: Ted Moore, *A Man for All Seasons*
Original Score: John Barry, *Born Free*
Adapted Score: Ken Thorne, *A Funny Thing Happened on the Way to the Forum*
Song: "Born Free," *Born Free*, m: John Barry, l: Don Black
Art Direction/B&W: Richard Sylbert, *Who's Afraid of Virginia Woolf?*
Art Direction/Color: Jack Martin Smith, Dale Hennesy, *Fantastic Voyage*
Costume Design/B&W: Irene Sharaff, *Who's Afraid of Virginia Woolf?*

Costume Design/Color:
Elizabeth Haffenden, Joan
Bridge, *A Man for All Seasons*
Editing: *Grand Prix*
Sound: *Grand Prix*
Sound Effects: *Grand Prix*
Special Visual Effects: *Fantastic
Voyage*
Short/Cartoon: *Herb Alpert and
the Tijuana Brass Double
Feature* (John and Faith Hubley)
Short/Live Action: *Wild Wings*
(British Transport Films, Edgar
Anstey)
Documentary/Feature: *The War
Game* (BBC Prod. for the British
Film Institute, Peter Watkins)
Documentary/Short: *A Year
Toward Tomorrow* (Office of
Economic Opportunity)
Foreign-Language Film: *A Man
and a Woman* (France)
Irving G. Thalberg Award:
Robert Wise
**Jean Hersholt Humanitarian
Award:** George Bagnall
Special Awards:
Y. Frank Freeman
Yakima Canutt, for achievements
as a stuntman and for developing
safety devices to protect stuntmen
everywhere

Golden Globes
Picture (Drama): *A Man for All
Seasons*
Picture (Comedy/Musical): *The
Russians Are Coming, The Russians
Are Coming*
**English-Language Foreign
Film:** *Alfie*
Foreign-Language Film: *A Man
and a Woman* (France)
Actor (Drama): Paul Scofield, *A
Man for All Seasons*
Actor (Comedy/Musical): Alan
Arkin, *The Russians Are
Coming, The Russians Are
Coming*
Actress (Drama): Anouk Aimée,
A Man and a Woman

Actress (Comedy/Musical):
Lynn Redgrave, *Georgy Girl*
Supporting Actor: Richard
Attenborough, *The Sand
Pebbles*
Supporting Actress: Jocelyne
LaGarde, *Hawaii*
Director: Fred Zinnemann, *A
Man for All Seasons*
Screenplay: Robert Bolt, *A Man
for All Seasons*
Original Score: Elmer Bernstein,
Hawaii
Original Song: "Strangers in the
Night," *A Man Could Get Killed*,
m: Bert Kaempfert, l: Charles
Singleton, Eddie Snyder
**Most Promising Newcomer
(Male):** James Farentino, *The
Pad and How to Use It*
**Most Promising Newcomer
(Female):** Camilla Sparv, *Dead
Heat on a Merry-Go-Round*
World Film Favorite (Male):
Steve McQueen
World Film Favorite (Female):
Julie Andrews
Cecil B. DeMille Award:
Charlton Heston

Directors Guild of America
Director: Fred Zinnemann, *A
Man for All Seasons*

New York Film Critics
Circle
Picture: *A Man for All Seasons*
Foreign Film: *The Shop on Main
Street*
Actor: Paul Scofield, *A Man for
All Seasons*
Actress: Elizabeth Taylor, *Who's
Afraid of Virginia Woolf?*, Lynn
Redgrave, *Georgy Girl* (tie)
Director: Fred Zinnemann, *A
Man for All Seasons*
Screenplay: Robert Bolt, *A Man
for All Seasons*

**** *Blowup* SOC CAN '67
Michelangelo Antonioni, forced
in his first English-language

film to be commercial, came up
with both his most
entertaining (well, *that's* not
hard to believe) and his most
influential work—the father not
only of all the '60s youth movies
to follow but of the whole
paranoia-conspiracy genre (*The
Conversation*, *JFK*, every
thriller of the last 30 years). The
story of a Swinging London
fashion photographer (David
Hemmings) who discovers a
murder in some shots he took,
it holds up surprisingly well
considering how much it's
been imitated, and its kitsch-to-
chic ratio is about as low as
any film of its era.

National Society of Film Critics
Picture: *Blowup*
Actor: Michael Caine, *Alfie*
Actress: Sylvie, *The Shameless Old Lady*
Director: Michelangelo Antonioni, *Blowup*

National Board of Review
Best English-Language Film: *A Man for All Seasons*
Born Free
Alfie
Who's Afraid of Virginia Woolf?
The Bible
Georgy Girl
Years of Lightning, Day of Drums
It Happened Here
The Russians Are Coming, The Russians Are Coming
Shakespeare Wallah
Best Foreign-Language Film:
The Sleeping Car Murders
The Gospel According to St. Matthew
The Shameless Old Lady
A Man and a Woman
Hamlet

Actor: Paul Scofield, *A Man for All Seasons*
Actress: Elizabeth Taylor, *Who's Afraid of Virginia Woolf?*
Supporting Actor: Robert Shaw, *A Man for All Seasons*
Supporting Actress: Vivien Merchant, *Alfie*
Director: Fred Zinnemann, *A Man for All Seasons*

Photoplay Gold Medal Awards
Gold Medal: *The Russians Are Coming, The Russians Are Coming*
Most Popular Male Star: David Janssen
Most Popular Female Star: Barbara Stanwyck

British Academy Awards
Film: *Who's Afraid of Virginia Woolf?*
British Film: *The Spy Who Came in from the Cold*
Actor (British): Richard Burton, *Who's Afraid of Virginia Woolf?*, *The Spy Who Came in from the Cold*
Actor (Foreign): Rod Steiger, *The Pawnbroker*
Actress (British): Elizabeth Taylor, *Who's Afraid of Virginia Woolf?*
Actress (Foreign): Jeanne Moreau, *Viva Maria!*
Screenplay: David Mercer, *Morgan!—A Suitable Case for Treatment*

• *A Man and a Woman* AAW CAN
One of the big date movies of
the '60s—and next to *Hawaii*
or *Thoroughly Modern Millie* I
don't doubt that to many people
it looked like the last word in
chic. Today it looks like a
pretend movie, the kind of fake

foreign film someone might put together for use (as a putdown) in a Hollywood movie—generically pretty shots from beer commercials and Hallmark cards, randomly (and sometimes alarmingly) cut together the way someone who'd never seen a foreign film might imagine foreign films were edited, and accompanied by vapidly irritating music (*Marienbad*-like organ crossed with dentist's office Muzak). Gad.

Cannes Film Festival
Palme d'Or: *A Man and a Woman* (Claude Lelouch, France), *The Birds, the Bees and the Italians* (Pietro Germi, Italy)
20th Anniversary Prize: Orson Welles, for *Chimes at Midnight* and for his contribution to world cinema
Special Jury Prize: *Alfie* (Lewis Gilbert, UK)
Actor: Per Oscarsson, *Hunger* (Sweden)
Actress: Vanessa Redgrave, *Morgan!—A Suitable Case for Treatment* (UK)
Director: Sergei Yutkevich, *Lenin in Poland* (USSR)
Best First Film: *Blazing Winter* (Mircea Muresan, Romania)
Special Mention: Totò, *Big Birds, Little Birds* (Italy)
Palme d'Or/Short Film: *Skater Dater* (Noel Black, USA)
International Critics Prize: *Young Törless* (Völker Schlöndorff, West Germany), *La Guerre Est Finie* (Alain Resnais, France)

**** *The Battle of Algiers* VEN
One of the first films to try making a realistic subject matter more vivid by filming it as if it were a documentary (another one, Kevin Brownlow's *It Happened Here*, played Cannes the same year). After everything from *Medium Cool* to *Spinal Tap* to a million shaky-cam commercials, you might not expect it to hold up at all, but Gillo Pontecorvo's account of the growth of Algerian resistance to French rule in the '50s is still an absorbing, perceptive political thriller.

Venice Film Festival
Golden Lion: *The Battle of Algiers* (Gillo Pontecorvo, Italy)
Special Jury Prize: *Yesterday's Girl* (Alexander Kluge, West Germany), *Chappaqua* (Conrad Rooks, USA)
Special Homage: Robert Bresson, *Au Hasard, Balthasar* (France)
Actor: Jacques Perrin, *Quest* (Spain), *Half a Man* (Italy)
Actress: Natalia Arinbasavora, *The First Teacher* (USSR)
International Critics Prize: *The Battle of Algiers*

*** *Cul-de-Sac* BER
Roman Polanski's only film to win a major festival's top prize is a minor but amusing and edgy black comedy, sort of an art-film version of *Key Largo* (or a comic version of his own *Knife in the Water*). Nutty writer Donald Pleasance and wife Françoise Dorléac (Catherine Deneuve's sister) find their island retreat invaded by a pair of comic-menacing gangsters (Lionel Stander, Jack MacGowran).

Berlin Film Festival
Golden Bear: *Cul-de-Sac* (Roman Polanski, UK)
Silver Bear: *Off-Season for Foxes* (Peter Schamoni, West Germany)
Actor: Jean-Pierre Léaud, *Masculin-Feminin* (France), special award to Lars Passgard, *Manhunt* (Sweden)
Actress: Lola Albright, *Lord Love a Duck* (USA)
Director: Carlos Saura, *The Hunt* (Spain)
Special Mention: Satyajit Ray, for *Nayak* [*The Hero*] and his body of work
International Critics Prize: *Seasons of Love* (Florestano Vancini, Italy), and in honor of [the late] Max Ophüls for his body of work (in Retrospektiven)

Harvard Lampoon Movie Worsts
Ten worst pictures:
Is Paris Burning?
Hurry Sundown
The Oscar
The Fortune Cookie
The Bible
A Countess from Hong Kong
The Blue Max
Fantastic Voyage
Torn Curtain
Penelope
The Kirk Douglas Award to the

Worst Actor: George Peppard, *The Blue Max*
Worst Actress: Ursula Andress, *Casino Royale*
Worst Supporting Actor: John Huston, *The Bible*
Worst Supporting Actress: Leslie Caron, *Is Paris Burning?*
The OK-Doc-Break-the-Arm-Again Award (for the most flagrant example of miscasting): John Huston as the voice of God in *The Bible*
Der Otto: Awarded annually to Otto Preminger for his yearly excursions into the tawdry, the sordid, and the silly. This year for his direction of *Hurry Sundown*
The Piltdown Mandible (presented annually for the lamest explanation of scientifically improbable phenomena): This year to the producers of *Fantastic Voyage* for assuming that the molecules which made up the submarine would not re-expand to normal size simply because said submarine had been devoured by a white corpuscle; and to the lone cow in *The Bible* who supplied an estimated 974,000 gallons of milk to all the animals on the Ark for forty days and forty nights
The Merino Award: To the two Merinos on the Ark in *The Bible*

Box Office (Domestic Rentals)

1	*Thunderball*	$26,000,000	UA
2	*Dr. Zhivago*	15,000,000	MGM
3	*Who's Afraid of Virginia Woolf?*	10,300,000	WB
4	*That Darn Cat*	9,200,000	Disney
5	*The Russians Are Coming, The Russians Are Coming*	7,750,000	UA
6	*Lt. Robin Crusoe, USN*	7,500,000	Disney
7	*The Silencers*	7,000,000	Col
8	*Torn Curtain*	7,000,000	Uni
9	*Our Man Flint*	6,500,000	Fox

10	A Patch of Blue	6,300,000	MGM

Other films of note:

11	The Ugly Dachshund	6,000,000	Disney
12	The Wild Angels	5,500,000	American Int'l
18	Fantastic Voyage	4,500,000	Fox
25	Bambi [reissue]	3,900,000	Disney
27	The Singing Nun	3,590,000	MGM
31	Darling	3,360,000	Embassy
32	The Spy Who Came in from the Cold	3,100,000	Par
51	Dr. Goldfoot and the Bikini Machine	1,900,000	American Int'l
67	The Last of the Secret Agents?	1,000,000	Par
72	Where the Spies Are	995,000	MGM
82	A Man and a Woman	350,000	Allied Artists
	[through 1970:	5,600,000]	

The height of the spy craze—Thunderball at #1, a Matt Helm movie at #7, one of Hitchcock's last examples of the genre at #8, the first of many Bond spoofs at #9, the most serious example of the genre at #32, and even more spoofs farther down the list. Meanwhile, at #12 is a harbinger of the future—Roger Corman's The Wild Angels, with Peter Fonda. Corman's first film to play the Venice Film Festival was also his biggest hit to date—and the first real indication that the movie audience was about to fracture into over- and under-30 contingents.

Gebert's Golden Armchairs

Crowther was right to push for *Virginia Woolf?*, the highbrows were right to champion *Blowup* . . . but funny, I find the conservative choice the most satisfying of the bunch thirty years later.

Best American Film: *A Man for All Seasons*
Best Foreign Film: *Blowup*
Best Actor: Richard Burton, *Who's Afraid of Virginia Woolf?*
Best Actress: Elizabeth Taylor, *Who's Afraid of Virginia Woolf?*
Best Director: Michelangelo Antonioni, *Blowup*

1967

In the Heat of the Night is famous in Oscar lore as the movie that, thanks to the Academy's chickenheartedness, robbed *Bonnie and Clyde* (or, in other accounts, *The Graduate*) of its rightful Oscar and place as the first Best Picture of the New Hollywood. The problem with that is, while *The Graduate* may have picked up a couple of minor awards (including the comedy Golden Globe, for which it obviously didn't compete with *Night*), there wasn't a *single* awards group that named *Bonnie and Clyde* the best film of the year. The only one that might have, the National Society of Film Critics, picked Bergman's *Persona* over *B&C* by a 2–1 margin and placed Rod Steiger far ahead of Hoffman (four votes) and Beatty (two). (Remember that each critic gets three votes, so those aren't even necessarily first-choice votes.)

Bosley Crowther is said to have prevented the New York Critics Circle from picking it by sheer force of personality. The *Times* account, which usually detailed each round of the voting, is curiously vague that year—but membership hadn't changed *that* much yet from the group that had voted for *Ben-Hur* and *My Fair Lady*, and I wonder. Oscar—and Crowther—were hardly alone in finding *Bonnie and Clyde* more than they could stomach in '67.

Academy Awards

**** *In the Heat of the Night*
AAW GLO NYC
*** Rod Steiger AAW GLO NYC SOC BAA
In any other year, *In the Heat of the Night* would have been an uncontroversial, even laudable choice—no mere race feelgood movie like *Guess Who's Coming To Dinner*, but a superbly well-crafted police drama, sharply acted from top to bottom and with a feel for the stultifying, time-has-stopped atmosphere of a small town that today's hyperthyroid thrillers couldn't even imagine (one exception: Carl Franklin's *One False Move*). The three-star rating for Steiger as the sheriff is only because he was better elsewhere: it's an accent winner—but one of the better ones.

Picture
In the Heat of the Night (UA, Walter Mirisch)
Bonnie and Clyde (Warner Bros.–Seven Arts, Warren Beatty)
Doctor Dolittle (20th Century–Fox, Arthur P. Jacobs)
The Graduate (Embassy, Nichols-Turman, Lawrence Turman)
Guess Who's Coming to Dinner (Columbia, Stanley Kramer)

Actor
Rod Steiger, *In the Heat of the Night*
Warren Beatty, *Bonnie and Clyde*
Dustin Hoffman, *The Graduate*
Paul Newman, *Cool Hand Luke*
Spencer Tracy, *Guess Who's Coming to Dinner*

** ** Katharine Hepburn in *Guess Who's Coming to Dinner*   AAW BAA '68**
The movie that asks the question, Would you let a black Nobel Prize candidate marry your bubbleheaded white daughter, and wouldn't you wonder why he'd want to? A dismayingly accurate picture of what it would have been like if Hepburn had had a '50s TV sitcom like Donna Reed's (Wally, you must stop hitting the Beavah, really you must), and a mere copout for an Academy that couldn't see its way clear to honoring either Bancroft's Mrs. Robinson or English veteran Edith Evans in a little film like *The Whisperers* (the year's main female award-getter, but not, alas, on video for review).

Actress
Katharine Hepburn, *Guess Who's Coming to Dinner*
Anne Bancroft, *The Graduate*
Faye Dunaway, *Bonnie and Clyde*
Dame Edith Evans, *The Whisperers*
Audrey Hepburn, *Wait Until Dark*

Supporting Actor
George Kennedy, *Cool Hand Luke*
John Cassavetes, *The Dirty Dozen*
Gene Hackman, *Bonnie and Clyde*
Cecil Kellaway, *Guess Who's Coming to Dinner*
Michael J. Pollard, *Bonnie and Clyde*

Supporting Actress
Estelle Parsons, *Bonnie and Clyde*
Carol Channing, *Thoroughly Modern Millie*
Mildred Natwick, *Barefoot in the Park*
Beah Richards, *Guess Who's Coming to Dinner*
Katharine Ross, *The Graduate*

Director
Mike Nichols, *The Graduate*
Richard Brooks, *In Cold Blood*
Norman Jewison, *In the Heat of the Night*
Stanley Kramer, *Guess Who's Coming to Dinner*
Arthur Penn, *Bonnie and Clyde*

Original Screenplay: William Rose, *Guess Who's Coming to Dinner*
Adapted Screenplay: Stirling Silliphant, *In the Heat of the Night*
Cinematography: Burnett Guffey, *Bonnie and Clyde*
Original Score: Elmer Bernstein, *Thoroughly Modern Millie*
Adapted Score: Alfred Newman, Ken Darby, *Camelot*
Song: "Talk to the Animals," *Doctor Dolittle*, ml: Leslie Bricusse
Art Direction: John Truscott, Edward Carrere, *Camelot*
Costume Design: John Truscott, *Camelot*
Editing: Hal Ashby, *In the Heat of the Night*
Sound: *In the Heat of the Night*
Sound Effects: *The Dirty Dozen*
Special Visual Effects: *Doctor Dolittle*
Short/Cartoon: *The Box* (Brandon Films, Fred Wolf)

Short/Live Action: *A Place to Stand* (Ontario Dept. of Economics and Development, made for Expo '67)
Documentary/Feature: *The Anderson Platoon* (French Broadcasting System, Pierre Schöndörffer)
Documentary/Short: *The Redwoods*
Foreign-Language Film: *Closely Watched Trains* (Czechoslovakia)
Irving G. Thalberg Award: Alfred Hitchcock
Jean Hersholt Humanitarian Award: Gregory Peck
Special Award: Arthur Freed, for distinguished service to the Academy and the production of six top-rated Awards telecasts

Golden Globes
Picture (Drama): *In the Heat of the Night*
Picture (Comedy/Musical): *The Graduate*
English-Language Foreign Film: *The Fox*
Foreign-Language Film: *Live for Life* (France)
Actor (Drama): Rod Steiger, *In the Heat of the Night*
Actor (Comedy/Musical): Richard Harris, *Camelot*
Actress (Drama): Dame Edith Evans, *The Whisperers*
Actress (Comedy/Musical): Anne Bancroft, *The Graduate*
Supporting Actor: Richard Attenborough, *Doctor Dolittle*
Supporting Actress: Carol Channing, *Thoroughly Modern Millie*
Director: Mike Nichols, *The Graduate*
Screenplay: Stirling Silliphant, *In the Heat of the Night*
Original Score: Frederick Loewe, *Camelot*
Original Song: "If I Should Ever Leave You," *Camelot*, m: Frederick Loewe l: Alan Jay Lerner
Most Promising Newcomer (Male): Dustin Hoffman, *The Graduate*
Most Promising Newcomer (Female): Katharine Ross, *The Graduate*
World Film Favorite (Male): Paul Newman
World Film Favorite (Female): Julie Andrews
Cecil B. DeMille Award: Kirk Douglas

Directors Guild of America
Director: Mike Nichols, *The Graduate*
D. W. Griffith Award: Alfred Hitchcock
Honorary Lifetime Member: Darryl F. Zanuck

New York Film Critics Circle
Picture: *In the Heat of the Night*
Foreign Film: *La Guerre Est Finie*
Actor: Rod Steiger, *In the Heat of the Night*
Actress: Edith Evans, *The Whisperers*
Director: Mike Nichols, *The Graduate*
Screenplay: David Newman, Robert Benton, *Bonnie and Clyde*
Special Award: Bosley Crowther

***** *Persona* SOC
An actress (Liv Ullmann) breaks down on stage and refuses to speak; a nurse (Bibi Andersson) is recruited to look after her. The masterpiece of Ingmar Bergman's post–*Wild Strawberries* period, film-as-therapy at its most probing, serious, and hypnotic—even if,

at the end, it turns out to be Bergman's 8½, his self-defeating acknowledgment that it's all only a movie.

National Society of Film Critics

Picture: *Persona*
Actor: Rod Steiger, *In the Heat of the Night*
Actress: Bibi Andersson, *Persona*
Supporting Actor: Gene Hackman, *Bonnie and Clyde*
Supporting Actress: Marjorie Rhodes, *The Family Way*
Director: Ingmar Bergman, *Persona*
Screenplay: David Newman, Robert Benton, *Bonnie and Clyde*
Cinematography: Haskell Wexler, *In the Heat of the Night*

National Board of Review

Best English-Language Film:
Far from the Madding Crowd
The Whisperers
Ulysses
In Cold Blood
The Family Way
The Taming of the Shrew
Doctor Dolittle
The Graduate
The Comedians
Accident
Best Foreign-Language Film:
Elvira Madigan
The Hunt
Africa Addio
Persona
The Great British Train Robbery
Actor: Peter Finch, *Far from the Madding Crowd*
Actress: Edith Evans, *The Whisperers*
Supporting Actor: Paul Ford, *The Comedians*
Supporting Actress: Marjorie Rhodes, *The Family Way*
Director: Richard Brooks, *In Cold Blood*

Photoplay Gold Medal Awards

Gold Medal: *The Dirty Dozen*
Most Popular Male Star: Paul Newman
Most Popular Female Star: Barbara Stanwyck

British Academy Awards

Film: *A Man for All Seasons*
British Film: *A Man for All Seasons*
Actor (British): Paul Scofield, *A Man for All Seasons*
Actor (Foreign): Rod Steiger, *In the Heat of the Night*
Actress (British): Edith Evans, *The Whisperers*
Actress (Foreign): Anouk Aimée, *A Man and a Woman*
Screenplay: Robert Bolt, *A Man for All Seasons*
Robert Flaherty Documentary Award: *To Die in Madrid* (Frederic Rossif, France)

Cannes Film Festival

Palme d'Or: *Blowup* (Michelangelo Antonioni, UK)
Special Jury Prize: *Accident* (Joseph Losey, UK), *I Even Met Happy Gypsies* (Aleksandar Petrovic, Yugoslavia)
Actor: Odded Kotler, *Three Days and a Child* (Israel)
Actress: Pia Degermark, *Elvira Madigan* (Sweden)
Director: Ferenc Kósa, *Ten Thousand Days* (Hungary)
Screenplay: Alain Jessua, *The Killing Game/Comic-Strip Hero* (France), Elio Petri and Ugo Pirro, *We Still Kill the Old Way* (Italy)
Best First Film: *Le Vent des Aurés*, Mohammed Lakhdar Hamina (Algeria)
Tribute: to the work of Robert Bresson
International Critics Prizes: *Accident* (Joseph Losey, UK), *Earth in Revolt* (Glauber Rocha,

Brazil), *I Even Met Happy Gypsies*

***** ***Belle de Jour*** VEN
Blankly beautiful Belle (Catherine Deneuve) looks to be as uncomplicated a creature as any bourgeois Parisian housewife; in fact that pretty exterior conceals a startlingly baroque fantasy life that leads her into a side career as a prostitute, with devastating results for the men in her life. Sort of what an *Emmanuelle* film would be like if it were directed by someone with a real point of view; the masterpiece of Luis Buñuel's later career is a work of cool comic perfection, with Deneuve the greatest stone face since Buster Keaton.

Venice Film Festival
Golden Lion: *Belle de Jour* (Luis Buñuel, France)
Special Jury Prize: *La Chinoise* (Jean-Luc Godard, France), *China Is Near* (Marco Bellochio, Italy)
Actor: Ljubisa Samardzic, *Dawn* (Yugoslavia)
Actress: Shirley Knight, *Dutchman* (UK)
Best First Film: *Mahlzeiten* [*The Insatiable*] (Edgar Reitz, West Germany)
International Critics Prize: in competition, *China Is Near*; out of competition, *Rebellion* (Masaki Kobayashi, Japan)
Italian Critics/Pasinetti Prize: in competition, *Belle de Jour*; out of competition, *Mouchette* (Robert Bresson, France)

Berlin Film Festival
Golden Bear: *Le Départ* (Jerzy Skolimowski, Belgium)

Silver Bear: *La Collectionneuse* (Eric Rohmer, France)
Actor: Michel Simon, *The Two of Us* (France)
Actress: Edith Evans, *The Whisperers* (UK)
Director: Zivojin Pavlovic, *The Rats Awaken* (Yugoslavia)
Screenplay: Michael Lentz, *Every Year Again* (Ulrich Schamoni, West Germany)
International Critics Prize: *Every Year Again*

Harvard Lampoon Movie Worsts
Ten worst pictures:
Guess Who's Coming to Dinner
Valley of the Dolls
Up the Down Staircase
One Million Years B.C.
The Comedians
Reflections in a Golden Eye
Thoroughly Modern Millie
Doctor Dolittle
The Fox
Carmen Baby
Kirk Douglas Award for Worst Actor: Richard Burton, *Doctor Faustus*, *The Comedians*
Natalie Wood Award for Worst Actress: Raquel Welch, *One Million Years B.C.*, *The Biggest Bundle of Them All*, *Bedazzled*
The OK-Doc-Break-the-Arm-Again Award (for the most flagrant example of miscasting): to Charlton Heston, for portraying a human being in *Planet of the Apes*
The Piltdown Mandible (to the most obviously and unabashedly spurious scientific phenomena): *One Million Years B.C.*, for the contemporaneous existence of Raquel Welch and a passel of dinosaurs, an unscientific juxtaposition redounding entirely to the credit of the dinosaurs
The Tedium Is the Medium Citation (to the worst student

film): Tim Hunter's *Desire Is the Fire*

The Tin Pan (to the most obnoxious movie song): Leslie Bricusse's "Talk to the Animals" in *Doctor Dolittle*, for bloodcurdling anthropomorphism

The Merino Award: To the Pushme-Pullyou in *Doctor Dolittle*, who is, as we take it, a distant cousin to merinos, and at any rate leads just as tenuous an existence

Box Office (Domestic Rentals)

1	*The Dirty Dozen*	$18,200,000	MGM
2	*You Only Live Twice*	16,300,000	UA
3	*Casino Royale*	10,200.000	Col
4	*A Man for All Seasons*	9,200,000	Disney
5	*Thoroughly Modern Millie*	8,500,000	Uni
6	*Barefoot in the Park*	8,250,000	Par
7	*Georgy Girl*	7,330,000	Col
8	*To Sir With Love*	7,200,000	Col
9	*Grand Prix*	7,000,000	MGM
10	*Hombre*	6,500,000	Fox
Other films of note:			
13	*El Dorado*	5,950,000	Par
14	*Blowup*	5,900,000	MGM
18	*In Like Flint*	5,000,000	Fox
22	*In the Heat of the Night*	4,450,000	UA
	[through 1970:	11,000,000]	
24	*The Trip*	4,025,000	American Int'l
27	*The Taming of the Shrew*	3,540,000	Col
36	*One Million Years B.C.*	2,500,000	Fox
41	*For a Few Dollars More*	2,270,000	UA
46	*A Fistful of Dollars*	2,060,000	UA

Dueling Bonds at #2 and #3, but the top film of the year was the movie that introduced to the screen a new level of violence, a cast of murderous antiheroes, and a callous, sardonic attitude toward mayhem that would quickly prove infectious. No, not Bonnie and Clyde—The Dirty Dozen. *It's a schizophrenic year, with a Julie Andrews musical and Liz & Dick in Shakespeare competing against such unexpected hits as Antonioni's vision of Swinging London in* Blowup, *Roger Corman's vision of tripping Frisco, a minor TV star named Eastwood in two Westerns shot in Spain by Italians, and Raquel Welch in a brontosaurus-skin bikini in Hammer's extremely scientifically accurate* One Million Years B.C.

Gebert's Golden Armchairs

Bonnie and Clyde and *The Graduate* both deserve their reputations as movies that mark the line between the old Hollywood and the new one. *Bonnie and Clyde* is the more original and unnerving of the two—a movie that takes on the relationship between movie-star glamour and the glamorization of violence and dares us not to adore its killers. (We'd soon get over the moral problem, and the guns and the heroes have been getting bigger and more beautiful ever since.) *The Graduate*'s achievement is smaller (and also somewhat mixed in its legacy)—it popularized in the movies the nasty caricature-humor that sketch comedians, like director Mike Nichols in his earlier career, had been pioneering for a decade in live venues. The difference between it and later *Saturday Night Live* movies is the comic precision of Bancroft and Hoffman's performances (that *Rain Man*–like half-a-beat out of sync with the rest of the world—"Would you happen to know . . . where the old . . . make-out king . . . is getting married?") One is characterization—the other is just attitude.

Best American Film: *Bonnie and Clyde*
Best Foreign Film: *Belle de Jour*
Best Actor: Dustin Hoffman, *The Graduate*
Best Actress: Anne Bancroft, *The Graduate*
Best Director: Arthur Penn, *Bonnie and Clyde*

1968

The Academy hid behind *Oliver!*'s chorus line of urchins as its symbolic defense against youthful rebellion; but Cannes '68 actually fell apart in the chaos of a nationwide youth uprising that began, appropriately enough, in the world of film when the French government attempted to fire the legendary film archivist, Henri Langlois. Langlois had founded the Cinémathèque Française in 1936, and run it for many years as a shoestring operation, supposedly paying his staff every Friday out of a bag of crumpled franc notes. By the time the Cinémathèque had become a significant government institution, Langlois' methods were no longer tolerable to the bureaucrats above him, and in 1968 he was fired.

Every film personality in France rallied to the side of a man who, whatever the quirks of his working methods, had done more than anyone else living for the cause of film preservation. Within a short time there was the astonishing spectacle of police squaring off against a group of marchers including the likes of François Truffaut, Jeanne Moreau, Simone Signoret, and Yves Montand, while filmmakers worldwide telegraphed their support and threatened to withdraw their films. Faced with this, the government backed down—also withdrawing its funding of the Cinémathèque at the same time. But the world's first celebrity riot quickly encouraged uprisings against Vietnam, university policies, and other things, and by the time Cannes opened in May the students of the Sorbonne had taken to the streets and millions of workers were on strike.

Flames engulfed the beach on Opening Night—but that had nothing to do with Langlois, it was just a re-creation of the Burning of Atlanta in honor of yet another reissue of *Gone With the Wind*. For the Langloisistes, the festival was a symbol of cinematic officialdom that had to be brought to a halt, and at the Palais, Truffaut urged that the festival must close— "Everything that has a shred of dignity and importance is stopping in France." Truffaut, et al. were opposed in overthrowing the festival, ironically enough, by Iron Curtain filmmakers, for whom the festival wasn't a symbol of repression but a rare taste of Western freedom. Many younger filmmakers also resented the fact that their more wealthy and famous colleagues wanted to deny them the chance for their films to be shown—and the proletariat who served Cannes' hotels and restaurants weren't thrilled by this upper-class uprising, either.

In the end a shut-down proved inevitable—everything else in France had; and it was the younger filmmakers who became the main beneficiaries of the post–May '68 reforms, with the creation of the Directors Fortnight for new filmmakers.

Academy Awards

*** *Oliver!* AAW GLO
I am not someone who particularly thought that David Lean's 1948 *Oliver Twist* cried out for a chorus line of urchins singing "You've got to pick a pocket or two." It's enough to make you wonder about the artistic statute of limitations on misery (so a hundred years are enough to make the horrors of Victorian poverty and child labor sufficiently quaint to spawn a musical . . . that's it, I'm writing *Gettysburg!*). But if you can accept the very idea, it's an extremely solid and well-made musical—as the fact that it was utterly ransacked by the recent stage hit *Les Misérables* demonstrates.

Picture
Oliver! (Columbia, Romulus, John Woolf)
Funny Girl (Columbia, Ray Stark)
The Lion in Winter (Avco Embassy, Martin Poll)
Rachel, Rachel (Warner Bros.–Seven Arts, Paul Newman)
Romeo and Juliet (Paramount, B.H.E.–Verona–De Laurentiis)

** Cliff Robertson in *Charly* AAW BOR
A sci-fi *Rain Man*, with Robertson as a retarded man whose I.Q. is raised to genius levels—temporarily. Robertson is fair enough, though it's the part that won the Oscar. The movie, however, has dated terribly—Ralph Nelson, whose direction in *Lilies of the Field* was as eager to please as a puppy, clearly saw a lot of foreign films in the meantime, and there's not a single irritating cliché of '60s filmmaking he misses (dig that crazy split-screen!)—plus an ice-cold tone that comes off as smug and arrogant.

Actor
Cliff Robertson, *Charly*
Alan Arkin, *The Heart Is a Lonely Hunter*
Alan Bates, *The Fixer*
Ron Moody, *Oliver!*
Peter O'Toole, *The Lion in Winter*

**** Katharine Hepburn in *The Lion in Winter* AAW BAA
Clearly the most deserved of Hepburn's record four Oscars—though I could easily think of four of hers that are better yet than this waspish, dried-up wife and Queen (*Summertime*, *Holiday*, *Philadelphia Story*, *Adam's Rib* . . . wait, I can think of four more. . . .).

**** Barbra Streisand in *Funny Girl* AAW GLO HAR
Presenting the Anti-Andrews—an American musical star with all the confidence, stage presence and lung power of Sister Julie herself, but with a New York sense of humor, too. She takes a place in Oscar history as the thirteenth and last player to be directed to an Oscar by William Wyler—a line stretching back to Walter Brennan in *Come and Get It* through *Jezebel*, *Mrs. Miniver*, *The Best Years of Our Lives*, and *Ben-Hur*; and, given the slower pace today's star directors work at, a record that will probably never be broken (second place? Kazan, a mere nine).

Actress
Katharine Hepburn, *The Lion in Winter*
Barbra Streisand, *Funny Girl* (tie)
Patricia Neal, *The Subject Was Roses*
Vanessa Redgrave, *Isadora*
Joanne Woodward, *Rachel, Rachel*

Supporting Actor
Jack Albertson, *The Subject Was Roses*
Seymour Cassel, *Faces*
Daniel Massey, *Star!*
Jack Wild, *Oliver!*
Gene Wilder, *The Producers*

Supporting Actress
Ruth Gordon, *Rosemary's Baby*
Lynn Carlin, *Faces*
Sondra Locke, *The Heart Is a Lonely Hunter*
Kay Medford, *Funny Girl*
Estelle Parsons, *Rachel, Rachel*

Director
Carol Reed, *Oliver!*
Anthony Harvey, *The Lion in Winter*
Stanley Kubrick, *2001: A Space Odyssey*
Gillo Pontecorvo, *The Battle of Algiers*
Franco Zeffirelli, *Romeo and Juliet*

Original Screenplay: Mel Brooks, *The Producers*
Adapted Screenplay: James Goldman, *The Lion in Winter*
Cinematography: Pasqualino De Santis, *Romeo and Juliet*
Original Score: John Barry, *The Lion in Winter*
Adapted Score: John Green, *Oliver!*
Song: "The Windmills of Your Mind," *The Thomas Crown Affair*, m: Michel Legrand, l: Alan and Marilyn Bergman
Art Direction: John Box, Terry Marsh, *Oliver!*
Costume Design: Danilo Donati, *Romeo and Juliet*
Editing: *Bullitt*
Sound: *Oliver!*
Special Visual Effects: Stanley Kubrick, *2001: A Space Odyssey*
Short/Cartoon: *Winnie the Pooh and the Blustery Day* (Walt Disney)
Short/Live Action: *Robert Kennedy Remembered*
Documentary/Feature: *Journey into Self* (Western Behavioral Sciences Institute)
Documentary/Short: *Why Man Creates* (Saul Bass)
Foreign-Language Film: *War and Peace* (USSR)
Jean Hersholt Humanitarian Award: Martha Raye
Special Awards:
John Chambers, make-up, *Planet of the Apes*
Onna White, choreography, *Oliver!*

*** *The Lion in Winter* GLO DGA NYC BOR HAR
Oscar's honest enthusiasm for a bouncy musical looks better today than the consensus choice of this Broadway-bitchy drama, more middlebrow and heavy-handed than the earlier film in which Peter O'Toole played King Henry II, *Becket*. With O'Toole, Hepburn as his unloved and embittered wife Eleanor of Aquitaine, and no less than Anthony Hopkins, Timothy Dalton, and Nigel Terry in early or debut roles as their three scheming sons, star power is its best attribute.

Golden Globes
Picture (Drama): *The Lion in Winter*
Picture (Comedy/Musical): *Oliver!*
English-Language Foreign Film: *Romeo and Juliet*
Foreign-Language Film: *War and Peace* (USSR)
Actor (Drama): Peter O'Toole, *The Lion in Winter*
Actor (Comedy/Musical): Ron Moody, *Oliver!*
Actress (Drama): Joanne Woodward, *Rachel, Rachel*
Actress (Comedy/Musical): Barbra Streisand, *Funny Girl*
Supporting Actor: Daniel Massey, *Star!*
Supporting Actress: Ruth Gordon, *Rosemary's Baby*
Director: Paul Newman, *Rachel, Rachel*
Screenplay: Stirling Silliphant, *Charly*
Original Score: Alex North, *The Shoes of the Fisherman*
Original Song: "The Windmills of Your Mind," *The Thomas Crown Affair*, m: Michel Legrand, l: Alan and Marilyn Bergman

Most Promising Newcomer (Male): Leonard Whiting, *Romeo and Juliet*
Most Promising Newcomer (Female): Olivia Hussey, *Romeo and Juliet*
World Film Favorite (Male): Sidney Poitier
World Film Favorite (Female): Sophia Loren
Cecil B. DeMille Award: Gregory Peck

Directors Guild of America
Director: Anthony Harvey, *The Lion in Winter*

New York Film Critics Circle
Picture: *The Lion in Winter*
Foreign Film: *War and Peace*
Actor: Alan Arkin, *The Heart Is a Lonely Hunter*
Actress: Joanne Woodward, *Rachel, Rachel*
Director: Paul Newman, *Rachel, Rachel*
Screenplay: Lorenzo Semple, Jr., *Pretty Poison*

*** *Shame* SOC BOR '69
In its first nine years the National Society gave Ingmar Bergman three Best Film prizes—and his star Liv Ullmann three actress awards (plus another to Bibi Andersson). This Kafkaesque drama of refugees Ullmann and Max Von Sydow traveling through an unnamed, wartorn land is not on a par with the previous year's *Persona*; the first half might be, but the second, in which they wander mutely through a land littered with corpses, is so nihilistic as to be completely alienating—and more evidence

of a burnout that fortunately turned out to be only temporary.

National Society of Film Critics
Picture: *Shame*
Actor: Per Oscarsson, *Hunger*
Actress: Liv Ullmann, *Shame*
Supporting Actor: Seymour Cassel, *Faces*
Supporting Actress: Billie Whitelaw, *Charlie Bubbles*
Director: Ingmar Bergman, *Shame, Hour of the Wolf*
Screenplay: John Cassavetes, *Faces*
Cinematography: William A. Fraker, *Bullitt*
Special Awards: *Warrendale, A Face of War*, for documentary features; *Yellow Submarine*, for animated feature

National Board of Review
Best English-Language Film:
The Shoes of the Fisherman
Romeo and Juliet
Yellow Submarine
Charly
Rachel, Rachel
The Subject Was Roses
The Lion in Winter
Planet of the Apes
Oliver!
2001: A Space Odyssey
Best Foreign-Language Film:
War and Peace
Hagbard and Signo
Hunger
The Two of Us
The Bride Wore Black
Actor: Cliff Robertson, *Charly*
Actress: Liv Ullmann, *Hour of the Wolf, Shame*
Supporting Actor: Leo McKern, *The Shoes of the Fisherman*
Supporting Actress: Virginia Maskell, *Interlude*
Director: Franco Zeffirelli, *Romeo and Juliet*

Photoplay Gold Medal Awards
Gold Medal: *Rosemary's Baby*
Most Popular Male Star: Steve McQueen
Most Popular Female Star: Debbie Reynolds

British Academy Awards
Film: *The Graduate*
Actor: Spencer Tracy, *Guess Who's Coming to Dinner*
Actress: Katharine Hepburn, *Guess Who's Coming to Dinner, The Lion in Winter*
Supporting Actor: Ian Holm, *The Bofors Gun*
Supporting Actress: Billie Whitelaw, *The Twisted Nerve, Charlie Bubbles*
Director: Mike Nichols, *The Graduate*
Screenplay: Calder Willingham, Buck Henry, *The Graduate*
Short Animated Film: *Pas de Deux* (Norman McLaren, Canada)

Venice Film Festival
[NOTE: Official awards suspended 1969–79]
Golden Lion: *Artists Under the Big Top, Disoriented* (Alexander Kluge, West Germany)
Special Jury Prize: *Le Socrate* (Robert Lapoujade, France), *Nostra Signora del Turchi* (Carmelo Bene, Italy)
Actor: John Marley, *Faces* (USA)
Actress: Laura Betti, *Teorema* (Italy)

Berlin Film Festival
Golden Bear: *Ole Dole Doff* (Jan Troell, Sweden)
Silver Bear: *Innocence Unprotected* (Dusan Makavejev, Yugoslavia), *Come l'Amore* (Enzo Muzii, Italy)
Actor: Jean-Louis Trintignant, *The Man Who Lies* (France-Czechoslovakia)

Actress: Stéphane Audran, *Les Biches* (France)
Director: Carlos Saura, *Peppermint Frappé* (Spain)
First Film: *Signs of Life* (Werner Herzog, West Germany)
Documentary: *Portrait of Orson Welles* (François Reichenbach, France)
International Critics Prize: *Innocence Unprotected*, tribute to Asta Nielsen

Harvard Lampoon **Movie Worsts**
Ten worst pictures:
The Lion in Winter
Ice Station Zebra
Rosemary's Baby
Star!
The Boston Strangler
Candy
Barbarella
You Are What You Eat
The Seagull
Boom!
Kirk Douglas Award for Worst Actor: Sidney Poitier, *For Love of Ivy*
Natalie Wood Award for Worst Actress: Barbra Streisand, *Funny Girl*
Worst Supporting Actor: Rod Steiger, *No Way to Treat a Lady*
Worst Supporting Actress: Ewa Aulin, *Candy*
The Merino Award: To the cast of *The Green Berets*

Box Office (Domestic Rentals)

1	*The Graduate*	$39,000,000	Embassy
2	*Guess Who's Coming to Dinner*	25,100,000	Col
3	*Gone With the Wind*	23,000,000	MGM
4	*Bonnie and Clyde*	20,250,000	WB
5	*Valley of the Dolls*	20,000,000	Fox
6	*The Odd Couple*	18,500,000	Par
7	*Planet of the Apes*	15,000,000	Fox
8	*Rosemary's Baby*	12,300,000	Par
9	*The Jungle Book*	11,500,000	Disney
10	*Yours, Mine and Ours*	11,000,000	UA
Other films of note:			
11	*The Green Berets*	8,700,000	WB
12	*2001: A Space Odyssey*	8,500,000	MGM
	[through 1970:	14,501,000]	
15	*Camelot*	6,600,000	WB
18	*In Cold Blood*	5,600,000	Col
21	*Hang 'Em High*	5,000,000	UA
25	*The Good, the Bad, and the Ugly*	4,500,000	UA
28	*Wild in the Streets*	4,000,000	American Int'l
31	*Doctor Dolittle*	3,500,000	Fox
37	*Barbarella*	2,500,000	Par
42	*Elvira Madigan*	2,100,000	Cinema V
74	*Star!*	1,300,000	Fox

The audience cracked in half—under 30, the biggest hit was The Graduate; *over 30, it was yet another reissue of* Gone With the Wind, *this time blown up (inappropriately) to 70mm proportions. Just off the top ten, and coming in well below that other sci-fi movie with apes in it, was the film that would go on to become the longest-running success of its year—2001. Its initial reviews ranged from respectfully baffled to patronizing, but college kids hipped to it as an acid trip in celluloid form and kept it playing for over a decade. Way down at #74 is the year's biggest disaster—Julie Andrews in Star!, which did so poorly in its original three-hour cut that, like Heaven's Gate, it was pulled from release and reedited. Add to that the disappointing performances of Camelot and Doctor Dolittle, and studio executives had a lot of reason to be nervous about all the musicals they were making.*

Gebert's Golden Armchairs

For the award groups it was a year for Broadway sophistication on screen, but for anyone looking back, it was a year for genius-auteurs making visually extravagant widescreen trip films: Kubrick's landmark *Lawrence of Jupiter* and Sergio Leone's 2½-hour commercial for his western wear boutique, *Once Upon a Time in a Head Full of Western Imagery*.

By the time he'd survived the blacklist and played Tevye on stage for five years, Zero Mostel was too big a comic presence for the movies, and most of his performances are more frightening than funny; Mel Brooks' first film is shapeless enough that Mostel's overbearing persona can fill it out without destroying it. As a director John Cassavetes had only one trick—capturing, with exact but wearying precision, the feeling of hanging out with drunks long after you wanted to go home—but *Faces* at least has a pair of solid, un–self-indulgent performances from John Marley as a worldly adman and Gena Rowlands as a bimbo who's not so bimboish after all. (So of course Oscar went and nominated co-stars Seymour Cassel and Lynn Carlin. Go figure.)

Best American Film: *2001: A Space Odyssey*
Best Foreign Film: *Once Upon a Time in the West*
Best Actor: Zero Mostel, *The Producers*
Best Actress: Gena Rowlands, *Faces*
Best Director: Stanley Kubrick, *2001: A Space Odyssey*

1969

How did the Academy come to choose *Midnight Cowboy* instead of *Butch* (or *Anne of the Thousand Days* or God knows what)? The answer is simple: the membership was suddenly expanded with an infusion of younger voters, more in tune with the youth culture (and East Coast critical thinking). While a *True Grit* or *Patton* would still win here and there, I think it's safe to say that this was the only reason we had winners like *Cowboy*, Jackson in *Women in Love*, and Fonda in *Klute* over the next few years—otherwise we might very well be talking about winners like *Airport*, *Fiddler on the Roof*, Janet Suzman in *Nicholas and Alexandra* . . . or even *Love Story*.

Academy Awards

***** Midnight Cowboy
AAW DGA BAA
Briton John Schlesinger's portrait of the needy friendship between two NYC losers—a failed Texas gigolo and a tubercular little runt. At the time, while generally admiring, reviewers complained about how snide some of Schlesinger's satire was; that goes unnoticed now, but what seems remarkable today is how tender it all is—forget whether a *studio* would finance it today, would any handsome young *actor* today dare play a character so pathetic, so needy, so emotionally naive and open and lost? (Yes, one: River Phoenix in *My Own Private Idaho*, a character obviously inspired by Voight's here.) One of Oscar's proudest moments was choosing *Cowboy*—at that point, only a critical hit, and largely unknown to the general public—as Best Picture over a perfectly respectable crowd-pleaser like *Butch Cassidy and the Sundance Kid*.

Picture
Midnight Cowboy (UA, Jerome Hellman)
Anne of the Thousand Days (Universal, Hal B. Wallis)
Butch Cassidy and the Sundance Kid (20th Century–Fox, Hill-Monash, John Foreman)
Hello, Dolly! (20th Century–Fox, Ernest Lehman)
Z (Cinema V, Reggane Films–O.N.C.I.C., Jacques Perrin, Hamed Rachedi)

*** John Wayne in *True Grit*
AAW GLO
No *Searchers*—hell, it may not even be *McLintock!*—and even the Academy probably only gave it to Wayne because Voight and Hoffman canceled each other out, but what the hell. It's fun watching the Duke play the Martin-Mitchum drunk part from *Rio Bravo/El Dorado*, and he deserved one, though *The Shootist* would have

been the ideal combination of sentiment, merit—and dignity.

Actor
John Wayne, *True Grit*
Richard Burton, *Anne of the Thousand Days*
Dustin Hoffman, *Midnight Cowboy*
Peter O'Toole, *Goodbye, Mr. Chips*
Jon Voight, *Midnight Cowboy*

**** Maggie Smith in *The Prime of Miss Jean Brodie*
AAW BAA
An unconventional Scottish teacher who at first seems to be a marvelous inspiration to her pupils turns out to be a bundle of crypto-fascist neuroses, and spawns the student who brings her down. Sort of *Lord of the Flies* crossed with a Jeeves and Wooster novel; at a time when American actresses seemed terminally spaced out, Smith's crisp tragicomic precision as the dotty schoolteacher clearly cowed the Academy as firmly as Miss Brodie did her pupils.

Actress
Maggie Smith, *The Prime of Miss Jean Brodie*
Geneviève Bujold, *Anne of the Thousand Days*
Jane Fonda, *They Shoot Horses, Don't They?*
Liza Minnelli, *The Sterile Cuckoo*
Jean Simmons, *The Happy Ending*

Supporting Actor
Gig Young, *They Shoot Horses, Don't They?*
Rupert Crosse, *The Reivers*
Elliott Gould, *Bob & Carol & Ted & Alice*

Jack Nicholson, *Easy Rider*
Anthony Quayle, *Anne of the Thousand Days*

Supporting Actress
Goldie Hawn, *Cactus Flower*
Catherine Burns, *Last Summer*
Dyan Cannon, *Bob & Carol & Ted & Alice*
Sylvia Miles, *Midnight Cowboy*
Susannah York, *They Shoot Horses, Don't They?*

Director
John Schlesinger, *Midnight Cowboy*
Costa-Gavras, *Z*
George Roy Hill, *Butch Cassidy and the Sundance Kid*
Arthur Penn, *Alice's Restaurant*
Sydney Pollack, *They Shoot Horses, Don't They?*

Original Screenplay: William Goldman, *Butch Cassidy and the Sundance Kid*
Adapted Screenplay: Waldo Salt, *Midnight Cowboy*
Cinematography: Conrad Hall, *Butch Cassidy and the Sundance Kid*
Dramatic Score: Burt Bacharach, *Butch Cassidy and the Sundance Kid*
Musical Score: Lennie Hayton, Lionel Newman, *Hello, Dolly!*
Song: "Raindrops Keep Fallin' on My Head," *Butch Cassidy and the Sundance Kid*, m: Burt Bacharach; l: Hal David
Art Direction: John DeCuir, Jack Martin Smith, *Hello, Dolly!*
Costume Design: Margaret Furse, *Anne of the Thousand Days*
Editing: *Z*
Sound: *Hello, Dolly!*
Special Visual Effects: *Marooned*
Short/Cartoon: *It's Tough to Be a Bird* (Walt Disney, Ward Kimball)

Short/Live Action: *The Magic Machines* (Fly-By-Night Prods., Joan Keller Stern)
Documentary/Feature: *Arthur Rubinstein—The Love of Life*
Documentary/Short: *Czechoslovakia 1968* (U.S. Information Agency)
Foreign-Language Film: *Z* (France-Algeria)
Jean Hersholt Humanitarian Award: George Jessel
Special Award: Cary Grant

Golden Globes
Picture (Drama): *Anne of the Thousand Days*
Picture (Comedy/Musical): *The Secret of Santa Vittoria*
English-Language Foreign Film: *Oh! What a Lovely War*
Foreign-Language Film: *Z* (France-Algeria)
Actor (Drama): John Wayne, *True Grit*
Actor (Comedy/Musical): Peter O'Toole, *Goodbye, Mr. Chips*
Actress (Drama): Geneviève Bujold, *Anne of the Thousand Days*
Actress (Comedy/Musical): Patty Duke, *Me, Natalie*
Supporting Actor: Gig Young, *They Shoot Horses, Don't They?*
Supporting Actress: Goldie Hawn, *Cactus Flower*
Director: Charles Jarrott, *Anne of the Thousand Days*
Screenplay: John Hale, Bridget Boland, Richard Sokolove, *Anne of the Thousand Days*
Original Score: Burt Bacharach, *Butch Cassidy and the Sundance Kid*
Original Song: "Jean" *The Prime of Miss Jean Brodie*, ml: Rod McKuen
Most Promising Newcomer (Male): Jon Voight, *Midnight Cowboy*
Most Promising Newcomer (Female): Ali McGraw, *Goodbye, Columbus*

World Film Favorite (Male): Steve McQueen
World Film Favorite (Female): Barbra Streisand
Cecil B. DeMille Award: Joan Crawford

Directors Guild of America
Director: John Schlesinger, *Midnight Cowboy*
D. W. Griffith Award: Fred Zinnemann

**** Z AAW GLO NYC SOC CAN
The best real-life political film since *The Battle of Algiers*, a thrilling, crusading account of an honest magistrate (Jean-Louis Trintignant) investigating the supposedly accidental death of an opposition leader (Yves Montand) in Greece. With obvious parallels for an America in which suspicious political assassinations had become increasingly frequent, Costa-Gavras' film became the biggest non–sex-related foreign film hit of all time.

***** Jon Voight in *Midnight Cowboy* NYC SOC
A great performance in a great film—*Taxi Driver* with a heart to break.

New York Film Critics Circle
Picture: *Z*
Actor: Jon Voight, *Midnight Cowboy*
Actress: Jane Fonda, *They Shoot Horses, Don't They?*
Supporting Actor: Jack Nicholson, *Easy Rider*
Supporting Actress: Dyan Cannon, *Bob & Carol & Ted & Alice*

Director: Constantin Costa-Gavras, *Z*
Screenplay: *Bob & Carol & Ted & Alice* [award given to film, not writers]

National Society of Film Critics
Picture: *Z*
Actor: Jon Voight, *Midnight Cowboy*
Actress: Vanessa Redgrave, *The Loves of Isadora*
Supporting Actor: Jack Nicholson, *Easy Rider*
Supporting Actress: Sian Phillips, *Goodbye, Mr. Chips*; Delphine Seyrig, *Stolen Kisses*
Director: François Truffaut, *Stolen Kisses*
Screenplay: Paul Mazursky, Larry Tucker, *Bob & Carol & Ted & Alice*
Cinematography: Lucien Ballard, *The Wild Bunch*
Special Awards: Ivan Passer, for *Intimate Lighting*, a first film of great originality
Dennis Hopper, *Easy Rider*, as director, co-writer and co-star

National Board of Review
Best English-Language Film:
They Shoot Horses, Don't They?
Ring of Bright Water
Topaz
Goodbye, Mr. Chips
The Battle of Britain
The Loves of Isadora
The Prime of Miss Jean Brodie
Support Your Local Sheriff
True Grit
Midnight Cowboy

Best Foreign-Language Film:
Shame
Stolen Kisses
The Damned
La Femme Infidèle
Adalen '31
Actor: Peter O'Toole, *Goodbye, Mr. Chips*

Actress: Geraldine Page, *Trilogy*
Supporting Actor: Philippe Noiret, *Topaz*
Supporting Actress: Pamela Franklin, *The Prime of Miss Jean Brodie*
Director: Alfred Hitchcock, *Topaz*

British Academy Awards
Film: *Midnight Cowboy*
Actor: Dustin Hoffman, *Midnight Cowboy, John and Mary*
Actress: Maggie Smith, *The Prime of Miss Jean Brodie*
Supporting Actor: Laurence Olivier, *Oh! What a Lovely War*
Supporting Actress: Celia Johnson, *The Prime of Miss Jean Brodie*
Director: John Schlesinger, *Midnight Cowboy*
Screenplay: Waldo Salt, *Midnight Cowboy*

*** *if....* CAN
Don't like *Miss Jean Brodie* or the musical remake of *Goodbye, Mr. Chips*? Watch Malcolm McDowell take a machine-gun to *his* public school. A British youth film—just about exactly what you'd get by crossing *Easy Rider* with *Chariots of Fire*—which got a bit too much credit for inventing all the French New Wave tricks it borrows (including the use of both color and black-and-white, which, as with *A Man and a Woman*, was probably a budgetary matter rather than an artistic one).

Cannes Film Festival
Palme d'Or: *if....* (Lindsay Anderson, UK)
Special Jury Prize: *Adalen 31* (Bo Widerberg, Sweden)

Jury Prize: *Z* (Costa-Gavras, France)
Actor: Jean-Louis Trintignant, *Z*
Actress: Vanessa Redgrave, *Isadora* (UK)
Director: *Antonio das Mortes* (Glauber Rocha, Brazil), *All My Countrymen* (Vojtech Jasny, Czechoslovakia)
First Film: *Easy Rider*, Dennis Hopper (USA)
[Short Film Special Jury Prize to *La Pince à Ongles*, Jean-Claude Carrière (France)]
Technical Prize: *All My Countrymen*
International Critics Prize: *Andrei Rublev* (Andrei Tarkovsky, USSR)

Berlin Film Festival
Golden Bears: *Early Years* (Zelimir Zilnik, Yugoslavia)
Silver Bears: *Greetings* (Brian DePalma, USA), *I Am an Elephant, Madam* (Peter Zadek, West Germany), *A Quiet Place in the Country* (Elio Petri, Italy), *Made in Sweden* (Johan Bergenstråhle, Sweden), *Brazil Year 2000* (Walter Lima, Jr., Brazil)
International Critics Prize: to the Yugoslavian entries; tribute to Luis Buñuel

Harvard Lampoon Movie Worsts
Ten worst pictures:
Easy Rider
Medium Cool
Putney Swope
Bob & Carol & Ted & Alice
Topaz

The Maltese Bippy
True Grit
John and Mary
Hello, Dolly!
Last Summer
Kirk Douglas Award for Worst Actor: Peter Fonda, *Easy Rider*
Natalie Wood Award for Worst Actress: Jane Fonda, *Spirits of the Dead*, and for marrying Roger Vadim
The OK-Doc-Break-the-Arm-Again Award (for the most flagrant example of miscasting): Omar Sharif, *Che!*
The Uncrossed Heart (to the least promising young performer): Goldie Hawn, *Cactus Flower*
The Piltdown Mandible (to the most obviously and unabashedly spurious scientific phenomena): *Krakatoa, East of Java*, since Krakatoa, by all recent accounts, is a good 200 miles west of Java
The OhGodohGod, the Lights, the Shapes, the Colors Award (to that movie which makes us glad we have lungs to inhale with): To the revival of Walt Disney's *Fantasia*
The On-a-Clear-Day-You-Can-See-Fall-River Citation (for the most stereotyped New England scenery): *Alice's Restaurant*, whose Stockbridge, Mass., was just like *Life* magazine said it would be
The Merino Award: To the accompaniment of dull thuds produced by beating a dead sheep, to Andy Warhol's *Blue Movie*, filmed entirely in lurid aqua-merino

Box Office (Domestic Rentals)

1	*The Love Bug*	$17,000,000	Embassy
2	*Funny Girl*	16,500,000	Col
	[through 1971:	24,600,000]	
3	*Bullitt*	16,400,000	WB
4	*Butch Cassidy and the Sundance Kid*	15,000,000	Fox

	[through 1971:	26,200,000]	
5	Romeo and Juliet	14,500,000	Par
6	True Grit	11,500,000	Par
7	Midnight Cowboy	11,000,000	UA
8	Oliver!	10,500,000	Col
	Goodbye, Columbus	10,500,000	Par
10	Chitty Chitty Bang Bang	8,700,000	UA
Other films of note:			
11	Easy Rider	7,200,000	Col
	[through 1971:	16,200,000]	
12	I Am Curious (Yellow)	6,600,000	Grove Press
13	Where Eagles Dare	6,560,000	MGM
14	The Lion in Winter	6,400,000	Embassy
19	Finian's Rainbow	5,100,000	WB
23	The Wild Bunch	4,200,000	WB
	Star! [reissue]	4,200,000	Fox
27	Alice's Restaurant	3,500,000	UA
32	Yellow Submarine	3,000,000	UA
45	Paint Your Wagon	2,200,000	Par
58	Inga	1,800,000	Cinemation

With hits like The Love Bug, Chitty Chitty Bang Bang *and* True Grit, *1969 was the last big year of the family film, though under-thirties flocked to* Easy Rider *(easily the year's most profitable film) and dirty old men of all ages flocked to the X-rated Swedish import,* I Am Curious (Yellow)—*which spawned such a flood of softcore Swedish Helgas and Ingas that one British sex-film-maker, Radley Metzger, actually made a film in Swedish and dubbed it back into English, just so it would seem Scandinavian.* Funny Girl *introduced a new musical star and* Oliver! *also did well; but a two-hour cut of* Star! *released in January still didn't recover its costs, and neither did* Finian's Rainbow *or* Paint Your Wagon. *So either the musical was a surefire box office genre, or it was dead—your choice.*

Gebert's Golden Armchairs

Twenty-five years on, Sam Peckinpah's *The Wild Bunch* seems the greater and grander work, the greatest American film on one of the great American themes (or maybe even two— the nature of violence, and the corruption of the American frontier and frontiersman). But that's not to fault the Academy's choice at all—*Midnight Cowboy* was the movie of the moment, and an important landmark in Hollywood realism and the way urban life, in particular, was depicted on screen.

Best American Film: *The Wild Bunch*
Best Foreign Film: *Z*
Best Actor: Jon Voight, *Midnight Cowboy*
Best Actress: Maggie Smith, *The Prime of Miss Jean Brodie*
Best Director: Sam Peckinpah, *The Wild Bunch*

1970

Berlin broke down in controversy paralleling Cannes' collapse two years earlier. The cause was a film by West German Michael Verhoeven (not to be confused with the director of *Showgirls*; this Verhoeven's best-known success would be *The Nasty Girl* 20 years later). *O.K.* was loosely based on an actual 1966 incident in which a group of American G.I.s kidnapped, raped, and finally murdered a South Vietnamese girl.

The American delegation, led by director George Stevens (*Shane*, etc.), objected strongly to the film and attempted to have it removed, invoking a rule which stated that competing films should "contribute to the understanding and friendship between the peoples of different nations." That rule may have been a diplomatic necessity during the Cold War, when countries were liable to pull out at the slightest offense, but by 1970 it was a relic which could be used to bar virtually any film of political or social import.

Now it was the only Eastern European juror, Yugoslavian director Dusan Makavejev, who stood up for free speech, organizing a press conference in which he and other dissenting jurors pledged to resign if the jury chose to act as censors by disqualifying the Verhoeven film. Accusations flew back and forth and the situation grew increasingly ugly, with festival founder Dr. Alfred Bauer and the other officials offering their resignations to the Berlin Senate. A number of films were withdrawn by their producers—including Fassbinder's *Why Does Herr R. Run Amok?*, which might well have become the first film from the new German cinema to take a Golden Bear. Finally, four days after the controversy began, the festival announced that the competition would be cancelled, for the only time in Berlin's history.

The story has an interesting footnote. The controversy over *O.K.* scuttled an American version of the same story then in development at Columbia—which might have been Hollywood's first anti–Vietnam War film. But 19 years later, the incident was finally filmed as *Casualties of War* by Brian DePalma—and though by then no one remembered the fact or *O.K.*, DePalma had been present throughout the abortive 1970 Berlinale with an early independent film, *Dionysus in 1969*.

Academy Awards

*** *Patton* AAW DGA BOR
**** **George C. Scott** AAW
GLO NYC SOC BOR
A standard war biopic, in the
Tora! Tora! Tora! vein, runs
into two amazing pieces of
luck—first, an energetic young
screenwriter named Coppola
who fills it with some of the same
war-is-hell-and-I-love-the-
smell-of-napalm stuff that would
go into his later *Apocalypse
Now*, and then a brilliant, too-
big-for-the-movies actor who
understands perfectly how to play
the part so that it becomes both
the best pro-war and the best
anti-war movie of the year.

Picture
Patton (20th Century–Fox, Frank
McCarthy)
Airport (Universal, Ross Hunter)
Five Easy Pieces (Columbia, BBS
Productions)
Love Story (Paramount, Howard
G. Minsky)
M*A*S*H (20th Century–Fox,
Aspen, Ingo Preminger)

Actor
George C. Scott, *Patton*
Melvyn Douglas, *I Never Sang for
My Father*
James Earl Jones, *The Great White
Hope*
Jack Nicholson, *Five Easy Pieces*
Ryan O'Neal, *Love Story*

*** **Glenda Jackson in** *Women
in Love* AAW NYC SOC
BOR
Watch Ken Russell's film of the
D. H. Lawrence novel—a
respectable and fairly
restrained, if practically by
definition unsuccessful, attempt
to get Lawrence's passion and
philosophical heavy-lifting on
screen—and you may wonder
why Jackson came away with
all the acting prizes: Alan Bates
is the one who seems to most
get into the Lawrencian spirit,
while among the females
Eleanor Bron steals it as a
wicked parody of Lady Ottoline
Morrell (complete with
interpretive dance). The answer,
I guess, is that (1) the idea of
a squinty-eyed duck like
Jackson being the romantic lead
in a major movie, and (2) the
idea of a movie heroine being
healthily interested in sex,
especially intellectually, were
both so startling that she was the
first real feminist character up
for a Best Actress Oscar—even
if her character would quickly be
surpassed in that regard. (P.S.
And (3) they had all just seen
her as *Elizabeth R* on PBS.)

Actress
Glenda Jackson, *Women in Love*
Jane Alexander, *The Great White
Hope*
Ali MacGraw, *Love Story*
Sarah Miles, *Ryan's Daughter*
Carrie Snodgress, *Diary of a Mad
Housewife*

Supporting Actor
John Mills, *Ryan's Daughter*
Richard Castellano, *Lovers and
Other Strangers*
Chief Dan George, *Little Big Man*
Gene Hackman, *I Never Sang for
My Father*
John Marley, *Love Story*

Supporting Actress
Helen Hayes, *Airport*
Karen Black, *Five Easy Pieces*
Lee Grant, *The Landlord*
Sally Kellerman, *M*A*S*H*
Maureen Stapleton, *Airport*

Director
Franklin J. Schaffner, *Patton*
Robert Altman, *M*A*S*H*
Federico Fellini, *Fellini Satyricon*
Arthur Hiller, *Love Story*
Ken Russell, *Women in Love*

Original Screenplay: Francis
Ford Coppola, Edmund H.
North, *Patton*
Adapted Screenplay: Ring
Lardner, Jr., *M*A*S*H*
Cinematography: Freddie
Young, *Ryan's Daughter*
Score: Francis Lai, *Love Story*
Song Score: The Beatles, *Let It
Be*
Song: "For All We Know,"
Lovers and Other Strangers,
m: Fred Karlin, l: Robb Royer,
James Griffin
Art Direction: Urie McCleary,
Patton
Costume Design: Nino Novarese,
Cromwell
Editing: *Patton*
Sound: *Patton*
Special Visual Effects: *Tora!
Tora! Tora!*
Short/Cartoon: *Is It Always Right
to Be Right?* (Stephen and Nick
Bosustow)
Short/Live Action: *The
Resurrection of Broncho Billy*
(University of Southern
California, directed by John
Carpenter)
Documentary/Feature:
Woodstock (Michael Wadleigh)
Documentary/Short: *Interviews
with My Lai Veterans* (Joseph
Strick)
Foreign-Language Film:
*Investigation of a Citizen Above
Suspicion* (Italy)

Irving G. Thalberg Award:
Ingmar Bergman
**Jean Hersholt Humanitarian
Award:** Frank Sinatra
Special Awards:
Lillian Gish
Orson Welles

Golden Globes
Picture (Drama): *Love Story*
Picture (Comedy/Musical):
M*A*S*H
**English-Language Foreign
Film:** *Women in Love*
Foreign-Language Film: *Rider
on the Rain* (France)
Actor (Drama): George C. Scott,
Patton
Actor (Comedy/Musical): Albert
Finney, *Scrooge*
Actress (Drama): Ali MacGraw,
Love Story
Actress (Comedy/Musical):
Carrie Snodgress, *Diary of a
Mad Housewife*
Supporting Actor: John Mills,
Ryan's Daughter
Supporting Actress: Karen
Black, *Five Easy Pieces*,
Maureen Stapleton, *Airport*
Director: Arthur Hiller, *Love
Story*
Screenplay: Erich Segal, *Love
Story*
Score: Francis Lai, *Love Story*
Song: "Whistling Away the
Dark," *Darling Lili* m: Henry
Mancini, l: Johnny Mercer
**Most Promising Newcomer
(Male):** James Earl Jones, *The
Great White Hope*
**Most Promising Newcomer
(Female):** Carrie Snodgress,
Diary of a Mad Housewife
World Film Favorite (Male):
Clint Eastwood
World Film Favorite (Female):
Barbra Streisand
Cecil B. DeMille Award: Frank
Sinatra

Directors Guild of America

Director: Franklin Schaffner, *Patton*

**** *Five Easy Pieces* NYC

M*A*S*H gets away with its mockery today because the targets are as worth nailing as ever (military pomposity, religious hypocrisy, etc.). *Five Easy Pieces*, on the other hand, is a more uncomfortable piece, because the targets of rebellious youth Jack Nicholson are somewhat sympathetic to begin with—Karen Black's Okie girlfriend may be uneducated, but she's a decent person and doesn't deserve his condescension; even the waitress who won't serve him toast and the pompous academic who doesn't watch TV deserve more slack than they get from the self-righteous Nicholson. His character, in short, is sort of a jerk—and the one thing that saves *Five Easy Pieces* is that even then it understood that, and didn't make the mistake that nearly every other youth movie did of thinking young equaled right.

New York Film Critics Circle

Picture: *Five Easy Pieces*
Actor: George C. Scott, *Patton*
Actress: Glenda Jackson, *Women in Love*
Supporting Actor: Chief Dan George, *Little Big Man*
Supporting Actress: Karen Black, *Five Easy Pieces*
Director: Bob Rafelson, *Five Easy Pieces*
Screenplay: Eric Rohmer, *My Night at Maud's*

National Society of Film Critics

Picture: *M*A*S*H*
Actor: George C. Scott, *Patton*
Actress: Glenda Jackson, *Women in Love*
Supporting Actor: Chief Dan George, *Little Big Man*
Supporting Actress: Lois Smith, *Five Easy Pieces*
Director: Ingmar Bergman, *The Passion of Anna*
Screenplay: Eric Rohmer, *My Night at Maud's*
Cinematography: Nestor Almendros, *The Wild Child*, *My Night at Maud's*
Special Awards: Donald Richie and the Film Dept. of the Museum of Modern Art, for their Japanese film retrospective
Daniel Talbot of the New Yorker Theatre

National Board of Review

Best English-Language Film:
Patton
Kes
Women in Love
Five Easy Pieces
Ryan's Daughter
I Never Sang for My Father
Diary of a Mad Housewife
Love Story
The Virgin and the Gypsy
Tora! Tora! Tora!
Best Foreign-Language Film:
The Wild Child
My Night at Maud's
The Passion of Anna
The Confession
This Man Must Die
Actor: George C. Scott, *Patton*
Actress: Glenda Jackson, *Women in Love*
Supporting Actor: Frank Langella, *Diary of a Mad Housewife*, *The Twelve Chairs*
Supporting Actress: Karen Black, *Five Easy Pieces*
Director: François Truffaut, *The Wild Child*

British Academy Awards
Film: *Butch Cassidy and the Sundance Kid*
Actor: Robert Redford, *Butch Cassidy and the Sundance Kid*, *Tell Them Willie Boy Is Here*, *Downhill Racer*
Actress: Katharine Ross, *Butch Cassidy and the Sundance Kid*, *Tell Them Willie Boy Is Here*
Supporting Actor: Colin Welland, *Kes*
Supporting Actress: Susannah York, *They Shoot Horses, Don't They?*
Director: George Roy Hill, *Butch Cassidy and the Sundance Kid*
Screenplay: William Goldman, *Butch Cassidy and the Sundance Kid*

*** *M*A*S*H* GLO SOC CAN
Interesting how quickly times change: Robert Altman's Vietnam comedy (come on, there wasn't long hair like that in Korea) still looks as rambunctious and liberating as ever—except now it seems so *sexist*, in ways that even *Animal House* eight years later doesn't.

Cannes Film Festival
Palme d'Or: *M*A*S*H* (Robert Altman, USA)
Special Jury Prize: *Investigation of a Citizen Above Suspicion* (Elio Petri, Italy)
Jury Prize: *Falcons* (István Gaál, Hungary), *The Strawberry Statement* (Stuart Hagmann, USA)
Actor: Marcello Mastroianni, *Drama of Jealousy/The Pizza Triangle* (Italy)
Actress: Ottavia Piccolo, *Metello* (Italy)

Direction: John Boorman, *Leo the Last* (UK)
Best First Film: *Hoa-Binh* (Raoul Coutard, France)

Harvard Lampoon Movie Worsts
Ten worst pictures:
Love Story
Airport
Patton
Joe
Soldier Blue
Getting Straight
The Strawberry Statement
Little Fauss and Big Halsey
Julius Caesar
The Statue
Kirk Douglas Award for Worst Actor: Elliott Gould, for *Getting Straight* and for dumping Barbra Streisand
Natalie Wood Award for Worst Actress: Ali MacGraw, *Love Story*
Worst Supporting Actor: Jon Voight, *Catch-22*
Worst Supporting Actress: Ruth Gordon, *Where's Poppa?*
The OK-Doc-Break-the-Arm-Again Award (for the most flagrant example of miscasting): Dean Martin, who soberly piloted a 707 to a belly-landing in *Airport*
Prease Get Off Tojo Award: Darryl Zanuck, *Tora! Tora! Tora!*
The It-Can't-Happen-Here Award (presented to that film that shot a sequence which is geographically closest to The Lampoon Castle): *Love Story*, for showing the American public that the nicest things about Harvard are Cambridge winters, low-rent housing, Winthrop House, and leukemia
The Harvard Independent (to that film noted for its ignominious failure as both art and

politics): *The Strawberry
Statement*
The Merino Award: To the

frumpy housewife from a
frumpy movie, *Airport*, Maureen
O. Stapleton

Box Office (Domestic Rentals)

1	*Airport*	$37,650,796	Uni
2	*M*A*S*H*	22,000,000	Fox
3	*Patton*	21,000,000	Fox
4	*Bob & Carol & Ted & Alice*	13,900,000	Col
5	*Woodstock*	13,500,000	WB
6	*Hello, Dolly!*	13,000,000	Fox
7	*Cactus Flower*	11,300,000	Col
8	*Catch-22*	9,250,000	Par
9	*On Her Majesty's Secret Service*	9,000,000	UA
10	*The Reivers*	8,000,000	National General

Other films of note:

12	*Beneath the Planet of the Apes*	7,250,000	Fox
14	*Z*	6,750,000	Cinema V
21	*The Computer Wore Tennis Shoes*	5,500,000	Disney
22	*Cotton Comes to Harlem*	5,200,000	UA
23	*Getting Straight*	5,100,000	Col
24	*Beyond the Valley of the Dolls*	5,100,000	Fox
30	*Kelly's Heroes*	4,182,000	MGM
47	*Darling Lili*	3,250,000	Par
63	*House of Dark Shadows*	1,836,000	MGM
82	*Night of the Living Dead*	1,000,000	Image Ten

*The big news in 1970 was what wasn't on the chart—the mightiest of all studios, MGM. In 1970 it produced no hit higher than number 30, and sadly sold off its lot and its props, entering into the living death it has endured under Kirk Kerkorian ever since. Otherwise, 1970 demonstrates the split between the over-30 and the under-30 audience in its most graphic form—Patton vs. M*A*S*H, Airport's planeload of squares vs. Bob & Carol's bed full of swingers. While Elliott Gould was the year's hot new star, his ex-wife, Barbra Streisand, would have longer-lasting success—traditional enough for Broadway yet hip enough for the kids, she was the one female star who managed to remain a top draw through an otherwise male-dominated decade, mainly due to consistently smart career choices. On the other hand, the Era of Julie Andrews was officially declared over when* Darling Lili *flopped even bigger than* Star!

Gebert's Golden Armchairs

   *M*A*S*H* is the most
innovative movie of the year,
both in attitude and Altman's
quirky directorial style (it's one
of the few comedies that actually
has a directorial style—usually
that's not a good thing), and Sally

Kellerman is a sexy comic
villainness—The Prime of Miss
Hotlips Houlihan. But Arthur
Penn's *Little Big Man* is the movie
with the biggest generosity of
spirit and vision—more proof,
after *The Wild Bunch*, that the
best movies about the '60s were

those set closer to the 1860s. Andrei Tarkovsky's *Andrei Roublev* was made in '66 but shelved by Soviet authorities until it appeared at Cannes this year; determined to out-Bergman Bergman and out-Antonioni Antonioni, Tarkovsky made some of the most visually gorgeous, maddeningly slow and pretentious films of the '70s and '80s, but his second film, a grim pageant of medieval life in the *Seventh Seal* vein, finds a perfect combination of visual grandeur and narrative intensity.

Best American Film: *Little Big Man*
Best Foreign Film: *Andrei Roublev*
Best Actor: George C. Scott, *Patton*
Best Actress: Sally Kellerman, *M*A*S*H*
Best Director: Robert Altman, *M*A*S*H*

1971

How far had the New York Critics Circle (and the movies) gone since the deposing of King Bosley? A mere four years later, it voted its top award to a film which, far more than *Bonnie and Clyde*, deserved the words of condemnation Bosley Crowther had applied to that film: "a cheap piece of baldfaced slapstick comedy that treats the hideous depredations of that sleazy, moronic pair as though they were as full of fun and frolic as the jazz-age cut-ups in *Thoroughly Modern Millie*." The vote for *Clockwork Orange* does, however, prove that the group had not yet replaced King Bosley with Queen Pauline (who was predictably offended by the film's aesthetics rather than its violence); her candidates—*The Conformist* and *McCabe and Mrs. Miller*—came in well behind *Clockwork*, *The Last Picture Show*, *The French Connection*, and *Sunday, Bloody Sunday*.

Academy Awards

*** *The French Connection*
AAW GLO DGA
**** Gene Hackman AAW
GLO NYC BOR BAA '72
A terrific car chase, a fine, trendsettingly unglamorous performance by the most consistently superb American actor of the last three decades— but why does the whole movie seem to be in such a bad mood? Pissed-off isn't synonymous with realism.

Picture
The French Connection (20th Century–Fox, D'Antoni-Schine-Moore)
A Clockwork Orange (Warner Bros., Hawk Films, Stanley Kubrick)
Fiddler on the Roof (UA, Mirisch-Cartier)
The Last Picture Show (Columbia, BBS Productions)

Nicholas and Alexandra
(Columbia, Sam Spiegel)

Actor
Gene Hackman, *The French Connection*
Peter Finch, *Sunday, Bloody Sunday*
Walter Matthau, *Kotch*
George C. Scott, *The Hospital*
Topol, *Fiddler on the Roof*

***** Jane Fonda in *Klute*
AAW GLO NYC SOC
Forget that she's playing an unfeminist, classic-Oscar-bait part (a prostitute). After warm-ups like Christie in *Darling* and Jackson in *Women in Love*, Fonda plays the first truly modern woman on screen—a needy yet tough, sexy yet cynical, smart and manipulative woman, the sum of all the sex kittens she'd played before plus all the experience and cynicism that Fonda herself had gained along the way. A great performance,

with the kind of improvisational, personal-discovery qualities associated more with John Cassavetes' films than murder mysteries—she seems to be opening up new territories for other actresses to explore in every scene (Diane Keaton, you take the neurotic tics; Streep and Weaver, you get the no-bullshit attitude).

Actress
Jane Fonda, *Klute*
Julie Christie, *McCabe & Mrs. Miller*
Glenda Jackson, *Sunday, Bloody Sunday*
Vanessa Redgrave, *Mary, Queen of Scots*
Janet Suzman, *Nicholas and Alexandra*

Supporting Actor
Ben Johnson, *The Last Picture Show*
Jeff Bridges, *The Last Picture Show*
Leonard Frey, *Fiddler on the Roof*
Richard Jaeckel, *Sometimes a Great Notion*
Roy Scheider, *The French Connection*

Supporting Actress
Cloris Leachman, *The Last Picture Show*
Ellen Burstyn, *The Last Picture Show*
Barbara Harris, *Who Is Harry Kellerman, and Why Is He Saying Those Terrible Things About Me?*
Margaret Leighton, *The Go-Between*
Ann-Margret, *Carnal Knowledge*

Director
William Friedkin, *The French Connection*

Peter Bogdanovich, *The Last Picture Show*
Norman Jewison, *Fiddler on the Roof*
Stanley Kubrick, *A Clockwork Orange*
John Schlesinger, *Sunday, Bloody Sunday*

Original Screenplay: Paddy Chayefsky, *The Hospital*
Adapted Screenplay: Ernest Tidyman, *The French Connection*
Cinematography: Oswald Morris, *Fiddler on the Roof*
Art Direction: John Box, *Nicholas and Alexandra*
Costume Design: Yvonne Blake, Antonio Castillo, *Nicholas and Alexandra*
Sound: *Fiddler on the Roof*
Original Score: Michel Legrand, *Summer of '42*
Scoring Adaptation: John Williams, *Fiddler on the Roof*
Song: "Theme from *Shaft*," *Shaft*, ml: Issac Hayes
Editing: *The French Connection*
Special Visual Effects: *Bedknobs and Broomsticks*
Short/Animated: *The Crunch Bird*
Short/Live Action: *Sentinels of Silence*
Documentary/Feature: *The Hellstrom Chronicle* (David L. Wolper, Walon Green)
Documentary/Short: *Sentinels of Silence*
Foreign-Language Film: *The Garden of the Finzi-Continis* (Italy)
Special Award: Charles Chaplin, for the incalculable effect he has had in making motion pictures the art form of this century

Golden Globes
Picture (Drama): *The French Connection*

Picture (Comedy/Musical):
Fiddler on the Roof
**English-Language Foreign
Film:** *Sunday, Bloody Sunday*
Foreign-Language Film: *The
Policeman* (Israel)
Actor (Drama): Gene Hackman,
The French Connection
Actor (Comedy/Musical): Topol,
Fiddler on the Roof
Actress (Drama): Jane Fonda,
Klute
Actress (Comedy/Musical):
Twiggy, *The Boy Friend*
Supporting Actor: Ben Johnson,
The Last Picture Show
Supporting Actress: Ann-
Margret, *Carnal Knowledge*
Director: William Friedkin, *The
French Connection*
Screenplay: Paddy Chayefsky,
The Hospital
Score: Isaac Hayes, *Shaft*
Song: "Life Is What You Make
It," *Kotch*, m: Marvin Hamlisch,
l: Johnny Mercer
**Most Promising Newcomer
(Male):** Desi Arnaz, Jr., *Red Sky
at Morning*
**Most Promising Newcomer
(Female):** Twiggy, *The Boy
Friend*
World Film Favorite (Male):
Charles Bronson, Sean Connery
World Film Favorite (Female):
Ali MacGraw
Cecil B. DeMille Award: Alfred
Hitchcock

Directors Guild of America
Director: William Friedkin, *The
French Connection*

*** *A Clockwork Orange*
NYC HAR
Stanley Kubrick's state-of-the-
art in screen violence 1971
was exciting, vibrant
filmmaking—and it was
morally dubious in the extreme,

pushing Anthony Burgess'
moralistic novel to the point
where it unmistakably
encouraged us to laugh and
cheer Alex on in his murders and
rapes.

New York Film Critics
Circle
Picture: *A Clockwork Orange*
Actor: Gene Hackman, *The
French Connection*
Actress: Jane Fonda, *Klute*
Supporting Actor: Ben Johnson,
The Last Picture Show
Supporting Actress: Ellen
Burstyn, *The Last Picture Show*
Director: Stanley Kubrick, *A
Clockwork Orange*
Screenplay: Peter Bogdanovich,
Larry McMurtry, *The Last
Picture Show*; Penelope Gilliatt,
Sunday, Bloody Sunday

National Society of Film
Critics
Picture: *Claire's Knee*
Actor: Peter Finch, *Sunday,
Bloody Sunday*
Actress: Jane Fonda, *Klute*
Supporting Actor: Bruce Dern,
Drive, He Said
Supporting Actress: Ellen
Burstyn, *The Last Picture Show*
Director: Bernardo Bertolucci,
The Conformist
Screenplay: Penelope Gilliatt,
Sunday, Bloody Sunday
Cinematography: Vittorio
Storaro, *The Conformist*
Special Award: *The Sorrow and
the Pity*

National Board of Review
Best English-Language Film:
Macbeth
The Boy Friend
*One Day in the Life of Ivan
Denisovich*
The French Connection
The Last Picture Show

Nicholas and Alexandra
The Go-Between
King Lear
Peter Rabbit and Tales of Beatrix
   Potter
Death in Venice
Best Foreign-Language Film:
Claire's Knee
Bed and Board
The Clowns
The Garden of the Finzi-Continis
The Conformist
Actor: Gene Hackman, The
French Connection
Actress: Irene Papas, The Trojan
Women
Supporting Actor: Ben Johnson,
The Last Picture Show
Supporting Actress: Cloris
Leachman, The Last Picture
Show
Director: Ken Russell, The
Devils, The Boy Friend

British Academy Awards
Film: Sunday, Bloody Sunday
Actor: Peter Finch, Sunday,
Bloody Sunday
Actress: Glenda Jackson, Sunday,
Bloody Sunday
Supporting Actor: Edward Fox,
The Go-Between
Supporting Actress: Margaret
Leighton, The Go-Between
Director: John Schlesinger,
Sunday, Bloody Sunday
Screenplay: Harold Pinter, The
Go-Between
**Robert Flaherty Documentary
Award:** The Hellstrom
Chronicle (Walon Green, USA)
Academy Fellow: Sir Alfred
Hitchcock

Cannes Film Festival
Palme d'Or: The Go-Between
(Joseph Losey, UK)
25th Anniversary Prize:
Luchino Visconti, for Death in
Venice [Italy] and for his body of
work
Special Jury Prize: Taking Off

(Milos Forman, USA), Johnny
Got His Gun (Dalton Trumbo,
USA)
Jury Prize: Love (Károly Makk,
Hungary), unanimously, with
special mention for its lead
actresses, Lili Darvas and Mari
Törőcsik; Joe Hill (Bo Widerberg,
Sweden)
Actor: Riccardo Cucciolla, Sacco
and Vanzetti (Italy)
Actress: Kitty Winn, The Panic
in Needle Park (USA)
Best First Film: Per Grazia
Ricevuta (Nino Manfredi, Italy)
Technical Prize: The Hellstrom
Chronicle (Walon Green, USA)
International Critics Prize:
Johnny Got His Gun

***** The Garden of the Finzi-
Continis AAW BER**
In Fascist-era Italy, a fabulously
wealthy and ancient aristocratic
Jewish family believe
themselves above the
indignities and dangers that
their fellows are increasingly
subject to. De Sica's best film
in many years evokes a
beguiling, Gatsbyesque vision
of a world about to be
destroyed—though it doesn't
equal either the emotional or
the stylistic complexity of The
Conformist, its contemporary
in both production and subject
matter.

Berlin Film Festival
Golden Bear: The Garden of the
Finzi-Continis (Vittorio De
Sica, Italy)
Silver Bear: The Decameron
(Pier Paolo Pasolini, Italy)
Actor: Jean Gabin, Le Chat
(France)
Actress: Shirley MacLaine,
Desperate Characters (USA),
Simone Signoret, Le Chat

Screenplay: Frank D. Gilroy, *Desperate Characters* (USA)
Cinematography: Ragnar Lasse-Henriksen, *Love Is War* (Norway)
First Film: *Ang: Lone* (Franz Ernst, Sweden)
International Critics Prize: no prize to films in competition; instead, tribute paid to *W.R.— Mysteries of the Organism* (Dusan Makavejev, Yugoslavia), *Anaparastassi* (Theo Angelopoulos, Greece) and *Argentina, May 1969* (Argentina) in the Forum of Young Cinema

Harvard Lampoon Movie Worsts

Ten worst pictures:
A Clockwork Orange
Carnal Knowledge
Summer of '42
Fiddler on the Roof
The Last Movie
T. R. Baskin
Kotch
Willard
The Music Lovers
Dealing
Kirk Douglas Award for Worst Actor: Jack Nicholson, *Carnal Knowledge*

Natalie Wood Award for Worst Actress: Candice Bergen, *T. R. Baskin*
H. J. Heinz Laurel Clot (to the film that makes most extensive use of the company's various vegetable derivatives): *Dirty Harry*
The Beast of Buchenwald Award (to those actors who most thoroughly degrade themselves in order to pull in the paycheck, a handsomely tooled lampshade): Ernest Borgnine, *Willard*
The Tar Baby (in recognition of Hollywood's continued exploitation of the black market): To MGM for giving us *Shaft*
The Ayn Rand Award (to that writer whose bad books made worse movies): Michael Crichton, *The Andromeda Strain*
The Bosley (to that film critic whose writing consistently explores the farthest limits of bad taste): To the entire New York Film Critics Circle for naming *Clockwork Orange* best film of the year
The Merino Award: Murino eye drops for making Malcolm McDowell see the light in *Clockwork Orange*

Box Office (Domestic Rentals)

1	*Love Story*	$50,000,000	Par
2	*Little Big Man*	15,000,000	National General
3	*Summer of '42*	14,000,000	Fox
4	*Ryan's Daughter*	13,400,000	MGM
5	*The Owl and the Pussycat*	11,500,000	Col
6	*The Aristocats*	10,100,000	Disney
7	*Carnal Knowledge*	11,300,000	Avco Embassy
8	*Willard*	9,347,000	Cinerama*
9	*The Andromeda Strain*	8,200,000	Uni
10	*Big Jake*	7,500,000	National General

*Not *in* Cinerama, of course—just released by Cinerama Releasing Corp.

Other films of note:

11	*The Stewardesses*	6,418,170	Sherpix
12	*Shaft*	6,100,000	MGM
	The French Connection	6,100,000	Fox
	[through 1972:	27,500,000]	
14	*Klute*	6,000,000	WB
24	*Sweet Sweetback's Badasssss Song*	4,100,000	Cinemation
	Escape from the Planet of the Apes	4,100,000	Fox
26	*Billy Jack*	4,000,000	WB
30	*Bananas*	3,500,000	UA
53	*Willy Wonka and the Chocolate Factory*	2,000,000	Par
64	*The Abominable Dr. Phibes*	1,500,000	American Int'l

What can you say about a movie that takes the oldest clichés of movie romance and wraps them up in a long-haired, blue-jeaned package? I don't know, I was only ten then, and the only movie on this list that I saw in first run was The Aristocats. *Dustin Hoffman, Barbra Streisand, and Jack Nicholson all cemented their newfound stardom this year; blaxploitation took off; and the X-rated hit of the year was* The Stewardesses—*in 3-D. (A reissue of* House of Wax *quickly followed, naturally—the only other thing I remember seeing in a theater that year.)*

Gebert's Golden Armchairs

Everybody noticed that Peter Bogdanovich had pulled off a remarkable feat of directorial alchemy in filling John Ford's western landscapes with Antonioni's emptiness in the sad, hard-beautiful *The Last Picture Show*. Fewer noticed its third great influence—it was the sharpest film about class differences in America since Orson Welles' *The Magnificent Ambersons*, even coming complete with a sexually frustrated middle-aged woman in Cloris Leachman's coach's wife. At the other end of the Antonioni-influence scale, Bernardo Bertolucci took a fairly ordinary anti-Fascist drama (about a minor functionary who wants a respectable job in the Mussolini regime so that, among other things, he can deny his homosexual impulses to himself) and, with the help of the great cinematographer Vittorio Storaro and production designer Ferdinando Scarfiotti, gave it an intoxicating jolt of Art Deco style and color.

Best American Film: *The Last Picture Show*
Best Foreign Film: *The Conformist*
Best Actor: Gene Hackman, *The French Connection*
Best Actress: Jane Fonda, *Klute*
Best Director: Bernardo Bertolucci (and company), *The Conformist*

1972

Having caused a delectable Cannes scandal with *Viridiana*, Luis Buñuel perhaps never dreamed that he could do the same for the Oscars, but he got his chance when *The Discreet Charm of the Bourgeoisie* received an Oscar nomination for Best Foreign-Language Film. Buñuel came to Los Angeles, where he was feted at lunch by a Who's Who of Hollywood directors including Ford, Hitchcock, Cukor, Wyler, and Wilder. Shortly after, asked by a journalist if he thought his film would win the Oscar, he deadpanned, "Of course. I've already paid the twenty-five thousand dollars they wanted. Americans may have their weaknesses, but they do keep their promises." Shocked by this stunning revelation of behind-the-scenes manipulation, the international press erupted, demanding to know the details of the supposed Oscar fix. Buñuel, taken aback, admitted it was only a joke; the press relented, the storm died down . . . and then he won.

Academy Awards

***** *The Godfather* AAW
GLO DGA NYC
*** **Marlon Brando** AAW
GLO
A great American epic about the seductiveness of power and control that proved so seductive that its makers, horrified, immediately felt the need to turn around and make its antidote, *Godfather II*. Part of what horrified them was how easily Brando's Don Corleone became a part of the culture (Godfather's pizza, we'll make you an offer you can't refuse, delivery in 30 minutes or a horse's head in your bed)—a sign, perhaps, that it was more a catchy bunch of mannerisms than a fully inhabited Brando character. There was more

warmth in it the second time, in *The Freshman*.

Picture
The Godfather (Paramount, Albert S. Ruddy)
Cabaret (Allied Artists, ABC Pictures, Cy Feuer)
Deliverance (Warner Bros., John Boorman)
The Emigrants (Warner Bros., Svensk Filmindustri, Bengt Forslund)
Sounder (20th Century–Fox, Radnitz/Mattel, Robert B. Radnitz)

Actor
Marlon Brando, *The Godfather*
Michael Caine, *Sleuth*
Laurence Olivier, *Sleuth*
Peter O'Toole, *The Ruling Class*
Paul Winfield, *Sounder*

**** **Liza Minnelli in**
Cabaret AAW GLO BAA
At the time people said Minnelli was even better than her mom

had been, because she was just as much of a show-stopper and song-belter in a piece that was even, like, relevant and said something, man, unlike those old MGM musicals. Let's just say that for once she was as good as Mom was in *The Pirate* or *A Star Is Born.*

Actress
Liza Minnelli, *Cabaret*
Diana Ross, *Lady Sings the Blues*
Maggie Smith, *Travels with My Aunt*
Cicely Tyson, *Sounder*
Liv Ullmann, *The Emigrants*

Supporting Actor
Joel Grey, *Cabaret*
Eddie Albert, *The Heartbreak Kid*
James Caan, *The Godfather*
Robert Duvall, *The Godfather*
Al Pacino, *The Godfather*

Supporting Actress
Eileen Heckart, *Butterflies Are Free*
Jeannie Berlin, *The Heartbreak Kid*
Geraldine Page, *Pete 'n' Tillie*
Susan Tyrrell, *Fat City*
Shelley Winters, *The Poseidon Adventure*

Director
Bob Fosse, *Cabaret*
John Boorman, *Deliverance*
Francis Ford Coppola, *The Godfather*
Joseph L. Mankiewicz, *Sleuth*
Jan Troell, *The Emigrants*

Original Screenplay: Jeremy Larner, *The Candidate*
Adapted Screenplay: Mario Puzo, Francis Ford Coppola, *The Godfather*
Cinematography: Geoffrey Unsworth, *Cabaret*

Original Score: Charles Chaplin, Raymond Rasch, Larry Russell, *Limelight*
Scoring Adaptation: Ralph Burns, *Cabaret*
Song: "The Morning After," *The Poseidon Adventure*, ml: Al Kasha, Joel Hirschhorn
Art Direction: Rolf Zehetbauer, *Cabaret*
Costume Design: Anthony Powell, *Travels with My Aunt*
Editing: *Cabaret*
Sound: *Cabaret*
Visual Effects: *The Poseidon Adventure*
Short/Animated: *A Christmas Carol* (ABC, Richard Williams)
Short/Live Action: *Norman Rockwell's World . . . An American Dream*
Documentary/Feature: *Marjoe* (Howard Smith, Sarah Kernochan)
Documentary/Short: *This Tiny World*
Foreign-Language Film: *The Discreet Charm of the Bourgeoisie* (France)
Jean Hersholt Humanitarian Award: Rosalind Russell
Special Awards:
Edward G. Robinson, Renaissance man
Charles S. Boren, leader for 38 years of the industry's enlightened labor relations and architect of its policy of nondiscrimination

**** *The Discreet Charm of the Bourgeoisie* AAW SOC
The closest thing Buñuel ever made to a crowd pleaser, a delicious joke of a film with a dreamlike structure (*The Exterminating Angel* turned inside out)—a group of friends try to meet for dinner, but always seem to get

interrupted by something ever more strange.

Golden Globes
Picture (Drama): *The Godfather*
Picture (Comedy/Musical): *Cabaret*
English-Language Foreign Film: *Young Winston*
Foreign-Language Film: *The Emigrants, The New Land* (Sweden)
Actor (Drama): Marlon Brando, *The Godfather*
Actor (Comedy/Musical): Jack Lemmon, *Avanti!*
Actress (Drama): Liv Ullmann, *The Emigrants*
Actress (Comedy/Musical): Liza Minnelli, *Cabaret*
Supporting Actor: Joel Grey, *Cabaret*
Supporting Actress: Shelley Winters, *The Poseidon Adventure*
Director: Francis Ford Coppola, *The Godfather*
Screenplay: Francis Ford Coppola, Mario Puzo, *The Godfather*
Score: Nino Rota, *The Godfather*
Song: "Ben," *Ben*, m: Walter Scharf, l: Don Black
Most Promising Newcomer (Male): Edward Albert, *Butterflies Are Free*
Most Promising Newcomer (Female): Diana Ross, *Lady Sings the Blues*
World Film Favorite (Male): Marlon Brando
World Film Favorite (Female): Jane Fonda
Cecil B. DeMille Award: Samuel Goldwyn

Directors Guild of America
Director: Francis Ford Coppola, *The Godfather*
D. W. Griffith Award: William Wellman, David Lean

Honorary Life Member: David Lean

New York Film Critics Circle
Picture: *Cries and Whispers*
Actor: Laurence Olivier, *Sleuth*
Actress: Liv Ullmann, *Cries and Whispers, The Emigrants*
Supporting Actor: Robert Duvall, *The Godfather*
Supporting Actress: Jeannie Berlin, *The Heartbreak Kid*
Director: Ingmar Bergman, *Cries and Whispers*
Screenplay: Ingmar Bergman, *Cries and Whispers*
Special Award: *The Sorrow and the Pity*, best documentary

***** Al Pacino in *The Godfather*   SOC BOR
The great central performance in *The Godfather* isn't Brando's but Pacino's—an unknown actor, hired despite the producer's fear that he was too short, who dominates the picture like the cold heart of darkness. Only the National Society of Film Critics recognized him as the real star of the picture, with a comfortable 28–21-point lead over Brando (no other picture mattered, and the Circle's pick of Olivier came in tied for eleventh place—odd, the memberships weren't *that* different).

National Society of Film Critics
Picture: *The Discreet Charm of the Bourgeoisie*
Actor: Al Pacino, *The Godfather*
Actress: Cicely Tyson, *Sounder*
Supporting Actor: Joel Grey,

Cabaret; Eddie Albert, *The Heartbreak Kid*
Supporting Actress: Jeannie Berlin, *The Heartbreak Kid*
Director: Luis Buñuel, *The Discreet Charm of the Bourgeoisie*
Screenplay: Ingmar Bergman, *Cries and Whispers*
Cinematography: Sven Nykvist, *Cries and Whispers*
Richard and Hilda Rosenthal Foundation Awards:
For a film which, although not sufficiently recognized by public attendance, has nevertheless been an outstanding achievement: *My Uncle Antoine*
For a person working in cinema whose contribution to film art has not yet received due public recognition: Ivan Passer, director of *Intimate Lighting*; Robert Kaylor, director of *Derby*

National Board of Review
Best English-Language Film:
Cabaret
Man of La Mancha
The Godfather
Sounder
1776
The Effects of Gamma Rays on Man-in-the-Moon Marigolds
Deliverance
The Ruling Class
The Candidate
Frenzy
Best Foreign-Language Film:
The Sorrow and the Pity
The Emigrants
The Discreet Charm of the Bourgeoisie
Chloë in the Afternoon
Uncle Vanya
Actor: Peter O'Toole, *Man of La Mancha*, *The Ruling Class*
Actress: Cicely Tyson, *Sounder*
Supporting Actor: Al Pacino, *The Godfather*; Joel Grey, *Cabaret*

Supporting Actress: Marisa Berenson, *Cabaret*
Director: Bob Fosse, *Cabaret*

British Academy Awards
Film: *Cabaret*
Actor: Gene Hackman, *The French Connection*, *The Poseidon Adventure*
Actress: Liza Minnelli, *Cabaret*
Supporting Actor: Ben Johnson, *The Last Picture Show*
Supporting Actress: Cloris Leachman, *The Last Picture Show*
Director: Bob Fosse, *Cabaret*
Screenplay: Paddy Chayefsky, *The Hospital*; Peter Bogdanovich, Larry McMurtry, *The Last Picture Show*
Academy Fellow: Freddie Young

Cannes Film Festival
Palme d'Or: *The Working Class Goes to Heaven* (Elio Petri, Italy), *The Mattei Affair* (Francesco Rosi, Italy); the Jury wishes to underline the exceptional quality of Gian Maria Volonté's performances in both films
Special Jury Prize: *Solaris* (Andrei Tarkovsky, USSR)
Jury Prize: *Slaughterhouse-Five* (George Roy Hill, USA)
Actor: Jean Yanne, *We Will Not Grow Old Together* (France)
Actress: Susannah York, *Images* (USA)
Direction: Miklós Jancsó, *Red Psalm* (Hungary)
International Critics Prize: *Avoir 20 ans dans les Aures* (Rene Vautier, France)

• *The Canterbury Tales* BER
After the success of *Fellini Satyricon*, producer Alberto Grimaldi talked Pier Paolo Pasolini into devoting what turned out to be the rest of his

short life to a sort of X-rated *Masterpiece Theater*—nudity-filled versions of bawdy and pornographic classics including *The Decameron*, *The Arabian Nights*, and the Marquis de Sade's *Salo*. Since Pasolini's strength was gritty neorealism rather than Fellini's exotic visuals, in retrospect he seems like the wrong man for the job—and since Chaucer's jokes wouldn't exactly slay them in the Catskills these days, *The Canterbury Tales* minus its poetry is just bare butts and old goats mugging it up. Whatever its interest as a midnight-movie taboo-breaker back in the days of sexual liberation, it plays like poor late-night Europorn on Cinemax today.

Berlin Film Festival

Golden Bear: *The Canterbury Tales* (Pier Paolo Pasolini, Italy)
Silver Bear: *The Hospital* (Arthur Hiller, USA)
Actor: Alberto Sordi, *Detenuto in Attesa di Giudizio* [*Why*] (Italy)
Actress: Elizabeth Taylor, *Hammersmith Is Out* (UK)
Director: Jean-Pierre Blanc, *The Spinster* (France)
Special Prize for Artistic Originality: Peter Ustinov [actor-director of *Hammersmith Is Out*]
International Critics Prize: *The Audience* (Marco Ferreri, Italy), *Family Life* (Ken Loach, UK)

Harvard Lampoon Movie Worsts

Ten worst pictures:
Last Tango in Paris
The Candidate
The Getaway
Sounder
Deliverance
Play It As It Lays
The Emigrants
What's Up, Doc?
Man of La Mancha
The Man
Kirk Douglas Award for Worst Actor: Robert Redford, *The Candidate*
Natalie Wood Award for Worst Actress: Ali MacGraw, *The Getaway*
The Uncrossed Heart (to the least promising young performer): Cybill Shepherd, who has now gone through two major films without once opening her eyes
The Great Ceremonial Hot Dog (to the worst scene of the movie season): Carol Burnett, for her stunning impersonation of Charlie the Horse doing *Medea* in the bereavement scene of *Pete 'n' Tillie*
The Well-It-Sure-Is-Different Award (to the most chicly incomprehensible film): *Fellini's Roma*
The-Black-Symbolizes-Death, See? Award (to the worst student film): Jean Pignozzi, *Hamburger*
The Victor Mature Memorial Award (to the most embarrassing line of dialogue since Richard Burton was asked at the foot of the cross in *The Robe*, "Is this your first crucifixion?"): *Nicholas and Alexandra*, for a young Trotsky's angry reproach to the father of Modern Communism, "Lenin, you've been avoiding me!"
The Bosley (to that film critic whose writing consistently explores the farthest limits of bad taste): To Pauline Kael, whose hysterical encomium loosed Bertolucci's *Last Tango* on an all-too-trusting world

The Merino Award: Marino
Schneider in *Last Tango in Paris*

Box Office (Domestic Rentals)

1	*The Godfather*	$81,500,000	Par
2	*Fiddler on the Roof*	25,100,000	UA
3	*Diamonds Are Forever*	21,000,000	UA
4	*What's Up, Doc?*	17,000,000	WB
5	*Dirty Harry*	16,000,000	WB
6	*The Last Picture Show*	12,750,000	Col
7	*A Clockwork Orange*	12,000,000	WB
8	*Cabaret*	10,885,000	Allied Artists
9	*The Hospital*	9,000,000	UA
10	*Everything You Always Wanted to Know About Sex*	8,500,000	UA

Other films of note:

12	*The Cowboys*	7,000,000	WB
21	*Joe Kidd*	5,250,000	Uni
24	*Play It Again, Sam*	5,000,000	Par
27	*Fritz the Cat*	4,600,000	Cinemation
28	*Conquest of the Planet of the Apes*	4,500,000	Fox
31	*Superfly*	4,000,000	WB
35	*Shaft's Big Score*	3,675,000	MGM
86	*Blacula*	1,200,000	American Int'l

The Godfather *finally became the first movie to break* Gone With the Wind'*s record—and stay ahead of it. As third choice for the title role after Laurence Olivier and Burt Lancaster, Marlon Brando had only been paid $50,000—plus a piece of the profits which, it was estimated, would eventually amount to $16 million (the movie only cost twelve). Clint Eastwood wasn't even third choice for the part of "Dirty" Harry Callahan—it had previously been turned down by Frank Sinatra, Robert Mitchum, and—remember, this was the era of blaxploitation—Bill Cosby. (You're thinking, were there six Jell-O pudding pops in the fridge, or only five?) With a comedy and an Oscar-caliber drama in the top ten, Peter Bogdanovich looked like the most promising filmmaker of the '70s, and Woody Allen had his highest-ranking hit ever this year with a comedy about sex.*

Gebert's Golden Armchairs

Best American Film: *The Godfather*
Best Foreign Film: *The Discreet Charm of the Bourgeoisie*

Best Actor: Al Pacino, *The Godfather*
Best Actress: Liza Minnelli, *Cabaret*
Best Director: Francis Ford Coppola, *The Godfather*

1973

How influential was Pauline Kael in her heyday? It wasn't for nothing that other critics made jokes like calling Brian DePalma "A Filmmaker by Pauline Kael." Comparing the San Francisco Film Festival showing of Bernardo Bertolucci's *Last Tango in Paris* to the premiere of Stravinsky's "The Rite of Spring," her fervent rave and subsequent campaigning singlehandedly earned it a *Time* cover, acting awards from both critical groups and even an Oscar nomination for the actor you'd have thought the Academy had had enough of the previous year, Marlon Brando. All this, mind you, for a movie that was rated X—and included at least one act that most Academy voters probably wouldn't have admitted they knew existed.

Academy Awards

*** ***The Sting*** AAW DGA BOR
There's a bit of a sentiment among buffs these days that *The Sting* was a weak Best Picture choice between two *Godfather*s. But charm is an underrated quality, and considering that Oscar's likely other choice was *The Exorcist* (which looks downright silly today—people passing out and throwing up at *that*?), what the Nixon-era recession was to the Great Depression, *The Sting* is to '30s escapist classics—an imitation, but convincing enough.

Picture
The Sting (Universal, Tony Bill, Michael and Julia Phillips)
American Graffiti (Universal, Lucasfilm/Coppola Company)
Cries and Whispers (New World, Svenska Filminstitutet–Cinematograph AB Prod.)
The Exorcist (Warner Bros., William Peter Blatty)

A Touch of Class (Avco Embassy, Brut Prods., Melvin Frank)

*** **Jack Lemmon in *Save the Tiger*** AAW HAR
The end of the rope for a World War II vet and garment factory owner, fed up with a crappy, hypocritical Watergate-era America. Writer Steve Shagan's relentlessly downbeat, ugly view of America is overblown and often pretentious, but it has its teeth into the same thing *Network* and *Taxi Driver* did more successfully a few years later—and after *Glengarry Glen Ross*, it's the best showcase for Lemmon's patented whining middle-aged loser act. Though you have to wonder about the sincerity of director John G. Avildsen, who went straight from *Joe* and this to announcing morning again in America with *Rocky*. . . .

Actor
Jack Lemmon, *Save the Tiger*
Marlon Brando, *Last Tango in Paris*

Jack Nicholson, *The Last Detail*
Al Pacino, *Serpico*
Robert Redford, *The Sting*

*** Glenda Jackson in *A Touch of Class* AAW GLO
What passes for dazzlingly sophisticated romantic comedy in 1973 would have been just a little above average twenty years earlier, but Oscar seems so tickled to find that Glenda Jackson can do comedy too that it's ready to declare her Katherine Hepburn (although I like *Hopscotch* a little better).

Actress
Glenda Jackson, *A Touch of Class*
Ellen Burstyn, *The Exorcist*
Marsha Mason, *Cinderella Liberty*
Barbra Streisand, *The Way We Were*
Joanne Woodward, *Summer Wishes, Winter Dreams*

Supporting Actor
John Houseman, *The Paper Chase*
Vincent Gardenia, *Bang the Drum Slowly*
Jack Gilford, *Save the Tiger*
Jason Miller, *The Exorcist*
Randy Quaid, *The Last Detail*

Supporting Actress
Tatum O'Neal, *Paper Moon*
Linda Blair, *The Exorcist*
Candy Clark, *American Graffiti*
Madeline Kahn, *Paper Moon*
Sylvia Sidney, *Summer Wishes, Winter Dreams*

Director
George Roy Hill, *The Sting*
Ingmar Bergman, *Cries and Whispers*

Bernardo Bertolucci, *Last Tango in Paris*
William Friedkin, *The Exorcist*
George Lucas, *American Graffiti*

Original Screenplay: David S. Ward, *The Sting*
Adapted Screenplay: William Peter Blatty, *The Exorcist*
Cinematography: Sven Nykvist, *Cries and Whispers*
Original Score: Marvin Hamlisch, *The Way We Were*
Scoring Adaptation: Marvin Hamlisch, *The Sting*
Song: "The Way We Were," *The Way We Were*, m: Marvin Hamlisch, l: Alan and Marilyn Bergman
Art Direction: Henry Bumstead, *The Sting*
Costume Design: Edith Head, *The Sting*
Editing: *The Sting*
Sound: *The Exorcist*
Short/Animated: *Frank Film* (Frank Mouris)
Short/Live Action: *The Bolero*
Documentary/Short: *Princeton: A Search for Answers*
Documentary/Feature: *The Great American Cowboy* (Kieth Merrill)
Foreign-Language Film: *Day for Night* (France)
Irving G. Thalberg Award: Lawrence Weingarten
Jean Hersholt Humanitarian Award: Lew Wasserman
Special Awards:
Henri Langlois for his devotion to the art of film, his massive contributions in preserving its past and his unswerving faith in its future
Groucho Marx

Golden Globes
Picture (Drama): *The Exorcist*
Picture (Comedy/Musical): *American Graffiti*

Foreign-Language Film: *The Pedestrian* (West Germany)
Actor (Drama): Al Pacino, *Serpico*
Actor (Comedy/Musical): George Segal, *A Touch of Class*
Actress (Drama): Marsha Mason, *Cinderella Liberty*
Actress (Comedy/Musical): Glenda Jackson, *A Touch of Class*
Supporting Actor: John Houseman, *The Paper Chase*
Supporting Actress: Linda Blair, *The Exorcist*
Director: William Friedkin, *The Exorcist*
Screenplay: William Peter Blatty, *The Exorcist*
Score: Neil Diamond, *Jonathan Livingston Seagull*
Song: "The Way We Were," *The Way We Were*, m: Marvin Hamlisch, l: Alan and Marilyn Bergman
Documentary: *Visions of Eight*
Most Promising Newcomer (Male): Paul LeMat, *American Graffiti*
Most Promising Newcomer (Female): Tatum O'Neal, *Paper Moon*
World Film Favorite (Male): Marlon Brando
World Film Favorite (Female): Elizabeth Taylor
Cecil B. DeMille Award: Bette Davis

Directors Guild of America
Director: George Roy Hill, *The Sting*
Honorary Life Member: Charles Chaplin

*** Marlon Brando in *Last Tango in Paris* NYC SOC
Pauline Kael marveled at "how deep down [Brando] goes and what he dredges up" as the middle-aged wreck engaging in sex-power games with a nubile stranger. You can still easily see what amazed Kael and at least impressed others then—the first time a star of Brando's caliber had gone in for this kind of Cassavetes-style improvisation, taking it much further and much more personally into his own macho pathology. You could have believed that it marked the end of the phoniness of acting and the beginning of a new acting age, the second Brando revolution. But it's much harder to see, now, that Brando really reached a great deal of truth—what he improvises isn't especially profound (in fact, it's often childishly vulgar). And since then we've seen his improvisations nearly derail another movie that hoped in vain that he could find its heart of darkness (*Apocalypse Now*—we won't even go into *The Missouri Breaks*), and watched Brando himself disappear, like Garbo, beneath his size and self-indulgent whimsy.

New York Film Critics Circle
Picture: *Day for Night*
Actor: Marlon Brando, *Last Tango in Paris*
Actress: Joanne Woodward, *Summer Wishes, Winter Dreams*
Supporting Actor: Robert De Niro, *Mean Streets*
Supporting Actress: Valentina Cortese, *Day For Night*
Director: François Truffaut, *Day for Night*
Screenplay: George Lucas, Gloria Katz, Willard Huyck, *American Graffiti*

*** *Day for Night* AAW NYC SOC BAA

François Truffaut's valentine to moviemaking is a sort of *Sunny Boulevard*—no morbid fantasies here, just the workaday, sometimes ridiculous business of getting a movie down on film. Like other movies about movies (e.g., *The Player*) a bit overrated by movie reviewers, but certainly one of Truffaut's best later works.

National Society of Film Critics

Picture: *Day for Night*
Actor: Marlon Brando, *Last Tango in Paris*
Actress: Liv Ullmann, *The New Land*
Supporting Actor: Robert De Niro, *Mean Streets*
Supporting Actress: Valentina Cortese, *Day for Night*
Director: François Truffaut, *Day for Night*
Screenplay: George Lucas, Gloria Katz, Willard Huyck, *American Graffiti*
Cinematography: Vilmos Zsigmond, *The Long Goodbye*
Special Award: Robert Ryan, *The Iceman Cometh* [posthumous]
Richard and Hilda Rosenthal Foundation Awards: For a film which, although not sufficiently recognized by public attendance, has nevertheless been an outstanding achievement: *Memories of Underdevelopment* For a person working in cinema whose contribution to film art has not yet received due public recognition: Daryl Duke, director of *Payday*

National Board of Review

Best English-Language Film:
The Sting

Paper Moon
The Homecoming
Bang the Drum Slowly
Serpico
O Lucky Man!
The Last American Hero
The Hireling
The Day of the Dolphin
The Way We Were
Best Foreign-Language Film:
Cries and Whispers
Day for Night
The New Land
The Tall Blond Man With One Black Shoe
Alfredo, Alfredo
Traffic
Actor: Al Pacino, *Serpico*; Robert Ryan, *The Iceman Cometh*
Actress: Liv Ullmann, *The New Land*
Supporting Actor: John Houseman, *The Paper Chase*
Supporting Actress: Sylvia Sidney, *Summer Wishes, Winter Dreams*
Director: Ingmar Bergman, *Cries and Whispers*
Special Citations:
American Film Theatre and Ely Landau
Woody Allen, for his script *Sleeper*
Walt Disney Productions for *Robin Hood*
Paramount, for *Charlotte's Web*

British Academy Awards

Film: *Day for Night*
Actor: Walter Matthau, *Pete 'n' Tillie*, *Charley Varrick*
Actress: Stéphane Audran, *The Discreet Charm of the Bourgeoisie*, *Just Before Nightfall*
Supporting Actor: Arthur Lowe, *O Lucky Man!*
Supporting Actress: Valentina Cortese, *Day for Night*
Director: François Truffaut, *Day for Night*
Screenplay: Luis Buñuel, Jean-

Claude Carrière, *The Discreet Charm of the Bourgeoisie*
Academy Fellow: Grace Wyndham Goldie

Cannes Film Festival

Palme d'Or: *Scarecrow* (Jerry Schatzberg, USA), *The Hireling* (Alan Bridges, UK), underlining the exceptional performances by Sarah Miles [in *The Hireling*], Al Pacino and Gene Hackman [in *Scarecrow*]
Special Jury Prize: *The Mother and the Whore* (Jean Eustache, France)
Jury Prize: *Sanitarium Under the Hour Glass* (Wojciech Has, Poland), *The Invitation* (Claude Goretta, Switzerland)
Actor: Giancarlo Giannini, *Love and Anarchy* (Italy)
Actress: Joanne Woodward, *The Effects of Gamma Rays on Man-in-the-Moon Marigolds* (USA)
First Film: *Jeremy* (Arthur Barron, USA)
Special Prize: *La Planète Sauvage* [*Fantastic Planet*] (Rene Laloux, France)
Technical Prize: Ingmar Bergman, *Cries and Whispers* (Sweden), for his use of color to serve thought
International Critics Prize: *The Mother and the Whore*, *La Grande Bouffe* (Marco Ferreri, France)

Berlin Film Festival

Golden Bear: *Distant Thunder* (Satyajit Ray, India)
Special Jury Silver Bear: *Where There's Smoke There's Fire* (André Cayatte, France)
Silver Bears: *The Revolution of the Seven Madmen* (Leopoldo Torre Nilsson, Argentina), *The Tall Blond Man With One Black Shoe* (Yves Robert, France), *The Experts* (Norbert Kückelmann, West Germany), *All Nudity Will Be Punished* (Arnaldo Jabor, Brazil), *The 14* (David Hemmings, UK)
International Critics Prize: in competition, *Blood Wedding* (Claude Chabrol, France); Forum: *Lo Stagionale* (Switzerland); *Days of 36* (Theo Angelopolous, Greece)

Harvard Lampoon Movie Worsts

Ten worst pictures:
The Great Gatsby [NOTE: the second version of this novel to merit this honor; see 1949]
Day of the Dolphin
Jonathan Livingston Seagull
The Seven-Ups
A Touch of Class
Blume in Love
The Way We Were
The Exorcist
Save the Tiger
American Graffiti
Kirk Douglas Award for Worst Actor: Jack Lemmon, *Save the Tiger*
Natalie Wood Award for Worst Actress: Barbra Streisand, *The Way We Were*
Worst Supporting Actor: Dustin Hoffman, *Papillon*
Worst Supporting Actress: Dyan Cannon, *Shamus*, *The Last of Sheila*
The OK-Doc-Break-the-Arm-Again Award (for the most flagrant example of miscasting): Mia Farrow as Daisy Buchanan, *The Great Gatsby*
The Handlin Oscar (to the film which most distorts history): *Hitler: The Last Ten Days*
The Curse-of-the-Living-Corpse Award: Lucille Ball, *Mame*, in which her actual age was cleverly concealed by a paper towel taped over the camera lens; someone should saw this lady in half and count the rings
The Tin Pan (to the most

obnoxious movie song): Paul
McCartney, "Live and Let Die"
**The Charles Manson Memorial
Scalpel** (for the clumsiest job of
cutting): *O Lucky Man!*, whose
shooting script was first

published as a deck of flashcards
by Educational Playthings
Best Argument for Vivisection:
Jonathan Livingston Seagull
The Merino Award: To the
Mexican actor and comedian
ordinaire Mario Moreno

Box Office (Domestic Rentals)

1	*The Poseidon Adventure*	$40,000,000	Fox
2	*Deliverance*	18,000,000	WB
3	*The Getaway*	17,500,000	National General
4	*Live and Let Die*	15,500,000	UA
5	*Paper Moon*	13,000,000	Par
6	*Last Tango in Paris*	12,625,000	UA
7	*The Sound of Music [1973 only]*	11,000,000	Fox
8	*Jesus Christ Superstar*	10,800,000	Uni
9	*The World's Greatest Athlete*	10,600,000	Disney
10	*American Graffiti*	10,300,000	Uni
Other films of note:			
11	*The Way We Were*	10,000,000	Col
12	*Lady Sings the Blues*	9,050,000	Par
13	*Mary Poppins [1973 only]*	9,000,000	Disney
17	*Walking Tall*	8,500,000	Cinerama
18	*Jeremiah Johnson*	8,350,000	WB
19	*Billy Jack [1973 only]*	8,275,000	WB
	[total 1973–74 only:	14,000,000]	
20	*High Plains Drifter*	7,125,000	Uni
28	*Enter the Dragon*	4,250,000	WB
30	*Battle for the Planet of the Apes*	4,000,000	Fox
40	*The Chinese Connection*	3,400,000	National General
43	*Cleopatra Jones*	3,250,000	WB
52	*Pat Garrett and Billy the Kid*	2,700,000	MGM
65	*Black Caesar*	2,000,000	American Int'l
65	*Coffy*	2,000,000	American Int'l

There were new action stars in everyone from Burt Reynolds to Pam Grier and Bruce Lee this year, but the most interesting from a business perspective was a one-(well, two-) hit wonder, Tom Laughlin. Laughlin sued Warner Bros. over what he regarded as their mishandling of his 1971 Billy Jack, *and won the right to re-release it his way. His way turned out to be a nickelodeon-era practice called four-walling— in which the distributor rents the theater outright and keeps all the ticket money— combined with saturation TV and newspaper advertising which, like Hercules 14 years before, created the atmosphere of a limited-time, must-see event. Moving from town to town (mostly in the sticks), Laughlin quadrupled* Billy Jack's *box office take, inspired the big studios to try the same thing with reissues of* Jeremiah Johnson *(whose conventional release is shown here) and* The Exorcist, *spawned an entire genre of family-oriented exploitation films from companies like Sunn Classic International* (The Adventures of the Wilderness Family! In Search of the Historic Jesus! One week only!), *and in general, proved P. T. Barnum right.*

Gebert's Golden Armchairs

If *Nashville* is Robert Altman's most overrated movie, *The Long Goodbye* is the most underrated. True, Elliott Gould's Philip Marlowe is a joke who hardly bears any relation to Raymond Chandler's detective, but on the other hand, it gets the rot-under-the-palm-trees atmosphere of Chandler's work better than any other movie adaptation does. And Sterling Hayden's partly improvised performance, as the sexually and creatively impotent Hemingwayesque author who can't remember if he committed the murder, digs as deep into middle-aged male desolation as *Last Tango*—without the sensationalism. Also mining something of the same territory as *Last Tango* is Jean Eustache's *The Mother and the Whore*, a Special Jury Prize–winner at Cannes. It's best described as *My Dinner With Andre* filmed on the scale of *Lawrence of Arabia*—3½ hours of fascinating, exhausting, and seductive Parisian café conversation, mainly between bullshit-*artiste extraordinaire* Jean-Pierre Leaud and the two women he's involved with.

Best American Film: *The Long Goodbye*
Best Foreign Film: *The Mother and the Whore*
Best Actor: Sterling Hayden, *The Long Goodbye*
Best Actress: Glenda Jackson, *A Touch of Class*
Best Director: Robert Altman, *The Long Goodbye*

Life Achievement Awards: The American Film Institute Life Achievement Award and The Film Society of Lincoln Center Tributes

Given the chance to inaugurate the John F. Kennedy Center for the Performing Arts with a film festival, the American Film Institute had somehow failed to find out that the opening choice, Costa-Gavras' *State of Siege*, was an attack on U.S. policies—and something of a justification for political assassination, a particularly unfortunate thing to advocate in a theater named for John F. Kennedy. Days before the event, AFI director George Stevens, Jr. yanked it, setting off a firestorm of controversy and a wave of cancellations from producers with films in the festival.

The Life Achievement Award may have been in the works before the festival fiasco, but it took on new urgency in the AFI's state of siege. A party honoring the grand master of American cinema, John Ford, was the answer. With Danny Kaye a surprising but classy choice for host, no less than Peter

Bogdanovich in charge of picking the clips, and President and Mrs. Nixon in attendance along with numerous Hollywood stars, the AFI's first Life Achievement Award broadcast was a hit with both viewers and critics, and quickly became the organization's most visible activity.

Each year since, an aged Hollywood star or director has been trotted out to receive the tributes of other aged colleagues and of the younger powers-that-be of today's Hollywood. While the formula remains high-toned, in some ways the AFI broadcasts have become as morbidly fascinating as the Oscar telecast. The life expectancy of AFI honorees has not been great—Ford, for one, died the same year as his—and for every unforgettable moment such as Ingrid Bergman warmly embracing Alfred Hitchcock as she presents him with the famous key from *Notorious*, there is another straight out of *Sunset Boulevard* (such as an enfeebled Hitchcock asking Cary Grant who Sean Connery is, 15 years after Connery made *Marnie* for him). The irony of young Hollywood titans paying tribute to filmmakers like Orson Welles or Billy Wilder, for whom they have done nothing to help find financing for their last projects, hasn't gone unnoticed, either—not least by Sir David Lean, who came very near to lecturing his audience on that subject.

After twenty years the AFI had given its award to most of the surviving figures of Hollywood's golden age—with the exception of one refusenik, Katharine Hepburn—and the formula was beginning to seem more than a bit tired. To enliven the proceedings, in 1994 the AFI decided to honor a star who still had some of his own hair—Jack Nicholson. Hosted by Warren Beatty (who joked that the next year's recipient would be Macaulay Culkin), and with the likes of Dennis Hopper, Candice Bergen, Bob Dylan, and Kareem Abdul-Jabbar among the presenters and guests, the Nicholson tribute was the liveliest AFI show in years, and will no doubt serve as a model in the years to come.

The Film Society of Lincoln Center is in many ways the hipper, more intellectual mirror image of the AFI. Its magazine *Film Comment* has always been cheeky and smart where the AFI's (now-defunct) *American Film* was stodgy and safe; its New York Film Festival, founded in 1963, is the intellectually ambitious trendsetter and reputation-maker that the AFI's various film presentations have wanted to be. And where the AFI's Life Achievement Award has gone to strictly the most unimpeachable and uncontroversial Hollywood names, the tribute of the Film Society of Lincoln Center has been more likely to go to more iconoclastic figures such as Federico Fellini and Robert Altman. (Which is not to say that many of the same people haven't been honored by both groups.) Instead of a TV broadcast, the Lincoln Center tributes generally include an appreciative career retrospective piece or two in *Film Comment*. Here, for the first time, are the Film Society of Lincoln Center's honorees for comparison side by side with the better-known AFI ones.

	AFI	**Lincoln Center**
1972		Charles Chaplin
1973	John Ford	Fred Astaire
1974	James Cagney	Alfred Hitchcock
1975	Orson Welles	Paul Newman and Joanne Woodward
1976	William Wyler	
1977	Bette Davis	
1978	Henry Fonda	George Cukor
1979	Alfred Hitchcock	Bob Hope
1980	James Stewart	John Huston
1981	Fred Astaire	Barbara Stanwyck
1982	Frank Capra	Billy Wilder
1983	John Huston	Sir Laurence Olivier
1984	Lillian Gish	Claudette Colbert
1985	Gene Kelly	Federico Fellini
1986	Billy Wilder	Elizabeth Taylor
1987	Barbara Stanwyck	Sir Alec Guinness
1988	Jack Lemmon	Yves Montand
1989	Gregory Peck	Bette Davis
1990	David Lean	James Stewart
1991	Kirk Douglas	Audrey Hepburn
1992	Sidney Poitier	Gregory Peck
1993	Elizabeth Taylor	Jack Lemmon
1994	Jack Nicholson	Robert Altman
1995	Steven Spielberg	Shirley MacLaine

1974

Has any director in history ever had as good a year as Francis Coppola's 1974? From a particularly strong American field at Cannes including *The Last Detail*, Altman's *Thieves Like Us* and Spielberg's *The Sugarland Express*, *The Conversation* emerged to win a Palme d'Or generally considered deserved. *The Conversation* was no great hit, but back home *The Godfather, Part II* opened to business approaching that of its phenomenal predecessor. *G-2* got generally good reviews, and Pauline Kael called it "thematically richer, more shadowed, fuller" and "a Bicentennial picture that doesn't insult the intelligence." But despite her admiration maybe there was something of a backlash against *The Godfather*'s incredible commercial success; *The Conversation* was the only one to pick up a critical prize, from the National Board of Review.

Oscar nominated both of them for Best Picture—the first time anybody had had two pictures against each other since John Ford in 1940 (when there were ten nominee slots). Spurred on by the DGA, in the end Oscar followed popular taste more than critical opinion—and got it right.

Academy Awards

***** *The Godfather, Part II*
AAW
Coppola and Puzo's brilliant attack on everything people misunderstood *The Godfather* to stand for (family loyalty, order, old-fashioned respect, and manners). In the past we see the octopus-arms of the Mafia start to entangle and corrupt the New World; in the present we see Michael Corleone turn on his family, destroying it in the name of saving it.

Picture
The Godfather, Part II
(Paramount, Francis Ford Coppola, Gray Frederickson, Fred Roos)

Chinatown (Paramount, Robert Evans)
The Conversation (Paramount, Francis Ford Coppola)
Lenny (UA, Marvin Worth)
The Towering Inferno (20th Century–Fox/Warner Bros., Irwin Allen)

**** Art Carney in *Harry and Tonto* AAW GLO
As an old man with a cat and not much else in the world, Carney gives a low-key, quietly believable performance in what has to be the least trendy of Paul Mazursky's movies—and therefore one that has aged very well. But it's a sentimental choice (of someone who was a TV favorite, for that matter, not a movie star) in a year filled with more important work.

Actor
Art Carney, *Harry and Tonto*
Albert Finney, *Murder on the Orient Express*
Dustin Hoffman, *Lenny*
Jack Nicholson, *Chinatown*
Al Pacino, *The Godfather, Part II*

***** Ellen Burstyn in *Alice Doesn't Live Here Anymore***
AAW BAA '75

There was just a brief moment in recent Hollywood history when a middle-aged actress could find wonderful, fully developed character parts—and Ellen Burstyn got nearly all of them. (The only one she missed was Cloris Leachman's in *The Last Picture Show*, because she was already in it—and I think her casually amoral social-climber is a richer role than Leachman's Oscar-winning wallflower.) Martin Scorsese is usually thought of as a man's director, but there's a small collection of terrific female parts in his work, too, and Burstyn's funny, utterly believable, and sympathetic waitress/single mom suggests that he could have found an equally successful career away from the mean streets.

Actress
Ellen Burstyn, *Alice Doesn't Live Here Anymore*
Diahann Carroll, *Claudine*
Faye Dunaway, *Chinatown*
Valerie Perrine, *Lenny*
Gena Rowlands, *A Woman Under the Influence*

Supporting Actor
Robert De Niro, *The Godfather, Part II*
Fred Astaire, *The Towering Inferno*
Jeff Bridges, *Thunderbolt and Lightfoot*
Michael V. Gazzo, *The Godfather, Part II*
Lee Strasberg, *The Godfather, Part II*

Supporting Actress
Ingrid Bergman, *Murder on the Orient Express*
Valentina Cortese, *Day for Night*
Madeline Kahn, *Blazing Saddles*
Diane Ladd, *Alice Doesn't Live Here Anymore*
Talia Shire, *The Godfather, Part II*

Director
Francis Ford Coppola, *The Godfather, Part II*
John Cassavetes, *A Woman Under the Influence*
Bob Fosse, *Lenny*
Roman Polanski, *Chinatown*
François Truffaut, *Day for Night*

Original Screenplay: Robert Towne, *Chinatown*
Adapted Screenplay: Francis Ford Coppola, Mario Puzo, *The Godfather, Part II*
Cinematography: Fred Koenekamp, Joseph Biroc, *The Towering Inferno*
Original Score: Nino Rota, Carmine Coppola, *The Godfather, Part II*
Scoring Adaptation: Nelson Riddle, *The Great Gatsby*
Song: "We May Never Love Like This Again," *The Towering Inferno*, ml: Al Kasha, Joel Hirschhorn
Art Direction: Dean Tavoularis, *The Godfather, Part II*
Costume Design: Theoni V. Aldredge, *The Great Gatsby*
Editing: *The Towering Inferno*
Sound: *Earthquake*
Visual Effects: *Earthquake*

Short/Animated: *Closed Mondays* (Will Vinton)
Short/Live Action: *One-Eyed Men Are Kings*
Documentary/Feature: *Hearts and Minds* (Peter Davis, Bert Schneider)
Documentary/Short: *Don't*
Foreign Language Film: *Amarcord* (Italy)
Jean Hersholt Humanitarian Award: Arthur B. Krim
Special Awards: Howard Hawks, a master American filmmaker
Jean Renoir, a genius through silent film, sound film, feature, documentary, and television

*** **Gena Rowlands in** *A Woman Under the Influence*
GLO BOR
Rowlands is good as a woman who has a nervous breakdown, but the movie is perhaps the ultimate test for lovers or haters of John Cassavetes' improv-until-you're-exhausted style—and who would throw a party for his wife on her first day home from the nuthouse?

Golden Globes
Picture (Drama): *Chinatown*
Picture (Comedy/Musical): *The Longest Yard*
Foreign Film: *Scenes from a Marriage* (Sweden)
Actor (Drama): Jack Nicholson, *Chinatown*
Actor (Comedy/Musical): Art Carney, *Harry and Tonto*
Actress (Drama): Gena Rowlands, *A Woman Under the Influence*
Actress (Comedy/Musical): Raquel Welch, *The Three Musketeers*
Supporting Actor: Fred Astaire, *The Towering Inferno*

Supporting Actress: Karen Black, *The Great Gatsby*
Director: Roman Polanski, *Chinatown*
Screenplay: Robert Towne, *Chinatown*
Score: Alan Jay Lerner, Frederick Loewe, *The Little Prince*
Song: "(Benji's Theme) I Feel Love," *Benji*, m: Euel Box l: Betty Box
Documentary: *Beautiful People*
Most Promising Newcomer (Male): Joseph Bottoms, *The Dove*
Most Promising Newcomer (Female): Susan Flannery, *The Towering Inferno*
World Film Favorite (Male): Robert Redford
World Film Favorite (Female): Barbra Streisand
Cecil B. DeMille Award: Hal B. Wallis

Directors Guild of America
Director: Francis Ford Coppola, *The Godfather, Part II*
Honorary Life Member: Lew Wasserman

*** *Amarcord*   AAW NYC BOR
A flavorful slice of '30s Italian life from the era when that kind of nostalgic filmmaking was first hitting the scene. Fellini's least pretentious and, as a result, best-liked film in some years is no masterpiece, but it's very enjoyable—and it makes for fascinating contrast with his much more intense neorealist *I Vitelloni* (1953), which covered roughly the same period in his life.

**** Jack Nicholson in *Chinatown*, **and in *** *The Last Detail*** GLO NYC SOC BAA

Nicholson had as good a pair of showcases as any actor could hope for that year— charismatically Bogart-like and old-movie glamorous in *Chinatown*, and homelied-up for a character part as the profane M.P. with a heart of gold in *The Last Detail* (both written, incidentally, by his pal from Roger Corman days, Robert Towne). Both are very good, but the movie-star part is the rarer and more valuable thing than the character role.

New York Film Critics Circle

Picture: *Amarcord*
Actor: Jack Nicholson, *Chinatown*, *The Last Detail*
Actress: Liv Ullmann, *Scenes From a Marriage*
Supporting Actor: Charles Boyer, *Stavisky*
Supporting Actress: Valerie Perrine, *Lenny*
Director: Federico Fellini, *Amarcord*
Screenplay: Ingmar Bergman, *Scenes from a Marriage*
Special Award: Fabiano Canosa, for his innovative programs at the First Ave. Screening Room

National Society of Film Critics

Picture: *Scenes from a Marriage*
Actor: Jack Nicholson, *Chinatown*, *The Last Detail*
Actress: Liv Ullmann, *Scenes From a Marriage*
Supporting Actor: Holger Löwenadler, *Lacombe, Lucien*
Supporting Actress: Bibi

Andersson, *Scenes From a Marriage*
Director: Francis Ford Coppola, *The Godfather, Part II*, *The Conversation*
Screenplay: Ingmar Bergman, *Scenes from a Marriage*
Cinematography: Gordon Willis, *The Godfather, Part II*, *The Parallax View*
Special Award: Jean Renoir

National Board of Review

Best English-Language Film:
The Conversation
Murder on the Orient Express
Chinatown
The Last Detail
Harry and Tonto
A Woman Under the Influence
Thieves Like Us
Lenny
Daisy Miller
The Three Musketeers
Best Foreign-Language Film:
Amarcord
Lacombe, Lucien
Scenes from a Marriage
The Phantom of Liberty
The Pedestrian
Actor: Gene Hackman, *The Conversation*
Actress: Gena Rowlands, *A Woman Under the Influence*
Supporting Actor: Holger Löwenadler, *Lacombe, Lucien*
Supporting Actress: Valerie Perrine, *Lenny*
Director: Francis Ford Coppola, *The Conversation*
Special Citations:
Special effects in *The Golden Voyage of Sinbad*, *Earthquake*, and *The Towering Inferno*
The film industry for increasing care in subsidiary casting in many films [presumably this means more minority casting]
Robert G. Youngson for his 25-year work with tasteful and intelligent compilation of films

People's Choice Awards
Favorite Picture: *The Sting*
Favorite Movie Actor: John Wayne
Favorite Movie Actress: Barbra Streisand

British Academy Awards
Film: *Lacombe, Lucien*
Actor: Jack Nicholson, *The Last Detail, Chinatown*
Actress: Joanne Woodward, *Summer Wishes, Winter Dreams*
Supporting Actor: John Gielgud, *Murder on the Orient Express*
Supporting Actress: Ingrid Bergman, *Murder on the Orient Express*
Director: Roman Polanski, *Chinatown*
Screenplay: Robert Towne, *Chinatown, The Last Detail*
Academy Fellow: Sir David Lean

**** The Conversation BOR CAN
Critics who were sick of godfathers tended to drift toward the austerity and uncommerciality of Coppola's other '74 film, which remakes *Blowup* Watergate style—Gene Hackman is the bugging expert not sure what the conversation he recorded means, or who's listening to him. A strong and disturbing but admittedly derivative drama, and if it's almost as successful as *Godfather II* on its own terms, its terms are not as ambitious or profound.

Cannes Film Festival
Palme d'Or: *The Conversation* (Francis Ford Coppola, USA)
Special Jury Prize: *Arabian Nights* (Pier Paolo Pasolini, Italy)
Jury Prize: *Cousin Angelica* (Carlos Saura, Spain)
Actor: Jack Nicholson, *The Last Detail* (USA)
Actress: Marie José Nat, *Les Violons du Bal* (France)
Screenplay: *Sugarland Express*, [directed by] Steven Spielberg [written by Hal Barwood, Matthew Robbins, from Spielberg's story] (USA)
Special Mention: Charles Boyer as Baron Raoul in *Stavisky* (France)
Technical Prize: *Mahler* (Ken Russell, UK)
International Critics Prize: in competition, *Ali: Fear Eats the Soul* (R. W. Fassbinder, West Germany), *Lancelot du Lac* (Robert Bresson, France) [award refused]

*** The Apprenticeship of Duddy Kravitz BER
A flavorful slice of '40s Canadian Jewish life from the era when that kind of ethnic-nostalgic filmmaking was first hitting the scene, with Richard Dreyfuss as a What-makes-Sammy-run? type. What made Berlin cough up a prize, though, was probably the character played by Denholm Elliott—a pretentious, drunken documentary filmmaker who "won a prize at Venezuela." They *might* have known the type.

Berlin Film Festival
Golden Bear: *The Apprenticeship of Duddy Kravitz* (Ted Kotcheff, Canada)
Special Jury Silver Bear: *L'Horloger de St-Paul* [*The Clockmaker*] (Bertrand Tavernier, France)
Silver Bears: *In the Name of the*

People (Ottokar Runze, West Germany), *Little Malcolm and His Struggle Against the Eunuch* (Stuart Cooper, UK), *Still Life* (Sohrab Shahid Saless, Iran), *Bread and Chocolate* (Franco Brusati, Italy), *Rebellion in Patagonia* (Hector Olivera, Argentina)
International Critics Prize: *Still Life; To Proxenio Tis Annas* (Greece)

Harvard Lampoon Movie Worsts

Ten worst pictures:
Lenny
S*P*Y*S
Harry and Tonto
Airport 1975
Blazing Saddles
The Night Porter
The Trial of Billy Jack
Murder on the Orient Express
Daisy Miller
The Front Page
Kirk Douglas Award for Worst Actor: Burt Reynolds, *The Longest Yard*
Natalie Wood Award for Worst Actress: Julie Andrews, *The Tamarind Seed*
The Exhausted Udder (presented by the Dairy Farmers Assn. in recognition of attempts to milk every penny possible from a marketable idea)**:** To the producers of *Our Time*, *Macon County Line*, *The Lords of Flatbush*, and *Buster and Billie* for trying to eke piquancy from an era as colorless as the tag on a pair of overlaundered pedal pushers
The Victor Mature Memorial Award (to the most embarrassing line of dialogue)**:** George Kennedy's astute remark in *Earthquake*, "Earthquakes bring out the worst in people."
The Curse-of-the-Living-Corpse Award: Gloria Swanson, an actress only slightly older than the mountains she is imperiled above in *Airport '75*
The Merino Award: Maureen O. McGovern, the curtailing of whose adipose warbling in *The Poseidon Adventure* and now *The Towering Inferno* excuses in part the effects of the disasters that follow

Box Office (Domestic Rentals)

1	*The Sting*	$68,450,000	Uni
2	*The Exorcist*	66,300,000	WB
3	*Papillon*	19,750,000	Allied Artists
4	*Magnum Force*	18,300,000	WB
5	*Herbie Rides Again*	17,500,000	Disney
6	*Blazing Saddles*	16,500,000	WB
7	*The Trial of Billy Jack*	15,000,000	WB
8	*The Great Gatsby*	14,200,000	Par
9	*Serpico*	14,100,600	Par
10	*Butch Cassidy and the Sundance Kid* [1974 only]	13,820,000	Fox
Other films of note:			
12	*Airport 1975*	12,310,000	Uni
13	*Dirty Mary, Crazy Larry*	12,068,000	Fox
14	*That's Entertainment!*	10,800,000	MGM
16	*The Longest Yard*	10,100,000	Par

17	*Jeremiah Johnson [four-wall reissue only]*	10,000,000	WB
20	*Thunderbolt and Lightfoot*	8,500,000	UA
21	*Chinatown*	8,433,000	Par
24	*Earthquake*	7,900,000	Uni
	[through 1975:	32,000,000]	
30	*Death Wish*	5,850,000	Par
33	*Andy Warhol's Frankenstein*	4,700,000	Bryanston
72	*Animal Crackers*	1,595,000	Par

The Exorcist *and* The Sting *fought it out all year, but in the end the Satanic cultural sensation lost out at both the box office and the Oscars to the easygoing con-man comedy with the '60s' most reliable male star, Paul Newman, and his pal Bob, who was about to become the '70s' biggest name. With three films in the top ten, Redford became the first star to pull off that trick since Bing Crosby in 1946; and* The Sting *shifted into high gear a nostalgia craze that found expression in everything from* That's Entertainment! *and a Marx Bros. reissue to Mel Brooks' western parody and an all-dressed-up-but-no-place-to-go film of* The Great Gatsby.

Gebert's Golden Armchairs

For *Godfather II,* Oscar nominations went to Pacino, De Niro as young Vito (who won), Lee Strasberg as Hyman (cough) Roth and Michael V. Gazzo as the last survivor of Vito's era. But not to John Cazale, poor Fredo, the true central character in *Godfather II*—the un-vicious brother who decides that he's had enough of "this Sicilian thing" (as Diane Keaton's Kay puts it at one point), and has to die for it. *Ali: Fear Eats the Soul* was shown at Cannes, but it would be another couple of years before the amazingly prolific West German director Rainer Werner Fassbinder would be known in the U.S. *Ali* is his 40-films-in-15-years career in a nutshell: a sort-of-remake of Douglas Sirk's 1955 *All That Heaven Allows,* with a frumpy hausfrau and a bisexual Arab immigrant in place of Jane Wyman and Rock Hudson, grungy realism in place of Hollywood glitz, and unlikely as it may seem from that description, even more throbbing emotion and sympathy than the original.

Best American Film: *The Godfather, Part II*
Best Foreign Film: *Ali: Fear Eats the Soul*
Best Actor: John Cazale, *The Godfather, Part II*
Best Actress: Ellen Burstyn, *Alice Doesn't Live Here Anymore*
Best Director: Roman Polanski, *Chinatown*

1975

One Flew Over the Cuckoo's Nest's Oscar sweep of the top four Oscars, the first since It Happened One Night, was the climax to 25 years of the best studio management post–Golden Age Hollywood had known: United Artists. Chairman Arthur Krim had taken over the near-bankrupt distributor from its remaining founder-owners, Chaplin and Pickford, in 1951—just as the breakup of the studio-owned theater chains and the postwar boom in independent production vastly increased the market and need for its services. UA's ubiquitous presence at the Oscars in the '50s was more due to its deals with enlightened independents like Burt Lancaster and Walter Mirisch than to its own homegrown projects, but by the 1960s it was known as the class act in town, and it followed Cuckoo's sweep by producing no less than three of 1976's Best Picture nominees (Network, Bound for Glory, and the winner, Rocky), and a third winner in Annie Hall the year after that. Not even MGM in the '30s had won three in a row.

It all unraveled in a matter of months. UA's parent, insurance conglomerate Transamerica, began to meddle; Krim and company resigned one day en masse and founded Orion; and the new management, eager to repeat UA's streak at the Oscars, made a fateful deal: agreeing to finance the next film of 1978's Oscar-winner, Michael Cimino's Heaven's Gate.

Academy Awards

**** *One Flew Over the Cuckoo's Nest* AAW GLO DGA LAC PEO '76
***** **Jack Nicholson** AAW GLO NYC SOC BOR
*** **Louise Fletcher** AAW GLO

Nobody argued with Milos Forman's film as a big-hearted version of Ken Kesey's novel about life in a mental asylum—or with Jack Nicholson's performance as the funny, cocky rebel without a chance McMurphy. (If he played Bogart in *Chinatown*, this is his Cagney part—and it seems to suit him even better.) But Louise Fletcher was widely thought to have won by default in a weak year for actresses (note that the critics' groups all found other candidates); many felt she was miscast as the totalitarian Nurse Ratched. I think she is miscast, but I think it's one of the most brilliant jobs of miscasting in movie history. It would have been easy to find actresses to play Ratched as Goering in starched white. But Czech émigré Forman understands that an evil system often comes with a human face, and Ratched is the nurturing, well-intentioned earth mother who couldn't be kinder—until you violate her sense of order, and she has to kill you.

Picture
One Flew Over the Cuckoo's Nest (UA, Fantasy Films, Saul Zaentz, Michael Douglas)
Barry Lyndon (Warner Bros., Hawk Films, Stanley Kubrick)
Dog Day Afternoon (Warner Bros., Martin Bregman, Martin Elfand)
Jaws (Universal, Richard D. Zanuck, David Brown)
Nashville (Paramount, ABC Entertainment-Weintraub-Altman)

Actor
Jack Nicholson, *One Flew Over the Cuckoo's Nest*
Walter Matthau, *The Sunshine Boys*
Al Pacino, *Dog Day Afternoon*
Maximilian Schell, *The Man in the Glass Booth*
James Whitmore, *Give 'em Hell, Harry!*

Actress
Louise Fletcher, *One Flew Over the Cuckoo's Nest*
Isabelle Adjani, *The Story of Adèle H*
Ann-Margret, *Tommy*
Glenda Jackson, *Hedda*
Carol Kane, *Hester Street*

Supporting Actor
George Burns, *The Sunshine Boys*
Brad Dourif, *One Flew Over the Cuckoo's Nest*
Burgess Meredith, *The Day of the Locust*

Chris Sarandon, *Dog Day Afternoon*
Jack Warden, *Shampoo*

Supporting Actress
Lee Grant, *Shampoo*
Ronee Blakley, *Nashville*
Sylvia Miles, *Farewell, My Lovely*
Lily Tomlin, *Nashville*
Brenda Vaccaro, *Jacqueline Susann's Once Is Not Enough*

Director
Milos Forman, *One Flew Over the Cuckoo's Nest*
Robert Altman, *Nashville*
Federico Fellini, *Amarcord*
Stanley Kubrick, *Barry Lyndon*
Sidney Lumet, *Dog Day Afternoon*

Original Screenplay: Frank Pierson, *Dog Day Afternoon*
Adapted Screenplay: Lawrence Hauben, Bo Goldman, *One Flew Over the Cuckoo's Nest*
Cinematography: John Alcott, *Barry Lyndon*
Original Score: John Williams, *Jaws*
Scoring Adaptation: Leonard Rosenman, *Barry Lyndon*
Song: "I'm Easy," *Nashville*, ml: Keith Carradine
Art Direction: Ken Adam, *Barry Lyndon*
Costume Design: Ulla-Britt Soderlund, Milena Canonero, *Barry Lyndon*
Editing: Verna Fields, *Jaws*
Sound: *Jaws*
Sound Effects: *The Hindenburg*
Visual Effects: *The Hindenburg*
Short/Animated: *Great* (Bob Godfrey)
Short/Live Action: *Angel and Big Joe*
Documentary/Feature: *The Man Who Skied Down Everest*
Documentary/Short: *The End of the Game*

Foreign Language Film: *Dersu Uzala* (USSR)
Irving G. Thalberg Memorial Award: Mervyn LeRoy
Jean Hersholt Humanitarian Award: Jules C. Stein
Special Award: Mary Pickford

Golden Globes

Picture (Drama): *One Flew Over the Cuckoo's Nest*
Picture (Comedy/Musical): *The Sunshine Boys*
Foreign Film: *Lies My Father Told Me* (Canada)
Actor (Drama): Jack Nicholson, *One Flew Over the Cuckoo's Nest*
Actor (Comedy/Musical): Walter Matthau, *The Sunshine Boys*
Actress (Drama): Louise Fletcher, *One Flew Over the Cuckoo's Nest*
Actress (Comedy/Musical): Ann-Margret, *Tommy*
Supporting Actor: Richard Benjamin, *The Sunshine Boys*
Supporting Actress: Brenda Vaccaro, *Jacqueline Susann's Once Is Not Enough*
Director: Milos Forman, *One Flew Over the Cuckoo's Nest*
Screenplay: Laurence Hauben, Bo Goldman, *One Flew Over the Cuckoo's Nest*
Score: John Williams, *Jaws*
Song: "I'm Easy," *Nashville*, ml: Keith Carradine
Documentary: *Youthquake*
Best Acting Debut (Male): Brad Dourif, *One Flew Over the Cuckoo's Nest*
Best Acting Debut (Female): Marilyn Hassett, *The Other Side of the Mountain*

Directors Guild of America

Director: Milos Forman, *One Flew Over the Cuckoo's Nest*

*** *Nashville* NYC SOC BOR
Another example of Pauline Kael's domination of the critical groups—after her rapturous pre-release review (based on a rough cut and a reading of the script!), a lot of critics tried very hard to see the Great American Film in Altman's 24-character panorama of life in country music's capital. But like most of his multi-character pieces, it varies from fine, poignant miniature portraits (Lily Tomlin and her deaf son and her husband who doesn't sign, Keenan Wynn at the hospital) to smug, one-dimensional satire (Geraldine Chaplin's pompous journalist)—and I'd argue *Short Cuts* has a better ratio of the former to the latter.

** **Isabelle Adjani in** *The Story of Adèle H* NYC SOC BOR
If you don't find the pouty-lipped Adjani dazzlingly beautiful, the odds are significantly reduced that you'll find her a great actress (since what she really is is modern French cinema's one Garbo-level glamour queen). And if you don't find her a great actress, it's not likely that you'll find her character in this Truffaut film—the daughter of Victor Hugo, who went *Fatal Attraction* for a soldier—particularly sympathetic or interesting.

New York Film Critics Circle

Picture: *Nashville*
Actor: Jack Nicholson, *One Flew Over the Cuckoo's Nest*
Actress: Isabelle Adjani, *The Story of Adèle H*
Supporting Actor: Alan Arkin, *Hearts of the West*
Supporting Actress: Lily Tomlin, *Nashville*
Director: Robert Altman, *Nashville*
Screenplay: François Truffaut, Jean Gruault, Suzanne Schiffman, *The Story of Adèle H*

National Society of Film Critics

Picture: *Nashville*
Actor: Jack Nicholson, *One Flew Over the Cuckoo's Nest*
Actress: Isabelle Adjani, *The Story of Adèle H*
Supporting Actor: Henry Gibson, *Nashville*
Supporting Actress: Lily Tomlin, *Nashville*
Director: Robert Altman, *Nashville*
Screenplay: Robert Towne, Warren Beatty, *Shampoo*
Cinematography: John Alcott, *Barry Lyndon*
Special Award: Ingmar Bergman's *The Magic Flute*, for demonstrating how pleasurable opera can be on film

Los Angeles Film Critics Association

Film: *Dog Day Afternoon, One Flew Over the Cuckoo's Nest*
Foreign Film: *And Now, My Love*
Actor: Al Pacino, *Dog Day Afternoon*
Actress: Florinda Bolkan, *A Brief Vacation*
Director: Sidney Lumet, *Dog Day Afternoon*
Screenplay: Joan Tewkesbury, *Nashville*

Cinematography: John Alcott, *Barry Lyndon*

National Board of Review

Best English-Language Film:
*Nashville, Barry Lyndon
Conduct Unbecoming
One Flew Over the Cuckoo's Nest
Lies My Father Told Me
Dog Day Afternoon
The Day of the Locust
The Passenger
Hearts of the West
Farewell, My Lovely
Alice Doesn't Live Here Anymore*
Best Foreign-Language Film:
*The Story of Adèle H
A Brief Vacation
Special Section
Stavisky
Swept Away*
Actor: Jack Nicholson, *One Flew Over the Cuckoo's Nest*
Actress: Isabelle Adjani, *The Story of Adèle H*
Supporting Actor: Charles Durning, *Dog Day Afternoon*
Supporting Actress: Ronee Blakely, *Nashville*
Director: Robert Altman, *Nashville*; Stanley Kubrick, *Barry Lyndon*
Special Citation: Ingmar Bergman's *The Magic Flute*, outstanding in its translation of opera to screen

People's Choice Awards

Favorite Picture: *Jaws*
Favorite Movie Actor: John Wayne
Favorite Movie Actress: Katharine Hepburn

British Academy Awards

Film: *Alice Doesn't Live Here Anymore*
Actor: Al Pacino, *The Godfather, Part II, Dog Day Afternoon*
Actress: Ellen Burstyn, *Alice Doesn't Live Here Anymore*

Supporting Actor: Fred Astaire, *The Towering Inferno*
Supporting Actress: Diane Ladd, *Alice Doesn't Live Here Anymore*
Director: Stanley Kubrick, *Barry Lyndon*
Screenplay: Robert Getchell, *Alice Doesn't Live Here Anymore*
Academy Fellow: Jacques Cousteau

Cannes Film Festival
Palme d'Or: *Chronicle of the Burning Years* (Mohammed Lakhdar Hamina, Algeria)
Special Jury Prize: *Every Man for Himself and God Against All/ The Mystery of Kaspar Hauser* (Werner Herzog, West Germany)
Actor: Vittorio Gassman, *Profumo di Donna* [*Scent of a Woman*] (Italy)
Actress: Valerie Perrine, *Lenny* (USA)
Director: Michel Brault, *Les Ordres* (Canada), Costa-Gavras, *Special Section* (France)
Special Mention: The Jury wishes to underline the quality and presence of Delphine Seyrig in young cinema
International Critics Prize: in competition, *Every Man For Himself and God Against All/The Mystery of Kaspar Hauser*; out of competition, *The Travelling Players* (Theo Angelopolous, Greece)

Berlin Film Festival
Golden Bear: *The Adoption* (Marta Mészáros, Hungary)
Special Jury Silver Bear: *Overlord* (Stuart Cooper, UK), *Dupont Lajoie* (Yves Boisset, France)
Actor: Vlastimil Brodsky, *Jacob the Liar* (East Germany)
Actress: Kinuyo Tanaka, *Sandakan 8* (Japan)

Director: Sergei Soloviev, *A Hundred Days After Childhood* (USSR)
Special Award/Silver Bear: Woody Allen, for his complete works
International Critics Prize: *In a Foreign Land* (Sohrab Shahid Saless, Iran/West Germany)

Harvard Lampoon Movie Worsts
Ten worst pictures:
Barry Lyndon
Tommy
At Long Last Love
The Other Side of the Mountain
The Hindenburg
The Day of the Locust
The Story of O
Mahogany
Shampoo
Once Is Not Enough
Kirk Douglas Award for Worst Actor: Ryan O'Neal, *Barry Lyndon*
Natalie Wood Award for Worst Actress: Diana Ross, *Mahogany*
The Bratwurst Award (to that juvenile actor or actress who most convincingly presents a strong argument for compulsory education): Jodie Foster, *Taxi Driver* [NOTE: Foster applied to Yale shortly thereafter]
The Wrong-Way Corrigan Memorial Flight Jacket (for worst direction): Steven Spielberg, *Jaws*, for turning *Moby Dick* into *King Kong* and attempting to pass this fish story off as great cinematic art
The Handlin Oscar (to the film which most distorts history): *The Wind and the Lion*, which was actually quite accurate if you can accept Sean Connery as a North African chieftain and Candice Bergen as having a mental edge over a five-year-old sufficient to be a governess

**The Victor Mature Memorial
Award** (to the most
embarrassing line of dialogue):
Gable and Lombard, for the
screen great's insouciant
commentary following the
incendiary demise of his beloved
in a plane crash, as he gazes
fondly over the twisted wreckage:

"She should have taken the
train."
The Roscoe Award: Karen Black,
who crawls the gamut of human
emotions in *The Day of the Locust*
and *Nashville*
The Merino Award: Marino
Berenson, whose name doesn't
even come close to sounding like
merino, *Barry Lyndon*

Box Office (Domestic Rentals)

1	*Jaws*	$102,650,000	Uni
2	*The Towering Inferno*	55,000,000	Fox
3	*Benji*	30,800,000	Mulberry Square
4	*Young Frankenstein*	30,000,000	Fox
5	*The Godfather, Part II*	28,900,000	Par
6	*Shampoo*	22,000,000	Col
7	*Funny Lady*	19,000,000	Col
8	*Murder on the Orient Express*	17,800,000	Par
9	*Return of the Pink Panther*	17,000,000	UA
10	*Tommy*	16,000,000	Col

Other films of note:

12	*Freebie and the Bean*	12,500,000	WB
15	*The Man with the Golden Gun*	9,500,000	UA
16	*The Great Waldo Pepper*	9,400,000	Uni
17	*Three Days of the Condor*	8,960,000	Par
21	*Part II Walking Tall*	8,000,000	American Int'l
27	*Nashville*	6,800,000	Par
34	*A Woman Under the Influence*	6,117,812	Faces Int'l
46	*Death Race 2000*	4,800,000	New World
49	*Love and Death*	4,500,000	UA
52	*Emmanuelle*	4,000,000	Col

*1975 is remembered mainly as the year that brought back the popcorn movie, not
only with the massively successful movie-movie* Jaws *(the first film to break $100
million in domestic rentals) but even in such a square polyester form as* The Towering
Inferno. *But 1975 was also important as the year that gave sequels respectability—
what would once have been called* Son of the Godfather *instead called itself* Part II,
*as if it had been planned that way all along and wasn't just a quick cash-in. (Parts
of it were based on bits of Puzo's book that hadn't been filmed in "Part I," but the
real justification for the title was in its quality.) When G-2 won the Best Picture Oscar
the sequel floodgates opened—beginning with* Part II Walking Tall, *the only one to
put the number before the title.*

Gebert's Golden Armchairs

After Fassbinder, the next exciting new filmmaker to appear on the scene from West Germany was a sort of hippie-mystic named Werner Herzog, most of whose films were indescribably strange and irrational. The best of them, based on the true story of a mysterious 19th-century idiot-savant called Kaspar Hauser, starred (in what turned out to be perfect typecasting) a disconnected street person known only as Bruno S.

Best American Film: *One Flew Over the Cuckoo's Nest*

Best Foreign Film: *Every Man for Himself and God Against All/ The Mystery of Kaspar Hauser*

Best Actor: Jack Nicholson, *One Flew Over the Cuckoo's Nest*

Best Actress: Lily Tomlin, *Nashville*

Best Director: Werner Herzog, *Every Man For Himself and God Against All*

1976

Barely half a decade after feminism hit the movies, the good roles for women had virtually dried up—Faye Dunaway, like Louise Fletcher the year before, practically won the Best Actress Oscar by default (it took two foreign-language performances to fill out the five nomination slots, the only time that's ever happened). And the Supporting Actress winner, Beatrice Straight, won for a role that would have been far too short for serious consideration in earlier years—her two-scene, five-minute and 56-second role as William Holden's wife is, in fact, the shortest Oscar-winning part ever. A mini-boom of female roles followed in 1977–78, but the reality has been tough times ever since for actresses, who can only marvel at the way predecessors like Davis, Crawford, and de Havilland dominated audience and Oscar attention in their day.

Academy Awards

** *Rocky* AAW GLO DGA LAC
Forget what it spawned—not merely Stallone's career and a zillion sequels, but an entire culture in which movies are only about trumped-up victories—and you *still* just have a near scene-for-scene ripoff of *Somebody Up There Likes Me*.

Picture
Rocky (UA, Irwin Winkler, Robert Chartoff)
All the President's Men (Warner Bros., Wildwood, Walter Coblenz)
Bound for Glory (UA, Robert F. Blumofe, Harold Leventhal)
Network (MGM/UA, Howard Gottfried)
Taxi Driver (Columbia, Tony Bill, Michael and Julia Phillips)

***** Peter Finch in *Network*
AAW GLO BAA '77**

**** Faye Dunaway in *Network* AAW GLO
Oscar rules don't allow posthumous nominations, so it took some pretty tight scheduling for Peter Finch to get a nomination and then die before the voting, so that he could have the predictable sentimental win. In Paddy Chayefsky's satire on TV's willingness to put on anything that gets ratings—dismissed as over the top then, and obviously dead-on today—Finch is very loud and pretty good, but William Holden, also nominated, is quiet and better. Dunaway, on the other hand, had no significant competition from her picture or any other, but she, too, was excellent. The exotically beautiful, vaguely distracted, and slack-jawed young woman of *Bonnie and Clyde* and even *Chinatown* had, out of nowhere, gained the focus and intensity

that made her perfect casting five years later as Joan Crawford.

Actor
Peter Finch, *Network*
Robert De Niro, *Taxi Driver*
Giancarlo Giannini, *Seven Beauties*
William Holden, *Network*
Sylvester Stallone, *Rocky*

Actress
Faye Dunaway, *Network*
Marie-Christine Barrault, *Cousin, Cousine*
Talia Shire, *Rocky*
Sissy Spacek, *Carrie*
Liv Ullmann, *Face to Face*

Supporting Actor
Jason Robards, *All the President's Men*
Ned Beatty, *Network*
Burgess Meredith, *Rocky*
Laurence Olivier, *Marathon Man*
Burt Young, *Rocky*

Supporting Actress
Beatrice Straight, *Network*
Jane Alexander, *All the President's Men*
Jodie Foster, *Taxi Driver*
Lee Grant, *Voyage of the Damned*
Piper Laurie, *Carrie*

Director
John G. Avildsen, *Rocky*
Ingmar Bergman, *Face to Face*
Sidney Lumet, *Network*
Alan J. Pakula, *All the President's Men*
Lina Wertmuller, *Seven Beauties*

Original Screenplay: Paddy Chayefsky, *Network*
Adapted Screenplay: William Goldman, *All the President's Men*
Cinematography: Haskell Wexler, *Bound for Glory*

Original Score: Jerry Goldsmith, *The Omen*
Scoring Adaptation: Leonard Rosenman, *Bound for Glory*
Song: "Evergreen (Love Theme from *A Star Is Born*)," *A Star Is Born*, m: Barbra Streisand, l: Paul Williams
Art Direction: George Jenkins, *All the President's Men*
Costume Design: Danilo Donati, *Fellini's Casanova*
Editing: *Rocky*
Sound: *All the President's Men*
Visual Effects: Carlo Rambaldi, *King Kong*; *Logan's Run* [special awards—not a tie]
Short/Animated: *Leisure* (Film Australia)
Short/Live Action: *In the Region of Ice* (American Film Institute)
Documentary/Feature: *Harlan County, U.S.A.* (Barbara Kopple)
Documentary/Short: *Number Our Days* (Lynne Littman)
Foreign Language Film: *Black and White in Color* (Ivory Coast)
Irving G. Thalberg Award: Pandro S. Berman

Golden Globes
Picture (Drama): *Rocky*
Picture (Comedy/Musical): *A Star Is Born*
Foreign Film: *Face to Face* (Sweden)
Actor (Drama): Peter Finch, *Network*
Actor (Comedy/Musical): Kris Kristofferson, *A Star Is Born*
Actress (Drama): Faye Dunaway, *Network*
Actress (Comedy/Musical): Barbra Streisand, *A Star Is Born*
Supporting Actor: Laurence Olivier, *Marathon Man*
Supporting Actress: Katharine Ross, *Voyage of the Damned*
Director: Sidney Lumet, *Network*

Screenplay: Paddy Chayefsky, *Network*
Score: Paul Williams, Kenny Ascher, *A Star Is Born*
Song: "Evergreen (Love Theme from *A Star Is Born*)," *A Star Is Born*, m: Barbra Streisand, l: Paul Williams
Documentary: *Altars of the World*
Best Acting Debut (Male): Arnold Schwarzenegger, *Stay Hungry*
Best Acting Debut (Female): Jessica Lange, *King Kong*
World Film Favorite (Male): Robert Redford
World Film Favorite (Female): Sophia Loren
Cecil B. DeMille Award: Walter Mirisch

Directors Guild of America
Director: John G. Avildsen, *Rocky*
Honorary Life Member: H. C. Potter

**** *All the President's Men*
NYC SOC BOR
Thrilling adaptation of Woodward and Bernstein's book about their Washington *Post* investigation of the Watergate break-in—though it's a little scary how easily Alan J. Pakula's film transmutes 1973's reality into 1976's subtly glamorized portrait of newspaper-detective work. (Check the statistics on how journalism-school enrollment went up in the late '70s—and then watch *Network* again to see the kind of stuff all those J-school grads wound up doing.)

***** Robert De Niro in *Taxi Driver* NYC SOC LAC
De Niro, fresh from playing Joe Kennedy (that is, Vito Corleone), now plays Lee Harvey Oswald. A brilliantly accurate and creepy portrait of an all-too-familiar American type, the murderous, semi-literate, self-righteous loner-crank itching for the big bang, half a turn out of whack with the rest of humanity, but making up for it with all the conversations going on in his head.

New York Film Critics Circle
Picture: *All the President's Men*
Actor: Robert De Niro, *Taxi Driver*
Actress: Liv Ullmann, *Face to Face*
Supporting Actor: Jason Robards, *All the President's Men*
Supporting Actress: Talia Shire, *Rocky*
Director: Alan J. Pakula, *All the President's Men*
Screenplay: Paddy Chayefsky, *Network*

National Society of Film Critics
Picture: *All the President's Men*
Actor: Robert De Niro, *Taxi Driver*
Actress: Sissy Spacek, *Carrie*
Supporting Actor: Jason Robards, *All the President's Men*
Supporting Actress: Jodie Foster, *Taxi Driver*
Director: Martin Scorsese, *Taxi Driver*
Screenplay: Alan Tanner, John Berger, *Jonah Who Will Be 25 in the Year 2000*

Cinematography: Haskell
Wexler, *Bound for Glory*

Los Angeles Film Critics Association
Film: *Network*, *Rocky*
Foreign Film: *Face to Face*
Actor: Robert De Niro, *Taxi Driver*
Actress: Liv Ullmann, *Face to Face*
Director: Sidney Lumet, *Network*
Screenplay: Paddy Chayefsky, *Network*
Cinematography: Haskell Wexler, *Bound for Glory*
Music: Bernard Herrmann, *Taxi Driver*
Special Prizes: Marcel Ophüls, for *The Memory of Justice*
Max Laemmle, for his many years of innovative programming of specialized motion pictures in Los Angeles

National Board of Review
Best English-Language Film:
All the President's Men
Network
Rocky
The Last Tycoon
The Seven-Per-Cent Solution
The Front
The Shootist
Family Plot
Silent Movie
Obsession
Best Foreign-Language Film:
The Marquise of O
Face to Face
Small Change
Cousin, Cousine
The Clockmaker
Actor: David Carradine, *Bound for Glory*
Actress: Liv Ullmann, *Face to Face*
Supporting Actor: Jason Robards, *All the President's Men*
Supporting Actress: Talia Shire, *Rocky*

Director: Alan J. Pakula, *All the President's Men*

People's Choice Awards
Favorite Picture: *One Flew Over the Cuckoo's Nest*
Favorite Movie Actor: John Wayne
Favorite Movie Actress: Barbra Streisand

British Academy Awards
Film: *One Flew Over the Cuckoo's Nest*
Actor: Jack Nicholson, *One Flew Over the Cuckoo's Nest*
Actress: Louise Fletcher, *One Flew Over the Cuckoo's Nest*
Supporting Actor: Brad Dourif, *One Flew Over the Cuckoo's Nest*
Supporting Actress: Jodie Foster, *Bugsy Malone*, *Taxi Driver*
Director: Milos Forman, *One Flew Over the Cuckoo's Nest*
Screenplay: Alan Parker, *Bugsy Malone*
Academy Fellow: Sir Charles Chaplin; Lord Olivier

Cannes Film Festival
Palme d'Or: *Taxi Driver* (Martin Scorsese, USA)
Special Jury Prize: *Cría Cuervos* [*Cría!*] (Carlos Saura, Spain), *The Marquise of O* (Eric Rohmer, France)
Actor: Jose Luis Gomez, *Pascual Duarte* (Spain)
Actress: Mari Törocsik, *Where Are You, Mrs. Dery?* (Hungary), Dominique Sanda, *The Inheritance* (France-Italy)
Director: Ettore Scola, *Brutti, Sporchi e Cattivi* [*Down and Dirty*; Italian title is a play on Leone's *Il Buono il Bruto il Cattivo*]
Technical Prize: Soundman Michel Fano, *Fang & Claw* (France)

International Critics Prize: *In the Course of Time [Kings of the Road]* (Wim Wenders, West Germany), *Strongman Ferdinand* (Alexander Kluge, West Germany)

** *Buffalo Bill and the Indians* BER

Robert Altman in his scattershot-sarcastic mode— yes, the beloved mode that brought us *Ready-to-Wear* and *A Wedding*. Some moments of amusement from Paul Newman as a fraudulent Buffalo Bill and a typically offbeat Altman cast (including *Tonight Show* writer Pat McCormick as Grover Cleveland!), but on the whole, a second-rate *Little Big Man* imitation, and not even the best of those—*The Life and Times of Judge Roy Bean*, also with Newman, is much better. One has to assume the Berlin jury was attempting to honor Altman for his overall work— unsuccessfully, as it turned out, since Altman declined the prize in protest over producer Dino DeLaurentiis's recutting of the film.

Berlin Film Festival
Golden Bear: *Buffalo Bill and the Indians* (Robert Altman, USA) [award declined]
Silver Bear: *Canoa* (Felipe Cazals, Mexico), *Baghe Sanguy* (Parviz Kimiavi, Iran)
Actor: Gerd Olschewski, *Lost Life* (West Germany)
Actress: Jadwiga Baranska, *Night and Days* (Poland)
Director: Mario Monicelli, *Caro Michele* [*Dear Michael*] (Italy)
First Film: *Azonositas* (Laszló Lugossy, Hungary)

Silver Bear/Short: *Trains* (Caleb Deschanel, USA)
International Critics Prize: *Long Vacations of '36* (Jaime Camino, Spain)

Harvard Lampoon Movie Worsts
Ten worst pictures:
A Star Is Born
The Enforcer
Murder by Death
Slapshot
The Omen
Lipstick
Mikey and Nicky
The Missouri Breaks
Car Wash
King Kong
Kirk Douglas Award for Worst Actor: Clint Eastwood, *The Enforcer*
Natalie Wood Award for Worst Actress: Barbra Streisand, *A Star Is Born*. Her performance should delight those who can't tell the difference between Eydie Gormé and Patti Smith
The Liquid-Paper-Correction-Fluid Award: Diana Ross, for her portrayal of a fashion model in *Sparkle*. We could have sworn the woman used to be white
The Volvo Trophy: Liv Ullmann in *Face to Face* as the Swedish import that always breaks down
The Golden Glob (for the pornographic movie that limps along most lamely): *How Funny Can Sex Be?*
The Roscoe Award: Margaux Hemingway, *Lipstick*
The Merino Award: *Shearings*, a horror film about radioactive sheep in the Mojave Desert

Box Office (Domestic Rentals)

1	*One Flew Over the Cuckoo's Nest*	$56,500,000	UA
2	*All the President's Men*	29,000,000	WB
3	*The Omen*	27,851,000	Fox
4	*The Bad News Bears*	22,266,517	Par
5	*Silent Movie*	20,311,000	Fox
6	*Midway*	20,300,000	Uni
7	*Dog Day Afternoon*	19,800,000	WB
8	*Murder By Death*	18,800,000	Col
9	*Jaws [reissue]*	16,077,000	Uni
10	*Blazing Saddles [reissue]*	13,850,000	WB

Other films of note:

11	*Lucky Lady*	12,107,000	Fox
12	*Taxi Driver*	11,600,000	Col
13	*The Outlaw Josey Wales*	10,600,000	WB
18	*Barry Lyndon*	9,100,000	WB
21	*Logan's Run*	8,700,000	MGM
26	*Family Plot*	6,825,000	Uni
37	*Monty Python and the Holy Grail*	5,170,000	Cinema V
104	*Won Ton Ton, the Dog That Saved Hollywood*	1,197,330	Par

People made fun of Pauline Kael when, in a 1980 essay, she first referred to the mid-'70s as a cinematic renaissance—but look at 1976's box office chart, especially nos. 1, 2, 7, and 12, and see if you don't agree that not only was Hollywood more adventurous then, audiences were, too. In fact, Cuckoo's Nest *was the last Best Picture Oscar–winner to rank #1 on the Box Office chart until* Forrest Gump. *The relative failure of the much-hyped* Lucky Lady *and the absolute failure of #104 demonstrated that the '30s nostalgia craze had run its course; and* Logan's Run, *the year's big sci-fi epic, made only $8.7 million at the box office, proving that in a post-Apollo world, sci-fi was dead as a box office genre. (And you want $10 million, Mr. Lucas, for your space adventure?)*

Gebert's Golden Armchairs

Swiss director Alain Tanner's *Jonah . . .* is a smart, sympathetically observed progress report on the people of the '60s, and what their idealism has come to after a few years of hard reality. That also makes it the film that spawned John Sayles' *Return of the Secaucus 7*, which spawned *The Big Chill*, which spawned *The Breakfast Club*, and *thirtysomething* and—well, one of the lessons of the '60s was that noble acts sometimes had unforeseen unfortunate consequences. . . .

Best American Film: *Network*
Best Foreign Film: *Jonah Who Will Be 25 in the Year 2000*
Best Actor: Robert De Niro, *Taxi Driver*
Best Actress: Faye Dunaway, *Network*
Best Director: Martin Scorsese, *Taxi Driver*

1977

Do festivals kill? That was the allegation some made after Cannes '77. Festival director Maurice Bessy was said to have all but promised the Palme d'Or to Italian producer Carlo Ponti for a glossy Sophia Loren–Marcello Mastroianni drama, *A Special Day*. Jury head Roberto Rossellini found far more to admire in another Italian film, *Padre Padrone*, which he felt carried on the ideals of neorealism—and over Bessy's adamant objections that *Padre Padrone* was too small and unimportant to win a Palme d'Or, the jury followed Rossellini. But the effort involved was so great, Rossellini's associates said, that when he suffered a fatal heart attack a few days later they blamed it on the strain of overruling Bessy.

Academy Awards

**** *Annie Hall* AAW DGA NYC SOC BAA
**** Diane Keaton AAW GLO NYC SOC BAA
Every once in a while someone writes a big book about how deep and philosophical Woody Allen's movies are. Allen no more put deep philosophy on screen than he did kung-fu, but what he did do—and more to the point, what Diane Keaton did by bringing to life on screen what he wrote—was something much more valuable. Together, they invented the modern romantic-comedy couple: two people who are culturally sophisticated (but *not* intellectual), witty in an offhand and believable manner, successful yet tinged with insecurity, and aiming for equality of the sexes without always living up to it (Allen is hardly the first man of his generation who, after wrestling with the dawn of feminism,

ultimately felt more comfortable living with a younger, more inexperienced woman rather than an equal of his own age).

Picture
Annie Hall (UA, Rollins-Joffe)
The Goodbye Girl (MGM/Warner Bros., Ray Stark)
Julia (20th Century–Fox, Richard Roth)
Star Wars (20th Century–Fox, Gary Kurtz)
The Turning Point (20th Century–Fox, Herbert Ross, Arthur Laurents)

** Richard Dreyfuss in *The Goodbye Girl* AAW GLO LAC BAA '78
As Neil Simon pieces go, this is one of the best (there, was that praise faint enough for you?), but it wasn't even Dreyfuss' best performance of the year—he's the human heart of *Close Encounters*, and merely a pretty standard supporting object-of-affection here. One fears that it was reciting Shakespeare that got him the statue, just as it did

for Ronald Colman in *A Double Life*, etc. . . .

Actor
Richard Dreyfuss, *The Goodbye Girl*
Woody Allen, *Annie Hall*
Richard Burton, *Equus*
Marcello Mastroianni, *A Special Day*
John Travolta, *Saturday Night Fever*

Actress
Diane Keaton, *Annie Hall*
Anne Bancroft, *The Turning Point*
Jane Fonda, *Julia*
Shirley MacLaine, *The Turning Point*
Marsha Mason, *The Goodbye Girl*

Supporting Actor
Jason Robards, *Julia*
Mikhail Baryshnikov, *The Turning Point*
Peter Firth, *Equus*
Alec Guinness, *Star Wars*
Maximilian Schell, *Julia*

Supporting Actress
Vanessa Redgrave, *Julia*
Leslie Browne, *The Turning Point*
Quinn Cummings, *The Goodbye Girl*
Melinda Dillon, *Close Encounters of the Third Kind*
Tuesday Weld, *Looking for Mr. Goodbar*

Director
Woody Allen, *Annie Hall*
George Lucas, *Star Wars*
Herbert Ross, *The Turning Point*
Steven Spielberg, *Close Encounters of the Third Kind*
Fred Zinnemann, *Julia*

Original Screenplay: Woody Allen, Marshall Brickman, *Annie Hall*

Adapted Screenplay: Alvin Sargent, *Julia*
Cinematography: Vilmos Zsigmond, *Close Encounters of the Third Kind*
Original Score: John Williams, *Star Wars*
Scoring Adaptation: Jonathan Tunick, *A Little Night Music*
Song: "You Light Up My Life," *You Light Up My Life,* ml: Joseph Brooks
Art Direction: John Barry, *Star Wars*
Costume Design: John Mollo, *Star Wars*
Editing: *Star Wars*
Sound: *Star Wars*
Sound Effects: Benjamin Burtt, Jr., for the creation of the alien, creature, and robot voices in *Star Wars* [special award]
Sound Effects Editing: *Close Encounters of the Third Kind*
Visual Effects: John Dykstra, Richard Edlund, *Star Wars*
Short/Animated: *Sand Castle* (National Film Board of Canada, Co Hoedeman)
Short/Live Action: *I'll Find a Way* (National Film Board of Canada)
Documentary/Feature: *Who are the DeBolts? And Where Did They Get Nineteen Kids?* (John Korty)
Documentary/Short: *Gravity Is My Enemy*
Foreign Language Film: *Madame Rosa* (France)
Irving G. Thalberg Award: Walter Mirisch
Jean Hersholt Humanitarian Award: Charlton Heston
Special Awards:
Margaret Booth, for her exceptional contribution to the art of film editing
Gordon E. Sawyer and Sidney P. Solow, for outstanding service and dedication to the Academy

** **The Turning Point** GLO BOR HAR**
Widely considered the favorite going into the Oscars—God knows why; a pretty good imitation of a '50s soap opera with some pretty ballet scenes thrown in, but silly stuff, worthwhile only as an employment program for high-powered middle-aged actresses.

Golden Globes
Picture (Drama): *The Turning Point*
Picture (Comedy/Musical): *The Goodbye Girl*
Foreign Film: *A Special Day* (Italy)
Actor (Drama): Richard Burton, *Equus*
Actor (Comedy/Musical): Richard Dreyfuss, *The Goodbye Girl*
Actress (Drama): Jane Fonda, *Julia*
Actress (Comedy/Musical): Diane Keaton, *Annie Hall*, Marsha Mason, *The Goodbye Girl*
Supporting Actor: Peter Firth, *Equus*
Supporting Actress: Vanessa Redgrave, *Julia*
Director: Herbert Ross, *The Goodbye Girl*
Screenplay: Neil Simon, *The Goodbye Girl*
Score: John Williams, *Star Wars*
Song: "You Light Up My Life," *You Light Up My Life*, ml: Joseph Brooks
World Film Favorite (Male): Robert Redford
World Film Favorite (Female): Barbra Streisand
Cecil B. DeMille Award: Red Skelton

Directors Guild of America
Director: Woody Allen, *Annie Hall*
Honorary Life Member: David Butler

New York Film Critics Circle
Picture: *Annie Hall*
Actor: John Gielgud, *Providence*
Actress: Diane Keaton, *Annie Hall*
Supporting Actor: Maximilian Schell, *Julia*
Supporting Actress: Sissy Spacek, *Three Women*
Director: Woody Allen, *Annie Hall*
Screenplay: Woody Allen, Marshall Brickman, *Annie Hall*

National Society of Film Critics
Picture: *Annie Hall*
Actor: Art Carney, *The Late Show*
Actress: Diane Keaton, *Annie Hall*
Supporting Actor: Edward Fox, *A Bridge Too Far*
Supporting Actress: Ann Wedgeworth, *Handle With Care*
Director: Luis Buñuel, *That Obscure Object of Desire*
Screenplay: Woody Allen, Marshall Brickman, *Annie Hall*
Cinematography: Thomas Mauch, *Aguirre: The Wrath of God*

*** **That Obscure Object of Desire** LAC**
Minor Buñuel film, his last, about an older man obsessed with a younger woman, of interest only because of its bizarre use of two actresses (Angela Molina and Carole Bouquet) to play the role. (Maria Schneider was originally hired, then fired; hiring *two* replacements for her somehow seemed the logical thing.)

Los Angeles Film Critics Association
Film: *Star Wars*
Foreign Film: *That Obscure Object of Desire*
Actor: Richard Dreyfuss, *The Goodbye Girl*
Actress: Shelley Duvall, *Three Women*
Supporting Actor: Jason Robards, *Julia*
Supporting Actress: Vanessa Redgrave, *Julia*
Director: Herbert Ross, *The Turning Point*
Screenplay: Woody Allen, Marshall Brickman, *Annie Hall*
Cinematography: Douglas Slocombe, *Julia*
Music: John Williams, *Star Wars*
Special Prize: Gary Allison, writer-producer of *Fraternity Row*

National Board of Review
Best English-Language Film:
The Turning Point
Annie Hall
Julia
Star Wars
Close Encounters of the Third Kind
The Late Show
Saturday Night Fever
Equus
The Picture Show Man
Harlan County, USA
Best Foreign-Language Film:
That Obscure Object of Desire
The Man Who Loved Women
A Special Day
Cría!
The American Friend
Actor: John Travolta, *Saturday Night Fever*
Actress: Anne Bancroft, *The Turning Point*
Supporting Actor: Tom Skerritt, *The Turning Point*
Supporting Actress: Diane Keaton, *Annie Hall*
Director: Luis Buñuel, *That Obscure Object of Desire*

Special Citations: Walt Disney Studios, for restoring and upgrading the art of animation in *The Rescuers*
Columbia Pictures, for special effects in *Close Encounters of the Third Kind*

People's Choice Awards
Favorite Picture: *Star Wars*
Favorite Movie Actor: John Wayne
Favorite Movie Actress: Barbra Streisand

British Academy Awards
Film: *Annie Hall*
Actor: Peter Finch, *Network*
Actress: Diane Keaton, *Annie Hall*
Supporting Actor: Edward Fox, *A Bridge Too Far*
Supporting Actress: Jenny Agutter, *Equus*
Director: Woody Allen, *Annie Hall*
Screenplay: Woody Allen, Marshall Brickman, *Annie Hall*
Academy Fellow: Sir Denis Forman, Fred Zinnemann

*** *Padre Padrone* CAN
Absorbing, simply told true story from the Taviani brothers (later to make *The Night of the Shooting Stars*), about a Sardinian peasant boy who was denied exposure to friends or school and kept a virtual prisoner of peasant ways by his tyrannical farmer father.

Cannes Film Festival
Palme d'Or: *Padre Padrone* (Paolo and Vittorio Taviani, Italy)
Actor: Fernando Rey, *Elisa, My Love* [*Elisa, My Life*] (Spain)
Actress: Shelley Duvall, *3 Women*

(USA), Monique Mercure, *J.A. Martin Photographe* (Canada)
First Film: Ridley Scott, *The Duellists* (UK)
Music: Norman Whitfield, *Car Wash* (USA)
Technical Prize: *Car Wash* (Michael Schultz, USA)
Homage: Peter Foldés, John Hubley [independent animators who died during 1977]
International Critics Prize: in competition, *Padre Padrone*, out of competition, *Nine Months* (Marta Mészáros, Hungary)

Berlin Film Festival
Golden Bear: *The Ascent* (Larissa Shepitko, USSR)
Special Jury Silver Bear: *The Devil, Probably* (Robert Bresson, France)
Silver Bears: *The Bricklayers* (Jorge Fons, Mexico), *A Strange Role* (Pál Sándor, Hungary)
Actor: Fernando Fernán Gómez, *The Anchorite*
Actress: Lily Tomlin, *The Late Show* (USA)
Director: Manuel Gutiérrez Aragón, *Black Litter* (Spain)
International Critics Prize: in competition, *The Ascent*, out of competition, *The Perfumed Nightmare* (Kidlat Tahimik, Philippines), special mention: Yilmaz Güney (Turkey)

Harvard Lampoon Movie Worsts
Ten worst pictures:
Looking for Mr. Goodbar
It's Alive
The Turning Point
A Nightful of Rain
New York, New York
Coming Home
Oh, God
Semi-Tough
The Goodbye Girl
The Gauntlet
Kirk Douglas Award for Worst Actor: Kris Kristofferson, *Semi-Tough*
Natalie Wood Award for Worst Actress: Marthe Keller, *Black Sunday*
The California Reich Award (awarded to those Hollywood producers who use mass slaughter for mass profit, who express a tacit "thank you" to Mr. Hitler and company every time they subject the moviegoing public to yet another unnecessary and unwanted account of the people and places of World War II): *MacArthur* and *A Bridge Too Far* [NOTE: the title of award comes from a documentary on neo-Nazi movements]
The Roscoe Award: Rudolph Nureyev, *Valentino*
The Merino Award: to the L.A. Rams in *Heaven Can Wait*

Box Office (Domestic Rentals)
1	*Star Wars [1977 only]*	$127,000,000	Fox
2	*Rocky*	54,000,000	UA
3	*Smokey and the Bandit*	39,744,000	Uni
4	*A Star Is Born*	37,100,000	WB
5	*King Kong*	35,851,283	Par
6	*The Deep*	31,000,000	Col
7	*Silver Streak*	27,100,000	Fox
8	*The Enforcer*	24,000,000	WB
9	*Close Encounters of the Third Kind*	23,000,000	Col
	[through 1978:	77,000,000]	
10	*In Search of Noah's Ark*	23,000,000	Sunn Classic

Other films of note:

11	*The Spy Who Loved Me*	21,200,000	UA
14	*The Pink Panther Strikes Again*	19,500,000	UA
15	*The Rescuers*	17,000,000	Disney
18	*Network*	14,500,000	MGM-UA
19	*Slap Shot*	14,497,000	Uni
20	*Fun With Dick and Jane*	14,000,000	Col
26	*Annie Hall*	12,000,000	UA
37	*Final Chapter: Walking Tall*	7,500,000	American Int'l
48	*Damnation Alley*	5,500,000	Fox

Few years mark so clear a change in the movie business as 1977, not only because the twin successes of Star Wars *and* Rocky *meant that the industry has lived from blockbuster to blockbuster ever since, but because they gave us our (post) modern movie world in which every picture ends not merely happily, as they did in the '40s, but on a note of supreme triumph and total victory. (Interesting question: Would even* Rocky *have the nerve to give us its he-lost-but-he-really-won ending now)? As for Mr. Lucas' picture, rumor has it that Fox thought their big sci-fi hit of the year would be* Damnation Alley, *and switched marketing money to* Star Wars *only when preview audiences went wild. Jane Fonda, last seen protesting a war and making avant-garde films with Godard, came home to begin a career as the top female star of the late '70s/early '80s, beginning with* Fun With Dick and Jane. *And the redneck crowd continued to demonstrate its power at the box office—Clint saw Burt race past him and decided maybe he better make himself one of them trucker comedies, too, while a four-walled Sunn Classic brought up the rear of the top ten.*

Gebert's Golden Armchairs

Bernardo Bertolucci's *1900* is a grand folly—as any movie which calls itself that and attempts to cover the first 45 years of this century would just about have to be. But even if it's kind of crazy, half-cocked-full-intensity Bertolucci is more exciting filmmaking than most other directors today at their best. *Close Encounters* went *Star Wars* one better by demonstrating that a special-effects movie could have a heart, too—and that a Spielberg movie could have a heart without overdosing on sugar.

Is it possible for a great American actor to go completely unknown even while working steadily? Apparently it is, if he's built like a Mac truck. Hulking, 300-pound Tim McIntire found more work as a voice (in cartoons and as the dog in *A Boy and His Dog*) than on-screen, but the two times he had parts with any meat to them at all—as DJ Alan Freed in *American Hot Wax* and as a redneck godfather in James B. Harris' little-seen prison picture *Fast-Walking*—he dominated the screen with De Niroesque intensity. In 1986, he died of a heart attack at age 42.

Best American Film: *Annie Hall*
Best Foreign Film: *1900*
Best Actor: Tim McIntire, *American Hot Wax*
Best Actress: Diane Keaton, *Annie Hall*
Best Director: Steven Spielberg, *Close Encounters of the Third Kind*

1978

With movies opening in a blitz of TV advertising on 2,000 screens at once these days, why do most Oscar contenders still follow the archaic pattern of getting reviewed in December but not opening until February or March?

Because of *The Deer Hunter*, the classic example of a commercially dubious movie which rode a protracted pre-Oscar buzz to both fortune and prizes. Under the canny direction of *Grease* promoter and disco society figure Allan Carr, Universal opened it in New York for one week in December—strictly restricting admission to critics and other glitterati. When the buzz started to build, Carr had it yanked—knowing that the cachet of being one of the select few to have seen it would make it irresistible cocktail party talk. They repeated the same trick in Los Angeles, this time restricting admission to Academy members, and again yanking it after a week (although a few especially influential members, like Steven Spielberg, got personal screenings later). As the film started to win awards, Universal sat on it, betting that no potential Oscar contender could ever look as good as one you couldn't see. By the time it finally went into general release in February, everyone "knew" that *The Deer Hunter* was a sure thing for Best Picture.

Academy Awards

**** *The Deer Hunter* AAW DGA NYC
Its picture of Vietnam combat is as much fantasy as *Rambo*'s—in fact, it comes straight from World War II movies—and nearly every 'Nam movie that followed has done that better. But no movie has done a better job of capturing the sense of blue-collar rage and betrayal that has obviously been a major feature of American politics since the war. And though the unwieldy dramatic sense that did in director Michael Cimino's *Heaven's Gate* is present here, too, there's so much electric acting that it makes you mourn the flame-out of his career: De Niro, quietly intense as the hero, an ethnic Gary Cooper; Walken, hollowed out like a tooth with pain; manic, over-the-top John Cazale in his last role; and an unshowy Streep, with her broken nose as unconventionally beautiful as a Russian icon of the madonna.

Picture
The Deer Hunter (Universal, EMI Films/Cimino)
Coming Home (UA, Jerome Hellman)
Heaven Can Wait (Paramount, Warren Beatty)

Midnight Express (Columbia, Casablanca-Filmworks, Alan Marshall, David Puttnam)
An Unmarried Woman (20th Century–Fox, Paul Mazursky, Tony Ray)

**** Jon Voight in *Coming Home* AAW GLO NYC SOC BOR CAN
** Jane Fonda in *Coming Home* AAW GLO LAC HAR
The first big Vietnam movie—beating *The Deer Hunter* by several months—is hardly a Vietnam movie at all, but rather a feminist consciousness-raising picture. And it's not much of that, either, since what mainly raises Army wife Jane Fonda's consciousness is the fact that husband Bruce Dern (try and guess what eventually happens to him) is lousy in bed, but wheelchair-bound vet Jon Voight brings her to orgasm. All the taste and care with which it is made can't hide the basic banality (and even offensiveness) of reducing the war to such glossily romantic terms—it's Mrs. Miniver on the Pill. Voight, nevertheless, is terrific as the vet turned against the war; Fonda isn't convincing as someone with a lowered consciousness, so her raising doesn't have much impact. Her own real story would have been much more interesting—under the same title, even.

Actor
Jon Voight, *Coming Home*
Warren Beatty, *Heaven Can Wait*
Gary Busey, *The Buddy Holly Story*

Robert De Niro, *The Deer Hunter*
Laurence Olivier, *The Boys from Brazil*

Actress
Jane Fonda, *Coming Home*
Ingrid Bergman, *Autumn Sonata*
Ellen Burstyn, *Same Time, Next Year*
Jill Clayburgh, *An Unmarried Woman*
Geraldine Page, *Interiors*

Supporting Actor
Christopher Walken, *The Deer Hunter*
Bruce Dern, *Coming Home*
Richard Farnsworth, *Comes a Horseman*
John Hurt, *Midnight Express*
Jack Warden, *Heaven Can Wait*

Supporting Actress
Maggie Smith, *California Suite*
Dyan Cannon, *Heaven Can Wait*
Penelope Milford, *Coming Home*
Maureen Stapleton, *Interiors*
Meryl Streep, *The Deer Hunter*

Director
Michael Cimino, *The Deer Hunter*
Woody Allen, *Interiors*
Hal Ashby, *Coming Home*
Warren Beatty, Buck Henry, *Heaven Can Wait*
Alan Parker, *Midnight Express*

Original Screenplay: Nancy Dowd, Waldo Salt, Robert C. Jones, *Coming Home*
Adapted Screenplay: Oliver Stone, *Midnight Express*
Cinematography: Nestor Almendros, *Days of Heaven*
Original Score: Giorgio Moroder, *Midnight Express*
Scoring Adaptation: Joe Renzetti, *The Buddy Holly Story*
Song: "Last Dance," *Thank God It's Friday*, ml: Paul Jabara

Art Direction: Paul Sylbert, *Heaven Can Wait*
Costume Design: Anthony Powell, *Death on the Nile*
Editing: *The Deer Hunter*
Sound: *The Deer Hunter*
Visual Effects: *Superman*
Short/Animated: *Special Delivery* (National Film Board of Canada)
Short/Live Action: *Teenage Father* (New Visions Inc. for the Children's Home Society of California, directed by Taylor Hackford)
Documentary/Feature: *Scared Straight!*
Documentary/Short: *The Flight of the Gossamer Condor*
Foreign Language Film: *Get Out Your Handkerchiefs* (France)
Jean Hersholt Humanitarian Award: Leo Jaffe
Special Awards:
Walter Lantz
Laurence Olivier
King Vidor
The Museum of Modern Art
　　Department of Film

Golden Globes
Picture (Drama): *Midnight Express*
Picture (Comedy/Musical): *Heaven Can Wait*
Foreign Film: *Autumn Sonata* (Sweden)
Actor (Drama): Jon Voight, *Coming Home*
Actor (Comedy/Musical): Warren Beatty, *Heaven Can Wait*
Actress (Drama): Jane Fonda, *Coming Home*
Actress (Comedy/Musical): Ellen Burstyn, *Same Time, Next Year*, Maggie Smith, *California Suite*
Supporting Actor: John Hurt, *Midnight Express*
Supporting Actress: Dyan Cannon, *Heaven Can Wait*

Director: Michael Cimino, *The Deer Hunter*
Screenplay: Oliver Stone, *Midnight Express*
Score: Giorgio Moroder, *Midnight Express*
Song: "Last Dance," *Thank God It's Friday*, ml: Paul Jabara
Best Acting Debut (Male): Brad Davis, *Midnight Express*
Best Acting Debut (Female): Irene Miracle, *Midnight Express*
World Film Favorite (Male): John Travolta
World Film Favorite (Female): Jane Fonda
Cecil B. DeMille Award: Lucille Ball

Directors Guild of America
Director: Michael Cimino, *The Deer Hunter*

*** **Ingrid Bergman in *Autumn Sonata*** NYC SOC BOR
The only collaboration between Ingrid and Ingmar Bergman comes off less like Ingrid starring in *Winter Light* than like Ingmar directing *Anastasia*; Ingrid is magnetic as ever but the story, about a famous violinist and her wallflower daughter (Liv Ullmann), is overly familiar.

New York Film Critics Circle
Picture: *The Deer Hunter*
Foreign Film: *Bread and Chocolate*
Actor: Jon Voight, *Coming Home*
Actress: Ingrid Bergman, *Autumn Sonata*
Supporting Actor: Christopher Walken, *The Deer Hunter*
Supporting Actress: Maureen Stapleton, *Interiors*

Director: Terrence Malick, *Days of Heaven*
Screenplay: Paul Mazursky, *An Unmarried Woman*

*** *Get Out Your Handkerchiefs* AAW SOC
Bertrand Blier's *Going Places* was a liberatingly scurrilous sex comedy about two lowlifes (Gérard Depardieu, Patrick Dewaere) who—this was the joke—were simultaneously reprehensible thugs, and dopey big babies. Five years later, Blier reunited Depardieu and Dewaere for a scrubbed-up, tamer middle-class version of the same thing—and won an Oscar.

National Society of Film Critics
Picture: *Get Out Your Handkerchiefs*
Actor: Gary Busey, *The Buddy Holly Story*
Actress: Ingrid Bergman, *Autumn Sonata*
Supporting Actor: Richard Farnsworth, *Comes a Horseman*, Robert Morley, *Who Is Killing the Great Chefs of Europe?*
Supporting Actress: Meryl Streep, *The Deer Hunter*
Director: Terrence Malick, *Days of Heaven*
Screenplay: Paul Mazursky, *An Unmarried Woman*
Cinematography: Nestor Almendros, *Days of Heaven*

Los Angeles Film Critics Association
Film: *Coming Home*
Foreign Film: *Madame Rosa*
Actor: Jon Voight, *Coming Home*
Actress: Jane Fonda, *Coming Home, Comes a Horseman, California Suite*

Supporting Actor: Robert Morley, *Who Is Killing the Great Chefs of Europe?*
Supporting Actress: Maureen Stapleton, *Interiors*, Mona Washbourne, *Stevie*
Director: Michael Cimino, *The Deer Hunter*
Screenplay: Paul Mazursky, *An Unmarried Woman*
Cinematography: Nestor Almendros, *Days of Heaven*
Music: Giorgio Moroder, *Midnight Express*

National Board of Review
Best English-Language Film:
Days of Heaven
Coming Home
Interiors
Superman
Movie Movie
Midnight Express
An Unmarried Woman
Pretty Baby
Girlfriends
Comes a Horseman
Best Foreign-Language Film:
Autumn Sonata
Dear Detective
Madame Rosa
A Slave of Love
Bread and Chocolate
Actor: Jon Voight, *Coming Home*; Laurence Olivier, *The Boys from Brazil*
Actress: Ingrid Bergman, *Autumn Sonata*
Supporting Actor: Richard Farnsworth, *Comes a Horseman*
Supporting Actress: Angela Lansbury, *Death on the Nile*
Director: Ingmar Bergman, *Autumn Sonata*

People's Choice Awards
Favorite Non-Musical Picture:
Animal House
Favorite Musical Picture:
Grease
Favorite Movie Actor: Burt Reynolds

Favorite Movie Actress: Olivia Newton-John
Favorite Supporting Actor: Jerry Reed
Favorite Supporting Actress: Stockard Channing

British Academy Awards
Film: *Julia*
Actor: Richard Dreyfuss, *The Goodbye Girl*
Actress: Jane Fonda, *Julia*
Supporting Actor: John Hurt, *Midnight Express*
Supporting Actress: Geraldine Page, *Interiors*
Director: Alan Parker, *Midnight Express*
Screenplay: Alvin Sargent, *Julia*
Academy Fellow: Sir Huw Weldon
Michael Balcon Award: Les Bowie, Colin Chilvers, Denys Coop, Roy Field, Derek Meddings, Zoran Perisic, Wally Veevers [British special effects technicians on *Superman*]

**** *The Tree of Wooden Clogs* CAN; '80: NYC BAA Three hours of the life of some Italian peasants. No social commentary like *1900*; no crafty peasant skullduggery like *Jean de Florette*; no great humanist insights like *Father Panchali*. Just the rhythms of day-to-day life; some may feel it's like watching paint dry, but I find its simplicity remarkably soothing—sort of the way some people come home from a hard day at the office and watch *Mister Rogers' Neighborhood*.

Cannes Film Festival
Palme d'Or: *The Tree of Wooden Clogs* (Ermanno Olmi, Italy)
Grand Jury Prize: *Bye Bye Monkey* (Marco Ferreri, Italy), *The Shout* (Jerzy Skolimowski, UK)
Camera d'Or: *Alambrista* (Robert M. Young, USA)
Actor: Jon Voight, *Coming Home* (USA)
Actress: Jill Clayburgh, *An Unmarried Woman* (USA), Isabelle Huppert, *Violette* (France)
Director: Nagisa Oshima, *Empire of Passion* (Japan)
[Short film Jury Prize co-won by *A Doonesbury Special* (John and Faith Hubley, Garry Trudeau, USA)]
International Critics Prize: *Man of Marble* (Andrzej Wajda, Poland), *The Smell of Wild Flowers* (Srdan Karanovic, Yugoslavia)

Berlin Film Festival
Golden Bear: to the Spanish entries as a whole: *The Trout* (José Luis García Sánchez), *Max's Words* (Emilio Martinez Lázaro), *Ascensor* (short; Tomás Muñoz)
Silver Bear: *A Queda* (Ruy Guerra, Nelson Xavier, Brazil)
Actor: Craig Russell, *Outrageous* (Canada)
Actress: Gena Rowlands, *Opening Night* (USA)
Director: Georgi Dyulgerov, *Advantage* (Bulgaria)
First Film: Octavio Cortázar, *The Teacher* (Cuba)
Tribute: Jerzy Kawalerowicz (Poland)
Special Mention: *Germany in Autumn* (collaborative film on modern West Germany by 12 filmmakers, including Alexander Kluge, Edgar Reitz, R. W. Fassbinder, Heinrich Böll, Volker Schlöndorff)
International Critics Prize: *The Happy Year of My Father* (Sándor Simó, Hungary)

U.S. Film Festival (Sundance)

Grand Jury Prize: *Girlfriends* (Claudia Weill)

Special Jury Prize: *The Whole Shootin' Match* (Eagle Pennell), *Martin* (George Romero)

Harvard Lampoon Movie Worsts

Ten worst pictures:

Sgt. Pepper's Lonely Hearts Club Band
Rabbit Test
Interiors
Superman
Foul Play
Up in Smoke
F. I. S. T.
Magic
Ice Castles

Same Time, Next Year
Kirk Douglas Award for Worst Actor: Warren Beatty, *Heaven Can Wait*'s triple threat (writer/director/idiot Ken-doll impersonator)

Natalie Wood Award for Worst Actress: We couldn't decide whether to give it to Jane Fonda for *Coming Home*, Jane Fonda for *Comes a Horseman*, or Jane Fonda for *Come the China Syndrome*. So we decided to give it to you, Jane, just for being you.

The Trinitron Memorial (for the most ungraceful transition from small screen to big): Farrah Fawcett-Majors, *Somebody Killed Her Husband*

The Merino Award: Meryno Streep, *Kramer vs. Kramer*

Box Office (Domestic Rentals)

1	*Grease*	$83,091,000	Par
2	*Saturday Night Fever*	71,463,000	Par
3	*Close Encounters of the Third Kind*	54,000,000	Col
4	*National Lampoon's Animal House*	52,368,000	Uni
5	*Jaws 2*	49,299,000	Uni
6	*Heaven Can Wait*	42,517,000	Par
7	*The Goodbye Girl*	41,000,000	Col
8	*Star Wars [1978 only]*	38,375,000	Fox
9	*Hooper*	31,500,000	WB
10	*Foul Play*	25,065,000	Par
Other films of note:			
11	*Revenge of the Pink Panther*	25,000,000	UA
12	*Up in Smoke*	21,271,000	Par
16	*High Anxiety*	17,040,000	Fox
18	*The Turning Point*	15,045,000	Fox
21	*Damien—Omen II*	12,050,000	Fox
23	*Julia*	11,300,000	Fox
31	*The Late Great Planet Earth*	9,656,000	Pacific Int'l
32	*F. I. S. T.*	9,500,000	UA
37	*Coming Home [1978 only]*	8,200,000	UA
	[through 1979:	13,389,000]	
50	*Corvette Summer*	6,250,000	MGM-UA

90   *Somebody Killed Her Husband*   1,850,000   Col

Easy Rider *was supposed to have signaled the arrival of the youth audience, but 1978 is the year the baby boomers really took over. Except for 41-year-old Warren Beatty, the box office was dominated by kids like John Travolta (24), John Belushi (29), Richard Dreyfuss (31), and Chevy Chase (a ripe old 35). The two veterans of TV's* Saturday Night Live *would prove to be the most influential comics of their time, as Chase's preppy-smartass sensibility and* Animal House's *gross-out, razz-the-grown-ups brand of humor quickly infected the entire culture. New stars who had trouble finding a second hit included Mark Hamill with* Corvette Summer, *Sylvester Stallone as a romanticized Hoffa in* F.I.S.T., *and TV sensation Farrah Fawcett-Majors in the instant-classic-bomb* Somebody Killed Her Husband.

Gebert's Golden Armchairs

Jill Clayburgh's only prize for Paul Mazursky's *An Unmarried Woman* was at Cannes, but I think there's no comparison between Fonda's G.I.'s-wife–turned–frizzy-haired-activist and Clayburgh's much subtler and richer transformation from middle-class wife in a genteel rut of a marriage to self-reliant woman on her own. In the 1930s, working-class audiences responded to caricatures of the upper classes and the Academy voted them Oscars; now middle-class audiences respond to caricatures of the working class and the Academy votes them Oscars, even when a much better movie about their own experience is right in front of them.

Best American Film: *The Deer Hunter*
Best Foreign Film: *The Tree of Wooden Clogs*
Best Actor: Jon Voight, *Coming Home*
Best Actress: Jill Clayburgh, *An Unmarried Woman*
Best Director: Michael Cimino, *The Deer Hunter*

1979

Apocalypse Now had already endured four years of production hell in a jungle, the firing of one star (Harvey Keitel) and the heart attack of his replacement (Martin Sheen), and a monsoon that destroyed the film's sets. Now Francis Coppola seemed determined to finish off its reputation by entering an uncompleted version as a work-in-progress at Cannes—something you just *didn't* do. Yet the reception to the film (which at that point ended with an epilogue in which Sheen returns to visit the Brando character's widow in America) was tremendously positive; Coppola, it was felt, had grabbed a tiger by the tail and made a great film.

So his next move was to hold a rambling, defensive press conference and denounce the press for having covered the ongoing story of the film's production troubles. That should have finished the film off at last; instead the press ate it up. Crazy Coppola with a great film was a great story—and a few days later, crazy Coppola as the first person ever to win a second Palme d'Or was an even better one.

Apocalypse Now came back to the U.S., opening after a wave of Vietnam films that had all entered production after it had, and its reviews ranged from respectful to awed. But a curious thing happened—the cultural moment for Vietnam epics seemed to have passed, and with Michael Cimino's *Heaven's Gate* enduring similar production troubles in Montana, maybe the moment for crazy-genius filmmakers had passed, too. When a cozy little film about ordinary life like *Kramer vs. Kramer* came along, critics and the Academy glommed onto it, and Coppola, who had left Cannes with an unprecedented prize and all the publicity in the world, found that it wasn't enough to get him another Best Picture Oscar.

Academy Awards

*** *Kramer vs. Kramer* AAW
GLO DGA NYC SOC LAC
*** **Dustin Hoffman** AAW
GLO NYC SOC LAC
Robert Benton's account of a single dad raising his kid is the first major sign of the '80s yuppie sentimentalization of fatherhood—presumably why the whole (male critical) world went gaga over it and over Hoffman's performance. Both of which are intelligent and carefully observed . . . but hardly the Bergman-quality *Scenes from a Toddlerhood* that some claimed.

Picture
Kramer vs. Kramer (Columbia,
Stanley R. Jaffe)
All That Jazz (Columbia/20th
Century–Fox, Robert Alan
Aurthur)
Apocalypse Now (UA, Omni
Zoetrope)
Breaking Away (20th
Century–Fox, Peter Yates)
Norma Rae (20th Century–Fox,
Tamara Asseyev, Alex Rose)

Actor
Dustin Hoffman, *Kramer vs.
Kramer*
Jack Lemmon, *The China
Syndrome*
Al Pacino, . . . *And Justice for All*
Roy Scheider, *All That Jazz*
Peter Sellers, *Being There*

****** Sally Field in *Norma
Rae*   AAW GLO NYC SOC
LAC BOR CAN**
A terrific true-life union-
organizing film from Martin Ritt
(*Hud, Sounder*)—the director
who made more movies about
ordinary America with less
Hollywood phoniness than
anybody. (This one makes
Silkwood look especially bad.)
Field has been all over the place
as an actress (not to mention
as a deliverer of Oscar
acceptance speeches), but
under Ritt's direction she gives
a smart, credibly down-to-
earth performance in a classic
gutsy-gal/no-makeup Oscar
part.

Actress
Sally Field, *Norma Rae*
Jill Clayburgh, *Starting Over*
Jane Fonda, *The China Syndrome*

Marsha Mason, *Chapter Two*
Bette Midler, *The Rose*

Supporting Actor
Melvyn Douglas, *Being There*
Robert Duvall, *Apocalypse Now*
Frederic Forrest, *The Rose*
Justin Henry, *Kramer vs. Kramer*
Mickey Rooney, *The Black
Stallion*

Supporting Actress
Meryl Streep, *Kramer vs.
Kramer*
Jane Alexander, *Kramer vs.
Kramer*
Barbara Barrie, *Breaking Away*
Candice Bergen, *Starting Over*
Mariel Hemingway, *Manhattan*

Director
Robert Benton, *Kramer vs.
Kramer*
Francis Coppola, *Apocalypse Now*
Bob Fosse, *All That Jazz*
Edouard Molinaro, *La Cage aux
Folles*
Peter Yates, *Breaking Away*

Original Screenplay: Steve
Tesich, *Breaking Away*
Adapted Screenplay: Robert
Benton, *Kramer vs. Kramer*
Cinematography: Vittorio
Storaro, *Apocalypse Now*
Original Score: Georges
Delerue, *A Little Romance*
Scoring Adaptation: Ralph
Burns, *All That Jazz*
Song: "It Goes Like It Goes,"
Norma Rae, m: David Shire,
l: Norman Gimbel
Art Direction: Philip Rosenberg,
Tony Walton, *All That Jazz*
Costume Design: Albert Wolsky,
All That Jazz
Editing: *All That Jazz*
Sound: Walter Murch,
Apocalypse Now

Sound Editing: Alan Splet, *The Black Stallion*
Visual Effects: H. R. Giger, Carlo Rambaldi, *Alien*
Short/Animated: *Every Child* (National Film Board of Canada, Derek Lamb)
Short/Live Action: *Board and Care*
Documentary/Feature: *Best Boy* (Ira Wohl)
Documentary/Short: *Paul Robeson: Tribute to an Artist*
Foreign-Language Film: *The Tin Drum* (West Germany)
Irving G. Thalberg Award: Ray Stark
Jean Hersholt Humanitarian Award: Robert Benjamin
Special Awards: Alec Guinness Hal Elias, for service to the Academy

Golden Globes

Picture (Drama): *Kramer vs. Kramer*
Picture (Comedy/Musical): *Breaking Away*
Foreign Film: *La Cage aux Folles* (France)
Actor (Drama): Dustin Hoffman, *Kramer vs. Kramer*
Actor (Comedy/Musical): Peter Sellers, *Being There*
Actress (Drama): Sally Field, *Norma Rae*
Actress (Comedy/Musical): Bette Midler, *The Rose*
Supporting Actor: Melvyn Douglas, *Being There*, Robert Duvall, *Apocalypse Now*
Supporting Actress: Meryl Streep, *Kramer vs. Kramer*
Director: Francis Coppola, *Apocalypse Now*
Screenplay: Robert Benton, *Kramer vs. Kramer*
Score: Carmine Coppola, Francis Coppola, *Apocalypse Now*
Song: "The Rose," *The Rose*, ml: Amanda McBroom

New Star of the Year (Male): Ricky Schroder, *The Champ*
New Star of the Year (Female): Bette Midler, *The Rose*
World Film Favorite (Male): Roger Moore
World Film Favorite (Female): Jane Fonda
Cecil B. DeMille Award: Henry Fonda

Directors Guild of America

Director: Robert Benton, *Kramer vs. Kramer*

New York Film Critics Circle

Picture: *Kramer vs. Kramer*
Foreign Film: *The Tree of Wooden Clogs*
Actor: Dustin Hoffman, *Kramer vs. Kramer*
Actress: Sally Field, *Norma Rae*
Supporting Actor: Melvyn Douglas, *Being There*
Supporting Actress: Meryl Streep, *Kramer vs. Kramer*, *The Seduction of Joe Tynan*
Director: Woody Allen, *Manhattan*
Screenplay: Steve Tesich, *Breaking Away*

National Society of Film Critics

Picture: *Breaking Away*
Actor: Dustin Hoffman, *Kramer vs. Kramer*, *Agatha*
Actress: Sally Field, *Norma Rae*
Supporting Actor: Frederic Forrest, *Apocalypse Now*, *The Rose*
Supporting Actress: Meryl Streep, *Kramer vs. Kramer*, *The Seduction of Joe Tynan*, *Manhattan*
Director: Robert Benton, *Kramer vs. Kramer*, Woody Allen, *Manhattan*
Screenplay: Steve Tesich, *Breaking Away*
Cinematography: Caleb

Deschanel, *Being There, The Black Stallion*

Los Angeles Film Critics Association
Film: *Kramer vs. Kramer*
Foreign Film: *Soldier of Orange*
Actor: Dustin Hoffman, *Kramer vs. Kramer*
Actress: Sally Field, *Norma Rae*
Supporting Actor: Melvyn Douglas, *Being There, The Seduction of Joe Tynan*
Supporting Actress: Meryl Streep, *Kramer vs. Kramer, The Seduction of Joe Tynan, Manhattan*
Director: Robert Benton, *Kramer vs. Kramer*
Screenplay: Robert Benton, *Kramer vs. Kramer*
Cinematography: Caleb Deschanel, *The Black Stallion*
Music: Carmine Coppola, *The Black Stallion*

National Board of Review
Best English-Language Film:
Manhattan
Yanks
The Europeans
The China Syndrome
Breaking Away
Apocalypse Now
Being There
Time After Time
North Dallas Forty
Kramer vs. Kramer
Best Foreign-Language Film:
La Cage aux Folles
The Tree of Wooden Clogs
The Marriage of Maria Braun
Nosferatu the Vampyre
Peppermint Soda
Actor: Peter Sellers, *Being There*
Actress: Sally Field, *Norma Rae*
Supporting Actor: Paul Dooley, *Breaking Away*
Supporting Actress: Meryl Streep, *Manhattan, The Seduction of Joe Tynan, Kramer vs. Kramer*
Director: John Schlesinger, *Yanks*

People's Choice Awards
Favorite Picture: *Rocky II*
Favorite Movie Actor: Burt Reynolds
Favorite Movie Actress: Jane Fonda
Favorite Young Performer: Kristy McNichol
Favorite Movie Song: "The Main Event," *The Main Event*

British Academy Awards
Film: *Manhattan*
Actor: Jack Lemmon, *The China Syndrome*
Actress: Jane Fonda, *The China Syndrome*
Supporting Actor: Robert Duvall, *Apocalypse Now*
Supporting Actress: Rachel Roberts, *Yanks*
Director: Francis Ford Coppola, *Apocalypse Now*
Screenplay: Woody Allen, Marshall Brickman, *Manhattan*
Robert Flaherty Documentary Award: *The Tree of Wooden Clogs*, Ermanno Olmi
Academy Fellow: Lord Grade
Michael Balcon Award: The Children's Film Foundation

***** *Apocalypse Now*   CAN The great Vietnam film, not least because—as Coppola said at Cannes, and as anyone who's watched the making-of documentary *Hearts of Darkness* can attest—"This movie isn't about Vietnam, it was Vietnam": all the technology and power in the world, going crazy in the jungle. If it made more sense, it wouldn't be as true.

*** *The Tin Drum* AAW CAN; '80: LAC BOR
Volker Schlöndorff's film clearly bites off more than it can chew in Gunter Grass' famous novel—but that bite, which tries to tell the story of postwar Germany through the surreal life of a hostile dwarf, is pretty fascinating nonetheless.

Cannes Film Festival
Palme d'Or: *Apocalypse Now* (Francis Coppola, USA), *The Tin Drum* (Volker Schlöndorff, West Germany)
Special Jury Prize: *Siberiade* (Andrei Konchalovsky, USSR)
Actor: Jack Lemmon, *The China Syndrome* (USA)
Actress: Sally Field, *Norma Rae* (USA)
Supporting Actor: Stefano Madia, *Caro Papà* (Italy)
Supporting Actress: Eva Mattes, *Woyzeck* (West Germany)
Director: Terrence Malick, *Days of Heaven* (USA)
Young Cinema Prize: *La Drôlesse* (Jacques Doillon, France)
Homage: Miklós Jancsó, for the body of his work
Camera d'Or: *Northern Lights* (John Hanson, Rob Nilsson, USA)
Technical Prize: *Norma Rae* (Martin Ritt, USA)
International Critics Prize: in competition, *Apocalypse Now*; out of competition, *Angi Vera* (Pal Gábor, Hungary), *Black Jack* (Ken Loach, UK)

Venice Film Festival
[NOTE: Official awards reinstated in 1980]
International Critics Prize: *La Nouba* (Assia Djebbar, Algeria), *Passe Montange* (Jean François Stevenin, France)
Italian Film Journalists Assn.:

Film: *Saint Jack* (Peter Bogdanovich, USA)
Actor: Evgeni Leonov, *Autumn Marathon* (USSR)
Actress: Nobuko Otowa, *The Strangling* (Japan)

Berlin Film Festival
Golden Bear: *David* (Peter Lilienthal, West Germany)
Silver Bear: *Alexandria—Why?* (Youssef Shahine, Egypt)
Actor: Michele Placido, *Ernesto* (Italy)
Actress: Hanna Schygulla, *The Marriage of Maria Braun* (West Germany)
Director: Astrid Henning-Jensen, *Winter-Born* (Denmark)
Cinematography: Sten Holmberg, *The Emperor* (Sweden)
Art Direction: Henning von Gierke, *Nosferatu the Vampyre* (West Germany)
Silver Bear for the entire film crew: *The Marriage of Maria Braun*
Golden Bear/Short: *Ubu* (Geoff Dunbar, UK)
International Critics Prize: in competition, *Albert: Why?* (Josef Roedl, West Germany), *My Way Home* (Bill Douglas, UK); in Forum, *The Movie Machine* (Silvano Agosti, Marco Bellochio, Sandro Petaglia, Stefano Rulli, Italy)

U.S. Film Festival (Sundance)
Grand Jury Prize: *Spirit of the Wind* (Ralph R. Liddle)
Special Jury Prize: *Northern Lights* (Rob Nilsson, John Hanson), *Over-Under, Sideways-Down* (Steve Wax, Eugene Corr, Peter Gessner)

Harvard Lampoon Movie Worsts
Ten worst pictures:
Manhattan

The Muppet Movie
The Amityville Horror
Apocalypse Now
10
All That Jazz
Rocky II
1941
The Rose
Star Trek: The Motion Picture
**Kirk Douglas Award for Worst
Actor:** Marlon Brando,
Apocalypse Now
**Jane Fonda Award for Worst
Actress:** Jane Fonda, *The Electric
Horseman* [award temporarily
renamed following Natalie
Wood's death]
**The Immoral, Illegal, and Fat
Award:** Linda Blair, *Roller
Boogie*
The Dark Bock Tankard (a

foamy mug of brew annually
drunk to the performer whose
name most resembles that of
Harvard's president, Derek Bok):
Bo Derek
Worst Movie Worst Award (for
the *Harvard Lampoon* Movie
Worst Award of the past forty
years which exemplifies their
smarmy, undignified and
scattershot approach): To the
1955 award to *Rebel Without a
Cause*: "Movie without a plot
... to prevent the perpetration of
further cinematic abominations,
let's pray lead actors (we use the
word perhaps too loosely) Sal
Mineo and James Dean meet
untimely deaths."
The Merino Award: Lauren
Mutton, *American Gigolo*

Box Office (Domestic Rentals)

1	*Superman*	$81,000,000	WB
2	*Every Which Way But Loose*	48,000,000	WB
3	*Rocky II*	43,049,274	UA
4	*Alien*	40,086,573	Fox
5	*The Amityville Horror*	35,000,000	American Int'l
	Star Trek [1979 only]	35,000,000	Par
	[through 1980:	56,000,000]	
7	*Moonraker*	33,934,074	UA
8	*The Muppet Movie*	32,000,000	ITC
9	*California Suite*	29,200,000	Col
10	*The Deer Hunter*	26,927,000	Uni
Other films of note:			
12	*The China Syndrome*	25,425,000	Col
13	*10*	25,000,000	Orion
14	*Apocalypse Now*		
	[1979 only]	22,855,657	UA
	[through 1980:	36,346,471]	
15	*Escape from Alcatraz*	21,014,000	Par
16	*Meatballs*	19,674,000	Par
18	*The In-Laws*	18,000,000	WB
19	*Manhattan*	16,908,439	UA
21	*The Jerk [1979 only]*	14,000,000	Uni
	[through 1980:	43,000,000]	
30	*Star Wars [1979 only]*	11,538,000	Fox
37	*Monty Python's Life of Brian*	9,500,000	WB

56	*1941 [1979 only]*	6,000,000	Uni
	[through 1980:	23,400,000]	

In its third year of release, Star Wars *fell all the way to #30, and no wonder. It finally had competition in the form of a host of special-effects-laden sci-fi–ish movies— not just* Star Trek, Superman, *and* Alien, *but also a hastily rewritten James Bond film, which, though one of the weakest, would prove to be the series' highest-grosser ever. (Adjusting for inflation, however,* Thunderball *would hold that title.) Three comedy stars of the '80s make their first appearances here: Dudley Moore, a last-minute replacement for George Segal, in the surprise hit* 10; *Steve Martin, debuting as The Jerk; and at #15, the low-budget Canadian tax-shelter movie which would introduce Chevy Chase's* Saturday Night Live *replacement, Bill Murray. Within two years Murray would become arguably the biggest ex-SNL movie star (only Eddie Murphy ever rivaled him); one reason might be that, unlike Aykroyd and Belushi, Murray steered clear of Steven Spielberg's only big flop,* 1941, *or* It's a Mad, Mad, Tora! Tora! Tora!

Gebert's Golden Armchairs

Apocalypse Now is the year's great movie, but in no small part it was saved in post-production by the brilliant sound designer Walter Murch—which is why it often feels more like other work of Murch's (e.g., *Romeo is Bleeding*) than other work of Coppola's. So it seems more right to honor a director whose picture didn't need saving—the legendary B movie director Don Siegel, whose last collaboration with Clint Eastwood is his best, the hard-as-an-iron-bar-and-tight-as-a-triple-bolt-lock prison picture *Escape from Alcatraz*. A lot of people would pick Robert Duvall for *Apocalypse*, and on another day I might be persuaded, but Peter Falk delivers a comic performance of delightful nuttiness in the Andrew Bergman–scripted *The In-Laws* (ah, those giant tsetse flies. . . .) And my foreign film choice is a *Taxi Driver*–like drama of a small-time gangster's descent into murderous madness, the Japanese *Vengeance Is Mine*, better than director Shohei Imamura's subsequent Cannes winner *The Ballad of Narayama*.

Best American Film: *Apocalypse Now*
Best Foreign Film: *Vengeance Is Mine*
Best Actor: Peter Falk, *The In-Laws*
Best Actress: Sally Field, *Norma Rae*
Best Director: Don Siegel, *Escape from Alcatraz*

1980

Cannes produced an unprecedented three-way tie—a shared Palme d'Or for *Kagemusha* and *All That Jazz* (which is like splitting a prize between *Hamlet* and an episode of *Lou Grant*), plus the officially "equal in stature" Special Jury Prize to *Mon Oncle d'Amérique*. This improbability was the result of political arm-twisting by retired-but-still-powerful former fest chief Robert Favre Le Bret—reportedly wanting to do something nice for Alain Resnais since he was felt to have been cheated of the Palme d'Or for *Je T'Aime, Je T'Aime*, when the '68 festival collapsed. It so incensed jury head Kirk Douglas that he refused to attend the announcement ceremony.

In fact, Favre le Bret may not have cared what Douglas thought; Cannes rumor has it that when Douglas was first invited to serve on a Cannes jury in 1970, he had intended to invite retired director Douglas Sirk, and a secretary unfamiliar with the director's name misread it as "Douglas, Kirk." . . .

Academy Awards

*** *Ordinary People* AAW GLO DGA NYC BOR
Obviously *Raging Bull* is the more accomplished work of art, but considering the number of people in Tinseltown who must have been waiting all their lives for a well-crafted film about an upper-middle-class family in therapy, it's no surprise Robert Redford's perfectly respectable and sensitively made film dominated the awards.

Picture
Ordinary People (Paramount, Wildwood, Ronald L. Schwary)
Coal Miner's Daughter (Universal, Bernard Schwartz)
The Elephant Man (Paramount, Brooksfilms, Jonathan Sanger)
Raging Bull (UA, Irwin Winkler, Robert Chartoff)

Tess (Columbia, Claude Berri, Timothy Burrill)

**** Robert De Niro in *Raging Bull* AAW GLO NYC LAC BOR
Martin Scorsese's drama of boxing, degradation, and redemption will do as the Scorsese masterpiece. But I think if you compare De Niro's performance here to the Scorsese-directed roles on either side of it—living with him inside the twitching brain of *Taxi Driver*, or sharing the starry-eyed delusions of his *King of Comedy*—there's something basically opaque about this performance, and it's Joe Pesci, as the human being among the LaMotta brothers, who becomes the focal point of the picture by default. Which is not to say that it might not be

the performance of a lifetime from anyone else, but it isn't De Niro's—and one suspects it was the 50 extra pounds that most impressed people.

Actor
Robert De Niro, *Raging Bull*
Robert Duvall, *The Great Santini*
John Hurt, *The Elephant Man*
Jack Lemmon, *Tribute*
Peter O'Toole, *The Stunt Man*

***** Sissy Spacek in *Coal Miner's Daughter* AAW GLO NYC SOC LAC BOR
That's quite a gutsy little performance you got there, ma'am. And you even did your own singing!

Actress
Sissy Spacek, *Coal Miner's Daughter*
Ellen Burstyn, *Resurrection*
Goldie Hawn, *Private Benjamin*
Mary Tyler Moore, *Ordinary People*
Gena Rowlands, *Gloria*

Supporting Actor
Timothy Hutton, *Ordinary People*
Judd Hirsch, *Ordinary People*
Michael O'Keefe, *The Great Santini*
Joe Pesci, *Raging Bull*
Jason Robards, *Melvin and Howard*

Supporting Actress
Mary Steenburgen, *Melvin and Howard*
Eileen Brennan, *Private Benjamin*
Eva Le Gallienne, *Resurrection*
Cathy Moriarty, *Raging Bull*
Diana Scarwid, *Inside Moves*

Director
Robert Redford, *Ordinary People*
David Lynch, *The Elephant Man*
Roman Polanski, *Tess*
Richard Rush, *The Stunt Man*
Martin Scorsese, *Raging Bull*

Original Screenplay: Bo Goldman, *Melvin and Howard*
Adapted Screenplay: Alvin Sargent, *Ordinary People*
Cinematography: Geoffrey Unsworth, Ghislain Cloquet, *Tess*
Score: Michael Gore, *Fame*
Song: "Fame," *Fame,* m: Michael Gore, l: Dean Pitchford
Art Direction: Pierre Guffroy, Jack Stevens, *Tess*
Costume Design: Anthony Powell, *Tess*
Editing: Thelma Schoonmaker [Powell], *Raging Bull*
Sound: *The Empire Strikes Back*
Visual Effects: Richard Edlund, Dennis Muren, *The Empire Strikes Back*
Short/Animated: *The Fly* (Ferenc Rofusz, Hungary)
Short/Live Action: *The Dollar Bottom*
Documentary/Feature: *From Mao to Mozart: Isaac Stern in China*
Documentary/Short: *Karl Hess: Toward Liberty*
Foreign-Language Film: *Moscow Does Not Believe in Tears* (USSR)
Special Award: Henry Fonda

Golden Globes
Picture (Drama): *Ordinary People*
Picture (Comedy/Musical): *Coal Miner's Daughter*
Foreign Film: *Tess* (France/UK)
Actor (Drama): Robert De Niro, *Raging Bull*
Actor (Comedy/Musical): Ray Sharkey, *The Idolmaker*

Actress (Drama): Mary Tyler Moore, *Ordinary People*
Actress (Comedy/Musical): Sissy Spacek, *Coal Miner's Daughter*
Supporting Actor: Timothy Hutton, *Ordinary People*
Supporting Actress: Mary Steenburgen, *Melvin and Howard*
Director: Robert Redford, *Ordinary People*
Screenplay: William Peter Blatty, *Twinkle Twinkle Killer Kane* [*The Ninth Configuration*]
Original Score: Dominic Frontière, *The Stunt Man*
Original Song: "Fame," *Fame*, m: Michael Gore, l: Dean Pitchford
Best Acting Debut (Male): Timothy Hutton, *Ordinary People*
Best Acting Debut (Female): Nastassja Kinski, *Tess*
Cecil B. DeMille Award: Gene Kelly

Directors Guild of America
Director: Robert Redford, *Ordinary People*
D. W. Griffith Award: George Cukor
Honorary Life Member: Joseph L. Mankiewicz

**** *Mon Oncle d'Amérique*
NYC CAN
The next time you wonder if there's anything to do in movies that hasn't been done before, see Alain Resnais' film, in which he interviews the behaviorist Henri Laborit— and then constructs a narrative, perfectly compelling in conventional terms, which also illustrates Laborit's behavioral notions. Maybe the 21st century will bring us an entire scientific-analytic genre of films like this one on a multitude of subjects—economics, psychology, Chomskian linguistics. Or, maybe, just more Pauly Shores.

New York Film Critics Circle
Picture: *Ordinary People*
Foreign Film: *Mon Oncle d'Amérique*
Actor: Robert De Niro, *Raging Bull*
Actress: Sissy Spacek, *Coal Miner's Daughter*
Supporting Actor: Joe Pesci, *Raging Bull*
Supporting Actress: Mary Steenburgen, *Melvin and Howard*
Director: Jonathan Demme, *Melvin and Howard*
Screenplay: Bo Goldman, *Melvin and Howard*
Cinematography: Geoffrey Unsworth, Ghislain Cloquet, *Tess*
Documentary: *Best Boy*

*** *Melvin and Howard* SOC
One of the critical cults that never percolated through to the general public was for Jonathan Demme, maker of winsome little comedies of Americana that were part Capra and Preston Sturges, part Robert Altman. The cult started with *Citizens Band/Handle With Care*, a drive-in comedy obviously modeled on *Nashville*, and built to a peak with his account of the supposed encounter between gas station attendant Melvin Dummar and Howard Hughes (Jason Robards). *Melvin and Howard*

is probably the best case to be made for him—but even it can be seen as New York critics going gaga over an L.A. hipster's vision of the vast country in-between which neither of them has ever seen.

National Society of Film Critics
Picture: *Melvin and Howard*
Actor: Peter O'Toole, *The Stunt Man*
Actress: Sissy Spacek, *Coal Miner's Daughter*
Supporting Actor: Joe Pesci, *Raging Bull*
Supporting Actress: Mary Steenburgen, *Melvin and Howard*
Director: Martin Scorsese, *Raging Bull*
Screenplay: Bo Goldman, *Melvin and Howard*
Cinematography: Michael Chapman, *Raging Bull*

Los Angeles Film Critics Association
Film: *Raging Bull*
Foreign Film: *The Tin Drum*
Actor: Robert De Niro, *Raging Bull*
Actress: Sissy Spacek, *Coal Miner's Daughter*
Supporting Actor: Timothy Hutton, *Ordinary People*
Supporting Actress: Mary Steenburgen, *Melvin and Howard*
Director: Roman Polanski, *Tess*
Screenplay: John Sayles, *Return of the Secaucus 7*
Cinematography: Geoffrey Unsworth, Ghislain Cloquet, *Tess*
Music: Ry Cooder, *The Long Riders*
Independent/Experimental Film: *Journeys to Berlin 1971*

(Yvonne Rainer), *Demon Lover Diary* (Joel De Mott)

National Board of Review
Best English-Language Film:
Ordinary People
Raging Bull
Coal Miner's Daughter
Tess
Melvin and Howard
The Great Santini
The Elephant Man
The Stunt Man
My Bodyguard
Resurrection
Best Foreign-Language Film:
The Tin Drum
Kagemusha
Knife in the Head
From the Life of the Marionettes
Eboli
Actor: Robert De Niro, *Raging Bull*
Actress: Sissy Spacek, *Coal Miner's Daughter*
Supporting Actor: Joe Pesci, *Raging Bull*
Supporting Actress: Eva Le Gallienne, *Resurrection*
Director: Robert Redford, *Ordinary People*

People's Choice Awards
Favorite Picture: *The Empire Strikes Back*
Favorite Movie Actor: Clint Eastwood
Favorite Movie Actress: Jane Fonda, Goldie Hawn
Favorite Young Performer: Brooke Shields
Favorite Movie Song: "Nine to Five," *Nine to Five*

British Academy Awards
Film: *The Elephant Man*
Actor: John Hurt, *The Elephant Man*
Actress: Judy Davis, *My Brilliant Career*
Director: Akira Kurosawa, *Kagemusha*

Screenplay: Jerzy Kosinski, *Being There*
Academy Fellow: Sir David Attenborough, John Huston
Michael Balcon Award: Kevin Billington

**** *Kagemusha* CAN
In old age, Akira Kurosawa seems to have moved into a timeless realm of his own where his samurai dramas ask the big questions that no one else even dares contemplate any more; he seems to walk with Shakespeare and the Greek dramatists, not mere 20th-century moviemakers. I might want to rank this a notch below *Ran* in its mastery of color and evocation of pity and terror, but who living would dare make such a judgment?

** *All That Jazz* HAR '79; CAN
The real problem isn't that Bob Fosse doesn't do *8½* as well as Fellini. It's that, shockingly, he doesn't do choreography as well as Bob Fosse. There isn't a first-rate number in the whole picture—especially not the smutty, sclerotic-erotic thing that ends with Ann Reinking telling Scheider/Fosse that it's his best work. (It is, however, Scheider's best work—the movie, that is, not that number.)

Cannes Film Festival
Palme d'Or: *All That Jazz* (Bob Fosse, USA), *Kagemusha* (Akira Kurosawa, Japan)
Special Jury Prize: *Mon Oncle d'Amérique* (Alain Resnais, France) [NOTE: The Jury declared this award to be of equal stature to the Palme d'Or]
Jury Prize: *The Constant Factor* (Krzysztof Zanussi, Poland)
Actor: Michel Piccoli, *A Leap Into the Void* (Italy-France)
Actress: Anouk Aimée, *A Leap Into the Void*
Supporting Actor: Jack Thompson, *Breaker Morant* (Australia)
Supporting Actress: Milena Dravic, *Special Treatment* (Yugoslavia), Carla Gravina, *La Terrazza* (Italy)
Screenplay: Ettore Scola, *Age and Scarpelli* [Agenore Incrocci, Furio Scarpelli], *La Terrazza*
Camera d'Or: *Histoire d'Adrien* (Jean-Pierre Denis, France)
Technical Prize: *Le Risque de Vivre* (Gerard Calderon, France)
International Critics Prize: in competition, *Mon Oncle d'Amérique*, out of competition, *Provincial Actors* (Agnieszka Holland, Poland)

** *Gloria* VEN
The archaic title of the award category ("Quality for the Masses"? Brother, where art thou?) hints at the archaic thinking behind art-house director John Cassavetes' attempt to make a '30s–Warner Bros.–style commercial thriller about a gun moll (Gena Rowlands, natch) taking a young witness on the lam with her. Totally synthetic and not especially exciting—and it doesn't speak well for the first Venice jury in 14 years that they lumped it with *Atlantic City*, a movie which evokes old

gangster movies to infinitely better effect.

Venice Film Festival
Golden Lion/Quality for the Masses: *Gloria* (John Cassavetes, USA), *Atlantic City* (Louis Malle, USA/Canada) (shared)
Golden Lion/Emerging Cinema: *O Megalexandros* [*Alexander the Great*] (Theo Angelopolous, Greece)
Golden Lion/First Film: *A Special Day* (Péter Gothár, Hungary) [not to be confused with 1977 Ettore Scola film]
Young Talent Award: *Opera Prima* (Fernando Trueba, Spain)
Special Jury Citations: *The Rescuer* (Sergei Soloviev, USSR), *The Other Woman* (Peter Del Monte, Italy), *Guns* (Robert Kramer, France), *Lena Rais* (Christian Rischert, West Germany)
International Critics Prize: *O Megalexandros* [*Alexander the Great*]
Italian Critics Awards: Pasinetti Prize: *Sons of the Wind* (Brahim Tsaki, Algeria); actor, George Burns, Lee Strasberg, Art Carney, *Going in Style* (USA); actress, Liv Ullmann, *Richard's Things* (UK)

*** *Heartland* BER SUN '81
Practically the Platonic ideal of the Sundance movie (where it won an award the year after its Berlin win), starting with the title: a matter-of-fact, unsensational account of Montana pioneer life, based on an actual pioneer woman's diaries. Nicely done in a low-key realist style, and quite satisfying.

Berlin Film Festival
Golden Bear: *Heartland* (Richard Pearce, USA), *Palermo oder Wolfsburg* (Werner Schroeter, West Germany)
Silver Bear: *No Child's Land* (Marco Ferreri, Italy-France)
Special Jury Mentions: script: *Düsman* (Yilmaz Güney, Turkey), *Korpinpolska* (Markku Lehmuskallio, Finland), *Rude Boy* (David Mingay, Jack Hazan, UK)
Actor: Andrzej Seweryn, *The Conductor* (Poland)
Actress: Renate Krössner, *Solo Sunny* (West Germany)
Director: István Szabó, *Confidence* (Hungary)
Jubilee Prize: Athol Fugard, for his work and dedication
International Critics Prize: in competition, *Solo Sunny* (Konrad Wolf, East Germany); out of competition, *Hungerjahre* (Jutta Brückner, West Germany); Forum, *On Company Business* (Allan Francovich, USA)

Harvard Lampoon Movie Worsts
Ten worst pictures:
Xanadu
Altered States
Blue Lagoon
Dressed to Kill
The Jazz Singer
9 to 5
Yanks
Fame
Flash Gordon
The First Family
Kirk Douglas Award for Worst Actor: Jack Nicholson, *The Shining*
Jane Fonda Award for Worst Actress: Shelley Duvall, *Popeye*
The Madison Oscar (presented to Walter Matthau every time he appears on screen without his trousers, flashing some hairy gam): Walter Matthau, *Little Miss Marker*

The Manischewitz Whine Award: the "Schmulke" goes this year to "Sir" Laurence Olivier for his performance in *The Jazz Singer*, another in a seemingly endless series of inexplicable aged Hebrew roles. Not since Meyer Lansky has one man done so much for the Jewish peoples

The Watergate Worst (for the most outrageous cover-up job of the year): John Hurt and his makeup man, *The Elephant Man*

The Merino Award: *Serial*, a tepid tale of doings and undoings in Marin County, California

Golden Raspberry Awards
Worst Picture: *Can't Stop the Music!*
Worst Actor: Neil Diamond, *The Jazz Singer*
Worst Actress: Brooke Shields, *The Blue Lagoon*
Worst Supporting Actor: (tie) John Adames, *Gloria*, Laurence Olivier, *The Jazz Singer*
Worst Supporting Actress: Amy Irving, *Honeysuckle Rose*
Worst Director: Robert Greenwald, *Xanadu*
Worst Screenplay: Bronte Woodward, Allan Carr, *Can't Stop the Music!*
Worst Song: title song, *The Man with Bogart's Face*

Box Office (Domestic Rentals)

#	Film	Rental	Studio
1	*The Empire Strikes Back*	$120,000,000	Fox
2	*Kramer vs. Kramer*	60,528,000	Col
3	*The Jerk*	43,000,000	Uni
4	*Airplane!*	38,000,000	Par
5	*Smokey and the Bandit [1980 only]*	37,600,000	Uni
	[through 1981:	61,055,000]	
6	*Coal Miner's Daughter*	36,000,000	Uni
7	*Private Benjamin*	33,500,000	WB
8	*The Blues Brothers*	31,000,000	Uni
9	*The Electric Horseman*	30,917,000	Col
10	*The Shining*	30,200,000	WB
Other films of note:			
11	*The Blue Lagoon*	28,456,000	Col
12	*The Black Hole*	25,000,000	Disney
14	*Urban Cowboy*	22,700,000	Par
17	*Caddyshack*	20,000,000	Orion/WB
20	*Friday the 13th*	16,500,000	Par
26	*Ordinary People*	13,000,000	Par
54	*Prom Night*	6,000,000	Avco Embassy
83	*Terror Train*	3,500,000	Fox
90	*Don't Go in the House*	2,698,862	Film Ventures
105	*Don't Answer the Phone*	1,750,000	Crown

Star Wars II *(or* V, *by George Lucas' counting scheme) became the first sequel since* Jolson Sings Again *to top the chart—though not the last. But the real news in 1980 was the amazing (and somewhat appalling) revival of the horror genre. Following the phenomenal success of* Halloween *(which didn't make* Variety's *chart for* *some reason, but did about $30 million), cheap, formulaic slasher films came out of the woodwork—starting with Paramount's Friday the 13th series, which the company treated like a shameful habit that it regretted all the way to the bank. What really fueled the slasher movie cycle was that it came at just the moment that home video rental was becoming a national habit. Slasher pictures were a perfect slumber party activity for teens (well, perfect in their minds), and in a video rental environment—where whatever you wanted was always out anyway—the fact that one was the same as the next was an asset rather than a liability.*

Gebert's Golden Armchairs

France's answer to De Niro, Gérard Depardieu, has given an award-worthy performance (if not two or three) nearly every year from this point on; my choice of Maurice Pialat's *Loulou* is merely one possibility among many. And let me inaugurate my "Worst Hit" award by honoring, from Paramount, the studio that brought you Lubitsch, Sturges, and Wilder, the picture that inaugurated the worst series in Hollywood history—*Friday the 13th*.

Best American Film: *Raging Bull*
Best Foreign Film: *Mon Oncle d'Amérique*
Best Actor: Gérard Depardieu, *Loulou*
Best Actress: Sissy Spacek, *Coal Miner's Daughter*
Best Director: Martin Scorsese, *Raging Bull*
Worst Hit: *Friday the 13th*

1981

The last real surprise Best Picture Oscar–winner, *Chariots of Fire* actually owed its success to a neat scam pulled at Cannes nearly a year before by Roger Ebert. At Cannes it had been shown in competition and received a standing ovation, but then—for reasons probably more cultural than aesthetic—it was savaged by the French press. Ebert instantly loved it, and he also knew that the press reaction could harm its chances for international release. So he rounded up the other American critics in attendance, lobbied them on behalf of his choice, and—apparently having studied his Chicago elections well—produced a nice, definitive-but-unsuspicious 6-out-of-11-vote victory for his favorite as the winner of the "American Critics Prize."

Now, this prize had never existed before, and it has never been given since. But apart from a couple of questions about why an award was being given before all the films had even been shown, the press took it with a straight face. And *Chariots of Fire* left Cannes not as a critical disaster, but as the winner of an "important" Cannes prize.

Academy Awards

*** *Chariots of Fire* AAW GLO BOR BAA
In retrospect it should have been obvious why the America of Ralph Lauren and *The Preppy Handbook* would go for *Rocky-meets-Masterpiece Theater* over its stuck-in-the-'70s competitors. Neither the inspirational masterpiece its admirers thought, nor the reactionary Empire propaganda its detractors claimed, it certainly looks no worse 15 years later than its major competitors—and a good deal better than any of the million other *Rocky* descendants.

Picture
Chariots of Fire (The Ladd Company/Warner Bros., Enigma, David Puttnam)
Atlantic City (Paramount, International Cinema Corporation, Denis Heroux)
On Golden Pond (Universal, ITC Films/IPC Films, Bruce Gilbert)
Raiders of the Lost Ark (Paramount, Lucasfilm, Frank Marshall)
Reds (Paramount, J.R.S., Warren Beatty)

*** Henry Fonda in *On Golden Pond* AAW GLO BOR
** Katharine Hepburn in *On Golden Pond* AAW HAR BAA '82
No one could begrudge Fonda his long-awaited Oscar (even Burt Lancaster, who already had

357

one), but that doesn't mean that seeing him say "Wanna suck face?" in this piece of feelgood dinner-theater Chekhov isn't a grisly embarrassment. He was better in a similar TV thing, *Summer Solstice*, with Myrna Loy. (Hell, he was better in *The Great Smokey Roadblock*.) Hepburn, on the other hand, already had three of the damn things, so I *can* begrudge her an Oscar for this instantly parodied part ("The loons! The loons!").

Actor
Henry Fonda, *On Golden Pond*
Warren Beatty, *Reds*
Burt Lancaster, *Atlantic City*
Dudley Moore, *Arthur*
Paul Newman, *Absence of Malice*

Actress
Katharine Hepburn, *On Golden Pond*
Diane Keaton, *Reds*
Marsha Mason, *Only When I Laugh*
Susan Sarandon, *Atlantic City*
Meryl Streep, *The French Lieutenant's Woman*

Supporting Actor
John Gielgud, *Arthur*
James Coco, *Only When I Laugh*
Ian Holm, *Chariots of Fire*
Jack Nicholson, *Reds*
Howard E. Rollins, Jr., *Ragtime*

Supporting Actress
Maureen Stapleton, *Reds*
Melinda Dillon, *Absence of Malice*
Jane Fonda, *On Golden Pond*
Joan Hackett, *Only When I Laugh*
Elizabeth McGovern, *Ragtime*

Director
Warren Beatty, *Reds*
Hugh Hudson, *Chariots of Fire*

Louis Malle, *Atlantic City*
Mark Rydell, *On Golden Pond*
Steven Spielberg, *Raiders of the Lost Ark*

Original Screenplay: Colin Welland, *Chariots of Fire*
Adapted Screenplay: Ernest Thompson, *On Golden Pond*
Cinematography: Vittorio Storaro, *Reds*
Score: Vangelis, *Chariots of Fire*
Song: "Arthur's Theme (Best That You Can Do)," *Arthur*, ml: Burt Bacharach, Carole Bayer Sager, Christopher Cross, Peter Allen
Art Direction: Norman Reynolds, *Raiders of the Lost Ark*
Costume Design: Milena Canonero, *Chariots of Fire*
Editing: *Raiders of the Lost Ark*
Sound: *Raiders of the Lost Ark*
Sound Effects Editing: *Raiders of the Lost Ark*
Make-up: Rick Baker, *An American Werewolf in London*
Visual Effects: Richard Edlund, Joe Johnston, *Raiders of the Lost Ark*
Short/Animation: *Crac* (Canada)
Short/Live Action: *Violet*
Documentary/Feature: *Genocide*
Documentary/Short: *Close Harmony*
Foreign-Language Film: *Mephisto* (Hungary)
Irving G. Thalberg Award: Albert R. "Cubby" Broccoli
Jean Hersholt Humanitarian Award: Danny Kaye
Special Award: Barbara Stanwyck

** Meryl Streep in *The French Lieutenant's Woman* GLO LAC BAA
The first of the films that would make Meryl Streep and her

retinue of accents the most acclaimed actress of her time—or the female Paul Muni, depending on your point of view. There's no question Streep has tremendous skill, but too often all that results is that she gives a bloodlessly perfect imitation of a human being; I would have said that she lacked the human touch that great movie stars need, until she finally played comedy in *Defending Your Life*—and absolutely glowed with good humor. (Maybe it was just a remarkable imitation of a great comedienne, but it fooled me.) Anyway, this adaptation of John Fowles' Victorian pastiche has double the problem, since exactly the same comments apply to co-star Jeremy Irons (except that he finally found himself in a horror movie, *Dead Ringers*, not a comedy); with that brainy pair for lovers and Harold Pinter for screenwriter, the ice never melts.

Golden Globes
Picture (Drama): *On Golden Pond*
Picture (Comedy/Musical): *Arthur*
Foreign Film: *Chariots of Fire* (UK)
Actor (Drama): Henry Fonda, *On Golden Pond*
Actor (Comedy/Musical): Dudley Moore, *Arthur*
Actress (Drama): Meryl Streep, *The French Lieutenant's Woman*
Actress (Comedy/Musical): Bernadette Peters, *Pennies from Heaven*
Supporting Actor: John Gielgud, *Arthur*
Supporting Actress: Joan Hackett, *Only When I Laugh*
Director: Warren Beatty, *Reds*
Screenplay: Ernest Thompson, *On Golden Pond*
Original Song: "Arthur's Theme (Best That You Can Do)," *Arthur*, ml: Burt Bacharach, Carole Bayer Sager, Christopher Cross, Peter Allen
New Star of the Year: Pia Zadora, *Butterfly*
Cecil B. DeMille Award: Sidney Poitier

Directors Guild of America
Director: Warren Beatty, *Reds*
D. W. Griffith Award: Rouben Mamoulian

*** *Reds* DGA NYC
Like everything Warren Beatty's done since *Bonnie and Clyde*, his epic, ambitious biography of the American Communist John Reed is a grand gesture that somehow seems to be running on half horsepower. The depiction of the Kafkaesque dead end of the Soviet revolution, typified by Jerzy Koszinski's maddeningly opaque *apparatchik*, is first-rate; the picture of Greenwich Village intellectual life, if not especially deep, is brightly bitchy. But the depiction of Reed and Bryant's home life, dog whining at the door as they hump away, and the invented scenes of Diane Keaton sledding to Finland to rescue Beatty from jail, are audience-pandering. You know, Warren, *The Godfather* managed to get by without a *dog*.

New York Film Critics Circle

Picture: *Reds*
Foreign Film: *Pixote*
Actor: Burt Lancaster, *Atlantic City*
Actress: Glenda Jackson, *Stevie*
Supporting Actor: John Gielgud, *Arthur*
Supporting Actress: Mona Washbourne, *Stevie*
Director: Sidney Lumet, *Prince of the City*
Screenplay: John Guare, *Atlantic City*
Cinematography: David Watkin, *Chariots of Fire*
Special Prizes: *Napoleon* [1926 French silent by Abel Gance, restored by Kevin Brownlow and David Gill]
The artistry and independent spirit of the Polish filmmakers Andrzej Wajda and Krzysztof Zanussi as demonstrated in their films

National Society of Film Critics

Picture: *Atlantic City*
Actor: Burt Lancaster, *Atlantic City*
Actress: Marília Pera, *Pixote*
Supporting Actor: Robert Preston, *S. O. B.*
Supporting Actress: Maureen Stapleton, *Reds*
Director: Louis Malle, *Atlantic City*
Screenplay: John Guare, *Atlantic City*
Cinematography: Gordon Willis, *Pennies from Heaven*

**** *Atlantic City* VEN '80 SOC LAC
***** Burt Lancaster AAW SOC NYC LAC BAA
The critics' fave was a far better old-age film and performance than Oscar-winner Henry

Fonda's—beautifully written (you should have seen the Atlantic Ocean then, kid) and acted, for all its warmth, with the icy self-control that was always Lancaster's most imposing characteristic. It was the L.A. critics who discovered it (it had won at Venice the year before, then sat on the shelf) and, in the first display of their growing influence, led it to at least Oscar attention, if not victory.

Los Angeles Film Critics Association

Film: *Atlantic City*
Foreign Film: *Pixote*
Actor: Burt Lancaster, *Atlantic City*
Actress: Meryl Streep, *The French Lieutenant's Woman*
Supporting Actor: John Gielgud, *Arthur*
Supporting Actress: Maureen Stapleton, *Reds*
Director: Warren Beatty, *Reds*
Screenplay: John Guare, *Atlantic City*
Cinematography: Vittorio Storaro, *Reds*
Music: Randy Newman, *Ragtime*
Independent/Experimental Film: *The Art of Worldly Wisdom* (Bruce Elder)
Life Achievement: Barbara Stanwyck
New Generation Prize: John Guare, writer of *Atlantic City*

National Board of Review

Best English-Language Film:
Chariots of Fire
Reds
Atlantic City
Stevie
Gallipoli
On Golden Pond
Prince of the City

Raiders of the Lost Ark
Heartland
Ticket to Heaven
Breaker Morant
Best Foreign-Language Film:
Oblomov
The Boat Is Full
The Last Metro
Contract
Pixote
Actor: Henry Fonda, *On Golden Pond*
Actress: Glenda Jackson, *Stevie*
Supporting Actor: Jack Nicholson, *Reds*
Supporting Actress: Mona Washbourne, *Stevie*
Director: Warren Beatty, *Reds*

People's Choice Awards
Favorite Picture: *Raiders of the Lost Ark*
Favorite Movie Actor: Burt Reynolds
Favorite Movie Actress: Sally Field, Jane Fonda
Favorite Young Performer: Brooke Shields

British Academy Awards
Film: *Chariots of Fire*
Actor: Burt Lancaster, *Atlantic City*
Actress: Meryl Streep, *The French Lieutenant's Woman*
Supporting Artist: Ian Holm, *Chariots of Fire*
Director: Louis Malle, *Atlantic City*
Screenplay: Bill Forsyth, *Gregory's Girl*
Robert Flaherty Documentary Award: *Soldier Girls* (Nicholas Broomfield, Joan Churchill, UK)
Academy Fellow: Abel Gance; Michael Powell; Emeric Pressburger
Michael Balcon Award: David Puttnam

***** *Man of Iron* CAN
The sort of film event that festivals live for—an epic about the Polish Solidarity movement, filmed with actual figures of the movement like Lech Walesa, and completed just hours before its Cannes premiere while the Jaruzelski government (shortly to declare martial law) watched nervously. Under the circumstances no festival jury could refuse it the Palme d'Or; but Andrzej Wajda's sequel to his 1977 *Man of Marble* is totally enthralling filmmaking anyway, an anti-Soviet film with all the passion and immediacy of the great Soviet films of the '20s. In a neat reversal of the previous film, which saw a crusading TV journalist investigate the death of a labor leader in a 1970 uprising, a burnt-out hack is sent by the party to produce a hatchet job on the dead man's son, now a Solidarity leader, and becomes our guide to the decade between the two uprisings.

Cannes Film Festival
Palme d'Or: *Man of Iron* (Andrzej Wajda, Poland)
Special Jury Prize: *Light Years Away* (Alain Tanner, Switzerland)
Actor: Ugo Tognazzi, *Tragedy of a Ridiculous Man* (Italy)
Actress: Isabelle Adjani, *Quartet* (UK-France), *Possession* (France-Germany)
Supporting Actor: Ian Holm, *Chariots of Fire* (UK)
Supporting Actress: Elena Solovei, *The Fact/Blood Type O* (USSR)
Screenplay: István Szábo, Peter Dobai, *Mephisto* (Hungary–West Germany)
Artistic Contribution to Poetics

of Cinema: John Boorman, *Excalibur* (UK)

Prize for Contemporary Cinema: *Looks and Smiles* (Ken Loach, (UK), *Neige* [*Snow*] (Juliet Berto, Jean-Henri Roger, France)

Tribute: To Ettore Scola, on the occasion of the premiere of *Passione d'Amore* (Italy)

Camera d'Or: *Desperado City* (Vadim Glowna, West Germany)

Technical Prize: *Les Uns et les Autres* [*Bolero—not* the Bo Derek film] (Claude Lelouch, France), for sound

International Critics Prize: competition, *Mephisto*; Critics' Week, *Malou* (Jeannine Meerapfel, West Germany)

American Critics Prize: *Chariots of Fire* (Hugh Hudson, UK)

Venice Film Festival

Golden Lion: *The German Sisters* (Margarethe von Trotta, West Germany)

Golden Lion/First Film: *Do You Remember Dolly Bell?* (Emir Kusturica, Yugoslavia)

Special Golden Lion: *Sogni d'oro* (Nanni Moretti, Italy), *They Don't Wear Black Tie* (Leon Hirszman, Brazil)

Cinematography: Georgij Rerberg, *Fall of the Stars* (USSR)

Mention for Historical Reconstruction: Anja Breien, *Witch Hunt* (Norway)

Mention: Jiri Menzel, for humor, taste and optimistic vitality, *Cuttings* (Czechoslovakia)

International Critics Prize: *The German Sisters, They Don't Wear Black Tie, Do You Remember Dolly Bell?*

Italian Critics Awards: Pasinetti Prize: *Prince of the City* (Sidney Lumet, USA); actor, Robert

Duvall, *True Confessions*; actress, Lili Terselius, *Witch Hunt*

Berlin Film Festival

Golden Bear: *Deprisa, Deprisa!* [*Hurry Hurry*] (Carlos Saura, Spain)

Silver Bear: *In Search of Famine* (Mrinal Sen, India)

Actor: Jack Lemmon, *Tribute* (USA), Anatoli Solonitsyn, *26 Days in the Life of Dostoevsky* (USSR)

Actress: Barbara Grabowska, *Fever* (Poland)

Screenplay and Direction: Markus Imhoof, *The Boat Is Full* (Switzerland)

Special Jury Mention: *Zigeunerweisen* (Seijun Suzuki, Japan), *The Spacious Land of Alexis Droeven* (Jean-Jacques Andrien, Belgium)

Golden Bear/Short: *History of the World in Three Minutes Flat* (Michael Mill, Canada)

Silver Bear/Short: *On Land, At Sea, and In the Air* (Paul Driessen, The Netherlands)

International Critics Prize: in competition, *The Boat Is Full*; *Köszönöm, megvagyunk* [*I'm All Right*] (Laszlo Lugossy, Hungary); in Forum, *Dialogue With a Woman Departed* (Leo Hurwitz, USA), *Killer of Sheep* (Charles Burnett, USA); tribute to Yilmaz Güney for his work

U.S. Film Festival (Sundance)

Grand Jury Prize: *Heartland* (Richard Pearce), *Gal Young 'Un* (Victor Nuñez)

Special Jury Prize: *Return of the Secaucus Seven* (John Sayles), *The Day After Trinity: J. Robert Oppenheimer and the Atomic Bomb* (Jon Else), *The War at Home* (Glenn Silber, Barry Brown)

Harvard Lampoon **Movie Worsts**
Ten worst pictures:
On Golden Pond
Tarzan, the Ape Man
Superman II
Stripes
History of the World, Part I
The Fox and the Hound
Arthur
Reds
The Great Muppet Caper [NOTE: Lisa Henson was president of the *Lampoon* that year]
Raiders of the Lost Ark
Kirk Douglas Award for Worst Actor: Warren Beatty, *Reds*
Jane Fonda Award for Worst Actress: Katharine Hepburn as the *Creature from the Golden Pond*
The Grouch Oscar (for the worst film performance by a puppet): Miss Piggy, *The Great Muppet Caper*
The Brian DePalma "It Takes a Thief" Award: To Francis Ford Coppola, Alfred Hitchcock, Brian DePalma, Michelangelo Antonioni, Franklin Schaffner, William Friedkin, the Kennedy family, and John Avildsen, all of whom were robbed by Brian DePalma during the making of *Blow Out*

Golden Raspberry Awards
Worst Picture: *Mommie Dearest*
Worst Actor: Klinton Spilsbury, *Legend of the Lone Ranger*
Worst Actress: (tie) Faye Dunaway, *Mommie Dearest*; Bo Derek, *Tarzan, the Ape Man*
Worst Supporting Actor: Steve Forrest, *Mommie Dearest*
Worst Supporting Actress: Diana Scarwid, *Mommie Dearest*
Worst Director: Michael Cimino, *Heaven's Gate*
Worst Screenplay: Frank Yablans, Frank Perry, Tracy Hotchner, Robert Getchell, *Mommie Dearest*
Worst Song: "Baby Talk," *Paternity*
Worst Score: John Barry, *Legend of the Lone Ranger*
Worst New Star: Klinton Spilsbury, *Legend of the Lone Ranger*
Career Achievement Award: Ronald Reagan

Box Office (Domestic Rentals)

1	*Raiders of the Lost Ark*	$90,434,000	Par
2	*Superman II*	64,000,000	WB
3	*Stir Crazy*	58,408,000	Col
4	*9 to 5*	57,850,000	Fox
5	*Stripes*	39,514,000	Col
6	*Any Which Way You Can*	39,500,000	WB
7	*Arthur*	37,000,000	WB
8	*The Cannonball Run*	35,378,000	Fox
9	*The Four Seasons*	26,800,000	Uni
10	*For Your Eyes Only*	25,439,479	MGM/UA
	Other films of note:		
12	*The Fox and the Hound*	18,000,000	Disney
15	*Flash Gordon*	16,100,000	Uni
17	*The Great Muppet Caper*	16,000,000	Uni
18	*Tarzan, the Ape Man*	15,642,396	MGM/UA
20	*Bustin' Loose*	15,300,000	Uni
31	*Halloween II*	10,500,000	Uni

43	*Friday the 13th, Part 2*	10,016,000	Par
53	*Hardly Working*	8,861,000	Fox
103	*Napoleon*	2,500,000	Zoetrope

With Raiders, *Lucas and Spielberg demonstrated that* Star Wars *was no fluke—and that* 1941 *was. Richard Pryor passed Dudley Moore and the Saturday Night Live bunch to rank as the hottest comedian of the moment, while Jerry Lewis managed to attract a respectable audience for a comeback film that billed him as "The Original Jerk." Bo Derek got crowds out for a* Tarzan *picture, but it was so awful—without a doubt the worst film ever released by MGM—that it left a legion of once-burnt—twice-shy fans and turned her instantly from dorm-poster goddess to showbiz punchline. And a silent film "presented" by Francis Ford Coppola managed to break into the lower reaches of the chart—but then Abel Gance's* Napoleon *was accompanied by a full orchestra (conducted by Carmine Coppola), and tickets went at concert-hall, not multiplex prices.*

Gebert's Golden Armchairs

My pick of the best British film of the year wouldn't be a film in the tradition of *Pygmalion* and *Brief Encounter*, like *Chariots*, but a film in the visuals-first—talk-later tradition of Hitchcock and Michael Powell—John Boorman's visionary, occasionally ridiculous, always fascinating Arthur film, *Excalibur*. The summer's best popcorn movie (I mean *Raiders*, not *Clash of the Titans*) looks better than its more serious fellow Oscar contenders—and it contains the best female performance of the year, albeit one given under duress: Karen Allen, fighting Steven Spielberg every step of the way to provide the only liberated female in any of his films.

Best American Film: *Raiders of the Lost Ark*
Best Foreign Film: *Excalibur*
Best Actor: Burt Lancaster, *Atlantic City*
Best Actress: Karen Allen, *Raiders of the Lost Ark*
Best Director: John Boorman, *Excalibur*
Worst Hit: *Tarzan, the Ape Man*

1982

Man of Iron, rushed wet from the lab under the noses of the Jaruzelski regime, had provided seemingly the ultimate example of how determined filmmakers in repressive regimes could be to get their films international exposure at Cannes. But it was topped the next year by the circumstances of Yilmaz Güney's *Yol*. Güney, Turkey's best-known actor-director, had been jailed in 1975 on an apparently trumped-up murder charge, though his popularity and influence were so great that he continued to be able to make films—writing detailed production notes for screenplays which were then shot on the outside by his assistants. That was how *Yol*, a story of five prisoners on furlough which would prove Güney's harshest attack on Turkish society, was shot—and when shooting was completed, his assistant smuggled the raw footage to Switzerland, while Güney escaped from prison and fled the country to edit it and present it at Cannes, where—amid some confusion over who precisely deserved the directorial credit—it won the Palme d'Or.

Academy Awards

*** *Gandhi* AAW GLO DGA NYC BOR BAA
**** **Ben Kingsley** AAW GLO NYC LAC BOR BAA
The Academy would have been truer to itself if it had bitten the bullet and honored Spielberg's *E.T.* for both its magic and its moneymaking. But at the heart of the workmanlike *Gandhi* was a remarkable performance—one of those middle-aged discoveries, like Sydney Greenstreet or Ray McAnally or Robert Prosky, who suddenly appears on screen with a lifetime of experience behind him and instant understanding of the medium, as if he'd been one of the movies' most reliable character actors for years. (Kingsley was actually only 39, but he seemed older.) Now we've seen him all over the place, and some of his tricks are familiar, but if a nobody who effortlessly carries an ambitious and talky 3½-hour epic on his shoulders doesn't rate an Oscar, who would?

Picture
Gandhi (Columbia, Indo-British Films, Richard Attenborough)
E.T. The Extra-Terrestrial (Universal, Steven Spielberg, Kathleen Kennedy)
Missing (Universal, PolyGram, Edward and Mildred Lewis)
Tootsie (Columbia, Mirage/Punch, Sydney Pollack, Dick Richards)
The Verdict (20th Century–Fox, Richard D. Zanuck, David Brown)

Actor
Ben Kingsley, *Gandhi*
Dustin Hoffman, *Tootsie*
Jack Lemmon, *Missing*
Paul Newman, *The Verdict*
Peter O'Toole, *My Favorite Year*

**** Meryl Streep in *Sophie's Choice* AAW GLO NYC SOC LAC BOR
Even a non-fan of Streep's accent parts would have to recognize this as the best of them. A superior soap opera about a damaged Holocaust survivor and her relationship with a self-destructive manic type (an electric Kevin Kline—the last we'd see of him like that until *A Fish Called Wanda*), professionally handled for tasteful tears by old pro Alan J. Pakula.

Actress
Meryl Streep, *Sophie's Choice*
Julie Andrews, *Victor/Victoria*
Jessica Lange, *Frances*
Sissy Spacek, *Missing*
Debra Winger, *An Officer and a Gentleman*

Supporting Actor
Louis Gossett, Jr., *An Officer and a Gentleman*
Charles Durning, *The Best Little Whorehouse in Texas*
John Lithgow, *The World According to Garp*
James Mason, *The Verdict*
Robert Preston, *Victor/Victoria*

Supporting Actress
Jessica Lange, *Tootsie*
Glenn Close, *The World According to Garp*
Teri Garr, *Tootsie*
Kim Stanley, *Frances*

Lesley Ann Warren, *Victor/Victoria*

Director
Richard Attenborough, *Gandhi*
Sidney Lumet, *The Verdict*
Wolfgang Petersen, *Das Boot*
Sydney Pollack, *Tootsie*
Steven Spielberg, *E.T. The Extra-Terrestrial*

Original Screenplay: John Briley, *Gandhi*
Adapted Screenplay: Costa-Gavras, Donald Stewart, *Missing*
Cinematography: Billy Williams, Ronnie Taylor, *Gandhi*
Original Score: John Williams, *E.T. The Extra-Terrestrial*
Song Score: Leslie Bricusse, Henry Mancini, *Victor/Victoria*
Song: "Up Where We Belong," *An Officer and a Gentleman,* m: Jack Nitzsche, Buffy Saint-Marie, l: Will Jennings
Art Direction: Stuart Craig, Bob Laing, *Gandhi*
Costume Design: John Mollo, Bhanu Athaiya, *Gandhi*
Editing: *Gandhi*
Sound: *Gandhi*
Sound Effects Editing: *E.T. The Extra-Terrestrial*
Make-up: *Quest for Fire*
Visual Effects: Carlo Rambaldi, Dennis Muren, *E.T. The Extra-Terrestrial*
Short/Animated: *Tango* (Film Polski, Zbigniew Rybczynski)
Short/Live Action: *A Shocking Accident*
Documentary/Feature: *Just Another Missing Kid* (Canada)
Documentary/Short: *If You Love This Planet* (National Film Board of Canada)
Foreign-Language Film: *Volver a Empezar [To Begin Again]* (Spain)

Jean Hersholt Humanitarian Award: Walter Mirisch
Special Award: Mickey Rooney

Golden Globes
Picture (Drama): *E.T. The Extra-Terrestrial*
Picture (Comedy/Musical): *Tootsie*
Foreign Film: *Gandhi* (UK)
Actor (Drama): Ben Kingsley, *Gandhi*
Actor (Comedy/Musical): Dustin Hoffman, *Tootsie*
Actress (Drama): Meryl Streep, *Sophie's Choice*
Actress (Comedy/Musical): Julie Andrews, *Victor/Victoria*
Supporting Actor: Louis Gossett, Jr., *An Officer and a Gentleman*
Supporting Actress: Jessica Lange, *Tootsie*
Director: Richard Attenborough, *Gandhi*
Screenplay: John Briley, *Gandhi*
Original Score: John Williams, *E.T. The Extra-Terrestrial*
Original Song: "Up Where We Belong," *An Officer and a Gentleman*, m: Jack Nitzsche, Buffy Saint-Marie, l: Will Jennings
New Stars of the Year: Ben Kingsley, *Gandhi*; Sandahl Bergman, *Conan the Barbarian*
Cecil B. DeMille Award: Laurence Olivier

Directors Guild of America
Director: Richard Attenborough, *Gandhi*
D. W. Griffith Award: John Huston
Honorary Lifetime Members: Elia Kazan, Robert Wise

New York Film Critics Circle
Picture: *Gandhi*
Foreign Film: *Time Stands Still*
Actor: Ben Kingsley, *Gandhi*

Actress: Meryl Streep, *Sophie's Choice*
Supporting Actor: John Lithgow, *The World According to Garp*
Supporting Actress: Jessica Lange, *Tootsie*
Director: Sydney Pollack, *Tootsie*
Screenplay: Murray Schisgal, Larry Gelbart, *Tootsie*
Cinematography: Nestor Almendros, *Sophie's Choice*

National Society of Film Critics
Picture: *Tootsie*
Actor: Dustin Hoffman, *Tootsie*
Actress: Meryl Streep, *Sophie's Choice*
Supporting Actor: Mickey Rourke, *Diner*
Supporting Actress: Jessica Lange, *Tootsie*
Director: Steven Spielberg, *E.T. The Extra-Terrestrial*
Screenplay: Murray Schisgal, Larry Gelbart, *Tootsie*
Cinematography: Philippe Rousselot, *Diva*

Los Angeles Film Critics Association
Film: *E.T. The Extra-Terrestrial*
Foreign Film: *The Road Warrior*
Actor: Ben Kingsley, *Gandhi*
Actress: Meryl Streep, *Sophie's Choice*
Supporting Actor: John Lithgow, *The World According to Garp*
Supporting Actress: Glenn Close, *The World According to Garp*
Director: Steven Spielberg, *E.T. The Extra-Terrestrial*
Screenplay: Murray Schisgal, Larry Gelbart, *Tootsie*
Cinematography: Jordan Cronenweth, *Blade Runner*
Music: James Horner and The Bus Boys, *48 HRS.*
Independent/Experimental

Film: *Chan Is Missing* (Wayne Wang)
Special Prize: Carlo Rambaldi

National Board of Review
Best English-Language Film:
Gandhi
The Verdict
Sophie's Choice
An Officer and a Gentleman
Missing
E.T. The Extra-Terrestrial
The World According to Garp
Tootsie
Moonlighting
The Chosen
Best Foreign-Language Film:
Mephisto
Das Boot
Three Brothers
Yol
Siberiade
Actor: Ben Kingsley, *Gandhi*
Actress: Meryl Streep, *Sophie's Choice*
Supporting Actor: Robert Preston, *Victor/Victoria*
Supporting Actress: Glenn Close, *The World According to Garp*
Director: Sidney Lumet, *The Verdict*

People's Choice Awards
Favorite Picture: *E.T. The Extra-Terrestrial*
Favorite Movie Actor: Burt Reynolds
Favorite Movie Actress: Jane Fonda, Katharine Hepburn
Favorite Young Performer: Brooke Shields

British Academy Awards
Film: *Gandhi*
Foreign-Language Film: *Christ Stopped at Eboli* [*Eboli*] (Francesco Rosi, Italy)
Actor: Ben Kingsley, *Gandhi*
Actress: Katharine Hepburn, *On Golden Pond*

Supporting Actor: Jack Nicholson, *Reds*
Supporting Actress: Rohini Hattangandy, *Gandhi*; Maureen Stapleton, *Reds*
Director: Richard Attenborough, *Gandhi*
Screenplay: Costa-Gavras, Donald Stewart, *Missing*
Robert Flaherty Documentary Award: *Burden of Dreams*, Les Blank
Academy Fellow: Andrzej Wajda
Michael Balcon Award: Arthur Wooster

*** *Missing*   CAN HAR
Solid if not groundbreaking Costa-Gavras film, based on a true story of an American father (Jack Lemmon) searching for the truth of what happened to his son in Chile following the U.S.-backed '73 coup there— and meeting with sinister obstruction from U.S. officials. A little *Z* nostalgia for the politically minded Cannes jury that picked this and *Yol*.

*** *Yol*   CAN
A grim, gritty, mature film about five Turkish prisoners on furlough and the things that happen to them on the outside, which serves as an attack both on the military regime in power at that time and, more surprisingly, on the oppression of women in that society.

Cannes Film Festival
Palme d'Or: *Missing* (Costa-Gavras, USA), *Yol* (Yilmaz Güney/Serif Gören, Turkey)
35th Anniversary Prize: Michelangelo Antonioni, for *Identification of a Woman* (Italy)

and for the spirit of search and research and contemporaneity in his work

Special Jury Prize: *La Notte di San Lorenzo* [*The Night of the Shooting Stars*] (Paolo and Vittorio Taviani, Italy)
Actor: Jack Lemmon, *Missing*
Actress: Jadwiga Jankowska-Cieslak, *Another Way* (Hungary)
Director: Werner Herzog, *Fitzcarraldo* (West Germany)
Screenplay: Jerzy Skolimowski, *Moonlighting* (UK)
Artistic Contribution: Bruno Nuytten (cinematography), *Invitation au Voyage* (France)
Camera d'Or: *To Die at 30* (Romain Goupil, France)
Technical Prize: Raoul Coutard (cinematography), *Passion* (France)
International Critics Prize: *Yol*; special awards to *Another Way* (Karoly Makk, Hungary), *Les Fleurs Sauvages* (Jean-Pierre Lefèbvre, Canada)

**** The State of Things   VEN
The state of the art film, circa 1982: unstructured but sharply observed, existential vignettes of a movie crew stuck on location after the money has run out, full of allusions and photographed in stark, Antonioniesque black-and-white. Close to a masterpiece (but so elliptical I hesitate to recommend it indiscriminately); I think it also won because it's the movie that's most like being stuck in a festival town after the festival has ended.

Venice Film Festival
Golden Lion: *The State of Things* (Wim Wenders, West Germany)
Golden Lion/First Film: *Taste of Water* (Orlow Seunke, Holland), *Sciopen* (Luciano Odorisio, Italy)
Special Jury Prize: *Imperative* (Krzysztof Zanussi, West Germany)
Artistic Contribution: Mikhail Ulijanov, star of *Private Life* (USSR)
Italian Critics Awards: Pasinetti Prize: *Imperative*; actor: Max Von Sydow, *Flight of the Eagle* (Sweden); actress, Susan Sarandon, *Tempest* (USA)

*** Veronika Voss   BER
Rainer Werner Fassbinder's first film to win a Berlin Bear—and the last film he completed before his death. A fitting choice in either case, because this tale of a doomed, drug-addicted actress is the protean director's best late-period film, the one that best combines the commercial slickness and cleverness of his later work with the depth of feeling of his great mid-'70s work—no doubt because he identified with his protagonist more than any other recent character.

Berlin Film Festival
Golden Bear: *Veronika Voss* (Rainer Werner Fassbinder, West Germany)
Silver Bear: *Shivers* (Wojciech Marczewski, Poland)
Actor: Michel Piccoli, *A Strange Affair* (France), Stellan Skärsgård, *Den enfaldige mördaren* [*The Simple-Minded Murderer*] (Sweden)
Actress: Katrin Sass, *Bürgschaft für ein Jahr* [*On Probation*] (East Germany)
Director: Mario Monicelli, *The Marquis of Grillo* (Italy)
Screenplay: Zoltán Fábri, *Requiem* (Hungary)

Special Mentions: *Absence of Malice* (Sydney Pollack, USA), *Fellows* (Iskra Babitch, USSR), *The Killing of Angel Street* (Donald Crombie, Australia) **International Critics Prize:** in competition, *Shivers*; in Forum, *Pastorale* (Otar Ioseliani, USSR)

U.S. Film Festival (Sundance)
Grand Jury Prize: *Street Music* (Jenny Bowen)
Special Jury Prize: *The Dozens* (Christine Dall, Randall Conrad), *Killer of Sheep* (Charles Burnett)

Harvard Lampoon Movie Worsts
Ten worst pictures:
Star Trek II: The Wrath of Khan
The Verdict
E.T. The Extra-Terrestrial
Gandhi
An Officer and a Gentleman
Missing
Tootsie
Rocky III
Annie
Conan the Barbarian [NOTE: Conan O'Brien was president of the *Lampoon* that year]
Kirk Douglas Award for Worst Actor: Clint Eastwood, *Firefox*, *Honkytonk Man*

Natalie Wood Award for Worst Actress: Meryl Streep, *Sophie's Choice*. Jonathan Winters could have done a better job with that accent.
The Worst Movie with the Most Number "3's" in the Title Citation: *Friday the 13th Part 3 in 3-D*
The Embarrassing *Lampoon* Graduates Certificate: *Airplane II: The Sequel*, written by two *Lampoon* grads [Note: actually, the writing credits only show one]

Golden Raspberry Awards
Worst Picture: *Inchon!*
Worst Actor: Laurence Olivier, *Inchon!*
Worst Actress: Pia Zadora, *Butterfly*
Worst Supporting Actor: Ed McMahon, *Butterfly*
Worst Supporting Actress: Aileen Quinn, *Annie*
Worst Director: (tie) Ken Annakin, *The Pirate Movie*; Terence Young, *Inchon!*
Worst Screenplay: Robin Moore, Laird Koenig, *Inchon!*
Worst Song: "Pumpin' and Blowin'," *The Pirate Movie*
Worst Score: *The Pirate Movie*
Worst New Star: Pia Zadora, *Butterfly*

Box Office (Domestic Rentals)

1	*E.T. The Extra-Terrestrial*	$187,000,000	Uni
2	*Rocky III*	63,450,045	MGM/UA
3	*On Golden Pond*	63,000,000	Uni
4	*Porky's*	53,500,000	Fox
5	*An Officer and a Gentleman*	52,000,000	Par
6	*The Best Little Whorehouse in Texas*	48,000,000	Uni
7	*Star Trek II: The Wrath of Khan*	40,000,000	Par
8	*Poltergeist*	36,175,949	MGM/UA
9	*Annie*	35,180,855	Col
10	*Chariots of Fire*	27,600,000	WB
	Other films of note:		
12	*First Blood*	24,000,000	Orion

13	*Conan the Barbarian*	23,000,000	Uni
18	*Richard Pryor Live on the Sunset Strip*	18,274,345	Col
25	*Blade Runner*	14,500,000	Ladd Co./WB
26	*The World According to Garp*	14,000,000	WB
	Fast Times at Ridgemont High	14,000,000	Uni
29	*Dead Men Don't Wear Plaid*	12,200,000	Uni
34	*The Road Warrior*	10,500,000	WB
44	*Night Shift*	8,000,000	Ladd Co./WB
54	*Making Love*	6,100,000	Fox
102	*Personal Best*	3,000,000	WB

E.T. *passed* Star Wars *to become the top grosser of all time, and with the Spielberg-produced (and, it was rumored, partly directed)* Poltergeist, *Big Steve became the first guy to land two new movies in the same top ten since Peter Bogdanovich in 1972. Sylvester Stallone, who had so far proven incapable of producing a hit in which he didn't play Rocky Balboa, finally found a new character—from here on, he would just be incapable of producing a hit in which he didn't play either Rocky Balboa or John Rambo. What isn't well-remembered is that Harrison Ford, the late '80s Mr. Versatile, originally had the same problem; he didn't play either Han Solo or Indiana Jones in* Blade Runner, *and as a result the expensive, downbeat sci-fi thriller was a box office disappointment. (And what else could that Schwarzenegger guy ever expect to play besides Conan the Barbarian—comedy?) In the wake of the much-protested* Cruising, *a mini–gay-movie wave (*Making Love, *Robert Towne's* Emmanuelle-*Meets-*Chariots of Fire, Personal Best*) failed to demonstrate that there was a gay audience (maybe they were all lip-syncing to* Annie*).*

Gebert's Golden Armchairs

Of all the movies Quentin Tarantino's mixmaster mind has borrowed from, the one that seems both the most obvious and the least commented upon is *Diner*—Barry Levinson's drama which posited the radical notion that young men actually could and would chatter up a storm about nothing in particular. It's the Anti-*Animal House*—not least because it gave Ellen Barkin a terrific female character to play in the wife who's waiting for feminism to be invented.

Speaking of *Animal House*, the worst hit of the year was John Belushi's last film, in which the *SNL* crowd took their sledgehammers to a clever comic novel, Thomas Berger's *Neighbors*.

Best American Film: *Diner*
Best Foreign Film: *The State of Things*
Best Actor: Ben Kingsley, *Gandhi*
Best Actress: Ellen Barkin, *Diner*
Best Director: Wim Wenders, *The State of Things*
Worst Hit: *Neighbors*

1983

The golden age of foreign films in America was the late 1950s and 1960s, when films like *La Dolce Vita* could show things that Hollywood dared not, and Oscar nominations routinely went to the *Never on Sunday*s and *Z*s of the world. So it may be surprising to learn that the most successful foreign-language film in Oscar history came as late as 1983, when Ingmar Bergman's valedictory *Fanny and Alexander* picked up six nominations, winning four: Cinematography, Art Direction/Set Decoration, Costume Design, and—in a rare attack of quality in this category—Foreign-Language Film. That triumph was preceded by a whole host of prizes from the other groups, of course, but though the film played at Venice, a Golden Lion was not among them—after coming close several times but never quite winning at the big two festivals, the perpetually nervous-stomached Bergman had taken a page from Hollywood, only screening his films out of competition.

Academy Awards

*** *Terms of Endearment*
AAW GLO DGA NYC LAC
**** **Shirley MacLaine** AAW GLO NYC LAC BOR
The good and bad of being a top-drawer TV sensibility transferred to the movies: on the plus side, James L. Brooks' first film has a sharp sense of comic characterization—especially in creating a three-dimensional part for a great, sometimes too-big-for-the-movies middle-aged actress that doesn't descend to the campiness of *The Turning Point* or *Whatever Happened to Madame Sousatzka*. On the minus side, there's no particular sense of movie structure or pacing—it's less a movie than a four-episode Nick at Nite *Mary Tyler Moore Show*

retrospective, followed by the last reel of *Love Story*.

Picture
Terms of Endearment (Paramount, James L. Brooks)
The Big Chill (Columbia, Carson Productions, Michael Shamberg)
The Dresser (Columbia, Goldcrest, Peter Yates)
The Right Stuff (Ladd Company/ Warner Bros., Irwin Winkler, Robert Chartoff)
Tender Mercies (Universal/AFD, EMI, Philip S. Hobel)

*** **Robert Duvall in** *Tender Mercies* AAW GLO NYC LAC
Duvall certainly deserved an Oscar for something, but I'm not sure that alcoholism and a Texas accent truly add up to a richer character than, say, his corrosively cynical and self-destructive cop in *True Confessions* (honored at

Venice the year before)—or if they just add up to an Oscar.

Actor
Robert Duvall, *Tender Mercies*
Michael Caine, *Educating Rita*
Tom Conti, *Reuben, Reuben*
Tom Courtenay, *The Dresser*
Albert Finney, *The Dresser*

Actress
Shirley MacLaine, *Terms of Endearment*
Jane Alexander, *Testament*
Meryl Streep, *Silkwood*
Julie Walters, *Educating Rita*
Debra Winger, *Terms of Endearment*

Supporting Actor
Jack Nicholson, *Terms of Endearment*
Charles Durning, *To Be or Not to Be*
John Lithgow, *Terms of Endearment*
Sam Shepard, *The Right Stuff*
Rip Torn, *Cross Creek*

Supporting Actress
Linda Hunt, *The Year of Living Dangerously*
Cher, *Silkwood*
Glenn Close, *The Big Chill*
Amy Irving, *Yentl*
Alfre Woodard, *Cross Creek*

Director
James L. Brooks, *Terms of Endearment*
Bruce Beresford, *Tender Mercies*
Ingmar Bergman, *Fanny and Alexander*
Mike Nichols, *Silkwood*
Peter Yates, *The Dresser*

Original Screenplay: Horton Foote, *Tender Mercies*
Adapted Screenplay: James L. Brooks, *Terms of Endearment*

Cinematography: Sven Nykvist, *Fanny and Alexander*
Original Score: Bill Conti, *The Right Stuff*
Song Score: Michel Legrand, Alan and Marilyn Bergman, *Yentl*
Song: "Flashdance . . . What a Feeling," *Flashdance,* m: Giorgio Moroder, l: Keith Forsey, Irene Cara
Art Direction: Anna Asp, *Fanny and Alexander*
Costume Design: Marik Vos, *Fanny and Alexander*
Editing: *The Right Stuff*
Sound: *The Right Stuff*
Sound Effects Editing: *The Right Stuff*
Visual Effects: Richard Edlund, Dennis Muren, Ken Ralston, Phil Tippett, *Return of the Jedi*
Short/Animated: *Sundae in New York* (Jimmy Picker)
Short/Live Action: *Boys and Girls*
Documentary/Feature: *He Makes Me Feel Like Dancin'* (Emile Ardolino)
Documentary/Short: *Flamenco at 5:15* (National Film Board of Canada)
Foreign-Language Film: *Fanny and Alexander* (Sweden)
Jean Hersholt Humanitarian Award: M. J. "Mike" Frankovich
Special Award: Hal Roach

Golden Globes
Picture (Drama): *Terms of Endearment*
Picture (Comedy/Musical): *Yentl*
Foreign Film: *Fanny and Alexander* (Sweden)
Actor (Drama): Tom Courtenay, *The Dresser,* Robert Duvall, *Tender Mercies*
Actor (Comedy/Musical): Michael Caine, *Educating Rita*
Actress (Drama): Shirley

MacLaine, *Terms of Endearment*
Actress (Comedy/Musical): Julie Walters, *Educating Rita*
Supporting Actor: Jack Nicholson, *Terms of Endearment*
Supporting Actress: Cher, *Silkwood*
Director: Barbra Streisand, *Yentl*
Screenplay: James L. Brooks, *Terms of Endearment*
Original Score: Giorgio Moroder, *Flashdance*
Original Song: "Flashdance . . . What a Feeling," *Flashdance*, m: Giorgio Moroder, l: Keith Forsey, Irene Cara
Cecil B. DeMille Award: Paul Newman

Directors Guild of America
Director: James L. Brooks, *Terms of Endearment*
D. W. Griffith Award: Orson Welles

***** *Fanny and Alexander*
AAW GLO NYC LAC BOR VEN
Despite the well-deserved Oscars for plushness, the film is no costume romp—this semi-fictionalized version of Bergman's own childhood, in which he turns it into a tale of children kept prisoner by an ogre (his ultrareligious father), has a backbone of cold Scandinavian steel under its well-dressed exterior.

New York Film Critics Circle
Picture: *Terms of Endearment*
Foreign Film: *Fanny and Alexander*
Actor: Robert Duvall, *Tender Mercies*

Actress: Shirley MacLaine, *Terms of Endearment*
Supporting Actor: Jack Nicholson, *Terms of Endearment*
Supporting Actress: Linda Hunt, *The Year of Living Dangerously*
Director: Ingmar Bergman, *Fanny and Alexander*
Screenplay: Bill Forsyth, *Local Hero*
Cinematography: Gordon Willis, *Zelig*

**** *The Night of the Shooting Stars* CAN '82 SOC
The story of an entire Italian village taking it on the lam during the dying days of World War II is turned into a sort of magic-realism fable by the Taviani brothers, whose faux-naïf style is at its most effective here.

National Society of Film Critics
Picture: *The Night of the Shooting Stars*
Actor: Gérard Depardieu, *Danton*, *The Return of Martin Guerre*
Actress: Debra Winger, *Terms of Endearment*
Supporting Actor: Jack Nicholson, *Terms of Endearment*
Supporting Actress: Sandra Bernhard, *King of Comedy*
Director: Paolo and Vittorio Taviani, *The Night of the Shooting Stars*
Screenplay: Bill Forsyth, *Local Hero*
Cinematography: Hiro Narita, *Never Cry Wolf*

Los Angeles Film Critics Association
Film: *Terms of Endearment*
Foreign Film: *Fanny and Alexander*

Actor: Robert Duvall, *Tender Mercies*
Actress: Shirley MacLaine, *Terms of Endearment*
Supporting Actor: Jack Nicholson, *Terms of Endearment*
Supporting Actress: Linda Hunt, *The Year of Living Dangerously*
Director: James L. Brooks, *Terms of Endearment*
Screenplay: James L. Brooks, *Terms of Endearment*
Cinematography: Sven Nykvist, *Fanny and Alexander*
Music: Philip Glass, *Koyaanisqatsi*
Independent/Experimental Film: *So Is This* (Michael Snow)
Special Prize: To the studios which restored and re-released *A Star Is Born* and *The Leopard*

National Board of Review
Best English-Language Film:
Betrayal
Terms of Endearment
Educating Rita
Tender Mercies
The Dresser
The Right Stuff
Testament
Local Hero
The Big Chill
Cross Creek
Yentl
Best Foreign-Language Film:
Fanny and Alexander
The Return of Martin Guerre
La Nuit de Varennes
La Traviata
The Boat People
Actor: Tom Conti, *Reuben, Reuben, Merry Christmas, Mr. Lawrence*
Actress: Shirley MacLaine, *Terms of Endearment*
Supporting Actor: Jack Nicholson, *Terms of Endearment*
Supporting Actress: Linda Hunt, *The Year of Living Dangerously*

Director: James L. Brooks, *Terms of Endearment*

People's Choice Awards
Favorite Picture: *Return of the Jedi*
Favorite Movie Actor: Clint Eastwood, Burt Reynolds
Favorite Movie Actress: Meryl Streep
Favorite Young Performer: Brooke Shields
Favorite Movie Song: "Flashdance," *Flashdance*

British Academy Awards
Film: *Educating Rita*
Foreign-Language Film: *Danton* (Andrzej Wajda, France)
Actor: Michael Caine, *Educating Rita*, Dustin Hoffman, *Tootsie*
Actress: Julie Walters, *Educating Rita*
Supporting Actor: Denholm Elliott, *Trading Places*
Supporting Actress: Jamie Lee Curtis, *Trading Places*
Director: Bill Forsyth, *Local Hero*
Screenplay (Original): Paul Zimmermann, *The King of Comedy*
Screenplay (Adapted): Ruth Prawer Jhabvala, *Heat and Dust*
Robert Flaherty Documentary Award: *Schindler* (Jon Blair, UK)
Academy Fellow: Sir Richard Attenborough
Michael Balcon Award: Colin Young

**** *The Ballad of Narayama*
CAN
The second version of a novel about the awfulness of life in a 19th-century Japanese peasant village, filmed here by the most uncompromisingly serious

of modern Japanese directors, Shohei Imamura. The sort of film which simply steamrollers festival juries—how do you argue *against* the movie in which the son has to carry Mom up the mountain to let her die of exposure, only to have Mom go rolling past him a few minutes later? Powerful and unrelenting, superbly well made, but . . . yow!

Cannes Film Festival

Palme d'Or: *The Ballad of Narayama* (Shohei Imamura, Japan)
Special Jury Prize: *Monty Python's The Meaning of Life* (Terry Jones, UK)
Jury Prize: *A Closed Case* (Mrinal Sen, India)
Actor: Gian Mario Volonté, *The Death of Mario Ricci* (Switzerland)
Actress: Hanna Schygulla, *Storia di Piera* (Italy)
Grand Prize For Creative Filmmaking [in lieu of Best Direction]: Robert Bresson, *L'Argent* (France), Andrei Tarkovsky, *Nostalghia* (Italy)
Camera d'Or: *The Princess* (Pal Erdöss, Hungary)
Technical Prize: *Carmen* (Carlos Saura, Spain)
Artistic Contribution: *Carmen*
International Critics Prize: in competition, *Nostalghia*; Directors' Fortnight, *Daniel Takes a Train* (Pal Sandor, Hungary)

Venice Film Festival

Golden Lion: *First Name: Carmen* (Jean-Luc Godard, France/Switzerland)
Special Jury Prize: *Biquefarre* (Georges Rouquier, France)
Actor: The cast of *Streamers*, Matthew Modine, Michael Wright, Mitchell Lichtenstein,

David Alan Grier, Guy Boyd, George Dzundza (USA)
Actress: Darling Legitimus, *Rue Cases Négres* [*Sugar Cane Alley/Black Shack Alley*] (Martinique-France)
First Film: Euzhan Palcy, *Rue Cases Négres* [*Sugar Cane Alley/Black Shack Alley*]
Technical Achievement: Cinematographer Raoul Coutard, sound engineer François Musy, *First Name: Carmen*
Career Award: Michelangelo Antonioni
International Critics Prize: *Fanny and Alexander* (Ingmar Bergman, Sweden), *Die Macht der Gefühle* [*The Power of Emotion*] (Alexander Kluge, W. Germany)
Italian Critics Awards: Pasinetti Prize: *Zelig* (Woody Allen, USA)

Berlin Film Festival

Golden Bear: *Ascendancy* (Edward Bennett, UK), *The Beehive* (Mario Camus, Spain)
Silver Bear: *A Season in Hakkari* (Erden Kiral, Turkey)
Actor: Bruce Dern, *That Championship Season* (USA)
Actress: Yevgenia Glushenko, *Love by Request* (USSR)
Director: Eric Rohmer, *Pauline at the Beach* (France)
Outstanding Single Achievement: Xaver Schwarzenberger (cinematographer and director), *The Silent Ocean* (Austria)
Special Mentions: *Strange Friends* (Xu Lei, China), *Land of Plenty* (Morten Arnfred, Denmark), *Nothing Left to Lose* (Vadim Glowna, West Germany)
Golden Bear/Short: *Dimensions of Dialogue* (Jan Svankmajer, Czechoslovakia)
International Critics Prize: in competition, *A Season in*

Hakkari, Pauline at the Beach;
Forum, *Ashes and Embers* (Haile
Gerima, USA-Ethiopia), *Busch
Sings* (Konrad Wolf, Rainer
Bredemeyer, East Germany)

U.S. Film Festival (Sundance)

Grand Jury Prize: *Purple Haze*
(David Burton Morris)
Special Jury Prize: *Dream On!*
(Ed Harker), *The Ballad of
Gregorio Cortez*
(Robert M. Young), *Chan Is
Missing* (Wayne Wang)

Harvard Lampoon Movie Worsts

Ten worst pictures:
Silkwood
Terms of Endearment
Mr. Mom
Sudden Impact
National Lampoon's Vacation
Broadway Danny Rose
Return of the Jedi
Twilight Zone: The Movie
Yentl
Flashdance
**Kirk Douglas Award for Worst
Actor:** Al Pacino, *Scarface*
**Natalie Wood Award for Worst
Actress:** Natalie Wood,
Brainstorm
**The Junior High Prom/
Thermonuclear Weaponry
Award:** *War Games*, just a
booming rehash of those Mickey
Rooney/Judy Garland movies,
with the small substitution for
the big barnyard show of global
nuclear apocalypse
**The Eli Yale Award for
Extracurricular Activities:** [Yale
students] Jennifer Beals,
Flashdance; Jodie Foster, *The
Hotel New Hampshire*
**The Title Most Overtly
Evocative of Genitalia While
Retaining a PG Rating Award:**
Octopussy
**The Charles M. Schulz
Overcommercialization
Award:** Stephen King

Golden Raspberry Awards

Worst Picture: *The Lonely Lady*
Worst Actor: Christopher Atkins,
A Night in Heaven
Worst Actress: Pia Zadora, *The
Lonely Lady*
Worst Supporting Actor: Jim
Nabors, *Stroker Ace*
Worst Supporting Actress: Sybil
Danning, *Chained Heat, Hercules*
Worst Director: Peter Sasdy, *The
Lonely Lady*
Worst Screenplay: John
Kershaw, Shawn Randall, *The
Lonely Lady*
Worst Song: "The Way You Do
It," *The Lonely Lady*
Worst Score: Charles Calello,
The Lonely Lady
Worst New Star: Lou Ferrigno,
Hercules
Career Achievement Award:
Irwin Allen

Box Office (Domestic Rentals)

1	*Return of the Jedi*	$165,500,000	Fox
2	*Tootsie*	94,571,613	Col
3	*Trading Places*	40,600,000	Par
4	*War Games*	36,595,975	MGM/UA
5	*Superman III*	36,400,000	WB
6	*Flashdance*	36,180,000	Par
7	*Staying Alive*	33,650,000	Par
8	*Octopussy*	33,203,999	MGM/UA
9	*Mr. Mom*	31,500,000	Fox

10	*48 HRS*	30,328,000	Par
Other films of note:			
11	*National Lampoon's Vacation*	29,500,000	WB
12	*Risky Business*	28,500,000	Geffen/WB
13	*The Verdict*	26,650,000	Fox
14	*Jaws 3-D*	26,439,000	Uni
15	*Never Say Never Again*	25,000,000	WB
18	*Gandhi*	24,364,472	Col
25	*The Big Chill*	16,814,095	Col
	[through 1984:	23,902,000]	
39	*Stroker Ace*	8,834,000	Uni
65	*The Man with Two Brains*	4,600,000	WB

Star Wars III (*or* VI) *became the first trequel (or whatever) to reach #1 (too bad they never made* Jolson Really Belts It Out This Time). *The movie musical wasn't dead—with musicals like* Flashdance *and* Staying Alive, *it just felt that way. Eddie Murphy's first movie,* 48 HRS., *set the pattern for a decade of white-black buddy-cop movies (not to mention movies in which cops crack wise and comedians shoot bad guys); his second one made him the hottest star of his day.* Risky Business *introduced a dazzling, sexy new star—but somehow Rebecca DeMornay never made it big, and it was Tom Cruise who went on to superstardom. With* The Verdict, *Paul Newman proved he could still pack 'em in, long after contemporaries like Hudson and Heston had packed it in, while Roger Moore (#8) actually outgrossed Sean Connery (#15) as dueling Bonds. Steve Martin and Burt Reynolds both seemed to be fading, and a screenwriting machine named John Hughes had back-to-back hits with two of his scripts,* Mr. Mom *and* National Lampoon's Vacation, *earning him the right to direct the next one himself.*

Gebert's Golden Armchairs

Terms of Endearment made money, which is why at the Oscars it coasted easily past the surprise-flop *The Right Stuff*, a hipster epic which is the last great film of the '70s. If Oscar stiffed *Stuff*, it didn't even notice the existence of *King of Comedy*, which looks more brilliant in its dissection of America's celebrity-mania with every passing year—not least because Sandra Bernhard has turned into her character (which makes Madonna Jerry Lewis—somehow, appropriate). How a chilly actor, a clinical director, and a Stephen King story about a zoned-out character added up to such an emotionally affecting piece as David Cronenberg's *The Dead Zone* is one of the small miracles of recent filmmaking. And at least you can say this for *Staying Alive*: it prevented director Sylvester Stallone from making *Saturday Night Fever III*, *IV*, and *V*.

Best American Film: *King of Comedy*
Best Foreign Film: *Fanny and Alexander*
Best Actor: Christopher Walken, *The Dead Zone*
Best Actress: Sandra Bernhard, *King of Comedy*
Best Director: Philip Kaufman, *The Right Stuff*
Worst Hit: *Staying Alive*

1984

If the Best Picture Oscar has gone to only a handful of comedies, comic performances have gotten even less respect—the Grouchos and Bob Hopes of the world can only hope for special awards in their dotage, and even comic actors like Jack Lemmon and Tom Hanks have been more likely to win for serious parts than funny ones. In 1984 the New York Film Critics Circle decided to try to do something about it, voting an out-and-out comic—Steve Martin—the Best Actor prize for his wonderfully dextrous comic turn in *All of Me* as a man, half of whose body is controlled by the spirit of a woman (Lily Tomlin, to be precise). A few days later the semi-overlapping membership of the National Society seconded the prize. And amid much anticipation, a month later the Oscar nominations . . . completely ignored Martin.

Academy Awards

*** *Amadeus* AAW GLO DGA LAC
**** **F. Murray Abraham** AAW GLO LAC
The movie itself is just an amusement park ride through Baroqueland, no more credible than old Hollywood yarns like *A Song to Remember* (though a good deal more entertaining, mainly because it isn't about tuberculosis). But Abraham has the role of a lifetime as mediocrity Antonio Salieri, and surely some of Salieri's keenly felt desperation and carefully stoked envy must have been Abraham's own, knowing that balding middle-aged Arab-American actors don't get more than one chance at the brass ring. . . .

Picture
Amadeus (Orion, Saul Zaentz)
The Killing Fields (Warner Bros., Goldcrest, David Puttnam)
A Passage to India (Columbia, G. W. Films Ltd., John Brabourne, Richard Goodwin)
Places in the Heart (Tri-Star, Arlene Donovan)
A Soldier's Story (Columbia, Caldix)

Actor
F. Murray Abraham, *Amadeus*
Jeff Bridges, *Starman*
Albert Finney, *Under the Volcano*
Tom Hulce, *Amadeus*
Sam Waterson, *The Killing Fields*

** **Sally Field in** *Places in the Heart* AAW GLO
Field is pretty much your basic *Waltons* farm wife in Robert Benton's Pottery Barn version of farm life, reasonably well-crafted but too polite and tasteful by half—until a great ending (sort of borrowed from *Our Town*, but startling and effective all the same). All three

of 1984's unexpected crop of Hollywood farm dramas nabbed Best Actress nominations that year, and not one of them can compare with Richard Pearce's independent Sundance winner *Heartland*—including Pearce's *Country*.

Actress
Sally Field, *Places in the Heart*
Judy Davis, *A Passage to India*
Jessica Lange, *Country*
Vanessa Redgrave, *The Bostonians*
Sissy Spacek, *The River*

Supporting Actor
Haing S. Ngor, *The Killing Fields*
Adolph Caesar, *A Soldier's Story*
John Malkovich, *Places in the Heart*
Noriyuki "Pat" Morita, *The Karate Kid*
Ralph Richardson, *Greystoke: The Legend of Tarzan, Lord of the Apes*

Supporting Actress
Peggy Ashcroft, *A Passage to India*
Glenn Close, *The Natural*
Lindsay Crouse, *Places in the Heart*
Christine Lahti, *Swing Shift*
Geraldine Page, *The Pope of Greenwich Village*

Director
Milos Forman, *Amadeus*
Woody Allen, *Broadway Danny Rose*
Robert Benton, *Places in the Heart*
Roland Joffé, *The Killing Fields*
David Lean, *A Passage to India*

Original Screenplay: Robert Benton, *Places in the Heart*

Adapted Screenplay: Peter Shaffer, *Amadeus*
Cinematography: Chris Menges, *The Killing Fields*
Original Score: Maurice Jarre, *A Passage to India*
Song Score: Prince, *Purple Rain*
Song: "I Just Called to Say I Love You," *The Woman in Red*, ml: Stevie Wonder
Art Direction: Patrizia Von Brandenstein, *Amadeus*
Costume Design: Theodor Pistek, *Amadeus*
Editing: *The Killing Fields*
Sound: *Amadeus*
Sound Effects Editing: *The River*
Make-up: Paul LeBlanc, Dick Smith, *Amadeus*
Visual Effects: Dennis Muren, et al., *Indiana Jones and the Temple of Doom*
Short/Animated: *Charade*
Short/Live Action: *Up* (Pyramid Films, Mike Hoover)
Documentary/Feature: *The Times of Harvey Milk*
Documentary/Short: *The Stone Carvers*
Foreign-Language Film: *Dangerous Moves* (Switzerland)
Jean Hersholt Humanitarian Award: David L. Wolper
Special Awards:
National Endowment for the Arts
James Stewart

Golden Globes
Picture (Drama): *Amadeus*
Picture (Comedy/Musical): *Romancing the Stone*
Foreign Film: *A Passage to India* (UK)
Actor (Drama): F. Murray Abraham, *Amadeus*
Actor (Comedy/Musical): Dudley Moore, *Micki & Maude*
Actress (Drama): Sally Field, *Places in the Heart*
Actress (Comedy/Musical): Kathleen Turner, *Romancing the Stone*

Supporting Actor: Haing S. Ngor, *The Killing Fields*
Supporting Actress: Peggy Ashcroft, *A Passage to India*
Director: Milos Forman, *Amadeus*
Screenplay: Peter Shaffer, *Amadeus*
Original Score: Maurice Jarre, *A Passage to India*
Original Song: "I Just Called to Say I Love You," *The Woman in Red*, ml: Stevie Wonder
Cecil B. DeMille Award: Elizabeth Taylor

Directors Guild of America
Director: Milos Forman, *Amadeus*
D. W. Griffith Award: Billy Wilder
Honorary Lifetime Member: Tom Donovan

*** *A Passage to India* GLO NYC BOR
*** **Peggy Ashcroft** AAW GLO NYC LAC BOR BAA '85
After Lean's career beached itself on megaproductions like *Doctor Zhivago* and *Ryan's Daughter*, he went 14 years before turning out a single final work—a surprisingly unpretentious and witty adaptation of E. M. Forster's novel about a young woman (Judy Davis) unhinged by the mysteries of India, and her commonsense employer (Ashcroft), who in her own quieter way is just as unsettled by the East.

***** **Steve Martin in *All of Me*** NYC SOC
The sight of Martin trying to drag Tomlin's half of his body

to a urinal is as good as anything in *Tootsie*—but maybe because *All of Me*, unlike *Tootsie*, didn't have a message about *relationships*, Oscar didn't bite.

New York Film Critics Circle
Picture: *A Passage to India*
Foreign Film: *A Sunday in the Country*
Actor: Steve Martin, *All of Me*
Actress: Peggy Ashcroft, *A Passage to India*
Supporting Actor: Ralph Richardson, *Greystoke: The Legend of Tarzan, Lord of the Apes*
Supporting Actress: Christine Lahti, *Swing Shift*
Director: David Lean, *A Passage to India*
Screenplay: Robert Benton, *Places in the Heart*
Cinematography: Chris Menges, *The Killing Fields*
Documentary: *The Times of Harvey Milk*

*** *Stranger Than Paradise*
SOC CAN SUN '85
Jim Jarmusch's not-quite-debut film (one earlier film, *Permanent Vacation*, has been quietly forgotten) was no masterpiece, but with its deliberately flat, black-and-white visuals, Downtown retro-trendiness and deadpan sense of humor, it was the first sign of any style in the American independent movement. Weird trivia: it was mostly shot on short ends (bits of leftover film) from Wim Wenders' *The State of Things*—a movie about a movie company shooting on the last of their short ends.

National Society of Film Critics

Picture: *Stranger Than Paradise*
Actor: Steve Martin, *All of Me*
Actress: Vanessa Redgrave, *The Bostonians*
Supporting Actor: John Malkovich, *Places in the Heart*, *The Killing Fields*
Supporting Actress: Melanie Griffith, *Body Double*
Director: Robert Bresson, *L'Argent*
Screenplay: Babaloo Mandel, Lowell Ganz, Bruce Jay Friedman, *Splash*
Cinematography: Chris Menges, *Comfort and Joy*, *The Killing Fields*
Documentary: *Stop Making Sense*

Los Angeles Film Critics Association

Film: *Amadeus*
Foreign Film: *The Fourth Man*
Actor: F. Murray Abraham, *Amadeus*, Albert Finney, *Under the Volcano*
Actress: Kathleen Turner, *Romancing the Stone*
Supporting Actor: Adolph Caesar, *A Soldier's Story*
Supporting Actress: Peggy Ashcroft, *A Passage to India*
Director: Milos Forman, *Amadeus*
Screenplay: Peter Shaffer, *Amadeus*
Cinematography: Chris Menges, *The Killing Fields*
Music: Ennio Morricone, *Once Upon a Time in America*
Independent/Experimental Film: George Kuchar, for his oeuvre
New Generation Prize: Alan Rudolph, writer-director of *Choose Me*
Life Achievement: Rouben Mamoulian
Special Prizes: Andrew Sarris,

for his unique and distinguished contribution to the art of film criticism; François Truffaut, for his extraordinary contribution to world cinema (posthumous)

National Board of Review

Best English-Language Film: *A Passage to India*
Paris, Texas
The Killing Fields
Places in the Heart
Mass Appeal
Country
A Soldier's Story
Birdy
Careful, He Might Hear You
Under the Volcano
Best Foreign-Language Film: *A Sunday in the Country*
Carmen
A Love in Germany
The Fourth Man
The Basileus Quartet
Actor: Victor Banerjee, *A Passage to India*
Actress: Peggy Ashcroft, *A Passage to India*
Supporting Actor: John Malkovich, *Places in the Heart*
Supporting Actress: Sabine Azéma, *A Sunday in the Country*
Director: David Lean, *A Passage to India*

People's Choice Awards

Favorite Picture: *Beverly Hills Cop*
Favorite Movie Actor: Clint Eastwood
Favorite Movie Actress: Meryl Streep

British Academy Awards

Film: *The Killing Fields*
Foreign-Language Film: *Carmen* (Carlos Saura, Spain)
Actor: Dr. Haing S. Ngor, *The Killing Fields*
Actress: Maggie Smith, *A Private Function*

Supporting Actor: Denholm Elliott, *A Private Function*
Supporting Actress: Liz Smith, *A Private Function*
Director: Wim Wenders, *Paris, Texas*
Screenplay (Original): Woody Allen, *Broadway Danny Rose*
Screenplay (Adapted): Bruce Robinson, *The Killing Fields*
Robert Flaherty Documentary Award: *28Up* (Michael Apted, UK)
Academy Fellow: Sir Hugh Greene, Sam Spiegel
Michael Balcon Award: Alan Parker, Alan Marshall

*** *Paris, Texas*   CAN
Old-fashioned and a bit overlong, but absorbing slice of Euro-arty Americana from Wim Wenders and playwright Sam Shepard, giving veteran character actor Harry Dean Stanton a meaty starring role as a Texas drifter heading for reconciliation with his peep-show worker ex-wife (Nastassja Kinski—yeah, I always saw them as a couple, didn't you?)

Cannes Film Festival
Palme d'Or: *Paris, Texas* (Wim Wenders, USA-France-West Germany)
Special Jury Prize: *Diary for My Children* (Marta Mészáros, Hungary)
Actor: Alfredo Landa, Francisco Rabal, *The Holy Innocents* (Spain)
Actress: Helen Mirren, *Cal* (UK-Ireland)
Director: Bertrand Tavernier, *A Sunday in the Country* (France)
Screenplay: Theo Angelopolous, Th. Valtinos, Tonino Guerra, *Voyage to Cytherea* (Greece)
Artistic Contribution: Peter Biziou (cinematography), *Another Country* (UK)
Special Prize: John Huston
Camera d'Or: *Stranger Than Paradise* (Jim Jarmusch, USA)
Technical Prize: *The Element of Crime* (Lars von Trier, Denmark)
International Critics Prize: in competition, *Paris, Texas*, *Voyage to Cytherea*; out of competition, *Memorias do Cacere* (Nelson Pereira dos Santos, Brazil)

** *A Year of the Quiet Sun*
VEN
Shortly after World War II, a middle-aged G.I. without much to go home to (the underrated Scott Wilson) falls for a shrinking-violet Polish widow, but can't convince her to take a chance on love. Sensitive, well-made, but terminally downbeat and low-wattage wallflower-romance, a throwback to '50s and '60s humanist foreign films like *Sundays and Cybèle* from a Polish director (Krzysztof Zanussi) who never quite broke into international ranks like Wajda, Holland, Kieslowski, et al.

Venice Film Festival
Golden Lion: *A Year of the Quiet Sun* (Krzysztof Zanussi, Poland-USA-West Germany)
Special Jury Prize: *Favorites of the Moon* (Otar Ioselliani, France)
Actor: Naseeruddin Shah, *Paar* (India)
Actress: Pascale Ogier, *Full Moon in Paris* (France)
First Film: *Sonatine* (Micheline Lanctot, Canada)

Technical Prize: *Noi tre* (Pupi
Avati, Italy)
International Critics Prize:
Heimat (Edgar Reitz, West
Germany), *Beyond the Walls* (Uri
Barbash, Israel)
Pasinetti Italian Critics Prize:
film: *A Year of the Quiet Sun*;
actor: Fernando Fernán Gómez,
Los Zancos (Spain); actress:
Claudia Cardinale, *Claretta*
(Pasquale Squitieri, Italy)

Berlin Film Festival
Golden Bear: *Love Streams* (John
Cassavetes, USA)
Special Jury Silver Bear: *Funny
Dirty Little War* (Hector Olivera,
Argentina)
Silver Bears: *Le bal* (Ettore
Scola, France/Italy); Monica Vitti
for *Flirt* (Roberto Russo, Italy);
Morgen in Alabama (Norbert
Kückelmann, West Germany);
Rembetico (Costas Ferris,
Greece)
Actor: Albert Finney, *The
Dresser* (UK)
Actress: Inna Churikova, *Front
Romance* (USSR)
International Critics Prize: in
competition, *Love Streams*,
Funny Dirty Little War;

Forum: *Nippon-koku
Furuyashiki-mura* (Shinsuke
Ogawa, Japan)

U.S. Film Festival (Sundance)
Grand Jury Prize: *Old Enough*
(Marisa Silver)
Special Jury Prize: *Last Night at
the Alamo* (Eagle Pennell), *Hero*
(Barney Platts-Mills, UK)

Golden Raspberry Awards
Worst Picture: *Bolero*
Worst Actor: Sylvester Stallone,
Rhinestone
Worst Actress: Bo Derek, *Bolero*
Worst Supporting Actor:
Brooke Shields (with a mustache),
Sahara
Worst Supporting Actress:
Lynn-Holly Johnson, *Where the
Boys Are '84*
Worst Director: John Derek,
Bolero
Worst Screenplay: John Derek,
Bolero
Worst Song: "Drinkenstein,"
Rhinestone
Worst Score: Peter Bernstein,
Elmer Bernstein, *Bolero*
Worst New Star: Olivia D'Abo,
Bolero, Conan the Destroyer

Box Office (Domestic Rentals)

1	*Ghostbusters*	$127,000,000	Col
2	*Indiana Jones and the Temple of Doom*	109,000,000	Par
3	*Gremlins*	78,500,000	WB
4	*Beverly Hills Cop*	58,000,000	Par
	[through 1985:	108,000,000]	
5	*Terms of Endearment**	50,250,000	Par
6	*The Karate Kid*	41,700,000	Col
7	*Star Trek III: The Search for Spock*	39,000,000	Par
8	*Police Academy*	38,500,000	WB
9	*Romancing the Stone*	36,000,000	Fox
10	*Sudden Impact**	34,600,000	WB
	Other films of note:		
11	*Footloose*	34,000,000	Par
	Splash	34,000,000	Touchstone

*Includes 1983 revenues

13	*Purple Rain*	32,000,000	WB
17	*Tightrope*	22,500,000	WB
18	*2010*	20,000,000	MGM/UA
19	*Yentl*	19,630,000	MGM/UA
20	*Revenge of the Nerds*	19,500,000	Fox
21	*Bachelor Party*	19,070,000	Fox
25	*The Terminator*	17,000,000	Orion
30	*Dune*	14,000,000	Uni
48	*Starman*	10,000,000	Col

When sci-fi special effects extravaganzas like Starman *and* Dune *suddenly go stale at the box office, who ya gonna call? A bunch of* Saturday Night Live *comedians to give us a whole new genre, the special effects comedy epic. The Hollywood musical—still dead, with* Purple Rain *and* Footloose *showing more life than Babs'* Yentl *(or* Tootsie on the Roof, *as it was inevitably dubbed). Nevertheless, with* Footloose *following in the lumbering steps of* Saturday Night Fever *and* Flashdance, *people started talking about "the Paramount musical" as a subgenre and Paramount as the hottest studio in town—just as its guiding lights, Barry Diller and Michael Eisner, departed. And who'd have guessed that the future held two Oscars in store for Tom Hanks, the lightly talented, reasonably pleasant, passably good-looking new star of* Splash *and—remember this one?—* Bachelor Party, *from the writing team that also gave us* Police Academy?

Gebert's Golden Armchairs

The Terminator's $7 million budget wouldn't have bought one big explosion on a picture like *The Last Action Hero* or *Waterworld*—or its own sequel. Without money you have to rely on the old B-movie virtues of narrative economy, clever plotting and relentless drive, and James Cameron's first (modest) hit is a textbook example—there aren't twenty wasted seconds in the whole picture. Alan Rudolph's wry comedy about the wounded in the love wars, *Choose Me*, is the best of that Altman protegé's dozen or so films, with a great been-around-the-block performance by Lesley Ann Warren (love that *Graduate*-parody last shot). Worst hit: Burt drags Clint down to his level in a grisly comedy-gangster thing—*Dirty Harry Meets Lucky Lady*.

Best American Film: *The Terminator*
Best Foreign Film: *A Passage to India*
Best Actor: Steve Martin, *All of Me*
Best Actress: Lesley Ann Warren, *Choose Me*
Best Director: James Cameron, *The Terminator*
Worst Hit: *City Heat*

1985

The perpetual rivalry between the Paulettes and the Sarrisites for control of the two New York critics' groups exploded into open nastiness at the National Society of Film Critics meeting in January—one of those literary feuds that become cocktail talk for weeks in New York and are of absolutely no consequence to the rest of the world.

The issue was Claude Lanzmann's 8½-hour Holocaust documentary *Shoah* for Best Film. For Pauline Kael, a critic whose highest artistic ideals were intimately bound up with moviegoing pleasure, a film which demanded such attention and patience—and which is, it must be admitted, deliberately slow and repetitive—left her feeling like Huck Finn in school on a beautiful day for fishing. She wrote a dismissive review (which a nervous *New Yorker* sat on for several weeks before sneaking it out in the issue between Christmas and New Year's). When *Shoah* was proposed for Best Film, Kael was one of several to impatiently remind its partisans that there *was* also a Best Documentary category, thank you, and *Shoah* would do just fine there.

Shoah partisans in turn made it clear that they regarded a vote for anything else as a sign of moral bankruptcy. This was war for the Paulettes—for thirty years they'd fought the battle of style over content against the Crowthers of the world, and damned if they'd be shamed into supporting something they didn't like now, just because it had important subject matter. By the third ballot, they were half-sarcastically touting *Pee-wee's Big Adventure* for Best Film—the ultimate insult, as related by Sarrisite J. Hoberman in a tell-all piece in the *Village Voice* a few weeks later that stopped just shy of accusing Kael of anti-Semitism. (Actually, there's high irony in that coming from Hoberman, probably the most dedicated auteurist of the French school in America—since one can easily imagine him at a Critics Circle meeting in the '60s, giving Bosley Crowther apoplexy by suggesting that *The Nutty Professor* was better than *Judgment at Nuremberg*.) In the end, the Paulettes narrowly won out; *Ran* won best film—and *Shoah* easily won Best Documentary.

Academy Awards

*** *Out of Africa* AAW GLO
Events in the early life of the
writer Isak Dinesen (Meryl
Streep), depicting her decision
to marry and settle on a coffee
plantation in Africa, and her
romance with a British flier,
Denis Finch-Hatton (played,
with absolutely no attempt at
Britishness, by Robert
Redford). Handsome and
intelligent, but careful rather
than passionate filmmaking,
aiming at prestige more than
romance—and ever so faintly
dull.

Picture
Out of Africa (Universal, Sydney
Pollack)
The Color Purple (Warner Bros.,
Steven Spielberg, Kathleen
Kennedy, Frank Marshall, Quincy
Jones)
Kiss of the Spider Woman (Island
Alive, H.B. Filmes/Sugarloaf,
David Weisman)
Prizzi's Honor (20th
Century–Fox, ABC Motion
Pictures, John Foreman)
Witness (Paramount, Edward S.
Feldman)

***** William Hurt in *Kiss of
the Spider Woman* AAW
LAC BOR BAA**
The whitest actor in Hollywood
adopts an orange rinse and a
lisping mince to play a Brazilian
hairdresser sharing a jail cell
with a revolutionary, and the
flamboyance and pathos make
him interesting and sympathetic

in a way he'd never been
before. Who knew that inside
Woody Harrelson, Julie Harris
was struggling to get out?

Actor
**William Hurt, *Kiss of the Spider
Woman***
Harrison Ford, *Witness*
James Garner, *Murphy's Romance*
Jack Nicholson, *Prizzi's Honor*
Jon Voight, *Runaway Train*

***** Geraldine Page in *The
Trip to Bountiful* AAW IND**
Horton Foote's 1950s teleplay
about an old woman going to
visit what's left of her old home
town. A sweet piece, if jes' a
li'l ol' bit heavy on the Texas
caricatures; Page (finally
winning an Oscar on her eighth
try, the female record) is sort
of like Barry Fitzgerald in
Going My Way—such a high-
powered actress playing such an
ordinary person that the tricks
can't help but show, but
affecting nonetheless.

Actress
**Geraldine Page, *The Trip to
Bountiful***
Anne Bancroft, *Agnes of God*
Whoopi Goldberg, *The Color
Purple*
Jessica Lange, *Sweet Dreams*
Meryl Streep, *Out of Africa*

Supporting Actor
Don Ameche, *Cocoon*
Klaus Maria Brandauer, *Out of
Africa*
William Hickey, *Prizzi's Honor*
Robert Loggia, *Jagged Edge*
Eric Roberts, *Runaway Train*

Supporting Actress
Anjelica Huston, *Prizzi's Honor*
Margaret Avery, *The Color Purple*
Amy Madigan, *Twice in a Lifetime*
Meg Tilly, *Agnes of God*
Oprah Winfrey, *The Color Purple*

Director
Sydney Pollack, *Out of Africa*
Hector Babenco, *Kiss of the Spider Woman*
John Huston, *Prizzi's Honor*
Akira Kurosawa, *Ran*
Peter Weir, *Witness*

Original Screenplay: Earl W. Wallace, William Kelley; story by William Kelley, Pamela Wallace, Earl W. Wallace, *Witness*
Adapted Screenplay: Kurt Luedtke, *Out of Africa*
Cinematography: David Watkin, *Out of Africa*
Score: John Barry, *Out of Africa*
Song: "Say You, Say Me," *White Nights*, ml: Lionel Richie
Art Direction: Stephen Grimes, *Out of Africa*
Costume Design: Emi Wada, *Ran*
Editing: *Witness*
Sound: *Out of Africa*
Sound Effects Editing: *Back to the Future*
Make-up: *Mask*
Visual Effects: *Cocoon*
Short/Animated: *Anna & Bella* (Cilia Van Dijk)
Short/Live Action: *Molly's Pilgrim*
Documentary/Feature: *Broken Rainbow*
Documentary/Short: *Witness to War: Dr. Charlie Clements*
Foreign-Language Film: *The Official Story* (Argentina)
Jean Hersholt Humanitarian Award: Charles "Buddy" Rogers
Special Awards: Paul Newman Alex North, in recognition of his

brilliant artistry in the creation of memorable music
John H. Whitney, for cinematic pioneering [computer animation]

Golden Globes
Picture (Drama): *Out of Africa*
Picture (Comedy/Musical): *Prizzi's Honor*
Foreign Film: *The Official Story* (Argentina)
Actor (Drama): Jon Voight, *Runaway Train*
Actor (Comedy/Musical): Jack Nicholson, *Prizzi's Honor*
Actress (Drama): Whoopi Goldberg, *The Color Purple*
Actress (Comedy/Musical): Kathleen Turner, *Prizzi's Honor*
Supporting Actor: Klaus Maria Brandauer, *Out of Africa*
Supporting Actress: Meg Tilly, *Agnes of God*
Director: John Huston, *Prizzi's Honor*
Screenplay: Woody Allen, *The Purple Rose of Cairo*
Original Score: John Barry, *Out of Africa*
Original Song: "Say You, Say Me," *White Nights*, ml: Lionel Richie
Cecil B. DeMille Award: Barbara Stanwyck

Directors Guild of America
Director: Steven Spielberg, *The Color Purple*
D. W. Griffith Award: Joseph L. Mankiewicz

*** Jack Nicholson in *Prizzi's Honor* GLO NYC SOC
Nicholson plays a thick-witted mobster, and his change of pace is amusing—but Clever Jack is the last person you would have cast as William Bendix if he weren't a big star,

and award groups are too ready to honor big stars simply for playing against type.

New York Film Critics Circle
Picture: *Prizzi's Honor*
Foreign Film: *Ran*
Actor: Jack Nicholson, *Prizzi's Honor*
Actress: Norma Aleandro, *The Official Story*
Supporting Actor: Klaus Maria Brandauer, *Out of Africa*
Supporting Actress: Anjelica Huston, *Prizzi's Honor*
Director: John Huston, *Prizzi's Honor*
Screenplay: Woody Allen, *The Purple Rose of Cairo*
Cinematography: David Watkin, *Out of Africa*
Documentary: *Shoah*

***** *Ran*   AAW NYC SOC LAC BOR BAA '86
Akira Kurosawa's recasting of *King Lear* as a struggle between an old shogun and three samurai sons, the main troublemaker egged on Macbeth-like by his power-mad wife (Mieko Harada, in a tour-de-force performance). A dazzling fusion of brilliant color and overwhelming drama, filmed with imperial command of the art form by a great director as the summation of his work—and perhaps the one lasting masterpiece of recent years.

National Society of Film Critics
Picture: *Ran*
Actor: Jack Nicholson, *Prizzi's Honor*

Actress: Vanessa Redgrave, *Wetherby*
Supporting Actor: John Gielgud, *Plenty, The Shooting Party*
Supporting Actress: Anjelica Huston, *Prizzi's Honor*
Director: John Huston, *Prizzi's Honor*
Screenplay: Albert Brooks, Monica Johnson, *Lost in America*
Cinematography: Takao Saito, *Ran*
Documentary: *Shoah*

Los Angeles Film Critics Association
Film: *Brazil*
Foreign Film: *Ran, The Official Story*
Actor: William Hurt, *Kiss of the Spider Woman*
Actress: Meryl Streep, *Out of Africa*
Supporting Actor: John Gielgud, *Plenty, The Shooting Party*
Supporting Actress: Anjelica Huston, *Prizzi's Honor*
Director: Terry Gilliam, *Brazil*
Screenplay: Terry Gilliam, Tom Stoppard, Charles McKeown, *Brazil*
Cinematography: David Watkin, *Out of Africa*
Music: Toru Takemitsu, *Ran*
Independent/Experimental Film: *Fear of Emptiness* (Rosa von Praunheim)
New Generation Prize: Laura Dern, actress in *Mask, Smooth Talk*
Life Achievement: Akira Kurosawa
Special Citation: *Shoah*

** *The Color Purple*   DGA BOR
*** *Whoopi Goldberg*   GLO BOR
Boy Wonder Spielberg's first attempt to make a "grown-

up" movie is actually a good deal more juvenile than *The Sugarland Express*, *Jaws*, or *Close Encounters*—blowing up Alice Walker's South into a big Hallmark card, handling the lesbian angle with kid gloves, and meandering as aimlessly as *Giant*. Goldberg's performance has a world of warmth to it, but the frame it's in is feelgood pandering.

National Board of Review
Best English-Language Film:
The Color Purple
Out of Africa
The Trip to Bountiful
Witness
Kiss of the Spider Woman
Prizzi's Honor
Back to the Future
The Shooting Party
Blood Simple
Dreamchild
Best Foreign-Language Film:
Ran
The Official Story
When Father Was Away on Business
La Chèvre
The Home and the World
Actor: Raul Julia, William Hurt, *Kiss of the Spider Woman*
Actress: Whoopi Goldberg, *The Color Purple*
Supporting Actor: Klaus Maria Brandauer, *Out of Africa*
Supporting Actress: Anjelica Huston, *Prizzi's Honor*
Director: Akira Kurosawa, *Ran*

People's Choice Awards
Picture: *Back to the Future*
Movie Actor: Sylvester Stallone
Movie Actress: Meryl Streep

British Academy Awards
Film: *The Purple Rose of Cairo*
Foreign-Language Film:

Colonel Redl (István Szabó, Hungary West Germany)
Actor: William Hurt, *Kiss of the Spider Woman*
Actress: Peggy Ashcroft, *A Passage to India*
Supporting Actor: Denholm Elliott, *Defence of the Realm*
Supporting Actress: Rosanna Arquette, *Desperately Seeking Susan*
Screenplay (Original): Woody Allen, *The Purple Rose of Cairo*
Screenplay (Adapted): Richard Condon, Janet Roach, *Prizzi's Honor*
Academy Fellow: Jeremy Isaacs
Michael Balcon Award: Sydney Samuelson
Special Award: Dilys Powell

**** ***When Father Was Away on Business*** CAN
A delightful dark horse winner at Cannes that sent the international press scrambling to find someone who'd actually *seen* it during the festival. It's mid-'50s Yugoslavia, and the business Father is away on is actually a jail term. The movie gives us a child's-eye view of the period, while also providing an adult's sardonic perspective on its excesses (as when the nervous boy accidentally mangles a Youth League speech, causing Dad to be grilled over the doctrinal implications of saying "The People are Tito" rather than "Tito is the People").

Cannes Film Festival
Palme d'Or: *When Father Was Away on Business* (Emir Kusturica, Yugoslavia)
Special Jury Prize: *Birdy* (Alan Parker, USA)

Jury Prize: *Colonel Redl* (István Szábo, Hungary-West Germany-Austria)
Actor: William Hurt, *Kiss of the Spider Woman* (USA)
Actress: Norma Aleandro, *The Official Story* (Argentina), Cher, *Mask* (USA)
Director: André Téchiné, *Rendez-Vous* (France)
Artistic Contribution: John Bailey (visual concept), Eiko Ishioka (production design), Philip Glass (musical score), *Mishima* (USA)
Career Achievement: James Stewart
Camera d'Or: *Oriane* (Fina Torres, Venezuela)
Technical Prize: *Insignificance* (Nicolas Roeg, UK)
International Critics Prize: in competition, *When Father Was Away on Business*; out of competition, *The Purple Rose of Cairo* (Woody Allen, USA), *Visages de femme* (Desiré Ecaré, Ivory Coast)

Venice Film Festival
Golden Lion: *Sans toit ni loi* [*Vagabond*] (Agnès Varda, France)
Special Jury Grand Prize: *Tangos: the Exile of Gardel* (Fernando Solanas, France-Argentina)
Special Jury Prize: *The Lightship* (Jerzy Skolimowski, USA)
Silver Lion/Actor: Gérard Depardieu, *Police* (France)
Special Mentions/Actress [no Silver Lion awarded]: Themis Bazaka, *The Stone Years* (Greece), Galya Novents, *Childhood Tango* (USSR), Sonja Savic, *Life Is Beautiful* (Yugoslavia)
First Film: *Dust* (Marion Hänsel, Belgium)
Special Golden Lions/Career Awards: Manoel de Oliveira, John Huston

Biennale Golden Lion/Career Award: Federico Fellini
International Critics Prize: in competition, *Sans toit ni loi* [*Vagabond*], out of competition, *Yesterday* (Radoslaw Piwowarsky, Poland)
Pasinetti Italian Critics Prize: film: *Tangos: the Exile of Gardel*; actor: Robert Duvall, *The Lightship*; actress: Barbara De Rossi, *Mamma Ebe* (Italy)

*** *Wetherby* BER
This intelligent example of the Glum Talky British Drama, from playwright-turned-director David Hare (*Plenty*), is a good showcase for Vanessa Redgrave as a woman trying to figure out why a very casual acquaintance blew his brains out in her kitchen, and remembering her own lost youthful lover (it's no *The Dead*, though).

Berlin Film Festival
Golden Bear: *Wetherby* (David Hare, UK), *Die Frau und der Fremde* (Rainer Simon, East Germany) (shared)
Silver Bear: *Flowers of Reverie* (Laszlo Lugossy, Hungary)
Actor: Fernando Fernán Gómez, *Stico* (Spain)
Actress: Jo Kennedy, *Wrong World* (Australia)
Director: Robert Benton, *Places in the Heart* (USA)
Outstanding Individual Contribution: Tolomush Okeyev, art direction, *The Descendant of the Snow Leopard* (USSR/Kirghiz)
Film of Outstanding Imagination: *Ronja rövardotter* (Tage Danielsson, Sweden)
Special Mention: *The Children* (Marguerite Duras, France);

Tarik Akan (actor), *The Wrestler*
(Turkey); Damiano Damiani,
The Pizza Connection (Italy)
International Critics Prize: in
competition, *Tokyo Saiban*
(Masaki Kobayashi, Japan); out of
competition, *Secret Honor*
(Robert Altman, USA), *Cabra
marcado para morrer* (Eduardo
Countinho, Brazil)

*** *Blood Simple* SUN
The Coen Bros.' first feature is an
outlandishly stylish, tongue-in-
cheek film student's idea of film
noir—the granddaddy of
*Reservoir Dogs, The Last
Seduction*, etc. Though if Sundance
really wanted to honor inventive,
stylish independent filmmaking
with a personal artistic vision, they
would have given a Grand Jury
Prize to a film by a buddy of the
Coens who worked on *Blood
Simple*—Sam Raimi's *Evil Dead
2*.

**U.S. Film Festival
(Sundance)**
Grand Jury Prize: *Blood Simple*
(Joel Coen)
Special Jury Prize: *The Brother
from Another Planet* (John Sayles),
Stranger Than Paradise (Jim
Jarmusch), *The Roommate* (Nell
Cox)

Independent Spirit Awards
Film: *After Hours*
Foreign Film: *Kiss of the Spider
Woman*
Actor: M. Emmet Walsh, *Blood
Simple*
Actress: Geraldine Page, *The Trip
to Bountiful*
Director: Joel Coen, *Blood Simple*,
Martin Scorsese, *After Hours*
Screenplay: Horton Foote, *The
Trip to Bountiful*
Cinematography: Toyomichi
Kurita, *Trouble in Mind*

Golden Raspberry Awards
Worst Picture: *Rambo: First
Blood Part II*
Worst Actor: Sylvester Stallone,
Rambo: First Blood Part II,
Rocky IV
Worst Actress: Linda Blair, *Night
Patrol, Savage Island, Savage
Streets*
Worst Supporting Actor: Rob
Lowe, *St. Elmo's Fire*
Worst Supporting Actress:
Brigitte Nielsen-Stallone, *Rocky IV*
Worst Director: Sylvester
Stallone, *Rocky IV*
Worst Screenplay: Sylvester
Stallone, James Cameron,
Rambo: First Blood Part II
Worst Song: "Peace in Our
Life," *Rambo II*
Worst Score: Vince DiCola, Bill
Conti, *Rocky IV*
Worst New Star: Brigitte
Nielsen-Stallone, *Rocky IV, Red
Sonja*
Career Achievement Award:
Scream Queen Linda Blair

Box Office (Domestic Rentals)

1	*Back to the Future*	$94,000,000	Uni
2	*Rambo: First Blood Part II*	80,000,000	Tri-Star
3	*Rocky IV*	65,000,000	MGM/UA
4	*Beverly Hills Cop* [1985 only]	50,000,000	Par
	[through 1985:	108,000,000]	
5	*Cocoon*	40,000,000	Fox
6	*The Goonies*	29,900,000	WB

7	*Witness*	28,000,000	Par
8	*Police Academy 2*	27,200,000	WB
9	*National Lampoon's European Vacation*	25,600,000	WB
10	*A View to a Kill*	25,200,000	MGM/UA

Other films of note:

11	*Fletch*	23,923,119	Uni
12	*Spies Like Us*	23,000,000	WB
13	*Pale Rider*	20,800,000	WB
17	*Pee-wee's Big Adventure*	18,100,000	WB
19	*Mad Max Beyond Thunderdome*	17,900,000	WB
21	*The Breakfast Club*	17,254,091	Uni
24	*St. Elmo's Fire*	16,343,197	Col
27	*Amadeus [1985 only]*	13,800,000	Saul Zaentz
	[through 1985:	22,825,938]	
31	*Teen Wolf*	12,873,723	Atlantic
42	*Weird Science*	9,477,917	Uni

Spielberg proved that he could also spawn hits as a producer with the delightful Back to the Future *and the painful* Goonies—*not to mention spawn imitations with Ron Howard's letter-perfect* Cocoon. *Sylvester Stallone managed the remarkable feat of being the top box office star in America at the same time that no one in America would have admitted to liking him or his movies. (Hang in there, Sly, some day the French will make it up to you.—Jerry) But if Sly couldn't manage to broaden his appeal, Harrison Ford finally did with a non–Indy-or-Han romantic thriller part,* Witness. *And amid all the gross-out comedies, there appeared a surprising mini-wave of youth chatfests inspired by* The Big Chill—The Breakfast Club, St. Elmo's Fire, *and* The Sure Thing.

Gebert's Golden Armchairs

Not a stellar year in Hollywood—hell, on another day *I* might vote for *Pee-wee's Big Adventure*—but Albert Brooks' *Lost in America* will likely have a place as one of the quintessential '80s films, to yuppies what *The Apartment* was to Organization Men. Klaus Maria Brandauer got an Oscar nomination for his two supporting roles in *Out of Africa*, but the dynamic German actor was best served full intensity in Istvan Szabo's crisp true-life tale of an Austro-Hungarian double agent (sort of *Mayerling* crossed with *The Conformist*). And the worst hit was a gooey Steven Spielberg–produced ripoff of himself with a cast of unspeakable brats (several of whom have, amazingly, gone on to later careers—if you can call Corey Feldman's a career).

Best American Film: *Lost in America*
Best Foreign Film: *Ran*
Best Actor: Klaus Maria Brandauer, *Colonel Redl*
Best Actress: Mieko Harada, *Ran*
Best Director: Akira Kurosawa, *Ran*
Worst Hit: *The Goonies*

1986

Like *Apocalypse Now*, *The Mission* arrived at Cannes as a "work in progress"—and like *Apocalypse Now*, it left with a Palme d'Or, which was almost immediately followed by rumors, spread by the European producer of a competing film in particular, that the prize had been all-but-guaranteed to the Roland Joffé film before the festival even began. Producer David Puttnam angrily denied this to the authors of the Cannes history *Hollywood on the Riviera*, saying (with some justice) that "The idea of bribing ten people plus [jury head] Sydney Pollack is so ludicrous as to be a joke." But it would also be ludicrous to deny that politics is ever in the air at Cannes. *The Mission* benefited from the accumulated prestige of Puttnam, star Robert De Niro, and director Joffé's previous *The Killing Fields* . . . and the desire, after several years of mostly obscure European winners, to accommodate Hollywood by picking something, *anything* more commercial than Tarkovsky's *The Sacrifice*.

Academy Awards

*** *Platoon*   AAW GLO DGA IND
After the high-flying artiness of *Apocalypse Now*, *The Deer Hunter*, et al., a welcome return to a realistic grunt's-eye-view of the Vietnam War—and also, one suspects, a welcome return to the clear lines between the good guys and the bad guys of World War II movies, which made it easier for Academy types to handle.

Picture
Platoon (Orion, Hemdale, Arnold Kopelson)
Children of a Lesser God (Paramount, Burt Sugarman, Patrick Palmer)
Hannah and Her Sisters (Orion, Rollins-Joffe, Robert Greenhut)
The Mission (Warner Bros.,

Goldcrest, Fernando Ghia, David Puttnam)
A Room with a View (Cinecom, Merchant Ivory)

*** **Paul Newman in *The Color of Money***   AAW BOR
A life-achievement Oscar for then–six-time-loser Newman; he's quite good, but given its pedigree (a sequel to *The Hustler* written by Richard Price and directed by Martin Scorsese), the movie should have been *great*—not just better than *Cocktail*.

Actor
Paul Newman, *The Color of Money*
Dexter Gordon, *'Round Midnight*
Bob Hoskins, *Mona Lisa*
William Hurt, *Children of a Lesser God*
James Woods, *Salvador*

*** **Marlee Matlin in *Children of a Lesser God*** AAW GLO
The first actual handicapped person to win an Oscar since Harold Russell (as well as the youngest Best Actress winner ever), Matlin had a further Oscar advantage in a stereotype-breaking part as a feisty, sexually aware deaf person. That said, the rather conventional material is not as good as *The Piano* (or that much better than *Johnny Belinda*) and she does not have Hunter's range or variety of expression.

Actress
Marlee Matlin, *Children of a Lesser God*
Jane Fonda, *The Morning After*
Sissy Spacek, *Crimes of the Heart*
Kathleen Turner, *Peggy Sue Got Married*
Sigourney Weaver, *Aliens*

Supporting Actor
Michael Caine, *Hannah and Her Sisters*
Tom Berenger, *Platoon*
Willem Dafoe, *Platoon*
Denholm Elliott, *A Room With a View*
Dennis Hopper, *Hoosiers*

Supporting Actress
Dianne Wiest, *Hannah and Her Sisters*
Tess Harper, *Crimes of the Heart*
Piper Laurie, *Children of a Lesser God*
Mary Elizabeth Mastrantonio, *The Color of Money*
Maggie Smith, *A Room With a View*

Director
Oliver Stone, *Platoon*
Woody Allen, *Hannah and Her Sisters*

James Ivory, *A Room With a View*
Roland Joffé, *The Mission*
David Lynch, *Blue Velvet*

Original Screenplay: Woody Allen, *Hannah and Her Sisters*
Adapted Screenplay: Ruth Prawer Jhabvala, *A Room With a View*
Cinematography: Chris Menges, *The Mission*
Score: Herbie Hancock, *'Round Midnight*
Song: "Take My Breath Away," *Top Gun*, m: Giorgio Moroder, l: Tom Whitlock
Art Direction: Gianni Quaranta, Brian Ackland-Snow, *A Room With a View*
Costume Design: Jenny Beavan, John Bright, *A Room With a View*
Editing: *Platoon*
Sound: *Platoon*
Sound Effects Editing: *Aliens*
Make-up: Chris Walas, Stephan Dupuis, *The Fly*
Visual Effects: Stan Winston, *Aliens*
Short/Animated: *A Greek Tragedy*
Short/Live Action: *Precious Images* (Chuck Workman)
Documentary/Feature: *Artie Shaw: Time Is All You've Got*; *Down and Out in America* (tie)
Documentary/Short: *Women—For America, for the World*
Foreign-Language Film: *The Assault* (The Netherlands)
Irving G. Thalberg Award: Steven Spielberg
Special Award: Ralph Bellamy

Golden Globes
Picture (Drama): *Platoon*
Picture (Comedy/Musical): *Hannah and Her Sisters*
Foreign Film: *The Assault* (The Netherlands)
Actor (Drama): Bob Hoskins, *Mona Lisa*

Actor (Comedy/Musical): Paul Hogan, *"Crocodile" Dundee*
Actress (Drama): Marlee Matlin, *Children of a Lesser God*
Actress (Comedy/Musical): Sissy Spacek, *Crimes of the Heart*
Supporting Actor: Tom Berenger, *Platoon*
Supporting Actress: Maggie Smith, *A Room With a View*
Director: Oliver Stone, *Platoon*
Screenplay: Robert Bolt, *The Mission*
Original Score: Ennio Morricone, *The Mission*
Original Song: "Take My Breath Away," *Top Gun*, m: Giorgio Moroder, l: Tom Whitlock
Cecil B. DeMille Award: Anthony Quinn

Directors Guild of America
Director: Oliver Stone, *Platoon*
D. W. Griffith Award: Elia Kazan

**** *Hannah and Her Sisters*
GLO NYC LAC

The deft handling of a complex multi-character plot and the host of fine performances (especially from Dianne Wiest and Michael Caine) earned critical favor. But the real reason for its relative success and acclaim was that it was Woody Allen's closest thing to a feelgood picture . . . and only Woody Allen could make a feelgood picture that includes Max von Sydow as a gloomy Swedish painter.

*** Bob Hoskins in *Mona Lisa* GLO NYC SOC LAC BAA
Like his later *The Crying Game*, Neil Jordan's *Mona Lisa* looks like a crime thriller but acts like something else—in this case,

a fairy tale, with Hoskins as the gutsy Cockney frog who saves a princess (Cathy Tyson as a black prostitute with more than a passing resemblance to Jaye Davidson—hmm).

New York Film Critics Circle
Picture: *Hannah and Her Sisters*
Foreign Film: *The Decline of the American Empire*
Actor: Bob Hoskins, *Mona Lisa*
Actress: Sissy Spacek, *Crimes of the Heart*
Supporting Actor: Daniel Day-Lewis, *My Beautiful Laundrette*, *A Room With a View*
Supporting Actress: Dianne Wiest, *Hannah and Her Sisters*
Director: Woody Allen, *Hannah and Her Sisters*
Screenplay: Hanif Kureishi, *My Beautiful Laundrette*
Cinematography: Tony Pierce-Roberts, *A Room With a View*
Documentary: *Marlene*

National Society of Film Critics
Picture: *Blue Velvet*
Actor: Bob Hoskins, *Mona Lisa*
Actress: Chloe Webb, *Sid and Nancy*
Supporting Actor: Dennis Hopper, *Blue Velvet*
Supporting Actress: Dianne Wiest, *Hannah and Her Sisters*
Director: David Lynch, *Blue Velvet*
Screenplay: Hanif Kureishi, *My Beautiful Laundrette*
Cinematography: Frederic Elmes, *Blue Velvet*
Documentary: *Marlene*

Los Angeles Film Critics Association
Film: *Hannah and Her Sisters*
Foreign Film: *Vagabond*
Actor: Bob Hoskins, *Mona Lisa*

Actress: Sandrine Bonnaire,
Vagabond
Supporting Actor: Dennis
Hopper, *Blue Velvet, Hoosiers*
Supporting Actress: Cathy
Tyson, *Mona Lisa*
Director: David Lynch, *Blue
Velvet*
Screenplay: Woody Allen,
Hannah and Her Sisters
Cinematography: Chris Menges,
The Mission
Music: Herbie Hancock, Dexter
Gordon, et al., *'Round Midnight*
**Independent/Experimental
Film:** *Magdalena Viraga* (Nina
Menkes), *Stands in the Desert
Counting the Seconds of His Life*
(Jonas Mekas)
New Generation Prize: Spike
Lee
Life Achievement: John
Cassavetes
Special Prizes: Rafigh Pooya, for
venturesome film programming at
the Fox International Theatre in
Venice, California
Chuck Workman and the
Directors Guild of America, for
the short *Precious Images*

National Board of Review
Best English-Language Film: *A
    Room With a View*
Hannah and Her Sisters
My Beautiful Laundrette
The Fly
Stand By Me
The Color of Money
Children of a Lesser God
'Round Midnight
Peggy Sue Got Married
The Mission
Best Foreign-Language Film:
Otello
Miss Mary
Ginger and Fred
Ménage
Men
Actor: Paul Newman, *The Color
of Money*

Actress: Kathleen Turner, *Peggy
Sue Got Married*
Supporting Actor: Daniel Day-
Lewis, *My Beautiful Laundrette,
A Room With a View*
Supporting Actress: Dianne
Wiest, *Hannah and Her Sisters*
Director: Woody Allen, *Hannah
and Her Sisters*

People's Choice Awards
Picture: *Top Gun*
Movie Actor: Clint Eastwood
Movie Actress: Meryl Streep

British Academy Awards
Film: *A Room With a View*
Foreign-Language Film: *Ran*
(Akira Kurosawa, Japan)
Actor: Bob Hoskins, *Mona Lisa*
Actress: Maggie Smith, *A Room
With a View*
Supporting Actor: Ray
McAnally, *The Mission*
Supporting Actress: Judi Dench,
A Room With a View
Director: Woody Allen, *Hannah
and Her Sisters*
Original Screenplay: Woody
Allen, *Hannah and Her Sisters*
Adapted Screenplay: Kurt
Luedtke, *Out of Africa*
**Robert Flaherty Documentary
Award:** *Shoah* (Claude
Lanzmann, France)
Academy Fellow: Steven
Spielberg
Michael Balcon Award: The
Film Production Executives

** *The Mission* CAN
With his second film (after *The
Killing Fields*), Roland Joffé
has some of the same problems
that Michael Cimino had
going from *The Deer Hunter* to
Heaven's Gate—a director whose
strength is vivid contemporary
realism can't find in a
historical setting the equivalent

details that will bring his story to life. This tale of a 16th-century New World mission full of good priests and Indians slaughtered by bad Conquistadors is, for all its spectacular Chris Menges cinematography and memorable Ennio Morricone score, as obvious as it sounds.

Cannes Film Festival
Palme d'Or: *The Mission* (Roland Joffé, UK)
Special Jury Prize: *The Sacrifice* (Andrei Tarkovsky, Sweden-France)
Jury Prize: *Thérèse* (Alain Cavalier, France)
Actor: Michel Blanc, *Tenue de Soirée* [*Ménage*] (France), Bob Hoskins, *Mona Lisa* (UK)
Actress: Barbara Sukowa, *Rosa Luxemburg* (West Germany), Fernanda Torres, *Love Me Forever or Never* (Brazil)
Director: Martin Scorsese, *After Hours* (USA)
Artistic Contribution: Sven Nykvist, cinematography, *The Sacrifice*
Palme d'Or/Short Film: *Peel* (Jane Campion, Australia)
Camera d'Or: Claire Devers, *Noir et Blanc* (France)
Technical Prize: *The Mission*
International Critics Prize: in competition, *The Sacrifice*; out of competition, *The Decline of the American Empire* (Denys Arcand, Canada)

***** *Summer* VEN
A dazzlingly light-fingered romantic comedy from Eric Rohmer, that peerless French chronicler of the deepest thoughts of shallow people. The main character, a twentysomething French yuppie and professional whiner, ought to be one of the most irritating characters in film history, since she mopes her way through a sunny summer vacation in the south of France. Finally, with only hours left in her vacation, she decides she's going to have a good time for once in her life—but can she do it in time? If you don't believe that Hitchcockian suspense can be built out of the progress of a shallow yuppie's emotions, well, here's the proof.

Venice Film Festival
Golden Lion: *Le rayon vert* [*Summer*] (Eric Rohmer, France)
Special Jury Prize: *Cuzaja, belaja i rjaboj* (Sergei Soloviev, USSR), *Storia d'Amore* (Francesco Maselli, Italy)
Actor: Carlo Della Piane, *Regalo di Natale* (Italy)
Actress: Valeria Golino, *Storia d'Amore* (Italy)
First Film: *La pelicula del rey* (Carlos Sorin, Argentina)
Special Prize: *X* (Oddvar Einarson, Norway)
Career Award: Paolo and Vittorio Taviani:
International Critics Prize: *Le rayon vert* [*Summer*], special mention, *Acta General de Chile* (Miguel Littin, Spain)

Berlin Film Festival
Golden Bear: *Stammheim* (Reinhard Hauff, West Germany)
Silver Bear: *The Mass Is Ended* (Nanni Moretti, Italy)
Silver Bear for harmonious composition: *Gonza the Spearman* (Masahiro Shinoda, Japan)
Actor: Tuncel Kurtiz, *The Smile of the Lamb* (Israel)

Actress: Charlotte Valandrey, *Red Kiss* (France/West Germany), Marcelia Cartaxo, *The Hour of the Star* (Brazil) (shared)
Director: Georgi Shengelaya, *A Young Composer's Odyssey* (USSR)
Outstanding Individual Contribution: Gabriel Beristain, cinematographer, *Caravaggio* (UK)
Special Mention: *Paso Doble* (Dan Pita, Romania)
Golden Bear/Short: *Tom Goes to the Bar* (Dean Parisot, USA)
International Critics Prize: in competition, *Stammheim*; out of competition, *Shoah* (Claude Lanzmann, France); special mentions, *Woman from the Provinces* (Andrzej Baranski, Poland), *A Time to Live and a Time to Die* (Hou Hsiao-hsien, Taiwan)

*** *Smooth Talk* SUN
What starts as an excellent naturalistic tale of a teenage girl (Laura Dern) suddenly takes a left turn into Big-Time Literary Conceit, in the form of a symbolic Dude in a Hot Car (Treat Williams) who tries to seduce and/or rape her by way of awakening in her a sense of the Dark Side of Sexuality. In other words, there's a reason that most Sundance dramas stuck to the business of small-scale naturalism rather than aiming for deeper meanings. (It was directed by a woman from a Joyce Carol Oates story, in case you were wondering.)

U.S. Film Festival (Sundance)
Grand Jury Prize: *Smooth Talk* (Joyce Chopra)

Special Jury Prize: *Parting Glances* (Bill Sherwood), *Seven Minutes in Heaven* (Linda Feferman), *The Great Wall Is a Great Wall* [*A Great Wall*] (Peter Wang)

Independent Spirit Awards
Film: *Platoon*
First Film: Spike Lee, *She's Gotta Have It*
Foreign Film: *A Room With a View*
Actor: James Woods, *Salvador*
Actress: Isabella Rossellini, *Blue Velvet*
Director: Oliver Stone, *Platoon*
Screenplay: Oliver Stone, *Platoon*
Cinematography: Bob Richardson, *Platoon*

Golden Raspberry Awards
Worst Picture: (tie) *Howard the Duck*, *Under the Cherry Moon*
Worst Actor: Prince, *Under the Cherry Moon*
Worst Actress: Madonna, *Shanghai Surprise*
Worst Supporting Actor: Jerome Benton, *Under the Cherry Moon*
Worst Supporting Actress: Dom DeLuise (in drag), *Haunted Honeymoon*
Worst Director: Prince, *Under the Cherry Moon*
Worst Screenplay: Willard Huyck, Gloria Katz, *Howard the Duck*
Worst Song: "Love or Money," *Under the Cherry Moon*
Worst Special Visual Effects: *Howard the Duck*
Worst New Star: the six guys in the duck suit, *Howard the Duck*

Box Office (Domestic Rentals)

1	*Top Gun*	$82,000,000	Par
2	*The Karate Kid, Part II*	56,936,752	Col
3	*"Crocodile" Dundee*	51,000,000	Par
4	*Star Trek IV: The Voyage Home*	45,000,000	Par
5	*Aliens*	42,500,000	Fox
6	*The Color Purple*	41,900,000	WB
	[total 1985–86:	47,900,000]	
7	*Back to School*	41,748,000	Orion
8	*The Golden Child*	33,000,000	Par
9	*Ruthless People*	31,000,000	Touchstone
10	*Out of Africa*	30,051,817	Uni
	[total 1985–86:	42,051,817]	

Other films of note:

12	*Down and Out in Beverly Hills*	28,100,000	Touchstone
15	*An American Tail*	22,000,000	Uni
18	*The Color of Money*	20,800,000	Touchstone
19	*Police Academy 3: Back in Training*	20,700,000	WB
22	*The Fly*	17,500,000	Fox
25	*Hannah and Her Sisters*	16,587,000	Orion
38	*The Great Mouse Detective*	11,000,000	Disney
43	*Howard the Duck*	9,811,908	Uni
46	*Nightmare on Elm Street 2*	8,900,000	New Line
	[total 1985–86:	12,130,291]	
50	*A Room With a View*	8,200,000	Cinecom

The mid-'80s' one undeniable old-fashioned superstar, Tom Cruise, was top gun in a weak year, the beginning of a mid-decade slump which saw nothing break the $100 million mark between Beverly Hills Cop *and* Batman. *Bette Midler seemed to emerge as the comedy star of the year, but her career since has been only slightly more impressive than Rodney Dangerfield's. How bad off was Disney's animation unit, circa '86? Well,* The Great Mouse Detective *did only half the business of the year's main cartoon mouse epic, the Spielberg–Don Bluth* American Tail, *and for that matter did exactly the business of a reissue of* Lady and the Tramp. The Little Mermaid *was on the drawing board, but it would be three more years before it would launch the animation renaissance that would see a Disney cartoon at or near the top every year.*

Gebert's Golden Armchairs

The way David Lynch has repeated himself in later (and lesser) work like *Wild at Heart* and *Twin Peaks* has taken some of the originality out of *Blue Velvet*'s blend of psychosexual weirdness and educational-film campiness. All I can say is, I saw it at its American premiere at the Telluride Film Festival, and it had the audience alternately rolling in the aisles and scared shitless. And for the next three days, you started every conversation, a little nervously, with "Did you see *Blue Velvet*, and what did *you* think?"

Dennis Hopper was a knockout (even the Academy, which almost completely ignored *Blue Velvet*, snuck him in under the guise of a nomination for *Hoosiers*). But the most original and moving actor's performance this year was in the least likely place—smart, spooky, funny Jeff Goldblum in the remake of *The Fly*, the disintegration of his personality as the insect brain took over making a surprisingly effective metaphor for drug addiction (among other things). *Peggy Sue Got Married* was a pretty synthetic straight version of *Back to the Future*, but Kathleen Turner found amazing reserves of feeling in it (watch her face when she gets a phone call from her dead grandmother). And the Richard Pryor *Toy* Award for Smart Career Management goes to red-hot Eddie Murphy for choosing, out of all the parts offered him, the utterly leaden *Golden Child*.

Best American Film: *Blue Velvet*
Best Foreign Film: *Summer*
Best Actor: Jeff Goldblum, *The Fly*
Best Actress: Kathleen Turner, *Peggy Sue Got Married*
Best Director: David Lynch, *Blue Velvet*
Worst Hit: *The Golden Child*

1987

Under the Sun of Satan may be a serious film from a highbrow author (Georges Bernanos, whose *Diary of a Country Priest* and *Mouchette* were filmed by Bresson), but its main claim to fame comes from the sort of high comedy achievement that only an international festival could manage. Cannes decided that for its own 40th anniversary, it would be proper to give the Palme d'Or to a French film—something that hadn't happened since *A Man and a Woman* in 1966.

Unfortunately, the only first-rate French auteur they could find was Maurice Pialat, best known for the disturbing family drama *A Nos Amours*—and a man whose on-the-set tyranny has left a trail of enemies in French cinema (though it's worth noting that Gérard Dépardieu and Sandrine Bonnaire were making their second and third films with him respectively). When the prize was announced, the customary booing reached near-record levels—to which Pialat replied with a couple of obscene gestures and the heartwarming acceptance speech, "If you don't like me, I can tell you, I don't like you either."

Academy Awards

**** *The Last Emperor* AAW GLO DGA
An unusually arty choice for Oscar—a typically gorgeous Bernardo Bertolucci epic-with-a-zero-at-its-center, John Lone as the emperor of China who was a pawn of the imperial court, then a pawn of the Japanese invaders, then a pawn of the Communists. Not especially innovative, but consistently absorbing and intelligent; the fact that none of the critics' groups went for it (when they had certainly been Bertolucci fans in the past) ought to have doomed its Oscar chances, so its win shows the renewed influence of a reformed, post-Pia Golden Globes.

Picture
The Last Emperor (Columbia, Hemdale, Jeremy Thomas)
Broadcast News (20th Century–Fox, James L. Brooks)
Fatal Attraction (Paramount, Stanley R. Jaffe, Sherry Lansing)
Hope and Glory (Columbia, John Boorman)
Moonstruck (MGM, Patrick Palmer, Norman Jewison)

**** Michael Douglas in *Wall Street* AAW GLO BOR PEO
As far back as his draft-dodger in *Hail, Hero!* in '69, Douglas has been the cinematic icon of every trend and trauma to afflict Baby Boomer males; I expect the announcement that

he's starring in Michael Crichton's *Prostate!* any day now. It's harder to pick the worst than the best of them; where worst gives you such stiff (so to speak) competition as *Basic Instinct*, *Falling Down*, and *Disclosure*, there's only one Gordon Gekko. Douglas' rip-snorting scenery chewing as the Boesky-like baron would be totally over the top if it wasn't, in fact, completely accurate to the type and the era.

Actor
Michael Douglas, *Wall Street*
William Hurt, *Broadcast News*
Marcello Mastroianni, *Dark Eyes*
Jack Nicholson, *Ironweed*
Robin Williams, *Good Morning, Vietnam*

**** Cher in *Moonstruck*
AAW GLO
Norman Jewison and writer John Patrick Shanley's comedy was the best old-fashioned comedy to come Oscar's way since *Tootsie*, and for once they should have just gone with their hearts and picked it over the obligatory historical epic. At least they did pick Cher, who was never more likable (a tougher feat than making her look gorgeous, which she was even before the makeover—oh, yeah, those three gray hairs, who'd look at *her* twice?)

Actress
Cher, *Moonstruck*
Glenn Close, *Fatal Attraction*
Holly Hunter, *Broadcast News*
Sally Kirkland, *Anna*
Meryl Streep, *Ironweed*

Supporting Actor
Sean Connery, *The Untouchables*
Albert Brooks, *Broadcast News*
Morgan Freeman, *Street Smart*
Vincent Gardenia, *Moonstruck*
Denzel Washington, *Cry Freedom*

Supporting Actress
Olympia Dukakis, *Moonstruck*
Norma Aleandro, *Gaby—A True Story*
Anne Archer, *Fatal Attraction*
Anne Ramsey, *Throw Momma from the Train*
Ann Sothern, *The Whales of August*

Director
Bernardo Bertolucci, *The Last Emperor*
John Boorman, *Hope and Glory*
Lasse Hallstrom, *My Life As a Dog*
Norman Jewison, *Moonstruck*
Adrian Lyne, *Fatal Attraction*

Original Screenplay: John Patrick Shanley, *Moonstruck*
Adapted Screenplay: Mark Peploe, Bernardo Bertolucci, *The Last Emperor*
Cinematography: Vittorio Storaro, *The Last Emperor*
Score: Ryuichi Sakamoto, David Byrne, Cong Su, *The Last Emperor*
Song: "(I've Had) the Time of My Life," *Dirty Dancing*, m: Franke Previte, John DeNicola, Donald Markowitz, l: Franke Previte
Art Direction: Ferdinando Scarfiotti, *The Last Emperor*
Costume Design: James Acheson, *The Last Emperor*
Editing: *The Last Emperor*
Sound: *The Last Emperor*
Sound Effects Editing: *RoboCop*

Make-up: Rick Baker, *Harry and the Hendersons*
Visual Effects: Dennis Muren, *Innerspace*
Short/Animated: *The Man Who Planted Trees* (Société Radio-Canada/Canadian Broadcasting Corporation, Frederic Back)
Short/Live Action: *Ray's Male Heterosexual Dance Hall*
Documentary/Feature: *The Ten-Year Lunch: The Wit and Legend of the Algonquin Round Table*
Documentary/Short Subject: *Young at Heart*
Foreign-Language Film: *Babette's Feast* (Denmark)
Irving G. Thalberg Award: Billy Wilder

**** *My Life As a Dog* GLO NYC IND
Perfectly charming Swedish film about a little boy in the '50s who feels so put upon that he identifies with Laika, the dog the Soviets sent into space. Perfect Cannes bait (UNICEF film, see 1953 for details); can't imagine why they didn't enter it.

Golden Globes
Picture (Drama): *The Last Emperor*
Picture (Comedy/Musical): *Hope and Glory*
Foreign Film: *My Life As a Dog* (Sweden)
Actor (Drama): Michael Douglas, *Wall Street*
Actor (Comedy/Musical): Robin Williams, *Good Morning, Vietnam*
Actress (Drama): Sally Kirkland, *Anna*
Actress (Comedy/Musical): Cher, *Moonstruck*
Supporting Actor: Sean Connery, *The Untouchables*

Supporting Actress: Olympia Dukakis, *Moonstruck*
Director: Bernardo Bertolucci, *The Last Emperor*
Screenplay: Bernardo Bertolucci, Mark Peploe, *The Last Emperor*
Original Score: Ryuichi Sakamoto, David Byrne, Cong Su, *The Last Emperor*
Original Song: "(I've Had) the Time of My Life," *Dirty Dancing*, m: Franke Previte, John DeNicola, Donald Markowitz, l: Franke Previte
Cecil B. DeMille Award: Clint Eastwood

Directors Guild of America
Director: Bernardo Bertolucci, *The Last Emperor*
D. W. Griffith Award: Robert Wise
Honorary Lifetime Member: Michael H. Franklin

*** Holly Hunter in *Broadcast News* NYC LAC BOR BER '88
Hunter's first big role established her as the Shirley MacLaine of her time—cute and vulnerable enough for the fogies to like her, smart and tough enough that non-fogies (like the Coen brothers, who wrote *Raising Arizona* for her—and used to share a house with her) can accept her as one of the boys.

New York Film Critics Circle
Picture: *Broadcast News*
Foreign Film: *My Life As a Dog*
Actor: Jack Nicholson, *The Witches of Eastwick, Ironweed, Broadcast News*
Actress: Holly Hunter, *Broadcast News*
Supporting Actor: Morgan Freeman, *Street Smart*

Supporting Actress: Vanessa Redgrave, *Prick Up Your Ears*
Director: James L. Brooks, *Broadcast News*
Screenplay: James L. Brooks, *Broadcast News*
Cinematography: Vittorio Storaro, *The Last Emperor*

National Society of Film Critics
Picture: *The Dead*
Actor: Steve Martin, *Roxanne*
Actress: Emily Lloyd, *Wish You Were Here*
Supporting Actor: Morgan Freeman, *Street Smart*
Supporting Actress: Kathy Baker, *Street Smart*
Director: John Boorman, *Hope and Glory*
Screenplay: John Boorman, *Hope and Glory*
Cinematography: Philippe Rousselot, *Hope and Glory*
Special Prize: Richard Roud, former director of the New York Film Festival

Los Angeles Film Critics Association
Film: *Hope and Glory*
Foreign Film: *Au Revoir les Enfants*
Actor: Steve Martin, *Roxanne*, Jack Nicholson, *The Witches of Eastwick, Ironweed*
Actress: Holly Hunter, *Broadcast News*, Sally Kirkland, *Anna*
Supporting Actor: Morgan Freeman, *Street Smart*
Supporting Actress: Olympia Dukakis, *Moonstruck*
Director: John Boorman, *Hope and Glory*
Screenplay: John Boorman, *Hope and Glory*
Cinematography: Vittorio Storaro, *The Last Emperor*
Music: Ryuichi Sakamoto, David Byrne, Cong Su, *The Last Emperor*

Documentary: *Weapons of the Spirit*
Independent/Experimental Film: *Mala Noche* (Gus Van Sant, Jr.)
New Generation Prize: Pedro Almodóvar
Life Achievement: Joel McCrea, Samuel Fuller
Special Citation: Film Forum Theatre

National Board of Review
Best English-Language Film:
Empire of the Sun
The Last Emperor
Broadcast News
The Untouchables
Gaby—A True Story
Cry Freedom
Fatal Attraction
Hope and Glory
Wall Street
Full Metal Jacket
Best Foreign-Language Film:
Jean de Florette and *Manon of the Spring*
My Life As a Dog
Au Revoir les Enfants
Tampopo
Dark Eyes
Actor: Michael Douglas, *Wall Street*
Actress: Lillian Gish, *The Whales of August*, Holly Hunter, *Broadcast News*
Supporting Actor: Sean Connery, *The Untouchables*
Supporting Actress: Olympia Dukakis, *Moonstruck*
Outstanding Juvenile Performance: Christian Bale, *Empire of the Sun*
Director: Steven Spielberg, *Empire of the Sun*

People's Choice Awards
Favorite Drama: *Fatal Attraction*
Favorite Comedy: *Three Men and a Baby*

Favorite Movie Actor: Michael Douglas
Favorite Movie Actress: Glenn Close
Favorite All-Time Movie Star: Clint Eastwood
Favorite All-Time Musical Star: Barbra Streisand
Favorite All-Time Movie Song: "Somewhere My Love (Lara's Theme)," *Dr. Zhivago*

British Academy Awards
Film: *Jean de Florette*
Foreign-Language Film: *The Sacrifice* (Andrei Tarkovsky, Sweden)
Actor: Sean Connery, *The Name of the Rose*
Actress: Anne Bancroft, *84 Charing Cross Road*
Supporting Actor: Daniel Auteuil, *Jean de Florette*
Supporting Actress: Susan Woolridge, *Hope and Glory*
Director: Oliver Stone, *Platoon*
Screenplay (Original): David Leland, *Wish You Were Here*
Screenplay (Adapted): Claude Berri, Gérard Brach, *Jean de Florette*
Academy Fellow: Federico Fellini
Michael Balcon Award: The Monty Python Team
Special Award: Reginald Collin

**** *Under the Sun of Satan*
CAN
Despite the derision it received at Cannes, it really did deserve its Palme d'Or. Gérard Depardieu is a priest who comes to believe that the battle between good and evil must already have been fought—and lost. A very grim but powerful drama in the model of Robert Bresson, and as good as all but his best.

Cannes Film Festival
Palme d'Or: *Under the Sun of Satan* (Maurice Pialat, France)
40th Anniversary Prize: *Intervista* (Federico Fellini, Italy)
Special Jury Prize: *Repentance* (Tengiz Abuladze, USSR)
Jury Prize: Souleymane Cisse, for *Yeelen [Brightness]* (Mali), Rentano Mikuni, for *Shinran: Path to Purity* (Japan)
Actor: Marcello Mastroianni, *Dark Eyes* (Italy)
Actress: Barbara Hershey, *Shy People* (USA)
Director: Wim Wenders, *Wings of Desire* (West Germany)
Artistic Contribution: Stanley Myers (musical score), *Prick Up Your Ears* (UK)
Tributes: Jean Simmons, Jane Russell
Camera d'Or: *Robinson, My English Grandfather* (Nana Dzordzhadze, USSR)
Technical Prize: *Le Cinema dans les Yeux* (Gilles Jacob, Laurent Jacob, France) [NOTE: Gilles Jacob is festival director of Cannes]
Youth Prize: *I've Heard the Mermaids Singing* (Patricia Rozema, Canada)
International Critics Prize: in competition, *Repentance*; out of competition, *Wish You Were Here* (David Leland, UK), *Wedding in Galilee* (Michel Khleifi, Belgium-France-Palestine)

*** *Au Revoir les Enfants*
LAC VEN
Rather too genteel Holocaust-era story from French director Louis Malle, about a Gentile boy's ill-fated friendship with a Jewish boy attending his school under a fake name. *Europa, Europa* covered similar territory

more imaginatively—and Malle's earlier *Lacombe, Lucien* tackled the period more powerfully.

Venice Film Festival
Golden Lion: *Au Revoir les Enfants* (Louis Malle, France)
Silver Lion: *Maurice* (James Ivory, UK), *Lunga vita alla Signora!* (Ermanno Olmi, Italy)
Special Jury Prize: *Hip, Hip, Hurrah* (Kjell Grede, Sweden-Norway-Denmark)
Actor: James Wilby, Hugh Grant, *Maurice*
Actress: Kang Soo-Yeon, *Contract Mother* (South Korea)
Screenplay: David Mamet, *House of Games* (USA)
Cinematography: Sten Holmberg, *Hip, Hip, Hurrah*
Music: Richard Robbins, *Maurice*
Art Direction: Luciano Ricceri, *The Gold-Rimmed Glasses* (Giuliano Montaldo, Italy)
Costumes: Nana Cecchi, *The Gold-Rimmed Glasses*
Career Award: Luigi Comencini, Joseph L. Mankiewicz
Italian Senate Prize: *Plumbum, or a Dangerous Game* (Vadim Abdraschitov, USSR)
Tribute: Miklós Jancsó
International Critics Prize: in competition, *Motherland Hotel* (Omer Kavur, Turkey), *Lunga vita alla Signora!*; out of competition, *Burglar* (Valeri Ogordnikov, USSR)
Italian Critics Prize: *House of Games* (David Mamet, USA), *Dragon Food* (Jan Schütte, West Germany)

*** *The Theme* BER
A successful but shallow Moscow playwright goes to a small town and meets a woman who is emotionally involved with two artists who *didn't* sell out—a long-dead village poet typifying the pure Russian artist, and a living writer who has decided to emigrate to Israel. The emigration theme was surely enough to get this 1979 film shelved until glasnost, but the most subversive thing about it is how little it differs from a Western film on the same subject (say, $8^{1}/_{2}$): there's not a word about the artist's duty to the People, just the eternal question of how the artistic temperament is corrupted by fame and success (capitalist or Communist varieties, it doesn't matter). A witty and most un-Soviet work.

Berlin Film Festival
Golden Bear: *The Theme* (Gleb Panfilov, USSR)
Special Jury Silver Bear: *The Sea and Poison* (Kei Kumai, Japan)
Actor: Gian Maria Volonté, *The Moro Affair* (Italy)
Actress: Ana Beatriz Nogueira, *Vera* (Brazil)
Director: Oliver Stone, *Platoon* (USA)
Outstanding Achievement: *The Year of Awakening* (Fernando Trueba, Spain), *Diary for My Children* (Marta Mészáros, Hungary)
Silver Bear for Handling of Theme: *Children of a Lesser God* (Randa Haines, USA)
Alfred Bauer Prize: *Bad Blood* (Leos Carax, France)
International Critics Prize: in competition, *The Theme*; Forum, *Siekierezada* (Witold Leszczynski, Poland), *The Lit Lantern* (Agasi Ajvazjan, USSR)

U.S. Film Festival (Sundance)

Grand Jury Prize: *Waiting for the Moon* (Jill Godmilow), *The Trouble with Dick* (Gary Walkow)
Special Jury Prize: *The River's Edge* (Tim Hunter), *Working Girls* (Lizzie Borden)

Independent Spirit Awards

Film: *The River's Edge*
First Film: Emile Ardolino, *Dirty Dancing*
Foreign Film: *My Life As a Dog*
Actor: Dennis Quaid, *The Big Easy*
Actress: Sally Kirkland, *Anna*
Supporting Actor: Morgan Freeman, *Street Smart*
Supporting Actress: Anjelica Huston, *The Dead*
Director: John Huston, *The Dead*
Screenplay: Neil Jimenez, *River's Edge*
Cinematography: Haskell Wexler, *Matewan*

Golden Raspberry Awards

Worst Picture: *Leonard Part 6*
Worst Actor: Bill Cosby, *Leonard Part 6*
Worst Actress: Madonna, *Who's That Girl?*
Worst Supporting Actor: David Mendenhall, *Over the Top*
Worst Supporting Actress: Darryl Hannah, *Wall Street*
Worst Director: Norman Mailer, *Tough Guys Don't Dance*, Elaine May, *Ishtar* (tie)
Worst Screenplay: Jonathan Reynolds, based on a story by Bill Cosby, *Leonard Part 6*
Worst Song: "I Want Your Sex," *Beverly Hills Cop II*
Worst Special Visual Effects: *Jaws: The Revenge*
Worst New Star: David Mendenhall, *Over the Top*
Career Achievement Award: Bruce (the rubber shark), *Jaws, Jaws 2, Jaws 3-D, Jaws 4-F*

Box Office (Domestic Rentals)

1	*Beverly Hills Cop II*	$80,857,776	Par
2	*Platoon*	66,700,000	Orion
3	*Fatal Attraction*	60,000,000	Par
4	*Three Men and a Baby*	45,000,000	Touchstone
5	*The Untouchables*	36,866,530	Par
6	*The Witches of Eastwick*	31,800,000	WB
7	*Predator*	31,000,000	Fox
8	*Dragnet*	30,138,699	Uni
9	*The Secret of My Success*	29,542,081	Uni
10	*Lethal Weapon*	29,500,000	WB
Other films of note:			
12	*The Living Daylights*	26,600,000	MGM/UA
13	*Dirty Dancing*	25,009,305	Vestron
14	*Robocop*	23,571,784	Orion
15	*Full Metal Jacket*	22,700,000	WB
25	*Planes, Trains & Automobiles*	18,000,000	Par
26	*Roxanne*	17,600,000	Col
28	*The Running Man*	16,000,000	Tri-Star
30	*No Way Out*	15,523,826	Orion
40	*Wall Street [1987 only]:*	13,000,000	Fox
	[total 1987–88:	21,200,000]	

| 66 | *Ishtar* | 7,400,000 | Col |
| 102 | *Who's That Girl?* | 3,200,000 | WB |

At last, movie stars! 1987 was the second year in a row in which nothing came anywhere near the magic $100 million mark, and Eddie Murphy seemed the only bankable star on the scene. But in fact, 1987 saw the first real hits of a pack of male actors who would go on to become the megastars of the tail end of the decade: Michael Douglas as quintessential yuppies in Fatal Attraction *and* Wall Street, *Kevin Costner as Elliot Ness and a guy with . . . No Way Out, Tom Hanks as Joe Friday's partner, Schwarzenegger in his first real action hit since* Conan, *Mel Gibson in the first of the* Lethal Weapons *. . . and, of course, Patrick Swayze. There was no female star to compare—certainly not Madonna, the answer no one cared about to the question* Who's That Girl?

Gebert's Golden Armchairs

The year's best-shot, best-written, best-edited, and most distinctive comedy was *Raising Arizona*, still the best thing done by those ultra-quirky tyros, the guys who make Stanley Kubrick look easygoing and sociable, Joel and Ethan Coen. An equally distinctive comic sensibility—unfortunately not really borne out by his subsequent work—was that of Japanese talk show host-turned-director Juzo Itami, whose *Tampopo*, a sort of free-flowing narrative about the joys of eating, was the year's most unexpected delight (Japanese comedy? What's next, Soviet musicals?). Anjelica Huston was lovely and poignant in her dad's last film, the beautiful miniature *The Dead*, based on James Joyce's story. And the Richard Pryor *Toy* Award for Smart Career Management again goes to Eddie Murphy for deciding, based I guess on *Top Gun* and *The Hunger*, that Tony Scott could direct comedy.

Best American Film: *Raising Arizona*
Best Foreign Film: *Tampopo*
Best Actor: Michael Douglas, *Wall Street*
Best Actress: Anjelica Huston, *The Dead*
Best Director: Joel and Ethan Coen, *Raising Arizona*
Worst Hit: *Beverly Hills Cop II*

1988

1988's Oscar telecast—you know, the one in which Snow White and Rob Lowe did their duet of Creedence Clearwater's "Proud Mary"—may have been the most famously awful in history, but did you know that it could have been even worse? Allan Carr's original plans called for Kurt Russell and longtime live-in Goldie Hawn to present the Best Director award (which they did)—and for Russell to surprise Hawn on camera with a proposal of marriage (which, thankfully, they merely joked about instead). Given that the show had already included Bruce Willis and Demi Moore's home movies of their new baby (as prelude to the Cinematography award), one can only contemplate what embarrassing personal celebrity events might have been shared with a billion squirming couch potatoes in the years to come. . . .

Academy Awards

*** *Rain Man* AAW GLO DGA PEO BER '89
**** **Dustin Hoffman** AAW GLO PEO
Affecting but curiously soft tale of a yuppie who gets in touch with his feelings through meeting—but never *quite* connecting with—his heretofore-unknown autistic older brother. Cruise has never been better, and Hoffman is fascinating in a performance obviously based on lots of research. But the script had bounced around Hollywood so long that it had picked up a lot of unnecessary elements (did they really need to go to Las Vegas?), and like so much of Barry Levinson's work, it seems perversely determined to avoid dramatic conflict (having ripped off the casino, does anyone really believe they'd be allowed to depart with a mild rebuke and a couple of hundred thousand dollars?).

Picture
Rain Man (United Artists, Guber-Peters Co., Mark Johnson)
The Accidental Tourist (Warner Bros., Lawrence Kasdan, Charles Okun, Michael Grillo)
Dangerous Liaisons (Warner Bros., Lorimar, Norma Heyman, Hank Moonjean)
Mississippi Burning (Orion, Frederick Zollo, Robert F. Colesberry)
Working Girl (20th Century–Fox, Douglas Wick)

Actor
Dustin Hoffman, *Rain Man*
Gene Hackman, *Mississippi Burning*
Tom Hanks, *Big*
Edward James Olmos, *Stand and Deliver*

Max von Sydow, *Pelle the Conqueror*

*** **Jodie Foster in *The Accused*** AAW GLO BOR
A woman in a bar is gang-raped on a pool table as the other patrons cheer the rapists on. A true-life case is here turned into a typical Hollywood courtroom drama, with the one interesting ethical issue (at what point does a spectator to a crime become an accessory if he does nothing to prevent it?) getting lost in one-woman-against-the-system clichés. It *is* by far the more deserved of Foster's two Oscars, and she's appropriately feisty and defiant, though in both cases she robbed a clearly superior candidate (Glenn Close in this case) and mainly got it for being a Yalie playing white trash.

Actress
Jodie Foster, *The Accused*
Glenn Close, *Dangerous Liaisons*
Melanie Griffith, *Working Girl*
Meryl Streep, *A Cry in the Dark*
Sigourney Weaver, *Gorillas in the Mist*

Supporting Actor
Kevin Kline, *A Fish Called Wanda*
Alec Guinness, *Little Dorrit*
Martin Landau, *Tucker: The Man and His Dream*
River Phoenix, *Running on Empty*
Dean Stockwell, *Married to the Mob*

Supporting Actress
Geena Davis, *The Accidental Tourist*
Joan Cusack, *Working Girl*

Frances McDormand, *Mississippi Burning*
Michelle Pfeiffer, *Dangerous Liaisons*
Sigourney Weaver, *Working Girl*

Director
Barry Levinson, *Rain Man*
Charles Crichton, *A Fish Called Wanda*
Mike Nichols, *Working Girl*
Alan Parker, *Mississippi Burning*
Martin Scorsese, *The Last Temptation of Christ*

Original Screenplay: Ronald Bass, Barry Morrow, Story by Barry Morrow, *Rain Man*
Adapted Screenplay: Christopher Hampton, *Dangerous Liaisons*
Cinematography: Peter Biziou, *Mississippi Burning*
Score: Dave Grusin, *The Milagro Beanfield War*
Song: "Let the River Run," *Working Girl*, ml: Carly Simon
Art Direction: Stuart Craig, *Dangerous Liaisons*
Costume Design: James Acheson, *Dangerous Liaisons*
Editing: *Who Framed Roger Rabbit*
Sound: *Bird*
Make-Up: *Beetlejuice*
Visual Effects: *Who Framed Roger Rabbit*
Sound Effects Editing: *Who Framed Roger Rabbit*
Short/Animated: *Tin Toy* (Pixar, John Lasseter)
Short/Live Action: *The Appointment of Dennis Jennings* (Dean Parisot, Steven Wright)
Documentary/Feature: *Hotel Terminus: The Life and Time of Klaus Barbie* (Marcel Ophüls)
Documentary/Short: *You Don't Have to Die*
Foreign-Language Film: *Pelle the Conqueror* (Denmark)

Special Awards:
Eastman Kodak, in recognition of
its fundamental contributions to
the art of motion pictures during
the first century of film
The National Film Board of
Canada, in recognition of its 50th
anniversary
**Special Award/Animation
Direction:** Richard Williams,
Who Framed Roger Rabbit

Golden Globes

Picture (Drama): *Rain Man*
Picture (Comedy/Musical):
Working Girl
Foreign Film: *Pelle the
Conqueror* (Denmark)
Actor (Drama): Dustin Hoffman,
Rain Man
Actor (Comedy/Musical): Tom
Hanks, *Big*
Actress (Drama): Jodie Foster,
The Accused; Shirley MacLaine,
Madame Sousatzka; Sigourney
Weaver, *Gorillas in the Mist*
Actress (Comedy/Musical):
Melanie Griffith, *Working Girl*
Supporting Actor: Martin
Landau, *Tucker: The Man and
His Dream*
Supporting Actress: Sigourney
Weaver, *Working Girl*
Director: Clint Eastwood, *Bird*
Screenplay: Naomi Foner,
Running on Empty
Original Score: Maurice Jarre,
Gorillas in the Mist
Original Song: "Let the River
Run," *Working Girl*, ml: Carly
Simon; "Two Hearts,"
Buster, m: Lamont Dozier, l: Phil
Collins
Cecil B. DeMille Award: Doris
Day

Directors Guild of America

Director: Barry Levinson, *Rain
Man*
Honorary Lifetime Member:
Sidney Lumet

New York Film Critics Circle

Picture: *The Accidental Tourist*
Foreign Film: *Women on the
Verge of a Nervous Breakdown*
Actor: Jeremy Irons, *Dead
Ringers*
Actress: Meryl Streep, *A Cry in
the Dark*
Supporting Actor: Dean
Stockwell, *Married to the Mob*,
Tucker: The Man and His Dream
Supporting Actress: Diane
Venora, *Bird*
Director: Chris Menges, *A World
Apart*
Screenplay: Ron Shelton, *Bull
Durham*
Cinematography: Henri Alekan,
Wings of Desire
Documentary: *The Thin Blue
Line* (Errol Morris)

National Society of Film Critics

Picture: *The Unbearable
Lightness of Being*
Actor: Michael Keaton,
Beetlejuice, Clean and Sober
Actress: Judy Davis, *High Tide*
Supporting Actor: Dean
Stockwell, *Married to the Mob*,
Tucker: The Man and His Dream
Supporting Actress: Mercedes
Ruehl, *Married to the Mob*
Director: Philip Kaufman, *The
Unbearable Lightness of Being*
Screenplay: Ron Shelton, *Bull
Durham*
Cinematography: Henri Alekan,
Wings of Desire
Documentary: *The Thin Blue
Line*
Special Prize: Pedro Almodóvar,
for his originality in films such
as *Women on the Verge of a
Nervous Breakdown* and *Matador*

Los Angeles Film Critics Association

Film: *Little Dorrit*
Foreign Film: *Wings of Desire*

Actor: Tom Hanks, *Big, Punchline*
Actress: Christine Lahti, *Running on Empty*
Supporting Actor: Alec Guinness, *Little Dorrit*
Supporting Actress: Geneviève Bujold, *Dead Ringers, The Moderns*
Director: David Cronenberg, *Dead Ringers*
Screenplay: Ron Shelton, *Bull Durham*
Cinematography: Henri Alekan, *Wings of Desire*
Music: Mark Isham, *The Moderns*
Documentary: *Hotel Terminus: The Life and Times of Klaus Barbie* (Marcel Ophüls)
Independent/Experimental Film: *The Last of England* (Derek Jarman), *Amerika* (Al Razutis)
New Generation Prize: Mira Nair, director of *Salaam Bombay!*
Life Achievement: Don Siegel

National Board of Review
Best English-Language Film:
Mississippi Burning
Dangerous Liaisons
The Accused
The Unbearable Lightness of Being
The Last Temptation of Christ
Tucker: The Man and His Dream
Big
Running On Empty
Gorillas in the Mist
Midnight Run
Best Foreign-Language Film:
Women on the Verge of a Nervous Breakdown
Pelle the Conqueror
Le Grand Chemin
Salaam Bombay!
A Taxing Woman
Actor: Gene Hackman, *Mississippi Burning*
Actress: Jodie Foster, *The Accused*

Supporting Actor: River Phoenix, *Running on Empty*
Supporting Actress: Francis McDormand, *Mississippi Burning*
Director: Alan Parker, *Mississippi Burning*
Documentary: *The Thin Blue Line*

People's Choice Awards
Favorite Drama: *Rain Man*
Favorite Comedy: *Big, Twins*
Favorite Dramatic Movie Actor: Dustin Hoffman
Favorite Comedy Movie Actor: Eddie Murphy
Favorite Dramatic Movie Actress: Meryl Streep
Favorite Comedy Movie Actress: Bette Midler
Favorite All-Time Movie: *Gone With the Wind*

British Academy Awards
Film: *The Last Emperor*
Foreign-Language Film: *Babette's Feast* (Gabriel Axel, Denmark)
Actor: John Cleese, *A Fish Called Wanda*
Actress: Maggie Smith, *The Lonely Passion of Judith Hearne*
Supporting Actor: Michael Palin, *A Fish Called Wanda*
Supporting Actress: Judi Dench, *A Handful of Dust*
Director: Louis Malle, *Au Revoir les Enfants*
Screenplay (Original): Shawn Slovo, *A World Apart*
Screenplay (Adapted): Jean-Claude Carrière, Philip Kaufman, *The Unbearable Lightness of Being*
Academy Fellow: Ingmar Bergman
Michael Balcon Award: Charles Crichton
Special Award: John Mills

** *Pelle the Conqueror* AAW
GLO CAN

The hard lives of a defeated old
farmer and his plucky young
son as migrant labor on a Danish
farm. As one would expect
from a Swedish adaptation of a
famous-in-Scandinavia 19th-
century novel about farmers,
Pelle is grim, convincingly
squalid and unsentimental, well-
made and well-acted—and
ultimately exasperating, since it
is guaranteed that given two
choices, the plot will inevitably
take the turn that results in the
most misery for its characters,
no matter how improbable.
The performances of Max von
Sydow and young Pelle
Hvenegaard (who was named
for the book!) could hardly be
bettered; Bille August's
direction is sensitive and
skilled; everything about this is
first-rate, except the material
itself.

Cannes Film Festival
Palme d'Or: *Pelle the Conqueror*
(Bille August, Sweden); the Jury
also wishes to emphasize Max von
Sydow's exceptional
contribution
Special Jury Prize: *A World
Apart* (Chris Menges, UK)
Jury Prize: Krzysztof
Kieslowski, for *A Short Film
About Killing* [from *The
Decalogue*] (Poland)
Actor: Forest Whitaker, *Bird*
(USA)
Actress: Barbara Hershey, Jodhi
May, Linda Mvusi, *A World Apart*
(collectively) (UK)
Director: Fernando Solanas,
South (Argentina)
Artistic Contribution: Peter

Greenaway, *Drowning by
Numbers* (UK)
Camera d'Or: *Salaam Bombay!*
(Mira Nair, India)
Technical Prize: *Bird*, for the
quality of its soundtrack

Venice Film Festival
Golden Lion: *The Legend of the
Holy Drinker* (Ermanno Olmi,
Italy)
Silver Lion: *Landscape in the
Mist* (Theo Angelopolous,
Greece)
Special Jury Prize: *Camp
Thiaroye* (Ousmane Sembène,
Senegal-Tunisia-Algeria)
Actor: Joe Mantegna and Don
Ameche, *Things Change* (USA)
Actress: Isabelle Huppert, *Story
of Women* (France); Shirley
MacLaine, *Madame Sousatzka*
Screenplay: Pedro Almodóvar,
*Women on the Verge of a
Nervous Breakdown* (Spain)
Cinematography: Vadim Jusov,
The Black Monk (USSR)
Music: Jose Maria Vitier, Gianni
Nocenzi, Milanes, *A Very Old
Man With Enormous Wings*
(Spain)
Career Award: Joris Ivens
International Critics Prize:
Little Vera (Vasili Pitchul,
USSR), *High Hopes* (Mike Leigh,
UK), mention to: *Hard Times*
(Joao Botelho, Portugal)

*** *Red Sorghum* BER
The first of cinematographer-
turned-director Zhang
Yimou's brilliantly colorful
Chinese period dramas, with
Gong Li as the woman who
takes over a farm producing
sorghum dye (lots of red
splashing about—imagine *The
Good Earth* directed by Michael
Powell). Good, but the two
similar films that followed from

Zhang and his star—*Ju Dou* and *Raise the Red Lantern*—were better yet.

Berlin Film Festival
Golden Bear: *Red Sorghum* (Zhang Yimou, China)
Special Jury Silver Bear: *Komissar* (Alexander Askoldov, USSR)
Actor: Jörg Pose, Manfred Möck, *Einer Trage des Anderen Last* ... (Lothar Werneke, East Germany)
Actress: Holly Hunter, *Broadcast News* (USA)
Director: Norman Jewison, *Moonstruck* (USA)
Silver Bear for Artistic Quality: *La Deuda Interna* (Miguel Pereira, Argentina)
Silver Bear for Visualizing History: *Matka Królów* (Janusz Zaorski, Poland)
International Critics Prize: in competition, *Komissar*, *Asya's Happiness* (Andrei Konchalovsky, USSR) [both Soviet films c. 1967, unreleased until 1988], *Matka Królów*; Forum, *Dani, Michi, Renato and Max* (Richard Dindo, Switzerland)

** *Heat and Sunlight* SUN Rob Nilsson's first film, *Northern Lights*, was a terrific, authentic independent film about radical organizers in the midwest in the 'teens, which won prizes at the second U.S. Film Festival and at Cannes. His three subsequent works have all been much more typical Cassavetes-influenced independent dramas, semi-improvised confessional depictions of midlife crisis. If the artistic and relationship problems of a California

photographer (Nilsson) with good bone structure appeal to you, you might find it involving, but—like Henry Jaglom's vaguely similar work—it seems too much like sitting through someone else's therapy. On the whole, this is what independent filmmaking used to be, and why it didn't find an audience.

U.S. Film Festival (Sundance)
Grand Jury Prize: *Heat and Sunlight* (Rob Nilsson)
Special Jury Prize: *The Brave Little Toaster* (Jerry Rees)

Independent Spirit Awards
Film: *Stand and Deliver*
First Film: Donald Petrie, *Mystic Pizza*
Foreign Film: *Wings of Desire*
Actor: Edward James Olmos, *Stand and Deliver*
Actress: Jodie Foster, *Five Corners*
Supporting Actor: Lou Diamond Phillips, *Stand and Deliver*
Supporting Actress: Rosanna De Soto, *Stand and Deliver*
Director: Ramon Menendez, *Stand and Deliver*
Screenplay: Ramon Menendez, Tom Musca, *Stand and Deliver*
Cinematography: Sven Nykvist, *The Unbearable Lightness of Being*

Golden Raspberry Awards
Worst Picture: *Cocktail*
Worst Actor: Sylvester Stallone, *Rambo III*
Worst Actress: Liza Minnelli, *Arthur 2: On the Rocks*, *Rent-a-Cop*
Worst Supporting Actor: Dan Aykroyd, *Caddyshack II*
Worst Supporting Actress:

Kristy McNichol, *Two Moon Junction*
Worst Director: (tie) Blake Edwards, *Sunset*, Stewart Raffill, *Mac and Me*
Worst Screenplay: Heywood Gould, *Cocktail*

Worst Song: "Jack Fresh," *Caddyshack II*
Worst New Star: Ronald McDonald as himself, *Mac and Me*

Box Office (Domestic Rentals)

1	Who Framed Roger Rabbit	$78,000,000	Touchstone
2	Coming to America	65,000,000	Par
3	Good Morning, Vietnam	58,103,000	Touchstone
4	"Crocodile" Dundee II	57,300,000	Par
5	Big	50,800,000	Fox
6	Three Men and a Baby [1988 only]	36,300,000	Touchstone
	[1987–88 total:	81,300,000]	
7	Die Hard	35,000,000	Fox
	Cocktail	35,000,000	Touchstone
9	Moonstruck	34,393,000	MGM/UA
10	Beetlejuice	33,200,000	WB
Other films of note:			
12	Twins [1988 only]	32,000,000	Uni
	[1988–89 total:	57,237,000]	
13	Rambo III	28,000,000	Tri-Star
17	Nightmare on Elm Street 4	22,000,000	New Line
18	Bull Durham	21,900,000	Orion
30	The Last Emperor [1988 only]	16,000,000	Col
	[1987–88 total:	19,000,000]	
48	Friday the 13th Part VII	9,100,000	Par
53	Halloween 4	8,550,000	Galaxy
74	Poltergeist III	5,899,000	MGM/UA
99	The Last Temptation of Christ	3,739,147	Uni

The sight of Bruce Willis with a gun drew snickers in the previews, but Die Hard *was a hit and wound up being the most-imitated movie of the late '80s; soon everyone was ripping off Willis' character, a blue-collar, family-oriented James Bond who cracked wise as he blew up stuff. The sight of Arnold Schwarzenegger in a gentle comedy likewise should have drawn derision, but* Twins *was a hit, too. For all its success,* Halloween *was never able to get a successful series launched, probably because it tried too many different things for sequel fans who wanted the same thrills over and over—as proven by the success of the completely indistinguishable* Friday the 13th *series. The failure of* Poltergeist III *likewise proved that people could spot a cheapo follow-up to a high-budget hit; among horror sequels the greatest success went to the comparatively clever* Nightmare on Elm Street *series, in which the budgets climbed steadily and each film was just different enough and just enough the same. (The director of this one went on to make—you guessed it—* Die Hard 2.*)*

Gebert's Golden Armchairs

The opposite of *Rain Man* in every way, David Cronenberg's ultra-creepy yet psychologically probing *Dead Ringers* is about twin brother gynecologists (Jeremy Irons and Jeremy Irons) who *don't* find each other—they sink together into psychopathology and death. Can't imagine why it wasn't just as big a hit as the Tom Cruise film. Tom Hanks seemed to be taking notes on Dustin Hoffman's Oscar-winning performance, too, but I think Forrest Gump doesn't begin to compare with his wonderful, imaginative performance as a ten-year-old in Tom Hanks' body in *Big*.

Jodie Foster was good in *The Accused*, but she was up against one of the few great female parts of our time—and it's as ridiculous that she beat Glenn Close's spectacularly reptilian seductress in *Dangerous Liaisons* as it was that Judy Holliday beat Bette Davis' Margo Channing. Wim Wenders' lovely poetic meditation on a divided Berlin, *Wings of Desire* suggested that maybe the age of European masterpieces wasn't dead after all. And a Golden Reindeer Dropping to *Scrooged*, Bill Murray's Grinch-spirited, You-guys-didn't-get-the-point-of-the-original-story-did-you? updating of *A Christmas Carol*.

Best American Film: *Dead Ringers*
Best Foreign Film: *Wings of Desire*
Best Actor: Tom Hanks, *Big*
Best Actress: Glenn Close, *Dangerous Liaisons*
Best Director: David Cronenberg, *Dead Ringers*
Worst Hit: *Scrooged*

1989

Spike Lee inaugurated what seems to be becoming a Cannes tradition when he badmouthed the festival after it picked *sex, lies, and videotape* over his *Do the Right Thing*. Lee accused the jury led by German director Wim Wenders (and including both Sally Field and Krzsyztof Kieslowski) of racism; Wenders replied that he had not found anything noble in Lee's film, to which Lee responded—with some justice—that he didn't know what was so noble about a pervert with a video camera, either.

Actually, Lee had just had incredible bad luck in going up against *sex, lies* for Wenders' attention, since the coolly perverse yuppie tale could hardly have been more to Wenders' taste. (Kieslowski's, too; I don't know about Field's.) The original jury chairman was supposed to be Francis Coppola, who might well have liked Lee's film better, but he dropped out and Wenders replaced him at the last minute.

Certainly the year's conversation piece, *Do the Right Thing* might have made it to the Oscars (where it might have made people more uncomfortable about voting for *Driving Miss Daisy*, and at least tipped the race to *Born on the Fourth of July*)— if the critical groups had backed it up. But in the meantime, the ever-ingenious Weinstein brothers at Miramax had cannily targeted the critics as their best Oscar hope for *My Left Foot*— and the Critics Circle bit, touting the Daniel Day-Lewis film as *their* discovery of the year. *My Left Foot* is certainly a well-made little drama—and next to *Do the Right Thing*, and after a decade of adventurous, provocative British films such as Day-Lewis' own *My Beautiful Laundrette*, this art-house triumph-of-the-human-spirit movie was about the most conservative, Oscar-friendly choice the group could have made short of *The Eleanor Roosevelt Story*. The spirit that triumphed, one is tempted to say, was the late Bosley Crowther's. . . .

Academy Awards

*** *Driving Miss Daisy*   AAW GLO BOR
***** **Jessica Tandy in** *Driving Miss Daisy*   AAW GLO BAA '90 BER '90
As cozy a depiction of pre–civil rights race relations as it is, *Daisy* isn't entirely without bite—actually, the scene where Daisy attends a dinner for Martin Luther King but can't see her way to inviting chauffeur Morgan Freeman to come inside nails Hollywood liberalism just about perfectly. And the acting is near perfection: Tandy's picture of querulous old age and

increasing dependency, and Freeman's outward Uncle Tom manner concealing an icy, resigned realism about his station.

Picture
Driving Miss Daisy (Warner Bros., Richard D. Zanuck, Lili Fini Zanuck)
Born on the Fourth of July (Universal, Ho & Ixtlan, A. Kitman Ho, Oliver Stone)
Dead Poets Society (Touchstone/ Silver Screen Partners IV, Steven Haft, Paul Junger Witt, Tony Thomas)
Field of Dreams (Universal, Lawrence Gordon, Charles Gordon)
My Left Foot (Miramax, Ferndale/ Granada, Noel Pearson)

*** Daniel Day-Lewis in *My Left Foot* AAW NYC SOC LAC BAA
It's easy to see why Oscar, with the memory of Day-Lewis' pair of opposites in *A Room With a View* and *My Beautiful Laundrette*, crowned him Mr. Versatility for his portrayal of a witty, self-reliant Irishman with cerebral palsy. At least one thing is clear: doing Shakespeare on film isn't a straight ticket to an Oscar any more—with or without a John Wayne imitation.

Actor
Daniel Day-Lewis, *My Left Foot*
Kenneth Branagh, *Henry V*
Tom Cruise, *Born on the Fourth of July*
Morgan Freeman, *Driving Miss Daisy*
Robin Williams, *Dead Poets Society*

Actress
Jessica Tandy, *Driving Miss Daisy*
Isabelle Adjani, *Camille Claudel*
Pauline Collins, *Shirley Valentine*
Jessica Lange, *The Music Box*
Michelle Pfeiffer, *The Fabulous Baker Boys*

Supporting Actor
Denzel Washington, *Glory*
Danny Aiello, *Do the Right Thing*
Dan Aykroyd, *Driving Miss Daisy*
Marlon Brando, *A Dry White Season*
Martin Landau, *Crimes and Misdemeanors*

Supporting Actress
Brenda Fricker, *My Left Foot*
Anjelica Huston, *Enemies, A Love Story*
Lena Olin, *Enemies, A Love Story*
Julia Roberts, *Steel Magnolias*
Dianne Wiest, *Parenthood*

Director
Oliver Stone, *Born on the Fourth of July*
Woody Allen, *Crimes and Misdemeanors*
Kenneth Branagh, *Henry V*
Jim Sheridan, *My Left Foot*
Peter Weir, *Dead Poets Society*

Original Screenplay: Tom Schulman, *Dead Poets Society*
Adapted Screenplay: Alfred Uhry, *Driving Miss Daisy*
Cinematography: Freddie Francis, *Glory*
Score: Alan Menken, *The Little Mermaid*
Song: "Under the Sea," *The Little Mermaid*, m: Alan Menken; 1: Howard Ashman
Art Direction: Anton Furst, *Batman*
Costume Design: Phyllis Dalton, *Henry V*
Editing: *Born on the Fourth of July*

Sound: *Glory*
Sound Effects Editing: *Indiana Jones and the Last Crusade*
Make-up: *Driving Miss Daisy*
Visual Effects: Dennis Muren, et al., *The Abyss*
Short/Animated: *Balance*
Short/Live Action: *Work Experience*
Documentary/Feature: *Common Threads: Stories from the Quilt* (Robert Epstein, Bill Couturie)
Documentary/Short: *The Johnstown Flood*
Foreign-Language Film: *Cinema Paradiso* (Italy)
Jean Hersholt Humanitarian Award: Howard W. Koch
Special Award: Akira Kurosawa

*** *Cinema Paradiso*   AAW GLO CAN BAA '90
A middle-aged filmmaker remembers the crusty old projectionist who ran the beloved movie theater in his Sicilian home town. Italy's answer to *The Last Picture Show* has enough charm and genuine nostalgic feeling to overcome somewhat heavy treatment (and the fact that Philippe Noiret's projectionist seems a genuinely alarming character).

*** *Born on the Fourth of July* GLO DGA
Oliver Stone's greatest hits in one package—part *Platoon*, part *Midnight Express*, part *The Doors*, and all sledgehammer.

Golden Globes
Picture (Drama): *Born on the Fourth of July*
Picture (Comedy/Musical): *Driving Miss Daisy*

Foreign Film: *Cinema Paradiso* (Italy)
Actor (Drama): Tom Cruise, *Born on the Fourth of July*
Actor (Comedy/Musical): Morgan Freeman, *Driving Miss Daisy*
Actress (Drama): Michelle Pfeiffer, *The Fabulous Baker Boys*
Actress (Comedy/Musical): Jessica Tandy, *Driving Miss Daisy*
Supporting Actor: Denzel Washington, *Glory*
Supporting Actress: Julia Roberts, *Steel Magnolias*
Director: Oliver Stone, *Born on the Fourth of July*
Screenplay: Ron Kovic, Oliver Stone, *Born on the Fourth of July*
Original Score: Alan Menken, *The Little Mermaid*
Original Song: "Under the Sea," *The Little Mermaid*, m: Alan Menken; 1: Howard Ashman
Cecil B. DeMille Award: Audrey Hepburn

Directors Guild of America
Director: Oliver Stone, *Born on the Fourth of July*
D. W. Griffith Award: Ingmar Bergman
Honorary Lifetime Member: Barry Diller, Sid Sheinberg, Elliott Silverstein

*** *The Story of Women*   VEN '88 NYC LAC BOR
Powerful, pointed drama about abortion from Claude Chabrol (a director not normally known for tackling social issues), which captures a perfect moment of hypocrisy: Isabelle Huppert plays a woman prosecuted for murder for having an abortion—during the

Vichy years, when, of course, the sanctity of life was at its highest in France.

*** **Michelle Pfeiffer in** *The Fabulous Baker Boys* GLO NYC SOC LAC BOR BAA
I liked Pfeiffer's rolling about on a piano as much as the next red-blooded male, but—well, the critics' groups really are a boys' club, aren't they?

New York Film Critics Circle
Picture: *My Left Foot*
Foreign Film: *The Story of Women*
Actor: Daniel Day-Lewis, *My Left Foot*
Actress: Michelle Pfeiffer, *The Fabulous Baker Boys*
Supporting Actor: Alan Alda, *Crimes and Misdemeanors*
Supporting Actress: Lena Olin, *Enemies—A Love Story*
Director: Paul Mazursky, *Enemies—A Love Story*
New Director: Kenneth Branagh, *Henry V*
Screenplay: Gus Van Sant, Daniel Yost, *Drugstore Cowboy*
Cinematography: Ernest Dickerson, *Do the Right Thing*
Documentary: *Roger & Me* (Michael Moore)

National Society of Film Critics
Picture: *Drugstore Cowboy*
Actor: Daniel Day-Lewis, *My Left Foot*
Actress: Michelle Pfeiffer, *The Fabulous Baker Boys*
Supporting Actor: Beau Bridges, *The Fabulous Baker Boys*
Supporting Actress: Anjelica Huston, *Enemies—A Love Story*
Director: Gus Van Sant, *Drugstore Cowboy*

Screenplay: Gus Van Sant, Daniel Yost, *Drugstore Cowboy*
Cinematography: Michael Ballhaus, *The Fabulous Baker Boys*
Documentary: *Roger & Me*

Los Angeles Film Critics Association
Film: *Do the Right Thing*
Foreign Film: *Distant Voices, Still Lives, The Story of Women*
Actor: Daniel Day-Lewis, *My Left Foot*
Actress: Andie MacDowell, *sex, lies, and videotape*; Michelle Pfeiffer, *The Fabulous Baker Boys*
Supporting Actor: Danny Aiello, *Do the Right Thing*
Supporting Actress: Brenda Fricker, *My Left Foot*
Director: Spike Lee, *Do the Right Thing*
Screenplay: Gus Van Sant, Daniel Yost, *Drugstore Cowboy*
Cinematography: Michael Ballhaus, *The Fabulous Baker Boys*
Music: Bill Lee, et al., *Do the Right Thing*
Documentary: *Roger & Me*
Animated Film: *The Little Mermaid*
Independent/Experimental Film: *The Long Weekend o' Despair* (Gregg Araki)
New Generation Prize: Laura San Giacomo, actress in *sex, lies, and videotape*
Life Achievement: Stanley Donen
Special Citation: The Margaret Herrick Library of the Academy of Motion Picture Arts and Sciences

National Board of Review
Best English-Language Film:
Driving Miss Daisy
Henry V
sex, lies, and videotape
The Fabulous Baker Boys

My Left Foot
Dead Poets Society
Crimes and Misdemeanors
Born on the Fourth of July
Glory
Field of Dreams
Best Foreign-Language Film:
The Story of Women
Camille Claudel
La Lectrice
Chocolat
The Little Thief
Actor: Morgan Freeman, *Driving Miss Daisy*
Actress: Michelle Pfeiffer, *The Fabulous Baker Boys*
Supporting Actor: Alan Alda, *Crimes and Misdemeanors*
Supporting Actress: Mary Stuart Masterson, *Immediate Family*
Director: Kenneth Branagh, *Henry V*
Documentary: *Roger & Me*
Special Awards: Robert Giroux, for six decades of distinguished efforts on behalf of film
Robert A. Harris, for the restoration of *Lawrence of Arabia*
Critics Andrew Sarris and Molly Haskell

People's Choice Awards
Favorite All-Around Movie: *Batman*
Favorite Drama: *Batman*, *Steel Magnolias*
Favorite Comedy: *Look Who's Talking*
Favorite Movie Actor: Tom Cruise
Favorite Movie Actress: Meryl Streep
World Favorite Movie Actor: Dustin Hoffman
World Favorite Movie Actress: Meryl Streep

British Academy Awards
Film: *Dead Poets Society*
Foreign-Language Film: *Life and Nothing But* (Bertrand Tavernier, France)
Actor: Daniel Day-Lewis, *My Left Foot*
Actress: Pauline Collins, *Shirley Valentine*
Supporting Actor: Ray McAnally, *My Left Foot*
Supporting Actress: Michelle Pfeiffer, *Dangerous Liaisons*
Director: Kenneth Branagh, *Henry V*
Screenplay (Original): Nora Ephron, *When Harry Met Sally*
Screenplay (Adapted): Christopher Hampton, *Dangerous Liaisons*
Academy Fellow: Sir Alec Guinness
Michael Balcon Award: Lewis Gilbert
Special Award: Leslie Hardcastle, Richard Williams

**** *sex, lies, and videotape*
CAN SUN IND
A welcome throwback to the days of '50s serious TV drama, but with up-to-the-minute kinks—and considerably sharper acting than is usually seen in American independent films (not to mention than had been seen before from the likes of Andie MacDowell or Peter Gallagher). Steven Soderbergh's was the first debut film to win a Palme d'Or since Henri Colpi's *Such a Long Absence* in '61—and an impressive and highly promising one it was, even though nothing that has followed (including the masterful *King of the Hill*) has equaled its success.

Cannes Film Festival
Palme d'Or: *sex, lies, and videotape* (Steven Soderbergh, USA)
Special Jury Prize: *Cinema Paradiso* (Giuseppe Tornatore, Italy), *Too Beautiful For You*, (Bertrand Blier, France)
Jury Prize: *Jesus of Montréal* (Denys Arcand, Canada)
Actor: James Spader, *sex, lies, and videotape*
Actress: Meryl Streep, *A Cry in the Dark* (USA)
Director: Emir Kusturica, *Time of the Gypsies* (Yugoslavia)
Artistic Contribution: *Mystery Train* (Jim Jarmusch, USA)
Camera d'Or: *My Twentieth Century* (Ildiko Enyedi, Hungary)
Technical Prize: *Black Rain* (Shohei Imamura, Japan)
International Critics Prize: in competition, *sex, lies, and videotape*; out of competition, *Yaaba* (Idrissa Ouédraogo, Burkino Faso)

Venice Film Festival
Golden Lion: *City of Sadness* (Hou Hsiao-hsien, Taiwan)
Silver Lions: *Recollections of the Yellow House* (Joao César Monteiro, Portugal), *Death of a Tea Master* (Ken Kumai, Japan)
Special Jury Prize: *And There Was Light* (Otar Ioselliani, France)
Actor: Marcello Mastroianni, Massimo Troisi, *What Time Is It?* (Italy)
Actress: Peggy Ashcroft, Geraldine James, *She's Been Away* (UK)
Screenplay: Jules Feiffer, *I Want To Go Home* (France)
Cinematography: Yorgos Arvanitis, *Australia* (Belgium/France/Switzerland)
Music: The cast of *Street Kids* (Italy)
Career Award: Robert Bresson

International Critics Prize: in competition, *The Decalogue* (Krzysztof Kieslowski, Poland); out of competition, *World Without Pity* (Eric Rochant, France)
Pasinetti Italian Critics Prize: film, *I Want To Go Home* (Alain Resnais, France); actor, Massimo Troisi, *What Time Is It?*; actress: Peggy Ashcroft, *She's Been Away*

Berlin Film Festival
Golden Bear: *Rain Man* (Barry Levinson, USA)
Silver Bear: *Avia's Summer* (Eli Cohen, Israel)
Special Jury Prize: *Evening Bells* (Wu Ziniu, China)
Actor: Gene Hackman, *Mississippi Burning* (UK)
Actress: Isabelle Adjani, *Camille Claudel* (France)
Director: Dusan Hanak, *I Love, You Love* (Czechoslovakia)
Outstanding Individual Achievement: Eric Bogosian, writer-actor, *Talk Radio* (USA)
Alfred Bauer Prize: *Sluga* (Vadim Abdraschitov, USSR)
Tribute: Jacques Rivette, for the charm, wit and fantasy of *Gang of Four*
International Critics Prize: *Gang of Four* (Jacques Rivette, France), *I Love, You Love*; Forum, *The Documentator* (István Darday, Györgi Szalai, Hungary), *Biglai Hámilchama Hahi* (Israel)
Honorary Golden Bear: Dustin Hoffman

*** *True Love* SUN
Annabella Sciorra plays a Bronx bride whose wearied wedding planner demeanor turns to astonished protest when she realizes the elaborate ceremony didn't turn her bridegroom

into Prince Charming. An Italian-American wedding is about as easy a subject for caricature as there ever was, but this promising debut for writer-director Nancy Savoca (*Dogfight, Household Saints*) manages to find characters in the caricatures—though it does show up the Sundance jury system that they picked this crowd pleaser, while the crowds picked the more provocative and, ultimately, successful *sex, lies, and videotape.*

Sundance Film Festival
Grand Jury Prize: *True Love* (Nancy Savoca)
Filmmakers Trophy: *Powwow Highway* (Jonathan Wacks)
Audience Award: *sex, lies, and videotape* (Steven Soderbergh)

Independent Spirit Awards
Film: *sex, lies, and videotape*
First Film: Michael Lehmann, *Heathers*
Foreign Film: *My Left Foot*
Actor: Matt Dillon, *Drugstore Cowboy*
Actress: Andie MacDowell, *sex, lies, and videotape*
Supporting Actor: Max Perlich, *Drugstore Cowboy*
Supporting Actress: Laura San Giacomo, *sex, lies, and videotape*

Director: Steven Soderbergh, *sex, lies, and videotape*
Screenplay: Gus Van Sant, Daniel Yost, *Drugstore Cowboy*
Cinematography: Robert Yeoman, *Drugstore Cowboy*

Golden Raspberry Awards
Worst Picture of the Decade: *Mommie Dearest*
Worst Actor of the Decade: Sylvester Stallone, *Cobra, Lock Up, Over the Top, Rambo II, Rambo III, Rhinestone, Rocky IV, Tango & Cash*
Worst Actress of the Decade: Bo Derek, *Bolero, Tarzan, the Ape Man*
Worst New Star of the Decade: Pia Zadora, *Butterfly, The Lonely Lady*
1989 Awards:
Worst Picture: *Star Drek V*
Worst Actor: William Shatner, *Star Drek V*
Worst Actress: Heather Locklear, *Return of the Swamp Thing*
Worst Supporting Actor: Christopher Atkins, *Listen to Me*
Worst Supporting Actress: Brooke Shields (as herself), *Speed Zone*
Worst Director: William Shatner, *Star Drek V*
Worst Screenplay: Eddie Murphy, *Harlem Nights*
Worst Song: "Bring Your Daughter to the Slaughter," *Nightmare on Elm Street 5*

Box Office (Domestic Rentals)

1	*Batman*	$150,500,000	WB
2	*Indiana Jones and the Last Crusade*	115,500,000	Par
3	*Lethal Weapon 2*	79,500,000	WB
4	*Honey, I Shrunk the Kids*	71,097,000	Disney
5	*Rain Man [1989 only]*	65,000,000	MGM/UA
	[1989–90 total:	86,000,000]	
6	*Back to the Future Part II*	63,000,000	Uni
7	*Ghostbusters II*	61,649,019	Col
8	*Look Who's Talking [1989 only]*	55,000,000	Tri-Star

	[1989–90 total:	68,365,000]	
9	Parenthood	48,600,000	Uni
10	Dead Poets Society	47,596,000	Disney
Other films of note:			
11	National Lampoon's Christmas Vacation	42,000,000	WB
12	When Harry Met Sally	41,976,751	Col
16	Field of Dreams	30,309,587	Uni
17	The Little Mermaid [1989 only]	30,000,000	Disney
	[1989–90 total:	40,227,000]	
21	Star Trek V: The Final Frontier	27,100,000	Par
36	Licence to Kill	16,662,000	MGM/UA
45	Do the Right Thing	13,043,257	Uni
53	sex, lies, and videotape	10,000,000	Miramax

Hollywood's megahit drought finally came to an end with two superheroes who smashed through the $100 million mark. Otherwise, sequelitis dominated the charts, with no less than four sequels in the top ten (and this top ten have in turn produced to date eight sequels, one live-action and two animated TV series). Even so, the top ten also found room for a Best Picture Oscar–winner about autism (blessed with the highest star wattage of any winner in recent years), a warm and gooshy comedy-drama about parenting (I mean the one that doesn't have babies that talk like Bruce Willis), and Robin Williams teaching Macbeth to preppies. Sign of the action times: even the worst Star Trek film to date found nearly twice the audience of the best James Bond film in many years, while Spike Lee demonstrated that losing at Cannes could be more profitable than winning (as sex, lies did) if you hyped the right thing.

Gebert's Golden Armchairs

Do the Right Thing (which L.A. picked) and Drugstore Cowboy, both the best realist and the best surrealist movie of the year (which the National Society picked), seem like clearly the best fiction films of the year. But Roger & Me is the the one I'd most like to see imitated—after decades of dull, objective documentaries by invisible authors, Michael Moore's hilarious, wonderfully unfair attack on General Motors is a reminder that the camera can be as mighty as the pen in the hands of someone with a point of view and a sense of humor.

Denys Arcand's Jesus of Montréal, which was what everyone expected to be the film that would send Spike Lee home disappointed from Cannes, is a grown-up delight—a film about a '60s-style theater troupe doing the Passion Play that draws witty, cheeky parallels between the earnest, committed actors and the Apostles (instead of a serpent in the desert, a lawyer offers Jesus a TV deal). And if you liked Michael J. Fox's mom trying to date him as a bobby-soxer at the malt shop in Back to the Future, you'll love her as an alcoholic middle-aged slut trying to bang him in the sequel to 1985's hit, apparently the first Steven Spielberg production written by Charles Bukowski.

Best American Film: *Roger & Me*
Best Foreign Film: *Jesus of Montréal*
Best Actor: Morgan Freeman, *Driving Miss Daisy, Glory*

Best Actress: Jessica Tandy, *Driving Miss Daisy*
Best Director: Gus Van Sant, *Drugstore Cowboy*
Worst Hit: *Back To the Future Part II*

The National Film Registry

Following the furor over colorization, in 1988 Congress passed the National Film Preservation Act, authorizing the Librarian of Congress to designate each year 25 "culturally, historically or aesthetically significant" films, all at least ten years old, which would be preserved in their original form by the Library of Congress. If a film on the list were exhibited or released on video in altered form, it would have to be preceded by a notice to that effect—or face a $10,000 fine. Representatives from the industry and groups such as the Directors Guild, the American Film Institute, and the National Society of Film Critics would make recommendations, though the final list would be chosen by the Librarian of Congress. The films honored would represent a governmental commitment to the cause of film preservation—and of artistic integrity.

The first 25 films announced in 1989 were mostly the obvious classics of the studio era, like *Gone With the Wind* and *On the Waterfront*—and including seven films owned by Ted Turner. The one surprise on the list was *The Learning Tree*, a little-known film by black director Gordon Parks, Sr., chosen presumably in the spirit of multiculturalism. Librarian of Congress James H. Billington prefaced the list (and anticipated the obvious criticisms) by saying "this list of 25 films is not a list of the best 25 American films. Film critics and scholars could not agree on such a list, and the Library of Congress would not embark on any such futile exercise. This is not Academy Awards night." Nevertheless, it was impossible to avoid seeing the list as a "Top 25" and second-guessing it—even the bill's sponsor complained that his favorite (*To Kill a Mockingbird*) hadn't made the cut.

A more substantial complaint was that sticking a notice at the beginning of a handful of well-known studio-made talkies hardly addressed the real preservation issues facing archives and film libraries. Subsequent lists have made more of an effort to go beyond Hollywood features and extend protection and recognition to more marginal areas of film, naming independent films, documentaries, cartoons, Yiddish-language and all-black films, and even a home movie—Abraham Zapruder's 8mm footage of John F. Kennedy's assassination.

Yet 25 films a year would still be a ridiculously small number to preserve; in reality the Library of Congress has been at the forefront of film preservation since long before 1989, and on a much broader scale than 25 films a year. If the National Film Registry accomplishes anything, it's not that it makes a serious dent in the preservation backlog on its own, but that it serves as a PR event to draw annual attention to the wealth and variety of our movie heritage, and to remind us how much more there is to preserve than the few gilt-edged studio classics. As *Chicago Tribune* critic and National Society of Film Critics representative Dave Kehr wrote, tongue only slightly in cheek, on the 1992 selection of the legendary no-budget B movie *Detour* (largely through his own efforts), "That [*Detour*] has now joined *Gone With the Wind*, *Casablanca* and *Citizen Kane* on the list of the first 100 titles deemed worthy of the protection of the U.S. government is a tribute to the democratic spirit that still rules this land. No matter how disadvantaged a movie may appear to be, no matter how abject and obscure its creator, it can still make good."

Titles are listed alphabetically; the names of directors or other identifying notes have been added only for films which are likely to be unfamiliar.

1989
The Best Years of Our Lives
Casablanca
Citizen Kane
The Crowd
Dr. Strangelove
The General
Gone With the Wind
The Grapes of Wrath
High Noon
Intolerance
The Learning Tree (1969, Gordon Parks, Sr.; first studio film directed by an African-American)
The Maltese Falcon
Mr. Smith Goes to Washington
Modern Times
Nanook of the North (1921 Eskimo documentary, Robert Flaherty)
On the Waterfront
The Searchers

Singin' in the Rain
Snow White and the Seven Dwarfs
Some Like It Hot
Star Wars
Sunrise
Sunset Boulevard
Vertigo
The Wizard of Oz

1990
All About Eve
All Quiet on the Western Front
Bringing Up Baby
Dodsworth
Duck Soup
Fantasia
The Freshman (1925, Harold Lloyd)
The Godfather
The Great Train Robbery (1903 Edison Co. one-reeler considered the first Western)

Harlan County, USA (labor documentary)
How Green Was My Valley
It's a Wonderful Life
Killer of Sheep (1978, black director Charles Burnett)
Love Me Tonight
Meshes of the Afternoon (1943 experimental film, Maya Deren)
Ninotchka
Primary (1960 cinema-vérité documentary on Kennedy campaign)
Raging Bull
Rebel Without a Cause
Red River
The River (1937 New Deal documentary, Pare Lorentz)
Sullivan's Travels
Top Hat
The Treasure of the Sierra Madre
A Woman Under the Influence

1991
The Battle of San Pietro (1945 war documentary, John Huston)
The Blood of Jesus (1941 all-black film, Spencer Williams)
Chinatown
City Lights
David Holzman's Diary (1968 independent film, Jim McBride)
Frankenstein
Gertie the Dinosaur (1914 animated cartoon, Winsor McCay)
Gigi
Greed
High School (1968 documentary, Frederick Wiseman)
I Am a Fugitive From a Chain Gang
The Italian (1915 immigrant drama produced by Thomas Ince)
King Kong
Lawrence of Arabia
The Magnificent Ambersons
My Darling Clementine
Out of the Past
A Place in the Sun

The Poor Little Rich Girl (1917, Mary Pickford)
The Prisoner of Zenda (1937)
Shadow of a Doubt
Sherlock, Jr.
Tevya (1939 Yiddish-language film)
Trouble in Paradise
2001: A Space Odyssey

1992
Adam's Rib
Annie Hall
The Bank Dick
Big Business (1929 Laurel and Hardy short)
The Big Parade
The Birth of a Nation
Bonnie and Clyde
Carmen Jones
Castro Street (1966 experimental film, Bruce Baillie)
Detour
Dog Star Man (1964 experimental film, Stan Brakhage)
Double Indemnity
Footlight Parade
The Gold Rush
Letter from an Unknown Woman
Morocco
Nashville
Night of the Hunter
Paths of Glory
Psycho
Ride the High Country
Salesman (1969 documentary by Albert and David Maysles)
Salt of the Earth (1954 independent labor drama made by blacklistees)
What's Opera, Doc?
Within Our Gates (1920 all-black silent, Oscar Micheaux)

1993
An American in Paris
Badlands
The Black Pirate (1926, Douglas Fairbanks)
Blade Runner
Cat People

The Cheat (1915, Cecil B. DeMille)

Chulas Fronteras (1976 documentary on Hispanic music and culture, Les Blank)

Eaux d'Artifice (1953 experimental film by Kenneth Anger)

The Godfather, Part II

His Girl Friday

It Happened One Night

Lassie Come Home

The Magical Maestro (1952 Tex Avery cartoon)

The March of Time: Inside Nazi Germany (1938 newsreel)

A Night at the Opera

Nothing But a Man (1964 independent film about black life, Michael Roemer)

One Flew Over the Cuckoo's Nest

Point of Order (1964 documentary of Army-McCarthy hearings, Emile deAntonio)

Shadows (1959, John Cassavetes)

Shane

The Sweet Smell of Success

Touch of Evil

Where Are My Children? (1916, by Lois Weber, most prominent silent woman director)

The Wind (1928, Victor Sjostrom)

Yankee Doodle Dandy

1994
The African Queen
The Apartment

The Cool World (1963 independent film, Shirley Clarke)

A Corner in Wheat (1909, D.W. Griffith Biograph short)

E.T. The Extra-Terrestrial

The Exploits of Elaine (1914 serial with Pearl White)

Force of Evil

Freaks

Hell's Hinges (1916, William S. Hart western)

Hospital (1970 documentary, Frederick Wiseman)

Invasion of the Body Snatchers (1956)

The Lady Eve

Louisiana Story (1948 Robert Flaherty documentary)

The Manchurian Candidate

Marty

Meet Me in St. Louis

Midnight Cowboy

A Movie (1958 experimental film by Bruce Conner)

Pinocchio

Safety Last

Scarface (1932)

Snow White (1933 Betty Boop cartoon with Cab Calloway, Max Fleischer)

Tabu

Taxi Driver

The Zapruder Film (home movie footage of the Kennedy assassination)

1990

The first Sundance to be attended by the press en masse turned out to be the black Sundance—the popular hit it produced was the Hudlin brothers' *House Party*, the art-house hit it produced was Charles Burnett's *To Sleep With Anger* (along the way converting his virtually unknown 1978 film, *Killer of Sheep*, into the Great Lost Classic of African-American cinema), and the jury prize went to the most obviously independent of the bunch, *Chameleon Street*. (Spike Lee, who founded the black indie scene singlehandedly, obviously had been attending the wrong festival.)

Venice has had a thing for Shakespeare since *Hamlet*, and 1990 brought the festival two offbeat adaptations of the Bard—an all-*cat* adaptation of Prokofiev's ballet of *Romeo and Juliet* (I just report 'em, folks, I don't make 'em up) with the voices of John Hurt and Vanessa Redgrave, and Tom Stoppard's *Rosencrantz and Guildenstern Are Dead*. The latter turned out to be a surprising and highly unpopular choice for the Golden Lion when it won over the strongest Venice field since the '60s, including *GoodFellas*, Jane Campion's *An Angel at My Table*, and *Mr. & Mrs. Bridge*. The prize was apparently the work of jury chief Gore Vidal, whose admiration for Stoppard's brainy ironies apparently had no trouble overcoming his lack of interest in modern-day gangsters, New Zealand coming-of-age tales—or the first-rate filming of a novel by an American writer of Vidal's own generation.

Academy Awards

*** Dances With Wolves AAW DGA GLO BOR BER *GoodFellas* is as obviously superior as *Taxi Driver* was to *Rocky*—but I think the Academy made the right choice anyway. I mean, by this point anyone who thinks the Oscars represent the voice of posterity needs to go watch *Cimarron* or *Gigi* a few more times. *GoodFellas* can take care of itself in that regard. But here was Kevin Costner, a brand-

new sex symbol star, who could have cranked out one *Bodyguard* or *Revenge* after another—and instead he bet the farm on an ambitious, pro-Indian three-hour western. They called this one "Kevin's Gate," too, just like *Waterworld*; and then it came out, and he'd pulled it off (in a way that his pal Larry Kasdan hadn't with *Silverado*). The New Age western, grand and romantic and self-deprecating (and one-sided and sometimes silly, sure—I'll call you Two

430

Socks, and you'll call me Dinner). It isn't a great film, but it is a good film and a grand gesture, and the best thing Hollywood could do with their silly statue was salute him for having the balls that so many suddenly-rich-and-adored young men and women in his position haven't had.

Picture
Dances With Wolves (Orion, Tig, Jim Wilson, Kevin Costner)
Awakenings (Columbia, Walter F. Parks, Lawrence Lasker)
Ghost (Paramount, Howard W. Koch, Lisa Weinstein)
The Godfather, Part III (Paramount, Zoetrope)
GoodFellas (Warner Bros., Irwin Winkler)

**** Jeremy Irons in *Reversal of Fortune*   AAW GLO SOC LAC
Jeremy Irons thanked David Cronenberg in his Oscar acceptance speech—recognizing not only that *Dead Ringers* was a better performance (or two), but, I suspect, that Cronenberg had finally taught him how to loosen up for the camera and not just be the tiresome Etonian sob sister of *The French Lieutenant's Woman* and *The Mission*. He's deliciously droll as the charmingly unspeakable Claus von Bülow in this odd but captivating hybrid—a TV movie-of-the-week with aspirations to be *Sunset Boulevard*.

Actor
Jeremy Irons, *Reversal of Fortune*

Kevin Costner, *Dances With Wolves*
Robert De Niro, *Awakenings*
Gérard Depardieu, *Cyrano de Bergerac*
Richard Harris, *The Field*

** Kathy Bates in *Misery*
AAW GLO
Bates is kind of fun as a psycho fan tormenting her favorite romance novelist—but I wouldn't say it's any more insightful or varied a caricature than the sort of work that Andrea Martin used to do every week on SCTV, say. And am I really the only person who could spot every one of director Rob Reiner's wheezing scares a mile away?

Actress
Kathy Bates, *Misery*
Anjelica Huston, *The Grifters*
Julia Roberts, *Pretty Woman*
Meryl Streep, *Postcards from the Edge*
Joanne Woodward, *Mr. & Mrs. Bridge*

Supporting Actor
Joe Pesci, *GoodFellas*
Bruce Davison, *Longtime Companion*
Andy Garcia, *The Godfather, Part III*
Graham Greene, *Dances With Wolves*
Al Pacino, *Dick Tracy*

Supporting Actress
Whoopi Goldberg, *Ghost*
Annette Bening, *The Grifters*
Lorraine Bracco, *GoodFellas*
Diane Ladd, *Wild at Heart*
Mary McDonnell, *Dances with Wolves*

Director
Kevin Costner, *Dances With Wolves*
Francis Ford Coppola, *The Godfather, Part III*
Stephen Frears, *The Grifters*
Barbet Schroeder, *Reversal of Fortune*
Martin Scorsese, *GoodFellas*

Original Screenplay: Bruce Joel Rubin, *Ghost*
Adapted Screenplay: Michael Blake, *Dances With Wolves*
Cinematography: Dean Semler, *Dances With Wolves*
Score: John Barry, *Dances With Wolves*
Song: "Sooner or Later (I Always Get My Man)," *Dick Tracy*, ml: Stephen Sondheim
Art Direction: Richard Sylbert, *Dick Tracy*
Costume Design: Franca Squarciapino, *Cyrano de Bergerac*
Editing: *Dances With Wolves*
Sound: *Dances With Wolves*
Sound Effects Editing: *The Hunt for Red October*
Make-up: *Dick Tracy*
Short/Animated: *Creature Comforts* (Aardman Animations Ltd., Nick Park)
Short/Live Action: *The Lunch Date* (Adam Davidson)
Documentary/Feature: *American Dream* (Barbara Kopple)
Documentary/Short: *Days of Waiting*
Foreign-Language Film: *Journey of Hope* (Switzerland)
Irving G. Thalberg Award: Richard D. Zanuck, David Brown
Special Awards: Sophia Loren
Myrna Loy

Golden Globes
Picture (Drama): *Dances With Wolves*

Picture (Comedy/Musical): *Green Card*
Foreign Film: *Cyrano de Bergerac* (France)
Actor (Drama): Jeremy Irons, *Reversal of Fortune*
Actor (Comedy/Musical): Gérard Depardieu, *Green Card*
Actress (Drama): Kathy Bates, *Misery*
Actress (Comedy/Musical): Julia Roberts, *Pretty Woman*
Supporting Actor: Bruce Davison, *Longtime Companion*
Supporting Actress: Whoopi Goldberg, *Ghost*
Director: Kevin Costner, *Dances With Wolves*
Screenplay: Michael Blake, *Dances With Wolves*
Original Score: Ryuichi Sakamoto, Richard Horowitz, *The Sheltering Sky*
Original Song: "Blaze of Glory," *Young Guns II*, ml: Jon Bon Jovi
Cecil B. DeMille Award: Jack Lemmon

Directors Guild of America
Director: Kevin Costner, *Dances With Wolves*
Honorary Lifetime Member: Gilbert Cates

***** *GoodFellas* AAW SOC LAC BAA VEN
Thirty years of one couple's life in the Mob, chronicled in colorful, exhilarating fashion—with its soundtrack of nonstop, perfectly chosen oldies, it's the MGM musical that Scorsese always wanted to make (all-singing, all-swaggering, all-killing). Though the action takes place in the '50s through the '70s, underneath there's a sly comment on '80s yuppie materialism here—Ray Liotta's

character has the beginnings of a moral sense, unlike his companions, and he never kills anyone himself, but both he and wife Lorraine Bracco are so seduced by the good life that they're willing to go along with practically anything to keep the cash flowing. An easy choice for the critics, the National Society in particular—it beat *Dances With Wolves* with 43 points . . . to *two*.

New York Film Critics Circle
Picture: *GoodFellas*
Foreign Film: *The Nasty Girl*
Actor: Robert De Niro, *GoodFellas, Awakenings*
Actress: Joanne Woodward, *Mr. & Mrs. Bridge*
Supporting Actor: Bruce Davison, *Longtime Companion*
Supporting Actress: Jennifer Jason Leigh, *Miami Blues, Last Exit to Brooklyn*
Director: Martin Scorsese, *GoodFellas*
New Director: Whit Stillman, *Metropolitan*
Screenplay: Ruth Prawer Jhabvala, *Mr. & Mrs. Bridge*
Cinematography: Vittorio Storaro, *The Sheltering Sky*

**** Anjelica Huston in *The Grifters* SOC LAC IND
This neo-*noir* can't decide if it's set in reality or in an old movie—by a stroke of bad luck, it's directed by the one British filmmaker alive (Stephen Frears) who *can't* seem to lose himself in empty stylistics. But at least it's a juicy piece for its actresses, Anjelica Huston

and Annette Bening, as two tough, heartless females (mom and girlfriend) fighting over con man/sap John Cusack.

National Society of Film Critics
Picture: *GoodFellas*
Foreign Film: *Ariel*
Actor: Jeremy Irons, *Reversal of Fortune*
Actress: Anjelica Huston, *The Grifters, The Witches*
Supporting Actor: Bruce Davison, *Longtime Companion*
Supporting Actress: Annette Bening, *The Grifters*
Director: Martin Scorsese, *GoodFellas*
Screenplay: Charles Burnett, *To Sleep With Anger*
Cinematography: Peter Suschitzky, *Where the Heart Is*
Documentary: *Berkeley in the Sixties*
Special Citation: Jean-Luc Godard, whose work has inspired, entertained and moved us for three decades

Los Angeles Film Critics Association
Film: *GoodFellas*
Foreign Film: *Life and Nothing But*
Actor: Jeremy Irons, *Reversal of Fortune*
Actress: Anjelica Huston, *The Grifters, The Witches*
Supporting Actor: Joe Pesci, *GoodFellas*
Supporting Actress: Lorraine Bracco, *GoodFellas*
Director: Martin Scorsese, *GoodFellas*
Screenplay: Nicholas Kazan, *Reversal of Fortune*
Cinematography: Michael Ballhaus, *GoodFellas*
Music: Ryuichi Sakamoto, *The Sheltering Sky*

Documentary: *Paris Is Burning*, *Pictures of the Old World*
Animated Film: *The Rescuers Down Under*
Independent/Experimental Film: *Tongues Untied* (Marlon Riggs)
New Generation Prize: Jane Campion, director of *Sweetie*
Life Achievement: Chuck Jones, Blake Edwards
Special Citation: Charles Burnett

National Board of Review
Best English-Language Film:
Dances With Wolves
Hamlet
GoodFellas
Awakenings
Reversal of Fortune
Miller's Crossing
Metropolitan
Mr. & Mrs. Bridge
Avalon
The Grifters
Best Foreign-Language Film:
Cyrano de Bergerac
Jesus of Montréal
The Nasty Girl
Monsieur Hire
Tie Me Up! Tie Me Down!
Actor: Robert De Niro, Robin Williams, *Awakenings*
Actress: Mia Farrow, *Alice*
Supporting Actor: Joe Pesci, *GoodFellas*
Supporting Actress: Winona Ryder, *Mermaids*
Director: Kevin Costner, *Dances With Wolves*

People's Choice Awards
Favorite All-Around Movie: *Pretty Woman*
Favorite Drama: *Ghost*
Favorite Comedy: *Pretty Woman*
Favorite Movie Actor: Mel Gibson
Favorite Movie Actress: Julia Roberts

British Academy Awards
Film: *GoodFellas*
Foreign-Language Film: *Cinema Paradiso* (Giuseppe Tornatore, Italy)
Actor: Philippe Noiret, *Cinema Paradiso*
Actress: Jessica Tandy, *Driving Miss Daisy*
Supporting Actor: Salvatore Cascio, *Cinema Paradiso*
Supporting Actress: Whoopi Goldberg, *Ghost*
Director: Martin Scorsese, *GoodFellas*
Screenplay (Original): Giuseppe Tornatore, *Cinema Paradiso*
Screenplay (Adapted): Nicholas Pileggi, Martin Scorsese, *GoodFellas*
Academy Fellow: Sir Paul Fox
Michael Balcon Award: Jeremy Thomas
Special Award: Dame Peggy Ashcroft, Leslie Halliwell

• *Wild at Heart* CAN
Festivals often give awards to a new film in order to honor a filmmaker's earlier work—and one has to hope that that was the reason David Lynch's ugly, trashy, white-trash-in-love story, in which Nicolas Cage merely repeats his *Raising Arizona* character, won a Palme d'Or.

Cannes Film Festival
Palme d'Or: *Wild at Heart* (David Lynch, USA)
Special Jury Prize: *The Sting of Death* (Kohei Oguri, Japan), *Tilai* (Idrissa Ouédraogo, Burkino Faso)
Jury Prize: *Hidden Agenda* (Ken Loach, UK)
Actor: Gérard Depardieu, *Cyrano de Bergerac* (France)
Actress: Krystyna Janda, *Interrogation* (Poland)

Director: Pavel Lounguine, *Taxi Blues* (France-USSR)
Artistic Contribution: *The Mother* (Gleb Panfilov, USSR-Italy)
Special Mention: to Manoel de Oliveira and Andrzej Wajda
Camera d'Or: *Freeze—Die—Come to Life* (Vitali Kanevsky, Russia)
Technical Prize: Pierre Lhomme (cinematography), *Cyrano de Bergerac*
International Critics Prize: in competition, *The Sting of Death* (Japan), other, *Swan Lake: The Zone* (Yuri Ilienko, USSR); special mention to Manoel de Oliveira

Screenplay: Helle Ryslinge, *Syrup* (Denmark)
Cinematography: Mauro Marchetti, *Boys on the Outside* (Italy)
Editing: Dominique Auvray, *No Fear No Die* (France)
Music: Valeri Milovanski, *The Sole Witness*
Career Awards: Miklós Jancsó, Marcello Mastroianni
Senate Gold Medal: *Raspad* (Mikhail Belikov, USSR)
International Critics Prize: *Mathilukal* (Adoor Gopalkirshnan, India), *The Station* (Sergio Rubini, Italy), *La Discrète* (Christian Vincent, France)

** *Rosencrantz and Guildenstern Are Dead*   VEN
Tom Stoppard's late '60s play was basically an absurdist stunt—follow the two minor dupes from *Hamlet* as they wander about Elsinore, oblivious to Shakespeare's play. The idea that *Hamlet* was going on, live, just out of earshot was amusing on stage—and filming it preserves the joke in amber, where it merely seems perverse to watch these guys instead of Hamlet, Polonius, et al.

Venice Film Festival
Golden Lion: *Rosencrantz and Guildenstern Are Dead* (Tom Stoppard, USA)
Special Jury Prize: *An Angel at My Table* (Jane Campion, New Zealand)
Actor: Oleg Borisov, *The Sole Witness* (Bulgaria)
Actress: Gloria Munchmeyer, *The Moon in the Mirror* (Chile)
Director: Martin Scorsese, *GoodFellas* (USA)

** *The Music Box*   BER
*** *Larks on a String*   BER
Berlin's first two post-Wall picks reflect a certain taking-stock of the two Germanys' pasts. Costa-Gavras' *Music Box* was inspired by American news stories about aged immigrants who suddenly turned out to have been Nazi criminals; it has nice Chicago-ethnic atmosphere, but since there's no point to the movie if prosecutor Jessica Lange doesn't uncover the worst about her dad (Armin Mueller-Stahl), there's not much suspense. *Larks on a String*, by the leading Czech purveyor of whimsy, Jiri Menzel (*Closely Watched Trains*), is an amusingly subversive comedy about workers in a scrap yard, poking fun at the contrast between grand Party rhetoric and the lackadaisical attitudes and work ethic of the workers. But it too would seem too minor for a festival prize

if not for the fact that it was actually made in 1969 and banned; Menzel spent nearly a decade before he was in the authorities' good graces again, and it would be hard to say that his subsequent work has had even this film's gentle bite.

Berlin Film Festival
Golden Bear: *The Music Box* (Costa-Gavras, USA), *Larks on a String* (Jiri Menzel, Czechoslovakia)
Silver Bear: *Coming Out* (Heiner Carow, East Germany)
Special Jury Prize: *The Weakness Syndrome* (Kira Muratova, USSR)
Single Performance: Iain Glen, *Silent Scream* (UK)
Ensemble: Jessica Tandy, Morgan Freeman, *Driving Miss Daisy* (USA)
Director: Michael Verhoeven, *The Nasty Girl* (West Germany)
Special Achievement Award: Xie Fei [director] for *Black Snow* (China)
Alfred Bauer Prize: *The Guard* (Aleksandr Rogoshkin, USSR)
Golden Berlin Camera/40th Anniversary Prize: Oliver Stone
International Critics Prize: *The Guard, Larks on a String, Spur der Steine* (Frank Beyer, East Germany [1966 film]); Forum, *Near Death* (Frederick Wiseman, USA)

*** *Chameleon Street* SUN Wendell B. Harris, Jr.'s low-budget account of the true adventures of one Douglas Street, a black con man who posed (with success in each case) as a surgeon, an African exchange student at Yale, and a lawyer for the Detroit Human Rights Commission, among other things. Dramatically a little uneven, but a sardonically funny account of the essential absurdity of the black man's position in a white-dominated society (and the semi-dangerous fun you could have subverting it).

Sundance Film Festival
Grand Jury Prize/dramatic: *Chameleon Street* (Wendell B. Harris, Jr.)
Grand Jury Prize/ documentary: *H-2 Worker* (Stephanie Black), *Water and Power* (Pat O'Neill)
Special Jury Prize: dramatic: *To Sleep With Anger* (Charles Burnett); recognition to documentary *Samsara: Death and Rebirth in Cambodia* (Ellen Bruno)
Cinematography: dramatic: Peter Deming, *House Party*; documentary: Maryse Alberti, *H-2 Worker*
Filmmakers Trophy: dramatic: *House Party* (Reginald Hudlin); documentary: *Metamorphosis: Man Into Woman* (Lisa Leeman)
Audience Award: dramatic competition: *Longtime Companion* (Norman René); documentary competition: *Berkeley in the Sixties* (Hark Kitchell)

Independent Spirit Awards
Film: *The Grifters*
First Film: Whit Stillman, *Metropolitan*
Foreign Film: *Sweetie*
Actor: Danny Glover, *To Sleep With Anger*
Actress: Anjelica Huston, *The Grifters*
Supporting Actor: Bruce Davison, *Longtime Companion*

Supporting Actress: Sheryl Lee Ralph, *To Sleep With Anger*
Director: Charles Burnett, *To Sleep With Anger*
Screenplay: Charles Burnett, *To Sleep With Anger*
Cinematography: Frederic Elmes, *Wild at Heart*

Harvard Lampoon Movie Worsts
Worst Movie: *Darkman*
Worst Actor: Patrick Swayze, *Ghost, Road House*
Worst Actress: Bette Midler, *Beaches*
Worst Soundtrack: *Pretty Woman*

Golden Raspberry Awards
Worst Picture: (tie) *The Adventures of Ford Fairlane, Ghosts Can't Do It*

Worst Actor: Andrew "Dice" Clay, *The Adventures of Ford Fairlane*
Worst Actress: Bo Derek, *Ghosts Can't Do It*
Worst Supporting Actor: Donald Trump (as himself), *Ghosts Can't Do It*
Worst Supporting Actress: Sofia Coppola, *Godfather III*
Worst Director: John Derek, *Ghosts Can't Do It*
Worst Screenplay: Daniel Waters, James Cappe, David Arnott, *The Adventures of Ford Fairlane*
Worst Song: "He's Comin' Back (The Devil!)," *Repossessed*
Worst New Star: Sofia Coppola, *Godfather III*

Box Office (Domestic Rentals)

1	*Ghost*	$94,000,000	Par
2	*Pretty Woman*	81,903,000	Disney
3	*Home Alone [1990 only]*	80,000,000	TriStar
	[1990–91 total:	*140,000,000]*	
4	*Die Hard 2*	66,500,000	Fox
5	*Total Recall*	65,000,000	Tri-Star
6	*Teenage Mutant Ninja Turtles*	62,000,000	New Line
7	*Dick Tracy*	59,526,000	Disney
8	*The Hunt for Red October*	58,500,000	Par
9	*Driving Miss Daisy*	49,500,000	WB
10	*Back to the Future Part III*	48,951,109	Uni
	Other films of note:		
13	*Days of Thunder*	40,000,000	Par
15	*Born on the Fourth of July*	36,789,030	Uni
20	*The Godfather, Part III [1990 only]*	28,000,000	Par
	[1990–91 total:	*38,000,000]*	
26	*Rocky V*	20,000,000	MGM/UA
31	*GoodFellas*	18,200,000	WB
40	*Edward Scissorhands [1990 only]*	13,000,000	TriStar
	[1990–91 total:	*27,500,000]*	
53	*Ernest Goes to Jail*	11,413,000	Disney
79	*My Left Foot*	7,000,000	Miramax
99	*Henry V*	4,900,000	Goldwyn
119	*Roger & Me*	3,000,000	WB

Don't they make movies for men anymore? A host of hyped-up actioners like Die Hard 2 *and* Total Recall *wound up taking a back seat to date movies like* Pretty Woman, Ghost, *and* Home Alone. *The latter increased the number of bankable kid stars to one, while* Pretty Woman *and* Ghost *increased the number of bankable female stars to two—or maybe three, since the latter seems to have done as much for supporting player Whoopi Goldberg's then-stalled career as it did for star Demi Moore's. The year's most oversold movie,* Dick Tracy, *arrived as something of an anticlimax to its ubiquitous marketing campaign, and made back only about half its cost; another noisy, expensive flop,* Days of Thunder, *actually did slightly better than its star's earnest try for an Oscar in* Born on the Fourth of July.

Gebert's Golden Armchairs

It was Costner's year, but it was Scorsese's film—and Joe Pesci's amazingly wild performance—that will last. Due for rediscovery someday is Debra Winger's risky, no-holds-barred performance as the woman who loses herself in sexual captivity in the desert in Bertolucci's (frankly, rather grueling) film of Paul Bowles' classic novel *The Sheltering Sky* (or *Last Tango in Morocco*). Michael Verhoeven's *The Nasty Girl*, a sharp satire about a German woman who pokes into her town's Nazi past, was the liveliest and smartest thing to come from that country since Fassbinder's death. And *Cadillac Man* is the epitome of the bad-idea–high-concept movie—hey, let's combine *Tin Men* and *Dog Day Afternoon* into the same movie, and Robin Williams will save us!

Best American Film: *GoodFellas*
Best Foreign Film: *The Nasty Girl*
Best Actor: Joe Pesci, *GoodFellas*
Best Actress: Debra Winger, *The Sheltering Sky*
Best Director: Martin Scorsese, *GoodFellas*
Worst Hit: *Cadillac Man*

1991

At the Oscars *The Silence of the Lambs* became only the third film ever to sweep all of the top prizes—though unlike *It Happened One Night* and *Cuckoo's Nest*, *Lambs*' triumphs mainly seem to have been by default. This gruesome, commercial thriller was ordinarily the sort of thing that wouldn't have gotten within miles of Oscar, even with its class cast. But the ball started rolling when critics' long-running admiration for Jonathan Demme carried it to a four-way New York Film Critics Circle win—even though a pumped-up, manipulative FBI thriller was pretty much the opposite of every laidback post-hippie thing Demme's previous work had been about.

The other groups didn't share New York's enthusiasm—L.A. liked *Bugsy* and Nick Nolte; while at the National Society, given a lack of enthusiasm for anything else, the avant-garde wing was able to push British filmmaker Mike Leigh's *Life Is Sweet* past *Thelma & Louise*, *Bugsy*, and *Naked Lunch*—and Hopkins placed well behind River Phoenix, Beatty, and Nolte. Going into the Oscars, Hopkins was no doubt a lock, but probably the biggest buzz was behind *JFK*. Then too many questions were raised about Oliver Stone's conspiracy theorizing (whatever the appeal of his filmmaking), and meanwhile *Bugsy*, the other contender, flopped at the box office. The vacuum at the top sucked *Lambs* upward—and Thelma and Louise canceled each other out in the Actress category to complete its triumph.

Academy Awards

*** *The Silence of the Lambs*
AAW DGA NYC BOR PEO
**** **Anthony Hopkins** AAW
NYC BOR BAA
** **Jodie Foster** AAW GLO
NYC BAA
Hopkins' Hannibal Lecter is a lot of fun, even if British actors are trained to do this sort of thing in their sleep (see Cushing, Peter), and it *is* the only Oscar given for making rude noises with your tongue and lips. (Jim Carrey, there's hope.) But was Foster's Southern accent and lamb-in-the-headlights naïveté worthy of an Oscar—in the year of Susan Sarandon's hardbitten, lived-in Thelma? She's not terrible—she's not much of anything, really (Wah wood he kul-lect the skiyins, Doc-tore Lec-tore?). It's a shallow part, played with exactly the jutjawed one-dimensional toughness required. There are a hundred other movie cops in recent years who were written and played with more complexity and

imagination—starting with William Petersen's damaged psycho-hunter in the other, little-seen Hannibal Lecter movie, *Manhunter*.

Picture
The Silence of the Lambs (Orion, Strong Heart/Demme)
Beauty and the Beast (Disney, Don Hahn)
Bugsy (TriStar, Mark Johnson, Barry Levinson, Warren Beatty)
JFK (Warner Bros., Camelot, A. Kitman Ho, Oliver Stone)
The Prince of Tides (Columbia, Barwood/Longfellow, Barbra Streisand, Andrew Karsch)

Actor
Anthony Hopkins, *The Silence of the Lambs*
Warren Beatty, *Bugsy*
Robert De Niro, *Cape Fear*
Nick Nolte, *The Prince of Tides*
Robin Williams, *The Fisher King*

Actress
Jodie Foster, *The Silence of the Lambs*
Geena Davis, *Thelma & Louise*
Laura Dern, *Rambling Rose*
Bette Midler, *For the Boys*
Susan Sarandon, *Thelma & Louise*

Supporting Actor
Jack Palance, *City Slickers*
Tommy Lee Jones, *JFK*
Harvey Keitel, *Bugsy*
Ben Kingsley, *Bugsy*
Michael Lerner, *Barton Fink*

Supporting Actress
Mercedes Ruehl, *The Fisher King*
Diane Ladd, *Rambling Rose*
Juliette Lewis, *Cape Fear*
Kate Nelligan, *The Prince of Tides*
Jessica Tandy, *Fried Green Tomatoes*

Director
Jonathan Demme, *The Silence of the Lambs*
Barry Levinson, *Bugsy*
Ridley Scott, *Thelma & Louise*
John Singleton, *Boyz N the Hood*
Oliver Stone, *JFK*

Original Screenplay: Callie Khouri, *Thelma & Louise*
Adapted Screenplay: Ted Tally, *The Silence of the Lambs*
Cinematography: Robert Richardson, *JFK*
Score: Alan Menken, *Beauty and the Beast*
Song: "Beauty and the Beast," *Beauty and the Beast*, m: Alan Menken, l: Howard Ashman
Art Direction: Dennis Gassner, *Bugsy*
Costume Design: Albert Wolsky, *Bugsy*
Editing: *JFK*
Sound: Gary Rydstrom, et al., *Terminator 2: Judgment Day*
Sound Effects Editing: *Terminator 2: Judgment Day*
Make-up: Stan Winston, Jeff Dawn, *Terminator 2: Judgment Day*
Visual Effects: Dennis Muren, Stan Winston, *Terminator 2: Judgment Day*
Short/Animated: *Manipulation*
Short/Live Action: *Session Man*
Documentary/Feature: *In the Shadow of the Stars*
Documentary/Short: *Deadly Deception: General Electric, Nuclear Weapons and Our Environment*
Foreign-Language Film: *Mediterraneo* (Italy)
Irving G. Thalberg Award: George Lucas
Special Award: Satyajit Ray, for his rare mastery of the art of motion pictures and for his profound humanitarian outlook

** *Bugsy* GLO LAC

As the smooth, self-inventing Bugsy Siegel, Warren Beatty was the most animated he'd been in years, and his first scene with Annette Bening, trading barbed wisecracks on a soundstage, crackles with sexual energy. There's the beginning of a really sharp, sexy tragicomedy here, and two hours later, you've still just seen the beginning of one.

Golden Globes

Picture (Drama): *Bugsy*
Picture (Comedy/Musical): *Beauty and the Beast*
Foreign Film: *Europa, Europa* (Germany/France)
Actor (Drama): Nick Nolte, *The Prince of Tides*
Actor (Comedy/Musical): Robin Williams, *The Fisher King*
Actress (Drama): Jodie Foster, *The Silence of the Lambs*
Actress (Comedy/Musical): Bette Midler, *For the Boys*
Supporting Actor: Jack Palance, *City Slickers*
Supporting Actress: Mercedes Ruehl, *The Fisher King*
Director: Oliver Stone, *JFK*
Screenplay: Callie Khouri, *Thelma & Louise*
Original Score: Alan Menken, *Beauty and the Beast*
Original Song: "Beauty and the Beast," *Beauty and the Beast*, m: Alan Menken, l: Howard Ashman

Directors Guild of America

Director: Jonathan Demme, *The Silence of the Lambs*
Documentary Director: Barbara Kopple, *American Dream*
D.W. Griffith Award: Akira Kurosawa

Honorary Lifetime Member: Charles Champlin

New York Film Critics Circle

Picture: *The Silence of the Lambs*
Foreign Film: *Europa, Europa*
Actor: Anthony Hopkins, *The Silence of the Lambs*
Actress: Jodie Foster, *The Silence of the Lambs*
Supporting Actor: Samuel L. Jackson, *Jungle Fever*
Supporting Actress: Judy Davis, *Naked Lunch, Barton Fink*
Director: Jonathan Demme, *The Silence of the Lambs*
New Director: John Singleton, *Boyz N the Hood*
Screenplay: David Cronenberg, *Naked Lunch*
Cinematography: Roger Deakins, *Barton Fink*
Documentary: *Paris Is Burning*

***** River Phoenix in *My Own Private Idaho* SOC VEN IND

River Phoenix's sweet, achingly vulnerable portrait of a narcoleptic hustler in Gus Van Sant's off-the-wall combination of *Midnight Cowboy* with *Henry V* will undoubtedly become the center of his posthumous cult.

National Society of Film Critics

Picture: *Life Is Sweet*
Foreign Film: *The Double Life of Véronique*
Actor: River Phoenix, *My Own Private Idaho*
Actress: Alison Steadman, *Life Is Sweet*
Supporting Actor: Harvey Keitel, *Bugsy, Thelma & Louise, Mortal Thoughts*

Supporting Actress: Jane Horrocks, *Life is Sweet*
Director: David Cronenberg, *Naked Lunch*
Screenplay: David Cronenberg, *Naked Lunch*
Cinematography: Roger Deakins, *Barton Fink*
Documentary: *Paris Is Burning*
Experimental Film: *Archangel* (Guy Maddin)
Special Citation: For film preservation, to Peter Delpeut for his compilation film, *Lyrical Nitrate* (The Netherlands)

Los Angeles Film Critics Association
Film: *Bugsy*
Foreign Film: *La Belle Noiseuse*
Actor: Nick Nolte, *The Prince of Tides*
Actress: Mercedes Ruehl, *The Fisher King*
Supporting Actor: Michael Lerner, *Barton Fink*
Supporting Actress: Jane Horrocks, *Life Is Sweet*
Director: Barry Levinson, *Bugsy*
Screenplay: James Toback, *Bugsy*
Cinematography: Roger Deakins, *Barton Fink*, *Homicide*
Music: Zbigniew Preisner, *Europa, Europa, The Double Life of Véronique, At Play in the Fields of the Lord*
Documentary: *American Dream*
Animation: *Beauty and the Beast*
Independent/Experimental Film: *All the Vermeers in New York* (Jon Jost)
New Generation Prize: John Singleton, director of *Boyz N The Hood*
Life Achievement: Vincent Price, Elmer Bernstein
Special Citation: The National Film Board of Canada, on its 50th anniversary

National Board of Review
Best English-Language Film:
The Silence of the Lambs
Bugsy
Grand Canyon
Thelma & Louise
Homicide
Dead Again
Boyz N the Hood
Rambling Rose
Frankie and Johnny
Jungle Fever
Best Foreign-Language Film:
Europa, Europa
The Vanishing
La Femme Nikita
My Father's Glory and *My Mother's Castle*
Toto le Héros
Actor: Warren Beatty, *Bugsy*
Actress: Susan Sarandon, Geena Davis, *Thelma & Louise*
Supporting Actor: Anthony Hopkins, *The Silence of the Lambs*
Supporting Actress: Kate Nelligan, *Frankie and Johnny*
Director: Jonathan Demme, *The Silence of the Lambs*

People's Choice Awards
Favorite All-Around Movie: *Terminator 2: Judgment Day*
Favorite Drama: *The Silence of the Lambs*
Favorite Comedy: *City Slickers*
Favorite Dramatic Movie Actor: Kevin Costner
Favorite Dramatic Movie Actress: Julia Roberts
Favorite Comedy Movie Actor: Steve Martin
Favorite Comedy Movie Actress: Julia Roberts

MTV Movie Awards
Movie: *Terminator 2: Judgment Day*
Actor: Arnold Schwarzenegger, *Terminator 2: Judgment Day*
Actress: Linda Hamilton, *Terminator 2: Judgment Day*

Most Desirable Male: Keanu
Reeves, *Point Break*
Most Desirable Female: Linda
Hamilton, *Terminator 2:
Judgment Day*
Breakthrough Performance:
Edward Furlong, *Terminator 2:
Judgment Day*
Best Comedic Performance:
Billy Crystal, *City Slickers*
Best On-Screen Duo: Mike
Myers, Dana Carvey, *Wayne's
World*
Best Villain: Rebecca DeMornay,
The Hand That Rocks the Cradle
Best Action Sequence:
Terminator 2: Judgment Day
Best Kiss: Macaulay Culkin,
Anna Chlumsky, *My Girl*
Best Song: Bryan Adams,
"(Everything I Do) I Do It For
You," *Robin Hood: Prince of
Thieves*
Best New Filmmaker: John
Singleton, *Boyz N The Hood*
Lifetime Achievement Award:
Jason Vorhees, *Friday the 13th*
series

British Academy Awards
Film: *The Commitments*
Foreign-Language Film: *The
Nasty Girl* (Michael Verhoeven,
Germany)
Actor: Anthony Hopkins, *The
Silence of the Lambs*
Actress: Jodie Foster, *The Silence
of the Lambs*
Supporting Actor: Alan
Rickman, *Robin Hood: Prince
of Thieves*
Supporting Actress: Kate
Nelligan, *Frankie and Johnny*
David Lean Award/Director:
Alan Parker, *The Commitments*
Screenplay (Original): Anthony
Minghella, *Truly, Madly, Deeply*
Screenplay (Adapted): Dick
Clement, Ian La Frenais, Roddy
Doyle, *The Commitments*
Robert Flaherty Documentary

Award: *35 Up* (Michael Apted,
UK)
Academy Fellow: Sir John
Gielgud, David Plowright
Michael Balcon Award: Derek
Jarman
Special Award: Audrey Hepburn

*** *Barton Fink* CAN
Cannes' first Triple Crown
winner—and the Best Actor
prize is the hardest to figure out,
since, as the screenwriter with
Ben-Hur–sized writer's block,
Turturro is mainly the straight
man for the rest of the cast,
especially John Goodman's
bigger-than-life, charming-
alarming salesman with a line in
mysterious suitcases. (The
Oscars, on the other hand,
followed the L.A. critics in
nominating Michael Lerner,
admittedly hilarious as a Louis
B. Mayer lookalike.) Another
example of movie people going
excessively gaga over a movie
about movies; the Coens have
done better, but Cannes has done
worse.

Cannes Film Festival
Palme d'Or: *Barton Fink* (Joel
and Ethan Coen, USA)
Special Jury Prize: *La Belle
Noiseuse* (Jacques Rivette,
France)
Jury Prize: *Europa* [*Zentropa*]
(Lars von Trier, Denmark), *Hors
la Vie* (Maroun Bagdadhi,
Lebanon)
Actor: John Turturro, *Barton Fink*
Actress: Irene Jacob, *The Double
Life of Véronique* (France)
Supporting Actor: Samuel L.
Jackson, *Jungle Fever* (USA)
Director: Joel Coen, *Barton Fink*
[Short film prizes included Jury

Prize to *Push Comes to Shove* by Bill Plympton (USA)]

Camera d'Or: *Toto le Héros* (Jaco von Dormael, Belgium); special mentions to *Proof* (Jocelyn Moorhouse, Australia), *Sam and Me* (Deepa Mehta, Canada)

Technical Prize: Lars von Trier, *Europa* [*Zentropa*]

International Critics Prize: in competition, *The Double Life of Véronique* (Krzysztof Kieslowski, France); out of competition, *Riff-Raff* (Ken Loach, UK)

*** *Close to Eden (Urga)* VEN

A lumpen Russian truck driver meets a Mongolian herder living on the line between the Stone Age and the 20th century. What was intended as a heavy-handed attack on 20th-century civilization and progress (by a director with ties to Russian right-wing groups) seems, like its main character, to have been distracted by the landscape once it actually got to Mongolia. It's all the better for it; the result may be incoherent, but it's also beautiful, mysterious, and often surreally funny—sort of a Mongolian *Local Hero*.

Venice Film Festival

Golden Lion: *Urga* [*Close to Eden*] (Nikita Mikhalkov, USSR/France)

Special Jury Prize: *La divina comedia* (Manoel de Oliveira, Portugal)

Silver Lions: *Raise the Red Lantern* (Zhang Yimou, China/Hong Kong), *The Fisher King* (Terry Gilliam, USA), *J'entende plus la guitare* (Philippe Garrel, France)

Actor: River Phoenix, *My Own Private Idaho* (USA)

Actress: Tilda Swinton, *Edward II* (UK)

Special Golden Lion: Gian Maria Volonté for his performance in *Una storia semplice* (Italy)

Senate Gold Medal: *Germany Year Nine Zero*, (Jean-Luc Godard, France)

Oselle d'Oro: *Scream of Stone* by Werner Herzog (Germany), for the skill and courage of its theme, to the cast and crew; *Mississippi Masala* by Mira Nair (USA), for its subject and screenplay; *Germany Year Nine Zero* for the way sound conveys meaning in the film

Berlin Film Festival

Golden Bear: *House of Smiles* (Marco Ferreri, Italy)

Silver Bear: *The Judgment* (Marco Bellochio, Italy), *Satan* (Victor Aristov, USSR)

Actor: Maynard Eziashi, *Mister Johnson* (UK)

Actress: Victorio Abril, *The Lovers* (Spain)

Director: Ricky Tognazzi, *Ultra* (Italy), Jonathan Demme, *The Silence of the Lambs*

Outstanding Single Contribution: Kevin Costner, director-star, *Dances With Wolves*

International Critics Prize: in competition, *The Little Gangster* (Jacques Doillon, France); Forum, *The Wall* (Jurgen Bottcher, Germany)

** *Poison* SUN

There's certainly none of the old Sundance timidity about this debut feature from the maker of the underground hit *Superstar*, which told the story of Karen Carpenter's anorexia using Barbie and Ken dolls to play the

Carpenters. *Poison* combines three stories inspired by Jean Genet, all exploring the edge between (homo)sexuality, self-abnegation, and revulsion, and each filmed in a different style—a *Hard Copy*-like report on a masochistic six-year-old killer, a b&w parody of '50s sci-fi in which a researcher isolates the sex drive and mutates into a hideous monster, and a naturalistic story of homosexual love between two French prisoners. Audacious as hell, and certainly a vast stylistic advance on the one-joke, amateurish *Superstar*—but only the prison story goes much beyond an adolescent desire to shock, while the other two take on styles that have been parodied far better elsewhere (and the sci-fi story really pales next to David Cronenberg's work).

Sundance Film Festival
Grand Jury Prize/dramatic: *Poison* (Todd Haynes)
Grand Jury Prize/documentary: *Paris Is Burning* (Jennie Livingston), *American Dream* (Barbara Kopple)
Special Jury Recognition: *Straight Out of Brooklyn* (Matty Rich)
Filmmakers Trophy: dramatic: *Privilege* (Yvonne Rainer); documentary: *American Dream*
Waldo Salt Screenwriting Award: Hal Hartley, *Trust*, Joseph Vasquez, *Hangin' With the Homeboys*
Cinematography: dramatic: Arthur Jafa, *Daughter of the Dust*; documentary: *Christo in Paris* (David Maysles, Albert Maysles,

Deborah Dickson, Susan Froemke)
Audience Award: dramatic competition: *One Cup of Coffee* [*Pastime*] (Robin B. Armstrong); documentary competition: *American Dream*

**** *Rambling Rose* IND
Terrific independent film about a young Southern gal (Laura Dern) with a good heart and a world-class case of raging hormones, and the unsettling effect she has on the well-meaning family that takes her in—including the 13-year-old son. It sounds like softcore porn in the *Private Lessons* vein, but the wise, funny script by novelist Calder Willingham (who *really* wrote Kubrick's *Lolita*) and sensitive direction by the underrated Martha Coolidge make it one of the most grown-up films about sexuality ever made in America.

Independent Spirit Awards
Film: *Rambling Rose*
First Film: Matty Rich, *Straight Out of Brooklyn*
Foreign Film: *An Angel at My Table*
Actor: River Phoenix, *My Own Private Idaho*
Actress: Judy Davis, *Impromptu*
Supporting Actor: David Strathairn, *City of Hope*
Supporting Actress: Diane Ladd, *Rambling Rose*
Director: Martha Coolidge, *Rambling Rose*
Screenplay: Gus Van Sant, *My Own Private Idaho*
Cinematography: Walt Lloyd, *Kafka*
Music: *My Own Private Idaho*

Golden Raspberry Awards

Worst Picture: *Hudson Hawk*

Worst Actor: Kevin Costner, *Robin Hood: Prince of Dweebs*

Worst Actress: Sean Young (as the twin who survives), *A Kiss Before Dying*

Worst Supporting Actor: Dan Aykroyd, *Nothing But Trouble*

Worst Supporting Actress: Sean Young (as the twin who's murdered), *A Kiss Before Dying*

Worst Director: Michael Lehmann, *Hudson Hawk*

Worst Screenplay: Stephen E. DeSouza, Daniel Waters, *Hudson Hawk*

Worst Song: "Addams Groove," *The Addams Family*

Worst New Star: Vanilla Ice, *Cool as Ice*

Box Office (Domestic Rentals)

1	*Terminator 2*	$112,000,000	TriStar
2	*Robin Hood: Prince of Thieves*	86,000,000	WB
3	*City Slickers*	60,750,000	Col
4	*Home Alone [1991 only]*	60,000,000	TriStar
	[1990–91 total:	140,000,000]	
5	*The Silence of the Lambs*	59,882,870	Orion
6	*The Addams Family*	55,000,000	Par
7	*Dances With Wolves [1991 only]*	52,538,000	Orion
	[1990–91 total:	81,538,000]	
8	*Sleeping With the Enemy*	46,300,000	Fox
9	*The Naked Gun 2$\frac{1}{2}$*	44,200,000	Par
10	*Teenage Mutant Ninja Turtles II*	41,900,000	New Line
Other films of note:			
13	*Beauty and the Beast [1991 only]*	39,000,000	Col
	[1991–92 total:	69,415,000]	
20	*Boyz N the Hood*	26,700,000	Col
24	*New Jack City*	22,000,000	WB
27	*Thelma & Louise*	20,000,000	MGM/UA
40	*Jungle Fever*	15,674,000	Uni
45	*JFK [1991 only]*	14,000,000	WB
	[1991–92 total:	34,000,000]	
56	*Bugsy [1991 only]*	11,500,000	TriStar
	[1991–92 total:	21,000,000]	
76	*Hudson Hawk*	8,000,000	TriStar

Terminator 2 *cost close to $100 million (James Cameron claimed a mere $85 million and wished in print he'd had the other $15 million); even being the biggest hit of its year only pushed it a little past its cost. (Don't worry, they made it up overseas.) By comparison* Boyz N the Hood *cost less than ten, and with grosses over $50 million it became the most profitable movie of the year—as well as the black-directed hit that Spike Lee's movies had never quite been, kicking off a wave of angry rap movies about life N the hood. The summer's most talked-about movie, the feminist road movie* Thelma & Louise, *made a lot of noise but didn't do much business outside the big cities; as far as female-oriented actioners went, audiences much preferred* *the traditional damsel-in-distress antics of* The Silence of the Lambs *and* Sleeping With the Enemy, *which cemented Julia Roberts' stardom.*

Gebert's Golden Armchairs

Spike Lee had bad luck at Cannes again—not only was *Barton Fink* tailor-made for jury head Roman Polanski, but the jury also included two people Lee had dissed in public—*Mississippi Burning* director Alan Parker and blue-contact-lens-wearer Whoopi Goldberg. All the same, his was the best movie of a mediocre year. Watch it again and you'll find a surprisingly tender movie about a woman in love and a man in lust, hiding beneath the raucous comedy and controversy that Lee customarily stirs up in his pictures.

A Cannes runner-up, Jacques Rivette's portrait-of-the-artist-painting-a-portrait, *La Belle Noiseuse*, was the year's grandest art film, but it was another Palme d'Or–loser, Lars von Trier's weird-beyond-words *Zentropa* (aka *Europa*), a black-and-white fantasia on Nazis and trains, that had the kickiest style. *Zentropa*'s look was not lost on the future director of *Schindler's List*, who was represented this year by his incredibly cheesy-looking Nintendo-generation desecration of *Peter Pan*.

Best American Film: *Jungle Fever*
Best Foreign Film: *La Belle Noiseuse*
Best Actor: River Phoenix, *My Own Private Idaho*
Best Actress: Susan Sarandon, *Thelma & Louise*
Best Director: Lars von Trier, *Zentropa*
Worst Hit: *Hook*

1992

The Supporting Actor Oscar–winner from the previous year is always invited to give the Supporting Actress award (and vice versa). And so it was Jack Palance, looking as if he was feeling no pain, who read the nominees, including Vanessa Redgrave, the favorite for her marvelous bit in *Howards End*, and—alphabetically last—Marisa Tomei. Then Palance opened the envelope—and he said again the last name he had read, "Marisa Tomei, *My Cousin Vinny*."

So began one of the latest of Oscar rumors—that when it came time to read the winner, a shnockered Palance mistakenly repeated the name of a perky young actress in a minor comedy instead of the great Redgrave. There are plenty of reasons to doubt that that was the case—the mostly elderly Academy has honored cute young things before, and Redgrave's pro-Palestinian views are widely known and disliked in Hollywood. But the main reason is that one of the functions of the two guys from Price, Waterhouse is to stand in the wings and check the winners as they are announced. And if, say, Mr. Willis chooses to announce that Ms. Moore won when she in fact did not, they are supposed to stride to the podium and—regardless of the embarrassment it would cause—announce the correction.

Of course, since it's never happened, we don't know for sure that they really *would*. . . .

Academy Awards

**** *Unforgiven* AAW DGA SOC LAC
A powerful and grave western drama that many saw as a throwback to the revisionist westerns of the '70s, but which really belongs to the finest tradition of westerns which use the form for a probing moral examination of the uses of violence and its effects on the men who choose that way of life.

Picture
Unforgiven (Warner Bros., Clint Eastwood)
The Crying Game (Miramax, Palace Pictures, Stephen Woolley)
A Few Good Men (Columbia, Castle Rock)
Howards End (Sony Pictures Classics, Merchant Ivory)
Scent of a Woman (Universal, Martin Brest)

** Al Pacino in *Scent of a Woman* AAW GLO
Not even the best performance Pacino gave that *year*— *Glengarry Glen Ross*'s Ricky Roma would have had this guy

for lunch—and the hammiest Best Actor winner since . . . what? *The Lost Weekend*? *Disraeli*? Fun for a while, but two and a half hours on this wisp of a story—Phoo-ah!

Actor
Al Pacino, *Scent of a Woman*
Robert Downey, Jr., *Chaplin*
Clint Eastwood, *Unforgiven*
Stephen Rea, *The Crying Game*
Denzel Washington, *Malcolm X*

***** **Emma Thompson in *Howards End*** AAW GLO NYC SOC LAC BOR BAA
As the older of two independent sisters who willfully blinds herself to the unjust activities of the rich man (Anthony Hopkins) who wants to marry her, Thompson is never less than intelligent and keenly sensitive. But one scene, early in the picture, stands above all the others—when she meets Vanessa Redgrave, luminously sickly as Hopkins' dying first wife, and the greatest British actress alive decides to take Thompson for a run and see if the hot young kid everyone's talking about can hold her own. She does. . . .

Actress
Emma Thompson, *Howards End*
Catherine Deneuve, *Indochine*
Mary McDonnell, *Passion Fish*
Michelle Pfeiffer, *Love Field*
Susan Sarandon, *Lorenzo's Oil*

Supporting Actor
Gene Hackman, *Unforgiven*
Jaye Davidson, *The Crying Game*
Jack Nicholson, *A Few Good Men*

Al Pacino, *Glengarry Glen Ross*
David Paymer, *Mr. Saturday Night*

Supporting Actress
Marisa Tomei, *My Cousin Vinny*
Judy Davis, *Husbands and Wives*
Joan Plowright, *Enchanted April*
Vanessa Redgrave, *Howards End*
Miranda Richardson, *Damage*

Director
Clint Eastwood, *Unforgiven*
Robert Altman, *The Player*
Martin Brest, *Scent of a Woman*
James Ivory, *Howards End*
Neil Jordan, *The Crying Game*

Original Screenplay: Neil Jordan, *The Crying Game*
Adapted Screenplay: Ruth Prawer Jhabvala, *Howards End*
Cinematography: Philippe Rousselot, *A River Runs Through It*
Score: Alan Menken, *Aladdin*
Song: "Whole New World," *Aladdin*, m: Alan Menken, l: Tim Rice
Art Direction: Luciana Arrighi; Ian Whittaker, *Howards End*
Costume Design: Eiko Ishioka, *Bram Stoker's Dracula*
Editing: *Unforgiven*
Sound: *The Last of the Mohicans*
Sound Effects Editing: *Bram Stoker's Dracula*
Make-up: *Bram Stoker's Dracula*
Visual Effects: *Death Becomes Her*
Short/Animated: *Mona Lisa Descending a Staircase*
Short/Live Action: *Omnibus*
Documentary/Feature: *The Panama Deception* (Barbara Trent)
Documentary/Short: *Educating Peter*
Foreign Language Film: *Indochine* (France)
Jean Hersholt Humanitarian

Award: Audrey Hepburn, Elizabeth Taylor
Special Award: Federico Fellini

Golden Globes

Picture (Drama): *Scent of a Woman*
Picture (Comedy/Musical): *The Player*
Foreign Film: *Indochine* (France)
Actor (Drama): Al Pacino, *Scent of a Woman*
Actor (Comedy/Musical): Tim Robbins, *The Player*
Actress (Drama): Emma Thompson, *Howards End*
Actress (Comedy/Musical): Miranda Richardson, *Enchanted April*
Supporting Actor: Gene Hackman, *Unforgiven*
Supporting Actress: Joan Plowright, *Enchanted April*
Director: Clint Eastwood, *Unforgiven*
Screenplay: Bo Goldman, *Scent of a Woman*
Original Score: Alan Menken, *Aladdin*
Original Song: "A Whole New World," *Aladdin*, m: Alan Menken, l: Tim Rice
Cecil B. DeMille Award: Lauren Bacall

Directors Guild of America

Director: Clint Eastwood, *Unforgiven*
Documentary Director: Joe Berlinger, Bruce J. Sinfosky, *Brothers Keeper*
D. W. Griffith Award: Sidney Lumet
Honorary Lifetime Member: Arthur Hiller

*** *The Player* GLO NYC SUN

A glossy, highly enjoyable if not particularly profound poison-pen letter to Hollywood (which

of course made both director Robert Altman and writer Michael Tolkin hot commodities again). It only narrowly edged out *Unforgiven* at the New York Critics Circle voting, apparently because of an ironic screw-up—the wrong time for the meeting had been given to the Eastwood-leaning reviewers from, of all magazines, *Time*. . . .

***** *Raise the Red Lantern*
VEN '91 NYC SOC BAA

The fourth film of director Zhang Yimou (*Red Sorghum*, *The Story of Qui Ju*) is the best Chinese film yet to receive international attention and the first, to my mind, to deserve comparison with the greatest Asian films from Japan and India. Gong Li plays a student who becomes the fourth wife of a rich and wealthy landowner, moving into his huge, rambling compound and going slowly mad as she lives only to wait for the sign of his favor—the red lanterns that indicate that he will be spending the night in her house. There is perhaps some allegorical element here about the political situation in China, younger generations under the thumb of elderly tyrants, but Yimou's main interest is in the self-destructive politics that the powerless situation of the wives (and their maids) inevitably breeds.

New York Film Critics Circle

Film: *The Player*
Foreign-Language Film: *Raise the Red Lantern*
Actor: Denzel Washington, *Malcolm X*
Actress: Emma Thompson, *Howards End*
Supporting Actor: Gene Hackman, *Unforgiven*
Supporting Actress: Miranda Richardson, *The Crying Game*, *Damage*, *Enchanted April*
Director: Robert Altman, *The Player*
New Director: Allison Anders, *Gas Food Lodging*
Screenplay: Neil Jordan, *The Crying Game*
Cinematography: Jean Lapine, *The Player*
Documentary: *Brother's Keeper*

National Society of Film Critics

Film: *Unforgiven*
Foreign-Language Film: *Raise the Red Lantern*
Actor: Stephen Rea, *The Crying Game*
Actress: Emma Thompson, *Howards End*
Supporting Actor: Gene Hackman, *Unforgiven*
Supporting Actress: Judy Davis, *Husbands and Wives*
Director: Clint Eastwood, *Unforgiven*
Screenplay: David Webb Peoples, *Unforgiven*
Cinematography: Zhao Fei, *Raise the Red Lantern*
Documentary: *American Dream*
Special Citation: *Another Girl, Another Planet*, Michael Almereyda [experimental film shot on a Pixelvision children's b&w video camera]

Los Angeles Film Critics Association

Film: *Unforgiven*
Foreign Film: *The Crying Game*
Actor: Clint Eastwood, *Unforgiven*
Actress: Emma Thompson, *Howards End*
Supporting Actor: Gene Hackman, *Unforgiven*
Supporting Actress: Judy Davis, *Husbands and Wives*
Director: Clint Eastwood, *Unforgiven*
Screenplay: David Webb Peoples, *Unforgiven*
Cinematography: Zhao Fei, *Raise the Red Lantern*
Music: Zbigniew Preisner, *Damage*
Documentary: *The Threat*, *Black Harvest*
Animated Film: *Aladdin*
Independent/Experimental: Sadie Benning
Career Achievement: Budd Boetticher
New Generation Award: Carl Franklin, *One False Move*

National Board of Review

Best English-Language Film:
Howards End
The Crying Game
Glengarry Glen Ross
A Few Good Men
The Player
Unforgiven
One False Move
Peter's Friends
Bob Roberts
Malcolm X
Best Foreign-Language Film:
Indochine
Raise the Red Lantern
Tous les Matins du Monde [*All the Mornings of the World*]
Mediterraneo
Like Water for Chocolate
Actor: Jack Lemmon, *Glengarry Glen Ross*

Actress: Emma Thompson, *Howards End*
Supporting Actor: Jack Nicholson, *A Few Good Men*
Supporting Actress: Judy Davis, *Husbands and Wives*
Director: James Ivory, *Howards End*
Documentary: *Brother's Keeper*

People's Choice Awards
Favorite All-Around Movie: *A Few Good Men*
Favorite Drama: *A Few Good Men*
Favorite Comedy: *Home Alone 2: Lost in New York, Sister Act*
Favorite Movie Actor: Kevin Costner
Favorite Movie Actress: Whoopi Goldberg
Favorite Dramatic Movie Actor: Kevin Costner
Favorite Dramatic Movie Actress: Demi Moore
Favorite Comedy Movie Actor: Steve Martin
Favorite Comedy Movie Actress: Whoopi Goldberg

MTV Movie Awards
Movie: *A Few Good Men*
Actor: Denzel Washington, *Malcolm X*
Actress: Sharon Stone, *Basic Instinct*
Most Desirable Male: Christian Slater, *Untamed Heart*
Most Desirable Female: Sharon Stone, *Basic Instinct*
Breakthrough Performance: Marisa Tomei, *My Cousin Vinny*
Best Comedic Performance: Robin Williams, *Aladdin*
Best On-Screen Duo: Mel Gibson, Danny Glover, *Lethal Weapon 3*
Best Villain: Jennifer Jason Leigh, *Single White Female*
Best Action Sequence: *Lethal Weapon 3*

Best Kiss: Marisa Tomei, Christian Slater, *Untamed Heart*
Best Song: Whitney Houston, "I Will Always Love You," *The Bodyguard*
Best New Filmmaker: Carl Franklin, *One False Move*
Lifetime Achievement Award: The Three Stooges

British Academy Awards
Film: *Howards End*
Alexander Korda Award/British Film: *The Crying Game*
Foreign-Language Film: *Raise the Red Lantern* (Zhang Yimou, China)
Actor: Robert Downey, Jr., *Chaplin*
Actress: Emma Thompson, *Howards End*
Supporting Actor: Gene Hackman, *Unforgiven*
Supporting Actress: Miranda Richardson, *Damage*
David Lean Award/Director: Robert Altman, *The Player*
Screenplay (Original): Woody Allen, *Husbands and Wives*
Screenplay (Adapted): Michael Tolkin, *The Player*
Academy Fellow: Sydney Samuelson
Michael Balcon Award: Kenneth Branagh
Special Award: Dame Maggie Smith

*** *The Best Intentions* CAN
Four years after *Pelle the Conqueror*, Bille August became only the second director in history to win a second Palme d'Or (after Francis Coppola; Emir Kusturica has done it since). The fact is, though, the Palme d'Or was really for the film's screenwriter, Ingmar Bergman, who had never won

one himself. Bergman's *Fanny and Alexander* turned his early childhood into a kind of fable (with some significant fictionalizing); this goes back a few more years to recount, in entirely realistic and prosaic terms, the courtship and early marriage of his strong-willed, difficult (and, it would seem, manic-depressive) parents. Absorbing if heavy viewing, which also serves to demonstrate the difference between talent, taste, and high intelligence—all of which August clearly has—and genius, which is Bergman's sole property in the partnership.

Cannes Film Festival
Palme d'Or: *The Best Intentions* (Bille August, Sweden)
45th Anniversary Prize: *Howards End* (James Ivory, UK)
Special Jury Prize: *Stolen Children* (Gianni Amelio, Italy)
Jury Prize: *El Sol del Membrillo* [*The Dream of Light*] (Victor Erice, Spain), *An Independent Life* (Vitali Kanevsky, Russia)
Actor: Tim Robbins, *The Player* (USA)
Actress: Pernilla August, *The Best Intentions*
Director: Robert Altman, *The Player*
Camera d'Or: *Mac* (John Turturro, USA)
Technical Prize: *El Viaje* (Fernando Solanas, Argentina)

*** The Story of Qiu Ju VEN
Following his "red" trilogy—which, exceptional though it was, admittedly fit well within western ideas of colorful, exotic China—Zhang Yimou and his star Gong Li took on a contemporary subject (bureaucracy, basically, and one woman's fight against it) and a plainer, realistic style. Not as striking as the earlier works, but in its own way this sardonic comedy is just as interesting.

Venice Film Festival
Golden Lion: *The Story of Qiu Ju* (Zhang Yimou, China)
Silver Lions: *Jamón Jamón* (Bigas Luna, Spain), *Un Coeur en Hiver* [*A Heart in Winter*] (Claude Sautet, France), *Hotel de Lux* (Dan Pita, Romania)
Special Jury Prize: *Death of a Neapolitan Mathematician* (Mario Martone, Italy)
Actor: Jack Lemmon, *Glengarry Glen Ross* (USA)
Actress: Gong Li, *The Story of Qiu Ju*
Senate Medal: *Guelwaar* (Ousmane Sembène, Senegal)
Career Awards: Jeanne Moreau, Paolo Villaggio, Francis Ford Coppola
International Critics Prize: in competition, *Un Coeur en Hiver*, other, *Leon the Pig Farmer* (Vadim Jean, Gary Sinyor, UK)

** Grand Canyon BER
Lawrence Kasdan aims for Robert Altman (but ends up closer to Stanley Kramer Lite) in this drama of the lousiness and violence of modern life, with Kevin Kline and Danny Glover as white yuppie and black worker trying to relate across a social gulf. Kasdan seems sincere as hell, and as *The Accidental Tourist* and *The Big Chill* showed, he has a gift for grown-up comedy with a slight

edge of social comment—but if you're going to take on society as a theme, you need brass balls, and that's what separates the Altmans from the Altboys.

Berlin Film Festival
Golden Bear: *Grand Canyon* (Lawrence Kasdan, USA)
Silver Bear: *Sweet Emma, Dear Böbe* (István Szábo, Hungary)
Actor: Armin-Müller-Stahl, *Utz* (UK-Germany-Italy)
Actress: Maggie Cheung, *Ruan Ling Yu* [*Center Stage*] (Hong Kong)
Director: Jan Troell, *Il Capitano* (Sweden-Finland-Denmark)
Cinematography: *Beltenbros* (Pilar Miró, Spain)
First Film: *La Frontera* (Ricardo Larrain, Chile-Spain)
Alfred Bauer Prize: *Infinitas* (Marlen Kouziev, Russia)
Special Mention: Barbara Thummet in *Gudrun* (Hans W. Geissendörfer, Germany)
International Critics Prize: in competition, *A Tale of Winter* (Eric Rohmer, France); Forum, *La vie de Bohème* (Aki Kaurismäki, Finland), *Edward II* (Derek Jarman, UK); special mention: *Three Days* (Saruna Bartes, Lithuania)

** *In the Soup* SUN
One of the less wholesome trends in independent filmmaking is independent films about the travails of making an independent film—at least it took Fellini eight and a half movies to run out of subject matter, but the makers of films such as *Living in Oblivion*, *. . . And God Spoke*, and *Search and Destroy* all start at that point of insularity. (Maybe a year in the Peace Corps should be required for admittance to Sundance.) This one is made up of equal parts *Stranger Than Paradise* (the downtown scene and minimalist look), *Barton Fink* (with Steve Buscemi promoted from bellboy to Barton), and *The Freshman* (with Seymour Cassel taking over the Brando role as the nutty hood who, promising to raise money for Buscemi's film, turns the kid's life upside-down). Some hilarious moments, and old pro Cassel is really a blast, but the telltale sign is that all the characters apart from the filmmaker are simply caricatures. Okay for a first try, now get a life (and *then* make a movie).

Sundance Film Festival
Grand Jury Prize/dramatic: *In the Soup* (Alexandre Rockwell)
Grand Jury Prize/documentary: *A Brief History of Time* (Errol Morris), *Finding Christa* (Camille Billops, James Hatch)
Special Jury Prize/Artistic Excellence: *The Hours and Times* (Christopher Munch, UK), *My Crasy Life* (Jean-Pierre Gorin) [not to be confused with *Mi Vida Local/My Crazy Life*, shown at Sundance in 1994]
Special Jury Prize/Outstanding Performance: Seymour Cassel, *In the Soup*
Filmmakers Trophy: dramatic: *Zebrahead* (Anthony Drazan); documentary: *A Brief History of Time*
Waldo Salt Screenwriting Award: Neil Jimenez, *The Waterdance*

Cinematography: dramatic: Ellen Kuras, *Swoon* (Tom Kalin); documentary: Kathleen Beeler, Trinh T. Minh-ha, *Shoot for the Contents* (Trinh T. Minh-ha)
Audience Award: dramatic competition: *The Waterdance* (Neil Jimenez, Michael Steinberg); documentary competition: *Brothers Keeper* (Joe Berlinger, Bruce Sinofsky)

Independent Spirit Awards
Film: *The Player*
First Film: Neil Jimenez, Michael Steinberg, *The Waterdance*
Foreign Film: *The Crying Game*
Actor: Harvey Keitel, *Bad Lieutenant*
Actress: Fairuza Balk, *Gas Food Lodging*
Supporting Actor: Steve Buscemi, *Reservoir Dogs*
Supporting Actress: Alfre Woodard, *Passion Fish*
Director: Carl Franklin, *One False Move*
Screenplay: Neil Jimenez, *The Waterdance*
Cinematography: Frederic Elmes, *Night on Earth*
Music: *Twin Peaks: Fire Walk with Me* [Angelo Badalamenti]

Harvard Lampoon Movie Worsts
Ten worst pictures:
The Last of the Mohicans
A League of Their Own
[The authors then admitted they hadn't seen any other films and invented a number of typical-sounding '90s titles, including *Ballin': The Movie* and *Ebony & Ivy: The Lieutenant's Gonna Shit!*]
The Kirk Douglas' Son Award: Michael Douglas, *Basic Instinct*
Natalie Wood Award for Worst

Actress: Lorraine Bracco, *Medicine Man*
Special Midget Appreciation Award: Thank you, midgets
Worst Actor/Director/Producer/Writer: After 5 long years, someone finally manages to wrest this dubious honor from the clutches of Kevin Costner: Tim Robbins, *Bob Roberts*
Worst Blacksploitation Movie: *Mo' Money.* Damon Wayans comes up with the totally original concept of jive-talkin' black men looking for the fast buck. If he was a Native American, this would have been titled *Ugh, Wampum*
Worst Irishploitation Movie: *Far and Away*, with Tom Cruise. Thank you, midget

Golden Raspberry Awards
Worst Picture: *Shining Through*
Worst Actor: Sylvester Stallone, *Stop! Or My Mom Will Shoot*
Worst Actress: Melanie Griffith, *Shining Through*, *A Stranger Among Us*
Worst Supporting Actor: Tom Selleck, *Christopher Columbus: The Disco Version*
Worst Supporting Actress: Estelle Getty, *Stop! Or My Mom Will Shoot*
Worst Director: David Seltzer, *Shining Through*
Worst Screenplay: Blake Snyder, William Osborne, William Davies, *Stop! Or My Mom Will Shoot*
Worst Song: ''High Times, Hard Times,'' *Newsies*
Worst New Star: Pauly Shore, *Encino Man*

Box Office (Domestic Rentals)

1	*Home Alone 2 [1992 only]*	$102,000,000	Fox
	[estimated 1992–93 total:	120,000,000]	
2	*Batman Returns*	100,100,000	WB
3	*Lethal Weapon 3*	80,000,000	WB
4	*Sister Act*	62,420,000	TriStar
5	*Aladdin [1992 only]*	60,000,000	Disney
	[estimated 1992–93 total:	120,000,000]	
6	*Wayne's World*	54,000,000	Par
7	*A League of Their Own*	53,100,000	Col
8	*Basic Instinct*	53,000,000	TriStar
9	*The Bodyguard [1992 only]*	52,900,000	WB
	[estimated 1992–93 total:	76,000,000]	
10	*A Few Good Men [1992 only]*	52,000,000	Col
	[estimated 1992–93 total:	160,000,000]	
Other films of note:			
11	*Bram Stoker's Dracula*	47,200,000	Col
14	*Fried Green Tomatoes*	37,402,827	Uni
15	*Unforgiven [1992 only]*	36,000,000	WB
	[estimated 1992–93 total:	50,000,000]	
16	*White Men Can't Jump*	34,115,000	Fox
18	*Under Siege*	33,000,000	WB
29	*Malcolm X*	25,000,000	WB
41	*Passenger 57*	18,000,000	WB
62	*Hoffa [1992 only]*	9,300,000	Fox
	[estimated 1992–93 total:	14,000,000]	
66	*Howards End [1992 only]*	9,000,000	Sony
	[estimated 1992–93 total:	14,000,000]	
73	*The Player*	8,420,000	Fine Line

Despite mixed reviews in nearly every case, sequels dominated the box office in 1992, taking the top three spots (though note that if you throw in Aladdin's 1993 revenues, it ties for first place). Basic Instinct introduced a new female megastar in Sharon Stone, even though her record has been hit or miss (or quick and dead) since; the female-oriented sleeper hit of the year was Fried Green Tomatoes, which opened small in 1992 but played forever. Under Siege (Die Hard on a boat) made Steven Seagal look like a big star, and the really silly Passenger 57 (Die Hard in a plane) suggested that Wesley Snipes could make it as a straight action star without the aid of a white buddy (though his white-buddy movie, White Men Can't Jump, did even better). And Wayne's World launched a rash of Saturday Night Live character movies—which were really more video store fodder than serious attempts to get people to pay $7 to see two hours of Coneheads or Stuart Smalley.

Gebert's Golden Armchairs

Of the host of exciting action filmmakers to sprout up in Hong Kong since the late '70s, John Woo has come the closest to making a U.S. name—less because he's the best (I'd give that honor to Tsui Hark, when he's on) than because his films are the ones that are most like American actioners—except ten times more so. As *Hardboiled*, his *Die Hard*-in-a-baby-hospital, proves.

When Good Performers Happen to Bad Movies: Abel Ferrara's *Bad Lieutenant* really is a bad movie—imitation-Scorsese art house–violence porn with pretensions to Catholicism, sort of a *Last Tango You Motherf—*. But as a cop spiraling into hell, Harvey Keitel, finally getting to play De Niro's part in *Taxi Driver* after 15 years, gives such a powerful, emotionally raw performance that he'd earn the title of Hardest Workin' Man in Show Business if it wasn't taken. The only reason Michelle Pfeiffer took her part in *Love Field* was to get an Oscar nomination (which she did); long after that Oscar-bait soap opera is forgotten, her funny, imaginatively sexy-mousy Catwoman will still be treasured as the saving grace of the otherwise lumpy *Batman Meets Edward Penguinflippers*.

P.S. Note to Sharon—Next time the cinematographer spends 45 minutes setting up lights around your knees, it means the director has an even *worse* idea than usual how to spice up his dumb cop thriller.

Best American Film: *Unforgiven*
Best Foreign Film: *Raise the Red Lantern*
Best Actor: Harvey Keitel, *Bad Lieutenant*
Best Actress: Michelle Pfeiffer, *Batman Returns*
Best Director: John Woo, *Hardboiled*
Worst Hit: *Basic Instinct*

1993

Only one film, *GoodFellas*, had ever swept the three main critics' groups—and no film had ever done that and won the Best Picture Oscar as well, though *Unforgiven* might have been the first to take that quadruple crown if not for the reported screwup at the Critics Circle voting in 1992. The advance word on Steven Spielberg's *Schindler's List* was so strong, and the subject matter so compelling, that by the time it opened, its Oscar win seemed assured—but there was still the possibility that resentment of Steven Spielberg's box-office success would translate into a snub from the critics' groups, which could harm the film's chances as well. And at first that seemed to be what was happening, when both the New York and L.A. critics picked *Schindler* for film but *The Piano*'s Jane Campion for best director.

The test would be the most radical of the groups, the National Society, which included the few critics (such as the *Village Voice*'s J. Hoberman) who had dissented from the general praise. There were scattered votes for *Naked*, *The Age of Innocence* (written by an ex-member), and even (shades of *Pee-wee's Big Adventure*) *Groundhog Day* . . . but *Schindler* got a healthy 44 votes and 18-out-of-32 ballots majority to beat *The Piano* and *Short Cuts* on the first ballot. Then came Director . . . and the ratio, surprisingly, was almost identical, Spielberg again leading Jane Campion and Robert Altman to win on the first ballot. Only the question of whether his award should cite *Jurassic Park* as well was raised (and quickly shot down). Not long after this vote of confidence from the highbrows, Spielberg picked up the DGA award, and—probably against his own expectations—found himself holding a Best Director Oscar while his hair was still brown and his teeth real.

Academy Awards

***** *Schindler's List* AAW GLO DGA NYC SOC LAC BOR BAA
Jurassic Park, Spielberg's first non-sequel megahit since *E.T.*, was sort of the movie equivalent of Eric Clapton's *Unplugged* album—nice to see the old guy can still do it, but there's nothing you hadn't heard before. All the more reason to be impressed by his grand, unflinching Holocaust movie, proof that, Fitzgerald aside, occasionally there *are* second acts in American lives. Spielberg rose to his subject matter in every way, inventing not only a wholly new style for himself (if not the cinema)

but discovering unsuspected reservoirs of intelligence and sensitivity—not to mention the mordant insights into human nature that set Oskar Schindler's redemption into relief. Obliqueness, gravity, restraint, historical perspective, realism—these are not virtues Spielberg had been known for previously, but here he demonstrated mastery of them all. After some 14 films, many of them among the most popular films of their time, Steven Spielberg finally became a *mensch*.

Picture
Schindler's List (Universal, Amblin Entertainment, Steven Spielberg, Gerald R. Molen, Branko Lustig)
The Fugitive (Warner Bros., Arnold Kopelson)
In the Name of the Father (Universal, Hell's Kitchen Ltd., Jim Sheridan)
The Piano (Miramax, Jan Chapman & CIBY 2000, Jan Chapman)
The Remains of the Day (Columbia, Mike Nichols, John Calley, Merchant Ivory)

*** Tom Hanks in *Philadelphia* AAW GLO MTV BER '94
Hollywood tackles a bold new subject matter—and immediately turns it into a genre it can understand, the courtroom drama. With its explain-gay-life-to-me-like-I'm-four-years-old approach, the movie is likely to look like the *Gentleman's Agreement* of AIDS twenty years from now.

But Hanks gives a big-hearted, matter-of-factly fearless performance, and maybe there was something to its makers' claims that just having a star of his level say "I have AIDS" in his familiar scratchy voice did more to open a few minds than could a much better movie, like *Longtime Companion*, or the Sundance winner *Silverlake Life*, that only played to the already-convinced.

Actor
Tom Hanks, *Philadelphia*
Daniel Day-Lewis, *In the Name of the Father*
Laurence Fishburne, *What's Love Got to Do With It*
Anthony Hopkins, *The Remains of the Day*
Liam Neeson, *Schindler's List*

**** Holly Hunter in *The Piano* AAW GLO NYC SOC LAC BOR BAA CAN
Hunter's tour-de-force—as a 19th-century mute married off to one priggish New Zealand farmer but with the hots for another, rougher one—was sure award bait, and there's hardly a trophy between Cannes and Los Angeles that she didn't pick up. Taken with her scene-stealing good ol' gal in *The Firm*, she clearly had the best year of any American actress in years.

Actress
Holly Hunter, *The Piano*
Angela Bassett, *What's Love Got to Do With It*
Stockard Channing, *Six Degrees of Separation*

Emma Thompson, *The Remains of the Day*
Debra Winger, *Shadowlands*

Supporting Actor
Tommy Lee Jones, *The Fugitive*
Leonardo DiCaprio, *What's Eating Gilbert Grape*
Ralph Fiennes, *Schindler's List*
John Malkovich, *In the Line of Fire*
Pete Postlethwaite, *In the Name of the Father*

Supporting Actress
Anna Paquin, *The Piano*
Holly Hunter, *The Firm*
Rosie Perez, *Fearless*
Winona Ryder, *The Age of Innocence*
Emma Thompson, *In the Name of the Father*

Director
Steven Spielberg, *Schindler's List*
Robert Altman, *Short Cuts*
Jane Campion, *The Piano*
James Ivory, *The Remains of the Day*
Jim Sheridan, *In the Name of the Father*

Original Screenplay: Jane Campion, *The Piano*
Adapted Screenplay: Steven Zaillian, *Schindler's List*
Cinematography: Janusz Kaminski, *Schindler's List*
Score: John Williams, *Schindler's List*
Song: "Streets of Philadelphia," *Philadelphia*, ml: Bruce Springsteen
Art Direction: Allan Starski, Ewa Braun, *Schindler's List*
Costume Design: Gabriella Pescucci, *The Age of Innocence*
Editing: *Schindler's List*
Sound: Gary Rydstrom, *Jurassic Park*

Sound Effects Editing: Gary Rydstrom, *Jurassic Park*
Make-up: *Mrs. Doubtfire*
Visual Effects: Dennis Muren, Stan Winston, Phil Tippett, Michael Lantieri, *Jurassic Park*
Short/Animated: *The Wrong Trousers* (Aardman Animations, Nick Park)
Short/Live Action: *Black Rider* (Germany)
Documentary/Short: *Defending Our Lives*
Documentary/Feature: *I Am a Promise: The Children of Stanton Elementary School*
Foreign-Language Film: *Belle Epoque* (Spain)
Jean Hersholt Humanitarian Award: Paul Newman
Special Award: Deborah Kerr

Golden Globes
Picture (Drama): *Schindler's List*
Picture (Comedy/Musical): *Mrs. Doubtfire*
Foreign Film: *Farewell, My Concubine* (China–Hong Kong)
Actor (Drama): Tom Hanks, *Philadelphia*
Actor (Comedy/Musical): Robin Williams, *Mrs. Doubtfire*
Actress (Drama): Holly Hunter, *The Piano*
Actress (Comedy/Musical): Angela Bassett, *What's Love Got to Do With It*
Supporting Actor: Tommy Lee Jones, *The Fugitive*
Supporting Actress: Winona Ryder, *The Age of Innocence*
Director: Steven Spielberg, *Schindler's List*
Screenplay: Steven Zaillian, *Schindler's List*
Original Score: Kitaro, *Heaven and Earth*
Original Song: "Streets of Philadelphia," *Philadelphia*, ml: Bruce Springsteen

Cecil B. DeMille Award: Robert Redford
Special Achievement Award: *Short Cuts*

Directors Guild of America
Director: Steven Spielberg, *Schindler's List*
Documentary Director: Barbara Kopple, *Fallen Champ: The Untold Story of Mike Tyson*
D. W. Griffith Award: Robert Altman

**** David Thewlis in *Naked*
NYC SOC CAN
British filmmaker Mike Leigh's bleak-as-hell drama is a deliberately ugly, finally overbaked demonstration of the thesis that men are brutes and women are victims. But there's no denying the power of David Thewlis' spiteful homeless man, a frighteningly magnetic portrait of evil wit, brutality, and self-loathing.

New York Film Critics Circle
Film: *Schindler's List*
Foreign-Language Film: *Farewell, My Concubine*
Actor: David Thewlis, *Naked*
Actress: Holly Hunter, *The Piano*
Supporting Actor: Ralph Fiennes, *Schindler's List*
Supporting Actress: Gong Li, *Farewell, My Concubine*
Director: Jane Campion, *The Piano*
Screenplay: Jane Campion, *The Piano*
Cinematography: Janusz Kaminski, *Schindler's List*
Documentary: *Visions of Light: The Art of Cinematography*

National Society of Film Critics
Film: *Schindler's List*
Foreign-Language Film: *The Story of Qiu Ju*
Actor: David Thewlis, *Naked*
Actress: Holly Hunter, *The Piano*
Supporting Actor: Ralph Fiennes, *Schindler's List*
Supporting Actress: Madeleine Stowe, *Short Cuts*
Director: Steven Spielberg, *Schindler's List*
Screenplay: Jane Campion, *The Piano*
Cinematography: Janusz Kaminski, *Schindler's List*
Documentary: *Visions of Light: The Art of Cinematography*
Special Citation: Richard Wilson, Myron Meisel, Bill Krohn and Ed Marx, makers of *It's All True*, for their historic work in reassembling the footage from Orson Welles' "lost" 1942 Brazilian documentary *Rock Hudson's Home Movies*, by Mark Rappaport, for adroitly combining fictional narrative with essay to deconstruct Rock Hudson's screen image

***** Anthony Hopkins in *The Remains of the Day*
LAC BOR BAA
A literary conceit—the butler who was too stiff to be believed—comes brilliantly to life in Hopkins' performance, in which volcanic emotions roil and rumble beneath an implacable surface. Hannibal Lecter might eat his victims, but this guy could serve them without flinching.

Los Angeles Film Critics Association
Film: *Schindler's List*
Foreign Film: *Farewell, My Concubine*

Actor: Anthony Hopkins, *The Remains of the Day, Shadowlands*
Actress: Holly Hunter, *The Piano*
Supporting Actor: Tommy Lee Jones, *The Fugitive*
Supporting Actress: Anna Paquin, *The Piano*; Rosie Perez, *Fearless*
Director: Jane Campion, *The Piano*
Screenplay: Jane Campion, *The Piano*
Cinematography: Janusz Kaminski, *Schindler's List*; Stuart Dryburgh, *The Piano*
Music: Zbigniew Preisner, *Blue, The Secret Garden, Olivier Olivier*
Production Design: Allan Starski, *Schindler's List*
Documentary: *It's All True*
Animated Film: *The Mighty River*, Frederic Back
Independent/Experimental: Tom Joslin, Peter Friedman, *Silverlake Life: The View from Here*
Career Achievement: John Alton [cinematographer]
New Generation Award: Leonardo diCaprio, actor in *This Boy's Life, What's Eating Gilbert Grape*

National Board of Review
Best English-Language Film:
Schindler's List
The Age of Innocence
The Remains of the Day
The Piano
Shadowlands
In the Name of the Father
Philadelphia
Much Ado About Nothing
Short Cuts
The Joy Luck Club
Best Foreign-Language Film:
Farewell, My Concubine
El Mariachi
Un Coeur en Hiver
The Story of Qiu Ju

The Accompanist
Actor: Anthony Hopkins, *The Remains of the Day, Shadowlands*
Actress: Holly Hunter, *The Piano*
Supporting Actor: Leonardo diCaprio, *What's Eating Gilbert Grape*
Supporting Actress: Winona Ryder, *The Age of Innocence*
Director: Martin Scorsese, *The Age of Innocence*
Documentary: *The War Room*

People's Choice Awards
Favorite All-Around Movie: *Jurassic Park*
Favorite Drama: *The Firm*
Favorite Comedy: *Mrs. Doubtfire*
Favorite Dramatic Movie Actor: Tom Cruise
Favorite Dramatic Movie Actress: Julia Roberts
Favorite Comedy Movie Actor: Robin Williams
Favorite Comedy Movie Actress: Whoopi Goldberg

MTV Movie Awards
Movie: *Menace II Society*
Actor: Tom Hanks, *Philadelphia*
Actress: Janet Jackson, *Poetic Justice*
Most Desirable Male: William Baldwin, *Sliver*
Most Desirable Female: Janet Jackson, *Poetic Justice*
Breakthrough Performance: Alicia Silverstone, *The Crush*
Best Comedic Performance: Robin Williams, *Mrs. Doubtfire*
Best On-Screen Duo: Harrison Ford, Tommy Lee Jones, *The Fugitive*
Best Villain: Alicia Silverstone, *The Crush*
Best Action Sequence: *The Fugitive*
Best Kiss: Woody Harrelson, Demi Moore, *Indecent Proposal*
Best Song: Michael Jackson,

"Will You Be There," *Free Willy*
Best New Filmmaker: Steven Zaillian, *Searching for Bobby Fischer*
Lifetime Achievement Award: Richard Roundtree, the *Shaft* film series

British Academy Awards

Film: *Schindler's List*
Alexander Korda Award/British **Film:** *Shadowlands*
Foreign-Language Film: *Farewell, My Concubine* (Chen Kaige, China)
Actor: Anthony Hopkins, *The Remains of the Day*
Actress: Holly Hunter, *The Piano*
Supporting Actor: Ralph Fiennes, *Schindler's List*
Supporting Actress: Miriam Margolyes, *The Age of Innocence*
David Lean Award/Director: Steven Spielberg, *Schindler's List*
Screenplay (Original): Danny Rubin, Harold Ramis, *Groundhog Day*
Screenplay (Adapted): Steven Zaillian, *Schindler's List*
Short Film: *Franz Kafka's It's a Wonderful Life* (Ruth Kenley-Letts, Peter Capaldi)
Short Animated Film: *The Wrong Trousers* (Aardman Animations, Nick Park)
Academy Fellow: Michael Grade
Michael Balcon Award: Ken Loach
Special Award: Lord Attenborough [Richard], Thora Hird
Lifetime Achievement: Douglas Slocombe
Lloyd's Bank/Most Popular Film: *Jurassic Park*

**** The Piano CAN IND
Besides being the first woman director to win a Palme d'Or

(that is, if you don't count her own 1986 Short Film Palme d'Or), Jane Campion won a screenplay Oscar—rather ironically, because the writing is the movie's weakest aspect; the supposedly feminist film is a pure fairy tale. But her direction is magical—she can hardly compose a shot without showing us something we've never seen before. The writing will get better; the directing is there.

** *Farewell, My Concubine*
GLO NYC LAC BOR BAA CAN
Chen Kaige's '50s-style Peking-opera-soap-opera about a man loved by both a woman and a transvestite boyhood pal (yes, you read that right) during the upheavals of mid-century China. A big, splashy, somewhat grueling and mostly overrated Chinese *A Star Is Born*, with more melodrama and less real style than the work of Chen's former cinematographer Zhang Yimou.

Cannes Film Festival

Palme d'Or: *The Piano* (Jane Campion, Australia), *Farewell, My Concubine* (Chen Kaige, Hong Kong) (shared)
Special Jury Prize: *Faraway, So Close* (Wim Wenders, West Germany)
Jury Prize: *The Puppetmaster* (Hou Hsiao-hsien, Taiwan), *Raining Stones* (Ken Loach, UK) (shared)
Actor: David Thewlis, *Naked* (UK)
Actress: Holly Hunter, *The Piano*
Director: Mike Leigh, *Naked*

Palme d'Or/Short Film: *Coffee and Cigarettes (somewhere in California)* (Jim Jarmusch, USA)
Camera d'Or: *The Scent of Green Papaya* (Tran Anh Hung, France), special mention: *Friends* (Elaine Proctor, UK-France)
Technical Prize: *Mazeppa* (Jean Gargonne, Vincent Arnardi, France), special mention: short, *The Singing Trophy* (Grant Lahood, New Zealand)
International Critics Prize: in competition, *Farewell, My Concubine*; out of competition, *Child Murders* (Ildiko Szabo, Hungary); short, *The Debt* (Bruno de Almeida, USA)

**** *Short Cuts* VEN IND
After the fizzy apéritif that was *The Player*, this was the nine-course meal that signaled Robert Altman's return to top form. You could argue that the way Raymond Carver's short stories are intercut (which has a certain resemblance to channel-hopping) robs them of the thing short stories do best, which is to build single-mindedly to a moment of revelation. But taken purely as source material, they allow the movie to do what movies do best (and too rarely)—give a handful of appealing players, especially actresses, the opportunity to bring fully rounded characters to life on screen.

*** *Blue* VEN
The first of Kieslowski's "Three Colors" trilogy, a poem about a widow (Juliette Binoche), the sole survivor of her family's car crash who comes back to life by completing her husband's last symphony. Exquisite . . . but movies aren't poems.

Venice Film Festival
Golden Lion: *Short Cuts* (Robert Altman, USA), *Blue [Trois Couleurs: Bleu]* (Krzysztof Kieslowski, France) (shared)
Special Jury Prize: *Bad Boy Buddy* (Rolf De Heer, Australia/Italy)
Silver Lion: *Kosh ba Kosh* (Bakhtiar Khudoinazarov, Tadzhikistan)
Actor: Fabrizio Bentivoglio, *A Soul Torn in Two* (Italy)
Actress: Juliette Binoche, *Blue*
Supporting Actor: Marcello Mastroianni, *Un, Deux, Trois: Soleil* (France)
Supporting Actress: Anna Bonaluto, *Where Are You? I'm Here* (Italy)
Ensemble Cast: *Short Cuts*
Career Awards: Claudia Cardinale, Robert De Niro, Roman Polanski, Steven Spielberg

*** *The Wedding Banquet* BER
A Hollywood-style gimmick—gay Taiwanese-American yuppie marries Chinese woman, to get her a green card and make his parents think he's straight—is used more for exploring character than making cheap jokes in this nicely observed, low-key independent comedy-drama.

*** *Women from the Lake of Scented Souls* BER
The title sounds like an Asian ghost story à la *Ugetsu*, but it's actually a contemporary

feminist drama about a Chinese woman who gets her consciousness raised when a Japanese company starts buying her products. A little didactic, but with some interesting things to say (both good and bad) about women in both Chinese and capitalist societies.

Berlin Film Festival
Golden Bear: *The Wedding Banquet* (Ang Lee, Taiwan), *Women from the Lake of Scented Souls* (Xie Fei, China)
Silver Bear: *Arizona Dreams* (Emir Kusturica, USA)
Special Silver Bears: *The Sun of the Wakeful* (Temur Babluani, Georgia), *Samaba Traoré* (Idrissa Ouédraogo, Burkina Faso)
Actor: Denzel Washington, *Malcolm X* (USA)
Actress: Michelle Pfeiffer, *Love Field* (USA)
Blue Angel Prize for European Filmmaking: *Young Werther* (Jacques Doillon, France)
Wolfgang Staudte Film Prize: *Laws of Gravity* (Nick Gomez, USA)

**** *Ruby in Paradise* SUN
A lovely independent film about an uneducated but smart and self-reliant girl (Ashley Judd) trying to find her way in a tacky Florida resort town off-season. A throwback to the old Sundance of regional coming-of-age dramas—and close to the masterpiece of that school.

** *Public Access* SUN
An odd allegory about a stranger who comes to a small town and uses a public-access TV show to bring the town's

hidden anxieties and suspicions to a boil for his own secret purpose . . . a purpose *so* secret, in fact, that it's far from clear even once it's over. (I think it's trying to say something about media irresponsibility, but I'll entertain other suggestions.) The directorial debut of Bryan Singer, who subsequently made the twisty neo-*noir* thriller *The Usual Suspects*, this is similarly puzzling, darkly funny and overdirected within an inch of its life, but what it's *not* is particularly entertaining; Singer's talents were better served by that modest genre film than by this attempt at deeper meanings.

Sundance Film Festival
Grand Jury Prize/dramatic: *Ruby in Paradise* (Victor Nuñez), *Public Access* (Bryan Singer)
Grand Jury Prize/documentary: *Children of Fate: Life and Death in a Sicilian Family* (Andrew Young, Susan Todd, incorporating 1961 film by Robert M. Young, Michael Roemer), *Silverlake Life: The View From Here* (Peter Friedman)
Special Jury Prizes/dramatic: First Feature: *Just Another Girl on the I.R.T.* (Leslie Harris); Distinction: *Lillian* (David Williams)
Special Jury Prizes/documentary: Superb Technical Achievement: *Earth and the American Dream* (Bill Couturié); Merit: *Something Within Me* (Emma Joan Morris)
Filmmakers Trophy: dramatic: *Fly By Night* (Steve Gomer); documentary: *Something Within Me*

Waldo Salt Screenwriting Award: Tony Chan, Edwin Baker, *Combination Platter*
Cinematography: dramatic: Judy Irola, *An Ambush of Ghosts* (Everett Lewis); documentary: Andrew Young, Robert M. Young, *Children of Fate*
Freedom of Expression Award: *Silverlake Life*
Audience Award: dramatic competition: *El Mariachi* (Richard Rodriguez); documentary competition: *Something Within Me*

Independent Spirit Awards

Film: *Short Cuts*
First Film: Richard Rodriguez, *El Mariachi*
Foreign Film: *The Piano*
Actor: Jeff Bridges, *American Heart*
Actress: Ashley Judd, *Ruby in Paradise*
Supporting Actor: Christopher Lloyd, *Twenty Bucks*

Supporting Actress: Lili Taylor, *Household Saints*
Director: Robert Altman, *Short Cuts*
Screenplay: Frank Barhydt, Robert Altman, *Short Cuts*
Cinematography: Lisa Rinzler, *Menace II Society*

Golden Raspberry Awards

Worst Picture: *Indecent Proposal*
Worst Actor: Burt Reynolds, *Cop-and-a-Half*
Worst Actress: Madonna, *Body of Evidence*
Worst Supporting Actor: Woody Harrelson, *Indecent Proposal*
Worst Supporting Actress: Faye Dunaway, *The Temp*
Worst Director: Jennifer Chambers Lynch, *Boxing Helena*
Worst Screenplay: Amy Holden Jones, *Indecent Proposal*
Worst Song: "WHOOMP! There It Is," *Addams Family Values*
Worst New Star: Janet Jackson, *Poetic Justice*

Box Office (Domestic Grosses)

1	*Jurassic Park*	$338,929,640	Uni
2	*The Fugitive*	179,290,645	WB
3	*The Firm*	158,348,367	Par
4	*Sleepless in Seattle*	126,533,006	TriStar
5	*Aladdin [1993 only]*	118,899,051	Disney
	[estimated 1992–1993 total:	240,000,000]	
6	*Mrs. Doubtfire [1993 only]*	111,764,380	Fox
	[1993–94 total:	219,195,051]	
7	*Indecent Proposal*	106,614,059	Par
8	*In the Line of Fire*	102,314,283	Col
9	*Cliffhanger*	84,049,211	TriStar
10	*A Few Good Men [1993 only]*	78,211,341	Col
	[estimated 1992–93 total:	160,000,000]	
Other films of note:			
11	*Free Willy*	77,698,625	WB
17	*The Crying Game [1993 only]*	59,343,181	Miramax
	[estimated 1992–93 total:	65,000,000]	
20	*The Pelican Brief [1993 only]*	51,985,379	WB
	[1993–94 total:	100,768,056]	

23	*The Last Action Hero*	50,016,394	Col
76	*Like Water for Chocolate [1993 only]*	19,535,913	Miramax
89	*The Piano [1993 only]*	15,480,971	Miramax
	[1993–94 total:	40,157,856]	
110	*Manhattan Murder Mystery*	11,285,588	TriStar
187	*El Mariachi*	2,040,920	Col

Jurassic Park, Aladdin, *and* Free Willy *soaked up the kiddie market, but otherwise it was a surprisingly grown-up year, with a host of adult-oriented hits that—minus four-letter words and obligatory sex scenes—wouldn't have been out of place on 1959's list: just imagine* The Fugitive *with Kirk Douglas and Jimmy Stewart,* In The Line of Fire *with John Wayne and Peter Lorre,* A Few Good Men *reuniting Mister Roberts'* James Cagney and Jack Lemmon, *or Venetian Proposal with Cary Grant as the millionaire who offers Gig Young a million dollars to let him take wife Doris Day on a midnight gondola ride. (Matter of fact, we did get Mrs. Doubtfire in 1959: it was called* Some Like It Hot.*) Costing somewhere between $80 and $120 million,* The Last Action Hero *(1959 equivalent:* The Three Stooges Meet Hercules) *was the year's most notorious bomb; Sony started talking about selling Columbia, but star Arnold Schwarzenegger shrugged it off as a learning experience. And* Like Water for Chocolate *passed* La Dolce Vita, Z, *and* I Am Curious (Yellow) *to become the top-grossing foreign film of all time—and only one of three critical and financial hits carefully nurtured by the era's smartest marketers, the Weinstein brothers of Miramax, acquired that year by Disney.*

Gebert's Golden Armchairs

The Stephen King Award (for the bestselling author whose name on a marquee means "Stay Away!") goes to John Grisham's inaptly named *The Pelican Brief*, for taking a plot that would be transparent in 70 minutes (you don't introduce the President as a character if he's not guilty) and ladling it out over a butt-numbing 2:21.

Best American Film: *Schindler's List*
Best Foreign Film: *The Piano*
Best Actor: Anthony Hopkins, *The Remains of the Day*
Best Actress: Holly Hunter, *The Piano, The Firm*
Best Director: Steven Spielberg, *Schindler's List*
Worst Hit: *The Pelican Brief*

1994

Much of this book has shown that Oscar's final choices are really decided by the awards that precede it—but every once in a while Oscar goes its own way. *Pulp Fiction* could hardly have had more encouragement—beginning at Cannes, where even Quentin Tarantino assumed that *Red* was a lock for the Palme d'Or, and that the usual Cannes hints to stick around for the award ceremony meant only that he would win Best Director or that Samuel Jackson would win another Cannes acting prize. Instead, a jury led by Clint Eastwood (which in retrospect should have been a clue) gave the ex-video clerk a Palme d'Or, to be echoed over the coming months by three of the four main critics' groups and dozens of ten-best lists.

But *Pulp Fiction* was an indie release from Miramax—at the best of times an upstart in Oscar's eye, and at the moment a major irritant, since they were suing the Academy over its exclusion of *Red* from the foreign-language category for not being Swiss enough. And in the meantime, *Gump* had made $300 million. In modern Hollywood, even a movie as relentlessly feelgood and audience-pandering as *Gump* qualifies as something daring (it is true, it does *not* end with Tom Hanks blowing away drug kingpins with an Uzi), and by the time of the Golden Globes, it was a foregone conclusion that Hollywood would congratulate itself for finding $300 million worth of buttons to push with *Gump*.

Interestingly, it was the distributor, not the movie, that was mainly responsible for the Academy's other controversial snub of the year as well. *Hoop Dreams* was undoubtedly an extremely well-crafted documentary about inner-city life and basketball—but despite the claims of a certain pair of Chicago-based TV critics, it was *not* so obviously the best documentary of its time that any other choice was unimaginable. (In Chicago, basketball permeates life so completely that even the Best Documentary Oscars can't escape it.) After all, the previous January a Sundance jury had picked *Freedom on My Mind* (one of the eventual Oscar nominees) over *Hoop Dreams*—without inciting a national controversy.

What wrecked *Hoop Dreams*' chances in the documentary category was that its distributor campaigned for a Best Picture nomination—Fine Line chief Ira Deutchman going so far as to say in the trades that "the documentary Oscar doesn't mean anything." No doubt true . . . but the words of a man who wants the publicity of controversy more than he wants a gold-plated statuette.

Academy Awards

• *Forrest Gump* AAW DGA GLO BOR PEO
** **Tom Hanks** AAW GLO SAG BOR PEO
There are lots of reasons to dislike this feelgood historical fantasy, in which everything about the last 30 years that *didn't* matter happens to Tom Hanks (I mean, who thinks of the invention of the "Shit Happens" bumpersticker as a key cultural event, anyway?), while everything that *did* matter—the peace movement, feminism, etc.—is turned into something bad that happens to Robin Wright. (*Stripper-folksingers*? Where the hell did they get *that*? About the only place in America that women *weren't* treated as bimbos in 1965 was the folk-singing movement.) But say you could put its anti-counterculture politics aside. You'd still have a movie that wanders aimlessly for hours to no particular purpose, and then shamelessly drags in AIDS to give itself a tearjerk ending. I can see a sozzled Academy giving it Best Picture—but Best *Editing* (against *Hoop Dreams*, no less)? Yeah, I couldn't have cut a *minute* from it.

As for Hanks, God knows whatever the movie has is in his performance, but I think the singsong accent and stupefied look dampen down his natural charm, and the performance has grown monotonous by the time the damnable thing is (finally) over.

Picture
Forrest Gump (Paramount, Wendy Finerman, Steve Tisch, Steve Starkey)
Four Weddings and a Funeral (Gramercy Pictures, Working Title, Duncan Kenworthy)
Pulp Fiction (Miramax, Band Apart/Jersey Films, Lawrence Bender)
Quiz Show (Hollywood Pictures, Robert Redford, Michael Jacobs, Julian Krainin, Michael Nozik)
The Shawshank Redemption (Columbia, Castle Rock, Niki Marvin)

Actor
Tom Hanks, *Forrest Gump*
Morgan Freeman, *The Shawshank Redemption*
Nigel Hawthorne, *The Madness of King George*
Paul Newman, *Nobody's Fool*
John Travolta, *Pulp Fiction*

*** **Jessica Lange in** *Blue Sky* AAW GLO LAC
What a terrible time for actresses—where three out of five Best Picture nominees produced a Best Actor nomination, the entire ranks of the Best Actress category had to be dug up among otherwise-ignored genre films (*The Client*)

and failed Best Picture aspirants (*Nell*, *Tom & Viv*), and the winner was a movie that had sat on the shelf since 1991— which means, effectively, that 1994 produced no Best Actress winner at all. It's easy to see why this blew all the other little women away—it's the one full-blooded movie star part, a *Rose Tattoo* next to the likes of *Nell*. As a nymphomaniacal Army wife in the Kennedy era, Lange dresses like Bardot and Monroe, does a topless water ballet for a fleet of helicopters, has a knock-down fight with hubby Tommy Lee Jones, and does a mad scene—and that's just the first 20 minutes.

Actress
Jessica Lange, *Blue Sky*
Jodie Foster, *Nell*
Miranda Richardson, *Tom & Viv*
Winona Ryder, *Little Women*
Susan Sarandon, *The Client*

Supporting Actor
Martin Landau, *Ed Wood*
Samuel L. Jackson, *Pulp Fiction*
Chazz Palminteri, *Bullets Over Broadway*
Paul Scofield, *Quiz Show*
Gary Sinise, *Forrest Gump*

Supporting Actress
Dianne Wiest, *Bullets Over Broadway*
Rosemary Harris, *Tom & Viv*
Helen Mirren, *The Madness of King George*
Uma Thurman, *Pulp Fiction*
Jennifer Tilly, *Bullets Over Broadway*

Director
Robert Zemeckis, *Forrest Gump*
Woody Allen, *Bullets Over Broadway*

Quentin Tarantino, *Pulp Fiction*
Robert Redford, *Quiz Show*
Krzysztof Kieslowski, *Red*

Original Screenplay: Quentin Tarantino; story by Quentin Tarantino, Roger Avary, *Pulp Fiction*
Adapted Screenplay: Eric Roth, *Forrest Gump*
Cinematography: John Toll, *Legends of the Fall*
Score: Hans Zimmer, *The Lion King*
Song: "Can You Feel the Love Tonight?" *The Lion King*, m: Elton John, l: Tim Rice
Art Direction: Ken Adam, *The Madness of King George*
Costume Design: Lizzy Gardiner, Tim Chappel, *The Adventures of Priscilla, Queen of the Desert*
Editing: *Forrest Gump*
Sound: *Speed*
Sound Effects Editing: *Speed*
Make-up: Rick Baker, *Ed Wood*
Visual Effects: *Forrest Gump*
Short/Animated: *Bob's Birthday* (Channel Four/National Film Board of Canada)
Short/Live Action: *Franz Kafka's It's a Wonderful Life* (Peter Capaldi, Ruth Kenley-Letts), *Trevor* (Peggy Rajski, Randy Stone) (tie)
Documentary/Feature: *Maya Lin: A Strong Clear Vision* (Freida Lee Mock)
Documentary/Short: *A Time for Justice* (Southern Poverty Law Center)
Foreign-Language Film: *Burnt by the Sun* (Russia)
Irving G. Thalberg Award: Clint Eastwood
Jean Hersholt Humanitarian Award: Quincy Jones
Special Award: Michelangelo Antonioni

Golden Globes
Picture (Drama): *Forrest Gump*
Picture (Comedy/Musical): *The Lion King*
Foreign-Language Film: *Farinelli* (Belgium)
Actor (Drama): Tom Hanks, *Forrest Gump*
Actor (Comedy/Musical): Hugh Grant, *Four Weddings and a Funeral*
Actress (Drama): Jessica Lange, *Blue Sky*
Actress (Comedy/Musical): Jamie Lee Curtis, *True Lies*
Supporting Actor: Martin Landau, *Ed Wood*
Supporting Actress: Dianne Wiest, *Bullets Over Broadway*
Director: Robert Zemeckis, *Forrest Gump*
Screenplay: Quentin Tarantino, *Pulp Fiction*
Original Score: Hans Zimmer, *The Lion King*
Original Song: "Can You Feel the Love Tonight?" *The Lion King*, m: Elton John, l: Tim Rice
Cecil B. DeMille Award: Sophia Loren

Directors Guild of America
Director: Robert Zemeckis, *Forrest Gump*
Documentary Director: Steve James, *Hoop Dreams*
D. W. Griffith Award: James Ivory
Honorary Lifetime Member: Sheldon Leonard

Screen Actors Guild
Actor: Tom Hanks, *Forrest Gump*
Actress: Jodie Foster, *Nell*
Supporting Actor: Martin Landau, *Ed Wood*
Supporting Actress: Dianne Wiest, *Bullets Over Broadway*

★★★★ *Red* NYC SOC LAC IND

Though it went home empty-handed at Cannes, the third of Krzysztof Kieslowski's *Trois Couleurs* was the unanimous foreign-film choice of the three main critics' groups—a sign of critical excitement at having found a new European auteur-genius in the Fellini-Bergman mode (well, actually closer to Resnais and Jacques Rivette, but it isn't a time to be picky). A shockingly aged and unshaven Jean-Louis Trintignant plays a retired judge who is also some sort of pervert, spending most of his time in his broken-down house listening, God-like (or movie-director-like?) to the intimate conversations of his neighbors until a model he chanced to meet draws him out. The air of chicly aimless noodling that afflicted *Blue* isn't exactly gone, but this is really *cool* chicly aimless noodling, a great director inviting us into his head to sit around unshaven listening to all the conversations going on.

New York Film Critics Circle
Film: *Quiz Show*
Foreign-Language Film: *Red*
Actor: Paul Newman, *Nobody's Fool*
Actress: Linda Fiorentino, *The Last Seduction*
Supporting Actor: Martin Landau, *Ed Wood*
Supporting Actress: Dianne Wiest, *Bullets Over Broadway*
Director: Quentin Tarantino, *Pulp Fiction*

New Director: Darnell Martin, *I Like It Like That*
Screenplay: Quentin Tarantino, *Pulp Fiction*
Cinematography: Stefan Czapsky, *Ed Wood*
Documentary: *Hoop Dreams*
Special Award: Jean-Luc Godard

National Society of Film Critics
Film: *Pulp Fiction*
Foreign-Language Film: *Red*
Actor: Paul Newman, *Nobody's Fool*
Actress: Jennifer Jason Leigh, *Mrs. Parker and the Vicious Circle*
Supporting Actor: Martin Landau, *Ed Wood*
Supporting Actress: Dianne Wiest, *Bullets Over Broadway*
Director: Quentin Tarantino, *Pulp Fiction*
Screenplay: Quentin Tarantino, *Pulp Fiction*
Cinematography: Stefan Czapsky, *Ed Wood*
Documentary: *Hoop Dreams*
Special Citation: *Satantango* (Bela Tarr, Hungary), *The Pharoah's Belt* (Lewis Klahr)

Los Angeles Film Critics Association
Film: *Pulp Fiction*
Foreign Film: *Red*
Actor: John Travolta, *Pulp Fiction*
Actress: Jessica Lange, *Blue Sky*
Supporting Actor: Martin Landau, *Ed Wood*
Supporting Actress: Dianne Wiest, *Bullets Over Broadway*
Director: Quentin Tarantino, *Pulp Fiction*
Screenplay: Quentin Tarantino, *Pulp Fiction*
Cinematography: Stefan Czapsky, *Ed Wood*
Music: Howard Shore, *Ed Wood*
Documentary: *Hoop Dreams*

Animated Film: *The Lion King*
Independent/Experimental: John Maybury, *Remembrance of Things Fast*
Career Achievement: Billy Wilder
Special Achievement for Film Criticism: Pauline Kael
New Generation Award: John Dahl, *Red Rock West*, *The Last Seduction*

National Board of Review
Best English-Language Film: *Forrest Gump*, *Pulp Fiction* (tie)
Quiz Show
Four Weddings and a Funeral
Bullets Over Broadway
Ed Wood
The Shawshank Redemption
Nobody's Fool
The Madness of King George
Tom & Viv
Heavenly Creatures
Best Foreign-Language Film:
Eat Drink Man Woman
To Live
Strawberries and Chocolate
Red
Queen Margot
Actor: Tom Hanks, *Forrest Gump*
Actress: Miranda Richardson, *Tom & Viv*
Supporting Actor: Gary Sinise, *Forrest Gump*
Supporting Actress: Rosemary Harris, *Tom & Viv*
Special Award/Ensemble Acting: *Ready-to-Wear*
Director: Quentin Tarantino, *Pulp Fiction*
Documentary: *Hoop Dreams*
Family Film: *The Lion King*
TV Movie: *The Last Seduction*

People's Choice Awards
Favorite All-Around Movie: *Forrest Gump*
Favorite Drama: *Forrest Gump*
Favorite Comedy: *The Santa Clause*

Favorite Dramatic Movie Actor:
Tom Hanks
**Favorite Dramatic Movie
Actress:** Jodie Foster
Favorite Comedy Movie Actor:
Tim Allen
**Favorite Comedy Movie
Actress:** Whoopi Goldberg

MTV Movie Awards
Movie: *Pulp Fiction*
Actor: Brad Pitt, *Interview With
the Vampire*
Actress: Sandra Bullock, *Speed*
Most Desirable Male: Brad Pitt,
Interview With the Vampire
Most Desirable Female: Sandra
Bullock, *Speed*
Breakthrough Performance:
Kirsten Dunst, *Interview With
the Vampire*
Best Comedic Performance: Jim
Carrey, *Dumb and Dumber*
Best On-Screen Duo: Keanu
Reeves, Sandra Bullock, *Speed*
Best Villain: Dennis Hopper,
Speed
Best Action Sequence: *Speed*
Best Dance Sequence: John
Travolta, Uma Thurman, *Pulp
Fiction*
Best Kiss: Jim Carrey, Lauren
Holly, *Dumb and Dumber*
Best Song: Stone Temple Pilots,
"Big Empty," *The Crow*
Best New Filmmaker: Steve
James, *Hoop Dreams*
Lifetime Achievement Award:
Jackie Chan

British Academy Awards
Film: *Four Weddings and a
Funeral*
**Alexander Korda Award/
British Film:** *Shallow Grave*
Foreign-Language Film: *To Live*
(Zhang Yimou, China)
Actor: Hugh Grant, *Four
Weddings and a Funeral*
Actress: Susan Sarandon, *The
Client*

Supporting Actor: Samuel L.
Jackson, *Pulp Fiction*
Supporting Actress: Kristin
Scott Thomas, *Four Weddings
and a Funeral*
David Lean Award/Director:
Mike Newell, *Four Weddings
and a Funeral*
Screenplay (Original): Quentin
Tarantino, Roger Avary, *Pulp
Fiction*
Screenplay (Adapted): Paul
Attanasio, *Quiz Show*
Academy Fellow: Billy Wilder
**Lloyd's Bank/Most Popular
Film:** *Four Weddings and a
Funeral*

**** *Pulp Fiction* NYC LAC
BOR MTV CAN IND
The difference between, say,
GoodFellas and *Pulp Fiction*
is that *GoodFellas* is a
brilliantly virtuoso,
electrically acted gangster black
comedy with something to say
about materialism and
morality—and *Pulp Fiction* is
a brilliantly virtuoso,
electrically acted gangster
black comedy. But nobody is
having more fun at the
moment playing with genres
and audiences' heads than
Quentin Tarantino—and in the
land of the blind and the bland,
one-eyed hipsters are king. Like
GoodFellas, an easy pick for
the critics—in fact, it enjoyed
almost exactly the same
victory at the National Society:
41 points to 2 for *Gump*.

Cannes Film Festival
Palme d'Or: *Pulp Fiction*
(Quentin Tarantino, USA)
Special Jury Prize: *Burnt by the
Sun* (Nikita Mikhalkov, Russia-

France), *To Live* (Zhang Yimou, Hong Kong-China)
Jury Prize: *Queen Margot* (Patrice Chereau, France)
Actor: Ge You, *To Live*
Actress: Virna Lisi, *Queen Margot*
Director: Nanni Moretti, *Caro Diario [Dear Diary]* (Italy)
Screenplay: Michel Blanc, *Dead Tired* (France)
Camera d'Or: *Coming to Terms With the Dead* (Jacques Audiard, France); special mention, *The Silences of the Palace* (Moufida Tlatli, Tunisia-France)
Technical Prize: Special effects director Pitof, *Dead Tired*
International Critics Prize: in competition, *Exotica* (Atom Egoyan, Canada); out of competition, *Bab El-Oued City* (Merzak Allouache, Algeria)

*** *Before the Rain* VEN

If you're most American film school graduates, you try to raise money to make an independent film about your own life as an aspiring independent filmmaker. If you're an American film school graduate who happens to be from the Macedonian region of the former Yugoslavia, you raise the money to make a film about your homeland's strife—and if the cinematography is occasionally too exotically picturesque, and your main character, a world-weary photojournalist, has a whiff of cliché about him, the subject matter is meaty and urgent and authentic enough to forgive the minor sins that would sink your fellow students' projects.

Venice Film Festival

Golden Lion: *Before the Rain* (Milcho Manchevski, Macedonia), *Vive l'Amour* (Tsai Ming-liang, Taiwan) (shared)
Special Jury Prize: *Natural Born Killers* (Oliver Stone, USA)
Silver Lion: *Heavenly Creatures* (Peter Jackson, New Zealand), *Little Odessa* (James Gray, USA), *The Bull* (Carlo Mazzacurati, Italy)
Actor: Xia Yu, *In the Heat of the Sun* (Jiang Wen, China)
Actress: Maria de Madeiros, *Two Brothers My Sister* (Portugal)
Supporting Actor: Roberto Citran, *The Bull*
Supporting Actress: Vanessa Redgrave, *Little Odessa*
Direction: Gianni Amelio, *Lamerica* (Italy)
Cinematography: Wong Kar-Wai, Christopher Doyle, *Ashes of Time*
Screenplay: Bigas Luna, Cuca Canals, *The Tit and the Moon* (Spain)
Career Awards: Al Pacino, Susi Cecchi D'Amico, Ken Loach
Senate Gold Medal: *The Life and Extraordinary Adventures of Private Ivan Chonkin* (Jiri Menzel, Czech Rep.)
International Critics Prizes: *Before the Rain*, *Vive l'Amour*
Pasinetti Italian Critics Prizes: film, *Lamerica*; actor: Rade Serbedzija, *Before the Rain*; actress: Juliette Lewis, *Natural Born Killers*

*** *In the Name of the Father* BER

Daniel Day-Lewis plays an Irish hippie who was in the wrong place at the wrong time, and found himself—and his entire family—thrown into jail for an IRA bombing on what the British police knew was faulty evidence. A well-made docudrama, but like Day-Lewis' and director Jim Sheridan's *My Left Foot*, very conventional, old-fashioned filmmaking which was wildly overrated by critics (and Oscar) and given credit for a level of realism and a depth of characterization which just isn't there. Compare with Ken Loach's *Ladybird, Ladybird*, shown at the same festival, to see *real* British realist filmmaking from the proletarian trenches.

Berlin Film Festival
Golden Bear: *In the Name of the Father* (Jim Sheridan, UK-Ireland)
Silver Bear/Jury Prize: *Strawberry and Chocolate* (Tomas Gutierrez Alea, Cuba-Mexico-Spain)
Silver Bear: *The Year of the Dog* (Semyon Aranovich, Russia-France)
Actor: Tom Hanks, *Philadelphia* (USA)
Actress: Crissy Rock, *Ladybird, Ladybird* (UK); special mention to Rosie Perez, *Fearless* (USA)
Director: Krzysztof Kieslowski, *White* [*Trois Couleurs: Blanc*]
Cinematographer: Yang Wei, *Sparkling Fox* (Hong Kong-China)
Outstanding Single Achievement: Alain Resnais, *Smoking/No Smoking* (France)
Special Mention for Entertainment: *Dear Goddam Friends* (Mario Monicelli, Italy)
Blue Angel Prize for European Filmmaking: *Law of Courage* (Alessandro di Robilant, Italy)
International Critics Prizes: competition, *Ladybird, Ladybird* (Ken Loach, UK);

Forum, *Tigrero* (Aki Kaurismäki, Finland); special mention, Tomas Gutierrez Alea

Sundance Film Festival
Grand Jury Prize/dramatic: *What Happened Was* (Tom Noonan)
Grand Jury Prize/documentary: *Freedom on My Mind* (Connie Field, Marilyn Mulford)
Special Jury Prizes: acting: Sean Nelson, *Fresh* (Boaz Yakin), Alicia Witt, Renee Humphrey, *Fun* (Rafal Zielinski); technical excellence: *Coming Out Under Fire* (Arthur Dong)
Filmmakers Trophy: dramatic: *Clerks* (Kevin Smith), *Fresh* (Boaz Yakin); documentary: *Theremin—An Electronic Odyssey* (Steven M. Martin)
Waldo Salt Screenwriting Award: Tom Noonan, *What Happened Was*
Cinematography: dramatic: Greg Gardiner, *Suture* (Scott McGehee, David Siegel); documentary: Morten Sandtroen, *Colorado Cowboy: The Bruce Ford Story* (Arthur Elgort)
Freedom of Expression Award: *Dialogues With Madwomen* (Allie Light), *Heart of the Matter* (Gini Reticker, Amber Hollibaugh)
Short Films: *Family Remains* (Tamara Jenkins), *Avenue X* (Leslie McCleave)
Audience Awards: dramatic: *Spanking the Monkey* (David O. Russell); documentary: *Hoop Dreams* (Steve James)

Independent Spirit Awards
Film: *Pulp Fiction*
First Film: David O. Russell, *Spanking the Monkey*
Foreign Film: *Red*
Actor: Samuel L. Jackson, *Pulp Fiction*

Actress: Linda Fiorentino, *The Last Seduction*
Supporting Actor: Chazz Palminteri, *Bullets Over Broadway*
Supporting Actress: Dianne Wiest, *Bullets Over Broadway*
Debut Performance: Sean Nelson, *Fresh*
Director: Quentin Tarantino, *Pulp Fiction*
Screenplay: Quentin Tarantino, Roger Avary, *Pulp Fiction*
First Screenplay: David O. Russell, *Spanking the Monkey*
Cinematography: John Thomas, *Barcelona*
Someone to Watch Award: Lodge Kerrigan, writer-director, *Clean, Shaven*

Harvard Lampoon Movie Worsts

Ten Worst Films:
Forrest Gump
Reality Bites
Philadelphia
The Lion King
Speed
True Lies
Four Weddings and a Funeral
Schindler's List ["Spielberg had one purpose in making this film: to craft a movie so heart-rending it could not possibly appear in the Movie Worsts"]
It Could Happen to You
The Crow
Kirk Douglas Award for Worst Actor: Eric Stoltz as a Harvard student in *Naked in New York*
Natalie Wood Award for Worst Actress: Moira Kelly as a Harvard student in *With Honors*
Juliette Lewis Understudy Worst Actress Award: Patricia Arquette, *True Romance*
The From Milton Berle's Private Joke File Award (to the comedy that should have stayed private): *The Mask.* Too bad the computers couldn't write the jokes

just like they randomly selected Jim Carrey from a demographic data set to be a movie star
Merino Award: Dan Marino, *Ace Ventura, Pet Detective*

Golden Raspberry Awards

Worst Picture: *Color of Night*
Worst Remake or Sequel: *Wyatt Earp*
Worst Actor: Kevin Costner, *Wyatt Earp*
Worst Actress: Sharon Stone, *Intersection, The Specialist*
Worst Supporting Actor: O.J. Simpson, *The Naked Gun 33$\frac{1}{3}$*
Worst Supporting Actress: Rosie O'Donnell, *Car 54, Where Are You?, The Flintstones, Exit to Eden*
Worst Screen Couple: (tie) Sylvester Stallone, Sharon Stone, *The Specialist*, and Tom Cruise, Brad Pitt, *Interview With the Vampire*
Worst Director: Steven Seagal, *On Deadly Ground*
Worst Screenplay: Tom S. Parker & Jim Jennewein, Steven E. DeSouza, Lowell Ganz & Babaloo Mandel, Mitch Markowitz, Dava Savel, Brian Levant, Michael Wilson, Ai Aidekman, Cindy Begel, Lloyd Garver, David Silverman, Stephen Sustarsic, Nancy Steen, Neil Thompson, Daniel & Joshua Goldin, Peter Martin Wortman, Robert Conte, Jeffrey Reno, Ron Osbourne, Bruce Cohen, Jason Hoffs, Kate Barker, Gary Ross, Rob Dames, Lenny Ripps, Fred Fox, Jr., Lou Diamond, David Richardson, Roy Teicher, Richard Gurman, Michael J. DiGaetano, Ruth Bennett, *The Flintstones*
Worst Song: "Marry The Mole," *Thumbelina*
Worst New Star: Anna Nicole Smith, *The Naked Gun 33$\frac{1}{3}$*

Box Office (Domestic Grosses)

1	*The Lion King*	$298,879,911	Disney
2	*Forrest Gump [1994 only]*	298,096,620	Par
	[through 4/95:	327,838,708]	
3	*True Lies*	146,260,993	Fox
4	*The Santa Clause*	134,560,221	Disney
5	*The Flintstones*	130,522,921	Uni
6	*Clear and Present Danger*	121,715,132	Par
7	*Speed*	121,248,145	Fox
8	*The Mask*	118,644,781	New Line
9	*Mrs. Doubtfire [1994 only]*	107,430,221	Fox
	[1993–1994 total:	219,195,051]	
10	*Maverick*	101,631,272	WB

Other films of note:

11	*Interview With the Vampire*	100,006,585	WB
13	*Schindler's List*	91,077,929	Uni
14	*Philadelphia*	76,878,958	Sony
15	*Ace Ventura, Pet Detective*	72,217,936	New Line
16	*Star Trek Generations*	70,432,156	Par
17	*Stargate*	68,228,515	MGM/UA
19	*Pulp Fiction [1994 only]*	62,391,023	Miramax
	[through 4/95:	103,052,237]	
20	*Dumb and Dumber*	59,072,700	New Line
	[1994 only]		
	[through 4/95:	124,232,357]	
23	*Four Weddings and a Funeral*	52,700,832	Gramercy
37	*Tombstone*	39,648,712	Disney
53	*Wyatt Earp*	25,052,000	WB
59	*Quiz Show*	21,840,003	Disney

Stupidity beat brains hands down in 1994: Gump *became a cultural sensation,* Jim Carrey *went from critical pariah to comic genius in record time,* Nell *made Oscar's shortlist (if no money), and even* Speed *and* Pulp Fiction *had heroes who were not exactly Charles Van Doren. By comparison, the smart, funny* Quiz Show, *whose hero was Charles Van Doren, was a box office disappointment despite its great reviews; its makers were counting on Ralph Fiennes becoming the thinking woman's hot new British sex symbol, but that position had already been filled by Hugh Grant, whose major vehicle,* Four Weddings and a Funeral, *was only a modest hit in America but worldwide by far the most successful British film ever made, taking in something like $250 million. Elsewhere, the twin successes of* Stargate *and* Star Trek's *Not Ready for the Big Screen Players proved that even lamentably awful sci-fi is still better box office than westerns.*

Gebert's Golden Armchairs

Tarantino *nearly* gets my directing prize just for being the only person so far to direct a Quentin Tarantino screenplay without burying it under a ton of irritating music video stylistics. Oscar's supporting winners both seemed better than any of the year's lead performances: Dianne Wiest's hilarious theater phony in Woody Allen's best comedy in ages, and Martin Landau's magnificent effort to prove the impossible—that you can give an emotionally rich, deeply moving performance while talking the whole time like Bela Lugosi.

Best American Film: *Pulp Fiction*

Best Foreign Film: *Red*

Best Actor: Martin Landau, *Ed Wood*

Best Actress: Dianne Wiest, *Bullets Over Broadway*

Best Director: Krzysztof Kieslowski, *Red*

Worst Hit: *Flintstones Happy Meal: The Movie*

1995

There aren't supposed to be surprise hits at Sundance anymore—supposedly everybody who's anybody has already seen everything that's anything before the festival even begins. But *The Brothers McMullen* proved that the promise of Sundance for unknown filmmakers still holds; the $28,000 film about Long Island Irish Catholic men, made by and starring former *Entertainment Tonight* staffer Edward Burns, arrived as a reject from other festivals and left as a Fox pickup and the talk of Park City. In earlier days an independent film as pleasant and deliberately unstylish as this one might have seemed a textbook example of too-unadventurous Sundance regional filmmaking; it's a sign of how healthy the indie scene is today that not everything *has* to be cutting-edge—and, in fact, a sweet little film like this seems like a relief next to all the trendy Tarantino wannabes. (Though if it seems a little pat toward the end, that may be because the version that played at Sundance was nearly forty minutes longer than what Fox finally released.)

Cannes Film Festival

Palme d'Or: *Underground* (Emir Kusturica, Bosnia)

Special Jury Prize: *Ulysses' Gaze* (Theo Angelopoulos, Greece)

Jury Prize: *Don't Forget You're Going to Die* (Xavier Beauvois, France)

Actor: Jonathan Pryce, *Carrington* (UK)

Actress: Helen Mirren, *The Madness of King George* (UK)

Director: Mathieu Kassovitz, *Hate* (France)

Screenplay: Christopher Hampton, *Carrington*

Camera d'Or: *The White Balloon* (Jafar Panahi, Iran)

Technical Prize: *Shanghai Triad* (Zhang Yimou, Hong Kong); mention to *Denise Calls Up* (Harold Salwen, USA)

International Critics Prize: in competition, *Land and Freedom* (Ken Loach, UK), *Ulysses'Gaze*; out of competition, *The White Balloon*

Venice Film Festival

Golden Lion: *Cyclo* (Tran-Anh Hung, France-Vietnam)

Special Jury Prize: *God's Comedy* (Joao Cesar Monteiro, Portugal), *The Star Man* (Giuseppe Tornatore, Italy)

Actor: Goetz George, *The Deathmaker* (Germany)

Actress: Sandrine Bonnaire, Isabelle Huppert, *A Judgment in Stone* (France)

Supporting Actor: Ian Hart, *Nothing Personal* (Ireland)

Supporting Actress: Isabella Ferrari, *Diary of a Poor Young Man* (Italy)

Oselle d'Oro: *In the Bleak Midwinter* (Kenneth Branagh, UK), *Maborosi no hikari* (Hirokazu Koreeda, Japan), *Det yani dokhtar* (Abdolfazl Jalili, Iran)

Senate Gold Medal: *Pasolini: An*

Italian Crime (Marco Tullio
Giordana, Italy)
International Critics Prize:
Cyclo, Beyond the Clouds
(Michelangelo Antonioni, Wim
Wenders, France-Italy-
Germany)

Berlin Film Festival
Golden Bear: *Fresh Bait*
(Bertrand Tavernier, France)
Special Jury Silver Bear: *Smoke*
(Wayne Wang, USA), mention
to Harvey Keitel
Actor: Paul Newman, *Nobody's
Fool* (USA)
Actress: Josephine Siao, *Summer
Snow* (Hong Kong)
Director: Richard Linklater,
Before Sunrise (USA)
Silver Bears: visual design: *Blush*
(Li Shaohong, Hong
Kong–China), *The Play for a
Passenger* (Vadim
Abdraschitov, Russia); special
mentions to *Midaq Alley* (Jorge
Fons, Mexico), *Sh'chur* (Shmuel
Hasfari, Israel), *Moon Shadow*
(Alberto Simone, Italy)
**Blue Angel Prize for European
Filmmaking:** *Cross My Heart
and Hope to Die* (Marius Holst,
Norway)
International Critics Prize: in
competition: *Smoke*; Forum:
Citizen Langlois (Edgardo
Cozarinsky, France); Panorama,
Priest (Antonia Bird, UK);
mention to *Tokyo Kyodai* (Jun
Ichikawa, Japan)

Sundance Film Festival
Grand Jury Prize/dramatic: *The
Brothers McMullen* (Edward
Burns)

**Grand Jury Prize/
documentary:** *Crumb* (Terry
Zwigoff)
Jury Prize for Direction:
dramatic: James Mangold,
Heavy, Mathew Harrison, *The
Rhythm Thief*; documentary:
Michel Negroponte, *Jupiter's
Wife*
Filmmakers Trophy: dramatic:
Angela (Rebecca Miller);
documentary: *Black Is . . . Black
Ain't* (Marlon T. Riggs)
**Waldo Salt Screenwriting
Award:** Tom DiCillo, *Living in
Oblivion*
Cinematography: dramatic:
Ellen Kuras, *Angela*;
documentary: Maryse Alberti,
Crumb
**Special Recognition/Latin
Cinema:** *Eagles Don't Hunt
Flies* (Sergio Cabrera, Columbia),
mention: *Strawberry and
Chocolate* (Tomas Gutierrez Alea,
Juan Carlos Tobio, Cuba)
Freedom of Expression Award:
*When Billy Broke His Head . . .
and Other Tales of Wonder* (David
E. Simpson, Billy Golfus)
Short Films: dramatic: *The
Salesman and Other Adventures*
(Hannah Weyer), mention to:
Trevor (Peggy Rajski);
documentary: *Tom's Flesh* (Jane
Wagner, Tom diMaria), mention
to: *Nonnie & Alex* (Todd Field)
Audience Award: dramatic:
Picture Bride (Kayo Hatta);
documentary: *Ballot Measure 9*
(Heather MacDonald),
Unzipped (Douglas Keeve) (tie)

Appendix: Video Sources

Even though nearly every award-winner I review is on video, many readers may feel that they haven't got a chance of finding the lesser-known ones at their local video stores. One approach to the problem, of course, is to wave the book at your local store's manager and say, "Look, *The Tree of Wooden Clogs* won the Palme d'Or and a prize from the New York Critics Circle, why don't *you* have it?" Video stores will buy anything that has the word "Oscar" attached to it, and they could do worse than to start using the Palme d'Or and the Sundance prizes the same way. (And really smart ones will call their customers' attention to the fact—creating a Sundance section, say.)

Another answer is to use a mail-order service that rents videos through the mail. It's not cheap—with shipping, it usually runs around $10 a movie—but it's not that much more expensive than catching the latest Stallone flick at the multiplex, either, especially if you have like-minded friends to split the cost. The following companies all have reliable reputations, have been around since the dawn of video, and publish catalogs full of interesting choices:

Facets Multimedia
1517 West Fullerton Avenue
Chicago, IL 60614
1–800–5-FACETS

TLA Video
517 South 4th Street
Philadelphia, PA 19147
1–800–333–TLA1

Home Film Festival
P.O. Box 2032
Scranton, PA 18501
1–800–258–3456

Note that in the interests of carrying as many obscure titles as possible, these services may carry copies of foreign films in particular that skirt the edge of copyright law—and are sometimes of marginal quality as a result (even, in Facets' case, when better legal copies have since come out, unfortunately). It's always worth inquiring about the quality of a tape before you spend $10. That said, they're lifesavers and I couldn't have written this book without them.

I should also call attention to the large number of these award-winning films which have come out on laserdisc—often in editions that absolutely put VHS to shame, both because of better image and sound quality and because of extras like director commentaries and making-of supplements. In particular, the Voyager Co.'s Criterion Collection has put out many of the staples of the film festival/film society golden age in gorgeous, meticulously restored editions. If you're wondering whether laserdiscs are a viable format, include enough good titles, and are worth making the investment in, I can't think of any better answer than to point to the superb laserdisc editions of *Wild Strawberries*, *The 400 Blows*, *Black Orpheus*, *The Red Shoes*, *Sansho the Bailiff*, *Andrei Roublev*, and many other award-winners which are hardly household names. Check your local laser dealer or call Voyager at 1–800–446–2001.

Index of Award-Winning Personalities

The following index is designed to be more useful than a conventional page-reference index in helping you quickly find awards won by your favorite personalities. Awards are indicated by the year and the three-letter code for that award group—so that, for instance, **1961 AAW NYC, 1962 CAN** would indicate that the person had won an Academy Award and a New York Critics Circle citation in 1961, and a prize at Cannes in 1962. Then you can easily turn to the chapter for 1961 and scan, say, the Critics Circle listings to find the precise award as it was given.

While the index is not fully comprehensive, I have tried to include every person that even pretty serious film buffs might want to look up. You'll find nearly every actor and director who was ever nominated for an Oscar or who won an award from the other groups, along with the better-known figures in fields such as screenwriting, music, cinematography, set design, and special effects. Since general festival awards such as the Palme d'Or are usually considered to be awards for the filmmaker as well, these are also cited after directors' names. Generally speaking, it's only one-shots who are omitted; if you know that someone won a particular award and don't find them in the index, then that's a pretty good indication that that's *all* they ever won.

Academy Award nominations in acting and directing categories are indicated by AAN, and special Oscars are indicated by AAS—so that no one is led to think, for

instance, that Bob Hope won Best Actor five times.
Note that Oscar winners as indicated by "AAW" may
have received additional nominations as well, and that a win
is not necessarily in the obvious category—for instance,
Stanley Kubrick's "AAW" in 1968 is for *2001*'s special
effects, not its direction. Special or honorary awards from
groups besides the Academy are not indicated
separately, and it's always worth checking the listings
(especially in the cases of the Golden Globes and the
Directors Guild, both of which have a high proportion of
honorary awards) to see whether Ursula Andress *really*
won a Best Actress Globe—or merely Most Promising
Newcomer.

Key to Award Listings

AAW	Academy Award winner	**PEO**	People's Choice Awards
AAN	Academy Award nominee	**MTV**	MTV Movie Awards
AAS	Special Academy Award	**BAA**	British Academy Awards
GLO	Golden Globes	**CAN**	Cannes Film Festival
DGA	Directors Guild of America	**VEN**	Venice Film Festival
		BER	Berlin Film Festival
SAG	Screen Actors Guild	**SUN**	Sundance/U.S. Film Festival
NYC	New York Film Critics Circle		
SOC	National Society of Film Critics	**IND**	Independent Spirit Awards
LAC	Los Angeles Film Critics Association	**HAR**	Harvard Lampoon Movie Worsts
BOR	National Board of Review	**RAZ**	Golden Raspberry Awards
PHO	Photoplay Gold Medals	**AFI**	AFI Life Achievement Award
		LIN	Film Society of Lincoln Center tribute

Abdraschitov, Vadim   1987 VEN, 1989 BER, 1995 BER
Abraham, F. Murray   1984 AAW GLO LAC
Abril, Victoria   1991 BER
Adam, Ken   1975 AAW, 1994 AAW
Adams, Nick   1963 AAN
Addison, John   1963 AAW
Adjani, Isabelle   1975 AAN NYC

SOC BOR, 1981 CAN, 1989 AAN BER
Agutter, Jenny   1977 BAA
Aherne, Brian   1939 AAN
Aiello, Danny   1989 AAN LAC
Aimée, Anouk   1966 AAN GLO, 1967 BAA, 1980 CAN
Albert, Eddie   1953 AAN, 1972 AAN NYC

Auric, Georges   1946 CAN, 1952 VEN

Auteuil, Daniel   1987 BAA

Avati, Pupi   1984 VEN

Avildsen, John G.   1976 AAW DGA

Aykroyd, Dan   1988 RAZ, 1989 AAN, 1991 RAZ

Ayres, Lew   1948 AAN

Azéma, Sabine   1984 BOR

Babenco, Hector   1985 AAN

Bacall, Lauren   1992 GLO

Bacharach, Burt   1969 AAW GLO, 1981 AAW GLO

Baddeley, Hermione   1959 AAN

Bainter, Fay   1938 AAW, 1961 AAN

Baker, Carroll   1956 AAN GLO, 1964 HAR

Baker, Kathy   1987 SOC

Baker, Rick   1981 AAW, 1987 AAW, 1994 AAW

Baldwin, William   1993 MTV

Bale, Christian   1987 BOR

Balk, Fairuza   1992 IND

Ball, Lucille   1973 HAR, 1978 GLO

Ballard, Lucien   1969 SOC

Ballhaus, Michael   1989 SOC LAC, 1990 LAC

Balsam, Martin   1964 BOR, 1965 AAW

Bancroft, Anne   1962 AAW BOR BAA, 1964 AAN GLO BAA CAN, 1967 ANN GLO, 1977 AAN BOR, 1985 AAN, 1987 BAA

Bancroft, George   1928–9 AAN

Bankhead, Tallulah   1944 NYC

Bannen, Ian   1965 AAN

Barbera, Joseph: see William Hanna

Bardem, Juan Antonio   1955 CAN, 1956 VEN, 1958 CAN

Barnes, George   1940 AAW, 1952 GLO

Barreto, Lima   1953 CAN

Barrie, Barbara   1964 CAN, 1979 AAN

Barry, John [composer]   1966 AAW, 1968 AAW, 1981 RAZ, 1985 AAW GLO, 1990 AAW

Barrymore, Ethel   1944 AAW, 1946 AAN, 1947 AAN, 1949 AAN

Barrymore, Lionel   1928–9 AAN, 1930–1 AAW

Barthelmess, Richard   1927–8 AAN

Basehart, Richard   1951 BOR, 1956 BOR

Basevi, James   1943 AAW

Bass, Saul   1968 AAW

Basserman, Albert   1940 AAN

Bassett, Angela   1993 AAN GLO

Bates, Alan   1968 AAN

Bates, Kathy   1990 AAW GLO

Baxter, Anne   1946 AAW GLO, 1950 AAN, 1956 HAR

Baxter, Warner   1928–9 AAW

Beals, Jennifer   1983 HAR

Beatles, The (see also McCartney individually)   1970 AAW

Beaton, Cecil   1958 AAW, 1964 AAW

Beatty, Ned   1976 AAN

Beatty, Warren   1961 GLO HAR, 1967 AAN, 1975 SOC, 1978 AAN GLO HAR, 1981 AAW GLO DGA LAC BOR HAR, 1991 AAN BOR

Becker, Jacques   1947 CAN

Beery, Wallace   1929–30 AAN, 1931–2 AAN, 1934 VEN

Begley [Sr.], Ed   1962 AAW

Bel Geddes, Barbara   1948 AAN

Bellamy, Ralph   1937 AAN, 1986 AAS

Bellochio, Marco   1967 VEN, 1979 BER, 1991 BER

Benchley, Robert (including short subjects)   1935 AAW

Bendix, William   1942 AAN

Bening, Annette   1990 AAN SOC

Benjamin, Richard   1975 GLO

Benton, Robert   1967 NYC SOC, 1979 AAW GLO DGA SOC LAC, 1984 AAW NYC, 1985 BER

Berenger, Tom   1986 AAN GLO

Berenson, Marisa   1972 BOR, 1975 HAR

Beresford, Bruce   1983 AAN

Bergen, Candice   1971 HAR, 1975 HAR, 1979 AAN

Bergen, Edgar   1937 AAS

Bergman, Ingmar   1947 CAN, 1948 AAN, 1956 CAN, 1957 CAN, 1958 CAN VEN BER, 1959 BOR VEN, 1960 CAN, 1967 SOC, 1968 SOC, 1970 AAS SOC, 1972 NYC SOC, 1973 AAN BOR CAN, 1974 NYC SOC, 1975 SOC BOR, 1976 AAN, 1978 BOR,

Brooks, Albert 1985 SOC, 1987 AAN

Brooks, James L. 1983 AAW GLO DGA LAC BOR, 1987 NYC

Brooks, Mel 1963 AAW BAA [co-creator of cartoon], 1968 AAW

Brooks, Richard 1958 AAN, 1960 AAW, 1966 AAN, 1967 AAN BOR

Broughton, James 1954 CAN

Brown, Clarence 1929–30 AAN, 1930–31 AAN, 1935 VEN, 1943 AAN, 1945 AAN, 1946 AAN

Browning, Tod 1948 DGA

Bryan, Dora 1961 BAA

Brynner, Yul 1956 AAW BOR

Buchman, Sidney 1941 AAW

Bujold, Geneviève 1969 AAN GLO, 1988 LAC

Bullock, Sandra 1994 MTV

Bumstead, Henry 1962 AAW, 1973 AAW

Buñuel, Luis 1951 CAN, 1952 CAN, 1959 CAN, 1960 CAN, 1961 CAN, 1962 CAN, 1965 VEN, 1967 VEN, 1969 BER, 1972 SOC, 1973 BAA, 1977 SOC BOR

Buono, Victor 1962 AAN

Burke, Billie 1938 AAN

Burke, Johnny 1944 AAW

Burnett, Carol 1963 HAR, 1972 HAR

Burnett, Charles 1981 BER, 1982 SUN, 1990 SOC LAC SUN IND

Burns, George 1975 AAW, 1980 VEN

Burstyn, Ellen 1971 AAN NYC SOC, 1973 AAN, 1974 AAW, 1975 BAA, 1978 AAN GLO, 1980 AAN

Burton, Richard 1952 AAN, 1952 GLO, 1953 AAN, 1964 AAN, 1965 AAN, 1966 AAN BAA, 1967 HAR, 1969 AAN, 1977 AAN GLO

Buscemi, Steve 1992 IND

Busey, Gary 1978 AAN SOC

Buttons, Red 1957 AAW GLO

Byington, Spring 1938 AAN

Byrne, David 1987 AAW GLO LAC

Caan, James 1972 AAN

Cacoyannis, Michael 1962 CAN, 1964 AAN

Caesar, Adolph 1984 AAN LAC

Cagney, James 1938 AAN NYC, 1942 AAW NYC, 1955 AAN, 1974 AFI

Cahn, Sammy 1954 AAW, 1957 AAW, 1959 AAW, 1963 AAW

Caine, Michael 1966 AAN SOC, 1972 AAN, 1983 AAN GLO BAA, 1986 AAW

Calhern, Louis 1950 AAN

Cameron, James 1985 RAZ

Camus, Marcel 1959 CAN

Campion, Jane 1986 CAN, 1990 LAC IND, 1990 VEN, 1993 AAW NYC SOC LAC CAN

Cannon, Dyan 1969 AAN NYC, 1973 HAR, 1978 AAN GLO

Cannon, Robert (Bobe) (including cartoons by): 1950 AAW, 1951 BAA, 1956 BAA

Canonero, Milena 1975 AAW, 1981 AAW

Cantínflas 1956 GLO, 1960 GLO

Cantor, Eddie 1956 AAS

Capra, Frank 1932–3 AAN, 1934 AAW, 1936 AAW, 1938 AAW, 1939 AAN, 1941 DGA, 1943 NYC, 1946 AAN GLO, 1958 DGA, 1982 AFI

Carax, Leos 1987 BER

Cardiff, Jack 1947 AAW GLO, 1960 AAN GLO NYC BOR

Cardinale, Claudia 1984 VEN, 1993 VEN

Carey, Harry (Sr.) 1939 AAN

Carmichael, Hoagy 1951 AAW

Carné, Marcel 1938 VEN, 1946 VEN, 1953 VEN

Carney, Art 1974 AAW GLO, 1977 SOC, 1980 VEN

Caron, Leslie 1953 AAN BAA, 1962 BAA, 1963 AAN GLO, 1966 HAR

Carpenter, John 1970 AAW [short film dir. by]

Carradine, David 1976 BOR

Carradine, Keith 1975 AAW GLO

Carrey, Jim 1994 MTV HAR

Carrière, Jean-Claude 1969 CAN, 1973 BAA, 1988 BAA

Carroll, Diahann 1974 AAN

Cass, Peggy 1958 AAN

Cortese, Valentina 1973 NYC SOC BAA, 1974 AAN

Cosby, Bill 1987 RAZ

Costa-Gavras, Constantin 1969 AAN NYC CAN, 1975 CAN, 1982 AAW BAA CAN, 1990 BER

Costner, Kevin 1990 AAW GLO DGA BOR, 1991 PEO BER RAZ, 1992 PEO, 1994 RAZ

Cotten, Joseph 1949 VEN

Courtenay, Tom 1964 VEN, 1965 AAN, 1983 AAN GLO

Cousteau, Jacques-Yves 1946 CAN, 1956 AAW, 1959 AAW, 1964 AAW HAR, 1975 BAA

Coutard, Raoul 1970 CAN, 1982 CAN, 1983 VEN

Coward, Noel 1942 AAS

Crain, Jeanne 1949 AAN

Crawford, Broderick 1949 AAW GLO NYC

Crawford, Joan 1945 AAW BOR HAR, 1946 HAR, 1947 AAN, 1952 AAN, 1969 GLO

Crichton, Charles 1952 DGA, 1988 AAN BAA

Crichton, Michael 1971 HAR

Crisp, Donald 1941 AAW, 1955 DGA, 1956 DGA

Cronenberg, David 1988 LAC, 1991 NYC SOC

Cronenweth, Jordan 1982 LAC

Crosby, Bing 1944 AAW PHO, 1945 AAN PHO, 1946 PHO, 1947 PHO, 1948 PHO, 1950 HAR, 1954 AAN BOR, 1959 GLO HAR

Crosby, Floyd 1930–31 AAW, 1952 GLO

Crouse, Lindsay 1984 AAN

Crowther, Bosley 1953 DGA, 1967 NYC

Cruise, Tom 1989 AAN GLO PEO, 1992 HAR, 1993 PEO, 1994 RAZ

Crystal, Billy 1991 MTV

Cukor, George 1932–3 AAN, 1940 AAN, 1947 AAN, 1950 AAN, 1964 AAW GLO DGA, 1978 LIN, 1980 DGA

Culkin, Macaulay 1991 MTV

Curtis, Jamie Lee 1983 BAA, 1994 GLO

Curtis, Tony 1954 HAR, 1957 GLO, 1958 AAN PHO, 1960 GLO

Curtiz, Michael 1938 AAN, 1939

AAW [short film dir. by], 1942 AAN, 1943 AAW

Cusack, Joan 1988 AAN

Czapsky, Stefan 1994 NYC SOC LAC

Dafoe, Willem 1986 AAN

Dahl, John [director] 1994 LAC

Dahlbeck, Eva 1958 CAN

Dailey, Dan 1948 AAN

Dall, John [actor] 1945 AAN

Damiani, Damiano 1985 BER

Dandridge, Dorothy 1954 AAN

Dane, Clemence 1946 AAW

Daniels, William [cinematographer] 1948 AAW

Danning, Sybil 1983 RAZ

Darin, Bobby 1961 GLO, 1963 AAN

Darling, William 1943 AAW, 1946 AAW

Darwell, Jane 1940 AAW

Dassin, Jules 1955 CAN, 1957 CAN, 1960 AAN

Davidson, Jaye 1992 AAN

Davies, Valentine 1947 AAW

Davis, Bette 1935 AAW, 1937 VEN, 1938 AAW, 1939 AAN, 1940 AAN, 1941 AAN, 1942 AAN, 1950 AAN NYC, 1951 CAN, 1952 AAN, 1962 AAN PHO, 1973 GLO, 1977 AFI, 1989 LIN

Davis, Brad 1978 GLO

Davis, Desmond 1964 BOR

Davis, Geena 1988 AAN, 1991 AAN BOR

Davis, Judy 1980 BAA, 1984 AAN, 1988 SOC, 1991 NYC IND, 1992 AAN SOC LAC BOR

Davison, Bruce 1990 AAN GLO NYC SOC IND

Day, Doris 1951 PHO, 1957 GLO, 1959 AAN GLO PHO, 1962 GLO, 1988 GLO

Day, Richard 1942 AAW, 1951 AAW, 1954 AAW

Day-Lewis, Daniel 1986 NYC BOR, 1989 AAW NYC SOC LAC BAA, 1993 AAN

Deakins, Roger 1991 NYC SOC LAC

Dean, James 1955 AAN GLO, 1956 AAN GLO

de Broca, Philippe 1960 BER

Dee, Ruby 1961 BOR

Douglas, Michael 1987 AAW GLO BOR PEO, 1992 HAR

Dourif, Brad 1975 AAN GLO, 1976 BAA

Downey, Jr., Robert 1992 AAN BAA

Dreier, Hans 1945 AAW, 1950 AAW

Dressler, Marie 1930–1 AAW, 1931–2 AAN

Dreyfuss, Richard 1977 AAW GLO LAC, 1978 BAA

Dreyer, Carl 1947 VEN, 1955 VEN, 1965 VEN

Dukakis, Olympia 1987 AAW GLO LAC BOR

Duke, Patty 1962 AAW GLO, 1969 GLO

Dullea, Keir 1962 GLO

Dunaway, Faye 1967 ANN, 1974 AAN, 1976 AAW GLO, 1981 RAZ, 1993 RAZ

Dunn, James 1945 AAW

Dunne, Irene 1930–1 AAN, 1936 AAN, 1937 AAN, 1939 AAN, 1948 AAN

Dunnock, Mildred 1951 AAN, 1956 AAN

Duras, Marguerite 1985 BER

Durbin, Deanna 1938 AAS

Durning, Charles 1975 BOR, 1982 AAN, 1983 AAN

Duvall, Robert 1972 AAN NYC, 1979 AAN GLO BAA, 1980 AAN, 1981 VEN, 1983 AAW GLO NYC LAC, 1985 VEN

Duvall, Shelley 1977 LAC CAN, 1980 HAR

Duvivier, Julien 1937 VEN, 1939 VEN, 1946 VEN

Dykstra, John 1977 AAW

Dzundza, George 1983 VEN

Eagles, Jeanne 1928–9 AAN

Easdale, Brian 1948 AAW GLO, 1950 VEN

Eastwood, Clint 1970 GLO, 1976 HAR, 1980 PEO, 1982 HAR, 1983 PEO, 1984 PEO, 1986 PEO, 1987 GLO PEO, 1988 GLO, 1992 AAW GLO DGA SOC LAC, 1994 AAS

Eddy, Nelson 1941 HAR

Edlund, Richard 1977 AAW, 1980 AAW, 1981 AAW, 1983 AAW

Edwards, Blake 1988 RAZ, 1990 LAC

Eggar, Samantha 1965 AAN GLO CAN

Egoyan, Atom 1994 CAN

Ekberg, Anita 1955 GLO

Elliott, Denholm 1983 BAA, 1984 BAA, 1985 BAA, 1986 AAN

Elmes, Frederic 1986 SOC, 1990 IND, 1992 IND

Emerson, Hope 1950 AAN

Ephron, Nora 1989 BAA

Epstein, Julius J. and Philip G. 1943 AAW

Erice, Victor 1992 CAN

Errol, Leon 1937 AAN

Erwin, Stuart 1936 AAN

Etaix, Pierre (including short films by) 1962 AAW, 1963 BAA

Eustache, Jean 1973 CAN

Evans, Dame Edith 1959 BOR, 1963 AAN, 1964 AAN BOR, 1967 AAN GLO NYC BOR BAA BER

Ewell, Tom 1955 GLO

Fairbanks, Sr., Douglas 1939 AAS

Falk, Peter 1960 AAN, 1961 AAN

Farnsworth, Richard 1978 AAN SOC BOR

Farrow, John 1942 AAN NYC, 1956 AAW

Farrow, Mia 1964 GLO, 1973 HAR, 1990 BOR

Fassbinder, Rainer Werner 1974 CAN, 1978 BER, 1982 BER

Faye, Alice 1941 HAR

Fei, Xie 1990 BER, 1993 BER

Feiffer, Jules 1989 VEN

Fejos, Paul 1939 VEN

Fellini, Federico 1953 VEN, 1954 VEN, 1960 CAN, 1961 AAN, 1963 AAN, 1970 AAN, 1974 NYC, 1975 AAN, 1984 LIN, 1985 VEN, 1987 BAA, 1987 CAN, 1992 AAS

Fernandez, Emilio 1946 CAN, 1947 VEN, 1953 CAN

Ferrer, José 1948 AAN, 1950 AAW GLO, 1952 AAN

Ferreri, Marco 1960 VEN, 1972 BER, 1973 CAN, 1978 CAN, 1980 BER, 1991 BER

Feyder, Jacques 1936 VEN, 1938 VEN

Field, Sally 1979 AAW GLO NYC SOC LAC BOR CAN, 1981 PEO, 1984 AAW GLO

Fiennes, Ralph   1993 AAN NYC
  SOC BAA
Figueroa, Gabriel   1946 CAN, 1947
  VEN, 1948 GLO, 1949 VEN
Finch, Peter   1956 BAA, 1960 BAA,
  1961 BAA BER, 1971 AAN
  SOC BAA, 1976 AAW GLO,
  1977 BAA
Finlay, Frank   1965 AAN
Finney, Albert   1961 BOR, 1963
  AAN GLO VEN, 1970 GLO,
  1974 AAN, 1983 AAN, 1984
  AAN LAC BER
Fiorentino, Linda   1994 NYC IND
Firth, Peter   1977 AAN GLO
Fishburne, Laurence   1993 AAN
Fitzgerald, Barry   1944 AAW GLO
  NYC, 1949 HAR, 1952 HAR
Fitzgerald, Geraldine   1939 AAN
Flaherty, Robert   1934 VEN, 1937
  VEN, 1948 VEN
Fleming, Victor   1938 VEN, 1939
  AAW
Fletcher, Louise   1975 AAW GLO,
  1976 BAA
Flynn, Errol   1958 HAR
Foch, Nina   1954 AAN BOR
Fonda, Henry   1940 AAN, 1957
  BAA, 1978 AFI, 1979 GLO,
  1980 AAS, 1981 AAW GLO BOR
Fonda, Jane   1961 GLO, 1962 HAR,
  1969 AAN NYC HAR, 1971
  AAW GLO NYC SOC, 1972
  GLO, 1977 AAN GLO, 1978
  AAW GLO LAC BAA HAR,
  1979 AAN GLO PEO HAR,
  1980 PEO, 1981 AAN PEO, 1982
  PEO, 1986 AAN
Fonda, Peter   1969 HAR
Fontaine, Joan   1940 AAN, 1941
  AAW NYC, 1943 AAN, 1948
  HAR
Fontanne, Lynn   1931–2 AAN
Foote, Horton   1962 AAW, 1983
  AAW, 1985 IND
Forbes, Bryan   1960 BAA
Ford, Aleksander   1954 CAN
Ford, Glenn   1946 HAR, 1961 GLO
Ford, Harrison   1985 AAN, 1993
  MTV
Ford, John   1935 AAW NYC, 1939
  AAN NYC, 1940 AAW NYC,
  1941 AAW NYC, 1948 VEN,
  1952 AAW DGA VEN, 1953

  DGA, 1954 GLO, 1955 DGA,
  1958 BOR, 1973 AFI
Ford, Paul   1967 NYC
Foreman, Carl (awards given under
  pseudonym during
  blacklist):   1957 AAW BAA
Forman, Milos   1971 CAN, 1975
  AAW GLO DGA, 1976 BAA, 1984
  AAW GLO DGA LAC
Forrest, Frederic   1979 AAN SOC
Forsyth, Bill   1981 BAA, 1983 NYC
  SOC BAA
Fosse, Bob   1972 AAW BOR BAA,
  1974 AAN, 1979 AAN, 1980
  CAN
Foster, Jodie   1975 HAR, 1976 AAN
  SOC BAA, 1983 HAR, 1988
  AAW GLO BOR IND, 1991
  AAW GLO NYC BAA, 1994
  AAN SAG PEO
Fox, Edward   1971 BAA, 1977 SOC
  BAA
Fraker, William A.   1968 SOC
Franciosa, Anthony   1957 AAN
  VEN, 1959 GLO
Francis, Freddie   1960 AAW, 1989
  AAW
Franklin, Carl   1992 LAC, 1992
  MTV, 1992 IND
Franklin, Sidney   1942 AAS
Frears, Stephen   1990 AAN
Freed, Arthur   1967 AAS
Freeman, Morgan   1987 AAN NYC
  SOC LAC IND, 1989 AAN
  GLO, 1990 BER, 1994 AAN
Freleng, Friz (cartoons by)   1947
  AAW, 1955 AAW, 1957 AAW,
  1958 AAW, 1964 AAW
Fresnay, Pierre   1947 VEN
Freund, Karl   1937 AAW
Fricker, Brenda   1989 AAW LAC
Friedhofer, Hugo   1946 AAW, 1951
  VEN, 1957 GLO
Friedkin, William   1971 AAW GLO
  DGA, 1973 AAN GLO
Friedman, Bruce Jay   1984 SOC
Fuller, Samuel   1953 VEN, 1987
  LAC
Funicello, Annette   1960 HAR
Furlong, Edward   1991 MTV
Furse, Roger K.   1948 AAW
Furst, Anton   1989 AAW

Gabin, Jean   1951 VEN, 1954 VEN,
  1959 BER, 1971 BER

Gable, Clark   1934 AAW, 1935 AAN, 1939 AAN

Gabor, Zsa Zsa   1953 HAR, 1957 GLO

Gallone, Carmine   1935 VEN, 1937 VEN, 1938 VEN

Gance, Abel   1981 BAA

Ganz, Lowell, and Babaloo Mandel   1984 SOC, 1994 RAZ

Garbo, Greta   1929–30 AAN, 1935 NYC, 1937 AAN NYC, 1939 AAN, 1954 AAS

Garcia, Andy   1990 AAN

Gardenia, Vincent   1973 AAN, 1987 AAN

Gardner, Ava   1951 HAR, 1953 AAN

Garfield, John   1938 AAN, 1947 AAN

Garland, Judy   1939 AAS, 1954 AAN GLO, 1961 AAN GLO

Garmes, Lee   1931–2 AAW

Garner, James   1957 GLO, 1985 AAN

Garr, Teri   1982 AAN

Garson, Greer   1939 AAN, 1941 AAN, 1942 AAW, 1943 AAN, 1944 PHO, 1945 AAN PHO, 1960 AAN GLO BOR

Gassman, Vittorio   1975 CAN

Gaudio, Gaetano (Tony)   1936 AAW

Gaynor, Janet   1927-8 AAW, 1937 AAN

Gelbart, Larry   1982 NYC SOC LAC

Genn, Leo   1951 AAN

George, Chief Dan   1970 AAN NYC SOC

George, Gladys   1936 AAN

Gerima, Haile   1983 BER

Germi, Pietro   1951 VEN BER, 1962 AAW CAN, 1966 CAN

Getchell, Robert   1975 BAA, 1981 RAZ

Giannini, Giancarlo   1973 CAN, 1976 AAN

Gibbons, Cedric   1928–29 AAW, 1934 AAW, 1941 AAW, 1944 AAW, 1946 AAW, 1949 AAW, 1951 AAW, 1952 AAW, 1953 AAW, 1956 AAW

Gibson, Henry   1975 SOC

Gibson, Mel   1990 PEO, 1992 MTV

Gielgud, John   1953 BAA, 1964 AAN, 1974 BAA, 1977 NYC, 1981 AAW GLO NYC LAC, 1985 SOC LAC, 1991 BAA

Gilbert, Lewis   1966 CAN, 1989 BAA

Gilford, Jack   1973 AAN

Gilliam, Terry   1985 LAC, 1991 VEN

Gilliatt, Penelope   1971 NYC SOC

Gilroy, Frank D.   1971 BER

Gingold, Hermione   1958 GLO

Girardot, Annie   1965 VEN

Gish, Lillian   1946 AAN, 1970 AAS, 1984 AFI, 1987 BOR

Glass, Philip   1983 LAC, 1985 CAN

Gleason, Jackie   1961 AAN BOR

Gleason, James   1941 AAN

Glen, Iain   1990 BER

Glenville, Peter   1964 AAN

Glover, Danny   1990 IND, 1992 MTV

Glowna, Vadim   1981 CAN, 1983 BER

Godard, Jean-Luc   1960 BER, 1961 BER, 1962 VEN, 1965 BER, 1967 VEN, 1983 VEN, 1990 SOC, 1991 VEN, 1994 NYC

Goddard, Paulette   1943 AAN

Goldberg, Whoopi   1985 AAN GLO, 1990 AAW GLO BAA, 1992 PEO, 1993 PEO, 1994 PEO

Goldman, Bo   1975 AAW GLO, 1980 AAW NYC SOC, 1992 GLO

Goldman, James   1968 AAW

Goldman, William   1969 AAW, 1970 BAA, 1976 AAW

Goldsmith, Jerry   1976 AAW

Goldwyn, Samuel   1946 AAS, 1957 AAS, 1972 GLO

Golino, Valeria   1986 VEN

Golitzen, Alexander   1943 AAW, 1960 AAW, 1962 AAW

Gómez, Fernando Fernán   1984 VEN, 1985 BER

Gomez, Thomas   1947 AAN

Gordon, Dexter   1986 AAN LAC

Gordon, Ruth   1965 AAN GLO, 1968 AAW GLO, 1970 HAR

Goretta, Claude   1973 CAN

Gorin, Jean-Pierre   1992 SUN

Gosho, Heinosuke   1953 BER

Gossett, Jr., Louis   1982 AAW GLO

Gould, Elliott   1969 AAN, 1970 HAR

Grable, Betty   1941 HAR

Grahame, Gloria   1947 ANN, 1952 AAW

Granville, Bonita   1936 AAN

Grant, Cary   1941 AAN, 1969 AAS
Grant, Hugh   1987 VEN, 1994 GLO
   BAA
Grant, Lee   1951 AAN CAN, 1970
   AAN, 1975 AAW, 1976 AAN
Green, Guy   1947 AAW, 1960 BER
Greenaway, Peter   1988 CAN
Greene, Graham [writer]   1948 VEN,
   1949 BOR
Greene, Graham [actor]   1990 AAN
Greenstreet, Sydney   1941 AAN
Grey, Joel   1972 AAW GLO SOC
   BOR
Grier, David Alan   1983 VEN
Griffith, D. W.   1935 AAS, 1938
   DGA
Griffith, Hugh   1959 AAW BOR,
   1963 AAN
Griffith, Melanie   1984 SOC, 1988
   AAN GLO, 1992 RAZ
Griggs, Loyal   1953 AAW
Grusin, Dave   1988 AAW
Guare, John   1981 NYC SOC LAC
Guerra, Ruy   1964 BER, 1978 BER
Guerra, Tonino   1984 CAN
Guffey, Burnett   1953 AAW, 1967
   AAW
Guinness, Alec   1950 BOR, 1952
   AAN, 1957 AAW GLO NYC
   BOR BAA, 1958 VEN, 1977
   AAN, 1979 AAS, 1987 LIN,
   1988 AAN LAC, 1989 BAA
Guitry, Sacha   1937 VEN
Güney, Yilmaz   1977 BER, 1980
   BER, 1981 BER, 1982 CAN
Gwenn, Edmund   1947 AAW GLO,
   1950 AAN GLO, 1952 HAR

Haanstra, Bert   1958 BAA, 1959
   AAW [short film dir,. by], 1962
   BER, 1964 BER
Hackett, Joan   1981 AAN GLO
Hackford, Taylor   1978 AAW [short
   film dir. by]
Hackman, Gene   1967 AAN SOC,
   1970 AAN, 1971 AAW GLO
   NYC BOR, 1972 BAA, 1973
   CAN, 1974 BOR, 1988 AAN
   BOR, 1989 BER, 1992 AAW
   GLO NYC SOC BAA
Hagen, Jean   1952 AAN
Hall, Conrad   1969 AAW
Haller, Ernest   1939 AAW
Hallstrom, Lasse   1987 AAN
Hamilton, George   1959 GLO

Hamilton, Linda   1991 MTV
Hamlisch, Marvin   1971 GLO, 1973
   AAW GLO
Hammerstein II, Oscar   1941 AAW,
   1945 AAW
Hampton, Christopher   1988 AAW,
   1989 BAA, 1995 CAN
Hancock, Herbie   1986 AAW LAC
Hanks, Tom   1988 AAN GLO LAC,
   1993 AAW GLO MTV, 1994
   AAW GLO SAG BOR PEO BER
Hanna, William, and Joseph Barbera
   (including cartoons by)   1943
   AAW, 1944 AAW, 1945 AAW,
   1946 AAW, 1948 AAW, 1951
   AAW, 1952 AAW
Hannah, Darryl   1987 RAZ
Hanson, John   1979 CAN SUN
Harareet, Haya   1955 CAN
Harburg, E. Y. (Yip)   1939 AAW
Harding, Ann   1930–31 AAN
Hardy, Oliver: see Laurel & Hardy
Hare, David   1985 BER
Harlan, Veit   1942 VEN
Harper, Tess   1986 AAN
Harrelson, Woody   1993 MTV RAZ
Harris Barbara   1971 AAN
Harris, Julie   1952 AAN
Harris, Richard   1963 AAN CAN,
   1967 GLO, 1990 AAN
Harris, Rosemary   1994 AAN BOR
Harrison, Rex   1963 AAN BOR, 1964
   AAW GLO NYC
Hart, Ian   1995 VEN
Hartley, Hal   1991 SUN
Hartman, Elizabeth   1965 AAN GLO
Harvey, Anthony   1968 AAN DGA
Harvey, Laurence   1959 AAN, 1964
   HAR
Has, Wojciech   1973 CAN
Hathaway, Henry   1935 AAN
Hawks, Howard   1936 VEN, 1941
   AAN, 1948 DGA, 1974 AAS
Hawn, Goldie   1969 AAW GLO
   HAR, 1980 AAN PEO
Hawthorne, Nigel   1994 AAN
Hayakawa, Sessue   1957 AAN BOR
Hayes, Helen   1931–32 AAW, 1932
   VEN, 1970 AAW
Hayes, Isaac   1971 AAW GLO
Hayward, Susan   1947 AAN, 1949
   AAN, 1952 AAN GLO PHO,
   1955 AAN, 1956 CAN, 1958
   AAW GLO NYC, 1961 HAR

Hayworth, Rita　1949 HAR, 1958 HAR

Head, Edith　1949 AAW, 1950 AAW, 1951 AAW, 1953 AAW, 1954 AAW, 1960 AAW, 1973 AAW

Hecht, Ben　1927-8 AAW, 1935 AAW

Heckart, Eileen　1956 AAN GLO, 1972 AAW

Heckroth, Hein　1948 AAW

Heflin, Van　1942 AAW

Heifitz, Josef　1960 CAN

Hemingway, Mariel　1979 AAN

Hemmings, David　1973 BER

Henry, Buck　1968 BAA, 1978 AAN

Hepburn, Audrey　1953 AAW GLO NYC BAA, 1954 AAN GLO, 1959 AAN NYC BAA, 1961 AAN, 1964 BAA, 1967 AAN, 1989 GLO, 1991 BAA LIN, 1992 AAS

Hepburn, Katharine　1932–33 AAN, 1934 VEN, 1935 AAN, 1940 AAN NYC, 1942 AAN, 1951 AAN, 1955 AAN, 1956 AAN, 1959 AAN, 1962 AAN CAN, 1967 AAW, 1968 AAW BAA, 1975 PEO, 1981 AAW HAR, 1982 BAA PEO

Hermann, Bernard　1941 AAW, 1976 LAC

Hershey, Barbara　1987 CAN, 1988 CAN

Hersholt, Jean　1939 AAS, 1949 AAS, 1954 GLO

Herzog, Werner　1968 BER, 1975 CAN, 1982 CAN, 1991 VEN

Heston, Charlton　1959 AAW, 1961 GLO, 1962 HAR, 1966 GLO, 1967 HAR, 1977 AAS

Hickey, William　1985 AAN

Hill, George Roy　1969 AAN, 1970 BAA, 1972 CAN, 1973 AAW DGA

Hiller, Arthur　1970 AAN GLO, 1972 BER, 1992 DGA

Hiller, Wendy　1938 AAN, 1958 AAW, 1966 AAN

Hilton, James　1942 AAW

Hirsch, Judd　1980 AAN

Hitchcock, Alfred　1938 NYC, 1940 AAN, 1945 AAN, 1951 DGA, 1954 AAN DGA, 1960 AAN, 1967 AAS DGA, 1969 BOR, 1971 GLO BAA, 1974 LIN, 1979 AFI

Hoch, Winton　1948 AAW, 1949 AAW, 1952 AAW

Hoffman, Dustin　1967 AAN GLO, 1969 AAN BAA, 1973 HAR, 1974 AAN, 1979 AAW GLO NYC SOC LAC, 1982 AAN GLO SOC, 1988 AAW GLO PEO, 1989 PEO BER

Hogan, Paul　1986 GLO

Holden, William　1950 AAN, 1953 AAW, 1954 PHO, 1955 PHO, 1976 AAN

Holland, Agnieszka　1980 CAN

Holliday, Judy　1950 AAW GLO

Holliman, Earl　1956 GLO

Holloway, Stanley　1964 AAN

Holm, Celeste　1947 AAW GLO, 1949 AAN, 1950 AAN

Holm, Ian　1968 BAA, 1981 AAN BAA CAN

Homolka, Oscar　1948 AAN

Hope, Bob　1940 AAS, 1944 AAS, 1952 AAS, 1957 GLO, 1959 AAS, 1962 GLO, 1965 AAS, 1979 LIN

Hopkins, Anthony　1991 AAW NYC BOR BAA, 1993 AAN LAC BOR BAA

Hopkins, Miriam　1935 AAN

Hopper, Dennis　1969 SOC CAN, 1986 AAN SOC LAC, 1994 MTV

Horner, James　1982 LAC

Horrocks, Jane　1991 SOC LAC

Hoskins, Bob　1986 AAN GLO NYC SOC LAC BAA CAN

Houseman, John　1973 AAN GLO BOR

Howard, Leslie　1932–3 AAN, 1938 AAN VEN

Howard, Sidney　1939 AAW

Howard, Trevor　1958 BAA, 1960 AAN

Howe, James Wong　1955 AAW, 1963 AAW

Hsiao-hsien, Hou　1986 BER, 1989 VEN, 1993 CAN

Hubley, John and Faith (including cartoons by)　1959 AAW, 1962 AAW, 1966 AAW, 1977 CAN, 1978 CAN

Hudlin, Reginald　1990 SUN

Hudson, Hugh　1981 AAN CAN

Hudson, Rock　1956 AAN, 1957 BOR HAR, 1958 GLO, 1959

Jones, James Earl   1970 AAN GLO
Jones, Jennifer   1943 AAW GLO,
   1945 AAN, 1946 AAN, 1955
   AAN, 1955 PHO, 1956 HAR
Jones, Shirley   1960 AAW BOR
Jones, Terry   1983 CAN
Jones, Tommy Lee   1991 AAN, 1993
   AAW GLO LAC MTV
Jordan, Neil   1992 AAW NYC
Jost, Jon   1991 LAC [film dir. by]
Judd, Ashley   1993 IND
Julia, Raul   1985 BOR
Junge, Alfred   1947 AAW
Jurado, Katy   1952 GLO, 1954 AAN
Jurgens, Curt   1955 VEN

Kahn, Madeline   1973 AAN, 1974
   AAN
Kaige, Chen   1993 CAN
Kalatozov, Mikhail   1958 CAN
Kaminska, Ida   1965 CAN, 1966
   AAN
Kaminski, Janusz   1993 AAW NYC
   SOC LAC
Kane, Carol   1975 AAN
Kanevsky, Vitali   1990 CAN, 1992
   CAN
Kanin, Michael   1942 AAW
Kaper, Bronislau   1953 AAW
Karina, Anna   1961 BER
Kasdan, Lawrence   1992 BER
Kaufman, Boris   1954 AAW GLO
Kaufman, Phillip   1988 SOC BAA
Kaurismäki, Aki   1992 BER, 1994
   BER
Kautner, Helmut   1954 CAN, 1955
   BER
Kawalerowicz, Jerzy   1961 CAN,
   1978 BER
Kaye, Danny   1951 GLO, 1954 AAS,
   1958 GLO, 1981 AAS
Kazan, Elia   1947 AAW GLO NYC
   BOR, 1950 VEN, 1951 AAN
   NYC VEN, 1953 BER, 1954
   AAW GLO DGA NYC VEN,
   1955 AAN DGA CAN, 1956
   GLO, 1963 AAN GLO, 1982
   DGA, 1986 DGA
Keaton, Buster   1959 AAS
Keaton, Diane   1977 AAW GLO
   NYC SOC BAA, 1981 AAN
Keaton, Michael   1988 SOC
Kedrova, Lila   1964 AAW
Keitel, Harvey   1991 AAN SOC,
   1992 IND

Kellaway, Cecil   1948 AAN, 1967
   AAN
Keller, Marthe   1977 HAR
Kellerman, Sally   1970 AAN
Kelly, Gene   1945 AAN, 1951 AAS,
   1956 BER, 1980 GLO, 1985
   AFI
Kelly, Grace   1953 AAN GLO, 1954
   AAW GLO NYC BOR HAR,
   1955 GLO
Kendall, Kay   1957 GLO
Kennedy, Arthur   1949 AAN, 1951
   AAN NYC, 1955 AAN GLO,
   1957 AAN, 1958 AAN
Kennedy, George   1967 AAW, 1974
   HAR
Kern, Jerome   1936 AAW, 1941 AAW
Kerr, Deborah   1947 NYC, 1949
   AAN, 1953 AAN, 1956 AAN GLO,
   1957 AAN NYC PHO, 1958 AAN
   GLO, 1960 AAN NYC, 1993
   AAS
Kieslowski, Krzysztof   1988 CAN,
   1989 VEN, 1991 CAN, 1993
   VEN, 1994 AAN BER
King, Henry   1943 AAN, 1955 DGA
King, Stephen   1983 HAR
Kingsley, Ben   1982 AAW GLO
   NYC LAC BOR BAA, 1991
   AAN
Kinski, Nastassjia   1980 GLO
Kinugasa, Teinosuke   1954 CAN,
   1959 CAN
Kirkland, Sally   1987 AAN GLO
   LAC, 1987 IND
Kline, Kevin   1988 AAW
Kluge, Alexander   1966 VEN, 1968
   CAN, 1976 CAN, 1978 BER,
   1983 VEN
Knight, Shirley   1960 AAN, 1962
   AAN, 1967 VEN
Knox, Alexander   1944 AAN GLO
Kobayashi, Masaki   1963 CAN, 1965
   CAN, 1967 VEN, 1985 BER
Koch, Howard [writer]   1943 AAW
Kohner, Susan   1958 GLO, 1959
   AAN
Konchalovsky, Andrei   1979 CAN,
   1988 BER
Kopple, Barbara (including
   documentaries dir. by)   1976
   AAW, 1990 AAW, 1991 DGA
   SUN, 1993 DGA
Korda, Alexander   1934 VEN
Korda, Vincent   1940 AAW

Leighton, Margaret   1971 AAN BAA
Leisen, Mitchell   1951 BER
Leland, David   1987 BAA CAN
Lelouch, Claude   1966 AAW CAN,
    1981 CAN
Lemmon, Jack   1955 AAW, 1959
    AAN GLO BAA, 1960 AAN
    GLO BAA, 1962 AAN, 1972
    GLO, 1973 AAW HAR, 1979
    AAN BAA CAN, 1980 AAN,
    1981 BER, 1982 AAN CAN,
    1988 AFI, 1990 GLO, 1992 BOR
    VEN, 1993 LIN
Lenya, Lotte   1961 AAN
Leonard, Robert Z.   1929-30 AAN,
    1936 AAN
Lerner, Alan Jay   1951 AAW, 1958
    AAW, 1967 GLO, 1974 GLO
Lerner, Michael   1991 AAN LAC
LeRoy, Mervyn   1942 AAN, 1955
    DGA, 1956 GLO, 1975 AAS
Lester, Richard   1965 CAN
Leven, Boris   1961 AAW
Levine, Joseph E.   1963 GLO
Levinson, Barry   1988 AAW DGA,
    1989 BER, 1991 AAN LAC
Lewis, Jerry   1951 HAR, 1952 PHO
    HAR, 1961 HAR
Lewis, Juliette   1991 AAN, 1994
    VEN
Li, Gong   1992 VEN, 1993 NYC
Lindfors, Viveca   1962 BER
Lindtberg, Leopold   1946 CAN, 1951
    BER, 1953 VEN
Linklater, Richard   1995 BER
Lisi, Virna   1994 CAN
Lithgow, John   1982 AAN NYC
    LAC, 1983 AAN
Little Rascals: see Our Gang
Litvak, Anatole   1948 ANN DGA,
    1949 VEN
Lizzani, Carlo   1954 CAN
Lloyd, Christopher   1993 IND
Lloyd, Emily   1987 SOC
Lloyd, Frank   1928-29 AAW,
    1932-33 AAW, 1935 AAN
Lloyd, Harold   1952 AAS
Loach, Ken   1972 BER, 1979 CAN,
    1981 CAN, 1990 CAN, 1991
    CAN, 1993 BAA CAN, 1994
    VEN, 1995 CAN
Locke, Sondra   1968 AAN
Lockhart, Gene   1938 AAN
Locklear, Heather   1989 RAZ
Loesser, Frank   1949 AAW

Loewe, Frederick   1958 AAW, 1967
    GLO, 1974 GLO
Logan, Joshua   1955 AAN GLO
    DGA, 1957 AAN DGA
Loggia, Robert   1985 AAN
Lollobrigida, Gina   1960 GLO
Lombard, Carole   1936 AAN
Lord, Robert   1932-3 AAW
Loren, Sophia   1958 VEN, 1961
    AAN NYC BAA CAN, 1963
    GLO, 1964 AAN GLO, 1968
    GLO, 1976 GLO, 1990 AAS,
    1994 GLO
Losey, Joseph   1967 CAN, 1971
    CAN
Love, Bessie   1928-9 AAN
Lowe, Rob   1985 RAZ
Loy, Myrna   1990 AAS
Lubitsch, Ernst   1928-9 AAN,
    1929-30 AAN, 1943 AAN,
    1946 AAS
Lucas, George   1973 AAN SOC,
    1977 AAN, 1991 AAS
Luedtke, Kurt   1985 AAW, 1986
    BAA
Lukas, Paul   1943 AAW GLO NYC
Lumet, Sidney   1957 AAN DGA
    BER, 1975 AAN LAC, 1976
    AAN GLO LAC, 1981 NYC
    VEN, 1982 AAN BOR, 1988
    DGA, 1992 DGA
Lunt, Alfred   1931-2 AAN
Lupino, Ida   1943 NYC
Lynch, David   1980 AAN, 1986 AAN
    SOC, 1990 CAN
Lyne, Adrian   1987 AAN
Lyon, Sue   1962 GLO

McAnally, Ray   1986 BAA, 1989
    BAA
MacArthur, Charles   1935 AAW
McCambridge, Mercedes   1949
    AAW GLO, 1956 AAN
McCarey, Leo   1937 AAW, 1939
    AAN, 1940 AAN, 1944 AAW
    NYC, 1945 AAN
McCarthy, Kevin   1951 AAN GLO
McCartney, Paul   1973 HAR
McCormack, Patty   1956 AAN
McCrea, Joel   1987 LAC
McDaniel, Hattie   1939 AAW
MacDonald, Jeanette   1941 HAR,
    1948 HAR
McDonnell, Mary   1990 AAN, 1992
    AAN

1987 AAN CAN, 1989 VEN, 1990 VEN, 1993 VEN

Matlin, Marlee   1986 AAW GLO

Mattes, Eva   1979 CAN

Matthau, Walter   1966 AAW, 1971 AAN, 1973 BAA, 1975 AAN GLO, 1980 HAR

Mature, Victor   1953 HAR, 1955 HAR

Maxwell, Lois   1947 GLO

May, Elaine   1987 RAZ

Mayer, Louis B.   1950 AAS, 1951 DGA

Maysles, David and Albert   1991 SUN

Mazursky, Paul   1969 NYC SOC, 1978 NYC SOC LAC, 1989 NYC

Medeiros, Maria de   1994 VEN

Mellor, William C.   1951 AAW, 1959 AAW

Melvin, Murray   1962 CAN

Menges, Chris   1984 AAW NYC SOC LAC, 1986 AAW LAC, 1988 NYC CAN

Menjou, Adolphe   1930–1 AAN

Menken, Alan   1989 AAW GLO, 1991 AAW GLO, 1992 AAW GLO

Menzel, Jiri   1981 VEN, 1990 BER

Menzies, William Cameron   1927–28 AAW, 1939 AAS

Mercer, Johnny   1946 AAW, 1951 AAW, 1961 AAW, 1962 AAW, 1970 GLO, 1971 GLO

Merchant, Vivien   1966 AAN BOR

Mercouri, Melina   1960 AAN CAN, 1965 HAR

Meredith, Burgess   1962 BOR, 1975 AAN HAR, 1976 AAN

Merkel, Una   1961 AAN

Merman, Ethel   1953 GLO

Mészáros, Marta   1975 BER, 1977 CAN, 1984 CAN

Metty, Russell   1960 AAW

Midler, Bette   1979 AAN GLO, 1988 PEO, 1990 HAR, 1991 AAN GLO

Mifune, Toshiro   1961 VEN, 1965 VEN

Mikhalkov, Nikita   1991 VEN, 1994 CAN

Milestone, Lewis   1927–28 AAW, 1929–30 AAW, 1930–31 AAN

Miles, Sarah   1970 AAN, 1973 CAN

Miles, Sylvia   1969 AAN, 1975 AAN

Milland, Ray   1945 AAW GLO NYC BOR, 1946 CAN

Miller, Arthur [cinematographer]   1941 AAW, 1943 AAW, 1946 AAW

Miller, Seton   1941 AAW

Mills, Hayley   1959 BER, 1960 AAS GLO

Mills, John   1960 VEN, 1970 AAW GLO, 1988 BAA

Minnelli, Liza   1969 AAN, 1972 AAW GLO BAA, 1988 RAZ

Minnelli, Vincente   1947 CAN, 1950 DGA, 1951 AAN DGA, 1958 AAW GLO DGA

Mineo, Sal   1955 AAN, 1959 HAR, 1960 ANN GLO

Miranda, Isa   1949 CAN

Mirren, Helen   1984 CAN, 1994 AAN, 1995 CAN

Mister Magoo series   1954 AAW, 1956 AAW

Mitchell, Millard   1952 GLO

Mitchell, Thomas   1937 AAN, 1939 AAN

Mitchell, Yvonne   1954 BAA, 1957 BER

Mitchum, Robert   1945 AAN, 1960 BOR

Mizoguchi, Kenji   1952 VEN, 1953 VEN, 1954 VEN

Modine, Matthew   1983 VEN

Mohr, Hal   1935 AAW, 1943 AAW

Monicelli, Mario   1957 BER, 1959 VEN, 1976 BER, 1982 BER

Monroe, Marilyn   1952 PHO HAR, 1953 GLO PHO, 1959 GLO, 1961 GLO

Montand, Yves   1988 LIN

Montgomery, Robert   1937 AAN, 1941 AAN

Monty Python (see also Cleese, Gilliam, Jones, Palin individually)   1983 CAN, 1987 BAA

Moody, Ron   1968 AAN GLO

Moore, Demi   1992 PEO, 1993 MTV

Moore, Dudley   1981 AAN GLO, 1984 GLO

Moore, Grace   1934 AAN

Moore, Mary Tyler   1980 AAN GLO

Moore, Roger   1979 GLO

Moore, Ted   1966 AAW

Moore, Terry   1952 AAN, 1953 HAR

Moorehead, Agnes   1942 AAN NYC,

Oakie, Jack   1940 AAN

Oberon, Merle   1935 AAN

O'Brian, Hugh   1953 GLO

O'Brien, Edmond   1954 AAW GLO,
1964 AAN GLO

O'Brien, Margaret   1944 AAS

O'Connell, Arthur   1955 AAN, 1959
AAN

O'Connor, Donald   1952 GLO

O'Hara, Maureen   1960 HAR

O'Herlihy, Dan   1954 AAN

O'Keefe, Michael   1980 AAN

Olin, Lena   1989 AAN NYC

Oliver, Edna May   1939 AAN

Olivera, Hector   1974 BER, 1984
BER

Olivier, Laurence   1939 AAN, 1940
AAN, 1946 AAN AAS NYC
BOR VEN, 1948 AAW GLO
NYC VEN, 1955 BAA, 1956
AAN BER, 1960 AAN, 1965
AAN, 1969 BAA, 1972 AAN
NYC, 1976 AAN GLO BAA,
1978 AAN AAS BOR, 1980
HAR RAZ, 1982 GLO RAZ,
1983 LIN

Olmi, Ermanno   1961 VEN, 1978
CAN, 1987 VEN, 1988 VEN

Olmos, Edward James   1988 AAN
IND

Olson, Nancy   1950 AAN

O'Neal, Ryan   1970 AAN, 1975 HAR

O'Neal, Tatum   1973 AAW GLO

Ophüls, Marcel   1976 LAC

Ophüls, Max   1950 VEN, 1966 BER

Orry-Kelly   1959 AAW

Osborne, John   1963 AAW BAA

Oscarsson, Per   1966 CAN, 1968
SOC

Oshima, Nagisa   1978 CAN

O'Sullivan, Maureen   1962 HAR

O'Toole, Peter   1962 AAN BAA,
1964 AAN GLO, 1968 AAN
GLO, 1969 AAN GLO BOR,
1972 AAN BOR, 1980 AAN
SOC, 1982 AAN

Ouedraogo, Idrissa   1989 CAN, 1990
CAN

Ouspenskaya, Maria   1936 AAN,
1939 AAN

Our Gang (shorts by)   1936 AAW

Pabst, G. W.   1939 VEN, 1941 VEN,
1948 VEN

Pacino, Al   1972 AAN SOC BOR,
1973 AAN GLO BOR CAN,
1974 AAN, 1975 LAC
BAA, 1979 AAN, 1983 HAR,
1990 AAN, 1992 AAW GLO,
1994 VEN

Page, Geraldine   1953 AAN, 1961
AAN GLO BOR, 1962 AAN
GLO, 1966 AAN, 1969 BOR,
1972 AAN, 1978 AAN BAA,
1984 AAN, 1985 AAW IND

Pakula, Alan J.   1976 AAN NYC
BOR

Pal, George   1943 AAS

Palance, Jack   1952 AAN, 1953
AAN, 1991 AAW GLO

Palcy, Euzhan   1983 VEN

Palin, Michael   1988 BAA

Palmer, Lilli   1953 VEN

Palminteri, Chazz   1994 AAN IND

Pan, Hermes   1937 AAW

Panfilov, Gleb   1987 BER, 1990 CAN

Papas, Irene   1971 BOR

Parker, Alan   1976 BAA, 1978 AAN
BAA, 1984 BAA, 1985 CAN,
1988 AAN BOR, 1991 BAA

Parker, Eleanor   1950 AAN VEN,
1951 AAN, 1955 AAN

Parks, Larry   1946 AAN

Parsons, Estelle   1967 AAW, 1968
AAN

Paquin, Anna   1993 AAW LAC

Pasolini, Pier Paolo   1964 VEN, 1971
BER, 1972 BER, 1974 CAN

Passer, Ivan   1969 SOC

Pavan, Marisa   1955 AAN GLO

Paxinou, Katina   1943 AAW GLO

Paymer, David   1992 AAN

Pearce, Richard   1980 BER, 1981
SUN

Peck, Gregory   1945 AAN, 1946
AAN GLO, 1947 AAN, 1949
AAN HAR, 1950 GLO NYC,
1954 GLO, 1956 HAR, 1962
AAW GLO, 1967 AAS, 1968
GLO, 1989 AFI, 1992 LIN

Penn, Arthur   1962 AAN, 1967 AAN,
1969 AAN

Pennell, Eagle   1978 SUN, 1984 SUN

Peppard, George   1960 BOR, 1966
HAR

Perelman, S. J.   1956 AAW NYC

Perez, Rosie   1993 AAN LAC, 1994
BER

Perinal, Georges   1940 AAW

1974 GLO, 1976 GLO, 1977
GLO, 1980 AAW GLO DGA BOR,
1993 GLO, 1994 AAN

Redgrave, Lynn   1966 AAN GLO
NYC

Redgrave, Michael   1947 AAN BOR,
1951 CAN

Redgrave, Vanessa   1966 AAN CAN,
1968 AAN, 1969 SOC CAN,
1971 AAN, 1977 AAW GLO
LAC, 1984 SOC, 1985
SOC, 1987 NYC, 1992 AAN,
1994 VEN

Redman, Joyce   1963 AAN, 1965
AAN

Reed, Carol   1949 AAN DGA NYC
CAN, 1950 AAN, 1956 BER,
1968 AAW

Reed, Donna   1953 AAW

Reeves, Keanu   1991 MTV, 1994
MTV

Reinhardt, Gottfried   1956 BER

Reitz, Edgar   1967 VEN, 1978 BER,
1984 VEN

Remick, Lee   1962 AAN

Rennahan, Ray   1939 AAW, 1941
AAW

Renoir, Jean   1937 VEN, 1945 AAN
BOR, 1946 VEN, 1951 VEN,
1974 AAS SOC

Resnais, Alain   1961 VEN, 1966
CAN, 1980 CAN, 1989 VEN,
1994 BER

Revere, Anne   1943 AAN, 1945
AAW, 1947 AAN

Rey, Fernando   1977 CAN

Reynolds, Burt   1974 HAR, 1978
PEO, 1979 PEO, 1981 PEO,
1982 PEO, 1983 PEO, 1993 RAZ

Reynolds, Debbie   1955 HAR, 1956
BOR, 1958 PHO, 1963 HAR,
1964 AAN, 1968 PHO

Rice, Tim   1992 AAW GLO, 1994
AAW GLO

Rich, Matty   1991 SUN IND

Richardson, Miranda   1992 AAN
GLO NYC BAA, 1994 AAN
BOR

Richardson, Ralph   1949 AAN, 1952
GLO BOR BAA, 1962 CAN,
1984 AAN NYC

Richardson, Tony   1961 BAA, 1963
AAW DGA NYC BOR

Richter, Hans   1947 VEN

Rickman, Alan   1991 BAA

Riddle, Nelson   1974 AAW

Riefenstahl, Leni   1938 VEN

Riggs, Marlon T.   1990 LAC [film dir.
by], 1995 SUN

Riskin, Robert   1934 AAW

Ritt, Martin   1963 AAN, 1979 CAN

Ritter, Thelma   1950 AAN, 1951
AAN, 1952 AAN, 1953 AAN,
1959 AAN, 1962 AAN

Riva, Emmanuelle   1962 VEN

Rivette, Jacques   1989 BER, 1991
CAN

Roach [Sr.], Hal   1983 AAS

Robards [Jr.], Jason   1962 BOR
CAN, 1976 AAN NYC SOC
BOR, 1977 AAW LAC, 1980
AAN

Robbins, Jerome   1961 AAW AAS
DGA

Robbins, Tim   1992 GLO CAN HAR

Robert, Yves   1973 BER

Roberts, Eric   1985 AAN

Roberts, Julia   1989 AAN GLO, 1990
AAN GLO PEO, 1991 PEO,
1993 PEO

Roberts, Rachel   1960 BAA, 1963
AAN BAA, 1979 BAA

Robertson, Cliff   1968 AAW BOR

Robinson, Bruce   1984 BAA

Robinson, Edward G.   1949 CAN,
1972 AAS

Robson, Flora   1946 AAN

Robson, Mark   1949 DGA, 1957
AAN DGA, 1958 AAN

Robson, May   1932–33 AAN

Rocha, Glauber   1967 CAN, 1969
CAN

Rodgers, Richard   1945 AAW

Rodriguez, Richard   1993 SUN IND

Roeg, Nicolas   1985 CAN

Rogers, Charles "Buddy"   1985
AAS

Rogers, Ginger   1940 AAW

Rohmer, Eric   1967 BER, 1970 NYC
SOC, 1976 CAN, 1983 BER,
1986 VEN, 1992 BER

Romero, George   1978 SUN

Romm, Mikhail   1946 CAN

Rooks, Conrad   1966 VEN

Rooney, Mickey   1938 AAS, 1939
AAN, 1943 AAN, 1956 AAN,
1979 AAN, 1982 AAS

Rose, William   1955 BAA, 1967
AAW

Schulberg, Budd   1954 AAW
Schwarzenegger, Arnold   1976 GLO,
   1991 MTV
Schygulla, Hanna   1979 BER, 1983
   CAN
Scofield, Paul   1966 AAW GLO NYC
   BOR, 1967 BAA, 1994 AAN
Scola, Ettore   1976 CAN, 1980 CAN,
   1981 CAN, 1984 BER
Scorsese, Martin   1976 SOC CAN,
   1980 AAN SOC, 1985 IND,
   1986 CAN, 1988 AAN, 1990
   AAN NYC SOC LAC BAA
   VEN, 1993 BOR
Scott, George C.   1959 AAN, 1961
   AAN, 1970 AAW GLO NYC
   SOC BOR, 1971 AAN
Scott, Martha   1940 AAN
Scott, Ridley   1977 CAN, 1991 AAN
Seagal, Steven   1994 RAZ
Seastrom, Victor: *see* Sjöström, Victor
Seaton, George   1947 AAW GLO,
   1954 AAW DGA, 1961 AAS
Segal, Erich   1970 GLO
Segal, George   1964 GLO, 1966
   AAN, 1973 GLO
Selleck, Tom   1992 RAZ
Sellers, Peter   1959 BAA, 1964 AAN,
   1979 AAN GLO BOR
Selznick, David O.   1939 AAS
Sembéne, Ousmane   1988 VEN,
   1992 VEN
Semple, Jr., Lorenzo   1968 NYC
Sen, Mrinal   1981 BER, 1983 CAN
Sennett, Mack (including shorts
   produced by)   1931–32 AAW,
   1937 AAS
Seyrig, Delphine   1963 VEN, 1969
   SOC, 1975 CAN
Shaffer, Peter   1984 AAW GLO LAC
Shahine, Youssef   1979 BER
Shamroy, Leon   1942 AAW, 1944
   AAW, 1945 AAW, 1963 AAW
Shankar, Ravi   1957 BER
Shapiro, Stanley   1959 AAW
Sharif, Omar   1962 AAN GLO, 1965
   GLO, 1969 HAR
Sharkey, Ray   1980 GLO
Sharraff, Irene   1951 AAW, 1956
   AAW, 1961 AAW, 1963 AAW,
   1966 AAW
Shatner, William   1989 RAZ
Shaw, George Bernard   1938 AAW
Shaw, Robert   1966 AAN BOR
Shearer, Norma   1929–30 AAW,

   1930–31 AAN, 1934 AAN,
   1936 AAN, 1938 AAN VEN,
   1939 HAR
Sheldon, Sidney   1947 AAW
Shelton, Ron   1988 NYC SOC LAC
Shepard, Sam   1983 AAN
Shepherd, Cybill   1972 HAR
Shepitko, Larissa   1977 BER
Sheridan, Jim   1989 AAN, 1993 AAN
   BER
Sherman, Richard M. and Robert
   B.   1964 AAW
Sherwood, Robert   1946 AAW
Shields, Brooke   1980 PEO RAZ,
   1981 PEO, 1982 PEO, 1983
   PEO, 1984 RAZ, 1989 RAZ
Shinoda, Masahiro   1986 BER
Shire, David   1979 AAW
Shire, Talia   1974 AAN, 1976 AAN
   NYC BOR
Shirley, Anne   1937 AAN
Shore, Howard   1994 LAC
Shuftan, Eugene   1961 AAW
Sidney, George   1957 GLO, 1958
   DGA
Sidney, Sylvia   1973 AAN BOR
Siegel, Don   1945 AAW [short films
   dir. by], 1988 LAC
Sierck, Detlef: *see* Douglas Sirk
Signoret, Simone   1952 BAA, 1957
   BAA, 1958 BAA, 1959 AAW
   BOR CAN, 1965 AAN, 1971
   BER
Silliphant, Stirling   1967 AAW GLO,
   1968 GLO
Silverstone, Alicia   1993 MTV
Simon, Carly   1988 AAW GLO
Simon, Michel   1967 BER
Simon, Neil   1977 GLO
Simmons, Jean   1948 AAN VEN,
   1953 BOR, 1955 GLO, 1957
   GLO, 1969 AAN, 1987 CAN
Simpson, O. J.   1994 RAZ
Sinatra, Frank   1944 HAR, 1951
   HAR, 1953 AAW GLO, 1955
   AAN, 1957 GLO, 1960 HAR,
   1970 AAS GLO
Singleton, John   1991 AAN NYC
   LAC MTV
Sinise, Gary   1994 AAN BOR
Siodmak, Robert   1946 AAN, 1955
   BER
Sirk, Douglas   1935 VEN
Sjöberg, Alf   1946 CAN, 1951 CAN

Stoppard, Tom   1985 LAC, 1990 VEN

Storaro, Vittorio   1971 SOC, 1979 AAW, 1981 AAW LAC, 1987 AAW NYC LAC, 1990 NYC

Stowe, Madeleine   1993 SOC

Stradling, Harry   1945 AAW, 1964 AAW

Straight, Beatrice   1976 AAW

Strasberg, Lee   1974 AAN, 1980 VEN

Strathairn, David   1991 IND

Streep, Meryl   1978 AAN SOC HAR, 1979 AAW GLO NYC SOC LAC BOR, 1981 ANN GLO LAC BAA, 1982 AAW GLO NYC SOC LAC BOR, 1982 HAR, 1983 AAN PEO, 1984 PEO, 1985 AAN LAC PEO, 1986 PEO, 1987 AAN, 1988 AAN NYC PEO, 1989 PEO CAN, 1990 AAN

Streisand, Barbra   1968 AAW GLO HAR, 1969 GLO, 1970 GLO, 1973 AAN HAR, 1974 GLO PEO, 1976 AAW GLO PEO HAR, 1977 GLO PEO, 1983 GLO, 1987 PEO

Stroheim, Erich von   1950 AAN

Struss, Karl   1927–28 AAW

Sturges, John   1955 AAN DGA

Sturges, Preston   1940 AAW

Styne, Jule   1954 AAW

Sucksdorff, Arne   1954 CAN

Sukowa, Barbara   1986 CAN

Sullavan, Margaret   1938 AAN NYC

Surtees, Robert   1950 AAW GLO, 1951 GLO, 1952 AAW, 1959 AAW

Suzman, Janet   1971 AAN

Suzuki, Seijun   1981 BER

Svankmajer, Jan   1983 BER

Swanson, Gloria   1927–28 AAN, 1929–30 AAN, 1950 AAN GLO BOR, 1974 HAR

Swayze, Patrick   1990 HAR

Swinton, Tilda   1991 VEN

Sydow, Max von   1982 VEN, 1988 AAN CAN

Sylbert, Paul   1978 AAW

Sylbert, Richard   1966 AAW, 1990 AAW

Sylvie   1966 SOC

Szábo, István   1963 CAN, 1980 BER, 1981 CAN, 1992 BER

Tahimik, Kidlat   1977 BER

Tamblyn, Russ   1955 GLO, 1957 AAN

Tamiroff, Akim   1936 AAN, 1943 AAN GLO

Tanaka, Kinuyo   1975 BER

Tandy, Jessica   1989 AAW GLO, 1990 BAA BER, 1991 AAN

Tanner, Alain   1976 SOC, 1981 CAN

Taradash, Daniel   1953 AAW

Tarantino, Quentin   1994 AAW GLO NYC SOC LAC BOR BAA CAN IND

Tarkovsky, Andrei   1962 VEN, 1972 CAN, 1983 CAN, 1986 CAN

Tati, Jacques   1949 VEN, 1953 CAN, 1958 CAN

Taurog, Norman   1930–1 AAN, 1938 AAN VEN

Tavernier, Bertrand   1974 BER, 1984 CAN, 1995 BER

Taviani, Paolo and Vittorio   1962 VEN, 1977 CAN, 1982 CAN, 1983 SOC, 1986 VEN

Taylor, Elizabeth   1950 HAR, 1956 GLO, 1957 AAN, 1958 AAN, 1959 AAN GLO, 1960 AAW, 1963 HAR, 1966 AAW NYC BOR BAA, 1972 BER, 1973 GLO, 1984 GLO, 1986 LIN, 1993 AFI, 1992 AAS

Taylor, Lili   1993 IND

Taylor, Robert   1951 HAR, 1953 GLO

Taylor, Samuel   1954 GLO

Téchiné, André   1985 CAN

Temple, Shirley   1934 AAS, 1948 HAR, 1949 HAR, 1950 HAR

Teshigahara, Hiroshi   1964 CAN, 1965 AAN

Tesich, Steve   1979 AAW NYC SOC

Thewlis, David   1993 NYC SOC CAN

Thompson, Emma   1992 AAW GLO NYC SOC LAC BOR BAA, 1993 AAN

Thompson, Ernest   1981 AAW GLO

Thompson, J. Lee   1957 BER, 1961 AAN

Thompson, Jack   1980 CAN

Thorndike, Dame Sybil   1957 BOR

Three Stooges, The   1992 MTV

Thulin, Ingrid   1958 CAN

Thurman, Uma   1994 AAN MTV

Tidyman, Ernest   1971 AAW

Visconti, Luchino   1948 VEN, 1957
     VEN, 1960 VEN, 1963 CAN,
     1965 VEN, 1971 CAN
Vitti, Monica   1984 BER
Vlady, Marina   1963 CAN
Voight, Jon   1969 AAN GLO NYC
     SOC, 1970 HAR, 1978 AAW
     GLO NYC SOC BOR CAN, 1985
     AAN GLO
Volonté, Gian Maria   1972 CAN,
     1983 CAN, 1987 BER, 1991
     VEN

Wajda, Andrzej   1957 CAN, 1959
     VEN, 1978 CAN, 1981 NYC CAN,
     1982 BAA, 1990 CAN
Walas, Chris   1986 AAW
Walken, Christopher   1978 AAW
     NYC
Wallis, Hal B.   1938 AAW, 1943
     AAW, 1974 GLO
Walsh, Kay   1958 BOR
Walsh, M. Emmet   1985 IND
Walters, Charles   1953 AAN DGA
     CAN
Walters, Julie   1983 AAN GLO BAA
Wang, Wayne   1983 SUN, 1995 BER
Warden, Jack   1975 AAN, 1978 AAN
Warner, H. B.   1937 AAN
Warner, Harry M.   1938 AAS
Warner, Jack L.   1955 GLO, 1958
     AAS, 1964 DGA
Warren, Harry   1935 AAW, 1943
     AAW, 1946 AAW
Warren, Lesley Ann   1982 AAN
Washington, Denzel   1987 AAN,
     1989 AAW GLO, 1992 AAN
     NYC MTV, 1993 BER
Washington, Ned   1940 AAW, 1952
     AAW, 1961 GLO, 1963 GLO
Waters, Daniel   1990 RAZ, 1991
     RAZ
Waters, Ethel   1949 AAN
Waterston, Sam   1984 AAN
Watkin, David   1981 NYC, 1985
     AAW NYC LAC
Watson, Lucile   1943 AAN
Waxman, Franz   1950 AAW GLO,
     1951 AAW
Wayne, John   1949 AAN, 1950 PHO
     HAR, 1952 GLO, 1965 GLO,
     1969 AAW GLO, 1974 PEO,
     1975 PEO, 1976 PEO, 1977
     PEO

Weaver, Sigourney   1986 AAN, 1988
     AAN GLO
Webb, Chloe   1986 SOC
Webb, Clifton   1946 AAN GLO,
     1948 AAN, 1950 HAR
Wedgeworth, Ann   1977 SOC
Weir, Peter   1985 AAN, 1989 AAN
Welch, Raquel   1967 HAR, 1974
     GLO
Weld, Tuesday   1959 GLO, 1977
     AAN
Welland, Colin   1970 BAA, 1981
     AAW
Welles, Orson   1941 AAW, 1946
     HAR, 1952 CAN, 1959 CAN,
     1966 CAN, 1970 AAS, 1975 AFI,
     1983 DGA
Wellman, William   1937 AAW, 1949
     AAN, 1954 AAN DGA, 1972
     DGA
Wenders, Wim   1976 CAN, 1982
     VEN, 1984 BAA CAN, 1987
     CAN, 1993 CAN, 1995 VEN
Werker, Alfred L.   1949 DGA
Werner, Oskar   1965 AAN GLO
     NYC
Wertmuller, Lina   1976 AAN
Wexler, Haskell   1966 AAW SOC,
     1976 AAW SOC LAC, 1987 IND
Wheeler, Lyle   1939 AAW, 1946
     AAW, 1953 AAW, 1956 AAW,
     1959 AAW
Whitaker, Forest   1988 CAN
Whitelaw, Billie   1968 SOC BAA
Whitman, Stuart   1961 AAN
Whitmore, James   1949 AAN GLO,
     1975 AAN
Whitty, Dame May   1937 AAN, 1942
     AAN
Wicki, Bernhard   1961 BER
Widerberg, Bo   1965 BER, 1969
     CAN, 1971 CAN
Widmark, Richard   1947 AAN GLO
Wiest, Dianne   1986 AAW NYC SOC
     BOR, 1989 AAN, 1994 AAW
     GLO SAG NYC SOC LAC IND
Wilby, James   1987 VEN
Wilcox, Herbert   1937 VEN
Wilde, Cornel   1945 AAN, 1946
     HAR
Wilder, Billy   1945 AAW NYC, 1946
     CAN, 1950 AAW GLO DGA,
     1951 VEN, 1953 AAN DGA,
     1954 AAN GLO DGA, 1957
     AAN DGA, 1959 AAN, 1960

GLO DGA NYC, 1959 AAN
NYC BOR, 1960 AAN, 1966
AAW GLO DGA NYC BOR,
1969 DGA, 1977 AAN BAA

Zsigmond, Vilmos   1973 SOC, 1977
   AAW
Zukor, Adolph   1948 AAS

About the Author

Michael Gebert was born in Wichita, Kansas, in 1961, and attended the University of Kansas, where he was chairman of the film society from 1980 to 1983. As an undergraduate, he also curated two exhibits on rare books relating to the movies at the university's research library. In 1986 he founded probably the last new 16mm film society on Earth at the Wichita Art Association, where, among other things, he cooked Cajun food in the theater to accompany a documentary on Cajun culture. His writings on the entertainment industry and advertising have appeared in publications such as *Video Watchdog*, *Advertising Age*, and *Video Store*, and on the on-line feature "Film Scouts." He is also an advertising copywriter who has won many of the field's top national awards. He lives in Chicago with his wife and laserdisc collection; electronically he lives at DrMovieGuy @aol.com.

His inventive, off-the-wall humor made America laugh out loud in movies like *Big*, *Turner and Hooch*, and *A League of Their Own*. His charm and boyish good looks won over Darryl Hannah in *Splash* and Meg Ryan in *Sleepless in Seattle*. His genius for breathing life into a character made *Forrest Gump* a household name. And his haunting Oscar-winning performance in *Philadelphia* established him as one of today's hottest leading men.

Warm, witty and vulnerable, Tom Hanks is both the everyman we can all identify with and an actor with stunning star quality. Now, Roy Trakin traces Hanks' life and career in this honest, no-holds-barred biography.

TOM HANKS
JOURNEY TO STARDOM

ROY TRAKIN

There Will Never Be a Book on Streisand This Intimate . . .
until She Writes One Herself.

There has never been a star like Barbra Streisand—an artist of uncompromising vision who combines explosive flashes of talent with monumental outbursts of ego. Cold, brash, obsessively controlling, vain, insecure, devastatingly shy, she can also be sensual, warm, funny, and sizzling with sex appeal. But who is the real Streisand?

In this fascinating book, acclaimed biographer Randall Riese reveals all the faces of Barbra—plus behind-the-scenes insights into Barbra's personal life. It's Barbra as you've never seen her before.

Her Name Is

BARBRA

Randall Riese

"SIZZLING!" —*New York Post*

HER NAME IS BARBRA
Randall Riese
_____ 95391-7 $6.99 U.S./$7.99 Can.